I0796216
PUBLIC HOUSE AND LIVE MUSIC
SUNFLOWER
SUNFLOWER
NO TOPLESS BATHING
BOWES
BOWE'S 31
BOWE'S
THE KEEPERS ARMS
WALSHES
McCaffreys Bar
MACCARTHY'S
IRISH PUB OF THE YEAR 2016
THE OLD IRISH PUB
客乐我歌
THE OLD IRISH PUB · KARAOKE BAR · 客乐我歌
KARAOKE BAR

THE IRISH PUB
INVENTION & RE-INVENTION

GUINNESS

EDITED BY

MOONYOUNG HONG & PERRY SHARE

First published in 2025 by
Cork University Press
Boole Library
University College Cork
Cork
T12 ND89
Ireland

EU GPSR Authorised Representative: Sinéad Neville.
Email: corkuniversitypress@ucc.ie

Library of Congress Control Number: 2025942550
Distribution in the USA: Longleaf Services, Chapel Hill, NC, USA

ISBN 978-1-78205-066-7

Book design and typesetting, Anú Design, Tara
Printed in the UK by Bell and Bain Ltd, Glasgow

Dedicated to the memory of

Hong Hak-yong (1933–2025)

and Bernard V. Share (1930–2013)

GUINNESS
NEARY'S

Contents

Part II
Irish Pubs Abroad: Exporting and translating Ireland

Part III
Literary, Musical and Artistic Perspectives

Part IV
The Future of the Irish Pub

List of Figures and Tables

Tables

Notes on Contributors

Michael Cronin is 1776 Professor of French in Trinity College Dublin and Senior Researcher in the Trinity Centre for Literary and Cultural Translation. Among his recently published titles are *Eco-Translation: Translation and ecology in the age of the Anthropocene* (2017), *Irish and Ecology: An Ghaeilge agus an éiceolaíocht* (2019) and *Eco-Travel: Journeying in the age of the Anthropocene* (2022). He is a member of the Royal Irish Academy and a fellow of Trinity College Dublin.

Tracey Dalton is a lecturer on the BA Interior Design at the Technological University Dublin School of Art and Design. Tracey has a background in interior design practice since 1998 and has published on delivery, teaching and learning of interior design practice in the *Irish Journal of Academic Practice* (2016) and *Iterations* (2017). She is a PhD candidate at Kingston University, London. Her PhD research concerns the phenomenon of the Irish pub for export as a commodity, focusing on the 'Guinness Irish Pub Concept', created in 1992 by Guinness plc and McNally Design/Irish Pub Company, where Tracey worked in interior design practice from 1998 to 2005. Tracey has presented at conferences on her research topic at the Modern Interiors Research Centre at Kingston University, London, and TU Dublin School of Art and Design, along with the London Irish Centre, throughout her time researching for her PhD.

Eli Davies is a writer and researcher whose work focuses on the culture and politics of domestic life in Ireland and elsewhere. She completed an interdisciplinary PhD at Ulster University, exploring women's personal and cultural memories of the home during the Troubles. She has published widely for both academic and non-academic publications and her first solo-authored book *The Spinster Cookbook: Culture, politics and pleasure in the single woman's kitchen* will be published by The Indigo Press in 2026. She is now based in London but continues her research on gender, conflict and everyday life in Ireland.

Nicholas Grene is Emeritus Professor of English Literature at Trinity College Dublin and a member of the Royal Irish Academy. His books include *The Politics of Irish*

Drama (1999), *Yeats's Poetic Codes* (2008), *Home on the Stage* (2014), *The Theatre of Tom Murphy: Playwright adventurer* (2017), *Farming in Modern Irish Literature* (2021) and most recently, *Irish Theatre in the Twenty-First Century* (2024).

Moonyoung Hong is Assistant Professor in the School of English at the University of Hong Kong. She obtained her MPhil in Irish Writing and PhD in English at Trinity College Dublin. She is author of *Tom Murphy's Theatre of Everyday Space* (2025) and has published in *Irish Studies Review*, *Comparative Drama*, *Études Irlandaises* and *Review of Irish Studies in Europe (RISE)*. She is on the executive committee for the Irish Society for Theatre Research (ISTR).

James Little is Assistant Professor in Drama, Theatre and Performance at the Department of English Studies, University of Cyprus. His publications include *Samuel Beckett in Confinement: The politics of closed space* (2020), *The Making of Samuel Beckett's* Not I / Pas moi, That Time / Cette fois *and* Footfalls / Pas (2021) and – as co-editor – *Ireland: Interfaces and dialogues* (2022). He is co-editor of Bloomsbury's Global Perspectives in Irish Literary Studies book series and director of the UCY Irish Studies Collective.

Elizabeth Malcolm, MA, PhD, FRHistS, FASSA, worked at universities in Sydney, Dublin, Belfast and Liverpool before taking up a chair in Irish Studies at the University of Melbourne. She has published on topics such as drink and temperance, police and crime, mental health, women's history and Irish migration. Her latest book, co-authored with Dianne Hall, is *A New History of the Irish in Australia* (2019). She is currently writing a study of sexual violence and conflict in Ireland, 1100–1900, also with Professor Hall.

Kevin Martin is a former lecturer at the Institute of Technology Blanchardstown and the Castlebar campus of the Galway Mayo Institute of Technology. He is author of *Have Ye No Homes To Go To? The history of the Irish pub* (2016), *Complete Guide to Dublin Pubs* (2018), *A Happy Type of Sadness: A journey through Irish country music* (2018), *The Irish Whales: Olympians of Old New York* (2020) and *Emerald Emperors of the Ring: Irish and Irish American boxers in the United States* (forthcoming, 2026).

James McCauley is a lecturer in Marketing at the School of Culinary Arts and Food Technology at Technological University Dublin and doctoral candidate at the Atlantic Technological University in Sligo.

Sam McGrath wrote extensively for fifteen years on Dublin pub culture and social history for the Come Here To Me! blog. Two 'Best Of' collections were published in 2012 and 2017. His chapter on gay-friendly pubs has its origins in a 2013 article which became the second most read article in the website's history. He has also researched and written articles on the history of Dublin's 'early house' pubs, private member/club bars, after-hours shebeens and political 'drinking clubs'. Since 2017, he has been employed as an archivist with the Military Service (1916–1923) Pensions Collection, Military Archives.

Patricia Medcalf is a senior lecturer in Marketing and Advertising, Technological University Dublin, and is course leader on the Bachelor of Arts degree programme in Advertising and Marketing Communications. She is author of *Advertising the Black Stuff in Ireland 1959–1999: Increments of change* (2020): a study of the relationship between Guinness advertising and Irish society. She has published and presented on Guinness/advertising-related topics. Previously she worked as project director with corporate and brand identity specialists Brand Union (formerly known as The Identity Business).

Brenda Murphy is Professor of Media and Gender Studies, and is currently with the Department of Arts, at Southeast Technological University (SETU), Ireland. She was previously a founding member of the Department of Gender & Sexualities at the University of Malta. Her research focuses on gender representation in the media, and she is actively engaged in EU-funded projects as both an expert advisor and a research partner. She collaborates with the European Institute for Gender Equality (EIGE), COST Actions, and a range of international research initiatives. Since 2000, she has served as the National Coordinator for the Global Media Monitoring Project (GMMP) and has contributed to numerous European and global interdisciplinary projects on STEM education, gender in ICT, media portrayals of gender, and cultural representations in victimology. Her book *Brewing Identities: Globalisation, Guinness, and the Production of Irishness* was published with Peter Lang in 2015.

Brian J. Murphy is a senior lecturer at the School of Culinary Arts and Food Technology at the Technological University Dublin. He has published and presented on the role that place and story play in contemporary drink culture and on how food and drink locations communicate and engage with different audiences. A co-founder of the Dublin Gastronomy Symposium, Brian is also an active board member of the National Centre for Franco-Irish Studies, a research centre based at the Technological University Dublin. His first monograph, *Beyond Sustenance: An exploration of food and drink culture in Ireland*, was published in 2023.

Trish Murphy is a psychotherapist, teacher and trainer and currently serves as the director of student counselling in Trinity College Dublin. Trish writes a weekly column for *The Irish Times*. She has published two books: *The Challenge of Retirement* (2014) and *#Love: 21st-century relationships* (2016).

John O'Brien is a lecturer in Sociology and Criminology at University College Cork. His research interests lie in alcohol and other psychoactive substances; consumption; sociological theory; classical philosophy; Irish society; memory and commemoration. He is author of *States of Intoxication: The place of alcohol in civilisation* (2018).

Gwen Scarbrough is lecturer in Social Sciences at the Atlantic Technological University in Sligo. She completed her PhD 'The Irish Pub as a Third Place: A sociological exploration of people, place and identity' in 2008. 'New Places, Non-Places and the Changing Landscape of the Irish Pub' was published in M.P. Corcoran and P. Share (eds), *Belongings: Shaping identity in modern Ireland* (2008).

Perry Share is head of the School of Social Science and Humanities at Atlantic Technological University. He is a sociologist with a broad range of interests, from technology to education to food and eating. He is co-author of *A Sociology of Ireland* (2012) and of a number of publications in the sociology of food and drink. He is an Editorial Board member of the *European Journal of Food, Drink and Society* and was formerly external examiner on the MA in Gastronomy and Food Studies, Technological University Dublin.

Tom Spalding teaches at the Munster Technological University, Cork and is the author of several books on design history, specialising on Cork city where he has lived for many years. His book *Layers* (2013) concentrated on exploring the nature of nationalism as it has been displayed in the public realm. He has also written *Designed for Life: Architecture and design in Cork city, 1900–1990* (2025) and (with Daniel Breen) *The Cork International Exhibition 1902–1903: A snapshot of Edwardian Cork* (2014). He earned his PhD at the Technological University Dublin in 2021 with his thesis 'Intersections: Quotidian design and modernism(s) in Cork city, 1922–1969'.

Fintan Vallely is a musician, lecturer and writer in Irish traditional music. His books include the encyclopaedia *Companion to Irish Traditional Music* (1999, 2011, 2024), *Beating Time: The story of the Irish bodhrán* (2025), *Tuned Out: Protestant perceptions of traditional music in Northern Ireland* (2008). He teaches flute at Scoil Samhraidh Willie Clancy, has taught at NUI Maynooth, University of Ulster, Dundalk Institute of Technology and Trinity College Dublin, and was an organiser of major conferences on Irish traditional music – Crosbhealach an Cheoil 1996 and 2003, and NAFCo, 2012. (www.imusic.ie) He is an Adjunct Professor with the School of Irish, Celtic Studies and Folklore at University College Dublin, and in 2023 his work was honoured with TG4's lifetime achievement award, Gradam Saiol.

Katie Young is Assistant Professor of Cultural Geography in the School of Irish Studies at Concordia University. She received a PhD in Geography and Music from Royal Holloway, University of London in 2019, and undertook postdoctoral research at Mary Immaculate College in Limerick, Ireland where she examined experiences of music and migration in Cork and Galway's night spaces. Katie is the Canadian Co-Principal Investigator for Beyond Opposition, a European Research Council-funded research project based in the Geography Department at University College Dublin, Ireland. She has experience designing interactive arts-based public research activities, including the online website Music, Memory and the Night, the gallery exhibition From Canvas to Cassette, and the online exhibition Imperfect Utopias.

Acknowledgements

We would like to thank first and foremost all our contributors, for their patience and faith in the project. It has taken us almost four years since the day we first gathered over Zoom to discuss the importance of the Irish pub. Not only have we managed to work through the Covid-19 pandemic together but also have evolved ourselves, continuing to appreciate the pub on whatever path we happen to be.

Many thanks to the anonymous peer reviewers, who have reviewed our manuscript on multiple occasions, for their insights and feedback. Special thanks to Maria O'Donovan for her editorial support, to Aonghus Meaney for his rigorous copyediting, and all the staff at Cork University Press, for their enthusiasm and help in seeing through the collection.

We would like to mention Trinity Long Room Hub Arts and Humanities Research Institute, for their generosity in hosting the 'History of the Irish Pub' online St Patrick's Day event in 2021. Special thanks to Eve Patten, Ciaran O'Neill and Martina Mullin for making it happen. The panel discussion has become the basis for our interdisciplinary approach, and the participants have given us confidence in further research about the pub.

Thanks to Anne Marie Bolger and Máirtín Mac Con Iomaire of TU Dublin for recommending some of our excellent contributors.

The book would not have seen the light of day if it weren't for the institutional assistance from Trinity College Dublin (TCD) Trust, Atlantic Technological University (ATU), Sligo, and the School of English Small Projects Funds from the University of Hong Kong (HKU). Thank you for the financial and collegial support.

Thank you to the Irish Pub Company archive, Tourism Northern Ireland, National Museums in Northern Ireland Collection, Array Collective, Virtual Treasury of Ireland, Discover Ireland, the Guinness archives, EPIC The Irish Emigration Museum, Abbey Theatre archive and Druid Theatre, *The Irish Times*, *Irish Independent*, DublinByPub, Publin, TradFest archive, estate of Harry Aaron Kernoff, as well as other individual families who shared their works and stories, and the numerous photographers and artists for their generosity in allowing us to use the images, which has greatly enhanced the visual side of our book.

Thank you to Ciara Beale for helping us source the images, illustrations and clearing permissions.

Thank you to our family and friends: to Youngdo, Chang Moon, Kisan, Junga, Heeyoung, Hye Jeong, Youjin, Jinhyuk, Unhee, Hanwool, Brandon, Jenn, Holly, Claire, Angeliki, Dearbhaile, Patrick S., Callum, Tom, Fiona, Mairéad, Fergus, Féidhlim, Chris M. and Conor, for sharing many a pint with us. Thanks to Michelle, all the rest of the family and in memory of my father Bernard Share, who was something of a devotee of pubs and pints.

Chapter 1

Introduction: Inventing the Irish Pub

Moonyoung Hong and Perry Share

In October 2021, a nascent social movement emerged in response to the threatened remodelling of an 'iconic' Dublin public house – the Cobblestone in Smithfield. Facing incorporation into a new hotel development, the proposed transformation of this centre for Irish traditional music and oral culture was seen as a 'step too far' in a city that, on the face of it, was beginning to lose too much of what made it.[1]

The Cobblestone lies on a boundary of Dublin's 'drink tourism' district. This spans the inner city, from the adjacent Jameson distillery visitor centre on the northside, east to Pantibar and (also rescued from 'development') Nealon's, across to the southside of the river by way of the celebrated Mulligan's of Poolbeg Street and other celebrated 'Victorian' pubs such as Bowe's and the Palace, to the raucous drink palaces of Temple Bar, Dublin's best-known gay bar The George and the gilded Long Hall of South Great George's Street, thence to the Guinness Storehouse, Ireland's most-visited tourist destination. It extends to the 'new' Roe's and Pearse Lyons whiskey distilleries of James' Street, the nearby Guinness 'experimental' Open Gate, perhaps finishing at the Teeling distillery in the rapidly gentrifying Newmarket area of Dublin 8. A veritable history and geography of alcoholic drink, within which pubs feature strongly.[2]

Pubs – along with landscape, heritage and 'people' – have long been an Irish tourism product, and there is an undeniable irony in the disenchantment of a celebrated pub to facilitate the development of 'yet another' hotel. As well as occupying the core of Irish local society, pubs have, for many decades, also been a leading cultural export: first, organically, as Irish pubs emerged to serve local diasporic communities in towns and cities across the world, from Boston and Toronto, to Coventry and London, to Melbourne and Perth; then, more self-consciously, as specialised firms, often in partnership with brewers Guinness and Murphy's, manufactured, pre-packaged and sold an estimated 7,000-plus 'instant' Irish pubs into hundreds of global locations, from Nepal to Peru to Rovaniemi at the edge of the Arctic Circle.

This global 'product' draws on the long-established and widely recognised central place of the pub in Irish culture: reflected in popular discourse, political power

Figure 1.1 Protestors with placards at the Cobblestone pub. Photo by and courtesy of DublinByPub.

Figure 1.2 Snowy exterior of Oliver's Corner Irish Pub in Rovaniemi, Lapland, Finland. Photo by Christine Schmitt.

structures, streetscapes and vernacular architecture, literary and media sources and community practices. The 'traditional' pub, with its inevitable pint of stout, is a necessary stopping-off point and photo opportunity for every visiting US president or British royal and the topic of thousands of Instagram posts. Dublin, designated fourth UNESCO City of Literature in 2010, has recognised the interconnection between drink and literary creativity through the Literary Pub Crawl, offering a two-and-a-half-hour pub-centred odyssey in the virtual company of Oscar Wilde, James Joyce, Brendan Behan and Samuel Beckett.[3]

Every city, town and village in Ireland, as well as many a remote hillside or significant crossroads, is well-populated with pubs of many sorts – almost 7,500 north and south:[4] tourist pubs, food pubs, singing pubs, literary pubs, craft beer pubs, 'old man' pubs, classic 'Victorian' pubs, suburban beer barns, grocery shop pubs, 'early' houses, late bars, LGBTQIA+ pubs, sports bars, cocktail bars, hotel bars, racecourse bars, airport bars, listening bars, whiskey bars, even the odd (in both senses of the word) alcohol-free pub: 'one', as the saying goes, 'for everybody in the audience'.

Figure 1.3 United States President Barack Obama watches as First Lady Michelle Obama pulls a pint of stout under the guidance of Ollie Hayes (right), proprietor of the Ollie Hayes Pub in Moneygall, Ireland on 23 May 2011. Image source: Picryl.

As sociologists, anthropologists, geographers and social historians have demonstrated, pubs are intricately enmeshed within the texture of Irish society.[5] Over the past centuries they have been places of solace and of commerce; sites for the marking of life events from births to wakes; centres for sport, politics and romantic engagement. They have been life-affirming but also occasional locations for violence and crime.[6] Pubs have been important transportation nodes, bases for community-based organisations, and employment exchanges. Since the mid-twentieth century these economic and service functions have largely been taken over by more specialised and professionalised services and pubs have become part of the broader leisure, night-time economy and tourist industries, yet often important traces of these earlier purposes remain. Pubs remain, for example, a crucial element of social and friendship networks.[7]

As places of social interaction, pubs are both inclusive and exclusive. Like all social institutions, they are shaped by inequalities of class, gender, ethnicity, sexual identity and abledness. American sociologist Ray Oldenburg has captured the essence of the pub in his concept of 'the third place' – a space that is neither home nor work.[8] It is a public place, easily accessible, where one can relax, meet and interact. For Oldenburg, pubs, like other 'third places', are typified by their democratic and open nature: in theory, anyone can enter and participate in pub life. In practice, pubs can be more instrumental in shaping their clientele. Physical barriers, such as steps and heavy doors, or lack of accessible toilet facilities, can restrict access to all or parts of the building itself. Historically, women and children have been restricted to certain areas of pubs or excluded completely. As Curtin and Ryan found in a study of pubs and clubs in 1980s Ennis, they can be profoundly determinant and reflective of the class, occupation and status of their customers.[9] In more contemporary times the theming and symbolic construction of pubs acts as a subtler yet effective mechanism for the social sorting of customers by age, lifestyle, social identity and purchasing power.[10]

Pubs form an important if often taken-for-granted element of Ireland's built environment. In many villages and small towns, pubs – along with banks and courthouses – remain among the more substantial buildings, their family-name signage a marker of national and local identity. However grand or modest, pubs predominate on many Irish rural streetscapes. Individual pubs, such as the Covert in Westmeath, Horse and Jockey in Tipperary or the Silver Tassie in County Dublin, were important way-markers on major routes across the country. Along with imposing churches, large suburban pubs (such as Hill's, later the Submarine bar in Crumlin) arose with new housing developments around our cities, while several older urban centres (for example, Kilkenny or Sligo) consist of streets dominated by numerous pubs.

While a small number of Ireland's more iconic pubs are easily recognised in their exterior presentation (such as the much-photographed black and white façade of O'Donoghue's of Dublin's Merrion Row), visual analysis of pubs has tended to focus on interiors.[11] Tom Spalding traces this neglect to the lack of architectural archives and contemporaneous design commentary,[12] but it may reflect a broader reluctance to critically appreciate the everyday significance of the streetscapes of Ireland's smaller and larger towns and cities.[13] In some cases, as in the 'tied houses' of Murphy's brewery in Cork, there was an attempt to bring a regularity to the exterior of the pub,[14] while a few pubs across the country benefited from the attentions of noted Irish architects such as Sam Stephenson[15] and Michael Scott.[16]

Overall, pubs represent a distinctive, substantial yet relatively overlooked example of vernacular architecture in Ireland. They are an easily recognisable, if often unremarkable part of our surroundings and it is hard to imagine our streetscapes without them.[17] Contemporary trends in the number and distribution of pubs thus raise questions about Ireland's built environment – whether it is the management of popular 'drinking streets' such as Dublin's South William Street (a particular issue during the Covid-19 pandemic) or Cork's Washington Street, where there are significant concentrations of pubs (and drinkers) – or the challenge of how to best 'save' or repurpose the abandoned urban and rural pubs that are increasingly a part of many Irish settlements.

For the Irish pub – notwithstanding its privileged place in the Irish cultural firmament, as well as a history of dynamic adaptation – is seen as an institution under threat. Like so many other small family-based businesses, from hardware stores to grocery shops, as well as banks, post offices, newsagents and drapery stores, pubs are gradually disappearing from country roadsides, rural villages and urban streets.[18] A small town of ten or twelve pubs suddenly finds itself with just two or three. The combined forces of drink-driving legislation, the workplace smoking ban, changed licensing regulation, cheap supermarket alcohol and rising costs for insurance, rates and satellite TV services have been identified as key drivers of decline. Add to this the ever-rising value of urban property (a factor in the Cobblestone saga)

Figure 1.4 Exterior of Craic agus Ceol pub in Wellington Quay, Dublin, April 2020. Closed due to Covid-19 restrictions. Photo by and courtesy of CitySwift.

and the investment that ordinary people have made through furnishings, audio-visual technology and garden furniture to transform their homes into leisure and entertainment centres, and the future of the Irish pub does not look so bright.[19]

The Covid-19 pandemic of the early 2020s was in many cases the last straw for many struggling pubs, with its enforced closures, reliance on 'take-away pints', staggered re-openings, curfews and curtailments of who could do what, where and when. Many older publicans took the opportunity to hang up the bar towel and take retirement from a demanding role. Meanwhile the larger pub, restaurant and hotel chains and conglomerates have expanded their influence, perhaps pointing to a new structure for at least part of the industry.[20]

This book is – remarkably enough – the first full-length academic treatment of the phenomenon of the Irish pub in terms of its historic, literary, design, political, business, sociological and psychological dimensions. Its aim is to understand how the Irish pub as we know it today has been constructed – legislatively, historically, politically and socially, through written and visual texts, in the popular imagination, and as a lived reality. It borrows Doreen Massey's idea of the 'thrown-togetherness' of space – places that have been gathered and interwoven, a collection of stories, including the history, language, experiences and 'the wider power-geometries of space' as well as 'the non-meetings-up, the disconnections and the relations not established, the exclusions. All this contributes to the specificity of place'.[21] What is the history of the Irish pub? Who are the makers of this place, what are its functions, and what are the stories retold and/or untold? What makes an ordinary building that sells alcohol *the* Irish pub as we know, consume and experience it today? This book is an attempt to answer these questions by exploring the different forces that are interwoven in the pub space – forces simultaneously in operation and always in dialogue with one another.

While brewing practices go back to 4000 BC and records of brewers can be found in the twelfth century *Book of Leinster*,[22] one could argue that the Irish pub as we know it today is a modern invention that originated in the late seventeenth and eighteenth centuries. Drink shops had proliferated in the previous two centuries in the wake of English settlement near port towns and, later, as the result of industrialisation, where public coach networks, canals and then railways gave people access to a wider network of traffic and exchange. The precise origin of 'the pub' is difficult to trace as its role was constantly evolving, but scholars note that the term emerged in the seventeenth century, when distinctions between various drinking places became blurred. The inn, developed after the arrival of the Normans in the twelfth century, was a place that provided services for travellers, while the tavern, also from the Normans, was a place for wine merchants. Alehouses, or public alehouses, sold beer, but the distinction disappeared as the inn began to sell ales and both the tavern and alehouse offered lodging and various drinks. All these establishments were described in legal parlance and daily conversation as 'public house', abbreviated into 'pub' during the Victorian period.[23]

Diverse drinking and lodging establishments became systematised in this era, with active political control, reflected in frequent legislative interventions. Pubs became targets of state interest, and numerous laws and acts variously prohibited or promoted alcoholism by regulating or liberating the alcohol trade. This authoritative control contributed to the pub's successful survival and transition from traditional to commercial popular culture. The world witnessed significant commercialisation and modernisation of the 'drinks industry' in the eighteenth and nineteenth century: for example, between 1850 and 1875 Guinness sales increased by 600 per cent, across both domestic and export markets.[24] In Geneva, Schweppes commenced commercial production of soda water in 1783.[25]

Elizabeth Malcolm and Bradley Kadel have each explored the politics behind alcohol consumption and regulation and how resultant laws and legislative initiatives are tied to the economy and nationalism, particularly in the nineteenth century.[26] Diarmaid Ferriter further draws our attention to twentieth- and twenty-first-century problems associated with alcohol: excessive drinking was associated with child neglect, domestic violence, premature mortality, crime, poverty, psychiatric disorders and underage drinking: sources of concern for Irish governments, who at times failed to address these issues.[27]

In 2020, when pubs were at the centre of Covid-19 restrictions and the 'reopening' debate, Ferriter commented how 'there is little middle ground' when it comes to the pub trade in Ireland; it has been a 'cause for celebration and anguish' or 'indulgence and curse' as the title of his book, *Nation of Extremes*, suggests.[28] It is possible to establish an entire legal history related to alcohol consumption and the pub, and licensing is a lucrative branch of the law, but this volume looks at many different makers of the pub, notwithstanding the productive importance of the regulatory framework. By drawing on diverse sources, we challenge the underpinning binaries of the law, politics and health, going beyond their 'boon / evil' or 'wet / dry' frameworks, towards a more nuanced and holistic appreciation.

State control and private companies' marketing of pubs emblemise Henri Lefebvre's 'production of space', where space is both the 'locus of production' and 'itself, product and production'.[29] These social spaces are often tied to institutional and ideological superstructures and are politically instrumental in that they can facilitate the control of society. At the same time, 'space as products' serves various economic interests in that one can buy and sell place, as demonstrated by the 'Guinness Irish Pub Concept' in the 1990s, in which designers of the Irish Pub Company 'invented' diverse pub styles for export. This allows entrepreneurs and investors anywhere in the world to replicate them for business purposes.[30] In his article on Irish-themed bars, Mark McGovern argues that the pub is an example of cultural commodification and consumption of an imagined ethnic identity drawn from a pool of pre-existent signs and symbols.[31] This symbolic palette is generous, for the Irish pub is more than just a place of alcohol consumption; it is a community hub, a dancehall, a stage for performers, a concert hall for musicians, a gallery for artists,[32] a negotiating table for business people, and more.

The concept of 'invention' emphasises active human engagement and creation in the making of the pub. This volume sets out to investigate this construction rather than simply chronicling the inevitable changes that have occurred over the centuries. We challenge the notion of the 'traditional' Irish pub as fixed in time, and seek instead to explore its dynamism and conflict, the tension between the frozenness of the pub and its various movements, across and beyond the island of Ireland. All chapters engage with questions of authenticity, community, (Irish) identity, gender, sexuality and ethnicity, and how language and practice shape our ideas and experiences of the pub.

Re-inventing the Irish pub

If institutions – state and companies – show a 'top-down' approach in framing our understanding and experience of the pub, there have equally been forces that resist certain fixities surrounding the pub. The most standout example is gender. Pubs were regarded as a second home for many men and, before the 1960s, were almost exclusively for a male clientele. Some pubs had small rooms called 'snugs' or upscale 'lounges' for female customers, but most premises did not allow women to consume alcohol.[33] Much of this volume seeks to redress this imbalance; by exploring the role of female publicans, proprietors, bar-workers and consumers, and by incorporating female voices and writers, the book re-invents the Irish pub as a place of female agency and diversity.

The concept of reproduction follows Michel de Certeau's theories on everyday 'tactics'. Opposing the 'disciplinary' procedures and structures imposed by authorities, inhabitants 'make-do' with what is available, recreating the space according to their own needs and desires.[34] Pubs have fostered a community, be it political (trade unions, young men's societies and conspirators held meetings or used them as their headquarters), artistic and musical (writers, musicians and artists would frequent pubs to discuss their work or gather for readings and performances) or regional (many customers were often 'locals' and 'regulars' to their pubs). The everyday practice of frequenting the pub, gathering and talking has much greater significance than its surface triviality. An experiential account from a practising psychologist and psychotherapist included in this volume further testifies to the pub's positive function: it enables talking, emotional support and healing.

The pub exemplifies one of the ways that identities are contested and reformulated. To borrow Tim Edensor's words, the pub is a place where 'national landscape ideologies and popular sites of assembly and activity can be merged'.[35] Identity is continually reproduced, transgressed and negotiated in the everyday realm. In *Banal Nationalism* (1995), Michael Billig explores the routine and mundane reproduction of national identity as against the historical scholarship that has overemphasised extreme and overt displays of nationalism such as war.[36] This idea speaks to a host of other types of 'traditions' grounded in popular and vernacular cultural forms and practices. Thus, the ethnographic studies by our contributors in this volume are significant: their works document and inscribe these neglected 'traditions' often erased from the grand narratives of Ireland's history. For example, gay social life in the 1960s constitutes an alternative narrative to that of Éamon de Valera's Ireland or T.K. Whitaker's economic expansion. Private experiences of gay life around pubs were instrumental in the formation of public groups like the Irish Gay Rights Movement in the 1970s. Pubs are reservoirs of storytelling and oral history. Tracing stories through these pubs helps us forge a new kind of history, one that is inclusive and truer to people's lived experiences.

Another significance of this book's re-invention is the inclusion of diasporic experiences and migration. Irish pubs have long served diasporic communities in Britain, the United States, Canada, Australia, New Zealand and elsewhere. These movements across the globe with pubs as signposts demonstrate that pubs are not fixed entities, but that they travel and get 'translated' into different cultures. Contributors engage with these diasporic dialogues and movements that have solidified and challenged aspects of pub identity. The once exported pubs become re-imported into Ireland, as evident in the pubs in Dublin's Temple Bar. Hybridity rather than authenticity becomes a key factor in understanding pubs in this global era: these are places that can show through symbolic display that they are just 'Irish enough'.[37]

These extraterritorial or hybrid pubs raise an important question about Irish pubs in Northern Ireland. Belfast's most celebrated pub, the Crown Liquor Saloon, may owe more to English than Irish heritage. Pubs in Northern Ireland operate in a particular context, as they have inevitably reflected ongoing sectarian and political conflict; this erupted into more overt violence during the Troubles of the twentieth century. Although there are pubs that are marketed to tourists, pubs serving locals are almost inevitably divided into Catholic/nationalist or Protestant/unionist bars and thus became potential targets. Between 1969 and 1997, during the Troubles, the most atrocious bombing took place in a private establishment known as McGurk's bar. The

Gifts

KINGSTONS

THE IRISH TIMES

DUBLIN, MONDAY, DECEMBER 6, 1971

EMPIRE LOYALISTS CLAIM PUB BLAST

15 killed, 13 injured in worst ever explosion in Belfast

BOY (8) LONE WITNESS TO MAN PLANTING BOMB

Faulkner says insane fanatics responsible

NAMES OF VICTIMS

Ceasefire on India blocked by Russia

Figure 1.5 The McGurk's bar bombing, featured in *The Irish Times*. It was the deadliest attack in Belfast during the Troubles in Northern Ireland. *The Irish Times*, 6 December 1971.

attack took place on 4 December 1971, killing fifteen civilians and injuring seventeen, and was the highest death toll from a single incident in Belfast.[38] McGurk's bar was frequented by Catholics, and the bombing was carried out by the Ulster Volunteer Force, an Ulster loyalist paramilitary group. Whether the Red Lion pub bombing (perpetrated by the Provisional IRA) or Kelly's bar, pubs were subjected to bombing attacks from all sides. Even in these post-Good Friday Agreement days, tension and violence persist. It is within this political climate in Northern Ireland as well as the southern perception of the Troubles that any serious discussion of the pub should take place.

The Irish pub is an intersection of gendered, classed, sectarian and migrant space. It is crucial then that literature not only reflects but re-imagines the space that goes beyond the binaries of identities and tribal conflicts. In this book, literary scholars examine representations of pubs in Irish writing and performance, not only as social history, but also as capturing an artistic truth that expands our boundaries of reality, experience and consciousness. The texts, films and plays that are highlighted show pubs as a place of emotional profundity, exposing problems of depression, loneliness, alienation, addiction and violence, while pointing towards the possibility of reconciliation, regeneration and hope. Many Irish writers have engaged with the Irish

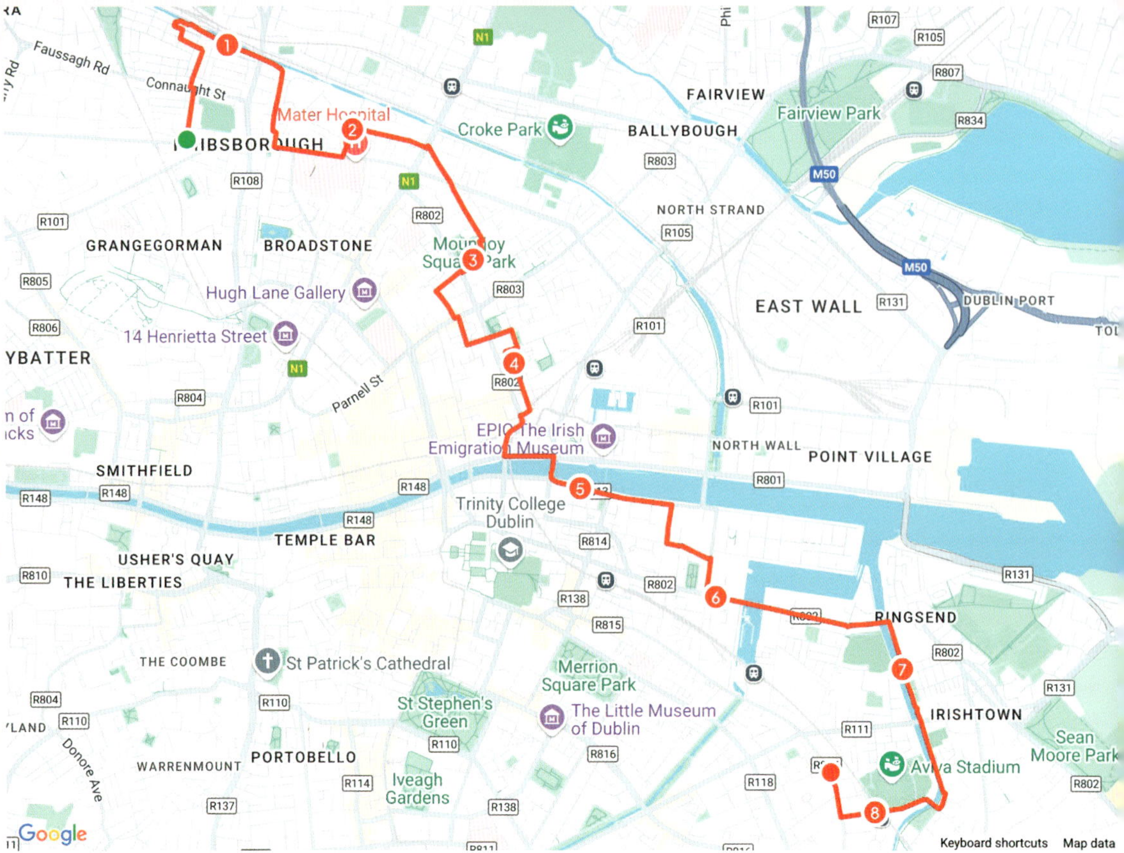

Figure 1.6 'How to Cross Dublin without Passing a Pub' on 'Map My Run' platform. Route created by Barry Sheehan.[39]

pub as the milieu for art and as itself literary and performative: we could list James Joyce, J.M. Synge, John McGahern, Paula Meehan, Tom Murphy, Conor McPherson, Roddy Doyle, Kevin Barry, Claire Keegan, Pat Murphy, Owen McCafferty, Nell McCafferty and Michael Magee. This would by no means include all those who have used the pub as setting, symbol or subject. Ordinary pub talk – with its storytelling, banter, dialogue and silences – constitutes a dramatic form for playwrights and a rich literary source for fiction writers. The pub occupies much of Irish literary life and imagination; Leopold Bloom in Joyce's *Ulysses* muses on the fact that you couldn't cross Dublin without passing a pub (a challenge subsequently taken up by computer programmers and artists), while Brendan Behan famously declared himself a 'drinker with a writing problem'. Irish writing's inextricable connection to the pub, whether in shaping the writer's life or their writing, is the basis for the re-invention of the pub.

Re-invention requires imagination; the pub fosters imagination and is itself re-imaginable through language and stories. If Brendan Behan has contributed to solidifying a stereotypical 'staged, drunk Irishman', other writers explored in this volume show other aspects of the pub, as a space of contestation and negotiation. In many ways, this volume itself is an act of re-imagination and further inventions. Rather than seeking or reproducing an imagined 'essence' of the Irish pub, we celebrate its diversity and its many manifestations and expressions. We trace patterns of historical continuity while exploring spatial variations.

If the pub is inextricably linked to the written tradition, it is also the case that Irish traditional music has strong associations with the institution. The dark silent interior of the pub was the perfect environment for acoustic music-making; many pubs (such as the Cobblestone) have welcomed musicians for organised and impromptu gatherings, which later gained economic value as they attracted drinks-purchasing listeners. Pub owners paid musicians, known as 'anchor' players, while also making themselves available to unpaid participants through 'sessions'. This practice was a development in the wake of the 1950s, when traditional music was re-popularised with the music revival.[40] Thus, the 'music pub' was invented as another product in the market to compete against other recreational spaces and media. At the same time, the value of the pub is not limited to contributing to the Irish economy; it has facilitated

Figure 1.7 Music session, Cobblestone pub. Photo by and courtesy of DublinByPub.

the cultural revival and passing down of tradition, as an active practice rather than as recordings in archives or a museum piece existing only in people's memory. The shared space of the pub as a musical venue has – like the idea of 'live music' – kept trad music (and, of course, other musical forms from rock to jazz) very much alive to this day.

Overview of the book

In Part I, 'Historical and Social Scientific Perspectives', Elizabeth Malcolm notes that contrary to the idea of a 'traditional' pub, retail drink outlets were always in a state of flux (Chapter 2). Examining the various liquor licensing laws in the 1630s, 1660s, 1790s and 1830s, Malcolm argues that it was the state's active control of the drink shops that led to this invention of the pub. A further proof of invention is the neglected roles of female publicans, who are rarely mentioned in history books or pub guidebooks; Malcolm excavates their stories from the late medieval periods and onwards, challenging the notion of the all-male (male-produced) pubs.

Tom Spalding and Gwen Scarbrough combine studies in interior design and anthropology to analyse the space and discourse surrounding women in pubs, which reflect 'segregation' and women's perceived roles in society (Chapter 3). In their focus on women's roles as proprietors, bar workers and consumers, Spalding and Scarbrough illuminate how women were controlled and contained, but equally how they took active roles within and beyond the patriarchal structures. Perry Share walks us through the current anthropological and sociological perspectives surrounding the pub (Chapter 4). From the under-explored concept of 'craic' to the power dynamics observed in the pub, Share sketches out the broader societal changes that the pubs reflect.

Sam McGrath provides us with an alternative oft-neglected history: the central role of certain pubs and bars in the gay social scene in Dublin over a fifty-year period from the founding of the Irish Free State in 1923 until the formation of the first Irish proto-gay rights group in 1973 (Chapter 5). These private stories themselves constitute a public history, one that deserves serious scholarly attention.

Trish Murphy sees the advantageous possibilities of the pub, as a space of therapy (Chapter 6). Murphy argues that the pub allowed a type of 'confessional', and in the process of being heard, without the fear of losing face, absolution was granted. It is not surprising then that, growing up in a pub, her professional skill as a psychotherapist was honed in this space.

Part II, 'Irish Pubs Abroad: Exporting and translating Ireland', further expands the boundaries of a place-bound Irish pub. The Irish pub is a global phenomenon, whether as an exportable commodity or a refuge for millions of the Irish diaspora across the globe. Tracey Dalton deconstructs the strategies employed by the 'Guinness Irish Pub Concept': the typologies, designs and methodologies developed by McNally Design/Irish Pub Company and Guinness (Chapter 7). Rather than a critique from the outside, Dalton, as an insider, presents us with the creativity and effort of those involved in the successful making of the Irish pub, which have helped build the reputation it has today.

Eli Davies takes us from the Irish pubs of the London diaspora to Belfast, where 'Irish' pubs are tinged with echoes of violence (Chapter 8). Sectarian conflict becomes a new axis of the pub's politics. Davies looks at cultural representations of the Irish pub in the North, including the 1981 film *Maeve* by Pat Murphy, writings by journalist Nell McCafferty, and short stories by Edna O'Brien. These different cultural sources recalibrate our understanding of pubs as a space of politics, outside and between the lines of laws and regulations.

Brenda Murphy takes several case studies of diasporic pubs (Irish pubs located outside of Ireland) to assess their function in identity shaping (Chapter 9). The pub offers support and a sense of belonging for the Irish community abroad which, at times, can be to the exclusion of others. This exclusion can be read along the lines of gender – like Spalding and Scarbrough – but crucially, for this chapter, along race. Murphy points to the importance of bearing in mind the multiple communities and multi-ethnic backgrounds when considering the Irish pub, which is always necessarily hybrid.

Michael Cronin explores how the pub travels around the world and how it 'translates' (both physically and symbolically) into the local spaces (Chapter 10). The target culture's different frames of meaning change the way the Irish pub is understood and consumed in these places. In this view, pubs exist in an eco-system; the pub-species adapt and transform depending on the environment and structures they are in.

The chapters in Part III, 'Literary, Musical and Artistic Perspectives', investigate the significance of literature, music and performance, the 'artistic' perspectives in comprehending the Irish pub. Nicholas Grene analyses short stories set in pubs by

James Joyce, John McGahern, Claire Keegan and Kevin Barry, which portray the pub-goers' desperation, frustration and impotence, and the different ways in which language expresses or fails to express what they feel (Chapter 11). The stories illustrate the varying psychological and emotional dynamics within the pub. Contrary to the optimism and fulfilment we saw in therapeutic pubs, in the stories the pub is a place of unresolved and inexpressible feelings.

James Little takes a feminist approach in literary criticism, providing us with close readings of Paula Meehan's poetry (Chapter 12). From Meehan's declaration of herself as a public poet, Little looks at how her poetry produces a 'counter-public sphere', reconfiguring the quintessential Irish public sphere – the pub – into a place where we hear the voices of traditionally marginalised children and women. In the process, Meehan's poems expose the many social ('public') issues in Ireland, including those of gender violence and addiction. Literary texts themselves can be a form of performance and intervention.

In Chapter 13, Moonyoung Hong explores dramatic representations and theatrical performances set in pubs. From J.M. Synge's *The Playboy of the Western World* (1907) – set in a shebeen in the west – to recent tours of Roddy Doyle's *Two Pints* across all pubs in Ireland (2017) and later on the Abbey stage in 2018, the chapter outlines a hundred years of pub drama history, and why pubs have become a popular setting for writers and theatre-practitioners. The pub itself is a performative space full of rich dialogue and storytelling; Irish playwrights have appropriated the pub, channelling the pub language into dramatic form, which became a unique trademark of Irish theatre.

Fintan Vallely gives us an account of how Irish traditional music has flourished in and been interconnected with the Irish pub (Chapter 14). As a practising musician, Vallely explains the appeal of the tiny pub, and why it was a perfect environment for performance. As well as fostering a musical community and renaissance, trad music contributed to the Irish economy, became commodified and was sold alongside the 'pub package'. Katie Young's chapter shows the changing makeup and diverse culture of these musicians and pub music. Black-and-Irish and Afrodiasporic musicians have turned the pubs into significant hubs for musical interactions and collaborations (Chapter 15). Focusing on musicians and musical collectives in Cork and Galway and their experiences in the pub, Young examines the different musical styles and influences as well as the political dimension of musical activism.

The contributors in Part IV, 'The Future of the Irish Pub', evaluate the current state of the pub following the Covid-19 pandemic, with a speculative look to the future. Author of *Have Ye No Homes To Go To? The history of the Irish pub* (2016), Kevin Martin explores the idea of a 'perfect pub' today. Starting from George Orwell and Ray Oldenburg's definitions, Martin revisits what makes a pub a pub, particularly an Irish pub, which is not necessarily defined by its materiality alone (Chapter 16). Martin discusses the intangible aspects – 'conviviality', 'authenticity', 'synergy' and other factors that attract people to visit a pub.

James McCauley has conducted research that focuses on contemporary rural publicans and draws on this to discuss the challenges that face rural pubs and their communities (Chapter 17). Brian Murphy and Patricia Medcalf present us with some of the ways that pubs are adapting to the rapidly changing circumstances (Chapter 18). With different advertisement regulations, pubs are finding alternative and inventive ways of promoting, communicating and interacting with their customers. Finally, John O'Brien revisits the pub as an ultimate symbol of collective identity, as exposed during Covid-19, and what it means to us as a community as we move further from the experience of a global pandemic (Chapter 19).

In the conclusion to the book (Chapter 20), we return to the spatial insights of Doreen Massey. We argue that the historical trajectory of the pub, from its beginnings in houses designed to serve both communities and travellers, to its contemporary and future role within the globalising industries of tourism, marketing and entertainment, can be understood at multiple spatial levels – from the global to the personal. We apply this analysis to current trends in the Irish pub experience, and how these are (or may not be) reflected in cultural representations. We argue that this volume ultimately generates as many questions as it answers – proving there is fertile ground for further pub research.

It might be argued that in some ways the pub acts as a microcosm of Irish life, reflective of both its conformity and diversity. In historiographical and literary terms, the pub has been strongly identified as a masculine stronghold, even a refuge, yet this is challenged by accounts of female agency and participation on both sides of the bar. Women have been, and continue to be, brewers, pub owners, barpersons, mixologists and pub designers, as well as customers and critical analysts. The increasing cultural diversity in Irish society is beginning to be reflected in pub culture with, for example, several central European and Brazilian-associated establishments emerging in larger urban centres, as well as a broad variety of LGBTQIA+ friendly pubs. Less positively, the Traveller community continues to experience discrimination in many pub settings, reflecting the broader societal picture.

If the pub is a microcosm, it contains markers of other societal structures and trends. It can be the venue for supportive or oppressive behaviour, for rich or impoverished communication, for the celebration or the undermining of identities. It is a site of unbridled commercialism, a venue for the display of corporate brands from sport to fashion to alcohol, but also a location for the enactment of non-monetised friendships, camaraderie and political expression. It is a rich cultural repository at the local and global levels and a place for potential innovation and exploration.

So, we encompass the Irish pub as a community resource, a literary phenomenon and a social driver, as well as a commodity in the global market. The book emphasises the intersectionality of history, sociology, architecture, politics, literature, psychology, music and arts, what these dialogues can offer, and how they have shaped our experience of space and place in our everyday life in the twenty-first century. The book uncovers some of the under-examined history of Ireland – gender and space, female writers and literary pubs, gay social life in the early twentieth century, stories of migration and multiculturalism, depression and alienation, the politics of music, social media and pubs – as a form of intervention, to re-invent the Irish pub as a more inclusive and creative space for what will, we hope, be a long and interesting future.

Part 1

Historical and Social Scientific Perspectives

Chapter 2

From Drink Shops to 'Traditional' Irish Pubs: Laws, Services and Invisible Women, c. 1400–1950

Elizabeth Malcolm

Introduction: a multitude of drink shops

It is commonplace these days to lament the decline of the Irish public house as if this space had existed largely unchanged across the centuries.[1] Yet shops retailing alcoholic drinks have taken many different forms in the past, the so-called 'traditional pub' being a relatively recent invention.[2] Reflecting their changing and often contested character, drink shops have operated under many names. These include taverns, inns, ale- or beer-houses, tippling houses, dram shops, tunable houses, tap-rooms, vintners, coffee houses, shebeens, spirit-grocer shops, refreshment rooms, drinking booths, gin palaces, public or lounge bars, and hotels. Such names refer to different spaces, often selling different types of alcohol, to different sorts of people, at different times in the past. The licensed pub, as we currently know it, is not the product of a continuous tradition that has evolved seamlessly. The term 'public house' first appeared in the late seventeenth century, but what is now considered the 'traditional' Irish pub only emerged during the late nineteenth century, having taken over some – although by no means all – of the functions of these earlier liquor retailers.[3] This means that, from a historical perspective, we should be wary of using the term 'pub' in its contemporary sense much before about 1850, for the word obscures the diversity of past retail outlets. Today's pub is certainly changing. But drink shops have always been contested spaces in Ireland and have always existed in a state of flux, being re-invented constantly in response to shifting circumstances, as their multiple names attest.

Most premises retailing liquor were run by individuals or families to serve their local communities and, despite claims to the contrary, those operating and staffing these premises were in some instances women. Later in this chapter we will explore the changing services provided by drink shops and the role of women in them. First, however, it is important to realise that all the various retail establishments listed above eventually came under tight state control or else they were suppressed. From the early seventeenth century onwards, successive British governments legislated to regulate and tax every facet of the Irish retail trade. To understand how this legislation shaped the emergence of the pub as it currently operates, we need to survey some key acts passed during the 1630s, 1660s, 1790s and 1830s.

Laws: How the state controlled drink shops and invented pubs

The first Irish licensing law, entitled an 'Act for Keepers of Alehouses to be Bound by Recognizance' (10 & 11 Chas I, c. 5), was passed by parliament in 1635 at the instigation of the English lord deputy, Thomas Wentworth.[4] The act's preamble complained of the 'many mischiefs' arising from the 'excessive number of alehouses ... [erected] in woods, bogs, and other unfit places ... and kept by unknown persons'. The main 'mischiefs' identified were that ale-houses had become 'receptacles for rebels and other malefactors', as well as for 'gamesters, and ... idle, disordered, and unprofitable livers'. Furthermore, ale-houses were 'not fitted or furnished to lodge or entertain travellers in any decent manner'.[5] Ale-houses were obviously perceived as both a political and a social threat, and this act aimed to transform them into a state asset. As well as discouraging rebels and other criminals, while facilitating law-abiding travellers, Wentworth hoped to raise substantial amounts of revenue for his master, Charles I, by charging ale-house keepers a licence fee. An aspiring drink seller was therefore required in future to apply to magistrates at quarter sessions for a licence. If deemed 'fit' to sell ale and beer, then he or she had to deposit a large bond guaranteeing their good behaviour, in addition to paying an annual licence fee. Their houses, clearly identified by a sign, stake or bush, were to sell good-quality ale or beer and to provide food and accommodation for travellers. The act, though, did not contain any mechanism for policing the behaviour of licensed ale-house keepers or for suppressing unlicensed retailers.[6]

While this act marked the first attempt by the crown to impose a national licensing system on Irish ale and beer sellers – English sellers having been licensed by statute since 1552 – it was very far from being the first regulation governing the supply of alcohol in Ireland. The early Brehon laws had, for instance, contained rules around the provision of mead and ale for the purposes of hospitality and feasting, as well as instructions for dealing with drunkenness.[7] After the arrival of the English in the late twelfth century, taverns proliferated in port towns. These were usually conducted by merchants, who sold imported French wines in their houses or traded them to Gaelic lords in exchange for hides, salted meat, fish and wheat. It is no coincidence

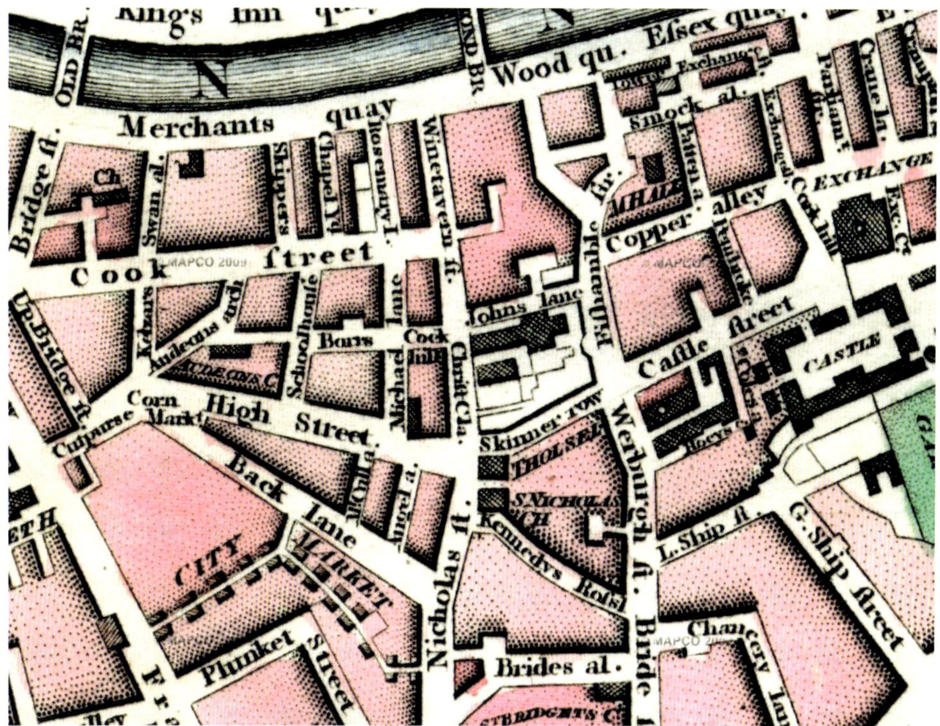

Figure 2.1 Winetavern Street on John Rocque's map of Dublin, 1756. L. Brown Maps and Charts Collection on Virtual Treasury of Ireland.

that one of medieval Dublin's most important streets, running from the cathedral down to the river and a wharf at Merchants' Quay, was called Wine or Winetavern Street.[8] Town corporations established by English royal charter were empowered to control the price, quality and amounts of ale or wine sold by ale-house or tavern keepers. Wealthy lords and monasteries employed brewers, and sometimes distillers, to provide drinks for the entertainment of their guests. But, during the late medieval period, most ale and whiskey continued to be produced on a domestic basis within families – largely by women – both for their own consumption and to help make up their rents.[9] Thus, by the early seventeenth century, many different groups had power over the supply of alcohol in Ireland. The 1635 act, however, marked the beginning of the development of an extensive body of national licensing legislation that in time would come to control all aspects of liquor retailing.

The duke of Ormond, Irish lord lieutenant during the 1660s, like his friend Wentworth before him, represented a king intent upon boosting his Irish revenues.

Consequently, in 1662, the 1635 act was repealed and replaced by an 'Act for the Improvement of His Majesty's Revenues upon the Granting of Licences for Selling Ale and Beer' (14 & 15 Chas II, c. 18). As its title suggests, this act substantially increased the cost of the annual fee for an ale-house licence. More significant, however, was another liquor licensing act passed in 1666 and entitled an 'Act for the Better Ordering of the Selling of Wines and Aqua Vitae' (17 & 18 Chas II, c. 19). Under this act, statutory licensing was extended, for the first time, from ale and beer sellers to the sellers of wine and whiskey. They too were now required to obtain a licence, although these licences were far more expensive than ale and beer licences.[10]

Whereas the 1635 act had contained no mechanism whereby retailers could be effectively policed, in 1662 customs and excise boards were established in Dublin. The revenue commissioners who headed these boards and their local agents, known as collectors and gaugers, assumed oversight of the drinks industry to ensure that commercial brewers and distillers obtained state licences, while merchants paid customs duties on wine imports.[11] The powers of the excise authorities were extended during the upheavals of Williamite Wars (1688–91) to the issuing of retail liquor licences as well, although this change was not confirmed by statute until 1737. But the revenue service, which was the largest civil employer in eighteenth-century Ireland, was renowned for its corruption and inefficiency.[12] Appointments made by the commissioners, most of whom were leading politicians, were often dictated by nepotism and patronage, with bribery being endemic.[13] Local communities frequently banded together to thwart revenue collectors, even though the latter were sometimes supported by the army. Unpopular collectors and gaugers lived in fear of assault, while anyone caught passing information to the revenue was likely to suffer the common fate of informers in Ireland: mutilation or death.[14]

Much alcohol was still made on an unlicensed domestic basis during the eighteenth century and, despite the efforts of the revenue service, the illicit trade appears to have expanded rather than contracted. Nonetheless, the taxes levied on commercial drink producers, importers and retailers became an increasingly substantial proportion of government income: by the 1780s, these taxes were producing upwards of one-third of all Irish revenue.[15] After 1750, three important developments contributed to the introduction of major new licensing laws at the end of the century. These were: a dramatic upsurge in the consumption of whiskey distilled illegally by a domestic industry based mainly in the north and west of the country; the appearance in towns of large commercial breweries like Guinness, which began production in Dublin in 1759; and the smuggling of wines and brandy from France and Spain along Irish coasts. By 1790, it was clear to Ireland's rulers that the drinks industry, although it had become an essential source of tax income, remained to a significant extent – and it appeared an increasing extent – beyond state control.[16]

The Irish authorities considered ale and beer, and wine as well, preferable drinks to whiskey. This was partly because brewing had become a prosperous and generally law-abiding industry, which enjoyed the support of many Protestant politicians, while wine was the favourite tipple of the upper classes.[17] Much illicit distilling, on the other hand, was carried on by poor Catholics in remote parts of the country, with the whiskey produced, known as poteen (Irish *poitín*), often being sold in unlicensed houses, known as shebeens (Irish *síbín*).[18] Furthermore, it was generally believed that ale and beer were nutritious and calming drinks, whereas 'ardent' spirits, like whiskey, not only damaged the physical health of their mainly lower-class consumers but could also excite their emotions to an alarmingly violent degree.[19]

Yet changes to liquor licensing in Ireland always took place within a political context – and this was certainly true of the 1790s.[20] The 1635 act, passed only six years before the 1641 rebellion, had been aimed to prevent dispossessed Irish lords and their followers gathering in ale houses to plot the overthrow of English rule and the recovery of their lands. Although the 1635 act had failed in this regard, the authorities during the 1790s had similar concerns and adopted similar tactics. They aimed to stop men getting drunk on whiskey in shebeens or small licensed shops, where, with their reason impaired and their emotions inflamed, they could be cajoled into joining agrarian secret societies, like the Defenders, or republican organisations, like the United Irishmen. Dissident groups did indeed make frequent use of drink shops for recruiting and planning purposes, sometimes with the encouragement of their proprietors. It has been estimated, for instance, that in Dublin during the 1790s around 10 per cent of United Irishmen were drink retailers. Meetings were usually held in inns and taverns, with copious amounts of alcohol being consumed, as Wolfe Tone's memoirs graphically reveal. Meanwhile, on the opposite side of the political fence, the Orange Order was established in 1795 at a beer-house operated by a founding member in Loughgall, County Armagh.[21]

The Irish parliament responded to concerns about the increasing consumption of spirits with a series of acts that aimed to reduce the number of whiskey retailers while encouraging beer drinking. The first act (31 Geo. III, c. 13), which was passed in 1791, has been described by E.B. McGuire in his history of Irish whiskey as a 'vicious attack on the poor man's "club"'. For, whereas upper-class males, like members of the exclusively Protestant parliament, had ready access to alcohol in their homes and clubs and were not exactly famous for their sobriety, the 1791 act was aimed specifically against drink retailers catering to the lower classes in both town and country. But, as well as class, considerations of politics and revenue also figured significantly in this act. Many of these small-scale sellers made a profit by supplying cheaper, illicitly distilled poteen. The act increased the costs of urban and rural retail licences substantially; aspiring licensees also now had to provide a certificate of good character from local magistrates before the excise would issue them with a licence; and all houses selling liquor had to contain at least two hearths. This latter requirement was intended to stop drink being sold in poor dwellings with only one hearth, like small rural cabins or rooms in urban working-class houses.[22]

A second liquor licensing act (32 Geo. III, c. 19), which followed in 1792, also aimed to promote beer in place of whiskey. Under its provisions, retail drink licences were only to be granted to those selling, in addition to spirits, 'good strong beer and ale' at 'reasonable prices'. Furthermore, while beer and ale could be sold at any time, spirits were not to be sold before sunrise each day or before 1 p.m. on a Sunday. However, these restrictions did not apply to coffee houses selling whiskey, presumably because they catered largely to middle- and upper-class consumers. Taverns retailing wine and inns offering accommodation were also required under the act to provide meals for their customers. Other acts (36 Geo. III, c. 2; 37 Geo. III, c. 45), passed during 1795–7, continued government efforts to foster the consumption of beer by removing taxes on beer production, while substantially increasing taxes on malt, which was used in distilling as well as brewing.[23]

Some of this legislation was deeply unpopular at the time: there were riots in Dublin in 1791 when the first bill aimed to suppress small whiskey shops was introduced into parliament. In the longer term, the acts were to prove counter-productive, for, rather than turning to beer as parliament had hoped, Irish drinkers shifted in ever growing numbers to illicitly distilled whiskey. Consequently, during the early nineteenth century, unlicensed shebeens selling illegal poteen proliferated.[24]

The legislation of the 1790s also saw the creation of what would later come to be known as an 'off-licence'. Grocer shops, licensed to sell imported products that included tea, coffee, sugar and tobacco, had been permitted to sell spirits without a liquor licence, but only for consumption off the premises. However, growing concern that grocers were turning a blind eye to illegal drinking in their shops led to the introduction of the spirit-grocer licence. This licence, which lasted until it was merged with other off-licences in 1910, was regulated by the 1791 and 1792 acts. A later 1825 act (6 Geo. IV, c. 81) consolidated these regulations, specifying that grocers could sell no more than two quarts of spirits[25] at any one time to a customer for consumption off the premises. But publicans, resenting the competition of spirit grocers, claimed that consumption on the premises was common, and after 1850 they took a leading role in a campaign to abolish the spirit-grocer licence. Grocers were alleged to have back rooms in their shops where drinkers – many of them women – secretly congregated.[26] The publicans' campaign partially succeeded when, under a major new licensing act passed in 1872 (35 & 36 Vict., c. 94), spirit grocers were required to secure a magistrates' good-character certificate before applying to the excise for a licence.[27]

Despite legislative attempts during the 1790s to curb whiskey consumption, in the decades before the Famine illicit distilling continued to thrive in remote rural areas.[28] Legislative changes in 1823 (4 Geo. IV, c. 94) gave a fillip to licensed distilling, which was centred on Dublin and Cork. Nevertheless, poteen remained cheaper and often of better quality than 'parliament' whiskey, and many drinkers naturally preferred it. An 1823 inquiry estimated that perhaps up to 60 per cent of the whiskey being consumed in Ireland was produced illegally. Much of this was sold in shebeens, but licensed drink retailers also often stocked poteen. Although they were forbidden to sell cheap liquor that had not paid excise duty, they had to compete with shebeens if their businesses were to survive, and many revenue men were willing to turn a blind eye to illegal sales after pocketing a bribe.[29] Beer drinking was more common in towns during the eighteenth century and continued so through the early nineteenth century. But, following the Famine, Guinness porter began its successful penetration of rural Ireland, which was where most of the population still lived, thereby offering substantial competition to whiskey, whether distilled illicitly or not.[30]

After 1800, from the state's point of view, the key to curbing the illegal production and sale of whiskey in Ireland became effective policing. Thus, stamping out the large illegal drink industry was a priority of the first national police forces. Armed and uniformed parties of revenue police were deployed from 1818 by the excise commissioners, specifically tasked with suppressing illicit distilling.[31] The paramilitary

Irish Constabulary, established in 1822, was quickly given dramatically increased powers to control drink shops and, in 1854, it took over the policing of illicit distilling as well.[32] Retail liquor licensing remained highly political, though. Licensing acts passed between the 1830s and 1860s were frequently directed against agrarian secret societies and dissident political groups that the authorities were convinced continued to use pubs as essential meeting and recruiting venues. This raft of new legislation included Perrin's Act (3 & 4 Wm IV, c. 68), passed in 1833, which restricted opening hours to between 7 a.m. and 11 p.m. The act also allowed magistrates to close drink shops in the event of a riot and constables to enter licensed premises during closing hours to investigate illegal drinking. In 1839 (2 & 3 Vict., c. 79), the police were empowered, having obtained a warrant from magistrates, to search any house whatsoever they suspected of being a shebeen. In 1836 (6 & 7 Wm IV, c. 38), it became illegal for retailers to display political emblems or to allow banned organisations to meet in their houses. To apply for or renew a liquor licence under this act, publicans now had to obtain a certificate of good character from the local police, in addition to the magistrates' certificate required since 1791. An 1854 act (17 & 18 Vict., c. 89) extended these powers when it permitted police inspectors to object to any individual being licensed to sell drink. This in effect handed police forces a veto power over licence applications.[33]

Some of these acts intended to curb licensed houses and to suppress unlicensed ones also contained provisions aimed at restricting the sale of alcohol out-of-doors at large gatherings, such as fairs, sports meetings and patterns, where booths or tents were usually erected to supply visitors with food and drink. By the 1836 licensing act (6 & 7 Wm IV, c. 38), drink sellers were ordered to close their booths between sunset and sunrise. Limiting drinking to daylight hours made it much easier for the police to control these events, and in some cases suppress them altogether. Under an 1862 act (25 Vict., c. 22), publicans were forced to take out what was called an 'occasional' licence to trade at fairs or horse races, with the hours fixed at between sunrise and one hour after sunset. However, if publicans were providing drink at large public dinners or balls, magistrates could extend their trading hours into the night (26 & 27 Vict., c. 33). Here, again, a class bias is apparent, with the licensing laws falling more onerously on working-class drinkers frequenting popular festivals than on the middle or upper classes attending formal banquets and balls.[34]

From the early seventeenth century onwards, first state licensing and then state policing increasingly determined who could sell liquor in Ireland, what could be sold, and where and when it could be sold. Between 1635 and 2000, it has been estimated that in total some 200 Irish liquor laws were passed. By the late nineteenth century, there were around fifteen distinctive liquor licences, with at least another nine being added during the twentieth century.[35] All this legislation reflected the fact that, for the state, while Irish drink shops provided a vital source of revenue, they were also perceived as a political and moral threat. Yet, for their customers, they had become an essential economic, social and cultural asset.

Services: drink shops, families and communities

Almost as numerous and complex as the liquor licensing laws were the functions that liquor retailers served in Ireland. By the late nineteenth century, pubs in England were largely tied houses. This meant that they were often purpose-built and were owned by large breweries, with their publicans being tenants obliged to sell the landlords' beers and vacate the premises when their leases expired. Irish pubs were different. Few were tied, except in Cork city where some breweries owned pubs.[36] In Ireland's other major cities, although elaborate, purpose-built premises known as

Figure 2.2 The Irish House (now demolished) in Wood Quay, Dublin, 1870. Courtesy of Paul Clerkin on archiseek.com.

'gin palaces' appeared after 1850, tied houses were largely unknown.[37] In rural areas and small towns, most pubs, like beer-houses and shebeens, were private homes, with one room converted into a bar.[38] Thus, whereas English pubs might be called 'The Crown', 'Queen's Head' or 'Prince of Wales', loudly proclaiming their brewery owners' loyalty and respectability, Irish pubs were usually known by the names of their licensees.[39]

Doherty's bar in Ardara, County Donegal, for example, was opened by Patrick Doherty in 1855 and was still being run by his descendants in 2002. Mone's in Keady, County Armagh, also dating to the 1850s and continuing under Mone family management into the twenty-first century, served at one time as a spirit-grocer shop and, simultaneously, as an undertaker's business. Often names were changed when a new licensee took over, although in many instances this did not necessarily mark a change in family ownership. In 1833, John O'Neill converted part of his house in Glasnevin, beside Dublin's newly opened cemetery, into a drink shop. But he soon

Figure 2.3 Exterior of John Kavanagh, Gravediggers pub in Glasnevin, Dublin. Photo by and courtesy of Niall Brady from discoverireland.ie.

transferred the business to his son-in-law, John Kavanagh, whose descendants continue to trade under that name, although the pub is also popularly known as 'The Gravediggers' (Fig. 2.3). Bohan's bar in Feakle, County Clare was started during the 1890s by Michael and Anne Fitzpatrick as a pub, grocery shop and tailoring business. Their daughter, Bridget, took over in 1927. But, because her husband Michael Bohan, as a policeman, was barred from holding a liquor licence, she continued to run the pub until her death in 1980, after which her son replaced her.[40]

As the above examples demonstrate, in many instances drink retailers did far more than just sell alcohol to customers for consumption in their shops. A variety of businesses were conducted on their premises and, furthermore, some of these retailers were women. In addition to spirit-grocers, large numbers of publicans in cities and towns took out grocers' licences. They recognised that supplying groceries, mainly to women, as well as alcohol, mainly to men, expanded their customer base and thus augmented their profits. Pubs in small towns sold produce supplied by local farmers, such as milk, eggs, butter and potatoes, in addition to tea, sugar and tobacco. Whereas male publicans usually worked behind the bar, their wives or daughters, as well as helping them there, also tended the grocery counter, which might be in the same room as the bar, with only a partition separating the two.[41] The grocery pub was for over a century an important and distinctive feature of the Irish retail liquor trade, but one now largely vanished, having been put out of business by the spread of supermarkets from the 1960s.[42]

Drink retailers served many other functions across the centuries, for diversification was not just profitable, in many cases it was both economically essential and legally required. During the eighteenth century, for instance, licensees were liable to have troops billeted in their houses; weddings could be celebrated on licensed premises until banned in 1753; accounts survive from the 1730s of Dublin taverns housing defendants awaiting trial; inns or hotels accommodated judges and barristers during the county assizes, as well as farmers on market days; and between 1846 and 1962, coroners' inquests could be conducted in pubs.[43] Studies of small towns in the late eighteenth century have shown that many drink retailers were crucial to the local economy because of their multiple functions: in addition to selling ale, beer or whiskey, they worked as maltsters, brewers, grocers and drapers.[44]

From the 1840s onwards, pubs often had post offices attached, which were usually managed by the women in the publican's family. To supplement their incomes, male publicans sometimes worked part-time during the late nineteenth century as farmers, blacksmiths, carpenters, tailors, undertakers or labourers. Although since 1735 drink retailers were barred from supplying drink on credit, after the Famine, publicans became important sources of credit and loans for small farmers. If a regular customer died, the publican might provide drink for the wake, while those who were undertakers would organise funerals. Farmers selling their produce at markets sealed deals over a pint in one of the many pubs that usually lined market squares. Drink sellers were also at the centre of much popular culture and recreation. They provided liquor at communal and family gatherings, like patterns, fairs, weddings and wakes, and they also promoted a variety of sports, from horse racing to cockfights and bull-baiting during the eighteenth century, to boxing and hurling matches during the nineteenth.[45]

Finally, some drink retailers, because of their important economic and social roles, became involved in local politics. Their houses might be used as headquarters by election candidates who plied potential voters with drink. During the eighteenth century, vintners and innkeepers served in civic roles in their towns; by the late nineteenth century, significant numbers of publicans were being elected to urban councils.[46] As one historian of the nineteenth-century retail drink trade has argued, pubs and their licensees 'built and disseminated networks of social power and political influence' throughout Ireland. An earlier historian had gone further, comparing the power of the publican in post-Famine rural Ireland to that of the parish priest.[47]

Drink shops primarily served the varied needs of their local communities, yet the success of many depended upon improvements in transportation. The number of long-distance travellers, requiring food, drink and accommodation on their journeys, increased substantially from 1700 onwards.[48] During the eighteenth century, the construction of turnpike roads and canals facilitated travel, giving rise to coaching inns in many towns and canal hotels along waterways; in the nineteenth century, the spread of railways saw the appearance of railway hotels near stations, as well as refreshment rooms selling alcohol on station platforms; and in the early and mid-twentieth century, pubs and hotels on major roads benefited from the patronage of the steadily growing numbers of motorists, travelling for business or pleasure. Moreover, between 1872 and 1953, so-called 'bona fide travellers', having covered at least three miles on a particular day, could expect to be able to drink on licensed premises at night or on a Sunday, outside legal trading hours.[49]

State licensing of drink retailers was, as we have seen, motivated in part during both the 1630s and the 1790s by fears that intending rebels were recruiting and plotting in ale-houses and whiskey shops. These fears continued through the nineteenth century and into the early twentieth century – and nor were they groundless. James S. Donnelly Jr, a leading historian of agrarian secret societies, commented that '[f]or as long as there had been Whiteboys in Ireland [that is, since the 1760s], the public house had been the most usual site for planning strategy and tactics'. In a study of the Rockite outbreak in Munster during the early 1820s, Donnelly listed a series of murders and assaults planned in drink shops by the followers of Captain Rock.[50] During the 1860s, Fenians also made extensive use of pubs in their recruiting, as the memoirs of one of their leading Dublin recruiters reveal. Meetings, according to John Devoy, were held especially in 'singing public houses', because, in these, 'casual visitors attracted no attention'.[51] Dublin pubs continued to harbour Fenians and also dissident Fenians during the 1880s. The notorious murders of the Irish chief secretary and under-secretary in the Phoenix Park in May 1882 were planned in several of the city's pubs. One was Wrenn's, opposite the gates of Dublin Castle, from where the assassins were able to monitor the comings and goings of British officials.[52]

Invisible women: the myth of the 'traditional' male pub

Many accounts of the 'traditional' Irish pub have represented it as an exclusively male space. Books about pubs have generally been written by men, and they have shown a marked tendency to ignore women. If women are mentioned, they are likely to appear as 'other': that is, in unflattering guises as either humourless critics of pubs or, if patrons, as prostitutes and drunkards.[53] Such writers have been far too quick, however, to accept that any woman frequenting a drink retailer's establishment was necessarily seen as an outsider or as morally compromised. There is a significant, but as yet little-known, story to be told about the history of women's involvement in the making, selling and consumption of alcohol in Ireland.

After the Famine, women's lives became more restricted as female paid employment opportunities contracted sharply. The increasingly powerful Catholic Church insisted that a woman's place was in the home, devoting herself wholly to the care of her family. And, while the church largely tolerated heavy male drinking, it demonised female drinkers.[54] As a result, the 'traditional' pubs of the century between the 1850s and the 1950s were widely perceived as male spaces, facilitating what has been termed 'homosocial exchange'.[55] In practice, though, few pubs excluded women entirely, whether as customers or staff. However, the belief that pubs have always been sanctuaries of masculinity has probably discouraged serious investigation of the role that women played in the Irish retail trade. In other countries, including major Irish diaspora countries, studies have shown significant involvement by women, including Irish immigrant women, in the running and staffing of pubs during the nineteenth and twentieth centuries.[56] But, in the absence of substantial research on Ireland, only a brief sketch of the history of women's roles can be offered here.[57]

In 1997, the sociologist Tanya Cassidy wrote that '[v]isions of drinking in Ireland which ignore women give not only an incomplete picture, but an inaccurate one'.[58] Cassidy was referring only to female drink consumers, yet the same could be said of producers and retailers as well. During the medieval period, as mentioned earlier, town merchants began selling casks of imported wine from cellars in their houses. These cellars gave rise to taverns, run by merchant-vintners and their wives – known as 'taverners' – which offered wine and food for consumption on the premises. But, during this period, women were probably best known for their skill in brewing ale. They were 'brewsters' or, as Dublin Corporation records spelt the word in 1470, 'brewesteres'. However, during the sixteenth and seventeenth centuries, as men became increasingly involved in brewing beer commercially, the male form of the word, 'brewer', came to dominate, covering both women and men. Brewing ale and baking bread were domestic tasks undertaken by women for their households, but in medieval towns some women, known as 'alewives', also became involved in selling ale.[59] Female engagement in domestic and commercial brewing, as well as retailing, continued for centuries.[60] In 1610, looking back on his years living in Dublin during the late sixteenth century and referring to the Winetavern Street area, the English soldier Barnabe Rich remarked that 'every householder's wife is a brewer'. As well as brewers, many of these women were also 'tavern keepers', even if their ale was, in Rich's opinion, 'hogwash'.[61] The English often criticised Irish ale and beer, probably because oats were used extensively in brewing, whereas in England barley was the primary ingredient.[62]

Dublin women continued to be prominent in the production and sale of drink through the seventeenth century, while in Cork women brewers were still active during the 1740s.[63] Late seventeenth-century wills show women engaged in commercial brewing. In 1686, for instance, a Cork woman was bequeathed brewing equipment by her father. When her brother, also a brewer, died about 1691, his wife, who was already working alongside him, took sole charge of the business.[64] Early eighteenth-century verse testifies not only to women's work as brewers, but as domestic distillers also. A poem from the 1740s praises the 'good Housewives' in prosperous Catholic farming families for teaching their daughters '[t]o brew and bake, spin and card'. But such women also 'shew'd the utmost skill' in distilling 'Good Iskebaha': that is, whiskey.[65]

Recipe books compiled by Irish women from the late seventeenth into the early nineteenth century frequently contain instructions on how to make sweet wines, liqueurs, mead and ale, while some big houses had special 'still rooms' where female servants made spirits.[66] Women also occasionally distilled spirits on a commercial basis.[67] The eighteenth-century records of the excise commissioners show that women not only made a great deal of alcohol, but they also sold it, ale especially.[68] Many were fined or even imprisoned for failing to pay state licence fees.[69] It is hardly surprising then to find that women were to the fore in some of the frequent violent clashes that occurred between local communities and revenue men.[70] In time, however, the growing popularity of hopped beer and the appearance during the late eighteenth century of large urban breweries owned and operated by men eventually saw the disappearance of the brewster and the alewife.[71] Yet women continued to operate and staff other types of drink shop into the twentieth century.

A number of eighteenth- and nineteenth-century paintings of the interiors of Irish inns, pubs and shebeens show women customers drinking and dancing, or women employees selling and serving alcohol.[72] In a study of the nineteenth-century Irish retail trade, Bradley Kadel noted that women were popularly associated with shebeens, while many beer-house keepers appear to have been women as well.[73] Illustrations representing shebeens certainly often portray their proprietors as female, as does Irish literature. For instance, a short story by William Carleton set in a shebeen in about 1830 features a woman as the establishment's 'excellent manager', whereas her husband, a 'good-humoured man', is mainly useful for attracting male customers.[74] Similarly, J.M. Synge's *The Playboy of the Western World*, first staged in 1907 and largely set in a 'very rough' County Mayo 'public house or shebeen', has a 'fat, jovial' male publican who spends much of his time drinking and talking with his friends, while his daughter manages the business and works behind the bar.[75] Many women were involved in those sectors of the trade that 'required little if any start-up capital or magisterial authorization'.[76] These were also the poorer and least well-documented sectors of the drinks industry, and the ones most likely to have engaged in illegal selling.

At the same time, it is important to remember that, as both Carleton and Synge demonstrate, drink retailing in Ireland was largely a family affair. This meant that numerous women who worked in licensed public houses were not listed as employees in surviving official records, such as censuses.[77] The pub licensee might have been a man, but his wife and daughters would almost certainly have worked alongside him in an unpaid capacity, either as barmaids selling drink or as shop assistants serving customers at the pub's grocery counter.[78] If the male publican died without a son ready to take over the family business, his widow or a daughter might well have transferred the licence into her name.[79] Lots of women worked and drank in Irish shops selling alcohol over the centuries but, to researchers blinded by the myth of the all-male pub, they have remained invisible.

Conclusion: dispelling the myth of the traditional pub

When considering the functions of the Irish pub, some scholars have found the German philosopher Jürgen Habermas' concept of the 'public sphere' relevant. This sphere or space was originally theorised by Habermas as an arena that developed in early modern western Europe in which private individuals could come together as a collective to critically discuss matters of common concern, formulate public opinion, and hold authoritarian regimes accountable to society through publicity. Habermas conceived of the 'public sphere' as distinct from the state and, indeed, as a mechanism intended to make the state more answerable to its subjects or citizens.[80]

In Ireland, however, the suppression of earlier, often unregulated, drink outlets, including shebeens, ale- or beer-houses and spirit-grocer shops, meant that the pub was a 'public sphere' originally invented by the British state and subsequently maintained by its Irish political successors on both sides of the border. The 'traditional' pub was created and curated by centuries of British licensing and policing legislation, not to facilitate the formation and expression of critical public opinion, but rather to contain and control it. Governments used pubs to monitor and regulate the behaviour of their mainly working-class patrons in order to suppress dissent. At the same time, via heavy taxation, pubs generated substantial amounts of much-needed revenue for official purposes. The state's aim of suppressing dissent was by no means always achieved, however. Indeed, the long history of political recruiting and organising in drink shops, between at least the seventeenth and the twentieth centuries, demonstrates how they could be subverted and exploited by revolutionary groups. Nor is it true, as often asserted, that pubs have invariably been gendered male: that is, operated exclusively by men for men. Since the medieval period, Irish women have always sold alcohol in a variety of different settings, including often in their own homes, while sometimes making it as well. The history of drink retailing in Ireland is far more complex and challenging in terms of politics and gender than the current nostalgic laments about the decline of the 'traditional' all-male pub would suggest.

Elizabeth Malcolm's Choice:

The Crown Liquor Saloon,

46 Great Victoria Street, Belfast

The only pub owned by the UK National Trust, the Crown is considered the best surviving example of a 'gin palace' in Ireland, and perhaps in Britain as well. First opened in 1826, it was extensively renovated in 1885, with elaborate Italianate stained glass and carved woodwork, plus ten snugs. It has featured in many films, notably Carol Reed's 1947 classic about the IRA, *Odd Man Out*. It was dangerous to drink in pubs in the North during the Troubles due to frequent bombings and shootings, and the Crown was damaged numerous times. It was directly opposite the Europa Hotel, notorious at the time as the most bombed hotel in Europe; and many of the hotel bombings blew out the Crown's windows. But when I lived in Belfast throughout the 1980s, I did drink there. Its nineteenth-century atmosphere gave one a – probably false – sense of security.

Figure 2.4 The Crown Liquor Saloon in Belfast. Photo by Brian Morrison and courtesy of Tourism Northern Ireland.

Chapter 3

Irish Pubs and Gender: Segmentation, Containment and Integration

Tom Spalding and Gwen Scarbrough

Spaces and places ... are gendered through and through![1]

Introduction

Irish pubs have traditionally been important social and community spaces. Throughout the twentieth century, rather than remaining culturally static, they have gone through a series of developments in terms of use and design. These changes provide insight into social transformations that occurred in Ireland during this time. In this chapter we examine how the pub has progressed through design phases that both mirrored and reinforced the position of women in Irish society. By using a case study that focuses on the structure, design and material culture of several public houses in Cork, this chapter will explore the relationship between gender and the Irish pub.[2]

The pub is what social geographer Stephen Daniels describes as a 'particular landscape' that has attained cultural status as a 'habitat of meaning'.[3] Comprehending experiences and meanings of the pub place encompasses concepts of human agency and discourses of power. Related to this conceptual agenda is the embodiment of place: Malpas views the people/place relationship as 'necessarily embedded in place, and in spatialised, embodied activity'.[4] Gender, for example, can be explored, performed, reproduced or subverted within the public realm of the pub. As well, the formative processes of the pub contribute to the construction and expression of gendered identities, in particular hegemonic masculinity.[5] For example, the use of alcohol in pub spaces operates as a meaningful signifier of gendered identities.[6] While gender is performed in pub spaces, the design, material culture and subsequent use of pub spaces also acts to regulate pub inhabitants.

For this discussion we have identified three historical approaches to design that mirror the relationships of gender, power and the Irish pub. These can be observed in the changing configurations and uses of pub spaces: segmentation, containment and controlled integration. These approaches are characterised by spatial practices within pubs that are embedded in the gendered norms of their times. Furthermore, the pattered use of material culture, space/place layout and the production of a gendered atmosphere throughout these periods reflect and shape pub inhabitants.[7]

For example, we consider how the layout of pub spaces influences, constructs and prohibits behaviour in relation to gender.[8]

Segmentation describes the use of pubs as primarily male spaces that allowed them to rigidly restrict and control access by women, if they were permitted at all, into small and controlled areas of pubs that were partitioned off: 'snuggeries' or 'snugs'. *Containment* refers to the period where women were allowed into snugs and the new 'lounge' bars that remained separate from the public bar and designed as more 'feminine' and welcoming to women and/or couples. *Controlled integration* describes most contemporary Irish pubs in which women have greater access to all areas of pub space, albeit subject to societal controls and expectations.

The chronological development of gendered space in the Irish pub

Historically the pub developed as an exclusively male territory, as it provided a unique location for the formation of the archetypal Irish (male) identity. Regular drinking among all-male groups defined a geography that was distinctly 'Irish' and 'male'.[9] Through the repeated use of alcohol, men mapped their identities onto pub spaces as they sought out sites of refuge from the domestic space or workplace that were largely absent of and denied to women. Pub space was usually demarcated not only by its absence of women, but also by masculinisation in terms of materiality and atmosphere.

Jane Rendell has suggested that space may be gendered in two different ways: that 'as well as being gendered through physical occupation – the different inhabitation of space by men and women – space is also produced as gendered through representation'.[10] Somewhat earlier Jos Boys had noted how architectural space can:

> reflect social relations … both symbolically – through imagery and 'appropriateness of place' for a particular activity – and in reality – through physical boundaries and the spatial relationships made between activities.[11]

While women's entry into pubs during the twentieth century was controlled (in terms of space) and sometimes restricted (in terms of time, or access at all), women had resisted exclusion and found ways to participate in Irish pub culture. While this case study particularly concentrates on Cork city, the themes we identified below

Figure 3.1 Miss Eileen Callanan, Callanan's bar, 24 George's Quay, Cork. Courtesy of the Crowley family.

were common across the country. Nevertheless, there were factors that made the Cork alcohol retail market unique and led to a situation where most pubs in the city were 'tied' to one of the city breweries – Murphy's or Beamish & Crawford – an economic model that was common in Britain, yet rare in Ireland.[12] Many of these Cork pubs were managed by women (Fig. 3.1).[13]

Becoming a tenant of one of the breweries held attractions for women. Prime among them was that most pubs had accommodation (sometimes generous) overhead for a family.[14] The business was relatively compatible with family life, and husbands generally did not help in the bar, but worked in a trade or in a factory. Hence the family had an opportunity to have two incomes. The weekly rent was small, so it was relatively easy for a woman to be her own boss. There were other socio-political factors that made running a pub attractive: professions, trades and security services were effectively closed to women and the civil service or teaching was not possible for married women until the early 1970s due to the 'marriage bar'. Hence, up to around 1970, running a pub was one of the few ways a woman could run a business, support a family and enhance her social capital. While female managers were rarer outside Cork, no doubt similar factors were at play in other parts of Ireland.

Irish society, as in other western cultures, began to experience gradual gender changes by the mid-twentieth century. As women slowly entered traditionally male professions and men experienced greater participation in domestic life, leisure time increased for both sexes and social life became more inclusive. As a result, women began to gain greater access to pub spaces, albeit at a much slower pace in rural areas. Cian Molloy notes that even in the 1970s 'it was still common enough to see women and children sitting outside a pub while husbands and fathers were drinking inside'.[15] Indeed, it appears that the main reason why pubs were changed was the rise of female customers, for example by the adoption of 'first class washroom facilities ... especially for the ladies'.[16] Through this engagement women became, in Mary McLeod's terms, 'vital actors contributing to a multiplicity of ... modes of occupation' of space as well as consumers.[17] In the early 1960s, the phenomenon was described in the trade press as 'an invasion'.[18]

Initially, the enclosed area of the snug was an acceptable location for women to occupy. In England, open-plan bars had begun 'to disappear from the 1850s onwards, partitioned into small compartments'.[19] These compartments also allowed women 'to separate themselves from men'.[20] Dickens gives an example of a snug in the Liverpool docks in 1860. After describing a musical performance by a young woman, the author takes care to explain that she was 'girl of a delicate prettiness' who '[k]ept herself select. Sat in the Snug, not listening to the blandishments of the [sailors]'.[21]

As in England, snugs were most often found in pubs in urban locales, but by no means in all or even most Irish public houses.[22] These small, contained spaces were located near an entrance, so women would not need to walk through or linger in the bar. Typically, the barman would enter the snug or use a side window so that the occupants could place an order, again preventing women from approaching the bar and the possibility of mixing with the predominantly male clientele.

As more women began to use pub spaces, a new strategy of 'containment' was adopted. This was manifested in the construction of lounge bars, continuing a trend that had started in the 1930s.[23] Purpose-built public bars during this period tended to be large, open drinking areas with substantial lounge bars (for women) off it.[24]

Such designs had been advocated by English pub designers such as Basil Oliver and E.B. Musman and, long before that, by late-Victorian social reformers.[25] The latter's concern was that snugs and small lounges allowed nefarious activities and, as seriously, that women could drink un-monitored.[26] A central horseshoe-shaped bar allowed a panoptical observation of the premises, with minimal staffing.

The public bar was retained as a space for men and generally continued to exclude women, while the lounge was feminised for the use of women and their partners, and later, families.[27] The lounge was maintained to a higher standard than the bar and was decorated to correspond with social conceptualisations of femininity. Comfort and cleanliness were of greater significance in the lounge area and a domestic atmosphere was evoked:

> A new trend has set in, the pubs of today are more often light and spacious with wide leather settees, carpets under foot, taped music playing or a television set interrupting the conversation; places where women are expected and catered for and where there is no snug. Probably, the pub itself is all lounge and has not a simple straightforward bar, where waiters circulated carrying trays laden with a bewildering variety of drinks.[28]

The pace of this modernisation increased in the mid-1960s, spreading to working-class urban areas and the countryside, to the extent that by 1966 a contributor to *The Irish National Vintner* could ask whether old-time public houses were 'almost extinct'.[29]

Today many pubs consist of mostly open areas and many of the older pubs have been remodelled and refurbished. This rebuilding of pubs has often involved the removal of the partition that separates lounge space ('feminine' space) from the bar ('masculine' space), resulting in larger gender-neutral areas. While this phenomenon should be welcomed, the publican's motivation was not egalitarian. The older layouts were more labour-intensive and limited turnover in relation to their size.

Women are now free to use all spaces of the pub, yet it is mostly men who dominate the bar while women and mixed-gender groups occupy sofas, stools or chairs with tables. In many pubs the layout of the bar and floorspace continues to frame and gender embodied encounters. As well, despite changing patterns of alcohol consumption, pub-based drinking continues to be largely male-dominated and pub and alcohol consumption remains a strong gender signifier.[30]

Cork pubs and gender 1920–2000

The following case study describes the three phases in the relationship between gender and spaces in the public house. We will examine, in some detail, the situation in Cork city, especially from the 1920s to the 1970s, through contemporary journalism, books and personal recollections. We draw upon interviews collected by ourselves and the Cork Folklore Project overseen by University College Cork. Examining a particular time and place allows us to generate a fine-grained study that reveals something of the relationships between social attitudes, alcohol, design and gender and provides directions for future study. The first systematic studies that touched on the relationship between social roles and structure and the Irish pub were conducted

Figure 3.2 Staff and customers, Kay O'Mahony's bar, Dominick Street, Cork, Interior, 1969, by William Harrington. Courtesy of Mr Michael Reidy.

by the American anthropologists Arensberg and Kimball in the 1930s and '40s, and we have continued their focus on the human experience and interest in narrative.[31]

The four Murphy sisters were the daughters of a farmer in Kilmichael, County Cork, and migrated to the city in the 1940s.[32] One, Mary, born in 1922, recounted how her siblings Kathleen, Ella and Nora each held a licence tied to Murphy's brewery. Kathleen had previously managed a city pub[33] and, according to Mary, the other women 'got pubs no bother' due to their solid reputations.[34] The prevalence of female publicans and barmaids in the city gave the trade an unusual character, nonetheless revelatory of gender relations (Fig. 3.2).[35] One customer explained how a maternal landlady would ensure that drinkers were dispatched on a Saturday evening for mass and then welcomed back: 'We'd be playing darts or cards, and when it's time for church, she'd hunt us out of the door and she would give us a tea leaf to chew on the way up to the [North] Chapel to take away the smell of the stout.'[36]

Family life and running a pub were not always compatible. The family of one woman who ran an 'early house' reported to the Cork Folklore Project how they would sometimes have to get dressed or take their breakfast in the 'snug', while their mother was pulling pints for thirsty dockers.[37] On occasion, they would share it with a worker shaking with delirium tremens – 'we would go out to school ... and there would be sing-songs going on in the bar'. Some women, including Collette Crowley, born into the trade in 1934 and who managed Callanan's bar on George's Quay, never really relished the role of landlady.[38]

The snug and segmentation

We have characterised 'segmentation' as the starting phase in the relationship between gender and the pub in Ireland. 'Respectable' women were welcomed in most city pubs in their snug or snugs,[39] and Cork bar owners seem to have still been keen on subdividing their premises into the early twentieth century.[40]

Cork snugs came in several forms. The most exclusive (in the sense of excluding others) were accessed directly from the street via a vestibule, and here customers were served from a hatch opening directly into the bar, perhaps shielded by a velvet curtain (Figs 3.3 and 3.4). Extant snugs feature frosted or patterned glass windows set in three-quarter height timber partitions and, as the street windows of the pub also featured opaque or textured glass,[41] it made it hard to know who was occupying the

THE CHANGE
DOWNLOAD THE GUINNESS Plus APP.
YOUR WELCOME PINT AND MORE IS WAITING.
EXTRAORDINARY. ON TAP.
BEAMISH
BEAMISH
GUINNESS
Natural Reflection
RUGBY CLUB

Figure 3.3 (opposite) Snug, Castle Inn, 99 South Main Street, Cork, Interior, 2019. Courtesy of Mr Michael O'Donovan (© Tom Spalding).

Figure 3.4 (right) Entrance to snug, Castle Inn, 99 South Main Street, Cork, 2019. Courtesy of Mr Michael O'Donovan (© Tom Spalding).

snug. In other cases, snugs were entered from the main bar, allowing the customer to be glimpsed by those in the bar. Some pubs were compartmentalised into a number of separate rooms and snugs.[42] Women could take a '*piscín*' of whiskey or a 'pony' of stout[43] in the snug, or be served drink into their own container for consumption off the premises.[44] The process was described by one woman thus: 'You went up to the hatch and you ordered your drink and the barman would deliver it to you, in case you might contaminate the poor men out in the bar with your womanly charms!'[45] According to one veteran publican, 'women were *only* allowed in snugs';[46] others' testimony states they were not exclusively for females but also used by clergymen, policemen,[47] judges,[48] men wishing to avoid someone or getting caught in a 'round',[49] or looking for privacy.[50]

The level of segregation between men and women in Cork appears to be less than in contemporaneous pubs in Lancashire,[51] where the pub continued to be dominated by men and male behaviour. In the case of the UK, Harrison argued that 'the woman's place in the pub is that part of it which is home from home, a better home from an ordinary worker's home'.[52] In Cork, the picture is more complex, and it was far from unknown for women to visit a public bar.

At the turn of the twentieth century, rather than being excluded from pubs, it appears that the abuse of alcohol by some women and girls, 'ranged along the bars' of licensed premises, was common in poorer areas of Cork.[53] According to one priest, 'gross intemperance of the parents' was leading to child neglect. Interestingly, the same man also laid the blame at the door of the tied-house system – the sheer number of pubs pitted publicans against each other in order to survive and encouraged them to serve inebriated customers.[54] Frank O'Connor writes of 'old women with pint pots under their tartan shawls',[55] and how in the 1910s 'shawly' women would mix with mourners in the bar after a funeral.[56] We should not overlook the strong influence of social class within these testimonies and how it interacts with gender. Respectable working-class women largely kept to the snug, while their less fortunate sisters could be less discriminating.

In the 1960s, Kealy's bar on Faulkner's Lane permitted women, albeit only in the snug,[57] but, depending on the venue, 'respectable' women could be found in a public bar. Mary Murphy remembered how, in the 1950s, two elderly friends, Mags and Queenie, would sit 'on wooden bottle crates in the main bar – they didn't have notions!'[58] A few pubs felt it necessary to put up notices reading 'No Women', which were actually intended to discourage prostitutes but also discouraged all female drinkers.[59] Cognisant of its maritime clientele, a 1969 review of one pub suggested that 'visiting women should be accompanied'[60] – in other words, unaccompanied women may be mistaken for sex workers. (These practices should be seen in the context of the narrative of 'the fallen woman' so prevalent in nineteenth-century discourse.)[61] Few pubs in Cork seem to have had an exclusive 'men only' policy. One example was Mackesy's which, after a refit in 1957, was 'still a man's pub. It still has the quiet dignity which time nor change can erase'.[62] Women could be dissuaded in subtler ways, such as not providing dedicated toilets for them.[63]

Invasion and containment

The interiors of many pubs were altered during the 1960s and, in our interview, Mary Murphy explained that by 1971 'older women continued to use the snug', but many now sat at the counter.[64] As previously mentioned, the 1960s had seen an 'invasion' of the pub by female drinkers. Not all males welcomed this. A Belfast journalist complained about their 'high-pitched chatter'; dogs [he added] 'were less trouble'.[65] According to the author and former director of Raidió Éireann, Maurice Gorham, the new lounges were 'plushed-up like a hotel lobby, [and] noisy with women's voices'.[66] However, just as snugs were not exclusively for women, lounges did not exclude men, but also catered for mixed groups or 'the man who wants to bring his wife out'.[67] As with the suspicion surrounding unaccompanied women in the public bar, single men in a lounge could be considered to be underplaying their gender role. While seated alone in a lounge Paul Durcan describes being subjected to the curiosity of drinkers in the public bar of Cissie Young's, a Cork bar, in 1971 in his poem '"Cissy Youngs" – to Rosa Alice Branco'.

The development of the lounge began in the 1930s as a way of enticing well-to-do women with disposable incomes, but by the 1960s it was as much a response to

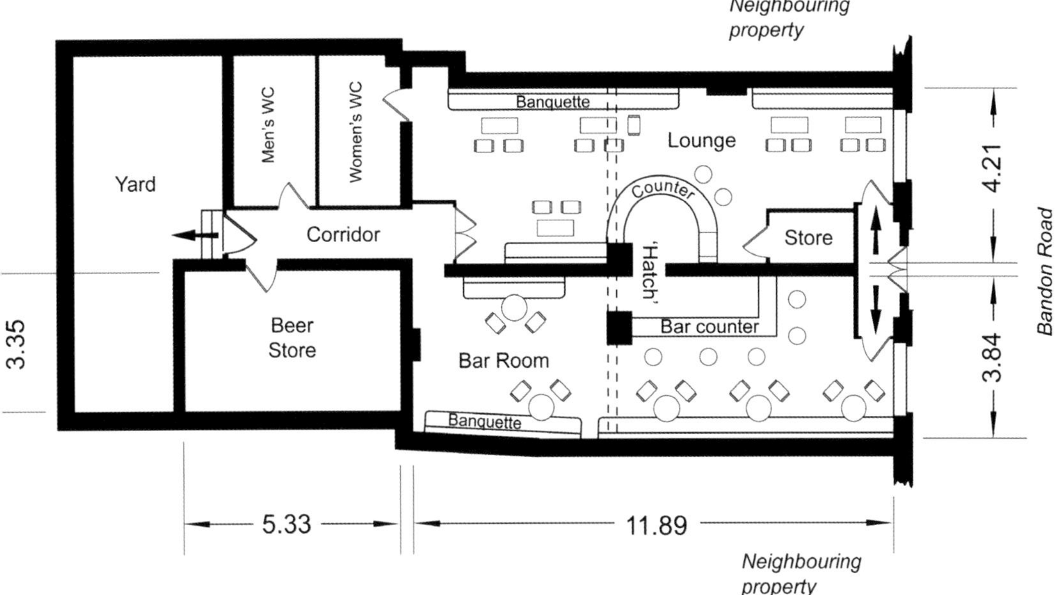

Figure 3.5 Plan, Cissie Young's, 80 Bandon Road, Cork, in 1969. Re-drawn in 2020 showing bar (top) and lounge (bottom). Courtesy of Mr Tom Lynch (© Tom Spalding).

demands from women for a comfortable environment. According to one lady, men might be happy with shabby surroundings, but women expected their drinks to be 'nicely served' in clean glasses by a 'man in an unobtrusive uniform … or a short white coat' and 'their surroundings to be in keeping with the trouble they have taken with their appearance'.[68] Jane Tate, a regular contributor to *The Licensed Vintner*, wrote in her *Female View of the Bar* column in 1967 that:

> as a lover of traditional things I feel I *should* love the old-style pubs … I do indeed love the *image they project*, but when it comes to going out for a drink with friends I invariably plump for a pub with the most modern décor, cosy chairs, interesting lights and plushy carpet [our emphasis].[69]

The adjective 'plush' (also used by Gorham) has strongly feminine associations, and the emphasis on pattern, texture and softness in many images of early lounges suggests they were intended to be understood as 'feminine' spaces (Fig. 3.6). Notwithstanding this, the modernisation of pubs did not automatically mean women were welcome. Kealy's bar retained a snug marked 'Ladies' after it was remodelled and was 'very much a man's pub' in the evenings.[70]

Figure 3.6 Illuminated sign, The Long Valley bar, 10 Winthrop Street, Cork. Courtesy of Mr Peadar Moynihan (© Tom Spalding).

Integration and the rise of the 'superpub'

By the 1990s the model whereby the Cork pub supported an individual resident family had declined. Ironically, the process of integrating female customers occurred after the management of the pubs themselves passed to male hands when the breweries sold their estates from the mid-1970s to the mid-1980s. Following this, many pubs were significantly altered, leading to the development of the 'superpub'. Cork examples include Cissie Young's, Bandon Road, where the bar and lounge of a former tied house were demolished and rebuilt as a large open-plan space around a central serving area around 1999,[71] and An Síol Broin, McCurtain Street, where two adjacent pubs were converted to one, around 2000.[72] In other cases, licences were transferred to commercial or industrial buildings, and large new venues created, such as the Bodega, 'the city's first "superpub"', on Cornmarket Street in 1996.[73]

These changes became widespread in Ireland by the late 1990s and coincided with the interest shown in pub design by corporations, such as the Guinness Group (see Chapter 7, this volume) and Murphy's. Despite these open designs, differences remained between the way women and men used bar spaces, the beverages they consumed and how much effort they put into their outfits prior to going out.[74] The process of integration is ongoing and the non-gendered toilets being installed today are logical extension of this.

There has also been a counter-movement in the last decade whereby new divisions or snugs have been installed.[75] This has been facilitated by miniaturised CCTV cameras and remote monitoring that allow surveillance of otherwise secluded areas. In 2020, Covid-19 provided a further impetus to this process.

Conclusion

There is considerable evidence that gender has played a key role in how pubs have operated and have been experienced, both historically and in contemporary Ireland. This chapter has outlined the spatial development of the Irish pub in Cork city as a gendered geography and posits that this development was typical throughout Ireland. In our work we have described the progression of the pub space as it has moved through several gendered design phases that we have categorised as segmentation, containment and integration. We argue that through time and space pub layout has reflected how the pub both mirrors social understandings of gender and acts as a site of reproduction.

Figure 3.7 'Pleasantly cosy, with basketwork light fittings … and hunting prints': Kealy's bar, Faulkner's Lane, Cork, after refit by Guinness & Co., 1966. Image 1968. Photo by and courtesy of Guinness Archives.

As found in several societies, the pub has been male-dominated due, in part, to alcohol consumption and drinking culture being synonymous with male culture and the reproduction of hegemonic masculinity.[76] In tandem with alcohol consumption, pub geographies from the mid-nineteenth century were often designed as exclusionary spaces, which were later reconstructed to manage women's access.[77] This configuration of space and its subsequent embodiment of male drinking culture acted to map gender onto the Irish pub.

Following this, we may understand snugs and lounges as representing these two ways of gendering. The available evidence suggests that snugs (at least in Cork) were austere and, in gender terms, one might suggest that they were 'masculine'. They were gendered 'female' by inhabitation. Lounges, on the other hand, were deliberately designed to attract and be enjoyed by women (Fig. 3.7).

While women's entry into pubs in the past has been limited in diverse ways, they often found ways to participate in Irish pub culture. The experience of female publicans and bar staff in Cork illustrates this point. Furthermore, it should be noted that women's experience of segmentation and containment within the pub geography intersected with other identities and was at times permeable. There is evidence that class and status also played a role in access into and use of pub spaces. The movement of middle- and upper-class women in the pub, for example, was restricted to the snug, while it appears some working-class women enjoyed greater freedom to drink at the bar. Experiences of rural women could also differ from those of women in urban areas, as reflected in the popularity of grocery counter pubs throughout the west of Ireland.

It was not coincidental that the increase in women's social and political powers in Ireland during the 1960s brought about greater access into the pub. As Burnett notes, the growth in women's participation in the pub was 'one of the unexpected results of the emancipation of women'.[78] Today women enjoy pub culture and alcohol consumption for similar reasons stated by men: for fun and entertainment, to socialise, to drink and to sometimes get drunk, to evade loneliness and alleviate boredom.[79] By allowing greater access to the pub and permitting women to become more active participants in the public arena, women can now, in many cases, comfortably use the pub. By the mid-1990s, at the time of the first superpubs, bars were the most popular place for Cork women to meet each other.[80]

Although pub culture has become more inclusive and women have gained greater access to the pub, it remains a predominantly male geography in which men continue to dominate bar spaces.

While there is no explicit social control over women concerning pub attendance, many women continue to feel restricted from participating in pub culture as men do. For example, going into a pub alone is accepted for men, whereas women who drink there unaccompanied, especially at the bar, still face a taboo. These attitudes suggest that women's behaviour is monitored and perceived differently than that of men. Additionally, solitary drinking, rowdiness, aggression and drunkenness are considered less acceptable in women than in men and can lead to stereotyping as 'loose', 'out-of-control' or as bad mothers. Although drinking in pubs has long been framed as a male pursuit, rising alcohol consumption among women, and greater social acceptability, has increased their presence in these venues. Yet women also report shouldering more of the burden of mitigating risks linked to public drinking – such as aggression, sexual assault and related threats – that can markedly shape their experience of pub culture.

Our work suggests that, while the modern open-plan pub is typically designed as a gender-neutral space, many changes remain superficial.[81] Despite the removal of partitions, first of the snug and then of the lounge, pubs continue to be in many ways exclusionary for many women.[82]

Tom Spalding's Choice:

Callanan's Bar,

24 George's Quay, Cork city

Callanan's has been in the management of the same family since 1935 when Eileen Callanan took over the licence on behalf of Murphy's brewery. Her husband, Robert, was a First World War veteran and a plasterer by trade, and the operation of the pub was to be Mrs Callanan's realm. As well as a small bar, the building offered accommodation in five bedrooms over the business, allowing Eileen to mind her growing family while supplementing Robert's earnings. In time her daughter Collette (1934–2023) took over the management of the bar and raised her own family 'over the shop'.

The history of the building is complex. Originally built in the 1780s on what was land newly reclaimed from the river Lee, it has operated as a pub since at least 1856. In 1901, it was purchased by Murphy's and (like most Cork city pubs) operated as a 'tied house'. In about 1914 the entire façade to George's Quay was taken down and rebuilt in a fashionable style by a local architect, J.F. McMullan. It retains a substantially unchanged Edwardian wooden interior including tables, bar counter, a snug and 'back bar' shelving. It is one of about six pubs in Cork which have largely original interiors.

Figure 3.8
Exterior of Callanan's. Photo by Tom Spalding.

Gwen Scarbrough's Choice:

Nancy's Bar,

Ardara, County Donegal

Figure 3.9 Exterior of Nancy's. Photo by Sarah McHugh.

I have been visiting Nancy's Pub in Ardara, County Donegal on occasion for the past two decades. It is a pub that draws you in and encourages you to return, to notice the small changes (the décor, the staff, the menu) but also to feel a sense of constancy.

Generations have cared for and added multiple layers of personality onto this pub. It's a textured place with soft lighting and a multitude of things to look at – mugs hanging off the low ceiling, photos and curious objects on the walls, curtains, cushions, dark knotty wood, copper, plaster, marble, stone, and creamy pints of Guinness. As a place to be well fed and find a session, it can envelop the visitor with such a sense of comfort and joviality that it can be difficult, once the evening comes to an end, to head out the door and take a step into the northerly winds of Donegal.

Chapter 4

The Irish Pub: Views from Social Science

Perry Share

Introduction

Many chapters in this volume suggest a relationship between the literary and visual manifestations of pubs and the social realities that may underpin them. But what do we know of these underlying social realities? What does the social scientific analysis of the pub have to tell us?

In Ireland, as in many cognate societies, such as Scotland, England and Australia, historians, particularly social historians, have contributed most to our knowledge of the pub.[1] Two books published in the 1990s provide important foundational knowledge of pubs in Ireland: Kearns' oral history of Dublin pubs to the mid-twentieth century focuses on the social aspects, while Ferriter extensively explored the often contradictory relationships between alcohol and Irish society.[2] A range of authors, including Kevin Martin and Cian Molloy, have created accessible popular histories of the Irish pub, with detailed accounts of many individual hostelries,[3] while among the often idiosyncratic outsiders' viewpoints we could list those by Britons Sybil Taylor and Pete McCarthy and the American Bill Barich.[4]

It has often been noted that sociologists have neglected serious analysis of the pub. This may be due to the pub's very ubiquity and pass-remarkableness. Like buses, convenience stores and street signs, they are part of our everyday, taken-for-granted world (until threatened or gone) and hardly worth worrying about. Their very integration into the daily patterns of social life has rendered them less visible, unlike, say, crime; struggles over gender, sexuality and religion; or the activities of politicians and the state.

Furthermore, the distinctive evolution of Irish sociology made pubs an unlikely focus of enquiry. The twin forces of a narrow 'Catholic sociology' and a state-sponsored social science harnessed to state-building and economic development have, as noted by a number of historians of Irish sociology, directed attention elsewhere: to questions of social cohesion and functioning, welfare and inequality, and public service delivery.[5] The everyday workings of existing Irish communities were a minority focus for a sociology that tended to address 'macro' issues of social change and 'modernisation'. When alcohol consumption was addressed, it was generally as a 'social problem' or as a reflection of some deeper societal malaise.[6]

Though (in my experience) practising sociologists have been no strangers to pubs, they seldom thought to study them in any detail. This was largely left, as we will see, to the anthropologists. This neglect is slowly changing, and researchers such as Scarbrough, McCauley and O'Brien (all represented in this book) have gradually expanded and deepened our sociological understanding. This 'cultural turn' in Irish sociology, as elsewhere, is the outcome of diverse societal and disciplinary influences, from the rise of global popular culture to feminist critiques of 'objectivist' social science, to a concern to engage a broader audience for research.

This chapter explores some anthropological and sociological accounts over the last century that show how Irish pubs, and how they have been interpreted, reflect broader societal changes. It points to work that describes and explains pubs as sites of social interaction, including the elusive phenomenon of 'craic'. While pubs are often seen as egalitarian settings, they are undeniably also shaped by hierarchy and inequality, and the chapter outlines issues in relation to the classical sociological variables of class, gender and ethnicity. It would be fair to say that social scientific perspectives do not reveal any 'hidden' aspects of the Irish pub, but they provide support and context for the more creative accounts of drama, visual art, poetry and prose.

The anthropological perspective

American anthropologist Adam Kaul finds himself in a communal drinking establishment – a pub – to better take his bearings of an exotic (to him) community. The study site is Doolin, County Clare, in the early 2000s. His location is rather untypical, Doolin being a heavily touristed town in the west of Ireland, famed for its multinational pub-based traditional music scene. But his 'thick description' is highly evocative:

> When you pull open the pub door, a blast of noise, cigarette smoke and body heat engulfs you and pulls you in. The collective low rumble of human voices is punctuated by the sharp sounds of clinking glasses and small explosions of laughter. Even on a sunny day, the light is dim enough indoors

> to force you to wait for your eyes to adjust before delving any further ... In order to get anywhere, you must sidle closely past people dearly clutching pints of lager or stout beer. When you catch the barman's eye you shout your order and a pint is pulled. Once purchased, you lift your drink gingerly over the tops of the heads of the people seated at the bar.[7]

This is a scene that would – apart from the indoor smoking – be familiar to any habitué of a busy Irish pub. Kaul's lively account of the evolution and meaning of the music scene in Doolin attests to the close connection between music performance and pubs. His analysis focuses on Gus O'Connor's pub, which began to attract domestic and international tourists and returning emigrants in the 1960s. A centre for the emergence and development of Doolin's music 'industry', O'Connor's also gave a job to the anthropologist while he engaged in his research. This meant he could observe first-hand the symbiotic relationship that existed between the pub and coach tour companies, as they deftly managed visits to maximise the benefit to all. Kaul shows how an understanding of the pubs (and the music) of Doolin can only be understood within a dynamic global culture.

Kaul was not the first visiting anthropologist to note the central role of the pub in the predominantly rural societies that attracted scholarly attention.[8] The pub often featured as a base for anthropologists' observations of community life, while publicans acted as key sources of information about the communities. For example, in a study of their correspondence, Anne Byrne notes that the celebrated and, within the tradition of Irish sociology and anthropology, highly influential Harvard University anthropologists Conrad Arensberg and Solon Kimball and their research team 'took regular refuge' in The Copper Jug in Ennis, a local 'public house, grocery and stable yard, for country people', where publican Edward Kerin was a regular research informant.[9] Unfortunately, they had little to say about the pubs themselves, focusing rather on the economic, social and political ties that underpinned all small rural businesses.[10]

More than half a century later, Australian anthropologist Adrian Peace revealed the importance of pubs to his research methodology: 'I hung around on boats, on farms, on street corners, and in other people's kitchens. Most of all, I hung around in bars mainly because so many other male residents did that too.'[11] Much of the lively social interaction in the coastal location he called Inveresk took place in the village's diverse pubs. There is no doubt that social interaction and talk in pubs has had an important, if under-documented, influence on our social scientific understanding of Irish communities – particularly western rural ones.

More broadly, the issue of alcohol has long been connected to arguments about the 'modernisation' of Irish society, a key theme of Irish social science throughout the twentieth century. Alcohol usage and modernity are counterpoised: as a society 'modernises' it is expected to reduce its consumption of alcohol. An early institution of Irish social science, the Dublin-based Statistical and Social Inquiry Society (SSIS), had a 'civilising' mission in relation to Irish social development and several papers on issues related to alcohol were read to the society in the mid-nineteenth century.[12] More recently John O'Brien has aligned the emergence of family-owned pubs with that of post-peasant rural society in the wake of the Land Wars of the nineteenth and early twentieth centuries.[13]

For much of the twentieth century, the west of Ireland was seen as a place in terminal decline, a victim of modernisation, plagued by emigration and depopulation and missing out on the economic development of the rest of the country. This feeling of decline was captured by British anthropologist Hugh Brody, who perceived an 'intense demoralisation' that stemmed from 'the breakdown of the communities, the devaluation of the traditional mores [and] the weakening hold of the older conceptions over the minds of young people in particular'.[14] Brody's study of (the pseudonymous) Inishkillane (conducted in the mid- to late 1960s) sought to describe and analyse these processes.

He describes O'Dwyer's bar, one of five in the village. It resonates with the classic 'old-timey' Irish pub, now re-created for the global market:

> The bar is panelled with tongue-and-groove varnished timber. There is a picture of an old steamship on one wall and religious icons on the others. The appearance is attractive; the bar has been well cared for for many years; it looks and feels old and weathered.[15]

Brody analyses the social interaction within O'Dwyer's. The community has many bachelor farmers, often dependent on remittances from family members abroad, and they, along with married farmers, dominate life in the bar. Women are marginalised in the pub setting and choose the village shop as their main public site of interaction.

Younger, unmarried farmers (all men) are at home in neither setting, a reflection of their now ambivalent position in Inishkillane society.[16] Those who choose to frequent the bar, with its symbolic link to the traditional life of the community, are making a statement about their commitment to the farming life; those who choose to socialise at the shop (a symbol of modernity with its array of brightly packaged goods) are more likely to exit the community.

Few women in the community drink alcohol and, on rare visits to the bar, 'will not even enter by the front door, preferring to go to the back of the house and come in through a kitchen entrance'.[17] Many young people have 'taken the [Pioneer] pledge' and are teetotal: less a rejection of alcohol per se than an identification with modernity – a challenge to a traditional way of life and those (traditional farmers) who pursue it. The farmers who 'do atypically farm in a businesslike manner' (the more capitalistically oriented farmers) also tend to steer clear of drinking at the bar. In short, Brody uses the village bars and shop as a synecdoche for the changes being wrought on the traditional rural community.

An acute observer of Irish community life in the 1980s was Australian anthropologist Chris Eipper, as revealed in his 1986 study *The Ruling Trinity*. Again, the target was a rural settlement in the west of Ireland: he located himself in Bantry, County Cork in 1975–7 to produce a complex account of the intermingling of social class, religion and business in the town, dominated economically by the local Gulf Oil refinery. Eipper's analysis included detailed consideration of the propertied middle class of shopkeepers, publicans and other small-business people. Often, such businesses overlapped: 'rural shopkeepers engaged in a varied range of activities which in addition to the shop or pub often included a farm, a sub-postmastership, an estate agency, a holiday guesthouse, a taxi service, or a fishing interest'.[18] As Arensberg had earlier noted, this extension of business interests into daily life gave the rural entrepreneur a position of some power as a patron and a broker within the community, as a supplier of services, favours, credit and employment, while 'the petty patron was imbued with a special, if limited, moral authority and prestige in the consciousness of country people'. Nevertheless, apart from the most prominent operators, publicans, like other small-business owners, 'were often no better off than wage workers and regarded themselves and were regarded by others as among "the ordinary people"'.[19]

Bantry's pubs provided an 'important base for a diffuse range of casual activities and meeting place for more formally organised groups. Quiz competitions were popular'. Some pubs were closely associated with specific groups: the Bantry Bay Hotel was the 'main drinking spot' for the local GAA club. One of Eipper's key concerns was to analyse the local power of the Catholic Church. He found that this did not extend to the realm of the pub, where 'the clergy had little influence … and had consistently attempted to weaken the links between alcoholic consumption and other leisure activities'.[20] The church promoted the formation of clubs that were independent of the pubs, but 'these efforts had only limited success, and then more with women than men, for the pubs were almost exclusively male clubs'.

The previously mentioned Adrian Peace was another Australian anthropologist to study a western Irish rural community: the fishing and farming village he called Inveresk, where he was based at various times in the 1980s and '90s. Pubs were a key part of the social life of the village: places both of connection and division. They were sites for family gatherings and inter-personal and inter-familial conflicts:

> [O]n one notorious occasion, a friendly darts match between teams from the pier's two public bars degenerated into a free-for-all because, as the teams lined up, it became evident that their composition mirrored some especially virulent rivalries between boat crews.[21]

On the other hand, 'among men, it is attendance at the bar which most facilitates social repair', and Peace describes how interpersonal or interfamilial issues (of which there were many in this particularly fractious community) were often resolved over a pint.

As in all Irish rural communities, there was a strong link between pubs and local sports clubs: 'presentation nights following weekend-long competitions had become a lucrative source of income for public house owners'.[22] Competition between publicans was strong and they needed to keep up with changing customer tastes and activities. This militates against the notion of a timeless pub tradition: rather, community pubs (as in Doolin, but unlike Inishkillane) continually changed to reflect broader trends in society.

Ireland of the 2020s has changed significantly since Eipper and Peace conducted their community studies. A key driver of change has been digital technology. In *Ageing with Smartphones in Ireland* Maynooth anthropologist Pauline Garvey teamed up with British anthropologist Daniel Miller to explore the relationship between technology and society in two middle-class Irish communities, as part of a broader multinational study. They learned much about the everyday social life of middle-aged and older people. A distinctive feature was how the pub has largely been supplanted by the café as a place to socialise and for social clubs and other groups to meet up:

> [T]raditionally the pub was central for men to meet people. For this age group, however, its role is much diminished. There is just one pub today in Cuan [pseudonym] where older men regularly go to watch horse racing after placing their bets and enjoy the banter that ensues. Quite a few men will go intermittently to pubs and it is entirely acceptable for them to go singly, and indeed to sit by themselves. Or they might meet to go as a group to participate in one of the several music 'sessions' and other pub activities … However, pubs are far less important to this age group than the cafés that have become the key site for friendship today.[23]

In these (sub)urban communities, sports clubs (yachting, golf, football) have also become places for men to meet. For the women, cafés are far more important than pubs. It is notable that at least some pubs are being refocused onto a younger clientele, with wholesale changes to décor, events and music. The shift from pub to café can be interpreted through a modernising lens: older people are choosing coffee and 'café society' largely for health reasons. It is contemporary cafés they frequent, rather than 'the old-fashioned tea shop'.[24] In a follow-up work, *The Good Enough Life*, Miller provides further evidence of how the pub has receded as a key social setting for the retired people that are the focus of his study.[25] That is not to say that pubs have lost all salience, but that there has been a decline in more excessive drinking:

> [A]lcohol consumption remains a major part of everyday life in Cuan, and the pubs are a key site for social activities, as are the sporting clubs. But the impression of a steep decline in alcoholism is reflected in the number of pub closures and the number of drinkers in each pub.[26]

Over the last century anthropologists have provided some fascinating glimpses into the place of pubs in Irish communities – predominantly rural ones. Pubs have been key institutions (for men, in any case) that provided an important site, along with churches, shops and other public locations, for social interaction, inclusion and exclusion. Also, publicans were people of some influence in local communities – influence that could be parlayed into social, economic and political power. Anthropology, with its traditions of close observation, longer term of engagement and 'thick description', is an ideal method to analyse pubs: it is a pity that its practitioners did not make even more of the opportunity to fully conduct an analysis of the institution. It is tempting to think there remains a lot of material in unpublished field notes!

Sociological perspectives

British sociologist Diane Watson, who helped to stimulate the contemporary sociological interest in pubs, notes that 'public drinking "houses" of one kind or another have been important sites of social, political and economic exchange in almost every type of society'.[27] In Ireland, as elsewhere, pubs and alcohol have been seen both as a social problem and as an expression of national identity: each society sees its own pub culture as 'unique'. Much sociological research has tended to reflect this dual perception – focusing either on 'problem' drinking, and its links with poor health, delinquency and other social problems, or on the role that drinking and alcohol play in relation to group, community or ethnic identity. A third sociological tradition seeks to explore the pub itself as a site of social interaction, shaped by broader structural elements such as gender and class.[28] The social research into alcohol misuse has surprisingly little to say about pubs per se, though they have been the site of much 'problem' drinking, so we will confine our account to the other questions.

The pub as 'third space'

According to Watson, the pub is an 'icon of the everyday' to which most people can relate. Pubs have much to do with habit and repetition: as expressed in the term 'regular'. They may offer continuity, regularity and order 'fundamental to [a] sense of place, of time and of security'.[29] In Irish society pubs have, as we have seen in the anthropological literature, been closely related to everyday community life. Conversely, perceived threats to the institution of the public house, whether through drink-driving legislation, the 'smoking ban' or changes in licensing laws, are often seen as an attack on the community or on popular practices.

American sociologist Ray Oldenburg has stressed the importance in modern societies of the so-called 'third place'.[30] This is a location that is *not* work and *not* home: a public place where people can easily meet, relax and interact. 'Third places' include not just pubs, but coffee bars, hairdressing salons, public libraries, children's playgrounds, amusement arcades and other similar but culturally specific locations. They are typified by their open, democratic nature, informality and ubiquity. For Oldenburg they are a major contributor to the maintenance of social capital and healthy community life. The concept of the 'third place' has become influential in sociological analysis of the pub and, as argued by Scarbrough, the Irish pub can be seen as the 'quintessential' third place.[31]

For Kearns, the pub is both 'epicentre' and 'a true microcosm of social life, reflecting the socio-economic ethos of its host community'.[32] Irish pubs, particularly those outside urban areas, often combined the sale of alcohol with other businesses, such as grocery sales, fuel supply, undertaking and drapery, and a few retain at least some of these multiple functions. The pub, and other related settings such as 'spirits grocers' (grocery shops that served alcohol, frequented by women) and social clubs (which may or may not have facilitated alcohol consumption), have long provided a non-domestic social space.[33] Publicans have played a central community role, such as providing financial services in the form of credit or loans, and have had other important economic impacts, for example in local sourcing of supplies and support for community organisations, such as the Gaelic Athletic Association (GAA).[34] The pub has served as a social support mechanism for men: for Kearns, an environment where 'they can openly share personal feelings about domestic life, work, health, finances and phobias'.[35] Pubs have also had an important function in maintenance of social cohesion and combating of loneliness, subject of an important UK report by Thurnell-Read.[36]

The pub provides for a particular type of freedom in modern industrial society, described by Britain's Mass Observation project in 1943 as 'the only type of public building used by large numbers of ordinary people where their thoughts and actions are not arranged for them'.[37] Socially, even geographically, pubs do occupy a space somewhere between 'work' and 'home'; their function, according to John Fiske and colleagues, is to 'mediate their opposition by a complex set of repudiations and incorporations of both'.[38] The pub can be a 'home away from home' or an extension of the workplace, but contains elements opposed to both those locations. Indeed, it has often been seen as a threat to the stability of these institutions and has consequently been heavily regulated.

For Fiske et al. the pub has provided a strong symbolic alternative to the home, in its décor and acceptance of deviant behaviour, such as swearing or drunkenness. These are features of the pub that, according to Thurnell-Read, many older people in Britain now find a barrier to enjoyment. In Ireland the gloomy and functional ambience of 1960s rural Limerick pubs was noted by McNabb, though he found the local farmhouses pretty uninspiring too; Curtin and Ryan said the same of urban Ennis pubs of the 1980s.[39] But as pubs have changed, in part to attract female customers, they have moved closer to the image of the home: with TV sets, sound systems, carpets, food and familiar adornments. For Fiske et al. this may change the symbolic function of the pub: 'erosion of the boundary between home and pub threatens to make the pub no longer a specialised privileged space, where anti-social behaviour is sanctioned'.[40] Indeed, there is now significant official pressure on publicans to restrict drunkenness and anti-social behaviour on licensed premises.

Notwithstanding expansion into food, coffee and even non-alcoholic drinks, pubs are pre-eminently places where alcohol is consumed. Significantly, a 'no-alcohol' pub, the Virgin Mary bar, survived just four years in Dublin, closing in 2023, though there has been a rapid expansion in the sales of low-alcohol beer in pubs, such as Guinness 0.0.[41] Alcohol helps to define the 'meaning' of pubs. In English-speaking countries and northern Europe, including Ireland, that alcohol has tended to be beer.[42] Fiske et al. suggest that beer 'is cheap, egalitarian, masculine, social and, when drunk in pubs, significantly differentiated from both home (family/wife) and work (boss)'.[43] This is not to suggest that in Ireland the consumption of spirits has not also been important. But, until relatively recently, more 'domesticated' drinks, such as wine or coffee, have not been an important element of Irish pub consumption.

When individuals enter a pub, they are purchasing more than a particular product. They are also accessing an experience or ambience, associated with desire, and the creation and expression of identity and lifestyle.[44] What is important is not so much the products consumed but the meanings attached to them. In the UK context Shaw draws on George Orwell's 'Moon Under Water' – an account of the fantasy ideal establishment – to explore the 'atmosphere' of a pub.[45] As Shaw notes, this is created through a 'subjective, difficult-to-grasp set of criteria' that may include the aural background and interior design, smell, level of business, demeanour of other customers, lighting, choice of drinks, food or absence of food, and so on.

The creation of atmosphere in the Irish pub setting has been explored in detail by Scarbrough. In her study of pubs in the north-west of Ireland, she pays particular attention to how pubs have responded to the identity-construction of patrons. Pubs, she notes, are in a continual process of re-invention, often to the dismay of regulars. They are frequently revamped in response to the changing tastes, activities and interests of potential customers. Pubs often shift from a 'traditional' ambience to one that is increasingly focused on a younger consumer with more disposable income, and to the important tourist market. These re-inventions can have complex effects: some lament the shift towards airier, more open-plan pubs, while these can be welcomed by other users. Scarbrough also notes how customers can re-personalise revamped pubs through the gradual re-accretion of meaningful bric-a-brac that adds to whatever fashionable pub design has been attempted.

For Scarbrough the greater challenge to the survival of the pub is the shift from place- to interest-based loyalties. Postmodern individuals have a greater interest in the creation of their personal identit(ies) and 'ego-casting' and this helps to shape their choice of pub environment. Within a world of social media, the choice of pub (or to use a pub at all) is tied up with the creation and maintenance of a particular personal image and self-identity, rather than a direct outcome of place or social group. Pubs are increasingly aware of this, and to be successful must respond in both the real and virtual worlds.

What's the 'craic'?

The essential attraction of Irish pubs can be found in the concept of *craic* – a quality of social interaction that every Irish person can recognise, albeit notoriously difficult to capture.[46] Commonly understood as 'fun' and enjoyment, it is much more than that and shares something with the concept of 'flow' as developed by social psychologist Csikszentmihalyi.[47] For Tom Inglis, craic is 'based on ritualistic self-surrender to the group, which in turn means that any overt display of individuality that threatens the solidarity of the group is likely to be censured'.[48] This reflects his rather gloomy view of Irish pub culture as a response to religious and social oppression.

From a more positive perspective, ethnographers, immersed in the environment, have made a good attempt to get to the nub of craic as experienced in pubs. For anthropologist Kaul:

> [T]he craic is collective experience: it is produced on those occasions when residents meet together in order to relax, to be at ease, to entertain themselves, and in the course of doing so they generate a special chemistry which distinguishes certain events from others. It marks them out as occasions to savour and recall' … [but] 'the craic is unpredictable … in that it is difficult to anticipate why certain events generate this pronounced sense of collective well-being when others do not.[49]

Craic is closely linked to space, as Kaul further elucidates:

> [E]specially during the summer months, drinking sessions are noisy, boisterous and entertaining: that much is par for the course. Yet without any kind of notice the word spreads that the atmosphere in one bar is promising. People begin to drift in its direction, conversation becomes intense, the noise level soars, the arrival of a band generates some singing, there are specific incidents and encounters which add to the rising level of good humour – all of which culminates in an exuberant, enthusiastic, and exhilarating display of camaraderie. At the end of the evening, the craic has been enjoyed by all, but no one can precisely say why in this particular bar on this particular night.[50]

Creation of this elusive conviviality is explored in the early 2020s context by ethnomusicologists Dillane and Raine in their study of Temple Bar TradFest: a long-standing pubs-based event created to encourage off-season visitors to this Dublin 'cultural quarter' and tourist hot-spot. Dillane and Raine are keen to challenge what they see as an increasingly unhelpful distinction between the 'authentic' (good) and the manufactured (bad), when it comes to both 'Irish pubs' and to 'traditional music'.[51] They stress the agency of participants in TradFest who are less concerned with issues of authenticity than they are to experience a particular type of conviviality – one they have come to expect from prior experience of Irish pubs, in other locations and/or online. As they put it:

Figure 4.1
TradFest poster, 2010. Courtesy of TradFest Archive.

> [T]here is a historically broad and deep lexicon of Irishness in material and sonic culture from which to draw in the creation of the specific ambience and experience locally, that is in dialogue with global flows and generating a contemporaneous experience of sorts.[52]

Physical space and aural soundtrack combine to create the convivial 'ambiance' or 'atmosphere' of the Temple Bar pub. They describe how 'the unfolding experience of space into sound pervades the sense of community or being part of a participatory crowd that is essential to the in-person pub-based conviviality experience'. Irish music and the recognisable interior architecture of the pub combine to create the anticipation of a particular type of 'Irish pub experience' where 'the conviviality of having a pint, chatting while listening to Irish music [is] the ultimate goal'.[53]

More cynically, pubs can deliberately seek to 'manufacture' craic. Boak and Bailey report that:

> while gaiety cannot be faked, it can be helped along. O'Neill's [English 'Irish pub' chain] staff were given a handbook containing Irish jokes they could trot out to cheer up glum-looking customers, and instructions on how to generate the right kind of *craic* for differing lunchtime and evening crowds.[54]

This is not unique to Irish pubs: Tutenges and Bøhling analyse how staff of drinking establishments in Denmark engage in sets of practices, involving encouragement of excess drinking and raucous behaviour, to ramp up enjoyability and conviviality within the context of the night-time economy.[55]

Social interaction in pubs

Pubs are not just atmospheric: they are, of course, the site of extensive social interaction. Much is overwhelmingly 'everyday' and routine, as revealed through participant observation studies such as those conducted by the British organisation Mass Observation in the 1940s, Gwen Scarbrough in Ireland and Thurnell-Read in the United Kingdom.[56] Aspects of pub life that have drawn sociologists' attention have been practices of reciprocity and ideologies of egalitarianism based, in part, on pubs' distinctive oral culture.

The ideology of egalitarianism and reciprocity is important to the experience of pubs. Kearns reports that the 'rounds system' was well entrenched in Ireland by the nineteenth century.[57] Reciprocating behaviour has been extensively discussed by Fiske and colleagues in the Australian context, where the 'shout' is an intrinsic part of pub culture.[58] Inglis – without reference to other English-speaking societies – sees in the strict rounds system evidence for Ireland's 'rule-bound' culture, part of a broader subservience to church and state. Egalitarianism, as expressed through such drinking practices, is for Inglis an expression of the desire to be accepted in the wider group. He maintains that pub drinking in Ireland has been closely associated with social control, unlike in other European cultures where alcohol is seen as a vehicle of celebration and relaxation.[59] Scarbrough found that, by the mid-2000s, the rounds system had become less universal, often only enforced at large-scale ceremonial events.[60] Perhaps this is more evidence of our 'modernity'?

Irish pubs have been noted for their oral culture: of the literary, storytelling kind (beloved of tourist brochures) and in the ritualised verbal abuse among participants, termed 'slagging' in Ireland. This activity may be interpreted as an egalitarian, levelling process, where pretentiousness and selfishness may be challenged; or it may be seen as an exercise of power, where a particular world view is enforced through verbal sanctions. In his celebrated work for the *Limerick Rural Survey*, sociologist Patrick McNabb deplored the process of 'taking a rise out of some person' and saw it as damaging to the (male) community.[61] Inglis sees in this process 'not so much a social problem but rather a practice by which the drinking group is maintained'.[62] For him, the traditional rural pub, with its dominant group of bachelor drinkers, was an associate of the church in the enforcement of a repressive social regime designed to protect private property and the family. This reflects Brody's interpretation of what was happening in Inishkillane pubs. Kearns, however, is more positive and argues that 'within the social dynamics of the pub each regular becomes valued for his distinctive personality and contributions to the group'.[63] It is not clear if he himself is engaged in a bit of light slagging here.

For all sociological analysts, the pub is recognisable as a semi-public but highly regulated social space with its own codes of behaviour. Pubs, like the world in which they exist, are hierarchical and ordered. As Thurnell-Read notes, pubs are not always egalitarian or accessible spaces.[64] Hierarchy can be expressed in the differences between pubs and through the geography of pubs themselves, for example as reflected in seating arrangements.[65] According to Kearns, 'the most coveted social niche in the life of many Dubliners is their status as a "regular" in their local pub ... regulars are the privileged pub elite. They form an inner social circle as secondary groups defer to them in seating and conversational status'.[66] Campbell and Phillips report similar findings for rural New Zealand pubs.[67] Brody created diagrams to indicate those at the 'centre' and on the 'margins' of pubs in Inishkillane.[68]

Class

Curtin and Ryan, in a study of Ennis clubs and pubs, argue that pubs both reinforce and reflect class inequalities. They detect a 'distinct class pattern in their usage' and can identify 'middle-class' and 'working-class' pubs, as well as a minority of 'mixed' ones.[69] People are drawn to a specific pub on the basis that it offers a 'forum for [the drinker's] particular cultural and leisure interests'. Echoing the findings of Mass Observation in 1940s Britain, they conclude that the local pub 'takes on the character of a semi-exclusive "club" where the "inner circle" or regulars are clearly distinguished from casual patrons'. The parameters that define a pub's clientele are shaped by those in the workplace and reflect broader ideas about group identity. The sets of meanings that define 'working-class' and 'middle-class' pubs emerge from the interaction between customers and the environment:

> The discreet middle-class bar, where the clientele speak in low educated tones of lofty issues, only recreates for the worker the formal rules of the workplace. He is not barred from these pubs and he can afford to buy his drink like the rest, but he cannot participate fully nor does he want to. 'Public' places such as pubs and lounge bars in this way become class specific according to 'informal' codes which are just as effective in shaping the character of social life in the town as were the 'formal' codes associated with 'members only' clubs of the 1930s.[70]

These distinctions are mirrored in Brody's analysis: in Inishkillane it is landed property rather than workplace relations that is the basis for differentiation. Eipper also noted clear class and political distinctions within the Bantry community: not surprisingly, the elite gravitated towards drinking sites such as the hotel and yacht club.[71]

As well as places of consumption, pubs are also places of work. While much of the literature on Irish pubs focuses on the familial pub proprietor, they are also places of employment. It has been estimated that up to 36,000 are employed in the pub sector in Ireland.[72] As we have seen in chapters 2 and 3, pubs often provided access to a paid livelihood for women, as well as requiring a lot of unpaid work. In rural areas it has been reported that a significant number of pubs are staffed by just one or two people.[73] In larger cities and towns, they have historically provided an opportunity for secure, unionised work, where the job of 'barman' involved an apprenticeship and potentially a lifelong career. There is evidence that this has changed. Sociologists James

Wickham and Alicja Bobek have identified that the pub workforce has increasingly come to rely on two other sources: students and recent immigrants, a process that started around the mid-1990s. Following a successful barmen's strike during the 1994 FIFA World Cup, employers began to replace unionised staff:

> Bar owners moved away from hiring experienced workers and started taking on young people (including students) who were looking for temporary jobs. Unions were no longer welcomed and career structures were gradually flattened. While the old staff often managed to continue with their good jobs, the new jobs became more casual and more flexible. The same trend, so some argue, then spread to hotels and restaurants.[74]

As in many sectors of the service economy, the work in pubs is now increasingly likely to be lower-paid, less secure and more casualised.[75] There is evidence that immigrant workers, in particular, experience lower levels of job satisfaction, particularly due to discriminatory and authoritarian personnel practices.[76]

Gender

> Pub culture is very important to men, particularly as their roles are challenged in modern society, often by women ... where else, if not to the pub, have many men to go to relax?[77]

Watson argues that 'what goes on in the pub is not separated from other areas of life but inextricably involved in it. Social relationships in the pub are intimately linked to social relationships outside and play a key role in reinforcing men's position of control and dominance in relation to wives and girlfriends'.[78] Sociologists have noted that pubs have tended, until recently, to exclude women and that they may be associated with gendered attitudes and behaviour that have operated to maintain male power, for example through joking and wordplay specifically demeaning to women.[79] This was revealed in a deprecating way by Sybil Taylor in a 1983 guide to Irish pubs:

> Women should be prepared for what is known as the 'Irish lep'. This is not a shortened version of 'leprechaun' but a form of brief, intense courtship

> crowned with a swift pounce-and-grapple. The 'lepee' is free to go on with it or to laugh it all away, as laughter is the universal oil for any type of troubled Irish water.[80]

It is hard to imagine that such casual sexual harassment would be so easily explained away today!

There are, as Clay Darcy notes, cross-cultural links between alcohol consumption and masculinity, and 'those men who manage to drink the most and retain control, demonstrate their bodily power and mastery'.[81] Taking the first alcoholic drink in a pub is seen as a 'coming of age'. In 1960s rural Limerick 'a young man was initiated when he took his first drink in a public house. This was a sign that he had grown up and was acceptable to the male community'.[82] Curtin and Ryan draw out the manifold connections between the workplace, the pub, sport and the development of what gender theorist Connell would refer to as 'hegemonic masculinity'.[83]

In many cultures, including Ireland, the pub has been recognised as a masculine domain. For Darcy, 'the historic domination of men within pub spaces may account for the significant cultural entwinement of alcohol in the ways in which Irish men socialise, communicate and form social hierarchies'.[84] McNabb reports that in rural Limerick of the 1960s, 'a respectable woman would never set foot inside one of these places unless there is a grocery shop attached. She certainly never drinks in the local bar'.[85] Molloy remarks that women were effectively excluded from most Irish pubs until the 1970s, more likely to be observed, along with children, outside pubs while male family members were inside, drinking. Eipper noted that by the 1970s 'young women' 'had begun to infiltrate "respectable" bars'.[86] Husbands more and more took their wives out for a drink together. These trends were changing the character of many of the pubs, but not weakening their links to other aspects of community life. While in 1989 Curtin and Ryan argue that Ennis pubs remained an almost exclusively male preserve, by the early 2000s Scarbrough can say that women participate extensively in pub life, even drinking pints, but that this participation remains circumscribed by notions of respectability and personal safety.[87]

Female drinking has been almost universally negatively perceived. From time to time there have been moral panics about female alcohol consumption. In the 1950s, according to Diarmaid Ferriter, 'pioneers writing about women were utterly unambiguous in asserting that females succumbing to drink were infinitely worse than drunken men, particularly in the context of the home'.[88] Women were traditionally confined to the snug or lounge and, until the 1980s, it was not unusual for pubs to refuse to serve women a pint of ale or stout, as opposed to a half-pint 'glass'. In recent decades concern has been raised about young women's excessive consumption, and the role of 'alcopops' and other sweetened spirit-based drinks in this.

Despite such societal disapproval, a commonly noted trend has been the ongoing feminisation of drinking spaces, led stylistically perhaps by the 'fern bars' of 1980s America.[89] Women are now welcomed into pubs and the nature of the spaces themselves has changed to accommodate this new market:

> [P]ubs have become carpeted and furnished. There are soft furnishings and household artefacts, magazines and newspapers, children's areas and tiled washrooms, all replicating, on a grander scale, elements of home and family life.[90]

Dunworth remarks that even 'old man' pubs have become attractive to any and all genders:

> The current obsession with pints, with Guinness and with the 'aesthetic' of an old man's pub must mean that there are only rare corners and bars that have not yet been discovered by the next generation of all-gender pint drinkers looking for that perfect pint for their next Instagram post or TikTok video.[91]

This process of equalisation of access and acceptance has been described extensively by Scarbrough in the Irish context in previous work and in this volume.[92] Such changes may be associated with Irish women's comparatively high level of alcohol consumption though other factors may be related to increased disposable income as well as to changes in women's status and the availability of new styles of drinks.[93] There have been significant changes in types of drink consumed in pubs, with a shift towards lighter beers (lagers) and white spirits, especially vodka and, more recently, gin. Consumption of such drinks was initially associated with women, but they have found increasing acceptance among males as well, suggesting that there has been a significant 'feminisation' of drinking.

Figure 4.2
Exterior of No Irish Pub. From Kristen Hartke, 'Kiss Off, You're Irish: In experiment, Detroit pub bans St Patrick's Day revelers', *The Salt* [NPR], 20 March 2018. Photo by Dan Margulis.

Ethnicity and cultural identity

For St Patrick's Day 2018, advertising professional Dan Margulis created the project and accompanying video 'No Irish Pub' to draw attention to the immigration experience of Irish Americans and contemporary immigration issues in the United States (Fig 3.2).[94] Inadvertently, the video can also lead us to think of the cultural identification of the 'Irish pub' itself. Some have argued that the global success of the Irish pub is a consequence of its specific ethnic marking. For Inglis this is partly due to craic, but also that 'the Irish are neutral, white and successful'.[95] Boak and Bailey suggest that Irish pubs' appeal (to the British) is in that they 'occupied a sweet spot between familiarity and foreignness', as they put it: 'near, and far away'.[96]

There are examples of Irish pubs outside Ireland that have been accused of racist practices: such as Hank's Olde Irish pub in Cape Town and some Boston pubs.[97] At the same time, the traditional Irish pubs of Woodside in the New York borough of Queens are adapting to greater ethnic diversity as the make-up of the local population changes.[98] There have also been cases reported to the Human Rights and Equality Commission in Ireland of racist exclusion from pubs and nightclubs: of both members of the Traveller community and of perceived racially different individuals and groups, such as Black African men.[99] There are certainly interesting questions to be asked about Irish pubs, 'Whiteness' and privilege.

A most significant change in Irish society over the last quarter century has been the shift towards an immigration economy and the resultant social, ethnic and cultural diversity. Ireland has seen significant waves of immigration from Poland, the Baltic states, Nigeria, Romania and Brazil, as well as numerous other source countries. This fundamental social change has been reflected in various ways, but with scant research on how it has changed pubs. In their study of London pubs, Knight and Montiero challenge the stereotypical 'Englishness' of the pub by drawing attention to pubs that have become associated with identifiable ethnic communities, for example from India ('Desi' pubs) or the Caribbean.[100]

There is little information on how pubs in Ireland have similarly become centres for sociability and exchange among immigrant groups. There is as yet no extended sociological research on how immigrant communities in Ireland make (or do not make) use of pubs. Few pubs appear to have identified or marketed themselves as 'ethnic': with occasional exceptions, such as the Biało-Czerwoni ('White-Red') pub in Limerick and the Czech Inn in Dublin's Temple Bar (both pubs have now closed or been re-branded). Pifko (then Pilsner Pub) in Usher's Quay, Dublin was a Slovak/Czech bar and restaurant, but had apparently ceased trading in 2024. At the turn of the millennium, Tierney described two now-defunct Dublin pubs that used varieties of 'ethnic' branding: the Zanzibar on Lower Ormond Quay and the Icon at Leopardstown racecourse – the former offered a generic 'African' experience (with waiting staff clad in 'Moroccan' costumes), while the latter was a short-lived visitor centre for Bailey's Irish Cream that provided a virtual tour of Irish landmarks and culture: a sort of Disneyfied 'Ireland-land'.[101]

Nevertheless, in a study of the friendship relationships of Polish people living in Cork, Stephens reports on the importance of pubs: in particular 'the relational interplay between emotions and pubs. Participants revealed that engagement within pub spaces played a significant role in their ability to develop friendships with Irish people'. Partly this was a consequence of the disinhibiting influence of alcohol:

> I like very much living in my town and Ireland, I find it hard to meeting the new people, but if you more drink, you don't have barrier to make

> friends here … For us, when going to pub in town, you drink a bit more, and you feel better talking, because first – alcohol, and the second is you and everyone else is getting funny, so is just having good time with friends, not serious talking when you have the bad English. So, I not feel bad there about bad English, if I was in more serious place, like office party, maybe it would be problem. For me, pub gives secure feeling as I can make friends with Irish people without feeling silly about my English.[102]

For Poles with a greater level of English fluency, and perhaps in different social situations, pubs were less important as a basis for friendship.

Conclusion

This chapter has touched on some of the key anthropological and sociological texts from the last ninety years to give some flavour of how social scientists have addressed the phenomenon of the Irish pub. There is no doubt that its ordinariness, ubiquity and everyday nature has militated against a more comprehensive analysis. As can be seen from other chapters in this volume, social research on Irish pubs is pushing into new areas, and hopefully this will continue to be the case. There are many issues to explore: for example, the impact of pub closure, especially in rural communities; cultural and ethnic diversity in pubs – on both sides of the counter; how the 'night-time economy' and global tourism are shaping pubs; and how pubs are visualised in urban and suburban planning: suburban pubs are markedly absent from sociological and cultural discourse. The Irish pub remains a fascinating subject for sociological and anthropological analysis and I look forward to the work that will no doubt emerge in the years ahead.

Perry Share's Choice:

Guinness Bar,

Dublin Airport, Terminal 1

Figure 4.3 Shamrock bar, Dublin Airport (1962), from Dublin Airport Brochure. Photo courtesy of brandnewretro.ie

'I'm very disappointed in you,' tutted the barman to the bearded Italian traveller. The cause of such regret: the young man had ordered an unmanly glass of Guinness in the eponymous bar in Dublin Airport. This gentle slagging struck me as distinctly pub-typical – but rather unexpected in what French anthropologist Marc Augé would term a classic 'non-place': an international airport terminal. 'But I've only got ten minutes,' responded the alarmed tourist, and was rewarded with a relieving grin from behind the bar.

Can an airport bar, especially one so unprepossessing in atmosphere or décor, constitute an Irish pub? In the halcyon days of air travel (pre-Ryanair), when flight was restricted to the important and the wealthy (others made do with the Dún Laoghaire mailboat, or stayed put), Dublin Airport sported an elegant cocktail bar and restaurant, drawing fashion-forward Dubliners to its renowned dinner dances. In those days the original airport building, an architecturally advanced structure preserved in aspic within today's sprawling airport complex, featured the Collar of Gold restaurant, reputedly one of Dublin's finest, as well as the Shamrock Lounge with its elegantly attired barmen. Rather than a non-place, Dublin Airport's eating and drinking facilities were the place to see and be seen.

Contemporary geographers of mobility, following Augé, see the airport as a place of flows and signs, of containing and releasing, of code and security.

Figure 4.4 Guinness bar, Dublin Airport Terminal 1, December 2023. Photo by Perry Share.

Figure 4.5 The 'snug', Guinness bar, Dublin Airport Terminal 1, December 2023. Photo by Perry Share.

It's a place where people occupy a holding pattern, tolerated with increasing levels of resignation, while waiting and wanting to be somewhere, anywhere, else. How can a pub, so closely associated with locale and immobility, thrive in such a context?

The unimaginatively if somewhat inevitably named Guinness bar in Terminal 1 is a joint venture between Diageo, the Dublin Airport Authority and Wright's of Howth, the erstwhile fishmongers who now operate many of the catering and retail concessions at the airport. It sits in a bare brick-lined box with once fashionable ('industrial style') exposed service ducts in the ceiling. Oversized Guinness 'barrels' support smallish round tables, with high stools, with some banquette seating. There is even a semi-circular area that claims to be a 'snug'. It sort of feels like a pub. Most tables are occupied by passengers with their assorted luggage. Cables snake from coveted power sockets to charge phones or laptops. Wall-mounted screens display imminent plane departures to cities far and further, as often as not sprinkled with delays of various duration.

Such delays are of course manna from heaven to the proprietors, as time wasted can so easily turn into time spent drinking pints, at any point of the day or night. As the geographers remark, real-world temporality tends to dissolve in this liminal non-space, and the bar opens at a convenient 4.30 a.m. After all, somewhere in the world, it's drinking time.

As befits its origins, the pint is excellent, reflected in more than one online video review, while the service is professional and genial, with no tolerance for anti-Irish queuing at the bar. Unsurprisingly, the drinks menu is strongly Diageo-tied. Thankfully, food is limited to a range of sandwiches from a vending machine while necessary crisps can be sourced from another nearby part of the Wright's shopping ecosystem.

On a recent visit a 'named storm' had led to general chaos in flight schedules across western Europe. Something of a party atmosphere reigned in the Guinness bar, as the lads' weekend trip to Manchester kicked off in style, while a high-stakes Premiership match played out dramatically on the big TV screen. The pints were lined up on the bar and the craic was approaching ninety. Yeh, this definitely felt like a pub! For the departing tourist, a last-stop reminder of what they were going to miss about Ireland; for the local, what better way to start a great holiday?

Chapter 5

Pubs and Gay Social Life in Dublin, 1923–73

Sam McGrath

Introduction

This chapter aims to provide an overview of the gay social scene in Dublin over a fifty-year period from the just-established Irish Free State in 1923 until the formation of the first proto-gay rights group in 1973. Its focus is the history, importance and legacy of public houses where gay men socialised – primarily Davy Byrnes, the Dawson Lounge, the Bailey, Bartley Dunne's and Rice's – in the Grafton Street and St Stephen's Green area of the south city centre. It will also highlight some of the hotel bars, restaurants, late-night cafés, private clubs and basement shebeens which were meeting points for a small social scene that was criminalised and underground.

It was a period in which there were no overtly Irish gay organisations, venues or publications. Men found each other through word of mouth and met secretly in pubs that were almost exclusively owned and staffed by heterosexuals. It is a difficult story to tell as the gay men who lived through these years have left few, if any, written accounts nor have they given interviews about their experience. Many married men had totally secret gay experiences, while countless others emigrated to more tolerant places due to the threat or experience of blackmail or arrest. This chapter, therefore, is based on new oral history interviews supported by contemporary records and publications.

The focus is on a community of gay men who had the opportunity to find each other and socialise in pubs in Dublin city. This was not a shared experience for others across the island. Those in rural areas or small towns often experienced lifelong isolation and loneliness while others married to conceal their sexuality. It is also important to note that the Dublin gay scene in this period was overwhelmingly comprised of men who were financially secure, and many were employed in sectors that were considered 'tolerant' for the time period – fashion, art, publishing, entertainment (television, radio, theatre) as well as the service industry (waiters, hairdressing, shop assistants). There was also a healthy number of art college and university students. The Dublin scene also contained a sizeable number (compared to the overall population) of Protestant and Jewish men.

With those caveats to one side, this chapter will shine a light on a bygone subterranean world of gay-friendly bars and venues that prevailed in an overwhelmingly conservative society that was unfriendly towards homosexuality. Despite this, many of the men – labelled illegal and immoral in the eyes of the law and church – enjoyed a healthy and happy social life in which they met lifelong friends and romantic partners.

1920s and 1930s

Creating a picture of the social lives of gay men in Dublin in the 1920s is difficult but the bars of central hotels provided discreet and often 'anonymous' spaces for middle-class gay men to meet. The Gresham on O'Connell Street and the Shelbourne on St Stephen's Green were probable early meeting points in the period.

For gay men involved in the arts, there was a fairly tolerant environment within the United Arts Club (established 1907) which had rooms, a bar and dining facilities at 3 Upper Fitzwilliam Street from 1920.[1] Their annual fancy dress Nine Arts Ball, initiated in 1925, involved many men who dressed up in drag as women, and vice

Figure 5.1 Interior shot of the Horseshoe bar, Shelbourne Hotel. Creating Agency: Fáilte Ireland. Photo by and courtesy of Barry Murphy.

Figure 5.2 Exterior of the Shelbourne Hotel, 1968. Dublin History Forum. Photographer unknown. Courtesy of Michael M. Wood.

versa. This was a rare chance for gay men and women to express themselves creatively in comparatively safe surroundings.

Another of the few progressive and bohemian social spaces in mid-1920s Dublin was the Studio Arts Club, 41 Harcourt Street, founded by Parisian Madame Daisy 'Toto' Bannard Cogley in late 1924 or early 1925. Known locally as Mrs Cogley's or Toto's Cabaret, the private cabaret and theatre space built up a membership of nearly 400.[2] It moved to the Little Theatre on 7 South William Street in 1927.[3] The following year, the Gate Theatre was co-founded by actors, producers and life partners Hilton Edwards and Micheál Mac Liammóir along with Gearóid Ó Lochlainn and the aforementioned Madame Cogley. The Gate and other Dublin theatres were relatively unprejudiced spaces and provided a certain sanctuary for gay men to socialise, network and find employment.

The world-renowned French restaurant Jammet's moved to 46 Nassau Street in 1926, coinciding with co-founder Michel Jammet transferring ownership to his son Louis and daughter-in-law Yvonne. Jammet's became a key gathering place for well-to-do artists, actors, literary figures and gay men. Yvonne, a landscape painter and sculptor, developed a close friendship with Edwards and Mac Liammóir. Dublin was a small city and there were healthy overlaps between the theatre, cabaret scene and a small selection of 'arty' pubs.

In the lead-up to the Eucharistic Congress in June 1932, the authorities imported several French pissoirs (urinals), which were placed in strategic points around the city centre including Eden Quay and Ormond Quay beside Capel Street Bridge. Given that they were put in place for an international Catholic gathering, it is somewhat ironic that they greatly increased the availability for gay men to meet for casual sexual encounters.[4] These locations were particularly busy, down through the decades, after the pubs closed.

Davy Byrnes

Davy Byrnes is the first documented pub to have an established gay clientele. Proprietor David 'Davy' Byrne (1860–1938), from Arklow, County Wicklow, took over a well-established licensed premises at 21 Duke Street in January 1889 and changed the name over the door to his own. In its early years, the pub advertised itself as the 'resort of athletes' and received 'extensive patronage' from footballers, athletes and cyclists.[5] Byrne was a member of the Bective Rangers rugby club, the Haddington Harriers athletics club and the Lyric Musical Society.[6]

The pub's association with artists, actors and literary types dates to its earliest years, with artist William Orpen sketching a scene of himself and his brother there in 1906. James Joyce refers to Davy Byrnes in his short story *Counterparts* (1914) and his renowned *Ulysses* (1922) in which fictional protagonist Leopold Bloom enjoys a gorgonzola sandwich and a glass of burgundy.

While the city's pubs were dominated by stout, ale and porter, Davy Byrnes stood out in the mid-1920s by importing 'genuine continental lager beer iced on draught' from Munich.[7] In the 'golden age of Davy Byrnes from about 1900 to the 1920s', the writer Charles Duff claimed that the premises was never 'uncomfortably crowded' and he lamented that 'in the old days you sat on any sort of old chair with a pint in front of you on a very plain table and *knew* there was no other pub quite like it'.[8] The writer Liam O'Flaherty celebrated proprietor Davy Byrne in 1929 as one of the 'few honourable' Irish publicans who tried to 'struggle against the tide of dirt, corruption and melancholy'. O'Flaherty described the pub as an 'excellent house ... where one may find good company and good liquor at any hour of the day or night'.[9]

A writer under the pen name 'Twenty-Seven' complained in the January 1933 issue of the Gate Theatre's magazine *Motley* that Dublin had a lack of meeting places for

Figure 5.3 Interior shot of Davy Byrnes bar, 1960. Unknown source.

the 'so-called arty element ... painters, playwrights, lesser poets, journalists, sculptors, actors, musicians, critics and causeurs'. The author concurred that the closest thing was Davy Byrnes where a 'few specimens can be found on occasions'.[10]

By the 1930s, Davy Byrnes was certainly the bar of choice for gay dancers, actors and stagehands from the Theatre Royal and other entertainment venues, according to Eileen Buckley who joined the theatre's dance troupe (the Royalettes) in 1937.[11] She affectionately used the term 'pansies' when speaking to interviewee Sean Leonard in the 1980s and said female dancers would joke to each other: 'be careful with him, he'll be asking you to Davy Byrne's next!'[12] Sean believed that if you were in the pub as a solo male in the period, 'a conversation could be struck up about a play or an art exhibition' to 'act as an opener to express interest'.[13]

The pub's association with the literary and art world grew in the decade. The writer Francis Stuart believed that he 'probably first met' Samuel Beckett 'in the now legendary back room of Davy Byrne's public house where a crowd of youngish men and women of all kinds, by no means all artists ... used to congregate'.[14] Edward Toner,

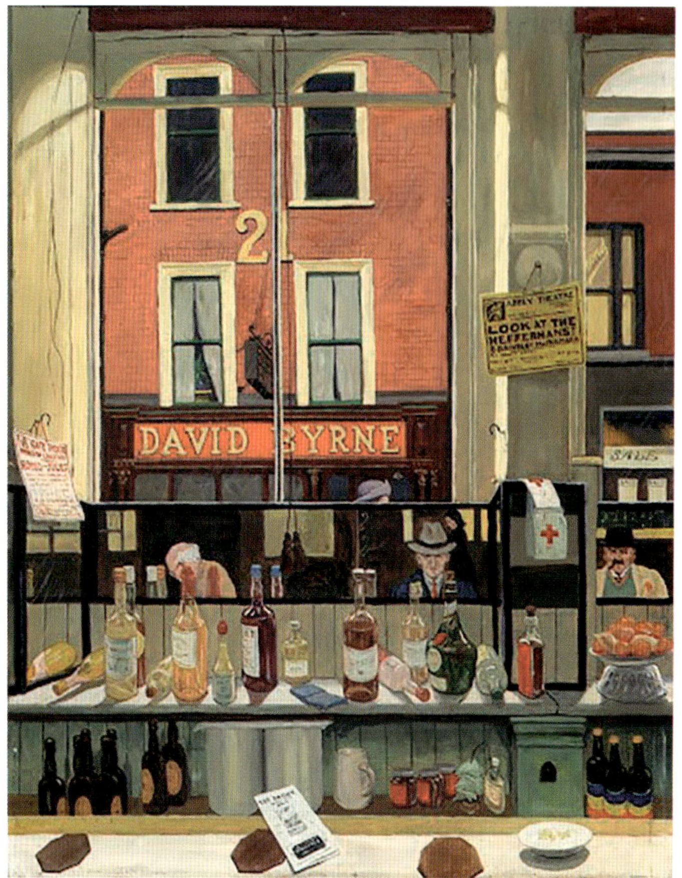

Figure 5.4
Harry Aaron Kernoff, *Davy Byrne's Pub, Dublin, from the Bailey* (1941). Photo by the National Gallery of Ireland (NGI.4677) and courtesy of the estate of Harry Aaron Kernoff.

a founding member of the Irish Film Society in 1936, spent most of his 'leisure time' as a student 'in the back "snug" … having an occasional pint and chatting about films'.[15]

Davy Byrnes was described in the 1930s as an 'informal club where men met to exchange and air their views'.[16] An unusual place where 'social distinctions were forgotten' and 'the professor and the professional man' could rub 'shoulders with the artisan' in the same space that 'the titled academician shared the next stool to the house painter.'[17] This was endorsed by Charles Duff who claimed that the 'old tavern had an atmosphere unique in Dublin … its clientele included men of the highest distinction and of a raggle-taggle disreputability'.[18]

The celebrated artist Harry Kernoff depicted the pub several times in his work and painted a scene of himself, proprietor Davy Byrne and Martin Murphy (Gate Theatre set designer) in 1936.

Following Davy Byrne's death in 1938, the pub was described by the *Irish Independent* as 'the rendezvous of many of those who figured in the political, artistic and sporting life of the country'.[19] *The Wicklow People* pronounced it simply as the 'meeting place of poets, painters and politicians'.[20]

Davy Byrne was buried in Glasnevin Cemetery alongside, as per the headstone, 'his friend Thomas Campbell' who had passed away eleven years previously.[21] This was a very unusual occurrence in 1930s Ireland and adds legitimate evidence to the rumours that Davy Byrne was himself gay.[22] The gravestone read:

In memory of David Byrne
Who died
On the 10th September 1938
And of his friend
Thomas Campbell
Who died
On the 10th March 1927

Dublin's first two high-class cocktail bars opened almost simultaneously in 1935. The Wicklow Hotel, Wicklow Street and the Royal Hibernian Hotel, Dawson Street had a reputation for attracting members of the Anglo-Irish landed gentry, the upper middle class and well-to-do gay men. George Buller, the bar manager of the Buttery cocktail bar in the Hibernian, had worked for many years in some of London's leading hotels[23] and was paired with Jack Lee, who had been a barman in the hotel since 1925.[24] The *Evening Herald* predicted that the Buttery would become 'a delightfully social centre for Dublin's fashionable circles'.[25] The Dolphin Hotel on East Essex Street opened its own cocktail lounge bar in August 1938.[26] This was followed by the Gresham Hotel on O'Connell Street in December 1939, which advertised a new basement bar 'fitted and furnished in the most complete and luxurious fashion'.[27]

1940s

The White Stag Group, an avant-garde art circle, relocated from London to Dublin in early 1940 during the Second World War.[28] The group was founded by two English artists, pacifists and occasional lovers – the bisexual Basil Rakoczi and gay Kenneth

Hall – who moved to Ireland to avoid conscription and London's restrictive war conditions. They were soon joined by several other Scottish and English painters and sculptors, who held joint exhibitions and social events in rented apartments in Lower Baggot Street.

One of the White Stag Group's patrons was landscape painter and sculptor Yvonne Jammet whose Jammet's restaurant was extremely popular in the 1940s with the affluent arts set. As well as the main restaurant and grill room, there was the Oyster bar at 1 Adam Court with an entrance from Grafton Street; the Burlington cocktail bar (managed by John O'Farrell); and two rooms for private parties – the Blue Bar and the Oak Room. The Smoke Lounge (also known as the back bar) was traditionally men-only and was known as a gay haunt.[29]

Author John Farrell has argued that 'the War years offered something of a boon to Ireland's gays as well as delivering a healthy influx of "Blitz Gaels" returning from London'.[30] Betty Chancellor, one of the Gate's leading actresses, said in a private letter that Dublin was devoid of fit fighting men because 'the place is full of drunken Blitz Gaels and Queens' (the latter term a clear euphemism for gay men).[31]

In the mid to late 1940s, the basement flat of 13 Fitzwilliam Place (known as The Catacombs) became an infamous after-hours spot and flop house for the city's bohemian set after the pubs closed. The leaseholder was Richard (Dickie) Wyman,[32] a tall, good-looking Englishman who had worked as a cocktail maker on a cruise liner and a nightclub manager in London. He moved to Dublin following the death of his British Army officer boyfriend in the war.[33] The Catacombs was renowned for its sexual licence, with Brendan Behan infamously recalling that it was a place where 'men had women, men had men and women had women'.[34] Michael O'Sullivan has argued that the Catacombs 'was the first place in Ireland that homosexuals could really mix freely in heterosexual company without incurring rancour or moral judgement'.[35]

While pubs were the most important place for socialising in the evening, there were several cafés that proved particularly popular with gay men for mixing during the daytime. Robert Roberts café on Grafton Street was a rendezvous spot for the art and literary set in the late 1940s. It also became a place where gay men from different social circles could find each other. Businessman and art collector Gordon Lambert, who was gay, 'kindled a lasting friendship' with another gay man, Cecil King (a publisher, later a painter), through his regular lunch visits. King 'drew him into his circle of artist friends' including Patrick Hennessy and his boyfriend Henry Robertson Craig. Historian Terry Clavin has remarked that Lambert, who had no background in the arts, 'was attracted initially by the tolerance this bohemian milieu afforded his sexuality'.[36] Actor Barry Cassin remembered the café as an important 'place for shop-talk' and where those working in the theatre could 'tap the grapevine for news of work'.[37] Actress Phyllis Ryan also recalled the 'informal "Green Room" of Roberts' as a place to share theatre gossip over coffee in the 1940s.[38] Bewley's Café, 78–79 Grafton Street, was a much-loved institution for all sections of Dublin society. It became a place for gay men to meet over coffee and from 1948 they were particularly well looked after by waitress Kathleen Toomey ('Tattens').[39]

Davy Byrnes, 1940s and 1950s

Davy Byrnes was sold in October 1941 for £10,000 to the Doran family, publicans of Marlborough Street.[40] Michael Carney, who joined the pub as a junior barman in about 1940, thought the Dorans were 'high falutin' people'.[41] They introduced a new decree that all staff had to 'wear a white vest and bowtie', which Carney thought was 'ridiculous'. In the 1940–2 period, Carney said that he served many of the 'literati' including writers (Brendan Behan and Patrick Kavanagh), painters (Seán O'Sullivan, Harry Kernoff and Cecil Salkeld), actors (Cyril Cusack, Denis O'Dea, Micheál Ó Briain, Eileen Crowe and Maureen Delaney) and playwright Lennox Robinson.

This period saw the painting of famous murals by Behan's father-in-law Cecil Ffrench Salkeld – 'Morning', 'Noon' and 'Evening' – depicting Davy Byrne, Bernard Shaw, Flann O'Brien and Micheál Mac Liammóir. Davy's walls in those years were also dotted with 'theatre playbills and other papers relating to drama and opera personalities'.[42] The Dorans renovated the interiors and reopened the pub as an upmarket, art deco cocktail bar in 1944.[43] Former barman Carney disapproved of the renovation job and 'almost cried' when he saw the new cocktail lounge that had replaced the 'historic backroom'.

In 1952, Charles Duff described Davy Byrnes as having the 'appearance of an American film set: glossy, modern, hygienic ... the atmosphere is cocktailish, the seats are most comfortable, the carpets soft'.[44] Davy's began to attract more foreign visitors as James Joyce's popularity as a writer grew. The journalist Seamus Kelly in a 1956 issue of *Holiday* magazine described the clientele as 'some of the younger

Figure 5.5 (above) Black and white postcard of Davy Byrnes. Photographer unknown, courtesy of Lennon Wylie.

Figure 5.6 (left) Photo of exterior of Davy Byrnes from 1950. Photographer unknown, courtesy of Ireland Old and New.

theatrical crowd and ... shrill ballet fanciers', which would seem to be a description of gay men.[45]

In an interview, Brian Ó Catháin was clear that the back room attracted gay men in the late 1950s, adding that 'eye codes' were critical as you had to 'make sure that there was no physical contact seen by the barmen'.[46] Ian Fox (b. 1941) agreed that 'the "gay side" of Davy Byrne's tended to be the room at the back' as it was 'more out of sight'.[47] The pub's three entrances – main one on Duke Street, side door at Duke Lane and via the Creation Arcade – made it easy for men 'cruising' to stroll in and out to see what the crowd was like.

In 1958, aspiring Belfast actor Willie Orr moved to Dublin to work as a stage designer at the Gate Theatre for a production of *The Way of the World*. This job was secured by his friend Henry Lynch Robinson, a famous Belfast architect, who had a great interest in theatre. Orr recalled in his memoir that Henry introduced him to a 'secret world' in Dublin 'of gay men meeting together in hotels and private clubs'.[48] Willie Orr told the author:

> I was welcomed into those circles in Dublin because I was a friend of [Henry's]. I remember there were hotels where the circle met, but I can't remember the names. Because of the law, a great deal of secrecy surrounded the meetings which were frequented by leading lawyers, bank managers, politicians as well as thespians – the Dublin elite. We met more generally in Davy Byrne's and Groome's across from the Gate but they were not specifically gay meeting places.[49]

The Dawson Lounge,[50] 25 Dawson Street, attracted a gay male clientele in the 1940s and 1950s. At the time, it was made up of separate bars across three levels – basement, ground floor and first floor. Today, only the basement bar remains and is well known for being the smallest pub in Dublin.

J.J. O'Hanlon was the proprietor throughout the 1930s and early 1940s.[51] In 1941, celebrated artist Desmond Rushton painted murals with scenes inspired by Omar Khayyam's Persian poem *Rubaiyat*.[52] An unnamed *Irish Independent* journalist admired 'the light colours, the delicate tracings of green, blue, and violet tempera against the creamy white walls', which would certainly have made it unusual by Dublin's pub standards.[53]

Figure 5.7 Entrance to Dawson Lounge. From the *Irish Independent*, 1976.

Harry Moore began to visit the pub in 1943 after he opened an electrical repair shop across the road. His son Dermod described the Dawson Lounge during the war years as 'a haven for the wild writers' set', but on the first floor his father found 'an oasis of calm, with a regular clientele of gentle, quiet men'.[54] It took a while before 'it dawned on him that they were gay'. They were 'discreet practically to the point of invisibility, but they were made welcome by the barman Simon'.[55]

In early 1951, the Dawson Lounge was bought by Arthur J. Gilligan for £14,000.[56] His son Arthur Jr described the Dawson's 'décor on the ground floor' to the author as 'reminiscent of a 1950s cocktail bar' with red leather plush banquettes and a carpeted floor which was later tiled.[57] The walls were painted 'a warm buttermilk tone' and had 'copper tinted mirrors'. The first floor had a more intimate lounge with a very small bar in the corner and there was another compact bar in the basement with storage.

Arthur Jr believes that the Dawson was unusual due to its décor and intimate size. It attracted a 'different clientele', including a 'cast of characters' composed of actors, writers, artists and others in the world of theatre and entertainment. The regulars called Arthur Sr 'Le Patron', which he enjoyed. Due to the Dawson's size, Arthur Jr believes that 'all people found solace in its intimate space' where their sexual orientation 'was never mentioned'.

The writer J.P. Donleavy, in the post-war period, described the pub's 'narrow stairs

Figure 5.8 Press advertisement for Dawson Lounge in *Irish Independent*, 30 September 1952.

down to its basement tiny bar' and an upstairs 'squeezed full' of 'resigned poets and painters, convicted and sentenced to Ireland for the rest of their lives'.[58]

One of the pub's famous patrons was Irish-American Kevin Monaghan (1916–89) who served with the US Army in Europe during the Second World War and settled in Dublin in the mid-1950s.[59] A painter and former professional piano player, he opened an antique shop at 43 Dawson Street and was described as an 'outrageously camp elderly gay man' by an interviewee who knew him in the 1980s. Another regular was Dubliner Paul Smith (1920–97), a gay man who started work for the Gate Theatre as a wardrobe/costume director in 1936 aged sixteen.[60] He published several well-received novels after he left Dublin in the 1950s. An advertisement in the *Irish Independent* in 1952 offered Dawson Lounge patrons 'the enjoyment of finest wines, spirits, snacks, savouries, coffee, etc. in the most congenial and comfortable surroundings'.[61] Two minor fires in the 1950s resulted in the closing of the street-level and first-floor bars. In February 1957, Arthur Sr bailed regular customer Brendan Behan out of jail at the behest of his wife Beatrice. Behan thanked him with a present and a note in Irish which read 'To Arthur from Brendan (with the) love of my heart'.[62]

Although its reputation as a gay-friendly bar seems to have flourished in the 1940s and 1950s, interviewee Ian Fox said 'the strange little Dawson Lounge' was 'quite popular' with a cliquey circle of older gay men into the early 1960s.[63] The Dawson was featured in the 1965 and 1967 editions of the gay travel publication *International Guild Guide*, but was removed by 1968. Arthur Sr retired in 1969 and died in 1974.[64]

The Bailey

The Bailey, 2–3 Duke Street, dates to the 1830s and was associated with many leading writers and political figures in the first half of the twentieth century. It attracted a middle-class gay crowd by the late 1950s but Ian Fox suspects that this was built on an earlier reputation.[65] The pub was purchased by artist and literary editor John Ryan in 1958, which coincided with Simon, the kindly barman from the Dawson Lounge, joining the team and taking many of the Dawson's gay crowd with him.[66] Interviewee Harold Clarke (b. 1938) fondly recalls Austin Doyle, formerly of the Dolphin Hotel,[67] who managed the Bailey's fish bar.[68] Doyle was the long-term boyfriend of Teddy Jacob, founder of Teddy's ice cream in Dún Laoghaire. Eddie Hernon, a waiter in the fish bar in the early 1960s, recalled that the Bailey was

> populated by mainly local businessmen. Night-time brought some students but very few in those early days. As I was based in the fish bar which was Austin's domain I did not have much contact with the main bar crowd. Simon was the barman, Christy was the cellarman … Austin was a beautiful young man and he knew it. He was the perfect gentleman, always impeccably turned out and stylish. [He] spoke several languages and was very popular … It was very lively on weekends with a business class of customers who frequented the Bailey [and] Davy Byrne's … I will never forget Austin Doyle strolling from Grafton Street … with [his] newspaper under his arm head held high and looking like Duke Street was his kingdom.[69]

Brian Ó Catháin, who became part of the gay scene in the late 1950s, described how the upstairs bar of the Bailey drew a selection of gay 'judges, lawyers and solicitors'.[70] He explained that Dublin

> was riddled by class so the judges didn't want to mingle with the lower classes in case they were outed. The usual procedure was that someone you knew would invite you to the Bailey and you were seen into the top bar. If you were

Figure 5.9 Exterior shot of the Bailey from an advertisement in the 1961 season programme of the Dublin Grand Opera Society. Special thanks to Andrew Percival. Courtesy of Opera in Ireland.

> presentable you would be introduced to one of them and then they would invite you to a party on one of their boats [in Dún Laoghaire]. You must remember that this wasn't 'rent', these people were just protecting themselves. All in all most of them were very friendly. At that time I didn't drink alcohol and a lot of these men protected me and others from spiked drinks.[71]

Brian's reference to 'spiked' drink is interesting but is not substantiated by other interviewees who had no first-hand or second-hand memories of 'spiked' drinks being a concern in the gay scene in the period.[72]

1960s–1970s
Bartley Dunne's

Bartley Dunne's, 32 Lower Stephen's Street, became Dublin's foremost gay-friendly bar in the 1960s and 1970s. Previously Hayden's, it was purchased in August 1941 by Bartholomew 'Bartley' Dunne Sr, a native Irish speaker from Kilconly, Tuam, County Galway. He had spent nearly forty years living and working in the pub trade in Manchester where he had been prominent in the Gaelic League and Irish politics.

Bartley Dunne's was a working-class, inner-city 'singing pub' frequented by locals from Mercer Street flats, students from the Royal College of Surgeons, theatregoers and actors from the Gaiety, and doctors, nurses and porters from nearby Mercer's Hospital.[73] It also built up a 'distinguished clientele' of international visitors including Dylan Thomas (Welsh poet), Sorley MacLean (Scottish Gaelic poet) and Valentine McEntee (Labour MP).[74]

Tony Carey, who visited in the mid-1950s as a young boy, remembered Bartley Sr in his 'pin-striped suit, waistcoat and white bib', who would drop him down a 'half-pint glass of diluted orange' while he minded the 'messages' for his mother in the hallway at the front door.[75]

There is some anecdotal evidence that Bartley Dunne's was attracting a gay clientele by the mid-1950s. Paddy Blair Mayne, the decorated Second World War veteran and rugby player, was a regular visitor in this period with his friend Carlos Kenny. Carlos' sister, journalist Mary Kenny, wrote that Bartley Dunne's was 'known

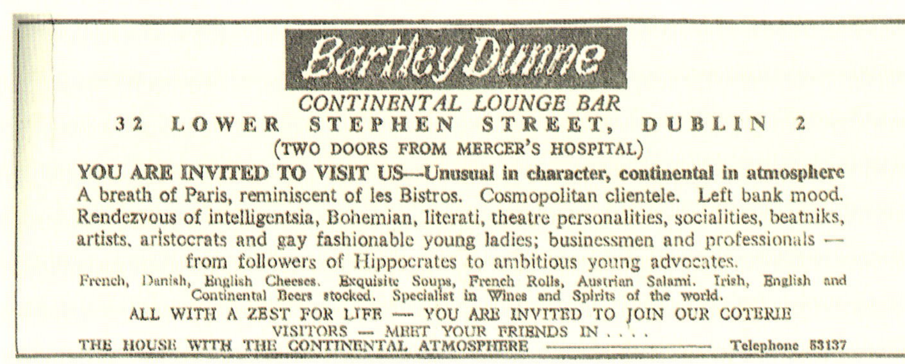

Figure 5.10 Advertisement for Bartley Dunne's, 1969, in *Publin '69: A selective guide to Dublin pubs* (Dublin: P.J. Publications, 1969).

Figure 5.11 Group of revellers at Christmas in Bartley Dunne's in the 1940s. Courtesy of Tony Carey. Sent to the author personally before his death in 2022.

as a gay bar' and described Mayne as a 'tormented homosexual seeking to escape 1950s Belfast'.[76] Mayne was killed in a car crash in 1955.

Bartley Sr, who presumably retired in the 1950s, died on 25 June 1961 aged eighty-five. The business was taken over by his two sons – Bartley Jr (known as Barry) and Gerard (known as Gerry) – who had been working in the pub for many years. The head barman was Albert 'Bertie' O'Rourke and another well-liked employee was Brian.[77] Bartley's extended its reputation as a gay-friendly bar in the late 1950s. Brian Ó Catháin recalled:

> I have fond memories of Bartley Dunne's in the late fifties. I remember Barry and Gerry well. In those days the curved corner near the entrance was bagged by the street girls and the rest was occupied by the 'boys' (this was long before the bar was extended). The barman Albert [Bertie] was liked by all the crowd, as was Gerry. Barry was a bit standoffish, though pleasant

> enough when he got to know you. There were always two gardaí outside at closing time. We soon learned that they were there to protect us from 'queer bashers' and not to take our names. There were some well-known actors as regulars, as well as writers and artists. [Actor] Paddy Bedford ('Diamond Lil') haunted the place.[78]

Brian's memory that gardaí used to frequently keep a watchful eye over patrons leaving Bartley Dunne's is not supported by other first-hand accounts. Willie Orr, who spent some time in Dublin around 1958, did not recall any specific homophobic attacks and believed 'there was much more fear of exposure among the affluent gay community'.[79] Tony O'Connell also did not recall any specific instances and believed such assaults became an issue in the 1970s and '80s when the community grew more visible.[80] Ian Fox did agree that the police 'would turn up occasionally' outside Bartley Dunne's and 'were friendly' but that 'homophobic behaviour on Grafton Street was only occasional … not too serious [and] mainly name-calling' in the 1960s.[81] Jeffrey Dudgeon, who was a university student in Dublin in the mid-1960s, believed that there 'were no anti-gay attacks at or near' Bartley Dunne's in those years but accepted that 'there may have been guards … sometimes' outside the public house at 'closing time'.[82] He pointed to Burgh Quay 'late at night' near the public toilets as being 'the only danger area in Dublin' for gay men and the scene of 'assaults and robberies'.[83]

Bartley Dunne's was refurbished in 1958,[84] a turning point in its transformation from a fairly conventional Dublin pub to a distinctive theatre/camp pub frequented by actors, bohemians and gay men. Jim Harkin (b. 1941) thought that the emergence of Bartley Dunne's was the 'best thing that ever happened on the gay scene. It changed everything. It was crazy, quite mad. There was nothing quite like it. It was more like a London King's Road pub'.[85] The 1962 international gay travel guide *Le Guide Gris* listed Bartley Dunne's with the simple description 'students and all'. In the same year an article in *Trinity News* made a coy reference to the bar:

> Were it not for their unfortunate influence in society, the public school products could be regarded as amusing anomalies, like beefeaters or debutantes, apart from the occasional occurrence of mistaken sexual identity, viz: Bartley Dunne's.[86]

Figure 5.12 Daggas (a Swedish student), Anita Casey, Barry Dunne (the proprietor) and Charlotte Leahy outside Bartley Dunne's, 1967/8. From 'Dublin Down Memory Lane' Facebook group by Charlotte Okonji.

The Dunne brothers built up a reputation for stocking exotic drinks from across the world. Barry later recalled to *The Irish Times* that 'there was a time when, if a customer wanted a particular drink and we didn't have it in stock, he got something else for free'.[87] The pub also had a well-stocked off-licence.

While never publicly describing itself as a homosexual or gay bar, the atmosphere in Bartley Dunne's was decidedly theatrical, with prints on the walls by Cézanne, Monet and Picasso as well as Parisian theatre posters and framed photographs of film stars. Famous for its dimly lit nooks and crannies, 'Non, Je Ne Regrette Rien' by Édith Piaf (1960) was played on repeat while Barry was known for addressing customers in 'camp' limited French and for his loud bellowing call at closing time. David Norris visited first in his late teens, *c.* 1961/2, and recalled in his memoir:

> It was an Aladdin's cave to me, its wicker-clad Chianti bottles stiff with dribbled candle wax, tea chests covered in red and white chequered cloths, heavy scarlet velvet drapes and an immense collection of multi-coloured

> liqueurs glinting away in their bottles. The place was (full) of theatrical old queens, with the barmen clad in bum-freezer uniforms.[88]

Another visitor, Patrick Fay, remembered the 'very bohemian atmosphere in the sixties' with 'red subdued lighting, alcoves, walls decorated with pictures of film stars'. The ladies' toilet had a figure of a man wearing a fig leaf with a sign: 'lift if you dare'. Curious women did so, unaware that it set off ringing bells in the bar and accompanying laughs among the regulars.[89]

Jeffrey Dudgeon, a Trinity College student from Belfast, first set foot in Bartley Dunne's in about 1965/6:

> It was deliberately bohemian. Candlelights and the snugs. Very dark lighting. Theatrical more than camp. [The] front part was totally gay in the sixties. The back part was not. When you think about it, there were about fifty gay men and women in the bar at most. Maybe a bit more at weekends.[90]

Artist Jim Fitzpatrick (b. 1944) worked in advertising in the late 1960s and was a regular in Bartley's at lunchtime. Not gay himself, he described it as 'the coolest hangout in Dublin. It was so glamorous but if you turned the lights on it was the seediest place you've ever seen! But it had style … it had a bit of a vibe … beatnik crew'.[91]

An early 1960s advertisement boasted of its 'unusual in character, continental atmosphere' and 'cosmopolitan clientele' of 'intelligentsia, bohemian, literati, theatre personalities, socialites, beatniks, artists, aristocrats and gay fashionable young ladies'. While the Dunne brothers always insisted to reporters that it was not a 'gay bar', it's hard to believe that they were not aware of the double entendre of the terminology used. Using language like 'unusual', 'continental', 'cosmopolitan', 'theatre' and 'gay' in a single advertisement for a bar was far from cryptic and almost certainly was broadcasting itself as a 'gay bar' to all those with even a basic understanding of gay double entendre and 'camp' culture.

Rice's

In April 1960, publican Robert 'Bobby' Rice, having sold his licensed premises at 86–87 Bride Street, bought Nolan's pub, at the corner of 141 St Stephen's Green and

Figure 5.13 Exterior shot of Rice's, 1984. Courtesy of 'Photos of Dublin'.

2 South King Street.[92] The exterior and interior of the pub had been comprehensively redesigned by architect Sam Stephenson two years previously.[93] Rice's had two bars on ground level with separate entrances. The 'front bar' opposite St Stephen's Green developed into a gay-friendly bar by the early 1960s.[94] Ian Fox called it a 'funny kind of pub' as it was a 'straight pub' up to and including six o'clock but turned into a 'gay pub' from about seven onwards with a 'totally different clientele'.[95]

In contrast to Bartley Dunne's, the pub was brightly lit and relatively small. It fit around twenty people sitting and roughly the same standing on busy evenings. Bobby and his brother Pat worked behind the bar. Bobby's wife Kathleen was there occasionally and was known as a tough lady; one interviewee had seen her clatter a customer across the head with his own shoe!

Tony O'Connell (b. 1943), who started visiting Rice's in 1965, remembers that if the owner 'Bobby was on duty and a non-gay couple came into the [front] bar he would usher them into the back lounge, lest they be contaminated'.[96] Its gay clientele was older, more middle class and attracted many from the worlds of theatre and broadcasting. A key group of regulars sat by the far window, which was nicknamed

Figure 5.14 Exterior shot of Nolan's pub, 1950s before it was taken over by Bobby Rice. From dublinforum.net.

the 'Royal Box'. Even in the late 1960s Rice's was sometimes called the 'geriatric ward' by younger gay men.[97]

By the early 1960s, the Bailey and Davy Byrnes were pubs where many gay men went in the afternoon/early evening – especially on the weekend – before finishing the night in Bartley Dunne's. *Le Guide Gris* described Davy Byrnes in 1962 as a 'quite notorious' and 'colourful' place populated by 'actors'.[98] However, there was some social division, with more affluent, older gay men preferring the refined surroundings of the Bailey and Davy Byrnes. Rice's was viewed as a mid-range option while Bartley Dunne's was looked down on, by some, as a bit too wild and 'rough and ready'. Interviewee Austin MacNally (b. 1944) told me, as an example, of one wealthy gay man named Paddy Barber who was a Davy Byrnes regular who would occasionally cross the threshold to Rice's but who would never set foot in Bartley Dunne's.[99]

Other Dublin pubs worth noting

The Metropole Long Bar opened in July 1942 in the downstairs of the Metropole Cinema and restaurant in O'Connell Street.[100] Five years later, the venue expanded with a new cocktail bar (the Adam Room) under the stewardship of Swiss barman Charles Farran, formerly of the Theatre Royal bar.[101] The Long Bar was a popular spot for visiting sailors and foreign servicemen. Interviewee Austin MacNally 'had many good times there in the sixties'.[102] The Long Bar was named in gay travel guides from 1962 until 1972 when trading ended.

The Tower bar, 33 Henry Street, was owned by George E. Brady from 1938.[103] It was the go-to spot for RTÉ Radio staff, based opposite in the General Post Office (GPO) from 1928 until the early 1970s. In 1950s advertisements placed in programmes for Rathmines & Rathgar Musical Society shows in the Gaiety Theatre, it boasted of its 'club atmosphere' and 'men only' policy. The Tower bar was listed in gay travel guides from 1968 to 1975 when it ceased business.[104]

Hotel bars continued to remain popular. The Shelbourne's Horseshoe bar attracted many gay visitors from across Ireland and further afield. Jim Harkin saw it as a 'great place for picking up posh Americans'.[105]

The Hibernian's Buttery was popular with the 'business gays' according to interviewee Austin

Figure 5.15 Advertisement for the Tower bar, 1958. Published in Rathmines & Rathgar Musical Society's programme for *Love from Judy*. Special thanks to Andrew Percival. Courtesy of Opera in Ireland.

Figure 5.16 External shot of the Hibernian Hotel, 1953. Courtesy of 'Photos of Dublin'.

MacNally. Ian Fox described it as 'very gay' and recalled that if barmen George Buller and Jack Lee 'liked you, you were grand [but] if they didn't, you'd have to wait half an hour to get served!'[106]

The Wicklow Hotel bar had a more bohemian atmosphere. Another interviewee, Brian Peppard, told the author that his social life in the late 1960s revolved around Bartley Dunne's, Rice's and the bar of the Wicklow Hotel.[107] The gay clientele was warmly welcomed here by barman Stephen Corcoran, from 1971, who later set up his own gay bar in Paris. Jim Harkin remembered Jammet's back bar as 'very, very gay' and as a spot where older 'gays' would take younger men on dates.[108] The United Arts Club continued to be an important social space with a 'good scattering' of gay men, according to Ian Fox. The Bailey's owner John Ryan described it somewhat uncharitably as a 'glorified after-hours pub'.[109]

Two interviewees referenced that Matt Smith's The Step Inn in Stepaside was popular to visit after the city centre pubs closed at 11.30 p.m. A 'bona-fide' house, it

Figure 5.17 Advertisement for the Hibernian Hotel's new American bar (The Buttery), 5 August 1935. Courtesy of *The Irish Times*.

utilised a legal loophole, dating back to early coaching days, that allowed a genuine 'bona-fide' traveller three miles (five in Dublin) from his place of residence to drink alcohol outside normal hours. Carloads of gay men would drive up to Stepaside after Bartley Dunne's closed, according to Austin MacNally.[110] Brian Ó Catháin also recounted that 'if you had a date with one of the Bailey crowd in their home or boat you usually ended up there for "afters". A lot of the guys from the city would come there after the pubs shut'.[111] This law was revoked in 1963.

Before the first gay discos in the early 1970s, there were very few places for gay men to socialise after the pubs shut besides private house parties. Maria Seligman, a middle-aged single Jewish lady who lived at 'Sunnyside', 175 Upper Rathmines Road in Dublin 6, made friends with many gay men and was renowned for opening her home to post-pub gatherings from the late 1960s to the mid-1970s.[112]

There were also a handful of restaurants and late-night cafés that were particularly popular with gay men after the pubs closed. The Manhattan was a 'greasy spoon' café that was opened in 1954 at 23 Harcourt Road by Englishman Reginald (Reg) Wiggins and his wife Mary Woods (Auntie May) from Fordstown, County Meath.[113] Tara, the granddaughter of Auntie May, agreed that the Manhattan was 'renowned for being a gay haunt' in the 1960s and early 1970s.[114] It opened from 10 p.m. to 4 a.m. but had no wine licence. Tara said that her grandmother welcomed anybody, irrespective of their sexuality or background: 'It didn't matter who you were. She didn't pre-judge anybody. Your money was welcome no matter who you were or what you were. I don't mean to sound that blunt about it but that's the easiest way of explaining it.'[115]

The Trocadero restaurant was opened in 1961 at 3 St Andrew's Street by Eddie Michaels (Liassides), known as 'Eddie the Greek'. It is unclear whether the business had any direct link to a restaurant of the same name that operated at 19 Kildare Street from late 1956 for less than a year. Eddie's 'Troc' became a well-known and established favourite of the theatre and entertainment world. In the early 1960s, Ian Fox recalled that 'it was cheap, very gay-friendly, opened late' and was popular with 'all the actors of the time … [and] the post theatre crowd'.[116] Known for its plush decor and simple, comforting cuisine, it attracted a significant gay clientele, which lasts to this day.

After establishing itself on Molesworth Street in 1959, Mrs Gaj's restaurant moved to a first-floor premises at 132 Lower Baggot Street in 1963. Harold Clarke called it a 'favourite place for gays',[117] while Jeff Dudgeon described Gaj's in the late 1960s as 'significantly gay [with] all sorts of bohemian types and Trotskyists'.[118] Tony O'Connell called it 'the best after-hours spot … good food … and a mixed clientele of a somewhat "bohemian" persuasion'.[119] Mrs Gaj's son Wladek explained that the 'acceptance of homosexuality in the restaurant was probably largely due to' his mother's personality, her 'open-mindedness' and 'progressive' politics'.[120] Unlike the Manhattan, Mrs Gaj's was able to serve wine with meals after hours. Wladek recalled his mother's 'kindness towards people and a great sense of humour'. There was an all-female staff that contributed to the 'liberal' atmosphere, consisting of Phyllis, Betty Day, Hope Armstrong and 'Mrs' Cooper. Wladek's memory of the late 1960s as a teenager was that 'there was no class "demarcation" at the time [and] many of the gay men were working-class'.

Wladek surmised that by the early 1970s 'the importance of Gaj's as an after-hours "gay" venue would have lessened' and 'especially as the war in the North commenced, things became even more politicised'.[121] The Irish Women's Liberation Movement was founded in the early 1970s and lesbian women started to frequent the restaurant in larger numbers. The 1972 *Le Guide Gris* described Gaj's as a 'place for late-night snacks after pub hours, mixed, colourfully conglomerate'.[122]

Figure 5.18 Advertisement for Gaj's restaurant in *Trinity News*, 11 May 1967.

Conclusion

This chapter set out to examine the history, geography and importance of Dublin pubs that were popular with gay men in Dublin over a fifty-year period from 1923 to 1973. It sought to shine a light on a small underground community who lived and socialised in relatively plain sight but were unable to publicly express their sexuality. Gay men in this period risked losing their jobs and ostracism from family and work colleagues if rumours circulated about their orientation. Threats of financial blackmail from unscrupulous people were a real and legitimate concern, with Harold Clarke remarking that it was 'always just below the surface'.[123] Being caught in an intimate situation with another man could lead to arrest, conviction and possible imprisonment. Between 1962 and 1972 there were 455 convictions of men in Ireland for crimes such as 'indecency with males' and 'gross indecency'.[124] Research carried out by Professor Diarmaid Ferriter found that between 1940 and 1978 an average of thirteen men a year were jailed for homosexual offences.[125] This was the atmosphere in which gay men in Ireland had to live.

Meeting places in Dublin for gay men were few and far between. There were certainly no pubs, bars or cafés advertising for custom with 'rainbow' flags or pink triangle symbols. There were no newspapers, magazines or books for the gay community to find out where to meet others. The first printed venue listings did not appear until the early 1960s, and they were marketed for middle-class American tourists, not locals. However, once you found details about the small number of gay-friendly pubs, they offered a warm and generally welcoming place for gay men. Pubs were much more important social outlets than they are today. Alcohol was generally cheaper and there were far fewer distractions at home for people in the evenings and on weekends. They were the key places for gay men to make friends and meet romantic partners. Harold Clarke told the author that he met his life partner in 1956 and was with him until he died in 2014. Interviewees Jim Harkin and Ian Fox met in Bartley Dunne's in 1966 in their mid-20s and have been happily together since then.

BeLonG To, an LGBT youth organisation in Ireland which caters for young people, produced a 'LGBTI+ Timeline – Ireland' which has a noticeably large gap of information between 1861 (Offences Against the Persons Act) and 1973 (establishment of the Sexual Liberation Movement). This chapter argues that there was a healthy, albeit underground, gay social scene in Dublin from the early 1920s to the early 1970s. Straddling the worlds of art, theatre, fashion, publishing and entertainment, the gay community was comprised of many influential writers, actors, poets, fashion designers, theatre set designers and television/radio employees.

Although the risk of blackmail and arrest was prevalent, many of the men remarked to the author that the scene was warm, inclusive and fun. This was in no doubt due to its small size (a few hundred men probably) and a feeling of camaraderie. 'It's one of those strange things in life,' Brian Ó Catháin told the author, 'when things were illegal it was far more interesting and definitely more friendly.'[126] Jim Harkin remembered a bustling social calendar in the 1960s: 'If you were twenty years old, tall, good-looking and you didn't have three different things you were invited to on a Saturday night – you weren't happening.'[127] These social gatherings in people's homes would generally take place after the pubs closed in flats and houses in Ranelagh, Rathmines, Terenure, Rathgar or Dalkey on the southside of the city. Several men were particularly known for throwing house and dinner parties, in upmarket suburbs like Dalkey, Rathgar, Terenure, Sandycove and Dún Laoghaire, including couple Teddy Jacob and Austin Doyle, Stanley Traynor, Karl Feldman, Tim Danaher, Torry Large, Harry Bieling and Ozzie Dixon.

The focus of research ends with the foundation of the Sexual Liberation Movement in 1973 and the Irish Gay Rights Movement (IGRM) the following year. The first gay discos organised in rooms at 21 Westland Row were soon followed by weekly dance events from late 1974 in the first-floor premises of the Good Karma restaurant, 4 Great Strand Street, with DJ Hugo McManus. These became the first events in Dublin where gay men could meet and socialise freely on their own terms. The gay-friendly bars mentioned in this chapter offered a relatively safe place to mix, but the gay community, it should not be forgotten, had to share the space with heterosexual customers, staff and management. None of the pubs ever publicly admitted they were important gay haunts and some even denied the associations as late as the mid-1980s.[128]

Rice's was closed and demolished in 1985. The Dunne family sold Bartley Dunne's in 1986 and the pub was pulled down in 1990. Davy Byrnes, the Bailey and the Dawson Lounge remain open today, but are no longer considered 'gay-friendly' spots to any great extent. The importance of these five pubs, and others, should be recognised as playing an important role in the social lives of gay men in the decades before the emergence of the gay rights movement.[129]

Sam McGrath's Choice:

The Lord Edward,

Christchurch Place, Dublin

The Lord Edward is one of the best pubs in Dublin city and has been a favourite of mine for the last fifteen years. I first visited as a fresh-faced college student in late 2008 at the start of the last great recession. Pints of Guinness were €4 which was considered fairly cheap even then. The pub was no-frills but comfortable and had a perfect mix of locals and the odd tourist.

Perched on the corner of Christchurch Place and Werburgh Place, The Lord Edward is technically in Dublin 8 but is spitting distance from its namesake Lord Edward Street in Dublin 2, a continuation of Dame Street and the city centre 'proper'. It stands opposite the substantial Christ Church Cathedral while a side entrance, beside the famous Burdock's fish and chips takeaway, faces St Werburgh's Church where the rebel Lord Edward FitzGerald (1763–98) himself is buried.

A five-storey over-basement building, the premises was designed by architect William Henry Byrne and was built in 1900 by builder H. & J. Martin at a cost of £4,081 for publican Thomas Cunniam from County Wicklow. It remained in the family's ownership for a hundred years. The pub's ground-floor lounge bar has a couple of exceptional window seats and a tiny little 'false snug'. The more open-plan cosy upstairs was once the family sitting room and has red plush seating and a fireplace, which perfectly sets the scene in wintertime. The third floor is currently vacant but was home to its famous seafood restaurant from 1967 to 2015. I have spent many happy evenings in the Lord Ed for birthday celebrations, farewell drinks, welcome-home drinks, pre-gig drinks and post-gig drinks. Long may it remain open and never change!

Figure 5.19 Exterior of The Lord Edward, Christchurch Place, Dublin. Photo by Angeliki Lima.

Chapter 6

The Irish Pub: Lived Experience and Therapeutic Value

Trish Murphy

Growing up in a pub in the west of Ireland was to be at the centre of the community, the place where everything happened and the therapeutic nerve centre from which all could be sorted. People were valued for their conversation, their songs, their wit and their friendliness – regardless (somewhat!) of the external roles they played in society and thus the pub offered a truly egalitarian possibility that was not otherwise available. The art of conversation was currency in such a venue and some of the best of Irish literature had its birth in the pub – in my case John B. Keane was the local bard in a rival pub only a few miles down the road.

As a therapeutic entity, the Irish pub offered *belonging* and as such fulfilled an essential aspect of Maslow's hierarchy of human needs. From this space, customers could go out into the world with a sense of place, of being accepted and of being part of something beyond themselves. It also offered a type of confessional where almost anything could be told over the settling pint. It was here that my psychotherapeutic skills were first honed and where men, in particular, could be given the space (sometimes hours or days) to unravel their story. There was always absolution, the slate would be wiped clean so that what was told the previous day could be put down to 'the drink' and the customer could continue on, saving face while also having been heard.

Irish pub: personal experience

I grew up in a small, family-run hotel in Abbeyfeale; it was on the main road from Limerick to Killarney and, while it was situated in the county of Limerick, it was in the diocese of Kerry and so its identity was always split – for rugby we were west Limerick and for Gaelic football we were firm Kerry supporters. As a small child in the sixties I experienced an expansion of the tourism industry and there were always buses stopping on the way to Killarney. I had bright red curly hair and I learned how to exploit this for the American tourists and often took off my shoes to complete

Figure 6.1 Leen's Hotel, Abbeyfeale, as it looked in the 1980s. Photo by Trish Murphy.

the picture of cute kid in need of gifts. It was the era of big bands and the dancehall in the town was always packed on Sunday nights, while people thronged into town on fair days, pay days and on any other possible occasion. Our place was where all the departed emigrants came to stay when they were visiting home and we got a glimpse of the far-flung world when these customers appeared in drainpipe jeans and non-beehive haircuts. Standing at the front door was to have access to the whole community – very little slipped past those who spent their time in this activity and the pastime was defended in William Foote Whyte's 1943 book *Street Corner Society*. I often wondered how anyone managed to have affairs with such scrutiny constantly turned on, but people are nothing if not ingenious!

Glamour came to the town in the form of the Rose of Tralee festival. The whole entourage would stop in the hotel for refreshments on the way to Tralee and I was usually dispatched to hold ashtrays, so that the artfully dangling cigarettes did not damage the carpets on the stairs and lobby. The women were impossibly elegant and beautiful, and their assigned male cohorts were handsome and well behaved (for the most part). These were occasions when I learned the names of drinks that I have never had use for since: Benedictine, Babycham, Cointreau and Drambuie. I'm sure the women picked them based on the colour matching their outfits. Colour was not

Figure 6.2 My twin brother and me, in my Shirley Temple phase. Courtesy of Trish Murphy.

the issue when I was behind the bar on a quiet weekday and a farmer asked me for a green chartreuse. I dutifully got a delicate little glass and handed it to him. He looked at me in disgust, saying, 'Girleen, it's not for me at all, 'tis for the dog', pointing to the greyhound beside him on the ground. Maybe not all of it was glamorous!

The Bachelor Festival in Ballybunion also provided a big event for the town. In contrast, this time the drinking was more serious and the craic was the whole point of the festival. There was a wildness to it that defied the still very conservative ethos of life in the seventies, but perhaps it also was a precursor to the later abandonment of restrictive societal mores. I remember leaving a note in the hotel kitchen as I left for college in Cork in the early hours: 'Gone back to college, bachelor in bed in room no. 10'! My parents, to their credit, never mentioned it to me later.

Conversations were the essence of life in the bar. You would never know where the conversation would take you or for how long it would last. Some themes lasted months, such as the long planning and execution of rescuing my bike when I had abandoned it in County Clare, having abruptly left an AnCO training course (when the mobile bank never arrived, and food became an issue for me). Many excursions left Abbeyfeale only to find themselves stranded in a pub in Tarbert or Ennistymon and the whole bike rescue had to be re-set again and again. These stories were re-hashed and re-told with relish and new bits added as new entrants to the rescue were brought into the story and the raconteur held court with new audiences.

Major discussions of the day got good airing in the bar. The AIDS virus, the divorce referendums, contraception, the rightness of women drinking pints, the scandal of Bishop Eamon Casey, church vs state, politics and the North were all legitimate topics. The best part of these discussions was that some people would swap sides following a discussion and become fervent proponents of the opposite of whatever position they had started out with – true democracy! I loved controversial topics as they made the time fly if I was working behind the bar, but my dad would sometimes sigh and say, 'Don't start on religion or politics as you know we'll be here all night.' As a true publican, he rarely showed his colours and everyone left feeling that their opinion was valued and needed. But he loved a good sing-song and these were regular occurrences, with everyone having their song or recitation that had to be inveigled out of them with pleas and begging. We were all shy to perform but of course gave in when the right amount of audience demand required it. I used to practise my song ('Blowing in the Wind') while peeling spuds in the yard – it causes me blushes of embarrassment to remember it now but at the time I thought I was great!

A young American walked into the bar one afternoon in the early eighties, said he was travelling for three months while he and his girlfriend waited for their HIV tests to come back – he stayed for the entire summer. It was no surprise if someone unexpectedly spent a night in the town (due to their car breaking down, a regular occurrence in those days, or some such). These unintended guests would be welcomed with open arms and after a night of stories and song they often returned year after year to reconnect with that sense of belonging. It helped that Ballybunion beach and golf club were only a half-hour away and the lakes of Killarney a little further. I was able to spend nights in those guests' homes around the world as I travelled on a shoestring in later years, and their children often took on the mantle of representing their parents' seat at the bar as time moved on.

The applications to psychotherapy

It was as a bar tender that I learned to listen, to follow the story and of course eventually to become an agony aunt: I write a problem page for a national newspaper and have been in training since knee-high. My career as a psychotherapist had its beginnings in the variety, depth and agony that was displayed as life played itself out on the other side of the counter every day. Customers' wins were celebrated and enjoyed by all but so too were the losses and griefs that are an inevitable part of life. The bar was a vehicle for support and consolation when death came to someone's door, and the sense of community it offered was genuine and available every day.

I was a couple of months into my psychotherapy training when I realised that my extended family was actually the pub community, and once that settled in I began to understand myself and my dad much better. Customers hung on for the late-night invite of 'we'll have one quiet one ourselves', as the last few customers sat by the fire and reflected on the day's events. To this day, I associate relaxation with the sacred quiet of a bar as the day ends. I can now rarely stay up that late, but it was a time when people spoke of real concerns, hopes and worries in a way that might not be so easy in the harsh light of day.

While all this sounds very therapeutic, it would be remiss not to address the alcohol abuse issues that arise. The serious drinkers were cared for with a quiet word, with someone to see the person home safely and a suggestion that they 'might have had enough now'. The other pubs often sent word that someone had left, and it would be better if they went home, and this would alert the community to try to make this happen. Inevitably, there was huge difficulty for someone who was trying to stay off alcohol, as the pub tended to be the gathering place and very little else was on offer in the town. Coffee culture was yet to arrive and there is no doubt those people suffered as their possible support was also their temptation.

As the health service began to provide more services for alcohol treatment, the culture has shifted to an awareness of professional support, and this is now factored into the response from the community. However, growing up in a local pub provided knowledge of the many factors that contribute to someone's problem drinking and showed how individual, couple and family psychotherapy all play a significant part in the recovery model. In fact, the more a community involves itself in being part of the solution, the higher the chance of success for the individual with the alcohol issue – for example a plan to encourage participation in a local sports or drama club, even at an organisational level. Many local clubs booked rooms in pubs to host meetings or events so the intimate knowledge of someone's issue could be delicately applied, allowing for the person to be treated with dignity.

Skills and principles

One of the great skills I learned was how to manage customers of all ages and dispositions when they were behaving badly. These skills of negotiation and conflict management came in handy when travelling alone and when working in detention centres and prisons – I never once got assaulted! I innately learned that to de-escalate a situation, body mirroring works: this included calm breathing, quiet voice, non-threatening stance and tensing and releasing muscles. Engaging with the person as a human being rather than as a nuisance was also a skill that was honed in the depths of an escalating situation late at night. This involved treating the person with dignity so that they could wake up the following morning without fear of shame. Attention, listening and validating were all aspects of managing a difficult situation that are core to the art of psychotherapy, as is the skill of challenging behaviour when the person is in a place to take it on board. Very often, a private word would happen in the days after a conflictual instance when boundaries and appropriate behaviour would be discussed with the person in question and a path laid out to return to the fold. As the pub is a communal space, the direction of acceptance by the community was headed by the pub owner and everyone knew that that reparation had happened, and life could continue as before.

Relating to a huge diversity of people was a skill learned in the pub and transferred easily into psychotherapeutic practice. The ability to start from where the person is at and to learn from them how they wanted to be communicated with was a core skill in pub life. A nod or a grunt was often enough to transfer a lot of information about needs and desires, and deciphering languages and cultures from gestures and smiles was also par for the course. As more and more tourists travelled to the west of Ireland, the publicans and their staff adapted to the diverse needs of customers and they worked to enlarge their welcome beyond their previous limits, again a transferable therapeutic skill.

Any successful pub holds the secrets of its customers close to its bosom, and this is something that is essential for psychotherapeutic work. It can be very tempting to show that you have insider information of a local but there is an honour badge of never playing this card in the pub business. In psychotherapy, that solemn vow to hold privately the client's story is sacrosanct and the profession would not survive without the public believing in this core element. One thing that psychotherapy has that the pub business does not have is monthly supervision, where these secrets and stories can be investigated for their effect on the bearer and on letting go the worries and concerns that often accompany holding secrets.

A common occurrence in both pub work and psychotherapy is where the customer/client can fall for the server/therapist, attributing all that is good to them. This may be partly due to the devotion, listening skills and non-judgemental approach of the person delivering the service. Learning how to recognise this as an outcome of good service and how to gently untangle the receiver from the illusion of being 'in love' is part of the pub server's skill set. Psychotherapy has titles such as 'transference' and 'countertransference' to describe similar situations, and a background in the pub business can fast track the budding psychotherapist in this area of learning. There is also the experience of the 'clingy' customer and the necessity to create boundaries, and to end the relationship appropriately, that has relevance for psychotherapy. The notion of co-dependency is relevant here as the psychotherapist must help the client leave them for participation in the real world of rough and tumble relationships.

Music is therapeutic, and participation in singing, even in the chorus, is known to free us up from our cares and woes. A pub that has a worn and used piano is a place where joy and connection can happen, and people can shed their self-consciousness for a little moment with Leonard Cohen (my choice) or a 'come all ye' (Irishism for a song everyone knows). These are moments of respite in a world where self-judgement is rampant, but it also offers the chance of taking the stage without too much fear of rejection.

Other skills developed in the pub were those of customer care and developing an entrepreneurial spirit. I saw no problem in setting up a bar in a bomb shelter in the Middle East in the early eighties, and I still have an ability to rustle up food for a large gang of people in twenty minutes or so. However, it is the skill of valuing a community, of accepting everyone as a customer of equal status, that sits closest to my heart, and this has formed the core of my working life. What I miss the most is the potential the pub offered – one never knew where the conversation would lead on any given night, and that was always thrilling.

The pub and the community were interchangeable, and, even now, if you go into a bar and sit at the counter, the possibilities it offers are intriguing. I often think that a pub in the late afternoon has an air of sacredness about it; with people sitting reading papers and the quiet undisturbed, it offers a sanctuary from the world. Then again, it also offers an opportunity for craic and a bit of mayhem …

Trish Murphy's Choice:

South Pole Inn,

Annascaul, County Kerry

Figure 6.3 The South Pole Inn in Annascaul. Photo by Trish Murphy.

It is the South Pole Inn in Annascaul, County Kerry. Nestled on the main road between Tralee and Dingle, it was owned by Antarctic hero Tom Crean, who bought the pub when he returned from his adventures with Captain Robert Scott and Sir Ernest Shackleton. Tom is buried in Ballinacourty graveyard and is a personal hero of mine: a gentle giant with awesome courage and fortitude. In the pub you can buy a book on his life story, get a t-shirt, drink Tom Crean beer and even see the one-man play on his life story if you are lucky! There is a cupboard that when opened reveals the Antarctic wind, and the voyages are detailed on the ceiling, as you sit cosily beside the fire with your toasted sandwich and good coffee!

Irish Pubs Abroad: Exporting and translating Ireland

Chapter 7

Exporting the Irish Pub: An interior designer's perspective, 1990–2010

Tracey Dalton

'Irishness' is self-consciously re-created in 'Irish pubs' through an over-the-top combination of visual symbolism, Irish music, festivals and food, and 'Irish' behavioural characteristics of relaxed informality. This last aspect involves a type of planned spontaneity. According to sociologist Eamonn Slater, 'designing the Irish pub seems to involve a necessary illusion: it should appear that no design has gone into it at all'.[1]

On a Friday morning in 1999, in the open-plan Dublin studio of McNally Design/Irish Pub Company, there is a buzz of activity. We see bodies on high stools, crouched over a sea of white drawing boards, lit by desk lamps, accompanied by the buzz of overhead fluorescents and Today FM on a transistor radio in the corner (Fig. 7.1). The design team are working frantically on hospitality design projects for the five o'clock deadline, to be collected by courier. Many are working on Irish pubs for export for the 'Guinness Irish Pub Concept'. Most are unaware of the origins of the concept, or have ever stopped to think about it. Such is the nature of a busy design office at the height of the 'Celtic Tiger' era in Ireland.[2] Some will be given a new brief on Monday morning, to design another Irish pub for the international market by the following Friday. Project managers will be heading off to far-flung places to oversee the construction and fitout of an Irish pub. Artists ('specialist painters') are home briefly, spending some time meeting with colleagues and preparing for the next trip overseas. They will spend most of their year away from Ireland, painting Celtic motifs in Gaelic-style pubs, or scripting an Oscar Wilde quote on a Victorian-style pub ceiling in Chicago, Dubai or Beijing. Sales and marketing representatives have a similar lifestyle, travelling to Sydney, then Tokyo, returning to Dublin to brief the design team, then turning around towards Dublin Airport a few days later to meet another client in some part of the world. At that moment, they look forward to the end of the day, gathering in the local pubs of Baggot Street that evening to reflect on the highs and lows of the week gone by, but, most of all, the craic they had getting it all together.

Figure 7.1 Author at McNally Design/Irish Pub Company design studio *c.* 2000. Courtesy of Tracey Dalton.

Introduction

This chapter[3] focuses on a little-seen perspective on the Irish pub for export, namely the experiences of the in-house designers of the Irish Pub Company, who created pubs for the 'Guinness Irish Pub Concept' (1992–2002) in the 1990s and 2000s as preferred supplier.[4] Interviews with in-house interior design practitioners of the period provide insights into how and why they designed the pubs as they did. The chapter will give a brief outline of the five typological styles offered, along with the turn-key methodology used by the 'Irish Pub Company'. Academic critiques, predominantly from a sociological, marketing and consumerist stance, looked at commodification of Irishness and the social, political and cultural landscape during the 'Celtic Tiger' era in Ireland. These writings (by Bill Grantham, Mark McGovern, Stephen Brown and Anthony Patterson, and Bill Barich) focused on the phenomenon of the Irish pub for export in the 1990s.[5] Their works help us understand the experiences and perceptions of in-house designers related to 'agency', 'authenticity', 'branding', 'postmodernism', 'theming' and 'taste'. The aim of this chapter is to get a seldom-seen perspective from those who 'lived through' the 'nine-to-five' experience of the design, packaging and construction of these pubs, and their personal insights into how interior design may have contributed to the success of the phenomenon.

Context

Witnessing cross-national popularity of Irish pubs at the 1989 Milan Fair[6] and at the Italia '90 FIFA World Cup, Guinness Brewing International saw an opportunity to increase sales worldwide. The 'Guinness Irish Pub Concept' (GIPC) was created in 1992, in partnership with the Irish Pub Company (IPC), a sister company of Dublin-based interior design firm McNally Design (formerly McNally Duffy Design). In 1991, IPC 'embarked on a countrywide research project on pub types and to learn why there was nothing quite like an Irish pub'.[7] Five styles of Irish pub were created from the research. Three were based on pre-existing styles: 'Victorian Dublin', 'Traditional Shop' and 'Country Cottage', while 'Brewery' and 'Gaelic', which did not pre-exist in Ireland, were invented for the international market, based on the Guinness brewery and history and Celtic folklore. The market was predominantly Germany and Italy in the early years of the concept, and subsequently the United States, when that market opened up in the late 1990s. 'Authentic' interior design, beverages, food, music and employment of staff of Irish origin were central to the concept, which was delivered using an in-house turn-key design-and-build methodology.[8] The 'Guinness Irish Pub Concept' became a worldwide phenomenon, in terms of global reach. By 1998, 1,800 pubs had been completed and were opening at a rate of one per day worldwide.[9] A global economic downturn in 2007 caused a decline in its popularity and subsequent liquidation of McNally Design / Irish Pub Company in 2009. It re-emerged in the mid-2010s and continues to survive, due to continuing demand for Irish pubs. Pub styles have been modernised and expanded from five to eight.[10]

The five original pub styles

Victorian Dublin

Surviving original Victorian pubs in Dublin were photographed and documented as reference material to capture the key elements of the interior and exterior for use by the design team.[11] These included the Long Hall, Doheny & Nesbitt's, Toner's, the International bar, the Stag's Head, Ryan's of Parkgate Street and McDaid's. These were described in GIPC marketing brochures as 'jewelled palaces' that 'matured with time, gathering the patina that made them all the more splendid and welcoming'.[12] The materiality of this style saw the use of polished mahogany, encaustic tiles, period-style fabrics, stained glass, bevelled and concave mirrors and polished brass.[13] This detailing and specification would be 'authentically' replicated in technical drawings by interior designers and architectural technicians. Spatial planning of the Victorian style pub was inspired by originals like the Long Hall, with 'hideaway hinge-windowed snugs' being placed adjacent to the bar and other areas of the pub, opening up for social gathering.[14]

Traditional Shop

Surviving examples of the 'Traditional Shop' style, one of the best examples being Morrissey's in Abbeyleix, County Laois (as seen in the IPC archive and marketing brochures), were used as reference material.[15] These pubs originated from the spirit grocer licences of the 1800s. This style is more often modelled on the rural town shop, with typical features of the pub being: rows of small drawers containing loose produce such as tea, sweets, and haberdashery; distressed timber flooring; painted joinery; bric-a-brac displays of 'products for sale', such as biscuit tins, breakfast cereal; and traditional alcoholic beverages such as Guinness and whiskey. Traditional advertising posters and signage would be a common feature, sourced from salvage or replicated from originals. These pubs were modelled as grocers, post offices, or even undertakers. The layout was more open plan than a Victorian pub, with a less polished finish, more colour, more light and a more casual atmosphere. Contemporary spatial planning principles for the hospitality industry would dictate a design for maximum seating capacity, differing from the originals, which would sometimes have had a spartan layout.

Country Cottage

The 'Country Cottage' style derived from traditional stone-built cottages prevalent in the eighteenth and nineteenth centuries. There was an emergence of these pubs, due to the ease in obtaining a liquor licence pre-1927.[16] A late 1990s 'Guinness Irish Pub Concept' brochure lists key features as 'whitewashed walls, stone floors, exposed roof timbers, stone fireplace, rough wood furniture' and 'family' bric-a-brac, which would be displayed on a wooden dresser. The design was 'aesthetically simple and largely unadorned'.[17] It evoked the rural home with the 'master of the house' becoming publican, their family name appearing on signage erected over the door. This trope of Irishness, an example of Urry's 'tourist gaze', appeared on the cover of IPC brochures, alongside Irish pubs, both existing and replicated (Fig. 7.2).[18] Gartlan's, Kingscourt, County Cavan was a surviving original used by the IPC and Guinness,

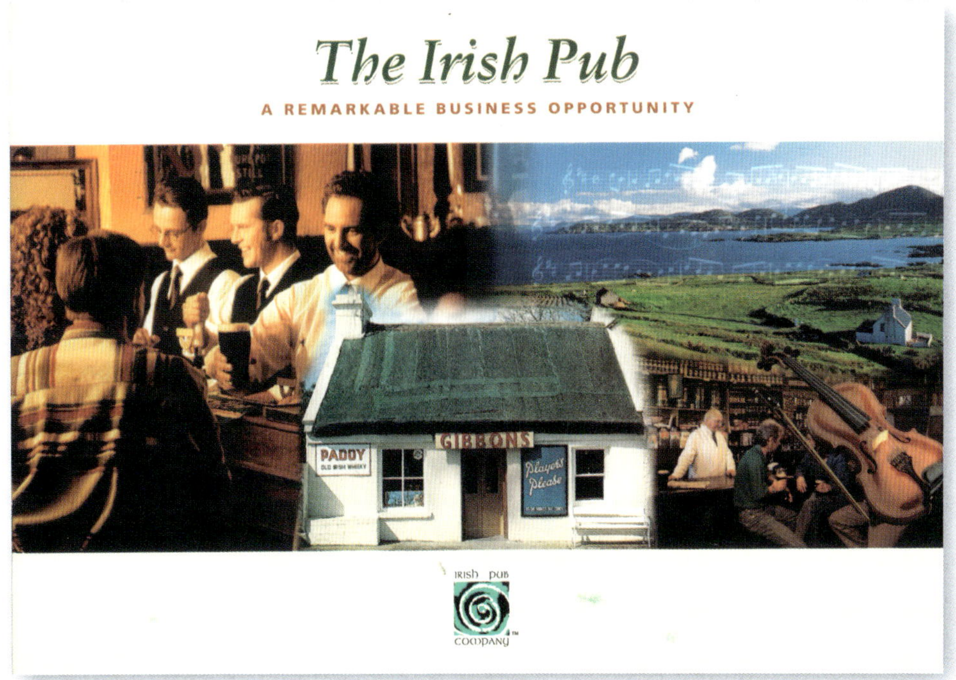

Figure 7.2 'The Irish Pub: A remarkable business opportunity' – an 'Irish Pub Company' promotional brochure cover page, *c.* 1995. Sourced from the 'Irish Pub Company' archive, 23 October 2018.

as an example of the style, in their 1990s brochures.[19] The layout placed a fireplace as a focal point and often included a performance area for the customary 'trad' music session. Authenticity of materiality, and the architecture of the building into which the pub was installed, influenced the success of this style.

Brewery

The 'Brewery' pub was inspired by the Guinness brewery, St James' Gate, and its eighteenth-century Georgian Dublin origins. It depicted interpretations of 'cobbled courtyards and vaulted ceilings crafted of stone and brick', wrought-iron metalwork and furniture made from repurposed oak barrels.[20] In contrast to the rise of the craft beer microbreweries post-2010, these were 'Brewery' in form, but not in function. They were adorned with polished copper kieves and brewing equipment, with copper and brass piping creating decorative patterns. Illustrations and graphics, along with photographic memorabilia and bric-a-brac aimed to depict the historical evolution of the Guinness brewery. The brewery-themed pub was created for the international market, with successful examples being 'Kilkenny Irish Pub', Berlin.[21] By the early 2000s the 'Guinness Irish Pub Concept' marketing brochure did not offer this style.

Gaelic

The 'Gaelic' style was also created for the international market and was not pre-existing in Ireland. It drew from the 'far-flung Gaelic tribes of Europe' and had an ethereal aesthetic with the use of 'delicate tapestries' and decorative Celtic patterns on walls and in metalwork.[22] This style enjoyed popularity in Germany and the United States, which had an interest in 'Gaelicism'.[23] In 1996, the Fadó brand was created for the US market with the Atlanta, Georgia flagship being the first to showcase all five styles.[24] The concept was also popular in the Middle and Far East from the late 1990s. Concepts drew from ancient storytelling, and a love of music and song. Joinery was 'rough-hewn', often crafted from midlands bog oak, creating an essence of authenticity among the trompe l'oeil murals and Celtic-patterned metalwork. The style tended to be used in a section of a pub that had other themes and it was also suited to dance spaces, with a connection to motifs used in Irish-dancing costumes.[25] Gaelic-style pub designs were sometimes hybridised, with pubs taking on a 'Gaelic/Raj' concept in India, for example. This was deemed acceptable in some quarters, in an era of theming and 'Disneyisation' in design.[26]

The turn-key methodology

The IPC applied a turn-key service[27] in the design and manufacture of the Irish pub for export. This is an iterative six-stage process, not dissimilar to that used in architectural practice across Ireland.[28] The IPC archive, and interviews with designers, sheds light on these six stages, and helps to show how and why the pubs were designed and constructed as they were. The six-stage turn-key service was delivered as follows:

1) Site visit: Sales and marketing managers travelled worldwide to meet with prospective and repeat clients to consult and take a design brief. In-house operations manuals provided key criteria on taking a client brief, focusing on specific requirements of international markets.
2) Concept design: Preliminary sketches and plans were produced by designers, giving early indications of the pub's potential design, on receipt of the brief (Fig. 7.3).

3) Detailed design: Design proposals presented a 'mood board', spatial plan, interior axonometric and an exterior shopfront drawing, accompanied by a walk-through written description of the proposed Irish pub (Figs 7.4 and 7.5). Colour-rendered perspective drawings also visually represented the pub design proposal (Fig. 7.6). This allowed the client to see the space in three-dimensional plan view, giving a sense of the concept and colour scheme. Generic plans and perspectives for each style were shown in promotional 'Guinness Irish Pub Concept' brochures throughout the 1990 to 2000 era to give prospective clients a taste of what the pub could look like (Fig. 7.7). The in-house quantity surveyor used the design proposal to provide a quotation to the prospective client.
4) Site preparation drawings: The project moved on to technical working drawings of the pub joinery (Figs 7.8 and 7.9). Designed 'packages' for flooring, lighting, metalwork, glass, furniture, specialist paint, signage, ironmongery and bric-a-brac were produced for all fixtures and fittings. *Interior Concepts* was an in-house catalogue which provided all items for these packages, with the company acting as agent between the suppliers and the client. This fulfilled the company promise of a turn-key service.

Figure 7.3 Preliminary sketch for a 'Gaelic' style pub proposal. Sourced from the 'Irish Pub Company' archive, 8 August 2018.

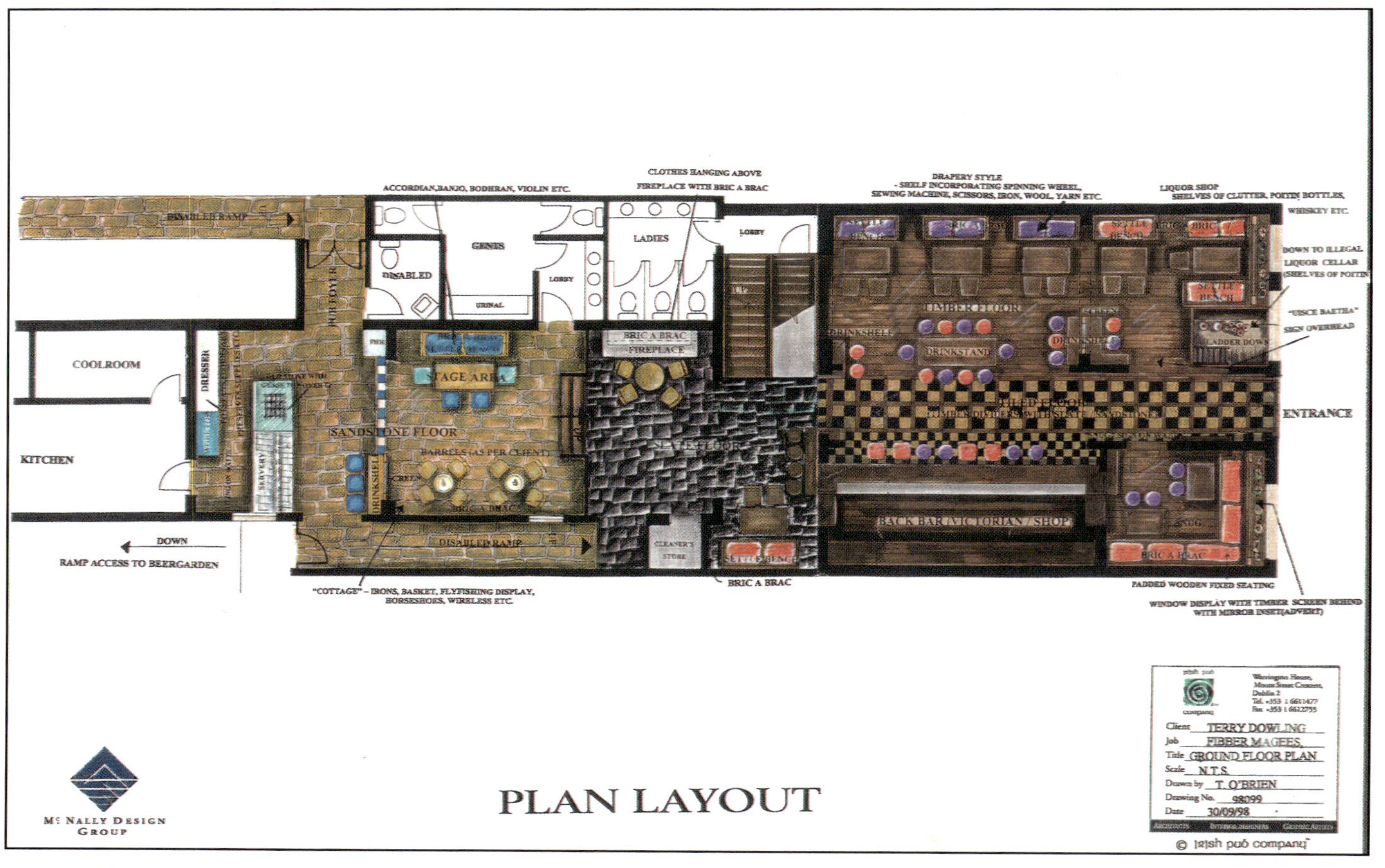

Figure 7.4 Proposal presentation for Fibber Magee's, Toowoomba, Queensland, Australia, with the Victorian-style area to the front and Cottage-style area to the rear. Created by Tracey Dalton for 'Irish Pub Company', 30 September 1998.

FIBBER MAGEES, TOOWOOMBA, QUEENSLAND

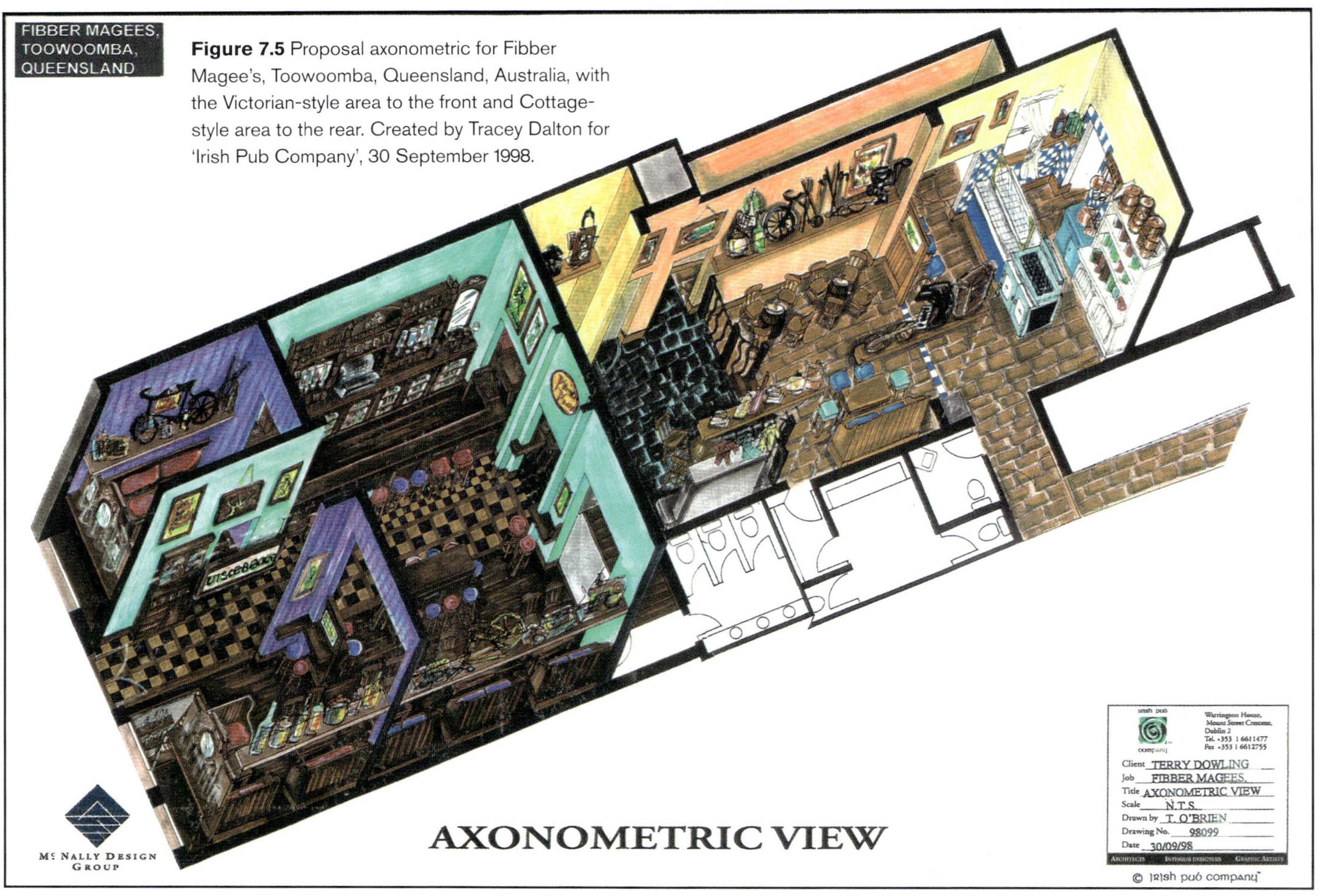

Figure 7.5 Proposal axonometric for Fibber Magee's, Toowoomba, Queensland, Australia, with the Victorian-style area to the front and Cottage-style area to the rear. Created by Tracey Dalton for 'Irish Pub Company', 30 September 1998.

Figure 7.6 Generic perspective of the Victorian pub style. Sourced from the 'Irish Pub Company' archive, 23 October 2018.

5) Manufacture and supply: In the 1990s, McNally Design / IPC had an in-house joinery and showroom, ILC Manufacturing, which employed in-house joiners who built and manufactured the pub interiors. This was slowly wound down post-2000 due to rising material and labour costs at the height of the Celtic Tiger era. The manufacture and supply processes were subcontracted to joinery firms in Ireland and overseas.
6) Shipping and fitout on site: The manufactured pub was loaded into a container and shipped to its destination. Contents were signed off by the project designer / manager who would oversee the construction and fitout (Fig. 7.10).

Interviews with the interior designers

Seven interior designers were interviewed individually, in June and July 2021, on their experiences of the design of the Irish pub for export for IPC. Duration of employment varied from two to fourteen years, spanning the period 1994 to 2012. Professional experience levels included one senior designer, four designers who progressed from junior to senior designers, and two designers who progressed from junior to middleweight designers. Interview questions covered the evolution of the 'Irish Pub Concept' from 1990 to 2010. The interviews took a retrospective look at 'agency',

THE GUINNESS IRISH PUB - IT'S TIME TO OPEN

Born of meticulous and painstaking attention to ornate decorative detail and an insistence on quality craftsmanship beloved of nineteenth century artisans, the Victorian pub -common in Dublin - harks back to the days when it was as vital to please the eye as the palate.

From the outside they shone like jewelled palaces, exquisite clusters of gas-fired and, later, new-fangled electric lamps glistening through patterned stained and cut-glass windows, highly-polished brass fittings adorning these splendid emporia both without and within.

Interiors were warm, rich and lavish: show-pieces of bevelled and gilded mirrors, of elaborate mosaics and terra cotta tiles, of decorative brass and finely-turned timbers imbued with lustrous depth by French-polishers. Fine-grained hardwoods were elaborately carved, turned on lathes or twisted into fantastic barley-sugar shapes ... the bar a mighty wooden slab over which might be poised an enamelled clock or behind which a cashier's booth modelled from panels of curved and filigreed glass ... the walls a rich resonance of dark wood and framed prints ... the cast-iron tables a triumph of that enterprising century's artistry and ingenuity.

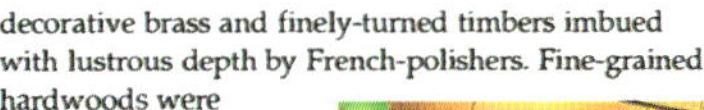

Such pubs matured with time, gathering with age a patina that made them all the more splendid and welcoming, their hideaway hinge-windowed snugs all the cosier, their sensual indulgences all the more enjoyable.

QUIET MAN, MADRID, SPAIN.

Centrally located on a high-turnover site which Guinness helped father-and-son co-proprietors Gregorio and Angel Monje find, this fine recreation of a rococo Victorian pub by Dublin architects Gemmel Griffin Dunbar is an excellent example of how Irish pub design has adapted to local circumstances.

IL BROLETTO, PAVIA, ITALY.

A building of character near the university was transformed into a Victorian-style pub redolent with mahogany and an unusual - and dominant - central bar. Able to comfortably seat 150, it has attracted a young, affluent and loyal clientele.

15

Figure 7.7 The 'Victorian Dublin' style option from a 'Guinness Irish Pub Concept' promotional brochure *c.* 1995. Sourced from the 'Irish Pub Company' archive, 23 October 2018.

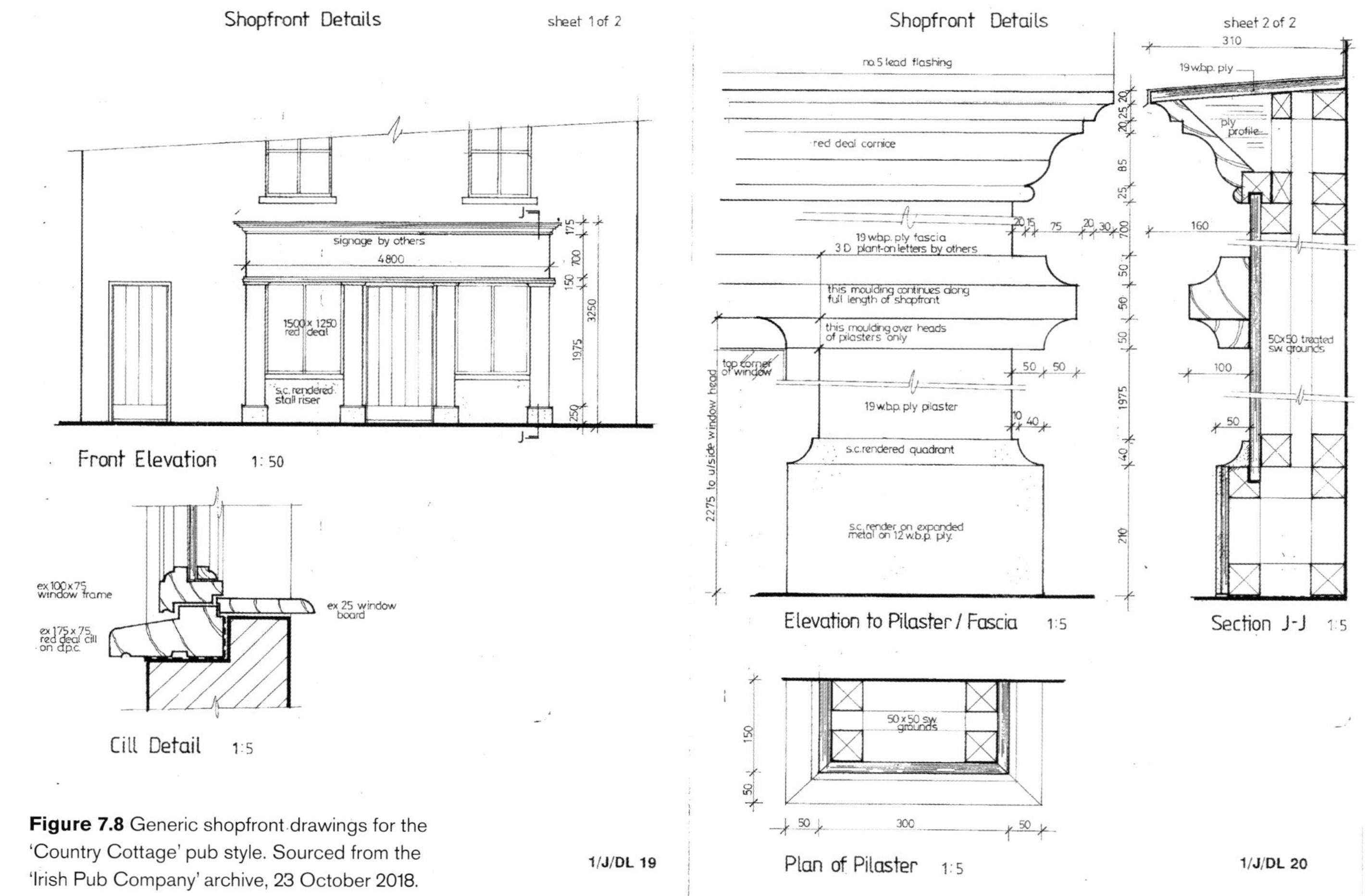

Figure 7.8 Generic shopfront drawings for the 'Country Cottage' pub style. Sourced from the 'Irish Pub Company' archive, 23 October 2018.

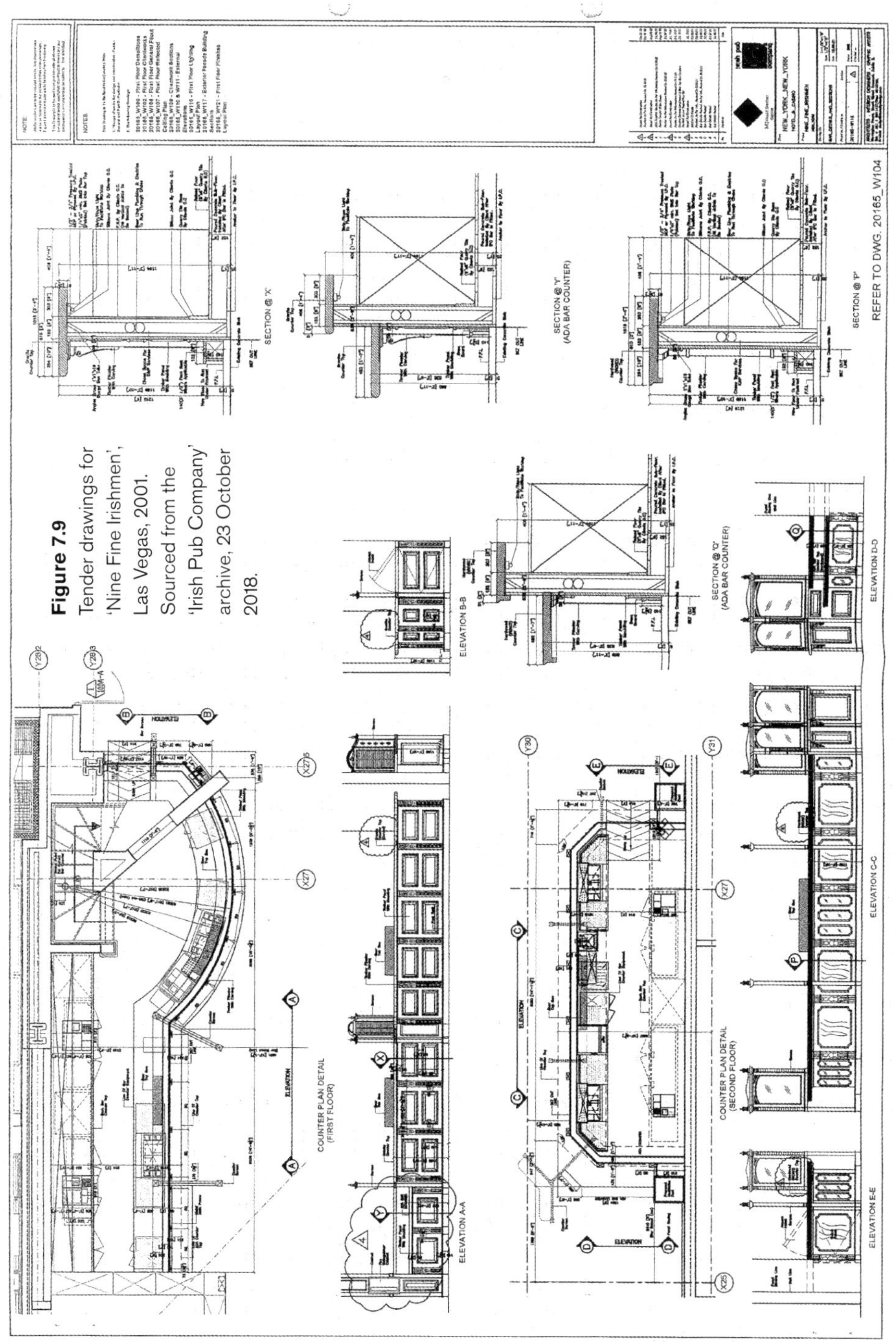

Figure 7.9 Tender drawings for 'Nine Fine Irishmen', Las Vegas, 2001. Sourced from the 'Irish Pub Company' archive, 23 October 2018.

Figure 7.10 Fitout photos of Fadó Chicago, December 1997. Sourced from the 'Irish Pub Company' archive,
18 December 2018.

'authenticity', 'branding', 'postmodernism', 'theming' and 'taste' from a contemporary (2021) lens. They took a design-centred approach and provide an opportunity to hear from those who were inside the concept creation during the period.

Findings

On 'agency'

The designer's role in the process, key projects they designed, and agency within the design process was investigated. All designers interviewed felt that they had agency to create what they wanted, within the parameters of the brief, in some form. Although underpinned by a process and a series of styles to adhere to, there was always room to 'put your own stamp' on the design of the pub. Contrary to a view within the critical literature that these pubs were largely identical, some believed a designer's individual style could be recognised in-house and that, as long as it was 'commercially viable', they had the freedom to do 'virtually anything'.

Experience determined levels of agency, with junior designers being instructed by a senior designer. The pubs were a team effort between designers and management. One junior designer observed: 'You were given guidance and you interpreted it. I had great respect for the people who were there designing … it was a lot of responsibility on them.' One designer referred to in-house research material as 'the Bible' to be adhered to, but there was agency in what was picked from it, although it was unnecessary to 're-invent the wheel'.

An experienced senior designer commented on agency in spatial planning, noting a necessity to adhere to principles, such as positioning of the bar and the 'snug': 'The snugs have to be connected to the bar, which has to be visible from the minute you walk in.' She notes being governed by rules but having scope to introduce different things and be a bit 'quirky'. Contrary to the academic critique of the commodification of the exported Irish pub, which implied that these were a homogenous, packaged version of what an Irish pub should be, some designers felt that whether 'Victorian', 'Brewery' or 'Gaelic', they saw them as all quite different.[29] Expert advice and direction was welcomed by most, from managing director Mel McNally, as he was 'the master of the concept'. On reflection, one junior designer differed on freedom of agency, observing that everything was closely monitored by those more senior and experienced, who 'would want to dictate'. In her opinion, the major design decisions were left to those in senior roles.

On 'authenticity'

Doreen Massey's 'thrown-togetherness' of space, where spatial forces are interwoven, always in dialogue with one another, acts as a metaphor for the evolution of the authentic surviving pubs in Ireland, over centuries.[30] They have evolved from their original functions such as the grocer, the undertaker, the post office and the living room. Adherence to the liquor licensing laws in the nineteenth and twentieth centuries, along with functional changes due to building regulations, health and safety requirements and the advent of a workplace smoking ban in 2004, has produced an organic arrangement, a 'thrown-togetherness' of materiality and space. Mike Featherstone also refers to the attraction of sites of 'ordered disorder', such as theme parks, malls and tourist attractions, which the Irish pub for export shares links with, on an experiential level.[31] This has resulted in an unplanned interior that has a charm which is difficult to put into words. This charm was 'bottled' by the 'Guinness Irish

Pub Concept', as a business opportunity for potential investors overseas, to increase Guinness sales. These pubs for export were designed to materially and spatially emulate the originals. This illusion of 'thrown-togetherness' was in reality a well-researched study of what makes an 'authentic' Irish pub. This could be said of the pre-1800s and Victorian pubs, planned and designed to contemporary standards and laws, and influenced by the pub owners and managers of the time. Perception of authenticity is subjective, influenced by life experience, education, nationality and culture. Caroline Muñoz and colleagues, in cross-cultural research on the perception of the importance of authenticity in the Irish pub, observed that it is a construct 'dependent on both marketers and consumers'.[32]

The in-house interior designers of IPC had nuanced views on authenticity. They believed the pubs they designed were authentic as they were 'born, bred and built in Ireland' by 'quality Irish joiners' and designers who 'grew up in Ireland' and 'knew Irish pubs'.[33] One designer felt they were as authentic as they could be, unless an original pub in Ireland was to be transplanted to another location.[34] She felt there was 'a huge effort put in, to make it as authentic as it could be'. This was achieved through use of materials such as stained glass, hardwood timbers, hand-sourced bric-a-brac and encaustic Victorian tiles, for example. She felt that company founder Mel McNally had his 'finger on the button' when it came to authenticity of materials and finishes.

Others questioned what defined authenticity. They believed that the Irish pub for export could never be like the local pub in Ireland, but that the design and atmosphere of an Irish pub 'travelled well'. One designer questioned whether pubs in Ireland are themselves always authentic and whether the tourist can distinguish one from another, noting that 'you would have to have a keen eye to spot the difference between a genuine Irish pub and a refurb, or a new Irish pub. If it was done right you'd be pretty hard pushed to find the difference'. She notes that even the 'genuine' pubs in Ireland have to be refurbished, such that what is defined as a refurbished or a 'new' pub is problematic, with a fine line between what is 'genuine', what is a refurbishment, or a new construction.

The export market and the customer's interpretation of what an Irish pub should feel like was also a determining factor, which meant a requirement to be a little bit more 'in your face', in the opinion of one designer, as a local pub in Ireland would have no theme or style to it. Another noted that it felt authentic when you walked into an Irish Pub Company pub compared to a pub 'that called itself an Irish pub, with maybe a flag or a few shamrocks' – which Blommaert and Varis have referred to as 'enough'

Irishness[35] – and that through design it managed to create a 'great atmosphere'.[36] One designer felt that it categorically could not be authentic unless original salvage was used, as opposed to authentic replication, regardless of the quality used.

Another differentiation is made by authenticity within styles, with most designers saying that the 'Victorian Dublin' and 'Traditional Shop' style were most authentic. A rich history behind a pub style gave it more authenticity, in one designer's opinion, as it was not 'just created from nothing'. The 'Cottage' style got mixed reactions, with one observation that 'designing from scratch, where it's all "cottagey" and pine', could not be authentic. While popular as an exported piece of 'Irishness', the designers who created them from a brief felt that these pubs were probably among the less convincing; they were often referred to as 'twee'. Most concurred that the 'Gaelic' and 'Brewery' styles were the least authentic as they did not have the 'proper historical footprint'. One designer believed that what potentially guaranteed authenticity of the 'Gaelic' pubs was the use of bespoke bog oak furniture pieces, crafted and sourced from the midlands. The 'Brewery' style got mixed opinions from the designers who created them, as it did not have a level of authenticity in the materials and relied on photos, graphics and other two-dimensional forms of storytelling. For others, it was their favourite style due to the pared-down industrial aesthetic and use of mixed metals, which made them appear more 'modern'.

The level of 'authenticity' may have been affected by the economic boom in Ireland in the 1990s to late 2000s. Construction and manufacturing costs escalated from the early 2000s.[37] One designer reflected that this was when the authenticity 'lost something, as we started to manufacture abroad' to reduce costs. This factor, along with a more multicultural design community in-house, may have influenced perceptions of authenticity and reflect the observations of Muñoz and her co-authors.[38]

On 'branding'

The 'Guinness Irish Pub Concept' enabled the phenomenal success of Irish pubs for export, which in turn increased sales of Guinness.[39] Brochures and other media promoting the GIPC were marketed to prospective and existing Irish pub owners in Europe. The focus on relatively standardised interior décor, one of the 'success factors' of the concept,[40] is an example of Ritzer's 'McDonaldisation' effect, whereby feelings of connection are fostered in the customer through similarity and familiarity of place, whether in an Irish pub in Italy, Spain or Ireland.[41] This directly contrasts with the idea of achieving authenticity through a 'thrown togetherness', also a key aspect of the concept. Designers commented on the increasing importance of branding, resulting in employment of in-house brand managers and graphic designers, from the late 1990s. Prior to this, interior designers had multitasked as graphic designers for uniforms, aprons, placemats, cutlery, crockery, signage and logos, even if not formally trained to do so. Interior branding within these pubs was evident on fixtures such as beer taps, mirrors, vintage posters and promotional material.

Irish 'chain' pubs were less common in Europe than in the United Kingdom or the United States, with the GIPC promoting the Irish pub as being unlike the English pub, many of which are 'tied' to breweries. The charm of the Irish pub is that most are family run and standalone.[42] One designer noted that branding in the European market became more important from the mid-1990s. The Australian market saw chains emerge, with 'P.J. Gallagher's' and 'P.J. O'Brien's' being two examples, where the success of a first pub prompted a chain to emerge in multiple locations. From 1996, the highly successful 'Fadó' chain ('long ago' in Gaelic) emerged in the United States.[43] The interior design of the flagship Fadó Irish pub, in Atlanta, Georgia, in 1995, showcased all five styles and provided a template which was used throughout the United States. It promoted a premium brand with 'Irish-made' fixtures and fittings. It was standard that uniforms and menus were branded in these chain pubs, which was not common practice in indigenous Irish pubs (but is becoming more prevalent today, in a brand and social media driven age).

On 'postmodernism'

The Irish pub for export was created at the height of the 'postmodern' era in architecture and design. This advocated the rejection of modernism and a return to versions of the past that took the form of stylised historic architecture, furniture and product design.[44] The designers of the IPC may have been influenced by their prior learning on contemporary visual culture in the 1980s and '90s, as most were design and architecture graduates of that time. Most designers did not see a connection between the creation of the pubs and contemporary architectural movements but reflected that this factor may have contributed to design decisions and the success of the concept. For one interior designer the architectural movement did not impact on interior design, which rather was pulled from several different sources as a response to the function of the environment, rather than as a response to modernity or any other style. Others saw the 'Irish pub' concept as a business opportunity first, feeling that it was in its own 'little bubble'. In hindsight, one designer observed that the concept was progressed during the 'postmodernist' era, as they were 'mass produced to a market', although she had not equated the 'Irish pub' concept with typical 'Las Vegas' and 'Disney' design methodologies.[45] Another, while aware that the concept was not 'fresh or new or exciting in the design world' (in Ireland) noted that this was not what it aimed to achieve; rather, contemporary design projects were taken care of by the McNally Design branch of the business.

Some designers noted that the Irish pubs have had longevity as they were not part of an era, such as 'modernism' or 'postmodernism', whereas more contemporary projects created by McNally Design had dated or were no longer in existence. They concurred that the concept creator, Mel McNally, may have been influenced by the 'postmodernist' emergence from the 1970s and into the 1980s.[46] Mark McGovern's 2002 paper on commodification of the Irish pub reports a 1997 statement by the IPC that the Irish pub 'emphasises the appeal of a "pre-modern" nostalgia ... and the way in which the Irish bar is, in some senses, about travelling in time as well as space'.[47] This echoes Featherstone's argument that postmodernist aesthetic ideals can be traced back to the mid-nineteenth century revivalist period, akin to the public fascination with theme parks and carnivals.[48] This correlates with observations from designers, who believed that the Irish pub for export was its own entity, not pretending to be a current or influential design concept. It transported the customer back in time, while simultaneously being time-less. As one designer sums it up:

> It is what it is, its own identity. However, if you pick and pull apart the individual areas within the Irish pub, you can see the design styles formed in it ... You can't pigeonhole it into an era of design, because all the elements that make up the Irish pub have their own identities and they pick from different eras.

On 'theming'

On visiting the 'Disneyland' theme parks in 1955, Julian Helavy, screenwriter and novelist, described 'a sickening blend of cheap formulas packaged to sell'.[49] Jean

Baudrillard, in his 1981 treatise *Simulacra and Simulation*, spoke of the blurring of real and themed environments, like 'Disneyland', where the themed environment is presented as imaginary in order to make us believe that the rest of the world is 'real'.[50] Umberto Eco later critiqued 'theming' of environments in his development of ideas on 'hyperrealism', arguing that we live in a world of the 'Absolute Fake', where imitations don't just imitate, but endeavour to be better than the original.[51] In *The Theming of America* (1997), Mark Gottdiener argues that, by infusing themed environments with symbolic meaning, businesses can transform mundane commodities into highly profitable experiences.[52] All of these arguments situate well with the goal of the GIPC to use the exported Irish pub as a profit-making vehicle for Guinness sales, by creating a themed environment even more 'real' than a 'real' pub in Ireland. This, in turn, affects tourists' perception and expectation of Ireland.

The Irish Pub Company's re-creation of the Irish pub is an example of a themed commodity, arguably an 'Absolute Fake', endeavouring, through design process, to be as 'authentic' as the originals. Designers were questioned on whether themed Irish pubs and themed spaces in general could achieve a desired authenticity. Responses proved to be varied, with some designers torn on the subject. One felt it depended on *how* themed the space was. She felt that the answer would have to be 'no' but did believe that some of the pubs were done so well, that within a few years, when the space had aged, 'you'd be hard pushed to know if it was a genuine Irish pub or a new one ... if it's designed and made well it can look authentic over a few years, once it's aged into itself, yes'. Another believed a themed space can never *be* authentic, but hoped that the Irish pubs they designed would be *viewed* as authentic. She expressed feelings of guilt in hindsight: 'maybe looking at it that way I feel a bit guilty ... it was our jobs for years ... you do put heart and soul into it. The intent for it to be authentic was there. When something is mass produced does it lose that?' Another designer reflected on the Irish pub for export in comparison to other themed interiors. While she wished it could be authentic, she concurred that a mass-produced product could not be. She compared the Irish themed pub to experiences of other themed hospitality spaces:

> If you walk into a diner, you feel like you're in a fifties American diner, or if you walk into a Hard Rock Café, it does feel like 'rock and roll', so I suppose themed bars can be authentic to the theme that they were portraying.

Theming styles were also infiltrated and influenced by the country or culture that the exported Irish pub was located in, reflecting Watson's findings on consumer perceptions of McDonald's restaurants in east Asia.[53] This was important to some designers' feelings on the topic of authenticity within theming: 'You had your different styles and depending on what locality they were in, they would pull on what was popular in the area, and if there was a link back to Ireland.' Another designer added that 'things have been filtered down from different cultures and colonialism in a country. Things do filter into the actual design of the Irish pub as a whole, as per the package of it being an Irish pub, having a little snug and stuff like that'.

On 'taste'

Pierre Bourdieu's 1979 study of the French bourgeoisie, *Distinction: A social critique of the judgement of taste*, suggested that whether one has 'good taste' or awareness of aesthetics is dependent on family background and education.[54] These criteria affect cultural, symbolic and social capital. This seemed a topic that should be examined with the interior designers, in light of the critical view of manufactured Irish pubs, which implies a lack of taste. Patterson and colleagues argue that the Irish pub for export is an 'invented tradition'[55] and a cynical commodification of Irishness:

> The typical Irish theme pub, with its garish green decor, pseudo-Gaelic invocations, 'thousand welcomes' doormats, shamrock-inscribed fittings, peat-burning fireplace … and general air of pseudo-hiberno bonhomie, cannot be considered indicative of today's Ireland, yesterday's Ireland, or any other Ireland this side of *The Quiet Man*. Irish theme pubs … are commercially-motivated commodifications of the Celtic Revival of the late-nineteenth century, which was itself a politically-motivated commodification – an invented tradition – of half-baked Irish pre-history.[56]

All designers interviewed had received an architecture-based design education in one of three Dublin-based institutes, as was the case for the majority of designers in the studio.[57] When the question of aesthetics, or taste, was put to them, they understood the question in different ways. One senior designer noted that the Irish pub has a 'more is more' maximalist aesthetic, that they believed was tastefully constructed by the IPC:

> They were crammed full of Irish artefacts, whether it was a library theme … the more books you had in it, the better, or whether it was a shop theme, you might have had all the washing powder boxes, or biscuit boxes and jars. They might not have been to everybody's taste. They were true to what they were supposed to be. So, whether they were tasteless or not … they were true to their authenticity of being an Irish pub. Victorian, Cottage, Shop style.

Another senior designer believed that the nature of the Irish pub derived from Irish culture, which rendered it different to the English pub. He interpreted this to a 'more casual' atmosphere which was 'a little bit more higgledy-piggledy'. The 'thrown-together' nature of the design was an advantage in guiding unknowing junior designers, new to the concept, through the design process. One thought 'it could suffer mistakes more easily' from designers with less experience: 'You could get a very good product from even somebody who maybe was just starting working in the business.'

Some former junior designers reflected that they were too young to appreciate the aesthetics of the Irish pub at the time and were lost in the machine of production: 'As far as taste … at that time, I wouldn't be interested in Irish pubs. I am now … When you go into the Long Hall, it's just it's so interesting. It's a different world. As a young person I wouldn't appreciate it.' Another concurred on the inexperience of youth: 'I think I probably wasn't confident enough at the time to question what I was doing … There was a lot of projects on the go … a lot of designers in our big studio, and you were just getting it out the door.' One believed that senior management and designers prescribed the various pub styles to be adhered to, and did not recall being trained, but inherently knew the aesthetic requirements for each, which came through in the furniture and finishes. Being caught up in the moment of a fast-moving, busy design studio did not leave time for reflection.

Conclusion

This chapter has engaged with the phenomenon of the Irish pub for export, from the perspective of the in-house interior designers from the Irish Pub Company, creator of the 'Guinness Irish Pub Concept' with Guinness Brewing Worldwide, in 1992. The chapter has uncovered perspectives previously neglected in the 'pub as global phenomenon' debate. A contextual overview explained the concept, along with description of the five styles of Irish pub created for the international market, and a brief description of the turn-key design methodology used. In-house interior designers were interviewed on their experiences in the creation of these pubs, in the 1990 to 2010 era. Some key topics from interviews – 'agency', 'authenticity', 'branding', 'postmodernism', 'theming' and 'taste' – have been highlighted to assess the interior designers' awareness of the overarching concept.

All designers interviewed believed they had agency in varying amounts depending on seniority, but were guided by management within the parameters of the turn-key design process.[58] There were conflicting views on authenticity, considered a core value of the Irish Pub Company in the creation of the Irish pub for export. This unearthed a conflict of conscience on whether a product can be authentic if it is mass-produced. They concurred that branding became increasingly important in the interior design of the pubs, resulting in the employment of brand experts post-2000, when pub chains had been created and developed in some markets. In hindsight, the designers did believe that the creation of the 'Guinness Irish Pub Concept' during the postmodernist era added to the success of the phenomenon worldwide, but debated whether the Irish pub for export sat within the movement. Most admitted that, at the time, they were not aware of its significance, but that management may have foreseen the zeitgeist. The designers were fully aware that the pubs were themed but believed that respectful attention to detail aimed to make them as authentic as they could be, while one designer expressed feelings of guilt at being part of the creation of a themed commodity. Regarding 'taste' and aesthetics, there were two main findings. Some believed they were inexperienced and didn't question whether the pubs were designed tastefully, whereas others concluded that the 'thrown togetherness' of the Irish pub facilitated the training of those more inexperienced and was sympathetic to mistakes made.

The overarching finding from the interviews was the feeling of nostalgia for a time that they all enjoyed. They worked in a fast-paced design studio with tight deadlines and high outputs. This was a fun environment and a training ground for young designers. Those who were there pre-1995 had knowledge of the overarching concept. Knowledge and precedent were passed down from management to senior and junior designers. A process was followed and the 'bigger picture' was not questioned. This study has provided an opportunity to understand in a more nuanced way how, in the Celtic Tiger era, the Irish pub was re-imagined for an international audience and helped to influence, in a broader way, portrayals of Irish identity.

Tracy Dalton's Choice:

The Welcome Inn,

Parnell Street, Dublin

Figure 7.11 The Welcome Inn, Dublin. Photo by Andy Sheridan.

The Welcome Inn is located on the corner of Parnell Street and Marlborough Street in Dublin. It has been closed for a long time now, but brings back fond memories of student days in the late 1990s. The pub interior hasn't changed since what Kevin Kearns referred to as the 'Formica Age' of the 1960s.[59] The pub was hit in the Dublin bombings of 1974, with the façade changing – the addition of bomb-proof concrete walls – but the interior never changed. One large room, it comprised of a distinctive red flock wallpaper (you would remember if you were a child of the seventies), black leatherette upholstered fixed seating, with low laminate tables and warm amber lighting. One quiet weekday afternoon I witnessed the black leatherette upholstery being replaced with the same black leatherette upholstery. Time stood still and that was the charm of The Welcome.

It was frequented by a mixed crowd of artists, students and locals. David Norris was even known to pop in now and again. One of the added benefits as a student was that bicycles were permitted at the rear, near the toilets, in full view of the whole pub. The bar was a one-man operation for many years, after the retirement of his parents, which resulted in sporadic openings and periods of closure. This made the pub feel more like an anomaly in the city centre – it seemed to belong in a rural town, with echoes of Friel's Philadelphia, Here I Come. It was often thought that the pub had closed for good, but a simple knock on the door would prove otherwise. The owner was friendly, quirky and welcoming, which added to the uniqueness of this pub. The atmosphere was relaxed, convivial, and conversation was always interesting, with the odd fancy dress party thrown in.

How a Home Should Be? Gender, identity and belonging in the Irish pubs in London, Dublin and Belfast

Eli Davies

Edna O'Brien's short story 'The Shovel Kings' describes the life of an Irish emigrant called Rafferty, via an unnamed female narrator who meets him in a north London Irish pub on St Patrick's Day.[1] Through the woman's account of their conversations, we learn of Rafferty's backstory, how he ended up in London with his father in the 1950s working on building sites, and his life in London since then. 'The Shovel Kings' is what Tony Murray has identified as a 'navvy narrative' – stories, novels and plays which chronicle the lives of male migrants from Ireland to Britain who worked in construction work in the 1950s and '60s. The pub in the story is Biddy Mulligan's in Kilburn, but when I first read it I pictured it as somewhere on Holloway Road. It was the summer of 2015 and I was living in Archway in the borough of Islington, within walking distance of several of the Irish pubs that dotted that road and where I'd spent a good deal of time in my adult life.

My Mayo-born grandmother Madge had died earlier that year, which had prompted a surge of romantic diasporic longing in me. I began to revisit the Irish literature I'd studied at school and university (some of which Madge had introduced me to), carving out time to re-read *Dubliners* between the community education classes I taught in Islington at that time. I'd lived in Dublin for a year in my early twenties and began trying to vaguely plot ways to live in Ireland again. I read about the approaching Easter Rising centenary commemorations and thought about how I could participate. O'Brien featured heavily in all this; there was *Saints and Sinners*, the collection that 'The Shovel Kings' comes from, but also her memoir *Country Girl* and an essay that appeared in a *Stinging Fly* issue of that year about the period in the 1960s when she first moved to London. O'Brien, unmistakeably Irish, was still somehow strongly connected to and placed in my city in a way that felt meaningful to me, particularly when I read that story.

The pub described in O'Brien's story, with its solitary old male drinkers sitting amid St Patrick's Day revelry, made me think of the pubs that have been a crucial part of my social life since I was a teenager. There is a particular mood evoked by the descriptions that reminds me of the times I spent in those places. Watching Ireland and Celtic matches in O'Rafferty's in Wood Green, the Sheephaven in Camden and the Black Horse in Archway; all-day sessions in McGovern's in Kilburn and the Red Lion in Walworth; popping into the Auld Shillelagh in Stoke Newington or Quinn's in Camden just for one and still being there six pints later; nights sat up at the bar in the Mother Red Cap in Archway, listening to covers bands and chatting to other punters, or a quick late drink in the Boston Arms on my way back from a night out. I've played game after game of pool, emptied my pockets into jukeboxes, bellowed out 'The Fields of Athenry' at the top of my voice and stood for the anthem at the end of the night. There are more – the Kingdom, the Inn on the Green, the Wishing Well, the Kingsland, the Faltering Fullback and a few others I don't remember the names of. Some of these places have closed and become flats, some of them have been spruced up, changed hands or gone downhill; some of them were never very good in the first place; some remain, and remain pretty good.

The Irish pub is a notorious expression of diasporic identity, its space representing various types of connection, longing and imaginings. Kathleen Heininge describes the diasporic Irish pub as 'the imagined community of those with connections (both physical and wishful) to Ireland' which then becomes a 'site for the contestation of Irish identity, and a determining factor in trying to assert a strange kind of authentic historical memory'.[2] In his discussion of 'The Shovel Kings', Tony Murray similarly draws on the complexity of the Irish pub, utilising Avtar Brah's concept of 'diasporic space' to acknowledge the conflicting emotions evoked by this place and the complicated relationships to national identity played out within it. Diasporic space is, according to Brah, 'where multiple subject positions are juxtaposed, contested, proclaimed or disavowed'.[3] In O'Brien's story, this is illustrated in part by both Rafferty and the narrator's slightly ambivalent responses to the St Patrick's Day celebrations they find themselves among. But this occurs as a trope in other literature of the Irish diaspora. The pub has a longstanding function in drama, for example, as a space for stories to be told and identity to be worked out, for example in David Ireland's *Cyprus Avenue* and Jimmy Murphy's *Kings of the Kilburn High Road*.

In this chapter I want to firstly explore how these diasporic dynamics intersect with those of gender. The academic Loic Wright, in an essay on the fiction of J.P Donleavy and Lee Dunne, explores the role of the pub in Ireland in the 'formation and regulation of local hegemonic masculinities in 20th century Ireland'.[4] My own relationship with Irish pubs and their masculinity has not been so straightforward. Using my experience of these spaces in London, Dublin and Belfast I want also to think about how those locations intersect with my own identity as a member of the Irish diaspora, an English woman, and the North of Ireland's history of colonisation and violence.

Part of what I always loved about London's Irish pubs was who they allowed me to be, amid an increasingly niche-marketed and commercialised drinking culture. They were sociable and fuss-free, I felt very at home in them and I found a similar home in pubs in Dublin. This, for a long time, was my predominant experience of the Irish pub. A complex space, for sure, and at times one in which those uneasy or conflicting emotions are present. But ultimately, for me, a safe space.

What it is about the position I occupied in those London Irish pubs that produced those feelings? And how did my relationship to pubs change when I moved to Belfast in 2018? Here my own identity shifted; I became an outsider, of course, but the space of the Irish pub itself – its function, meaning and what it represents – has different meanings in Belfast. It is a city with a history of violence, conflict and division in which arguably all public space is contested to varying degrees and the Irishness of the city and its inhabitants, and of the North of Ireland more broadly, has historically been challenged – often violently – *within* pubs. This mood of menace runs through the work of the great Belfast poet Ciaran Carson and I use his words later in the chapter to show how that threat is felt in the textures of everyday life, both during the Troubles and now.

And of course in these environments the presence and behaviours of women have always been challenged and policed, if not outright prohibited. My research into women's experiences of the Troubles, while focused primarily on domestic space, also brought to my attention the gendered dimensions of more public spaces. In Pat Murphy's 1981 film *Maeve*, for example, we can see both the difficulty and defiance prompted by the Irish pub for women protagonists, who argue about republican politics with older men in a local neighbourhood bar, or go out on a raucous night out with their female friends, risking harassment by the security forces in doing so. And in Nell McCafferty's eponymous account of the Derry woman Peggy Deery, nights out at the pub for Peggy provide an escape from her grief and the rigours of domestic labour, and here she can play around with who she is, away from her role as a long-suffering mother.

Figure 8.1 *The Druthaib's Ball* installation by Array Collective, Herbert Art Gallery and Museum, Coventry, 2021. Image by Garry Jones Photography.

So this chapter will also engage with the Irish pub as a space of possibility, a theme that has been brought to the fore by Belfast-based art collective Array and their Turner Prize-winning art installation *The Druthaib's Ball*, initially partly conceived as a wake for the centenary of Ireland's partition, a large part of which was their re-creation of a *síbín*, an illegal Irish drinking den. In this installation Array use the space of the Northern Irish pub to highlight the causes they engage with as activists as well as artists: fights for bodily autonomy, trans healthcare, Irish-language rights and quality mental health provision. They show that, while there undoubtedly remains an unease and even danger in many contemporary Northern Ireland drinking spaces, the pub can also be used to challenge many rigid gendered and sectarian distinctions.

Pubs and patriarchy

The gendered associations of pubs in general are well known. Up until relatively recently women were not allowed in many British and Irish pubs, and the lounge bar/public bar division was used to separate women from what were seen as 'unsuitable' surroundings. In her 1986 study *Patriarchy and Pub Culture*, Valerie Hey argues that pubs have served to enforce certain gendered public/private divisions whereby men can distance themselves from the domestic sphere; for her pubs form 'a paradigm of male domination made possible by female exclusion, control and oppression'.[5] Pubs are also a space for homosocial bonds to be formed and played out and Wright explores the particular ways that in Ireland pubs have become associated with various male rites of passage: buying drinks, taking up space, communicating with other men and a certain performance of heteronormative rituals in their relationships with women. So, there are undoubtedly certain types of hegemonic masculinity expressed by these spaces, and in the 'arenas for diasporic performance' of the London Irish pub this is given a further dimension. Here, away from Ireland, people often feel driven to demonstrate their connection to the home country through performances of national identity, via songs, sport and storytelling often connected to a 'masculinist nationalism'.[6]

In many ways Hey's 1980s account is quite dated, as she conceives the conventional pub as a kind of intrinsically masculine space. As well as underestimating the agency of women drinkers and the more complex positions they can occupy in this space, it also reinforces some gendered stereotypes around sport, behaviour and drinking itself. In the Republic of Ireland some of these stereotypes were literally enshrined in law until recently, as pubs were legally allowed to refuse a woman a pint of beer on the grounds it was 'unladylike', a practice that was officially outlawed by the Equal Status Act in 2000. In the early 1970s this law was challenged in a lively and playful feminist protest led by Nell McCafferty, when she and a

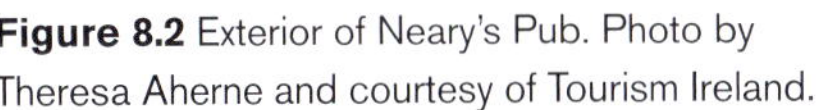
Figure 8.2 Exterior of Neary's Pub. Photo by Theresa Aherne and courtesy of Tourism Ireland.

group of women walked into the Dublin pub Neary's and each ordered a brandy. When the barman had lined these up on the bar they then asked for a single pint, and when it was refused they left the pub without paying for any of their drinks.

In a 2022 *Vogue* article by Claire Finney about a new 'feminist pub' in London, though, some stereotypes endure in what is conceptualised as a 'woman-friendly' drinking venue.[7] The managers of The Flower House pub in Marylebone describe the efforts they have made with the pub's décor, layout and menus to create a safe, comfortable space and in many respects this is important; there is no denying that the 'traditional' pub can often feel intimidating and male-dominated and it is crucial to expand our ideas of what a 'proper' pub is beyond dark corners, pints of beer, and old men propped up at the bar. But certain gendered clichés remain; as a woman who enjoys a solo trip to the pub I would object, for example, to Finney's assertion that there is 'something, well, male' about sitting in a pub alone. The article is illustrated with pictures of The Flower House's bright, floral wallpaper, and references to extensive wine and cocktail lists are cited as proof of the pub's woman-friendly credentials; but the argument that this is what makes a space attractive to women seems a little reductive, to put it charitably. For McCafferty and her comrades, they just wanted the right to drink what and where the men drank, if they so chose.

'Pure heaven': gender, politics and pool in the 1990s

I came of age as a drinker in the mid-1990s. I was aware of a certain type of gendered drinking culture emerging around me, whereby as a teenage girl/young woman I was expected to drink 'girly drinks' – white wine, alcopops or cocktails – and gravitate towards supposedly women-friendly spaces such as the chain bars All Bar One and Pitcher & Piano. This is partly a result of changes in the landscape of Britain's nightlife where such places aimed to attract more women through spatial design and increased choice in drinks.[8] But when I started going out with my older brothers and their friends, pubs became a kind of refuge from these ideas. I was, I felt, rebelling against a particular feminine notion of drinking in public as a woman, which seemed to involve sitting passively waiting for a man to buy you a drink in a small glass and a lot less fun than the big rounds of pints, games of pool and arguments over the jukebox that I saw my male counterparts engaged in.[9] Many of the pubs I had started going to were Irish – places, usually in north London, where my Celtic-supporting friends would go to watch Old Firm ties or where we would all gravitate to for Ireland football internationals (none of these places, it should be said, was an O'Neill's, the Irish pub chain which also emerged as a powerful market force in 1990s nightlife).

In these places I got to know the rituals and etiquette around round-buying, pool matches and rebel songs. My political ideals were developing around this time and, aided by my grandmother Madge and my 'A level' English teacher – both of whom possessed a serious, if at times slightly romantic, diasporic republicanism – these ideals began to include an attention to Irish literature and history, including partition, the Troubles and a belief in a united Ireland. This politics, combined with my love of the pub, found a perfect fit in the rowdy post-match drinking sessions in O'Rafferty's in Wood Green, where I learned all the words to 'Come Out Ye Black and Tans', 'Joe McDonnell' and 'The Fields of Athenry'.

Once, during a post-match afternoon drinking session in that pub, I was asked to referee a pool competition between the local London Irish lads. A guy called Dave gave me a piece of paper and a pen and asked me to note down names and scores as I watched them all compete against each other. I felt, that afternoon, as if I'd been admitted into some kind of sacred club. In hindsight, I can see I was still somewhat on the margins here – a ref rather than a player in that instance – but even so I liked who I was allowed to be at times like that. I enjoyed the seriousness with which sport was taken – the football of course, but also those pool games – and the apparent easy camaraderie that accompanied it, in which a commitment to generosity, good fun and collective allegiance appeared to be prized above all else. The simple, low-key conviviality of the London Irish pub is evoked in 'The Shovel Kings', as Rafferty describes the Aran pub he went to in the evenings during his early days in London: 'pure heaven, the warmth, the red table lamps, the talking and gassing, getting a pint, sitting down on a stool, without even exchanging a word'.[10]

That 'pure heaven' also conjures up the pubs I got to know when I lived in Dublin for a year, where there were stools up at mahogany bars, small cosy snugs, a friendly but business-like attention to a well-poured Guinness and no food beyond a packet of crisps or a toastie if you were lucky. When I returned to London, as I got older and the niche marketing of drinking evolved around me, Irish pubs offered me other things. The popularity of craft beer meant that many pubs became a venue for a type of connoisseurship, which changed the rhythms and behaviours around drinking. I enjoyed some of this, but there was a restlessness created by all that choice from which my locals, the Mother Red Cap and the Boston Arms, gave me an escape. In O'Brien's story, the pub in which Rafferty's friends host him at Christmas 'was how you imagine a home should be' and the quasi-domestic space evoked here reminds me of the easy hospitality offered by many of the places I frequented.[11] The first time I ever went to The Crown on Holloway Road I was alone after work on a Friday, carrying bags of my food shopping and a bit nervous about the reception I'd get in this new pub. My entrance was unremarked upon, I found a table, ordered a Guinness and a barman soon circulated with dishes of roast potatoes and sausages, which, apparently, was a Friday evening custom. It was all fine.

Whose pub? Drinking spaces and the Troubles

I did eventually make it back to Ireland and moved to the North in early 2017 to begin my PhD. The word 'stable' can never really be applied to the political situation in the northern statelet; even so it did seem that I had arrived at a particularly turbulent time. The Brexit vote had taken place not twelve months earlier and it was just after the 'cash for ash' scandal had been uncovered, revealing the incompetence and corruption of the majority governing Democratic Unionist Party's (DUP) renewable energy scheme. This prompted the resignation of Sinn Fein's then deputy first minister Martin McGuinness in January and the subsequent collapse of the Stormont power-sharing government. There has been no functioning government for most of the time I lived in Northern Ireland – and indeed for much of the time since the formation of those political institutions in 1998 – and at the time of writing there has only just been an end to the most recent political stalemate. Meanwhile, many of the 'post-conflict' dividends promised by the Good Friday Agreement and later St Andrew's Agreement have not been delivered; these include an Irish Language Act[12] and the dismantling of the notorious 'peace walls', barriers placed at the interface of Catholic and Protestant neighbourhoods supposedly to prevent violence (which have, in fact, increased both in number and height since 1998).[13] Northern Ireland remains deeply segregated, with high levels of deprivation, and tensions between and among communities persist, often manifesting themselves violently.

So, when republican songs and slogans are shouted out in a London Irish pub, there are different things at stake to when they are sung in the place where they originate, especially when the situation about which they were written remains contested and sometimes unresolved. A few months after I moved to Belfast, a friend and I went to a pub in a republican area close to where I was living, not too far outside the city centre. As I walked in, the space felt familiar. It reminded me of the London pubs where I'd spent so much time: the decor was plain and unfussy, there were framed GAA and Celtic football jerseys on the wall, and I was served an excellent pint of Guinness. My friend, from the North of Ireland himself, recognised two old friends of his sitting up at the bar soon after we arrived, and we joined them. They all talked away and, as I ordered my drink amid the wider hum of Belfast pub chatter, I became aware that, unlike in those old London haunts of mine, my accent marked me as an outsider.

Hearing me speak, a man sitting at the bar began to make conversation, asking me where I was from and what had brought me to Belfast, something that happened to me regularly. It is often people making harmless small talk in public situations – in taxis, on public transport, at work events, in pubs – but there is sometimes a kind of wariness. I answered this man's questions – explained my relationship to Belfast, that I had come over here to do my PhD but also that my parents used to live up on the north coast. I rattled through these facts and, at some point, without thinking, I used the term 'Northern Ireland'. He challenged me. 'Where?' he asked, and I instantly cursed myself for saying it, knowing full well that this is not a term you use in a republican pub (it's a term I'm often uncomfortable with myself). I apologised and corrected myself, but the mood of the conversation quickly changed. He began to quiz me about my relationship to Ireland, asking me what my relationship to the Irish community was when I lived in London, and as I talked about my nan, my Catholic schooling, the family connection in Mayo, I felt horribly as if he was testing me and that I was trying way too hard to prove myself in response.

I describe this experience not really to complain about how I was treated that night; there was no serious hostility towards me, the bar staff were fine with me and I don't think I was ever in danger at any point. It doesn't really surprise me when my English accent gets picked up on and I accept that it carries particular associations in particular spaces. Amid the long and complex history of England's colonial domination of Ireland, no English person can expect to sit neutrally outside of this power dynamic; Graham Dawson has pointed out how any person researching the Troubles should be sensitive of the fact that the Six Counties is 'one of the most heavily researched areas on the planet', which may also explain some of that wariness

I get.[14] But that night was important because it challenged certain ideas I had about the Irish pub and who I am inside it.

In fact, my experience that night was not unusual at all. It is almost a cliché to talk about how people in the North of Ireland love to fire questions at you when they first meet you, are always trying to figure out who you are and where you're from (there is a running joke I've heard from several Belfast friends that whenever you meet someone new at a social gathering, the first five minutes of conversation are always spent trying to work out the school friends or family members you know in common and that you can't relax until this is established). In a 2014 essay about the John Hewitt pub, writer Rosie Schaap, a New Yorker now based in Northern Ireland, describes an encounter with this tendency.[15] On her first visit to the Hewitt, a punter strikes up a conversation and asks her, in disarmingly direct fashion, 'Which are you then? Catholic or Protestant?' Schaap answers, 'Neither. I'm Jewish', and is reminded of Ciaran Carson's poem 'Belfast Confetti', in which he lists questions – 'What is / My name? Where am I coming from? Where am I going?' – to illustrate the danger that the 'fusillade of question marks' signals when the Troubles was at its height. Carson is a Belfast native and shows how such questions took a different, more subtle form when they were exchanged during the Troubles and among those from Belfast itself, with the consequences different and often more serious than for us outsiders.

In most Belfast city centre pubs these days, as Schapp argues, you are probably on much safer ground asking – and answering – those questions than you would've been in 1987 when Carson wrote his poem. But those echoes of violence are still there, and my encounter that night made me think more about the nature of the pub in the North of Ireland and question a lot of what I had taken for granted about the comfort and safety I thought I found there. I didn't realise at the time, but the bar I was in had been the target of loyalist violence during the Troubles, when it was bombed by the Ulster Volunteer Force in May 1974, an attack which killed five people, with another dying from his injuries several days later. This was part of a spate of loyalist attacks on Catholic nationalist spaces in the wake of the Sunningdale power-sharing agreement. There were three other attacks on Catholic-owned pubs in Belfast and Armagh during this time, killing six civilians in total, and pubs were the frequent target of violence throughout the conflict in both England and Ireland. Several of the conflict's worst and most notorious acts of paramilitary violence took place in pubs, including the McGurk's bar bombing in 1971, a UVF attack which killed fifteen Catholic men, women and children, the Greysteel massacre in October 1993, in which members of the UDA opened fire on a pub Halloween party, killing eight civilians, including two Protestants, and the Ballykelly bombing, in which the INLA targeted a pub frequented by British soldiers, killing eleven soldiers and six civilians. Pubs were also targets of violence outside of Northern Ireland during the Troubles; Biddy Mulligan's, the setting for 'The Shovel Kings', was itself the target of a UDA attack in 1975 and the Birmingham and Guildford pub bombings were among the worst and most notorious of those commonly attributed to the Provisional IRA's 'mainland campaign' (those two bombings did of course result in several wrongful convictions and lengthy campaigns to correct the resulting miscarriages of justice).

Carson's 'Belfast Confetti' gave the name to his 1989 collection of poetry and prose, in which several poems deal with the very real and concrete threat involved in going out for a drink.[16] In 'Last Orders', for example: 'how simple it would be for someone/ Like ourselves to walk in and blow the whole place, and/ ourselves, to Kingdom Come'. And in 'Barfly' there is the charged political geography of Belfast's drinking palaces. Pubs called The Crown and The Shamrock 'at opposite ends of the town'. Actual violence occurs in this poem rather than just its threat, again with the imagery of punctuation. 'Two punters walk in' and 'punctuate the lunchtime menu'.

These attacks challenge the idea of a pub as a place of refuge, safety, intimacy and community.[17] This in turn flags up the highly contested and segregated nature of public space in Northern Ireland generally during the conflict, by the mere fact that these spaces were attacked because of their association with a particular community. These dangers, real and imagined, are still alive to some extent in the contemporary North, with a study from Queen's University Belfast showing that people remain hesitant about going to unfamiliar bars and social spaces in a 'different' community.[18]

Pubs, protest, play and performance

There are obviously many other identities that intersect the binaries of Catholic/ Protestant and nationalist/unionist, both during the conflict and now. In her radical and formally inventive 1981 feminist film *Maeve*, Pat Murphy engages with the everyday gendered dangers of life in Belfast during the Troubles, and shows women in constant struggles for safety, freedom and self-determination in various spaces, including the pub.[19] The Maeve of the film's title is a young woman from a Catholic nationalist family in Belfast who has moved to London, though the film flits between different times and places. It shows the everyday operation of 'armed patriarchy', a term coined by Derry feminist and trade unionist Cathy Harkin to describe how the militarised nature of life in Northern Ireland heightened violence against women; after a night out in the pub one evening, for example, Maeve, her sister and their friends walk back home and they are stopped by a British Army patrol. Soldiers ask them to jump, a practice used ostensibly to check for weapons and explosives but shown clearly here as a way to dominate and humiliate women. We see how risky a night out for young women is after another evening in a local bar, and they talk about the strategies they have developed to keep themselves safer. 'Run like fuck when you get to the Shankill' one of them says as they leave. 'Take your shoes off,' another says. 'We'll get home quicker. We'll be quieter too.'

Another scene shows Maeve out drinking in a local pub with her father's friends, a lone woman in a group of older men; through their conversation we learn that Maeve's father went to prison in the cause of the republican movement, taking the blame for another man. Maeve openly rails against these men and their idea of political sacrifice for 'the movement' and points out the hard work that her mother did to keep things going at home in her father's absence. The pub in this context is a place in which patriarchal dynamics are made plain – Maeve's voice is dismissed and subtly undermined – but it is also a dialectical space in which she can challenge those dynamics, clearly and bravely, and claim a bit of territory for herself. The Irish pub in this film, then, is also a site of protest, play and disruption of norms. The young women on their night out, while clearly never free of physical danger, are prepared to take these risks for the sake of their fun, and there also is a great deal of joy in the scene, as they run giggling out of the bar, giddy on booze and music and their snatched freedoms.

There are similar snatched freedoms for women in Nell McCafferty's book *Peggy Deery*, which details the life and struggles during the Troubles of this working-class Catholic Derry woman, the only woman to be shot on Bloody Sunday.[20] Peggy battles with the daily grind of poverty and domestic labour in a war-torn Derry and her plight is made more difficult by the death of family members and the involvement of her children in armed republican struggle. McCafferty is unflinching in her portrayal of the family's hardship, but she is also at pains to show how and when Peggy regained some agency. She achieves this through accounts of her nights out at the pub with her friend Sandra; they dub their drinking double act 'Cagney and Lacey' and McCafferty describes their tastes, habits and tricks: 'Peggy liked Southern Comfort and white lemonade. Sandra liked Smirnoff vodka with ice cubes. Peggy sometimes managed to save on mixers by bringing her own bottle of white lemonade to the pubs.' Self-conscious of her wounded leg but encouraged by Sandra, Peggy uses these nights out to experiment with fashion, repurposing male military family objects for her outfits: 'Peggy's old flair for fashion returned, and her legendary ability to improvise. A lace nightdress, presented by one of her children, which she did not wish to waste in bed, was turned into a blouse. It was fastened at the waist with Paddy's dress-uniform IRA belt, converted for the occasion with white shoe-dye.' Again, we see women during the Troubles adopting small everyday practices of resistance and creativity to carve out space for themselves and using the setting of a night out in the pub to do so.[21]

The idea of the Irish pub as a space of both protest and play, like with that McCafferty-led feminist protest in Neary's, is kept very much alive by Belfast-based art collective Array in their 2021 Turner Prize-winning installation *The Druthaib's Ball*, comprised of a film exhibit and the recreation of a traditional Irish *síbín*. After its initial exhibition in Coventry where the Turner Prize was awarded, the installation travelled to Galway and returned 'home' in 2023 with an exhibition at the Ulster Museum in Belfast. The *síbín* is decorated with slogans and banners drawing attention to the political issues in Northern Ireland around which the collective campaign and organise: the lasting impact of the partition of Ireland, Irish language rights, reproductive healthcare, the North's mental health crisis and LGBTQ+ liberation. There are mirrors scrawled with slogans, a Red Hand of Ulster ashtray with a stubbed-out cigarette inside it, a beer called 'Southern Guilt' and a mocked-up version of the *Racing Post*, complete with listings for race meets and horse names which riff on political scandals and local references and in-jokes (my favourites included 'Buckfast Dream', 'No Rights for Anyone' and 'They Moved to Bangor and We Never Seen Them Again').

The use of the pub was deliberate, to draw out the contradictions and tensions of Northern society. Array member Sighle Bhreathnach-Cashell explained in an interview with *The Guardian*: 'Our pub is almost like a self-portrait of Northern Ireland. When tourists come to Northern Ireland, even English tourists, people always say how friendly the place is, sitting alongside the conflict. The irony of that is not lost on us. But we were also consciously thinking, "Let's make [our part of the show] a comfortable place, so that people can sit there and absorb it and take time

Figure 8.3 Front entrance to the Sunflower pub, Belfast, 2022. Photo by Brian Morrison and courtesy of Tourism Northern Ireland.

with it.”’[22] When I went to visit the exhibition myself I spent a long time just sitting at one of the pub tables, observing, reading, thinking (there's a lot to take in!) and also laughing (there is, as those horse names suggest, a lot of humour there too). In a 2022 *Irish Times* interview Array member Stephen Millar describes the various meanings held by the objects in the bar and the daily Northern Irish realities they represent. The red hand, for example 'is a constant in the psyche of all of us. That emblem is everywhere, our shared trauma belongs to all of us'.[23] Some of the echoes of violence I picked up on back in 2018 after my pub encounter are given a physical and material expression in the *síbín* and a safe space is provided to sit with them.

So while, in Belfast itself, many city-centre bars often work on a kind of studiously neutral positioning, the pub as a political space is also becoming something else. In 2013 in an interview in *Hospitality Ireland*, Colin Neill, chief executive of Pubs of Ulster, was keen to stress the value of the pub industry to tourism, saying that 'we don't do politics'. But politics is not just about sectarian binaries, it is about class, gender, sexual liberation, bodily autonomy, migrant rights; the John Hewitt pub that Schaap writes about, for example, is a social enterprise, set up and owned by Belfast Unemployed Resource Centre, which provides training and facilities to the unemployed and other socially and economically disadvantaged groups in the city. Queer politics are not far away in Union Street, which is now home to a couple of Belfast's best pubs, which sit close to a new LGBTQ+ resource centre.[24] And there is the Sunflower, a favourite post-protest gathering spot, its walls hung with pro-choice, migrant solidarity and internationalist paraphernalia and an event space that often plays host to feminist, queer and trade union fundraisers. It was actually the Sunflower – and my enthusiasm for good beer rather than rebel songs – which gave me my first introduction to Belfast drinking while still living on the north coast. I had recently joined the Belfast Women's Beer Collective Facebook group and came down to the city for one of their socials there in January 2018.

The Array *síbín* draws attention to the different identities, beyond the 'two communities', which are still frequently challenged and rejected in public space in

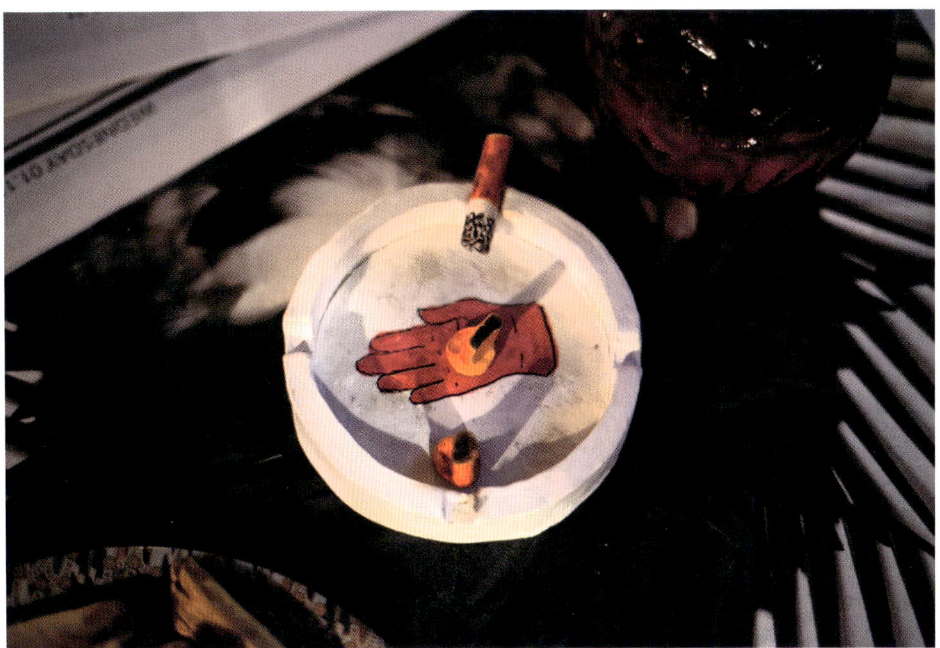

Figure 8.4 'Red Hand Ashtray' by Array Collective with ceramic cigarette butts by Rob Hilken as part of *The Druthaib's Ball* installation created for the Turner Prize 2021 now in the Ulster Museum Collection. Courtesy of National Museums in Northern Ireland collections.

the North of Ireland, often violently. In the programme for the Galway exhibit, Array explain that the *síbín* is both a space of resistance to and refuge from these various axes of oppression.

> [The *síbín*] embodies the complexities that distinguish our Northern Irish/Irish identities, honouring the personal experiences of existence and resistance, despite a litany of human rights abuses against us. Falling outside the sectarian dichotomies, which have dominated the collective memory of the North of Ireland for the last hundred years, has been dangerous, but the *síbín* is our shelter.[25]

The pub in various contexts has always had the capacity to provide such a shelter, as we have seen, but such realities are not straightforward. Speaking for myself, there are several pubs in Belfast that I love but hesitate about visiting alone. I hear conflicting stories about republican drinking spots in west Belfast, with some friends telling me to be wary, and others reassuring me I'll be fine, regaling me with a story of the warm reception a (male) cockney friend of theirs got, or telling me that that stuff doesn't matter anymore. This second-guessing is sometimes exhausting, but these anxieties are bigger than just myself and I have it easy in many ways: the Irish pub is not a neutral space for anybody and is still fraught with complexity, unease and danger for many people. The old motto 'whatever you say, say nothing' still holds true in many public spaces in the North of Ireland but the Array *síbín* offers a challenge to this. Inside it is held a multiplicity of voices and a space in which questions of identity and belonging can safely be raised without the pressure of them having to be resolved. Perhaps this is something to aim for.

Eli Davies' Choice:

The Auld Shillelagh,

Stoke Newington, London

Figure 8.5 The Auld Shillelagh. Photo by Jess Hand from *Time Out*.

The Auld Shillelagh in Stoke Newington has appeared on nearly every 'Best London Irish Pub' list going, so in many ways is an obvious choice. Unlike my other potential choices, though, the Shillelagh is *still* there. (My favourite north London Irish pub, the Mother Red Cap, closed in 2024.) Opened by Roscommon brothers Tom and Aonghus in the 1990s, it's a product of different diasporic movements than the places serving Irish migrants in the fifties and sixties but you'll still find many of those people in there, for the pub has many important and beautiful qualities of the old-school Irish pub. It has a cosy, confidential layout – the space is long, narrow and oak panelled – with plain and unfussy decor; it's a destination for London Irish communities to watch Gaelic games matches when they're on and there are framed GAA jerseys on the wall; at busy times there's the classic production line-style row of Guinnesses behind the bar and at quiet times they'll bring your pint to the table (an act that surprises some of my London friends). Stokey is an area that became fashionable way before the rest of the borough of Hackney and is now awash with fancy cafés and cocktail bars, but the beauty of the Shillelagh lies partly in how firmly it has resisted bowing to fashion: they've never served food, for example, and the drinks offering remains no-nonsense. It's a lively night spot, though, and there are posters dotting the place that nod to the music nights they sometimes run (when I lived round there they ran a regular David Bowie night) and their trad sessions. I love to drink there in the afternoon, pop in for one or two and read a book. The service is friendly and efficient and there's an air of calm, homely business about the place; if you want you'll probably be able to strike up a conversation with the bar staff or another punter, but otherwise nobody will pay you much attention. Perfect.

Discourses of Inclusion and Exclusion: Gender, race and point of origin in Irish pubs

Brenda Murphy

Introduction

Have you ever walked into an Irish pub – in Ireland or elsewhere – London, New York, Tokyo or Durban? How did you know how to 'be'? How to 'act'? How to 'navigate the space'? The discursive practices of any space carries rules of engagement in its legacy and in its everyday practices. How you enter; how and where you sit; how you speak to others in the pub; how you order; what you order – these are dictated by those rules and are performed by the consumer. Like any other space, the Irish pub demands an understanding of the rules of engagement, and it is overseen by a complex intersection of signifiers and signification around gender, class, and national and ethnic identity.[1] I anchor the discussion in this chapter around discourses of belonging and exclusion in a gendered space for women and men, and then expand that into spaces on belonging as outsiders and 'others' in London and New York.

Contextualising the Irish pub: thresholds and belonging

As you walk across the threshold of the Irish pub, you enter a space that is bounded and busy. The rules are complex, learned and contextualised in space and time. The role of the pub, and its rules of engagement, are inextricably bound. An understanding of the historical landscape and legacy is useful to contextualise the contemporary.

Between the 1900s and the 1950s, the role of a pub in Ireland would have been similar to Valerie Hey's description of the nineteenth-century London pub, where 'customers had access to newspapers, betting games, cock fighting arenas, political meeting places, debating societies, sporting venues and transport centres all in the context of company, social networks, and street and community gossip'.[2] In the late nineteenth and early twentieth centuries the pub was a place to gather and socialise and join a sing-song on a Saturday night. It functioned as a refuge from the often impoverished domestic space, offering light, heat and good company. To walk into that historical pub in Ireland required the drinker to be male, Irish, White and heterosexual. Most pubs were viewed as 'men only' and there were very few exceptions to the rule. Women in the pub space were compelled to follow other rules of engagement and were likely to fall into one of three categories: older and widowed, a prostitute, or bar staff.

Binaries of belonging

'Belonging' in the pub was demarcated architecturally, socially and culturally along a strict binary logic men:women, us:them, insiders:outsiders and, for women, an additional binary code prevailed around sexual availability and marital status in the madonna:whore dichotomy.[3]

By the 1960s and '70s the role of the pub began to shift slightly and the rules of engagement shifted too. The fortified boundaries of masculinity began to give way – and while to walk comfortably and without surveillance into a pub still required you to be male and a drinker, the multifunctionality of some pubs determined it to also be a 'grocery store, funeral parlour, concert hall, restaurant, bar, political forum, congenial meeting place, courting corner and, most of all, a place for talk'.[4] In fact, that multifunctioning pub – shop by day/pub by night – still exists in some very rural parts of Ireland and the 'shop pub' or 'grocery pub' has a long and meaningful role in the community.

Despite the rise of second-wave feminism internationally, women wishing to access the Irish pub were more likely to go to the pub under certain conditions – accompanied by a man, and/or expected to sit in the 'snug' or the lounge.[5] Indeed, the lounge was reminiscent of a room 'at home' in the domestic space and designed to replicate that space. The pub might even have two entrances: one leading directly to the bar, where the decoration would be minimal – uncarpeted floors and wooden seating; the other to the lounge, with fitted carpet, upholstered seating, fireplace and ornaments, where women only drank spirits or 'glasses', not pints.[6] Indeed, as recently as the late 1990s, if a woman ordered a pint of Guinness it was often refused, as women were only allowed to drink 'glasses' and advertising campaigns at the time reinforced this.

Regulating women: regulating men

In the 1980s and '90s the drinker in the pub, while still predominantly male, Irish,

White and heterosexual, had begun to give way to 'others'. A slackening of role and rule meant that both the pub itself, and the society it was in, was changing. While women were socially freer to move about in this space, many employed complex culturally and socially acceptable strategies to put themselves at ease and many described a discomfort about going into the pub alone.

Hey attributes this discomfort to the fact that the presence of women in the pub is still read as a statement of sexual availability. She goes on to suggest that it is still practically impossible for single women to consume pints of beer in a pub without their activity being read as a sexually deviant or defiant action:

> I would like to meet the woman who can unselfconsciously enter a strange public house alone. It is one of the consequences of a patriarchal control of female sexuality that we are prevented from 'popping into the local' for a social drink, unaccompanied.[7]

In the late 1990s women were still subtly reminded that the pub space was a male space and, according to one male respondent, 'women are usually brought into a pub rather than go into a pub'.[8] Women were still reporting that they were less than 100 per cent comfortable entering and sitting in the pub alone. They described the strategies they used to avoid sitting alone in the bar – arranging to meet friends outside the pub or waiting in their car until the rest of the group arrived. Many commented that it 'was not the done thing' to go to the pub alone, that 'there was a stigma attached to it'. The madonna:whore dichotomy was voiced clearly by women and, while on the first reading women were tolerated in the pub space, the ideology of 'outsider, insider' prevailed and the fear of judgement of sexual availability was acknowledged.

One of my favourite stories encapsulates the strategising and negotiating that women then engaged in to access the pub. Gráinne was a confident professional, living and working in Dublin, and described how she negotiated her space in the patriarchal pub.

> Gráinne: The only pub that I go to to have a drink on my own is Mulligan's[9] – 'cos of the good Guinness. For a pint of Guinness on my own … 'cos Mulligan's is renowned for its Guinness – so I can go and have a pint of Guinness.

BM: Do you feel you have a right to be in there?

Gráinne: I'm not known, barman don't come near me – I'm doing my crossword – [he won't] come up with 'so you've been stood up' whereas if it was another pub that wasn't so renowned for Guinness, I'd feel they were thinking you have been stood up.[10]

Gráinne did something very interesting. She selected a specific drink, and a pub renowned for serving it well, to justify her occupation of the pub space – the public space and the masculine space. Wearing the product – Guinness – as a 'badge of identity', she felt comfortable enough to sit alone, doing the crossword – reassured that no one would make assumptions about her use of the space. She had not been stood up, she was not waiting for a boyfriend and she was not a prostitute. She felt justified in being there, in this 'famous Guinness pub', because she was drinking Guinness. The consumption of the product enabled her to generate her own gendered identity and resist ideological constructs of what it is to be female in the pub space.

In London and New York

While the pub space incubates challenges and barriers for women in general, Irish women in London, New York and elsewhere experience a 'further problematised relationship' with the pub. Irish women in London and New York strive to access not just a 'male space' but a space that will afford them community and belonging, since the pub functions as a place where migrant communities can coalesce. Moments of 'exclusion' become ever more problematic. They are not just being excluded from a space that normally offers social, emotional and cultural support, they are being excluded from their 'surrogate Irish community'. As the diasporic pub carries a function of 'home away from home', it is critical that women are not excluded from this community of support, at a time and in a place that may be crucial for well-being.

Discursive practices surrounding the Irish as migrant consumers, and the Irish pub space

While the section above situates the pub's exclusionary practices around gendered borders, in this section I consider the pub 'abroad' (and I refer to the 'authentic pub'

– the pub owned by an Irish person or family, or the pub designated 'as Irish' by its drinkers as opposed to the Irish Pub Company commercial type). The 'authentic' Irish pub in London and New York has additional demands made of it. Alongside all the functions above – newspapers and other media, betting, political debates, sport, social networks, music, food, heat and good company – it is also a vital space for sourcing employment and crucial to social and community networks that function to provide news and connections 'from home', practical welfare and emotional support to the complex group of heterogeneous users.

I argue that the diasporic Irish pub 'abroad' plays a key role in supporting various expressions of Irish identity. Harnessing a binary logic of 'inclusion:exclusion', I examine the space and the discursive practices in and around moments of inclusion, against a backdrop of expressions around hybridity and authenticity. I also argue that we need to re-examine and re-address how we construct and utilise the term 'racism' and suggest that the terms 'difference' or 'difference in point of origin' would be more useful. Finally, I show that there are many varieties of inclusion and exclusion. In the authentic pub, abroad, we glimpse at a layering of 'other' where gender identities and national identities coalesce.

Practices of inclusion and exclusion around gender and race: expressions of hybridity and authenticity

> Cormac – not his real name – described an interview he attended some months earlier in an Irish pub in Boston. He attended the interview for a construction job and on arrival in the pub he was greeted in *Gaeilge* (Irish) – he wasn't a fluent Irish speaker but he managed to understand and reply and the entire interview was conducted in Irish. He didn't get the job because the company had an unwritten policy, which meant that they only recruited men from Connemara.[11]

Cormac's story encapsulates the main focus of this section: the Irish pub, in London and New York, provided a space where expressions of inclusion and exclusion were acted out. Bell and Valentine highlight this when they explore the various aspects of 'community'. They comment:

> We can instantly think of places where sharing food and drink helps bond us into a community – the local pub, or a street party, for example. But we must always be mindful of the fact that communities are about exclusion as well as inclusion.[12]

The pub space in London and New York is marked by ethnicity and, in very rare examples, some are willing to demarcate this space to accommodate more than one ethnic group. Indeed, pub clientele are usually adept at reading the ethnic semiotics of a pub, at least in their own locales. For example, I observed how the now defunct Atlantic bar, also known as Brady's, in Brixton was split into two halves: the Jamaican side, with one of its walls decorated with a mural of palm trees and parrots, and patrons heavily involved in games of dominoes; contrasted with the Irish side, which had nightly sessions of live Irish music, its patrons heavily involved in discussions about horseracing and watching Irish soccer games brought to them via the Irish satellite TV channel. There was a linking door between the two spaces but it was rarely used. These marked spaces of ethnicity underline one of the roles of the pub space, and this site for community, in-group membership and inclusion is also the site for exclusion.

I refer to the pub as a trope or generalised space, but when I spoke to respondents they often referred to particular pubs in their lived experiences. Their stories allow me to examine the complexities of 'Whiteness', hybridity and miscegenation, and authenticity, discussing 'the voice' of the diasporic Irish and exploring the power of 'points of origin'.

Cormac (above) described a moment of exclusion that had been unconsidered. It is not what Bronwyn Walter would refer to as White-on-White racism,[13] but it is a thought-provoking development, as it constructs a binary of 'us against us' – in this case, Irishman against Irishman.

Varieties of exclusion, varieties of racism

'Exclusion' or 'racism' is not merely a discussion about White people and people of colour residing in London or New York. It is also about other binary codes – White:White, people of colour:people of colour, and intra-group expressions of inclusion and exclusion. In the stories that follow, I unpack discourses of inclusion and exclusion found in Irish pub spaces in London and New York to organise and make sense of meanings around those practices. Practices that I organise as: (i) the Irish as the excluded 'other'; (ii) them and us – we, the Irish; you, the other; and (iii) us versus us – we, the Irish; us, the Irish.

Varieties of racism (i) The Irish as the excluded 'other'

Exploring 'community' demands an exploration of not just the members of the community but also of the non-members. While gathering stories in London and New York, I located racism as a lived experience. The 'racism' described was not acts of exclusion based on colour, but more likely to be what Mac an Ghaill describes as 'complex processes of social exclusion'.[14]

Anti-Irish expressions of exclusion: no dogs, Blacks or Irish

Being White in a White-power country doesn't automatically guarantee equality of relations; it simply blurs the power relation, suggesting one version of power, when, in fact, another version (usually the dominant power) is in place. The Irish in the UK do not occupy places of power, as they do in the United States; they are more likely to be disenfranchised, discriminated against, and bound up in a binary of 'White' and 'Black', where they are very definitely 'Black'.

Participants' experiences in the United Kingdom depended on which decade they arrived, and expressions of hostility towards them seemed proportionate to the level of political activity in Northern Ireland and specifically around the activity of the IRA in Britain. Frank described London in the 1970s as a hostile place. Any effort to secure accommodation was a nightmare because most landlords/landladies had notices warning 'No Irish, Blacks or dogs'. Two decades later in the early 1990s, as the IRA bombing campaign resumed, Tom, a building labourer in north London, described working as a truck driver and being 'booked twice and taken at gunpoint three times' by the police. He was afraid to speak as his accent would mark him as Irish.[15]

Many participants arrived in the United Kingdom and were surprised to discover 'they don't like us' and had never imagined that they might be perceived as 'other' in Britain. Likewise, traditional theoretical discourse has 'ignored' or 'regulated out' any discussion around White-on-White racism mainly due to prevailing discourses of colour racism. For Mac an Ghaill, the American model of race relations, where colour is a defining characteristic of racism, has continued to dominate British sociology and cultural studies, so that race and ethnic relations are discussed almost exclusively 'within a reductive model: that of the Black/White dualism, with its prescribed understanding of powerlessness/powerfulness that continues to interrupt and disrupt deeper understandings'.[16] Walter, in her 2001 work *Outsiders Inside*, addresses issues around the invisibility of Whiteness, where being White positions many groups, especially the Irish in Britain and the United States, in a place where they occupy a complex space of national exclusion and cultural invisibility.

The political tensions cannot be removed from the equation when we examine the Irish experience in the United Kingdom especially throughout the 1970s, '80s and '90s, and this is reflected in the reactions of both the Irish migrant and the British host. In fact, it was interesting to hear from respondents in New York, who had lived in both London and New York. Many commented that they were more likely to experience anti-Irish comments in London. Conor described negativity and offence in London when told to 'go home you dumb Mick'.[17]

Mac an Ghaill and Haywood argue that political and media discourses in Britain convey a contradictory message about the Irish: while proclaiming them 'the same as us', members of a larger British-Isles family, pervasive institutional mechanisms still exclude them from public life.[18] Respondents in New York reported a very different and more positive experience, although Avril did note that there were subtle forms of exclusion, commenting that 'there's a glass ceiling for every minority here, if you're not a WASP'.[19]

One of the earliest critics to consider the consequences of the dynamic of White-blindness in scholarship was Franz Fanon, in his 1952 work *Black Skin, White Masks*.[20] His work focused on racism and colonialism and dealt with the psychopathologies he encountered as a result of the psychological impact of racism upon Black people in France. He considered these pathologies of social relations and practices to be a direct result of colonial oppression. Later, Greenslade talks about the invisibility of the Irish in Britain and comments that 'one feature of Irishness in England is its relative invisibility' as 'English racism focuses upon colour of skin rather than ethnicity'.[21]

In the United States 'there is a growing realization that one cannot fully understand the existence of racism and racial inequality without paying close attention to the formation and maintenance of white racial identity',[22] and scholars are striving to recognise 'Whiteness' as a category, to strip it of its assumed power, and recognise those within it who are without power. Scholars focused on Irish migration to the United Kingdom are concerned with the use of the category of White, to position Irish migrants as White but not White, and maintain a status quo of 'disempowered White other'. While Ignatiev argues that the Irish Catholic became white by shifting from 'an oppressed race in Ireland' to become 'part of an oppressing race in America',[23] we could never say the same of the Irish experience in Britain.

Varieties of racism (ii) Them and us – we, the Irish; you, the other

While the Irish in London and New York experienced 'exclusion' to varying degrees, they were also aware of prevailing attitudes and sentiments among the Irish themselves towards other ethnic groups. They describe their own attitudes and the attitude of other Irish migrants. For example, in New York, the quest for cheap labour is a significant site for 'them and us' moments, as different minority groups (mostly 'illegals', those without a green card or work permit) battle over employment opportunities. One respondent, when asked about his experiences of discrimination, went on to say that the Irish, in his experience, were as bad if not worse than others for expressing racist sentiment.

It is useful to look to Lentin and McVeigh who, in the mid-2000s, mapped shifts in attitude in Ireland over the previous two decades.[24] They noted that in the mid-1990s 'Ireland was "remarkably free" of racism' – according to the European Parliament Second Committee of Inquiry into Racism and Xenophobia. It was certainly 'remarkably free' of concern about racism. Since then the Irish landscape has been reshaped as a result of new movements of migrants: retirees, return migrants, migrant workers, refugees and asylum-seekers. Lentin and McVeigh provide an annotated set of resources and a review on the nexus of racism, ethnicity and Irishness. They speak of 'Irish racism' as it began to be theorised by social scientists in the 1990s (with specific reference to Ireland, especially in light of new arrivals) and they work to fill a 'theoretical and pedagogical gap in speaking about the specificities of racism in the Irish context'. While working to develop the corpus, they acknowledge its newness, as racism and ethnicity are issues which had enjoyed little analysis or practice. They note that:

> [W]e have moved very quickly therefore from a situation in which very few people took the issue of racism in Ireland seriously – other than its victims of course – to one in which racism is a part of everyday discourse. Indeed, racism in Ireland in all its forms – from discrimination to murder – is now commonplace.[25]

While racism may be a relatively new phenomenon in Ireland, it would be unreasonable to suggest that prior to new arrivals the Irish expressed no racist tendencies. Irish migrants did display racist attitudes when they arrived in countries where they were seen and treated as White, and part of that privileged category, and they continue to do so. Exclusion is not limited in its expression, and it seems that those who experience exclusion go on to exclude others in an unending cycle. Racism, as expressed in the examples above, is clearly linked with difference of origin and ethnicity. The British landlady rejected Blacks and Irish as they both occupied a similar space of 'difference in point of origin'; and the Irish excluded 'others' in London and New York for the same reasons.

Varieties of racism (iii) Us versus us – we, the Irish; us, the Irish

While spending time in the diasporic pub to understand notions of identity, belonging, inclusion and exclusion, I located another form of exclusion which would not, under current discourses, be classed as racism, but is similar in every respect to the racist moments described above. This third variety of racism closes a circle as we return to Cormac's earlier story. While the term 'racism' does not automatically work when we consider us versus us, it is evidently a space where discrimination occurs. The manifestation of us versus us is not an expression of ethnocentrism because the in- and out-group members originate from shared ethnicity. Nor is it a case of horizontal racism, which occurs when members of a minority group adopt racist attitudes towards another minority group.

The binary *us versus us* suffers invisibility – we could call it discrimination instead of racism, but it behaves like racism because it is about 'point of origin' or 'place of origin' – where the roots of the discrimination are in the point of origin. We cannot simply substitute 'racism' for 'discrimination' or we lose the 'point of origin' as the root cause of the discrimination in the first place. To proceed, I have coined the phrase intra-racism to describe the actions and attitudes met. The discrimination that occurs is still based on 'point of origin', but here it is presenting itself in a way that is very different to the traditional paradigms. I document exclusion, of Irish, by Irish; where one Irish person is discriminating against another Irish person.

The first type of intra-racism (*Intra racism (i) 'What part are you from'?*) expressed itself in the form of exclusion, discrimination and 'unfair' advantage, based on one's point of origin in Ireland, where migrants were marked by which county they came from. The second type (*Intra racism (ii) 'Paddies' and 'narrowbacks', new migrants vs other generations*) originated from first-generation Irish who constructed themselves as 'authentic' while they constructed other generations of Irish as 'other'. This was also 'difference' based on point of origin; the second and other generations of Irish Americans were described as 'narrowbacks' and 'not authentic' because their point of origin was not Ireland – another including:excluding binary.

Intra racism (i) 'What part are you from'? or Cormac's story

Respondents in New York reported situations where they experienced 'intra-racism' or 'exclusion' based on *county* of origin rather than country of origin. Cormac's story above is a powerful example of the process of exclusion based on county of origin. His retold his interview experience of being excluded because he wasn't from Connemara. He described sitting in the Irish pub and drawing on remnants of his 'schoolboy Irish' to converse *as Gaeilge* as the interviews were conducted in Irish to eliminate 'outsiders' or non-Irish speakers. This exclusionary hiring policy occurred in the Irish pub space, exemplifying intra-racism along county boundaries.

Intra racism (ii) 'Paddies' and 'narrowbacks', new migrants vs other generations

A complex and interesting form of inclusion:exclusion among the Irish community was found between first-generation Irish and other-generation Irish in New York. This is expressed in a discursive practice of first-generation migrants (born in Ireland) versus second/other generations (born in America/Irish Americans). In the Starting Gate pub in Queens, Pat commented that 'the Irish Americans are the worst … they all consider themselves as Irish and then they see us, the real Irish, coming over'.[26] This tension around 'point of origin' was highlighted using the term 'narrowback', which was employed by first-generation speakers to describe second and other generations.

The term is derogatory and is used to describe an Irish American in a similar way that 'Paddy' is used by British speakers, when referring to all generations of Irish migrants. Another example of exclusion, which hinged on 'hybridity marking', was described by one first-generation Irish respondent, who articulated the schism between the 'authentic' and the 'hybrid'.

> Colin: It's a different culture. They're still Americans even though they call themselves Irish Americans. They're as American as an Italian-American, they are totally different from us. What annoys me is their stereotype[ical] view of Ireland ... half of them haven't been there.
>
> Peter: [they are] narrowbacks, like the Paddies in London.[27]

During discussions around Irish authenticity, first-generation speakers commented on and were dismissive of the validity of the claim to 'Irishness' by 'other' generations. These comments and, later, reactions from second and other generations raises the issue of 'authenticity' and 'hybridity'.

Homi Bhabha and others locate the discussion of hybridity and authenticity in the colonial discourses, and they locate their examples to the colonised 'other'. It is useful to locate it in contemporary spaces of migration too. According to Mac an Ghaill, it is helpful to import these terms when looking at immigrants outside the simple colonisation scenario. He cites Bhabha, who sees 'cultural translation and hybrid identities of metropolitan immigrants and minorities as disrupting older binaries of power relations between dominant colonisers and dominated colonised'.[28] Bhabha theorises that hybridity is represented as a new location of resistance to essentialist identities and associated political demands, and he employs this concept to challenge the assumption that 'national interest' is a meaningful analytical category. Lentin and McVeigh argue that, to understand racism, there is a need to 'theorise and resist two apparently contradictory trends – globalisation and the strengthening of the racist state'. They recognise that these are 'at the very core of the nexus of Irishness and racism'.[29]

Binary oppositions in action: paradoxes at play

When we talk about 'communities' we are talking about belonging and consequently exclusion. We talk about 'us' and consequently 'them', and the respondents' stories that I have retold in this chapter reveal that there are many versions and variations of exclusion in operation. To look at 'inclusion' and 'exclusion', and 'in-groups' and 'out-groups', it is possible to trace a complex set of binary oppositions, and several sets are immediately apparent from the data collected for this research.

While many other binaries exist in the Irish pub, gender and race remain key axes for these thresholds around belonging.[30] Earlier, I described the boundaries of the pub around gender, and then unpacked and renamed complex moments of exclusion around race, colour and 'point of origin'. Viewing these moments through a semiotic lens, and excavating the powerful binary codes at play, enables us to apply a cohesive lens to the conversation of inclusion and exclusion in the Irish pub in Ireland and abroad.

The oppositional paradigm of men:women is well-documented in Ireland and to a lesser extent in London and New York. In most pubs 'men' are given the status of 'in-group membership' while 'women' occupy the negotiated margins. In London and New York, the excluding binary 'one county in Ireland':'the rest of Ireland' is located, and in this opposition migrants from one county in Ireland can actively mark migrants from other counties in Ireland as 'other'. In-groups can be formed based on county borders, and so we find 'Galway' versus 'other counties', or 'Connemara' versus 'rest of Ireland', or 'Irish speakers' versus 'non-Irish speakers'. This exclusion is documented around recruitment for jobs in London and New York, and around sport, team identity (especially in New York) and sporting events in general.

The final binary opposition can be described as Irish:non-Irish. This is a complex binary because, within the category 'non-Irish', second- and other-generation Irish are located. Within this binary I also locate Irish Catholics and Protestants in Northern Ireland and Irish Protestants in the Republic. I have explored complex identity relations and examine the contested identities of these Irish groups in earlier work.[31]

Paradoxical belonging

The pub can and does function on many levels. All the evidence above suggests that the Irish pub, can, at times, be described as a construct where exclusions occur on many levels. The exclusions are complex and varied, and they function to support various expressions of Irish identity. To argue that the Irish pub space is necessarily exclusive of non-Irish people, and sometimes of Irish people from different counties or other religious groups, is complex and problematic. The Irish pub may also be a significant space for inclusion of people who are objects of exclusion elsewhere. This paradox of inclusion and group solidarity necessarily entails an out-group. And so, instead of talking in terms of the pub as a space where moments of racism occur, I argue that a more useful set of terms would enable a wider discussion around the occurrences of inclusion and exclusion.

Understandably, the respondents refer to their experiences as 'moments of racism' when they are the excluded party, and so I use the term 'racism' throughout this chapter. However, I argue that the varied forms of exclusion that I have identified in this chapter fall outside the scope and function of the term 'racism'. The examples of exclusion described by the respondents would remain unconsidered within the discourse of 'racism'. It would be more useful to locate a more accommodating term or set of terms to fully consider the complexities of these moments.

Mac an Ghaill takes the politics of identity, which he associates with materialism, and the politics of difference, which he associates with differentialism, and argues that, by looking to both approaches, a creative tension can be maintained.[32] Most importantly, he talks about a need to look at the wider occurrences of racism, not limiting the discussion to colour racism. I argue that, by moving beyond the confines of colour racism and recognising the existence of White-on-White, Black-on-Black, and intra-racism, a new term is needed. The term 'difference in point of origin' would be more useful than 'racism' and with this we could re-examine and re-address how we construct and deconstruct moments of inclusion and exclusion – including in pubs. Consequently, we would be able to piece together a more accurate picture which locates not only moments identified by the traditional definitions of racism, but also the other moments of exclusion that are described in this work.

Conclusion

The pub is a busy place – when located in Ireland it is most likely to perform its functions of social engagement and entertainment, with negotiated moments of gendered borders. When it is located abroad (London or New York) it still functions to inscribe social meaning (drinking, social exchange, information exchange, emotional support, location of employment); but it also provides a space for the performance of various discourses – bounded discourses around gender, race and ethnicity and, most interestingly in this case, around inclusion and exclusion. I described how the pub functions as a bounded space from a gendered perspective and serves as a powerful signifier for 'Irishness', 'Ireland' and 'home', and a site to articulate expressions of national identity.

The pub is a site where the Irish abroad locate 'affective support'. However, it is not only a site for the location of affective, economic, political and cultural support, nor only a space for expressions of community and the support of notions of ethnicity and identity: it is also a site for boundaries, inclusion and exclusion.

In 1987, anthropologist Gerald Mars examined the drinking cultures of longshoremen in Newfoundland, Canada and found examples of 'cohesion and division', 'insiderness and outsiderness' that became articulated through drinking practices.[33] The evidence of inclusion and exclusion becomes more profound when the ultimate 'them' and 'us' is explored. The ultimate 'them' and 'us' residing within the pub space is found under the umbrella of national identity; for the pub to successfully offer community to the migrant, it operates within this binary logic. One could argue that the value of 'the Irish pub' would be lost if the act of inclusion/exclusion did not occur. This is particularly observable in New York where respondents repeatedly describe their and others' attitudes towards 'other' ethnic groups.

Exclusion is necessary if communities are to exist and perform their task, and for Bell and Valentine 'communities are about exclusion as well as inclusion'.[34] I argue that this binary is especially pertinent in the case of pub spaces, which contain ethnic minority communities, because these spaces not only support membership groups but also sustain ethnic identity and subsequently they support the migrant's core identity.

I ask if this, the 'excluding' half of the including:excluding binary, is best described as 'racism' and I highlight the fact that the term 'racism' is a problematic one as it does not account for other kinds of exclusion that occur around 'point of origin'. I question whether some other expression would better help us understand what is going on – and while ethnocentrism and xenophobia are terms that might automatically be employed as alternatives, I argue that both are too extreme or blatant, not quite capturing the subtleties of exclusion that I set forth here. I propose that, instead of using the term 'racism', it may be useful to use another phrase such as 'difference of origin', so that we can construct the space for inclusion and exclusion, and the subtleties that accompany it, under other conditions and investigate them in terms of, or through the lens of, 'difference' instead.

Brenda Murphy's Choice:

McCormack's,

365 Third Avenue (between 26th and 27th Street), New York

Figure 9.1 Exterior of McCormack's bar. Illustration by Holly Furey.

Nestled in the heart of Manhattan on Third Avenue, McCormack's was a cherished Irish watering hole that stood as a testament to the city's rich history and cultural diversity. It was just a short stroll from Times Square and it served as a point of reference for many. Its warm, inviting atmosphere and hospitable staff were its signature, with Barry and Austin steering the ship. McCormack's offered Irish travellers, and NY locals, a welcoming respite from the bustle of a busy New York City.

Its iconic green and gold signage invited you in, and you were met with a warm atmosphere, chatty, smiling staff, classic pub food and a wide selection of drinks. For nearly two decades it served as a gathering place, a home from home, and a space for community to flourish – offering a quiet corner or a lively night out – to regulars and visitors alike.

Though McCormack's closed its doors in 2012, its legacy endures in the memories of the countless souls who passed through its doors, including doctoral students far from home seeking out a space to interview first- and other-generation Irish migrants. I raise a glass to good times and great company. As a testament to the enduring spirit of New York City, McCormack's remains a symbol of camaraderie, tradition and the simple pleasures of life.

The Road to McCarthy's Bar: Travel, translation and the Irish pub

Michael Cronin

Beth Crowe, the protagonist in Eimear Ryan's 2022 novel *Holding Her Breath*, agrees to have a drink with a group of students that includes her future lover, Justin, in a Dublin city centre pub. When she enters, the details are tantalisingly non-specific:

> Moving through the warm damp air of the pub, she scans the room for a group. She expects to see Sadie in a loose crush of chairs, to be able to sit beside her and admire Justin from across a table. But all she sees is Justin, sprawled in a corner seat with an empty glass in front of him, the ghost of a pint of stout still clinging to its edges.[1]

This is an Irish novelist describing an Irish pub, but it could be a pub anywhere. Only the tangential reference to 'stout' might indicate a tenuous connection to Ireland. For the locals, less (description) is more (evocative). For the globals, on the other hand, the travel writers from abroad who have dutifully explained Ireland to the world over the years, the pub needs a visual anchoring, a charting of its specificity, if only because the pub itself, in the contemporary moment, has become a standard part of Irish iconicity.[2] In this chapter, I want to explore how representations of the Irish pub in travel writing are driven partly by constraints that are particular to the genre of travel writing itself and partly by the need to engage in a form of translation that changes over time.

Sight

When Martin Heidegger claims that 'the fundamental event of the modern age is the conquest of the world as picture', he both subverts and amplifies the authority of the word. In the pre-modern world, the word of scriptural or classical authority was sacrosanct.[3] As scientific method evolves in the Renaissance, however, proof is not what you hold on authority but what you behold with your own eyes. Experiments allow others to see for themselves what has been affirmed. The experiment can be visibly reproduced over and over again. The Copernican and Newtonian revolutions would firmly establish ocularcentrism in western thinking, with observation becoming the touchstone of legitimacy in western science. Where the eye could not see, optical instruments (microscopes, telescopes) or visual metaphors stepped in.[4] Literacy and the advent of printing further strengthened visual and spatialised perceptions of experience.[5]

If seeing is believing, then travel writing in the new truth regime of scientific modernity has an even more crucial function, testing beliefs or assumptions about peoples and their environments against eyewitness reports from elsewhere. The word is both demoted by the visual and reinforced by the practical necessity of its truth claims. 'Sight-seeing' becomes a form of evidence gathering, proof that the traveller was there. However, for the sight to be seen, it must be recognised as such. Sight-seeing only makes sense if there is a 'sight' to be seen.

It is for this reason that Jonathan Culler has argued that tourism is a branch of semiotics: 'All over the world the unsung armies of semioticians, the tourists, are fanning out in search of the signs of Frenchness, typical Italian behaviour, exemplary oriental scenes, typical American thruways, traditional English pubs.'[6] It is telling that Culler, establishing his list at the beginning of the 1980s, references 'traditional English pubs' but makes no mention of the Irish pubs which have subsequently become such a feature of global cityscapes. In a sense, the Irish pub had not yet become a recognisable element in the international tourist lexicon; it was still an insufficiently developed sign.

Indeed, tracing the history of the first fifty years of the flagship publication of the Irish Tourism Board, *Ireland of the Welcomes*, we noted that the pub both as a subject of (verbal) commentary and an object of (photographic) description was almost wholly absent from the pages of the publication for much of the early part of its existence.[7] This was, in part, the result of a lingering nationalist hostility to tourism as an abject exercise in flunkeydom.[8] It was important to scotch any suggestion that welcoming visitors to Ireland involved a reversion to music-hall stereotype with craven natives capering around the gentry. Indeed, as early as 1916 (just over two weeks before the Easter Rising), George Bernard Shaw, writing on travel in Ireland for the magazine *The Car*, warned potential tourists against comic condescension:

> Irish people are, like most country people, civil and kindly when they are treated with due respect. But anyone who, under the influence of the stage

> Irishman and the early novels of Lever, treats a tour in Ireland as a lark, and the people as farce actors who may be addressed as Pat and Biddy, will have about as much success as if he were to paint his nose red and interrupt a sermon in Westminster Abbey by addressing music-hall patter to the dean.[9]

The trope of the drunken Irishman as national stereotype was one that the emerging state was keen to jettison, given its associations of laziness, fecklessness and tomfoolery. In 1960, Seán Lemass, addressing a community group in County Tipperary, railed against the ready association of the Irish and alcohol:

> One of the most persistent and irritating falsehoods about the Irish is that they are excessive consumers of alcoholic drink. The lie has gone very far afield. Even the BBC television service rarely, if ever, presents a play about Ireland without the characters moving around in clouds of alcoholic vapour.[10]

Other commentators, such as the American journalist Donal Connery, writing in 1970, questioned the usefulness of the Irish pub as an indicator of national character or attitudes:

> The pub is a booby-trap … for anyone trying to take a measure of Irish life. The fact is that the majority of adults hardly ever set foot in a pub. Most Irish females simply do not drink in public and may never touch a drop in their lives, and among the men there are more total abstainers than heavy drinkers … I will admit, as I write this, that it is painful to go against form and portray the Irishman as something other than a glorious drinker and an altogether devil of a fellow. None the less, there are far more homes than pubs in Ireland and it is in the homes that one must look for the Irishman as he is most of the time. Away from the conviviality of the pub he's revealed as someone who is extraordinarily ordinary. He leads a far simpler and certainly less sophisticated life than most Europeans.[11]

Travel

To understand the later development of the Irish pub as a cultural metonym in travel descriptions, it is useful to consider a mid-twentieth-century account of a visit to Ireland undertaken by Charles Graves, an English writer and journalist. In *Ireland Revisited* (1949), Graves notes that 'I could not begin to count the number of bars which I visited, mostly for information of course, during my tour', but they are hardly ever described in his account. He claims that 'I never once saw anyone drunk', and his principal interest in public houses is statistical. Graves observes, for example, that 'Bantry's chief characteristic remains the number of bars' and that 'Dingle has more bars in its little main street than any other town I have ever visited'.[12]

Graves, a sibling of the poet Robert Graves and erstwhile chronicler of English high society, devotes considerably more detail to descriptions of fine fare in the country's grander hotels and comments peevishly on the subject of bars, 'On my previous visit there was not an hotel in Dublin which had a cocktail bar ... The rest of Ireland, by the way, suffers considerably from the lack of refrigerators, and it is almost impossible to get ice to shake a cocktail'.[13] By his own admission, however, Graves does not allow his sense of entitlement to prevent him from going into many Irish bars ('I could not begin to count the number of bars') and he mentions several of them: Lenihan's in Galway, Honan's in Ennis, O'Donovan's in Bantry, O'Flynn's in Fermoy. But there is no careful depiction, no detailed portrayal; they are fleeting and anonymous backdrops for observations on the nature of haggling at livestock fairs or the behaviour of Spanish sailors in Irish port towns. There are pubs – many of them – in Ireland, but the Irish Pub, as a distinct, capitalised, semiotic entity, is not yet on view.

When Eric Newby and his wife Wanda embark on a cycling tour of Ireland in the late 1980s, the pubs are equally numerous. The difference, this time, is they are explicitly described, becoming an integral part of the structure of the narrative. In Sixmilebridge, the 'pub was huge, considering the size of the village. It had three bars, decorated with imitation half-timbering, wallpaper of a sultry tropical design and hue and glass cases containing stuffed, predatory animals'.[14] In McHugh's pub in Liscannor, not only the setting but the customers are sketched in:

> Inside, McHugh's was long, narrow and dark. Besides McHugh himself, a bright-eyed friendly man, and innumerable trophies won by his dogs at coursing, a sport in which he was a folk hero, the pub housed three men of indeterminate age with dark hair and thin, creased faces, all dressed in the dark suits the Irish use for working in the fields, caps and rubber boots.[15]

Publicans and their customers come to feature centre-stage as performing an essential narrative function in either dispensing information about Ireland or giving the reader the eye-witness, ocularcentric sense of being there as the journey unfolds. The procedure is made explicit in the bar of the Falls Hotel in Ennistymon: 'The bar was like the stage set for the first act of some interminable Irish equivalent of *A Month in the Country* with the players already in position for the rising of the curtain'.[16] Whole sections of speech are reported (in unfortunate, cringe-inducing, mock dialect) to enhance the vividness of scenes. Newby, for example, in Dunning's pub in Westport, is given a lecture by the barman on the pricing of whiskey in England and Ireland:

> I was treated to a fine technical discourse on the subject of comparative Irish and English whisky prices: 'And wat you get over dere, two English nips, at 75p English a nip, each nip's a sixth of a gill, dat's a third of a gill £1.50, and wat's more it comes outta litre bartle sploiced wid watter so dat de feller workin' de tap and fillin' it up is gettin' 68 nips from a bartle. Whereas, over here in Westport you're gettin' two Oirish tots, dat's quarter of a gill each, at £1 Oirish a tot, dat's £2 Oirish half a gill, but we're not sploicing it.[17]

The Irish pub in travel writing increasingly answers to the two contrary demands of fiction and truth. The fictional demand is the necessity to inject the story with narrative interest and strong characterisation, the sentimental turn in travel writing that brings it closer to prose fiction with the express purpose of holding the reader's attention through story.[18] The documentary demand is the need to offer plausible evidence of having been somewhere, the ever-present need to persuade doubters and nay-sayers that the traveller is not simply making it all up. The shift over four decades in the positioning of the Irish pub in the accounts of Graves and Newby points to a growing awareness of the usefulness of the pub in dealing with the fiction/truth dichotomy. The pub must be explicitly constructed as a repeated site of interest if it is to adequately fulfil its function.

Alongside the specific singling out of the pub as a privileged metonym in travel writing about Ireland, there is the parallel institutional framing of the pub as a distinctive heritage sign. No longer a legacy to be shunned but an inheritance to be embraced, the emporia of drinking culture are officially co-opted into the bucket lists of sights to be seen. Newby, in a Bord Fáilte tourist office on the banks of the

Grand Canal, finds a free copy of *A Visitor's Guide to Pubs in Dublin*. Sitting outside Healy's Black Lion Inn in Clondalkin, the English writer ironically alludes to the *Guide*'s classification of the pub: '"The in place," the *Guide* went on, "for the young and sporting fraternity," for which we undoubtedly qualified, if for nothing else, as a couple of elderly sports.'[19]

The ultimate consecration of the Irish pub as an object of tourist semiotics will be the publication in 2001 of Pete McCarthy's *McCarthy's Bar*. The book was an instant success, selling hundreds of thousands of copies and remaining in the bestseller lists in both Ireland and the United Kingdom for months. Scattered throughout the book are quixotic Rules of Travel. The Eighth Rule of Travel states, *Never Pass a Bar That Has Your Name On It* and McCarthy embraces the rule wholeheartedly, vowing to stop off in every pub bearing his family name.[20] The pub is no longer a secondary feature of a primary travel narrative but becomes the primary destination of the travel account itself.

Part of the object of the book is to try and arrive at an understanding of what defines the Irish pub as a separate or unique space. He attempts a definition, by way of contrast:

> [I]nstead of the depressingly corporate environment offered by pubs in the English countryside these days, where a retired estate agent or policeman presides over a muzak-polluted repro-furniture showroom in which furtive couples sit side by side eating microwave baked potatoes, in Ireland you can still find idiosyncratic, family-owned hovels with no food, or décor, that remain temples to hospitality, conversation and drink.[21]

In MacCarthy's bar in Castletownbere (Fig 9.1), the author finds himself caught up in an after-hours birthday party and later claims, 'I was in the dream Irish pub of the popular imagination – dimly lit, past midnight, shelves piled with obscure groceries, a buzz of conversation and a whoosh of energy coming off the crowd.'[22] Baby Hannah's pub in Skibbereen, described as a 'top-notch bar', is 'small and unadorned, with a solid fuel range in the corner, a tongue-and-groove ceiling, and sawdust on the floor, possibly left over from when they were fitting the tongue-and-groove ceiling ... the perfect bridge between past and present'.[23] For McCarthy, a writer preoccupied with translating travel experience into words, the experience of Irish pubs as pre-eminent venues for conversation is frequently an object of positive comment. There

Figure 10.1 Exterior of MacCarthy's bar, Castletownbere. Courtesy of MacCarthy's bar.

is the sense that the pub is not only a site of distraction and entertainment but also a place of instruction and enlightenment. Commenting on a 'perfect evening, in the perfect pub', McCarthy writes of a 'sharing of opinions, to be digested, rather than differences, to be confronted'.[24]

His positioning of the Irish pub is bound up with his own attempts at grappling with identity issues. He was born in the north of England to an English father and an Irish mother and his sense of Englishness is particularly fraught: 'now when I return to Ireland, I feel that I belong in a way that I have never belonged in the land of my birth. Even though I loved growing up in the North, England leaves me feeling detached: an outsider, an observer, in some way passing through'.[25] Passing through Irish pubs from Cork to Donegal becomes a way of teasing out a notion of potential community, an exploration of the vagaries of identity and belonging. When stopped by a customs officer in Holyhead at the outset of his travels, McCarthy wondered how he would explain that he 'planned to wander around for an unspecified length of time going into every pub I saw called McCarthy's … while trying to work out whether I was on some metaphysical level Irish'.[26] The semiotic labour of identifying the authentic Irish pub is paralleled by the ontological process of establishing an authentic sense of identity.

The convergent pressures of anxieties around representation and self make McCarthy acutely sensitive to evidence of the inauthentic, the dangers of faith in fakes. At a personal level, the unease is expressed in his doubts about his difference from other tourists and foreigners in Ireland and to what extent his Irish family connections give him a privileged claim on Irish identity. In the Castletownbere pub, he notes a bearded mandolin player who seemed 'the very essence of the traditional Irish musician'. As it turns out, he is German, and McCarthy notes: 'I found myself envying this outsider who's now an insider in a place where I desperately want to belong myself.'[27] Constantly questioning his own position within the community and the genuineness of his claims to belong, he nonetheless uses his insider/outsider liminality to chart the changing semiotic fortunes of the Irish pub itself.

Translation

Framing the nature of the English travel writer's observations requires a brief consideration of the notion of 'translation' to establish what is at play in his analysis. Translation is often construed as a specifically human, interlingual exercise. Kobus Marais, in his *A (Bio)Semiotic Theory of Translation*, details the theoretical origins of this narrowness of definition, a narrowness he attributes to a misreading.[28] The misreader, so to speak, is the Russian linguist Roman Jakobson, and the misread is the American semiotician C.S. Peirce. Jakobson, in his famous 1959 essay on translation, draws on the work of Peirce to argue that 'the meaning of any lingual sign is its translation into some further, alternative sign, especially a sign "in which it is more fully developed"'.[29] However, what Peirce actually wrote was: 'Conception of a "meaning" is, in its primary acceptation, the translation of a sign into another system of signs.'[30] In other words, the 'lingual' was Jakobson's addition. Hardly surprising coming from a linguist, but the baleful outcome has been an almost exclusive concentration on interlingual translation in subsequent understandings of what is meant by 'translation'. The generous inclusivity of Peirce's original definition of translation – which was a semiotic theory that would account for all signs, not just lingual ones – was lost. The problem was further compounded by Saussurean semiotics where again a linguist modelled all semiotic processes on human language. Marais offers a broader understanding of translation in his own definition:

> Translation is negentropic semiotic work (performed by an agent) in which any one or more of the components in a sign system or any one or more of the relationships between them are changed, or in which the relationship between the sign and its environment (time and/or space) is changed.[31]

McCarthy goes to great lengths to establish the 'sign system' of the Irish pub, locating those elements – hospitality, conversation, decorative unfussiness – that mark it out as distinct. What he is faced with on his journey through Ireland at the turn of the new millennium are two forms of translation – intrinsic and extrinsic – that become the object of repeated commentary. The *intrinsic translation* of the Irish pub consists of alterations to such establishments within Ireland itself to adapt to new target audiences, both domestic and international. The *extrinsic translation* is the *translatio*, the spatial translation of the Irish pub to destinations outside of the island of Ireland.

In terms of intrinsic translation, McCarthy is acutely sensitive to the role of signs in flagging change. He claims that '[t]he Second Rule of Travel in Ireland says: *The More Bright Primary Colours and Ancient Celtic Symbols Outside the Pub, the More Phoney the Interior*'.[32] In Killarney, the critique moves inside: 'I read my book and have a couple of pints in a cramped, dark, sawdust-strewn bar that I suspect used to be a spacious, bright, carpeted bar until the heritage refurbishers got a hold of it.'[33] The sawdust that was the accidental by-product of alterations in Skibbereen is now part of the calculated curation of vintage, translating the pub back to an imagined and carefully scripted past. The most vivid example of intrinsic translation is the small pub McCarthy encounters in the early pages of the book on his arrival in Cork city. It is described as 'a small, one-room, nicotine-stained place', and he is mostly struck by the smell of unwashed bodies and by finding that all the traditional musicians there are English.[34] In the closing pages of his account, he returns to the 'dingy pub' to find it is no more:

> The Shelbourn [*sic*], says the upmarket font on the black-tiled façade with, in tiny letters below it, An Siol [*sic*] Broin. The smoky atmospheric boozer has been devoured by a brand-new 'traditional' bar. Two estate agents and a woman from a management consultancy are sitting in the big new clear-glass window, sipping Malibu with Aqua Libra and cranberry juice, or at least that's how it looks from the street. I pop my head through the door.

> They're still putting the finishing touches to the décor. The new boards that have replaced the old boards are being stained down to look old. The place smells of sawdust and aftershave, instead of old stout and crusties.[35]

The semiotic labour in making sure that the new boards are 'being stained down to look old' is the paradoxical outcome of a kind of vintage modernisation where the existing pub must be translated into a new kind of visual language if it is to be credible as a traditional Irish pub. The old pub does not look old enough. It is no longer a question of writers seeking out the authentic Irish pub in the verbal signs of the travel narrative. The pub, both outside and in, must be rendered in the recognisable and constructed idiom of the 'traditional'.

For the Irish pub to function as part of the semiotic economy of tourism, the relationship of the sign to its environment must change, a putative past translated into the present, both signalling and annulling the passage of time. In a perverse reworking of ocularcentrism, the tourist tracks the visual evidence for the authenticity of the Irish bar, evidence which, in turn, is artificially constructed to meet a precise set of semiotic expectations. There is no point effecting a translation if the translation cannot be understood by the target audience; hence the need for the bright, primary colours, the ancient Celtic symbols, and the artfully stained floorboards.

If translation needs to be 'performed by an agent', per Marais among others, it is clear in McCarthy's mind who that agent ultimately is: the tourist. Tourist baiting has, of course, been a standard part of travel writing since the emergence of organised, mass travel in the nineteenth century.[36] The note of patrician disdain in Paul Fussell's obituary on travel writing between the two world wars is familiar: 'Because travel is hardly possible anymore, an inquiry into the nature of travel and travel writing between the wars will resemble a threnody, and I'm afraid that a consideration of the tourism that apes it will be like a satire.'[37] Hostility to the tourist is partly ontological. How do travel writers distinguish themselves from other travellers? How do they justify their own travelling practices over others? McCarthy, not surprisingly, uses one of Ireland's most popular travel destinations, Killarney, to vent his anti-tourist spleen. As he announces prior to his arrival in the town: 'After wandering in glorious, deserted landscapes, and being treated as long-lost family in fantasy small-town pubs, a dose of mainstream tourism would be good for the soul.'[38] McCarthy is not long into his stay in Killarney when he observes ruefully that when 'somewhere has more tourists than local people' then 'the game is up, and the balance has irrevocably shifted in favour of revenue, occupancy and the forces of darkness'.[39]

In the village of Cong, in County Mayo, where he finds not a single attractive pub and only a series of licensed premises that had 'been enlarged or brutalised in some way to cope with greater numbers of visitors', McCarthy concludes that 'a successful tourist industry can quickly turn into a parody of itself'.[40] The ultimate expression of the intrinsic translation performed by the tourist agent – translation as travesty – is for the English traveller to be found in the capital city, in the Temple Bar quarter:

> Plain, unadorned, authentic pubs, previously unchanged for decades, now reek of new wood and paint, as they're gutted and refurbished to conform to

Figure 10.2 Exterior of Temple Bar pub, Dublin. Artwork by and courtesy of Oney.

> the notion of Irishness demanded by the stag nights from Northampton and the conference delegates from Frankfurt who fill the streets, interchangeable in their smug fat smiles and Manchester United replica shirts.[41]

The bars of Temple Bar are both metonym and metaphor. Metonym because they are materially transformed to fit a legible 'notion of Irishness', and metaphor because they symbolically express the degraded metaphysics of Celtic Tiger Ireland, the cynical manipulation of ethnic branding for financial gain. However, just as McCarthy worries over whether he can ever be successfully translated into a version of Irishness, there is the equally pressing question as to whether the traveller can ever be successfully translated out of the condition of being a tourist. In determining his own criteria for 'authentic' pubs, his desire for 'plain, unadorned' originals, McCarthy is engaged in a form of semiotic exploration, the assembly of a sign system that can, of course, in turn become a template for a new generation of travellers, eager to discover pubs resembling the textual bars of the travel account.

Temple Bar as a site of intrinsic translation is also a portal to the world of extrinsic translation, the global export of the Irish pub – tourists flocking to an area to encounter simulacra of the Irish pubs dotted around the globe. McCarthy opens his book with a description of a raucous St Patrick's night spent in a pub bearing his name but it is only several pages in that the reader is told of the location of the bar: Budapest. Reading a business magazine in a hotel on the eve of his departure from Ireland, McCarthy spots an advertisement touting investment opportunities in Irish pubs abroad. He meets 'Paul from Marketing' and asks him, 'what is this Irishness they're selling?'[42] McCarthy lists different artistic icons (James Joyce, Oscar Wilde, Van Morrison, U2), a rebellious reputation and a highly developed drinking culture as potential components of this bankable Irishness, but the marketing executive argues it is none of the above as, in many countries where the pubs are established, knowledge of Ireland barely exists. What sells the Irish pub concept is:

> Sociability and warmth. People are buying into the concept of sitting down and talking to someone you haven't met before. We're creating an atmosphere that persuades people to go and frequent a pub in countries where they don't frequent pubs. We're changing habits.[43]

Paul admits that the Irish do not have a monopoly on hospitality, but claims that, 'we're unique in packaging and marketing it'. Behind the material translation of the Irish pub into different locations are the immaterial experiences of 'sociability and warmth', precisely those aspects of the Irish pub experience that McCarthy identifies as core in the course of his travels.

For the commodification ('packaging and marketing') to become effective, the semioticians need to do their work. The elements of an effective sign system need to be isolated and operationalised. The marketeer sees Irish pub translation as foreignising, not domesticating. The Irish pub is 'changing habits' in foreign locations rather than adapting to them. Like its interlingual equivalent, this form of intercultural translation is bringing new ideas, new modes of social behaviour and interaction, into the target cultures. Later, McCarthy visits a warehouse full of vintage bric-a-brac and avant-garde furniture. Paul tells him that '"[t]he old stuff's for overseas. The new stuff's for Ireland"'. The distinction, however, is not as clear as the pub vendor makes out. As McCarthy repeatedly illustrates with the intrinsic translation of the pub, the marshalling of a fabricated past is as crucial to its operations as the inclusion of the 'old stuff' in overseas extrinsic translation.

When the English writer tells of 'Ireland's well-marketed image of the Celt and the craic',[44] he could be describing the notion of 'nation branding' or brand nationalism.[45] The concept was first articulated in *The Boston Globe* where it was defined as 'shorthand for coordinated government efforts to manage a country's image, whether to improve tourism, investment, or even foreign relations'.[46] The 'nation brand' is one that marries positive associations to the profit imperative. These are associations that help bring foreign investment and tourists into a country while also acting as a stimulus to the sales of nationally-produced goods and boosting the international image of the country. The emphasis on image is seen to parallel the transition from modernist industrial production to postmodern consumption. As Volcic and Andrejevic argue:

> The promoters of nation branding market it as a powerful equalizer – a way that countries without the economic or military clout of superpowers can compete in the global marketplace. They claim that nation branding can help such nations to achieve greater visibility, attract tourists and foreign investors, expand exports, and promote their profile among the member

> states of various international organizations (such as the EU), all the while cultivating patriotism at home.[47]

The concert of nations becomes the global trading floor, each nation clamouring for competitive advantage as the notion of political sovereignty becomes subservient to market position or positioning. If one of the champions of Ireland's integration into the world economic order, Seán Lemass, was aghast at the association of the Irish and alcohol, his free trade successors have turned the public vice into a profitable virtue. The Irish pub as a distinct semiotic entity has become one of the international calling cards of small-state brand nationalism. McCarthy himself – while acknowledging the success of the Irish pub as a lynchpin of Irish self-promotion and to which he, ironically, contributes – is apprehensive for the future: 'The fear must be that the process will change the reality; that warmth and conviviality, like other resources, may turn out to be finite.'[48]

Anti-Eden

When the American writer and activist Rebecca Solnit travels to Ireland in the 1990s, she finds much in the way of warmth and conviviality accompanied by 'tea or beer, the twin elixirs which pour forth in such abundance to fuel and modify the national temperament'.[49] Solnit's great-grandparents came from Ireland and she became an Irish citizen in 1986. Like Pete McCarthy, one reason for her Irish journey is to puzzle through notions of identity and belonging. Unlike McCarthy, pubs are a more marginal presence in her account, as she seeks out less conspicuously male places of encounter.

The pub does, nonetheless, act as a crucible for Solnit's reflections on the nature of place and affiliation. In Doolin, in west Clare, she notes that though the village is famed for traditional music, the musicians in the pubs 'are hired people playing for an audience rather than each other'.[50] In a pub in Lisdoonvarna, Solnit discovers that the fiddler is German and the bodhrán player Welsh. As if parodying her own doubts about the authenticity of her musical pub experiences, a fellow American from the Midwest mansplains his way through his irritation at the number of tourists in Doolin and how to have a more genuine experience of Ireland. However, Solnit's pub visits in west Clare lead her thinking in a different direction. She wonders about the preoccupation with origin myths and the quest for origins in many western cultures:

> There is a peculiar authority granted to origins in this culture, perhaps itself originating in the story of the Garden of Eden. The authority of origins asserts that in the beginning things were as they should be, and therefore everything afterwards is an unravelling, a decline, a sullying of original purity. Thus the true Irishman for my midwesterner would not be the young rock and roll aficionado in the pub briefly paying his respects before setting off for Sydney but some crusty old Gaelic-speaking fisherman on the Aran islands … One could tell an anti-Eden myth in which it is destination rather than origin in which true identity lay: thus to be Irish is to be destined to emigrate, to love African-American music, to outmarry and mingle, and the true, ideal Doolin is only realized when one can hear several other languages in the pubs besides picturesque brogues and when musicians there get paid. In such a myth, impurity and hybridity would be the ideal form all things aspired to, borders would only exist to be crossed, the urge to go backwards towards the origins before things moved around and mingled would vanish.[51]

In a sense, the model of pub translation that Solnit is proposing is one that loses its preoccupation with source-text fidelity, a phobic loyalty to origin. The pub in Doolin is always already translated by the passage of visitors who alter the ethnic composition of the players and audiences, even if music's contribution to the construction of local community cannot be underestimated.[52] If conventional understandings of translation suppose a fixed and immutable source text of origin dutifully transferred into other target spaces and cultures, Solnit's anti-Eden myth proposes a notion of translation where the original is in a state of flux, constantly open to being modified by the translational practices of 'destination'. The pub is, after all, for the writers discussed in this chapter, a destination, not a point of origin.

As travel writing in the English language over the course of the twentieth century gradually constructs the notion of the Irish pub as a separate, intelligible, semiotic entity, it must acknowledge a necessary 'hybridity and impurity'. Just as texts regularly demand new translations to find new readerships, so the Irish pub is repeatedly translated by different travel writers into an idiom that is sensed to be more appropriate to its age and time. Both the intrinsic and extrinsic translations of the Irish pub are a dialogue with a myth of origin, a myth in constant tension with the anti-Edenic myth of destination. Whether this destination be domestic (intrinsic) or international (extrinsic), the idea of an idealised past for the Irish pub is constantly reworked by the changing values and preferences of the target audiences. The ghost of the pint of stout, in the opening passage from Eimear Ryan's novel, is there to remind us that origins are unsettling, haunting, always raising questions about absent causes. Translating the Irish pub into the words of the travel narrative has shown that there is no definitive translation, no version of the pub that remains unchanged over time, preserving the original, Ur-pub in the aspic of consecration. If moving around and mingling are often presented as core elements of the physical experience of the Irish pub, the moving around and mingling of representations are no less a feature of its symbolic expression. The pub may be a paradise for some but is an anti-Eden for many. And therein lies its salvation.

Michael Cronin's Choice:

Bowe's Pub,

Fleet Street, Dublin

Figure 10.3 Exterior of Bowe's pub. Photo by Angeliki Lima.

Three feet. This was the distance the ancient Celts felt separated heaven and earth. In places known as 'thin places', the ordinary and the miraculous were closer still. Only a whisper separated them. These thin places were scattered over the island – portals to the more than human – waiting to be revealed by a lost traveller or an addled soul. Nothing announced the presence of these places, camouflaged in the ordinariness of grass and stone. Bowes is one of the thin places. At the dark, fag-end of Fleet Street, far from the dollar hustle of Temple Bar, it lurks in the shadowlands of empty loading bays and bus rat runs. The entrance is more labyrinth than gateway. A succession of sharp turns before the veil is suddenly rendered and all is wood and soft, enduring, yellow light. The beetling bar stools give way to the chattering tables and chairs to the left and the back recess calls the musicians into its semi-circular embrace. Behind the bar, on the right, the whiskey bottles on the mirrored shelves multiply endlessly, the tantalising otherworlds of tipplers' possibility. The thin places are ideally seen at that liminal hour between light and dark when daylight consciousness dims and the world becomes fuzzy and uncertain. Bowes never opens before 5 p.m. Once you cross the threshold and enter into that parallel dimension of talk and elation, time fades to a distant point in the forgotten world of the everyday, the hidden entrance the surest sign that there is, thankfully, no escape from the wondrous.

Part 3

Literary Musical and Artistic Perspectives

Chapter 11

Grim Days in the Pub

Nicholas Grene

Go to the pub to enjoy yourself, to celebrate an occasion, to relax after work, to meet up with your friends; but don't go to cheer yourself up, to drown your sorrows, to get away from it all. Alcohol may be an initial stimulant, but beyond that it is a depressant, as all the websites on addiction will tell you.[1] If your mood is buoyant, it may help to keep you afloat, but if you are feeling sorry for yourself, you will end up sorrier still. The Irish pub has been exported around the world as a moveable site of jollity, *ceol agus craic*. The pub has been a standard setting for much Irish drama from Synge and O'Casey through to Tom Murphy, Marina Carr and Conor McPherson. It has by no means been all jollity, but it has been a site of social, sexual and political negotiation, lubricated by drink. Somewhat surprisingly, it does not seem to have figured so prominently in Irish short fiction; at least a glance through three modern anthologies, chosen more or less at random, shows relatively few stories with pubs as their central location.[2] The four writers considered in this chapter show Irish pubs very unlike the *ceol agus craic* export model. They are places of frustration and loss, of anomie and depression, where the sinking heart sinks further.

James Joyce, 'Counterparts'

The theme of Joyce's *Dubliners* is paralysis, as the author told his publisher before the book even appeared, and students have been repeating in dutiful essays ever since.[3] Recurrently through the stories, what is dramatised is the thwarted need to escape from the city, from the cultural milieu, above all from the hamstringing effects of the self. The boy in 'Araby' journeys across town to the bazaar on the southside which he has made into an oriental Other to the 'blind' North Richmond Street where he lives. The anticlimactic ending leaves 'a creature driven and derided by vanity; and my eyes burned with anguish and anger'.[4] Chandler, in 'A Little Cloud', daydreams of moving to London and a career as a poet: 'The English critics, perhaps, would recognise him

Figure 11.1 An older woman in an empty pub. Illustration by and courtesy of Oney.

as one of the Celtic school by reason of the melancholy tone of his poems.' But back at home, unable to still the crying of his baby, he is convinced it 'was useless, useless! He was a prisoner for life'.[5] Even more painful than 'A Painful Case', in which the uptight Mr Duffy recoils in revulsion from the potential of a developing relationship with Mrs Sinico, is the study of Farrington in 'Counterparts'.

Farrington is employed as a clerk in the law firm of Crosbie & Alleyne. His principal occupation is to copy out legal contracts by hand, the 'counterparts' of the story's title. Looking back from the time of Xerox machines and scanners, it is hard to imagine the sheer amount of mindless labour that went into this work. Although typewriters were already available, contracts had to be copied out long-hand because 'typewritten documents at the time of this story were not legally binding'.[6] An indication of the sheer volume of work involved can be gauged from the fact that

Farrington realises in despair, as he approaches the end of office hours, that he still has fourteen pages to copy on the contract demanded by his employer: that would have been fourteen foolscap pages, and a clean sheet needed every time a mistake was made.[7] As well as the counterparts of contracts, every letter that went out of the office had also to be copied by hand. When the correspondence in the 'Delacour case' is sent for, Farrington can only hope 'Mr Alleyn would not discover that the last two letters were missing'.[8] But of course he does, and this becomes the subject of another tirade against the negligent clerk.

The dynamics of the power structure in the office are obvious from the very opening of the story:

> The bell rang furiously and, when Miss Parker went to the tube, a furious voice called out in a piercing North of Ireland accent.
> —Send Farrington here!

The bell, like the voice that is heard through the intercom, is an angry sound of authority descending from on high into the lower office. And it is significant that the accent is Northern Irish. Terence Brown comments that it is likely that Crosbie and Alleyne 'is a Protestant firm',[9] and certainly the only Dublin family of Alleynes in the 1901 census was Church of Ireland.[10] It adds an extra dimension to Farrington's subaltern status that he is bossed by a Protestant from the Orange North of Ireland.

Farrington is a big man, as we see from his first appearance in the story. 'When he stood up he was tall and of great bulk'.[11] By contrast, Mr Alleyne, seen at his desk in the office to which Farrington has been summoned, is a little man, clean-shaven and bald. 'The head itself was so pink and hairless that it seemed like a large egg reposing on the papers.' The big-bodied clerk, standing in attendance before his seated employer, is conscious of their physical disparity, the very opposite of their social status: 'The man stared fixedly at the polished skull which directed the affairs of Crosbie & Alleyne, gauging its fragility'.[12] The image of the skull as an egg emphasises just how breakable it might be to a man of Farrington's size.

> A spasm of rage gripped his throat for a few moments and then passed, leaving after it a sharp sensation of thirst. The man recognised the sensation and felt that he must have a good night's drinking.[13]

There we have it. The need for a night out drinking is deflected violence, the consciousness of his powerless subordinate status driving him to the solace of alcohol and the comfort of the pub.

The pub will guarantee him congenial company. 'He knew where he would meet the boys: Leonard and O'Halloran and Nosey Flynn'.[14] Already on his way to Davy Byrnes, Farrington is rehearsing how to recast the final office humiliation into a triumph. Challenged on the missing letters from the Delacour file, he had tried to brazen it out, insisting that he had duly made the fair copies. 'Tell me,' said Alleyne with hyperbolic scorn, 'do you take me for a fool? Do you take me for an utter fool?' At this, Farrington's tongue 'found a felicitous moment. —I don't think, sir, that that's a fair question to put to me'. Of course, the brief pleasure of the retort is followed by the abject apology that is demanded of him, all the more abject because witnessed by Miss Delacour, the rich woman, who has 'smiled broadly' at the witticism.[15] She is included in his revised script:

> —So, I just looked at him – coolly, you know, and looked at her. Then I looked back at him again – taking my time, you know. *I don't think that that's a fair question to put to me*, says I.

And sure enough, it goes down very well with the familiar men he meets in the pub. Nosey Flynn says 'it was as smart a thing as ever he heard'.[16] It has to be repeated to O'Halloran and Paddy Leonard when they join the others, and later Higgins, as a fellow clerk, an eye-witness to the event, tells the story again playing all the parts himself. With the afflatus of the appreciative audience, the balloon of Farrington's ego soars upward.

'The barometer of his emotional nature was set for a spell of riot', after the very bad day at the office.[17] Unable to get an advance on his salary, Farrington is driven to pawning his watch, realising the six shillings that will guarantee him his 'spell of riot'. Paul Delaney charts the pub crawl that follows, with the details of the men's drinking and what it costs, from the cheapest 'g.p.' (glass = half-pint of porter), through the small whiskey, the 'tailor' which was three-quarters the size of a 'ball of malt', and 'specials', hot whiskeys with additions.[18] He analyses it in terms of 'homosocial consumption', involving a 'three-sided exchange of money, drink and talk'.[19] But, as Delaney also makes clear, Farrington, with his reckless six shillings in his pocket, pays for most of the drink, trying to buy the elation of the all-male camaraderie. What with the applause for his story and the lift of the alcohol, for a time he succeeds. But as the composition of the group shifts, and outsiders are included, the close, warm fug of drink and talk among the boys can no longer be sustained.

At the Scotch House, Farrington, Leonard and O'Halloran, the three remaining from the group, meet 'a young fellow named Weathers who was performing at the Tivoli as an acrobat and knockabout *artiste*'. This initially adds an element of the exotic and the erotic to the atmosphere, as Weathers promises 'to get them in behind the scenes and introduce them to some nice girls'.[20] Sure enough, two such girls appear at their next encounter in Mulligan's in Poolbeg Street, and Farrington is particularly struck with one of them. There is a distinct *frisson* as she leaves, when 'she brushed against his chair and said *O, pardon!* in a London accent'. But she does not even look back at him and Farrington is left with another source of frustration, his animus focused on Weathers who had so depleted his money with ordering 'whiskies and Apollinaris', expensive because including this foreign mineral water.[21] This leads on directly to the arm-wrestling challenge in which Farrington, the big man who stands as champion for Ireland, is twice defeated by the English 'stripling'.[22] The physical strength which he could not use against his Northern Irish employer in the office now proves impotent, even in the pub where men are men.

When 'Counterparts' was first composed, Stanislaus complimented his brother on the 'intercranial journey' of the story.[23] Readers do indeed live within Farrington's head, all the more remarkably so for the studied impersonality of the narration: he is identified at arm's length as 'the man' throughout much of the text. The effect is never more striking than in the opening sentence of the final section, as the pub and the cronies are left behind. 'A very sullen-faced man stood at the corner of O'Connell Bridge waiting for the little Sandymount tram to take him home'.[24] Farrington bitterly reviews his current state: 'He had done for himself in the office, pawned his watch, spent all his money, and he had not even got drunk.' This is the night after the night before. The home to which he 'loathed returning' is a cheerless place which he shares with five children and his wife, 'a little sharp-faced woman who bullied her husband when he was sober and was bullied by him when he was drunk'.[25] In this catch-as-catch-can circulation of power, we may expect the savage attack by the frustrated Farrington on his unfortunate child, counterparts in the home to employer and subordinate in the office, though it is no less shocking for that.[26] 'Counterparts',

Figure 11.2
James Joyce statue in Temple Bar, Dublin. Photo by Lisa Gygax.

one of the most merciless of the stories in *Dubliners*, dramatises the moods of the protagonist, under the whips and scorns of the workplace looking to the fantasies of the pub for reaffirmation, then taking revenge for their failure in brutal domestic violence.

John McGahern, 'Parachutes'

A mean domesticity is what Farrington returns to after his spell of riot, its meanness all the more aggravating for the failure of his debauch. Domesticity of what appears to be a more attractive sort has been on offer to the unnamed narrator of John

McGahern's 'Parachutes', and its rejection has led to the despairing state in which he finds himself at the start of the story, his lover having just broken off the relationship. He has been taken to a pre-Christmas dinner at the suburban home of her pregnant sister and brother-in-law. It is a conventionally festive meal but for the narrator, '[s]ome vague unease curdled the food and cheer in that small front room, was sharpened by the determined gaiety'.

> It was as if he were looking down a long institutional corridor; the child in the feeding chair could be seen already, the next child, and the next, the postman, the milkman, the van with fresh eggs and vegetables from the country, the tired clasp over the back of the hand to show tenderness as real as the lump in the throat, the lawnmowers in summer, the thickening waists. It hardly seemed necessary to live it.

When asked for his reaction to the visit, he says, 'It's the sort of house that would drive me crackers.'[27] Rejected by his lover, however, he bitterly regrets this road not taken, dreary as it had seemed to him. 'All the days would have to start without her':[28] that is the vista that is now ahead of him instead of the suffocating future of married life he had imagined.

McGahern's protagonist does not go looking for therapeutic release and relief as Farrington does, yet he also is in search of company. 'I went into the Stag's Head and then O'Neill's. Both bars were crowded. There was no-one there I knew'.[29] It is only when he moves to the bars off Grafton Street that he finds familiar faces, Claire and Paddy Mulvey, and Eamonn Kelly. 'Parachutes' was written in 1980 but, according to Denis Sampson, the 'very recognisable setting among the Dublin literati' can be dated to around 1960.[30] These are certainly very different sorts of drinkers than the lower-middle-class clerks of Joyce. In his stories, McGahern often drew on memories of his early days as a beginning writer in Dublin and the circles around Patrick Kavanagh who drank in McDaid's of Harry Street. A barely fictionalised version of Kavanagh himself features in 'My Love, My Umbrella' and 'Bank Holiday'. Figures who might have provided models for the Mulveys and Kelly include Anthony and Thérèse Cronin, and John Jordan.

Whoever might or might not be their real-life counterparts, these are literary journalists, currently without money for their drinks because the editor Halloran

Figure 11.3 Interior of McDaid's pub, Dublin. Courtesy of discoverireland.ie.

who 'owes us a cheque' has gone off without paying them.[31] The narrator, who one must assume has a regular salary like the then schoolteacher McGahern, buys rounds for all. But he does so in no mood of exhilarated abandon like Farrington. It is rather a measure of his despair: 'It was a sort of freedom to be rid of the money'.[32] Notwithstanding the presence of Claire Mulvey, this is a version of the homosocial group, at least in so far as it stands opposed to the love relationship. When asked why they had seen so little of him recently, the narrator explains with apologetic belittlement, 'I got mixed up with a girl'.[33] But despite such gestures of dismissal, the pub atmosphere cannot block out the memories of lost love that haunt him. He is there only because he can think of nowhere else to go: 'I was bewildered as to what I was doing here but even blinder still about possible alternatives'.[34]

He listens to the conversation around him with a sort of numbed distaste, making no effort to join in. We are given a sample of the self-consciously 'literary' language in Mulvey's question: 'Do you realise how rich the English language is, that it should have two words, for instance, such as "comprehension" and "apprehension", so subtly different in shading and yet so subtly alike?'.[35] The desultory talk, its aimless stories and mock hostilities, is stale and stagnant. As it comes towards closing time, even the illusion of communication is lost:

> Eamonn Kelly had begun an energetic conversation with himself, accompanied by equally vigorous gestures, a dumbshow of removing hat and gloves, handshakes, movements forward and back, a great muttering of

some complicated sentence, replacing of hat and gloves. The Mulveys had retreated into stewing silences.[36]

The drinking session goes on, nonetheless, courtesy of takeout bottles of stout in 'sugar bags', bought by the narrator and carried off to the Mulveys' home. The image which introduces this part is significant. 'Mulvey's house was in a terrace along the canal. A young moon lay in a little water between the weeds and cans and bottles'.[37] No *Moon in the Yellow River* this. If the central character had been appalled by the prospect of a settled middle-class suburban life, the bohemian version of home life is hardly much better.

> A red-eyed child in a nightdress met us. She was hungry. Claire Mulvey soothed her, started to get her some food from the cold press, and we took the sugar bags upstairs. There was no furniture of any kind in the room other than empty orange crates. There were plenty of books on the floor along the walls.[38]

In its less dramatic way, it is as grim as the scene in which Farrington beats his son.

The bottles are opened, the drinking continues until the narrator passes out. The next day, a Sunday, continues much as the day before. Mulvey tries, and fails, to write a review; the child is farmed out with neighbours and the party sets out again towards the pubs, Claire and Paddy quarrelling along the way. '"When we were first together I used to hate these rows"', she tells the narrator.

> 'I used to be ill afterwards, but Paddy taught me that there was nothing bad about them. He taught me that fights shouldn't be taken too seriously. They often clear the air. They're just another form of expression', she confided.[39]

This is Mulvey's philosophy – nothing need be taken too seriously. When the narrator reminds him of his previous praise for Halloran, whom he is now badmouthing, he laughs it off: 'Oh, I was just making him up … People need a great deal of making up. I don't see how they'd be tolerable otherwise. Everybody does it. You'll learn that soon enough'.[40] And so it goes on, the bitching, the bickering, and the stale talk of language and literature through another session in the pub, funded by an advance from the still absent Halloran.

As against this nauseating unreality comes the vision, as they sit with their drinks, looking out through the open door of the bar:

> The state was so close to dreaming that I stared in disbelief when I saw the first thistledown, its thin, pale parachute drifting so slowly across the open doorway that it seemed to move more in water than in air. A second came soon after the first had crossed out of sight, moving in the same unhurried way. A third. A fourth. There were three of the delicate parachutes moving together, at the same dreamlike pace across the doorway.[41]

Talk turns to the possible origin of these thistledowns in the heart of the city, improbable 'backyards and dumps around Grafton Street'. This is Mulvey's view, and characteristic, also, is his interpretation of the phenomenon: 'Just old boring rural Ireland strikes again. Even its principal city has one foot in a manure heap'.[42] For the narrator, the thistledown conjures up memories of his first meeting with his lost lover, the turning of their dance in the dancehall, the spectral parachutes a metaphor for memory itself. In its very visionary purity, it stands opposite to the tacky, urban pub world of drink, gossip and begrudgery in which the narrator has tried to lose himself through a long weekend.

Claire Keegan, 'Dark Horses'

Claire Keegan is an admirer of McGahern; her story 'Surrender', subtitled 'After McGahern', takes off from an incident in the author's *Memoir*. It may be as a sort of tribute to him that she sets 'Dark Horses' in an area of Cavan and Monaghan adjacent to McGahern's own home territory of Leitrim/Roscommon. Brady comes from Monaghan but buys his goods in Belturbet in the neighbouring county; the men in the bar listen to the news on the local radio station Northern Sound. The story was first published in *The Stinging Fly* in 2006, collected in *Walk the Blue Fields* (2007), but it is set back in pre-mobile phone days: Brady has to use a phone box to ring Leyden.[43] 'Counterparts' and 'Parachutes' are city stories, with a great choice of pubs in which to drink. The attraction of the pub crawl is the variety of venues, the chance of meeting up with strangers, as well as the company of the chosen friends. In 'Dark Horses' we are in a rural small town, where everyone knows everyone, exactly who they are and what their standing is within the closely observed community.

The central character Brady has a small farm; he used to eke out a living by working on a regular basis for the prosperous Leyden with his stable full of horses, his 'fine house on a hill' kept immaculately by his schoolteacher wife.[44] Brady, by contrast, is clearly on a downward slide, waking in the morning still half-dressed from the night before, looking out at a garden that has been let go to seed, and watching through cloud his farming neighbour McQuaid, 'walking through fields greener than his own ... herding, counting all the bullocks once again'.[45] Still, he has good intentions for the work before him: 'The two heifers need to be brought in and dosed. He must clear the drains, fell the ash in the lower field – and there's a good day's welding in the sheds before winter comes on strong'.[46] It is only when he runs short of cash to pay for the goods he needs for this work that he contacts Leyden, who owes him money, and whom he helps shoeing a horse.

The horse once shod, he follows Leyden into the town, parking behind 'The Arms'; the town is almost certainly Cavan and the bar the Farnham Arms Hotel.[47] The regulars are gathered in the bar, all men, picking horses for the next race, joshing with the barman, exchanging ritual intercounty jibes. It is companionable company, where it does not matter if the conversation occasionally drops. 'The silence is like every silence; each man is glad of it and glad, too, that it won't last'.[48] Brady is not the only one on a downward path: Norris 'has drunk two farms. Except for the slight shake in his hand, no one would ever know it'.[49] Leyden has a cheque cashed at the bar and Brady is paid. These were the days when there was no problem in having a third-party cheque cashed in a pub. Decorum requires Brady, once in funds, to stay for at least one more drink: 'The shoeing had put a thirst on him so Brady, not liking to leave with the money, orders another round'.[50]

Brady has fish and chips in the local diner and tries to remember where he parked the van. 'When he is walking past the hotel, he recognises a tune he cannot name. He stops to listen, then finds himself at the counter ordering a pint. The day is no longer his own'.[51] And so it goes. His neighbour McQuaid is there 'in a dark suit of clothes, with his wife'. They are ordering the hotel's full steak dinner, a measure of the farmer's settled prosperity. There is no condescension, though, but normal neighbourly courtesy in McQuaid ordering a pint to be delivered to Brady. Leyden, re-finding Brady at the bar, asks conventionally, but all too accurately, 'Have you no home to go to?' Assuming that Brady's depression is due to the poor state of his farm, he tries to reassure him with equally conventional folk wisdom. '"Pay no mind," he says. "Not a hate about it. The land'll be here long after we're dead and gone. Haven't we only the lend of it?"'.[52] He then sympathetically draws out the real cause of Brady's sorrow.

He, like the figure in 'Parachutes', is in mourning for a lost love. The story opens with his imagining her return: 'In the night, Brady dreams the woman back into his life again. She's out the yard with the big hunter, laughing, praising her dark horse'.[53] It is the same at the end of the day's drinking: 'As sleep is claiming him, she is already there, her pale hand on his chest and her dark horse is back again grazing his fields'.[54] They were brought together by horses, for which Brady has a passion but which, unlike the woman – she is never called anything else – he could not afford to own himself. He remembers their first meeting at another Cavan hotel, their dancing, their love-making. It brings the glimpse of a possible happy settled life for him. 'That morning, walking down the main street, buying milk and rashers, he felt like a man'.[55] It is an idea of manhood quite unlike the homosocial bonding of the pub. But after his lover has moved in with him, the horses that brought them together finally drive them apart. When she demands he share in the housekeeping, 'buy food, pay bills', 'take her out to dinner', he tells her to 'go fuck herself'; he threatens to 'put her horses out on the road', which is what he then literally does. Leyden, who has elicited this story, reacts, whether in shock or admiration: 'I didn't think you had it in you'.[56]

Brady's lover will not come back. The day in his life which the story dramatises will be succeeded by other such bleak days on the way down. The night out in 'Counterparts', disastrous as it is, is just another night out for Farrington. The weekend's drinking in 'Parachutes' brings no solace for the anguish of breakup, but it is felt as a single episode in the man's life. What differentiates Keegan's story further, though, is the warmth of its tone and the even distribution of its sympathy. Joyce etches in acid all of his characters, all the phases of action in 'Counterparts'. The pettiness and squalor of the literary coterie in 'Parachutes' is regarded with satiric disgust by the suffering lover. Keegan extends feeling to Brady in the isolation of his self-destructive remorse, little as he might seem to deserve it; at the same time, there is no censoring judgement on the pub culture she sketches in. Leyden is kindly and supportive, the atmosphere of the bar is genial enough. The day's drinking will do Brady no good, but that is his problem alone.

Kevin Barry, 'Breakfast Wine'

Joyce, McGahern and Keegan all use a single centre of consciousness as the lens for their storytelling. The style in all three is more or less realistic, from Joyce's 'scrupulous meanness', through the image-based observation of McGahern, to Keegan's textured rendering of the lived life. From the first sentence of 'Breakfast Wine', Kevin Barry filters his scene through a highly wrought style, a sort of comic baroque. 'They say it takes just three alcoholics to keep a small bar running in a country town and while myself and the cousin, Thomas, were doing what we could, we were a man shy and these were difficult days for Mr Kelliher, licensee of the North Star, Pearse Street.'[57] Published in 2007, it appears to be set more or less at that time, when Irish urbanisation was accelerating into a gallop. Brendan and Thomas, the two alcoholics that prop up the North Star, have benefited from the soaring market for country land on which city people could build second homes. No longer really farmers, they are '[s]ite farmers'.

> these had been good years for us. The land of the vicinity wasn't great, not by any stretch, but it had fine views of dreary hills, and the rivers were swollen with licey trout, and this was enough to draw people in. We sold them what space they wanted, having plenty to spare.[58]

This is expressive of the shrugging demoralisation of a rural community where land is worth far more for building than can be made from farming it, a polluted landscape where even the trout have lice.

The exact identity of the town is never made clear, somewhere in Tipperary, large enough for Pearse Street to be a backwater, 'a narrow, vague, nothing-much sort of street'.[59] The North Star is contrasted with a range of other local pubs, 'the low bars of Nicholas Street', 'the suede-smelling hush of the hotel's lounge bar', 'all the honky-tonks of the Castle Walk'.[60] It is just about hanging on at the bottom end of that range – this is before the following decade in which economic changes cut a swathe through Irish country pubs.[61] The only normal signs of life on Pearse Street are the lorries thundering past; since the introduction of 'traffic calming' on Castle Walk the drivers have been using it as a diversionary rat run.[62] These are dead-end lives in a dead-end place that we are invited to witness in 'Breakfast Wine'. The tiny routines of the bar are observed with a sort of manic particularity:

> He took the rag to the counter and worked the rag in small tight circles, worked it with the turn of the knot and the run of the grain, he was a man of precise small flourishes, Mr Kelliher, and these flourishes were a taunt to the world. Even in desperate times, they said, proper order shall be maintained.[63]

The desolate boredom of the long day is staved off by the exactly repeated formalities of ordering the drinks:

> 'Would you put on a pint for me, Mr Kelliher?'
> 'I would of course, Brendan.'
> 'Cuz?'
> 'I will so,' said Thomas.[64]

The pub, darkened behind its blinds, without any other customers besides the two cousins, with the only diversion the filling in of the *Irish Times* crossword, is its own castaway place.

Barry's style is shot through with playful parody. Brendan and Thomas are the stereotypical frustrated bachelors who hang about in any number of fictional Irish bars.

> We had no women. It was an awful lack in our lives. Mothers, daughters, lovers, wives, we had none of these at all, not a one between us, because women were at a premium in the county, and in truth we were hardly prizetakers.[65]

But that is about to change: 'The door opened up and glamour stepped in.' The template here might be Conor McPherson's *The Weir*, in which the ageing celibate men in the country pub wait in eager anticipation for the arrival of Valerie, the younger woman from Dublin. It is indeed a dramatic spectacle that appears in the North Star:

> Glamour carried itself with great elegance and ease. It was jewelled at the fingers and jewelled at the throat. It wore fine woollens and high leather boots and a green velvet cape, the texture such an excitement against machine-tanned skin.[66]

As she takes her place between the men on the high stools, the erotic effect is immediate: 'she crossed her long legs beneath the woollen folds. The electric rustling of nylons was heard, it went off like a crack of lightning in the premises, and a light sweat broke out on my forehead'.[67]

But the story is not going where a reader might expect: rivalry between the cousins for the favour of the glamorous newcomer, the possibility of a liaison with one of them or neither. Instead, we hear Josie's account of why she is there, escaping from a jealous husband who has tied her up with flex in the garage. '"This is what flex does," she said, and she shucked the cuffs of her sleeves to show the weals and raised welts, blistered yellow and furious red, and soft consoling noises were made'.[68] It is rather like the story that Valerie tells in *The Weir* to top and transform the ghost stories the men have recounted to impress her. Josie leaves, having polished off three of the 33cl bottles of cabernet sauvignon, the 'breakfast wine' of the title, 'and there was an intimation that there was shared history to come, that she too would become a familiar of the premises'. The story ends with a reversion to the wry irony of the opening line: 'So it was that the North Star was saved'.[69] The missing third alcoholic had been found.

These stories were written a full hundred years apart, a century in which Ireland completely changed, as it has changed again in the time since the most recent of them was published. There are no doubt still bullying employers and supervisors like Mr Alleyne in 'Counterparts', but no-one any longer has to carry out the poorly paid office drudgery of Farrington. Latter-day couples can limit the size of their families, so there need not be the five children in cramped conditions which contribute to his horror of home. Even though the real-life originals of the figures in 'Parachutes' may not be identifiable, the scene is quite clearly that of the Dublin literati of around 1960. By now, with new regulations on driving under the influence, you could hardly be so sure not to be pulled in by the guards driving home after a day's drinking as Brady is: 'It will be all right; the sergeant knows him; he knows the sergeant. He will not be stopped'.[70] Pubs like The North Star have lost the battle for survival. But these stories are not about the specifics of social history, catching the atmosphere of this time or that. They are concerned with the pub-goers' desperation, frustration and impotence, the different ways in which language expresses and fails to express what they feel. The stories dramatise the varying psychological and emotional dynamics of the pub, the neediness they serve and the unfulfilment they provide.

Nicholas Grene's Choice:

Phelan Licensed Grocer,

Ballinaclash, County Wicklow

Figure 11.4 Exterior of Phelan's. Photo by Moonyoung Hong.

It stands, as it has always stood, at the centre of the village, just across from our house, Phelan Licensed Grocer. When we first moved to Ballinaclash in 1952, it still nominally offered accommodation as well as groceries, wines, beers and spirits: 'Avonbeg Hotel' appeared on the bottles of Guinness it sold. You entered a tiny entrance hall – you still do – with on the left-hand side the grocery, the bar on the right. As a child I would never have dreamed of entering the pub part; I came in only for messages for my parents or to buy a twopenny, a fourpenny or (if really in funds, oh joy, oh rapture!) a sixpenny ice cream, cut from the block by the publican Fred Phelan. But the mirror behind the bar next door allowed me to see the men as they sat on their high stools nursing their pints: Peter Coffey with his crinkly smile, or the dark saturnine Tom Corrigan. It has been my 'local' now for over seventy years, but I have rarely taken a drink there, still inhibited by that child's sense of the bar as the forbidden space only to be peeked at in the mirror.

Paula Meehan's Pubs: From pub counter to counter-public sphere

James Little

Introduction: Meehan's counter-publics

In a 1998 interview with Luz Mar González Arias, Irish poet Paula Meehan[1] reflected on criticism of her female contemporaries for, as González Arias put it, 'writing the so-called "domestic poem"'. Meehan responded:

> They may criticise you or diminish your work for writing what they call 'domestic poems' but yet, if you write a public poem, or a poem that is perceived to be public, they freak out. When you decode what they are saying critically, basically what they say is 'get back in the kitchen, get back in the bedroom'.[2]

Meehan here attacks the gendered dynamics of participation in the literary public sphere, particularly in what she terms 'a public poem, or a poem that is perceived to be public'. The problematic relationship between the private and the public runs throughout Meehan's work, from her debut collection *Return and No Blame* (1984) – whose title poem is set in the kitchen of her Dublin father – to the more explicitly celestial consciousness of her most recent collections, *Geomantic* (2016) and *The Solace of Artemis* (2023). As Meehan outlined to Theo Dorgan, the public sphere and the poet's private life are never mutually exclusive: 'My poems, though they're autobiographical in one way, are public speech.'[3] Aside from her own statements on the matter, the idea of poetry as a form of public speech is also found in responses to Meehan's writing. 'The Statue of the Virgin at Granard Speaks', for instance, has been called 'perhaps the most notable public poem in recent Irish literary history'.[4] Elsewhere, Fintan O'Toole puts the matter succinctly: 'Meehan is unafraid of being a public poet.'[5]

This chapter ranges across Meehan's poetic career to show how the pub serves as a focal point for her engagement with the public sphere. Starting with the depiction of the interior of the public house in 'Tempus Fugit' (1984), it goes on to examine the pub as a site of exclusion in 'Buying Winkles' (1991), which is analysed in light of the gendered dynamics of the Irish pub space. In my third section, I analyse the pub as an important space for themes of addiction and abuse that permeate Meehan's oeuvre, focusing in particular on 'Thunder in the House' (2000). While analysis of Meehan's work has frequently highlighted the mapping of urban space as a key part of her aesthetic,[6] the pub as a centre of social life has yet to be given the attention it deserves.

As outlined in other contributions to this volume, the Irish pub is central to the nation's 'public sphere', Jürgen Habermas' concept of an arena where private individuals come together to discuss matters of public concern, chief among them being critique of the state. In Habermas' historically specific account – focusing mainly on the emergence and subsequent decline of the bourgeois public sphere in eighteenth-century Britain, France and Germany – such public discourse is rooted in real spaces of social interaction, such as the coffee house or *salon*.[7] Given its importance in Irish social life, it is no surprise that the Irish public house has likewise been seen as 'one of these institutions fostering "the public"' according to the sense in which Habermas defines it.[8]

Participation in the literary public sphere – and in the public sphere more generally – has not been a straightforward matter for Irish women. The same is true of entry into the Irish pub, even as it underwent significant change as Meehan (b. 1955) attended school and university in Dublin. Sociological research in England has shown how the tradition of the Victorian public house as a space of male homosocial interaction left its mark on twentieth-century pub culture, with the English pub remaining a male-dominated space despite increased custom from women.[9] The Dublin pub of the 1960s and '70s also retained its gender dynamics even as the clientele changed. In his oral history of the Dublin pub, Kevin Kearns describes how 'segregated pubs toppled like dominoes' during these two decades, though anecdotal evidence suggests that pub culture remained staunchly patriarchal, with Nell McCafferty describing routine refusals to serve women in Dublin pubs in an *Irish Times* article of 1977.[10]

Journalism such as McCafferty's can be seen as part of an Irish feminist 'counter-public sphere', Rita Felski's term for social movements emerging in the 1970s and '80s whose 'emancipatory project no longer appeals to an idea of universality but is directed toward an affirmation of specificity in relation to gender, race, ethnicity, age, sexual preference, and so on'.[11] Theorists of such counter-publics extend Habermas' concept of the public sphere, while also subjecting its universalist aspirations to critique. As Nancy Fraser points out, Habermas defines the bourgeois public sphere as 'an arena in which interlocutors would set aside such characteristics as differences in birth and fortune and speak to one another as if they were social and economic peers'. Fraser continues: 'The operative phrase here is "as if". In fact, the social inequalities among the interlocutors were not eliminated, but only bracketed.'[12] It is such inequalities that second-wave feminism brought to the fore, with writers such as McCafferty refusing to accept the idea that the Irish pub was a forum for all as long as women were being refused service there.

This chapter reads Meehan's poetry as part of this cultural movement, tracing the turn in her poems away from the pub counter, towards a feminist counter-public.[13] Perhaps unsurprisingly for a poet who has also worked as a playwright, the pub will be presented as a performance platform, a feature which the poems themselves take on and subvert in order to play their oppositional role in the public sphere.

Meehan's pub counter: 'Tempus Fugit'

'Tempus Fugit' – from Meehan's debut collection *Return and No Blame* – is one of her few poems actually set inside a pub, juxtaposing the intimate cosiness of a couple's night out against the key public debate of abortion access in 1980s Ireland. The poem consists of fourteen tercets, and the first twelve tell a well-worn tale of a heterosexual date in a Dublin bar.[14] The opening line sets a brightly optimistic tone, end-stopped for emphasis: 'They had come to the bar laughing.'[15] But the suspicion immediately arises: if they had come laughing, how did they leave? In what follows, it seems that any possible answer will come from the man's perspective: his story 'of tossing // And winning the throw' is what causes that opening laughter, and it is only he who speaks – albeit to himself – in eleven of the poem's forty-two lines. Moreover, the language used suggests this might not be the first watering-hole visited that evening: elevated thoughts such as 'Now we are knowing / All of our selves', with its awkwardly constructed continuous present, feels like a poor imitation of the direct translations of Irish-language dialogue from the years of the Gaelic Revival, while his self-directed description of the woman likewise sounds like a man with a pint trying to be a poet:

> You are lovely
> With the rain on your skin

One bead of which contains
The whole bar within.[16]

Given this high-flown talk, perhaps it is no wonder she leaves 'politely' for a bathroom break – though if there is a break in the relationship, he hardly seems to notice.[17] The pub as presented through this figure's eyes is far from the public sphere as envisioned by Habermas, where ideas about public policy can be exchanged and debated, but is rather a space of mercantilism, with its 'harsh cries // Of coin on coin, / Of brutal ads, / Of drowning sailors' ameliorated only by her presence. When she leaves, he has to reassure himself by thinking 'All this is normal'.[18] And, to the extent that this is male monologue in a public space, this is indeed true, so far.

It is then he notices the inscription on the pub clock which gives the poem its name:

Tempus Fugit. 'Latin'
He thought, 'Time yet for a few
Small ones perhaps,
Then her last bus is due.'[19]

The first word marked for speech is the clearest sign yet that the preceding self-talk has been a public performance, as public as the tale of the sports contest with which the poem opened. For who identifies a language to themselves when reading silently? Only Leopold Bloom is as helpful to his readers when signalling his misunderstanding of the words of a priest in James Joyce's *Ulysses*.[20] But it is Virgil's *Georgics*, rather than Meehan's compatriot's novel, which provides the inscription on this clock.[21] If 'time flies' – as in the standard translation of Virgil's tag – it is her time, not his, that now begins to take precedence: 'her last bus' sets the temporal limit to their date; he seems to have no such concerns about getting home.

The *Georgics* is ostensibly an agricultural manual, and this may explain some of the vocabulary in the toilet scene that follows, which switches to the woman's perspective. There, the other women are 'Powdered and pruned', the latter word denoting the clipping back of plants, organic growth managed by a controlling hand.[22] It may be of note here that Virgil's famous tag on time is preceded by lines outlining the importance of keeping bulls separated from female cattle and regulating the sexual activity of other animals.[23] With this in mind, the man's line about there being time for a few 'small ones' could be read as a comment on his date's reproductive capacity. Meehan – who studied Classics – here evokes the resonances between the regulation of animal sexuality by Roman farmers and the regulation of human reproduction in Ireland, which underwent a major change in the year before *Return and No Blame* was published. A 1983 referendum, approved by 'two-thirds of those who voted', inserted the Eighth Amendment into the Irish constitution, making abortion – which was already illegal – constitutionally forbidden in the Republic.[24] It is in this context that the woman's sight of 'A discarded foetus on the floor' must be read.[25] For Andrew J. Auge, this is 'a sight so horrible that she can assimilate it only by rendering it into a poetic image'.[26] However plausible, this horror has to be read into the poem, as there is no description of it in the closing tercet, which ends as follows: 'She will always swear she saw / A pale face staring, like a moon'.[27] Unlike the man's tale-telling at the outset, this concluding narrative provides no contextual follow-on, no resolution of the storyline. Instead, this unnamed woman's encounter with a foetus in the toilets of a public house draws attention to the fact that the most important public issues in Ireland are not always discussed in spaces associated with the public sphere. Indeed, it is the liminal space of a toilet cubicle which constitutes the most important 'public' space in 'Tempus Fugit'. Meehan's poem thus takes its stand in the public sphere, while drawing attention to the fact that the places of social and commercial intercourse may not be where we encounter issues of public concern. This pattern is followed in her other pub poems.

The pub as 'no go area': 'Buying Winkles'

Moving from the pub interior of 'Tempus Fugit', 'Buying Winkles' gives us the Dublin pub as viewed from without, through the eyes of a young girl sent by her mother to buy periwinkles from a street trader. To use the title of another poem from the same collection, the pub is presented here as a 'No Go Area'.[28] Mirroring the heavily gendered relationship between the public and private spheres of Irish society, this poem is structured around the division between interior and exterior space, with the mother's early warning serving as a reminder to her daughter about the dangers of the streets: 'Hurry up now and don't be talking to strange / men on the way'.[29] According to Mona Domosh and Joni Seager, 'Although most violence against women is actually perpetrated in the private spaces of home, it is those spaces defined as "public" that the majority of women fear most'.[30] Discussing Meehan's work in light of this statement, Kathryn Kirkpatrick reads the streets in Meehan's poetry as 'welcome respite' from domestic enclosure.[31] Yet, as Elisabeth Mahoney points out, there are also passages in her poems that present public spaces as sites of gender-based violence.[32] Take the final stanza of 'Night Walk':

> On Mount Street high heels clack,
> stumble in their rhythm, resume.
> *Let her too get home safe*, your prayer,
> not like that poor woman last night
> dragged down Glovers Alley, raped there,
> battered to a pulp. Still unnamed.[33]

By contrast, the girl in 'Buying Winkles' is 'all relief' to exit the darkened hallway of her home and get out onto Gardiner Street, with this the first in several contrasts between darkness and light. The phrase 'all relief' describes not only the emotions of the young girl but also points to how she stands out as a figure of light, a key theme which I will return to below. The moon, the stars, even the winkles themselves (when it rains) light her way through a city whose spaces are divided according to gender. While the women she describes and waves to are homebound, 'at sills' or 'lingering in doorways', the girl has to negotiate the male-dominated space of the street, 'and weave a glad path through / men heading out for the night'.[34] If we bear in mind the root of 'glad' in the Old English *glæd* ('originally in the sense "bright, shining"' (*OED*)), the theme of light associated with the girl is further reinforced.

Outside the Rosebowl bar (formerly located on the corner of Summerhill and Middle Gardiner Street), the girl meets the winkle-seller, though her attention is soon drawn to what is going on inside the pub:

> When the bar doors swung open they'd leak
> the smell of men together with drink
> and I'd see light in golden mirrors.
> I envied each soul in the hot interior.[35]

If we follow the north inner-city Dublin location and read the poem biographically, this scene would probably be set in the 1960s, when women were an increasing presence in Irish pubs. However, the description here shows a male-dominated bar, in line with the earlier gendered division of public and private space. So, alongside a perhaps understandable desire to escape inside from the Dublin weather, there seems to be something symbolic about the girl's desire to join the crowd of men in the public house, especially if we consider the fact that her story is told in the inherently public form of the poem. This girl does not just want to join the party, she wants to play her part in the public sphere. As we will see, the light she sees indoors is soon found reflecting from the shining winkles sold across a pram used as the woman's sales counter,[36] rather than the more established counter of the bar inside. The public sphere the young girl wishes to join is thus reshaped as an all-female counter-sphere through her exchange with the winkle-seller.

In stark contrast to the harsh sounds of pub trade in 'Tempus Fugit', the account of this exchange presents this trader more as a sage than a money-hungry merchant. When the protagonist asks her 'again' to show her how to extract the winkle from its shell, the seller is happy to engage in what seems to be a ritual instruction of the young girl. Indeed, the highlighted pronoun in 'I'd ask her again to show me the right way / to do *it*' suggests a kind of secret knowledge which is passed on. Removing a pin from her shawl, the woman demonstrates:

> Open the eyelid. So. Stick it in
> till you feel a grip, then slither him out.
> Gently, mind.[37]

Here, where we might expect another 'it', we have a 'him' designating the winkle. The men in the pub might be there for the night, but this woman has shown the young girl how to get another male out of his snug shell. It is notable that her final spoken piece of news is intended for the speaker's mother: 'Tell yer Ma I picked them fresh this morning',[38] reinforcing the idea of an all-female counter-public existing alongside the male-dominated public sphere.

Most of the poem can be read as a loosely structured iambic tetrameter, with the first stanza containing fourteen lines, the second and third seven each. The final stanza consists only of a tercet in iambic tetrameter, shortening the text's end to a point in a manner that resembles the shells of the winkles, or the 'newspaper twists' the girl carries them 'proudly home' in, 'like torches'.[39] Having negotiated the potentially dangerous street crowded with men, and caught a glimpse of the warm, golden pub interior they occupy in the Rosebowl, it is now the girl who brings home the light to her waiting mother in the form of the glistening shellfish. Again, rather than the space traditionally associated with the public sphere, it is an area adjacent to it where Meehan's characters find the most telling instances of social action.

'Dublin pubs and Dublin pain': 'Thunder in the House'

What has been described so far is a move away from the pub counter, towards a female-oriented public sphere which has its roots in more liminal urban spaces. It is from the outside that pubs are described in most of Meehan's poetry, as when she implores the artist–addressee of 'Before the Pubs Close' to capture the Dublin streetscape 'Before last orders and drunken cries / steal the breath the street is holding'.[40] In this way, pubs are part of Meehan's portrayal of the Dublin cityscape, albeit from a distance. In *Pillow Talk*, we read of 'Late / drinkers ... turfed from the bar' and 'closing-time vomit', giving glimpses of the underside of the warm bar-room glow observed in 'Buying Winkles', more reminiscent of the adjacent alley than the snug.[41]

The Dublin pub is an important locale for themes of addiction and substance abuse that run throughout Meehan's oeuvre. Addiction is particularly prevalent in *Painting Rain* (2009), which includes a poem dedicated to children of Dublin's north inner city who died from drug use ('Prayer for the Children of Longing'), another featuring a discussion of Samuel Taylor Coleridge's opiate use with recovered heroin addicts ('Teaching "Kubla Khan" to the FÁS Trainees at the Recovery through Art, Drama, and Education Project') and others which deal with deaths in the wake of drug use ('Common Sense'; 'Hectic'). Alcohol has its place in this poetic catalogue of addiction, from the derelict old man cradling his bottle like a breastfeeding mother in 'Intruders' (1984) to the drunken doctor, 'worse than useless', who prescribes pills to a suicidal mother in *Painting Rain*'s 'This Is Not a Confessional Poem'.[42] Given that the same collection's 'Quitting the Bars' is structured around the refrain 'Quitting's hard but staying sober's harder',[43] it is no great surprise that Meehan alliterates 'Dublin pubs and Dublin pain' elsewhere in *Painting Rain*.[44] But precisely what kind of pain is associated with the pub in Meehan's poetry? This final section focuses on a poem from *Dharmakaya* (2000), 'Thunder in the House', in which the pub is a kind of social slingshot that hurls its drunken customers back home, where they cause havoc.

One further crucial piece of framing context is needed before I discuss 'Thunder in the House' itself. For while its references to the pub are oblique, the poem which immediately precedes it leaves us in no doubt as to the causes of domestic disturbance. 'The Lost Twin' comprises a set of memories related to the speaker's sister, the last of which recalls a thirteen-year-old girl carrying 'her drunken mother home from the pub. Piggyback'.[45] As Seán Kennedy puts it in his analysis of Meehan's poetry, 'shame is nothing without an audience'. He continues: 'the internalization of shame is a social dynamic', which often takes place in the public sphere, alongside more traditionally Habermasian activities such as rational debate and critique of the state.[46] This is why the memory soon shifts to the image of 'Other children jeering' and the words they use: '*Locked. Sloshed. Pissed. Paralytic*'.[47] The sound of the drunken mother being insulted by the neighbouring children 'is merciless in the sunshine'.[48] But while her own child does show mercy – in the sense of giving relief to suffering by bringing her mother home safely – there is no such mercy from the upstairs neighbour's bouts of drunken violence in the poem which follows.

The title, 'Thunder in the House', is a phrase used by the speaker's mother to describe the sound of a man beating his daughter in an upstairs flat. But the second couplet – 'not Jesus moving wardrobes' – seems to suggest that an earlier explanation had it that the noise upstairs was Jesus 'shifting heaven's furniture to help his mam'.[49] Presumably, this is no longer believable for the poem's focalising narrator, whose rapidly growing awareness of the world beyond her flat includes meeting her heavily bruised twelve-year-old neighbour on the stairs. Instead of a heaven, the 'thunder in the house' makes the flat upstairs a 'hell', with the speaker and her family downstairs counted among the 'damned'.[50]

What does this domestic hellscape have to do with the public house? There is little discussion of the man's drinking, or of the fact that this is a spur to his violent behaviour. But such is the centrality of the pub to Irish social life that this context hardly needs to be mentioned. It exists as a shared cultural backdrop, so much so that a few bare hints will suffice. When the speaker mentions that the beatings would stop when 'he fell asleep // or headed out for more', for instance, the reader takes it for granted that he is going to the pub for 'more' alcohol.[51] When we are told that 'Fridays were the worst', we do not need to be reminded that this is when Irish pubs have traditionally been at their busiest, their coffers swelled with payday income, their customers unconcerned about getting up for work or mass the next morning.[52] The sense that there is an uncomfortable acceptance in the speaker's family (and in the wider community) of abusive behaviour is reflected in the weak-sounding clichés the parents use to respond to the violence:

> My mother had no answers, or if she knew,
> was leaving well enough alone. My own father
> got cranky and threatened *to settle his hash. God*
> *love her*, they'd say, she has nobody else.[53]

By contrast, the beatings themselves are almost wordless:

> She was curst and soundly whacked. Sometimes
> we could even hear the individual smack
> of his hand on her cheek. But rarely words. No.[54]

'No' is the only word the speaker has to describe what happens above. And, by avoiding her, 'no' is effectively what she says to her abused neighbour, who steals her message money, her hair slide and her blue scarf: 'I avoided her after that', the speaker tells us.[55]

The violence – and the attendant elliptical, inadequate explanations – only disappear when the girl does, 'one cold midwinter's day, // the year I lost faith in Santa'.[56] In this way, the failure to prevent – or even to describe – the abuse happening upstairs is bookended by two cultural figures, Jesus and Santa, both of whom require faith in order to function in society. With Jesus having been jettisoned as a means of making sense of a violent world by the mother early in the poem, Santa disappears from the belief system of the young girl at its conclusion. Yet she still sees the value in such stories, standing sentry on Gardiner Street, shouting back 'bulletins' of Santa-spottings to the 'younger children'.[57] This could be a somewhat disturbing ending, in which the poet-to-be becomes mythmaker for a younger audience, drawing their attention away from the 'thunder in the house', which is transformed in this winter scene to 'a fine fall of snow' coming from the plastered ceiling.[58] Yet again, however, the poem itself stands as a public intervention – however distanced – against domestic violence that the parents or the poet's younger self were unwilling or unable to carry out. In this way, as well as *describing* the public sphere, Meehan's poetry also *performs* as part of a counter-public sphere, calling out not only the state, but the way in which the public sphere itself is structured. From the self-absorbed performance of the man in 'Tempus Fugit', Meehan's poetry moves to play its own role in the public sphere.

Conclusion

In her reading of 'Thunder in the House', Kirkpatrick states that 'rather than havens, domestic interiors appear as traps' in Meehan's poems.[59] Generally speaking, the pub does not provide a haven for Meehan's protagonists – though there is one that almost does so. In 'Home', the closing poem of *Pillow Talk*, the nomadic speaker thinks she has found such a haven in the Sean Relig bar, Leitrim: 'I had come for the session, I stayed / for the vision and lore'. But then the landlord stops the session, so she decides to leave: 'When the jukebox blared out *I'd only four senses and he left me senseless*, / I'd no choice but to take to the road'.[60] While trad sessions generally offer music for free, a jukebox only operates on insertion of a coin.[61] So, here again, the pub as meeting place for cultural exchange is trumped by its position as a money-spinner in modern Ireland.

Tempting as the pub may sometimes be in her poems, it is not somewhere that Meehan's protagonists ever fully feel at home in, whether this is because of the accompanying oppression of women in the public sphere ('Tempus Fugit'), their exclusion from a key public space ('Buying Winkles'), or the havoc caused by pub life when a drunken parent returns home to their children ('The Lost Twin'; 'Thunder in the House'). In this way, Meehan's depiction of the Irish pub stands as an important counter-narrative to the backslapping descriptions of the public house in broader culture. Furthermore, the pub is crucial to her development as a poet. In moving away from depicting the pub counter, Meehan creates in her poetry a counter-public sphere, one in which a 'public poem, or a poem that is perceived to be public' can help to question the make-up of our public sphere.

James Little's Choice:

Walsh's,

Stoneybatter, Dublin

Figure 12.1 Walsh's pub. Photo by Paul O'Connell.

At the heart of a vibrant, diverse music and social scene in present-day Stoneybatter, Walsh's pub has a history that can tell us a great deal about the evolution of the pub and gendered space in modern Ireland. According to historian Kevin Kearns:

> Walsh's public house in Stoneybatter was probably the last truly segregated pub in Dublin. Tom Ryan, head barman at Walsh's for fifty years, still refused to seat women at the bar in 1988 when he confidently proclaimed, 'It's a male preserve. Men prefer to be on their own. I know this from experience. Women just wouldn't fit in.' Ironically, a woman owned the pub. In 1990 she sold the public house to new owners who opened the establishment to women on an equal basis – and Ryan decided the time had finally come to retire.[62]

Walsh's current barman tells me that the pub was in fact the second-last establishment in Dublin to refuse entry to women; he gives that dubious honour to a pub in Inchicore. A trip to Walsh's, preserved in pristine condition from those earlier days, gives us access to a space that has completely changed its social practice, if not the surroundings where people gather.

Chapter 13

The Stage Irish Pub: Irish pub drama, 1900–2020

Moonyoung Hong

Modern Irish theatre, characterised by its storytelling, long monologues and myths, has found its staple setting in the Irish pub, to the extent that it has become a trope. From the early peasant drama of J.M. Synge's *The Playboy of the Western World* (1907) and social realism of Sean O'Casey's *The Plough and the Stars* (1926) – both of which caused riots at the national theatre, the Abbey – to the most contemporary pub tour and dramatic adaptation of Roddy Doyle's *Two Pints* (2017), this chapter interrogates (problematic) ideas of 'Irishness', nationalism and modernity. It examines the links between two performative spaces – theatre and the pub – and their significance in Irish history and culture. As the contributors in this collection have noted, the idea of the pub as a 'third place' and liminal space, situated in-between the private-public, is a perfect setting for various dramas to unfold. Mark McGovern argues that the pub is an example of 'cultural commodification and consumption of the imagined ethnic identity drawn from a pool of pre-existent signs and symbols'.[1] Thus, if we consider the pub and the theatre as a kind of 'cultural industry', places of entertainment bound by monetary exchange, not only do they both participate in this cultural commodification, but they also offer possibilities where these identities can be challenged, contested and reformulated precisely of its liminal, performative and playful nature.

In the early to mid-twentieth century, Irish theatrical realism relied heavily on the audience's sense of place, which defined their Irish identity to the point of abstraction. This theatrical approach used familiar Irish spaces such as the 'west' and 'peasant kitchen' to establish a sense of comfort and familiarity.[2] The pub, as a recognisable and culturally significant setting, is a prime example of this technique. While the pub contributed to this sense of place, it equally offered a way to negotiate these established conventions. By discussing plays set in pubs from the early Abbey days and the literary movement to (post-)Celtic Tiger, (post-)Troubles, and contemporary pub dramas, I argue that this Irish sense of place anchored in pubs played out a crucial role in Irish theatre history. These plays include iconic John B. Keane's *The Field* (1965), urban pub in Tom Murphy's *The Blue Macushla* (1980), rural pubs in the Celtic Tiger era in Conor McPherson's *The Weir* (1997), the Northern Irish pub in Marie Jones' *The Blind Fiddler of Glenaduach* (1990), Owen McCafferty's *Quietly* (2012) and more contemporary commercialised pub dramas by Roddy Doyle, Enda Walsh and Bisi Adigun. These different contexts, locations and time periods allow for a diachronic and comparative analysis of the space. This comprehensive mapping offers new ways of examining individual and communal identities. Moreover, when the pub is staged, it functions as a meta-theatrical reflection on theatre and contributes to creating a 'lived' experience for the audience.

Early Abbey days: 1900s

In 1907, Lady Gregory told W.B. Yeats after the third act of Synge's *The Playboy of the Western World* that 'the play broke up in disorder at the word "shift"'.[3] In Act II, Pegeen uses the term scornfully to highlight the Widow's lack of proper undergarments, making her request for a penny's worth of starch seem absurd. However, the mention of the unmentionable item went unnoticed at that moment. It was only when Christy envisioned a group of selected women standing in their shifts that the audience erupted into chaos. *Playboy* takes place in a shebeen in Mayo. Christy, who is a murderer on the run, a liar and a skilled storyteller, becomes the town hero. Pegeen, the publican's daughter, falls in love with Christy, and portraying her and the women in the town as people with desire went against the morality of the nationalist audience and their image of Ireland (neither did violence or valorising parricide cancel out their anger). Pegeen's shebeen, where most of the action takes place, is a community space of the Mayoites, a transitory space for 'outsiders', and a transformative space of storytelling.[4] The play emphasises performative identity, Christy's storytelling and role-playing significantly impacting his identity. Synge's work, especially *Playboy*, received much attention, warning against the dangers of self-delusion, myths and ideologies that often obscure the realities of 'dirty deeds'.[5] Despite being part of the Irish literary revival, Synge remained ambivalent towards cultural nationalists' romanticism of the peasantry. As Charlotte McIvor and Patrick Lonergan point out, the play has – ironically – established a new trope of Irish theatre, by continuing to be restaged, appropriated and performed, critiquing Irish cultural realities along the way.[6]

Synge's pub in *Playboy* is distinctly Irish, not only because it is located in the west, which is often considered the 'authentic' place of Irish identity, or because of its use of Hiberno-English, but also due to its 'homeliness'. The play specifies the pub as a 'shebeen' – a term that originates from the Irish word *síbín*, first used in 1780–90 to refer to a private residence where homemade whiskey was sold illegally.[7] Poteen is sold on the premises and, although Michael in the play indicates that they have a licence – thus, a business establishment – the play at first shows that the pub is a homely place, a safe haven for Christy, with food, warm fire and lodging provided for him. Christy even refers to Pegeen as 'the woman of the house', with his stay seen as him belonging to her sphere of influence. The women in the play compete to take Christy to their own house, with Widow Quin offering to look after him at her own 'houseen' in Act II. The shebeen is not only a battleground for private relationships, but also serves as a microcosm and performative space, providing an ideal platform for social commentary. This in-betweenness has been accentuated in various productions, such as the Druid and Wildfire film version of *Playboy* (2005), where a minimal set was used with the ground covered in earth, and the interior resembling a disassembled

Figure 13.1 Presented as part of *DruidSynge* (2005), Druid and Wildfire Films have made the award-winning production of *The Playboy of the Western World* by J.M. Synge. Directed by Garry Hynes, starring Aaron Monaghan, Marie Mullen and Catherine Walsh. Photo by Keith Pattison. Courtesy of Druid Theatre.

and worn-out house (Fig 12.1). The pub setting allows for playing with the interior/exterior, insider/outsider, private/public axis, emphasising the impact that outsider Christy has on the locals, on both personal and communal levels.

While the reception of the play across different times and places (including contemporary audiences) will not be discussed in depth here, it is worth nothing that even though the play was heavily criticised in the early days, with Arthur Griffith commenting that it was 'a vile and inhuman story' told in the 'foulest language we have ever listened to from a public platform', when finally staged in the west of Ireland the audience was 'bored rather than annoyed', saying that 'you could see the like of that carry on any day in the pub'.[8] Wild as Synge's imagination may have been, the discrepancy between the projected image and the lived experience of the pub can be observed here.

Similar to the protests that followed the performance of *Playboy*, the audience was outraged by the commentary on their Irishness in O'Casey's *The Plough and the Stars*, which is set around the 1916 Rising. In the second act, the play employs a similar trope of a mass gathering, with a fight happening while Patrick Pearse's speeches are being delivered outside, but this time a prostitute named Rosie is present in the pub as well. This parallel between the backlash against *Playboy* and *Plough and the Stars* demonstrates the signifying and actualising power of the pub on the stage. The pub was often associated with degeneracy, and the words of Sighle Humphreys exemplify how the play was offensive. Humphreys, who fought in the War of Independence and the Irish Civil War, noted that the real objection to the play was the lack of respect for the tricolour:

> Bringing the republican flag, unfold[ed], into the public house ... a flag like that, you know, floating, it is always a sign of delight and victory and everything, but these publicans would not bring that into a public house ... That was the main objection ... to bring an unfold[ed] republican flag, which we worshipped at that time, into a public house.[9]

Humphreys uses the phrase 'public house' three times. Nationalism seems to have been sullied by the juxtaposition of the flag, the national symbol, with the pub. Furthermore, the staunch realism of these plays leaves little room for interpretation. Synge insisted that *Playboy* should not be taken as social realism, rather an 'extravaganza' of the 'psychic state'.[10] It is no coincidence that the plays that instigated hostility take place in a pub, since their verisimilitude and familiarity threatened the public's self-image, identity and values.

Land and property: John B. Keane's *The Field* (1965)

In the 1960s, Ireland underwent a significant transformation, marked by renewed economic policies introduced by the senior public servant T.K. Whitaker and the taoiseach, Seán Lemass. This period of rapid modernisation and industrialisation created a clash of values between those who sought to protect traditional ways of living tied to the country's past, and those embracing the new, cosmopolitan and exciting urban Ireland. This tension was particularly evident in rural Ireland. In John B. Keane's *The Field*, we see traces of the early theatrical realism of the Irish peasant plays; however, as Marie Hubert Kealy argues, 'Keane's themes of land, inheritance, marriage and emigration fit within the tradition of the folk plays', but 'his social stance differs from early writers'.[11] Keane explores personal problems – individuals' struggles within the technologising and modernising Ireland. The pub, in this context, becomes a 'cross section of village life'.[12]

The play opens with the stage direction: 'Action takes place in the bar of a public-house in Carraigthomond, a small village in the south-west of Ireland'.[13] Most guests are regulars, who discuss business, gossip and socialise, fostering a loyalty tinged with violence, self-interest and irrationality. Bull McCabe, a stubborn farmer who has rented and cared for a plot of land belonging to a widow, Maggie Butler, for years, decides to buy the land, believing he has the rights to it. When a Galwayman from England, William Dee, offers to purchase the land at a significantly higher price to build a factory, Bull grows desperate, threatening and conspiring with others to the extent that the villagers maintain silence over his murder of William.[14] Neither religion (represented by Fr Murphy) nor law (Sergeant Leahy) can intervene. The villagers adhere to their own morality and laws, grounded in their insular customs and close-knit community. This dynamic is not without its toxicity: at the beginning, Bull threatens and makes a deal with Mick Flanagan, the pub owner and property agent, to acquire the land at a low price. Bull warns Mick, 'There's a hundred relations of mine in this village and around it. Not one of them will ever set foot in this pub again if I say so.'[15] However, when faced with an alternative future in which the land would

Figure 13.2 *The Field*, 7 July 1987. Abbey Theatre Digital Archive at the University of Galway. Photo by Fergus Bourke. Courtesy of the Abbey Theatre Archive.

be 'cover[ed] … with concrete' so that William Dee can 'move in [his] machinery' to start his business,[16] it is understandable that Bull's love for the land – though motivated by greed – may be considered the lesser evil.

The pub presents a moral quandary for the audience. When Fr Murphy and the sergeant arrive at the pub seeking information, the audience becomes akin to witnesses in a courtroom. Having seen the murder (which occurs outside the pub) unfold on stage, the audience is complicit alongside the villagers. The sergeant remarks, 'Strange, isn't it, Mick, the way nobody knows anything about anything?'[17] This line implies dramatic irony, where the character remains unaware of what the audience knows. The pub is an ideal space to test out these various moral dilemmas at multiple levels – be it personal, communal or theatrical. Playing on the private / public, tradition / modernity, insider / outsider and rural / urban divides, the pub not only reflects Ireland's tumultuous transition and social condition in the 1960s, but also acts as a dynamic and theatrical experimental space where individuals and communities can process, confront and navigate the conflicting values and rapid changes that characterised this pivotal era. In the next section, I want to turn our attention to urban pubs of the 1970s and '80s, where even more boundaries are blurred.

Urban pub-scape: Tom Murphy's *The Blue Macushla* (1980)

In Tom Murphy's *Conversations on a Homecoming* (1985), Michael, a returned émigré, reunites with his old friends at a pub in the west of Ireland; the pub is called the White House, where the owner looks like John F. Kennedy. We get the sense that Irish culture has been eroded by Americanisation. The play exemplifies the disillusionment and hopelessness of the Irish situation, while questioning the concept of 'Irishness'. In an interview with Colm Tóibín, Murphy explains his attempt to balance and adapt everyday conversational speech to the unspoken rules of theatrical language, in order to express emotions that may not be linear or logical, and to dramatise ordinary people who are inarticulate.[18] *Conversations* is a realisation of ordinary people's language, with Murphy employing typical pub-talk as a dramatic form. These authentic 'conversations' in the pub are in contrast to the 'speeches', 'Puppetry, mimicry, and rhetoric!' that the character Tom despises.[19] It is interesting that when *The White House* (1972) – the original version of *Conversations* before being revised – was put to an actual performance, it received a critical response equivalent to that of the *Playboy* and *Plough and the Stars* riots.[20] When screened by RTÉ in 1977, Murphy's play was condemned by the media and various councils as 'scandalous filth', 'scurrilous and filthy', 'blasphemy', 'a gross insult to Christian principles', and 'obscene'.[21] This negative reception is foreseen by the play itself, such as when J.J. hangs a nude in the pub, provoking Fr Connolly to call it 'dirty' and 'bad'.[22] Tom even mocks the neighbours who complained about the pub's immoral and obscene influence on the people.[23] *Conversations* is the ultimate pub play set in the west of Ireland, which I have discussed elsewhere.[24] Thus, in this section, I want to discuss Murphy's *The Blue Macushla* (1980) as an example of an urban pub, set in Dublin in the late 1970s.

Influenced by American gangster movies, *The Blue Macushla* portrays the vibrant night-scene and changing landscape of Dublin, a place most radically and rapidly modernised, encapsulating the anomalies and cultural clashes people experienced as a consequence. In the 1970s, the owners of big companies could manage multiple entertainment venues and properties. Shane Butler and other researchers explore how the 'superpub' format developed from the different licensing legislations and policies. Superpubs are 'vast drinking emporia in urban areas',[25] which have the capacity to hold hundreds and thousands of customers, often with several bars and/or dance areas. In a 2013 report on Ireland's nightclub industry, Anthony Friel traces the origin of the nightclub to the 1935 Dance Hall Act. The distinction between pubs and clubs has become blurry, as many pubs now tend to be like nightclubs, offering drinks, small dance floor areas, lighting, DJs and live music. As observed in several studies, the nature of the club is ambivalent, reflecting the changing times and increased movement of capital. The context of the club should be regarded as a distinctively urban phenomenon. In *Consciousness and the Urban Experience* (1985), David Harvey describes the image of the city as a 'place of mystery, the site of the unexpected, full of agitations and ferments', as opposed to 'home', which is a space of familiarity, dullness and stasis.[26] While the pub is at the epicentre of everyday social space in Ireland, the inflow of global capital and the process of modernisation have brought about various entertainment venues competing in the leisure market as well as greater merging of these spaces.[27]

Fintan O'Toole eloquently captures the national mood of this period, marked by 'disintegration of Irish nationalism and the rise of Americanisation' as well as urbanisation:

> Throughout the sixties and into the seventies, rural Ireland in particular adapted its own self-image to American models, so that the thatched cottage was replaced by the hacienda-style bungalow and the popular music of the Irish countryside became a peculiar hybrid of sentimental Irish ballads and American country-and-western, often sung in lounge bars in a mock-American accent by bands dressed in cowboy suits.[28]

JFK is important in *Conversations*, but the question of Irish-American dependency – of borrowed styles and images – is even more central and explicit in *Macushla*. The poster for the play re-creates those images: its blue neon title, man with a cigarette and woman in a revealing dress with a gun in hand, all seem to borrow the tropes and stereotypes of a classic Hollywood action movie.

Murphy felt that he had 'absorbed' the 'national mood' of his time. He once commented in an interview: 'The Ireland I see around me is populated with gangsters, with robberies and murder and, most damagingly, with rumours about everyone in power. If the figureheads in our society are being whispered about, idealism really isn't possible for the ordinary citizen.' Moreover, 'I find it difficult to locate Raidió Éireann on my set because the DJs have replaced their own voices with that of a phony culture and it's impossible to distinguish them from those on any other station.'[29] The play works as a mirror, a satire on and critique of the time in which Murphy was living. The play not only critiques the Irish political situation in the 1970s, but also the nature of identity politics, in an attempt to reveal the universal theme of self-expression. In the play, both personal and national identities are shown as 'theatrical constructs'; Murphy uses meta-theatricality to disclose such identity politics.

The Blue Macushla is the name of the pub/nightclub in the play. Various public and private spaces make up the club and demonstrate the intricacy of the club as a liminal space. As the stage directions indicate:

> It always feels like night down here and, because of the gloom, *nothing is defined as yet*. … The idea is that we are in the belly of a club, in a basement or semi-basement. The club proper is off. Perhaps a half-window lets in a bit of light from the street. The lay-out – theoretical – is that EDDIE's office is one side and there is a bar on the other side (more properly, it is the back of the bar that serves the club); and there is access to the yard through the bar. And there is a piano somewhere at which one can rehearse a song. From the open space that is the middle, steps lead upstage to a landing; centre of the landing are swing-doors leading to the club. Turning right on the landing leads off to the 'Hospitality Room'; turning left to other quarters off (like, say, Roscommon's bedroom). The door to the exterior is a side-door; it probably leads to a lane: a staff-door.[30]

The space is multi-functional, undefined, ambiguous and dark, allowing for the mysterious plot to unfold. As the owner of the club, Eddie has robbed a bank to finance it, attributing the deed to Erin Go Bráth – a nationalist splinter group. The group chases down Eddie and forces him to join them. They use the bar as a base from which to pursue their own political agenda, one that involves torturing and interrogating a suspected British intelligence defector in the 'hospitality room'. The 'defector' turns out to be a young priest kidnapped by mistake, whom Eddie must shoot. Meanwhile, Eddie's best friend Danny, who has served a prison sentence for the crimes they both committed, returns to the club asking for his share. Danny gets romantically involved with Eddie's girlfriend, the singer Roscommon. She warns the newcomer Danny that '[p]eople aren't always what they seem'[31] and indeed, the countess with a fake foreign accent turns out to be Erin Go Bráth's Northern Irish agent. No. 1, the head of the group, is unveiled as an upper-class English woman. The young priest that Eddie appears to shoot in the opening scene is in fact the countess who has been put in his place. Pete, the pianist, turns out to be an undercover Special Branch agent working with a government minister. He resolves the whole situation, allowing Danny and Roscommon to go free. The club is a space of transaction, exchange and capital where vested interests in their disguised form conflict with one another. The space itself is divided into different 'splinters' to accommodate the different agendas. Beneath the façade of things, or at the most inner core, corruption and violence lie concealed in the hospitality room.

The multiple layering of performances is evident from the start. The play is set on St Patrick's Day and brass bands are marching just outside the club, while the actions inside are grim. The national celebration of St Patrick's Day is another form of performance, and its occurrence outside the club (off stage) further accentuates the absurdity of the situation. Such simultaneous performances inside and outside the club serve to undermine nationalist discourses. *Macushla* is, despite its box office disappointment, an important theatrical experiment for Murphy. The exaggerated performances and the changing structures of the everyday underworld in a modernising Ireland expose the comic mismatch in form, in experience and in sensibility. As one of the provisional titles for *Conversations*, 'Images', hints at, the borrowed American neon signs on an Irish pub in *Macushla* present a ridiculous veneer. It is therefore a play which further enriches our understanding of liminal spaces in seeing the movements and clashes of cultures and the ways they are blurred, transposed, and felt in people's everyday lives.

Post-Celtic Tiger pubs: Conor McPherson's *The Weir* (1997)

Conor McPherson's *The Weir* is set in an Irish pub in Leitrim in the 1990s, where a group of local men engage in storytelling to impress a new arrival, Valerie. They take turns to tell ghostly tales which expose individual hardships, hidden truths and trauma. The intimate atmosphere of the pub and the storytelling ultimately lead Valerie to reveal her own eerie experience of losing her child. McPherson's play is another example where people gather and talk about their personal experiences; by sharing their private matters in a public setting, the characters can come to terms with their past, their traumas and feel a sense of belonging and consolation. Like Tom Murphy, McPherson is known for placing an inarticulate monologist in front of the audience. In an interview, McPherson remarked: 'What I really look for as a writer is to try and weave a sense of inarticulacy into my characters, because I think, in reality, people are sometimes not articulate as a performer in a play … I try to evoke how difficult it is to communicate.'[32] His use of monologue places the audience as the intended listeners; the audience hears characters' confessions and anxieties, failed attempts at communication, as well as their hopes and aspirations. In *The Weir*, he exploits the theatrical pub space: characters perform their monologues both in front of the other characters and the audience. The pub becomes an expanded theatrical space where the audience engages in listening to the stories that the performer-as-character tells. The pub becomes a shared space between real people.

The pubs in all the plays we have explored thus far resemble actual pubs commonly seen around town, with props that re-create the historical nuances reminiscent of the time period and community. The photos that hang in the pubs likewise express the history and identity of each pub. They are a ghostly imprint, a record of the past, and serve as a presence on stage. Photographs also dot the landscape of *The Weir*. As Valerie talks about Finbar's explanation of 'the history of the place', everyone takes notice of the old black-and-white photographs of a nearby ruined abbey, images of people posing near a newly erected Electricity Supply Board (ESB) weir in 1951, and a town in a cove with mountains around it. McPherson's use of these specific images shows the changes that have happened outside the pub. Jim, for instance, says that '[t]his townland used to be quite important back a few hundred years ago … This was like the capital of the, the county'.[33] The exterior is brought into the interior of the set. Not only do the images add to the realistic setting, but as signifiers of something else they extend the space beyond what is displayed to the eye. The photographs in *The Weir* are a testament to what has been in the past, what has been lost and what has changed.

Even though the photographs and realistic props contextualise the pub space, in certain moments the audience finds itself in a space of no-where. In the programmes

Figure 13.3 Decadent Theatre Company's production of Conor McPherson's *The Weir* (1997), Pavilion Theatre, Dún Laoghaire, 16 July 2016. Directed by Andrew Flynn, stage design by Owen MacCarthaigh. Photo by Moonyoung Hong.

and posters from the 2016 Decadent production, a young girl in a white dress is seen drowning in dark water, an image that links to Valerie's traumatic story and shows the ghostly psychic state of the play. The most striking feature introduced in the Decadent production is the use of wind sound as the controlling force in the soundscape. When Jack arrives in the pub, a harsh sound is heard, and it is referred to as the wind from the north that is blowing against him. It evokes the cold and inhospitable environment outside the pub in contrast with the pub's warm and inviting interior. However, as the wind continues throughout the play after each uncanny story, it turns into a ghostly sound that transforms the pub into a haunted house. It no longer signifies the surrounding setting of the perceived space, but a liminal space that is somewhere between consciousness and imagination. The sound weaves different times, and the audience experiences a transcendent moment. Ben Brantley, who reviewed a 1999 production of the play, suggests that the 'moment arrives, and it's hard to say when because you've shed all sense of time, when you realize that you have strayed into territory that scrapes the soul'.[34] The sound defamiliarises the pub space and thereby contributes to the illusion or disillusion of the theatre world.

It must be said, however, that in all the plays, the women are marginalised, excluded, or appear as sex workers. In *The Weir*, Valerie, who is a blow-in, is the only woman in the pub; it is she who changes the pub into something spiritual and something more meaningful – which might suggest a traditional understanding of gender. In Synge's *Playboy*, neither is Pegeen the ideal feminine figure nor is Christy the macho man, and we see the performative aspect of gender at play. The portrayal of women in the pub so far has been problematic; it is important to consider the gendered aspect of the pub and how different productions and performances could intervene in subverting these representations and tropes.

Northern Ireland: Marie Jones' *The Blind Fiddler* (1990/2004) and Owen McCafferty's *Quietly* (2012)

The tropes we have seen so far – the storytelling, performances, monologues – that characterise Irish pub drama take on a different meaning and resonance in the context of Northern Irish politics, highlighting the complexities and tensions that underpin the region's historical struggles while also engaging with themes of identity, family and belonging. Belfast-born playwright Marie Jones' *The Blind Fiddler* (2004) is based on her one-act play *The Blind Fiddler of Glenadauch* (1990) produced by Charabanc Theatre Company. There are two central locations in the play: Lough Derg and Pat's pub. Kathleen, the protagonist, visits Lough Derg, following the path of her late father, Pat, who visited the island annually for thirty years. Lough Derg is a site that has inspired many Irish literary works, including Seamus Heaney's poem cycle *Station Island* (1995). Like Heaney, Jones employs the metaphor of religious rituals to explore the recurring nature of violence in Northern Ireland. The three-day Catholic pilgrimage becomes Kathleen's personal attempt to reconcile with her past, as she revisits memories featuring her father's pub. The scenes in the pub showcase a variety of characters – played by just four actors – and are accompanied by a live traditional score. These live music sessions blend theatre and Irish traditional music, highlighting Jones' collaborative approach to performance.

While it is easy to notice the parallels with the plays discussed above, there are subtle reminders of sectarian conflicts. In Act I, Mary, wife of Pat, the proprietor, is annoyed that music is played in the pub, when '[y]ou have bin told – no music in the pub'.[35] Part of this caution comes from Mary's fear that they would get arrested and lose their business: 'Can't you see that I'm scared? If we lose the Protestant customers we may close this pub.'[36] Pat also admits: 'This is a mixed pub, you have to keep everybody happy.'[37] The division, however, does not only pertain to religious or cultural conflict between Protestant and Catholic. As a child, Kathleen was captivated by her father's story of the Blind Fiddler, whose music made people forget their hunger. This romantic tale is firmly dismissed by Mary, who feels that it is unsuitable for a poor Catholic family in 1960s Belfast. Mary insists that their children become educated and climb the class ladder. Her priority is financial stability and getting a new address (a house on 'Cave Hill Road') rather than living above the pub. Kathleen explains: 'They shared each other's dreams at one time – Pat's Pub – but it wasn't enough … she wanted us kids out – away from all the stupid drunken fools … I wanted to know about him and his stories and his music, he desperately wanted me to know.'[38] As the next generation, Kathleen struggles to navigate between these diverging values and becomes perplexed by her father's compliance with her mother's demands. Mary's effort and sacrifice make her children successful; however, it also results in a generational divide: Pat's pub is bombed during the Troubles and both Mary and Pat fail to connect with their children. The play thus enacts a wake on stage. The plot device of trying to organise 'a week wake for Liam', who is not even dead (only anticipated) is, on a textual level, a comedic excuse to have a party; however, this performance bleeds out to include a shared live moment with the audience. As characteristic of many pub dramas, the stage becomes an extended pub space. As Pat tells the story of the Blind Fiddler of Glenadauch, '*The following is enacted by everybody, with music*' … which breaks into a '*Dance – a barn dance of folk dance*'.[39] It is on the surface a wake for Liam, but on stage it takes on a symbolic meaning – it is a form of grieving and celebration of the lost lives of many during the Troubles, but also of the dreams, romance, values and community that seem to vanish in face of the new and changing realities.

Unlike Jones' collaborative performances featuring traditional live music that focus more on the social realities of 1960s Belfast, the power of telling stories and conversation is most politically realised in Owen McCafferty's *Quietly* (2012). Ian and Jimmy meet in the pub to discuss an event from their teenage years when Ian, a member of the Ulster Volunteer Force, threw a bomb into the pub, killing Jimmy's father, who was watching a football match. The pub is a setting scarred by its past and memories, but the play hints at the possibility of reconciliation and peace through these characters. The story of pub bombings during the Troubles would have been familiar to the people in Northern Ireland, just as the pub in *Quietly* reflects these real conflicts. The setting of *Quietly*'s pub was modelled on the original design and décor of the Rose and Crown bar that McCafferty's father regularly visited. Like many of the pubs in the city, it was reduced to a charnel house when in 1972 the UVF bombed it in a sectarian attack.[40] In the case of the McGurk's bar bombing, families had to suffer from police and government officials attempting to cover up the atrocity, with the RUC initially claiming it had been carried out by the IRA. In 2011, John McGurk, one of the victims, described how he confronted the man who had killed his family.[41] The murderer refused to talk about any details of the bombing, and could only offer an apology for what he had done. Nothing much has progressed politically in Northern Ireland and the pub on stage replicates this reality.

Mark Phelan explains that McCafferty's plays focus on 'post-conflict' Northern Ireland, dealing with the aftermath of violence rather than the acts themselves.[42] The ordinary pub space in the theatre provides an alternative way to address the broader political stalemate. Consequently, the audience revisits the pub as a site of memory, attempting to address past tragedies as a lived experience.

The pub provides a flexible environment for the characters to address their wounded past. At first, Ian and Jimmy struggle with how to 'sort things out'.[43] When Ian enters the pub, Jimmy immediately threatens him, telling him that 'I'll kick you all over the fuckin street … a wouldn't stop until ya had no fuckin head left',[44] before wishing cancer upon him.[45] Gradually, however, they begin to share personal stories. When Jimmy reflects on a childhood memory about beating up a Protestant kid, he tells Ian, 'I've decided to make it easier for you – this is me playin my part in the truth and reconciliation process.'[46] After giving extended 'background information' as to the 'shite' and consequences of the inactivity of the reconciliation committee, Jimmy insists that a man 'must act on his own – take the initiative – save his own soul and that – so yes to answer your question again – yes it must be in fuckin public – the floor is yours'.[47] The debate as to whether the reconciliation process should proceed in private or public becomes important, as it addresses how to deal with a past that is personal and yet political. Furthermore, Jimmy tells Robert, the barman, that Robert was meant to hear the entire story. Both Robert and the audience become part of the 'peace process', making the performance a public occasion as they bear witnesses to the whole scene.

The characters recount the details of their stories and try to work out what happened by re-enacting their past. Jimmy insists that Ian articulates all the details of the story out loud: 'Say it – that's what you're here to do so fucking do it – say it – out loud – every fucking detail – I'll start you off – on the third of July nineteen seventy-four.'[48] He then recites all the names and ages of the victims. They go through the details and try to replicate what happened: 'Jimmy – in this bar – the one we are sittin in now – where were they sittin – (Moves to centre stage) – the bar was here – (Points upstage) – you ran in through the door there – (Points downstage) ... where did you throw the bomb?'[49] Their actions resemble those of investigators reconstructing a crime scene. Instead of dismissing the details and the people as statistics, they are genuinely attempting to recover the situation of that moment in time. As Ian says, 'There's more to the truth than facts.'[50] The point of this re-enactment 'is about us livin through this together'.[51]

After the truth recovery process through mutually experiencing the past, Ian apologises to Jimmy for what happened: 'I can't speak for the actions of a sixteen-year-old child – but I can speak for myself now – I'm sorry what happened.'[52] The meaning of apology is discussed in this conversation. They cannot travel back in time and even if they did they would not have listened to each other. Mature acknowledgement of the past allows for a deeper understanding; it is about talking and listening, about communicating with one another from different perspectives. The pub is important not only because it opens up the floor to the peace process, but because it is a place of consolation that functions as a haven for ordinary people. Jimmy imagines how the last moments of the victims may have been:

> I always like to think that it ended with a joke an a laugh – men havin a drink to help them ease the burden of the daily grind – an on top of that – Belfast in those days – a few drinks – a release – watchin the match an shootin the shit – maybe like they were in their own cave or something – protected from all the fuckin nonsense goin on in the outside world.[53]

Jimmy is consoled by thoughts that the men hanging out in the pub must have felt secure and relaxed amid the violence outside. The pub's 'playful' quality gives

Figure 13.4 Patrick O'Kane, Robert Zawadzki and Declan Conlon in the Abbey Theatre production of *Quietly* at Irish Repertory Theatre, New York. Photo by and courtesy of James Higgins.

the feeling of 'mutually withdrawing from the rest of the world and rejecting the usual norms'.[54] The pub space connects the different worlds of the past and present and allows for re-imagining and re-defining of the past; it sheds a light on the place otherwise scarred by its memory of violence.

While the shouting outside haunts the pub in the end, the sound of the World Cup match on the TV screen barely impinges on the silence and conversation that Jimmy and Ian maintain. In the Abbey production, some parts of the text, such as Jimmy's long monologue on page 31, were pared back, and were filled with long silences instead. The audience has to listen 'quietly' to their life stories amid the 'loud' narratives of the Troubles. By hearing them out, the audience becomes participants of the peace process. Without a political consensus or framework to deal with the past, the role of art and theatre becomes more important than ever. The theatre is a public space where audience becomes part of what is being performed. *Quietly*'s pub setting opens the floor to a reconciliation process reconstructed in the theatre and transforms the audience into witnesses.

Conclusion: Branching out – adaptations, musicals, touring pubs 2000–22

As space is limited, instead of providing in-depth analysis of all recent developments in Irish pub drama, I will conclude by briefly mentioning them. These plays showcase the cultural commodification of various Irish pub drama themes, as well as a commitment to engaging with the community and challenging norms through their performances. Enda Walsh's internationally acclaimed *Once: The musical* (2011) deals with issues of migration and failed aspirations with bittersweet sentimentality and music in the pub. In Martin McDonagh's *Hangmen* (2015), a dramatic hanging takes place in a pub and the play re-imagines 1960s England when the death penalty was abolished. Bisi Adigun's *The Paddies of Parnell Street* (2013) is adapted from Jimmy Murphy's *The Kings of the Kilburn High Road* (2007) and takes place in 'an African restaurant/bar ... a small stage with a few musical instruments – two small conga drums, a portable keyboard on a stand – and a few mike stands on it'.[55] The adaptation engages with ideas of diaspora, as the characters discuss their relationship to their homelands, and complicated identity (referring to themselves at one point as 'Black Paddy'). There are multiple performances, including singing and the use of various proverbs and sayings, as a way to discuss their past wounds. Adigun's Arambe Productions is also known for having adapted Synge's *Playboy* with an all-Black cast.[56] The pub serves as a platform to discuss not only emigration but also immigration and multi-directional migrations. Finally, Roddy Doyle's *Two Pints* (2017) is the epitome of Irish pub drama; it toured actual pubs across Ireland. Rather than the stage becoming a pub, in this case the pub becomes the stage, further blurring boundaries. It was restaged at the Abbey Theatre in 2018 and 2019, followed by tours around the United Kingdom and the United States. While this chapter has focused on representations of pubs on stage, these further branches suggest ways these performative spaces can become mutable and feed one another. Aspects that this chapter could not cover, for example, include theatrical personas such as Brendan Behan in the 1950s shaping the image of and discourse around the pub.

If liminality contests boundaries and binaries, then these plays demonstrate what it means to inhabit such a contested space. Since the 1920s, Ireland has undergone rapid changes that have involved wars, vast social and political reforms, economic growth and crisis, industrialisation and globalisation, and these changes are reflected in the places and spaces that people engage in. The pub on stage sets the emotional temperature of this period of rapid change in which characters feel displaced and unsettled. Characters are haunted by past memories and an uncertain future, and the plays expose these anxieties by exploring the ways people engage with the space. At the same time, theatre as a liminal space provides a release of these feelings, offering glimpses of hope. The flexibility and hybridity allow for a possible redemption, mature understanding, and communion. The performativity of the pub can even be traced back to Oliver Goldsmith's *She Stoops to Conquer* (1773), set in an alehouse, which involves farce, satire, role-playing and misrecognition. Furthermore, as we've seen in the case of Doyle's *Two Pints*, 'Irish pubs' have gained currency outside of Ireland, and have been radically transformed – and sometimes re-imported. Opportunities exist to see how pubs are represented in an international context. Theorising the pub space as a specific but abstract concept illuminates the evolving nature of the self and society. Singular or communal identities are constantly re-envisioned and re-configured in theatre, just as liminality represents a continual state of becoming. Irish drama's spaces are not fixed but mutable and, by exploring the definitive liminal space, the pub, we can come to understand the complex realities and emotions behind the narratives of modern Ireland and its people.

Moonyoung Hong's Choice:

Delaney's,

Hong Kong

Figure 13.5 Exterior of Delaney's in Hong Kong. Photo by Moonyoung Hong.

Opened in 1994, Delaney's was the first Irish pub in Hong Kong and at one time had three branches across the region: Delaney's Kowloon in Tsim Sha Tsui, Delaney's Pok Fu Lam in Cyberport, and Delaney's Wanchai. The Wanchai branch sadly closed in 2024. Each branch has a different emphasis and is localised to suit the neighbourhood. Kowloon (and Wanchai before it closed) has a more late-night bar vibe, broadcasting major sporting events, including rugby and football. The pub features Guinness advertisements, rugby jerseys and even a small replica of the 1916 Proclamation of the Irish Republic. Cyberport is more family-friendly, hosting children's birthday events, and its walls are decorated with black-and-white photographs of children playing rugby for the local club, Sandy Bay RFC (these children are now adults). As well as the 'atmosphere', Delaney's has embraced 'culinary sophistication': it imports Irish organic Hereford beef, Irish artisan farmhouse cheeses, Irish organic salmon, jet fresh Irish oysters, Barry's tea,

Achill Island sea salt, and more. Guinness is also imported straight from St James' Gate. Managed by Noel Smyth since 1995 and Peter Maxwell who joined in 2012 (initially coming 'on a holiday'), they have held the fort and spirit of Delaney's in their various iterations and locations for almost three decades now. Noel's trademark phrase – 'keep it Irish' – reminds customers of what the pub is really about: good humour, friendly atmosphere, fun and entertainment. Entering Delaney's transports you right back to Ireland – it has served as a refuge for many Irish expatriates in Hong Kong, and provides a taste of Ireland for Hong Kong residents and also tourists unfamiliar with the place.

Figure 13.6 Interior of Delaney's in Hong Kong. Photo by Moonyoung Hong.

Chapter 14

Traditional Music and the Appeal of 'the Pub'

Fintan Vallely

This chapter is an analytical assembly of observations on Irish-music pubs of which the writer has had direct experience from the earlier years of traditional music revival in the 1960s through to the Covid-19 era of the early 2020s. It does not deal with – and certainly does not imply as inferior – the tremendous range of other private and semi-public traditional-music-playing circumstances. Indeed, the greater number of these are in homes, halls, schools and music-organisation premises like those of Comhaltas Ceoltóirí Éireann (CCÉ) and the Cork, Dublin and Armagh Pipers' clubs. As regards music quality, the pub is just an alternative place to play, both semi-privately and publicly, but it has additional social merits and has often been the initiation point for the professional skills of many of today's best-known performers.

For me, the panorama of pub music spaces opens with music sessions in small, music-friendly bars in the town of Armagh, in Belfast, and in occasional *fleadh cheoil* host towns and villages. At the beginning of the timespan, many musicians did not drink alcohol, yet the physical features of the pub made it an attractive place for them to socialise with music.[1] In this performance-among-peers we had a palpable feeling of pride, for playing 'out' and being listened to with a music that previously had only been superficially acknowledged or heard at a distance from a stage in a *céilí* dance hall. We were hooked on the music, with a compulsion to learn more, find new tunes and get on top of the complexities. Some of us spent most of our waking moments in exhilarating, repetitive practice, and in our dreamtime wrestled with fingerings and notes, all the time aware of the infinity of just how much more we had to, or could, learn. None of this was a burden, and our playing was energised by the widespread opinion that being able to do that was considered culturally valuable, as well as being widely regarded as 'a gift'. Most homes did not have the privacy needed for total engagement, so outside venues were important, including kitchens and parlours, and the odd folk club which was generally a tea-and-sandwiches affair in a hall, and without drink. But pubs featured too, a consequence of the fact that some of the better older musicians, survivors from the numerous *céilí* bands of the earlier twentieth century, valued the relaxing comfort of a drink. And so, especially at *fleadhs*, we younger players had the occasion and approval to enter those mysterious adult venues, so formulating an indelible connection between music and 'the pub'.

Beer and smoke

Along with the first intense – but not unpleasant – musty whiff of stout and cigarette smoke experienced in a cosy pub interior came the rush of knowing that this was a most satisfying environment for music. Later, but gradually, other dimensions of pub life had to be dealt with, including awareness of the variety among publicans – the gracious and respectful one who was in awe of the music, the indifferent one for whom this was a business, not caring whether people socialised through music or talking, the mean one who begrudged the non-drinking players their seats despite them being part of the reason why drinking customers lingered. Among us were stoic temperance, non-drinking players who spoke little, and led tunes with well-mannered tuning and timing, others who grumbled at the proprietor's reluctance to part with a complimentary drink for musicians, and those whose only interest was leaping to the next tune and being vexed by the curtailment of the holy hour or closing time. Overlapping all this was the gratitude of the listeners whose expression of appreciation of the music was marked by the occasional unasked-for bottle of stout, the assumption being that we all drank. A most vivid memory of that was my playing in Club Uí Chonradh in Harcourt Street in Dublin, 1968, to which, still a Pioneer, I had gone to hear music, only to find none that night; but there I met the tremendous *sean-nós* singer Seán Ó Conaire who insisted that I play, to his great appreciation, and volunteered to dispose of my line of gifted drinks in return for introducing me to the music clubs and bars of Dublin. That was a valuable exchange that immersed me in the cosmos of the old 'big' airs and *sean-nós* singing, all organically fused with the environment of a bar.

The myriad functions of the pub

Once upon a time 'the pub' could be regarded as the main venue for male escape from children, clamour, economic crisis and domestic culpability. But in the 1960s, in many cases it took on the additional role of being a haven for indigenous music-making, singing and occasional step or 'half-set' dancing, and drew in female as well as male customers. Song does not seem to feature particularly in my recollections of these, for the main site for ballads was where money was in flux, among crowds at markets and sports events,[2] performed by perambulating specialists to eager audiences for whom the lyrics were news or carried meaning which could not be accessed otherwise: the street was the poor-person's concert hall. Like ballad song, dance music did not have sit-down audiences like it enjoys in modern times, rather it was part of community activity, and performed traditionally in homes, later in halls, for its primary purpose of facilitating dance. Yet music to be listened to did take place in pubs, but on a casual and impromptu basis, and sometimes with dancing too, as can be seen in nineteenth-century paintings. There are also stories recalling ballads in pubs, but music sessions as we know them with sit-down audiences are a post-1950 product.

Irish bars in places of exile – notably in American cities, prime among them being New York – did have music as a featured attraction, initially more associated with dance, catering for neighbourly, community needs which could not always be achieved otherwise in people's cramped, large-family, private dwellings. Music-performance formats in the New York bars, as reported in early- to mid-1900s accounts, were an evolving thing, as gleaned from information concerning the lives of leading musicians such as Michael Coleman, James Morrison, Paddy Killoran, Patsy Touhey and John McGrath.[3] They performed on audience-facing stages in Vaudeville-style formats; they were not playing for themselves in sessions as we now know them. But those Irish-bar circumstances were the prototype for the Irish-music session-pub that we know today.

Defining the space

It might be said that there were as many pubs in Irish towns as there were political opinions, as, for instance, could be seen in the town of Bailieborough, County Cavan, which in the early 1960s had more than thirty bars; Miltown Malbay in County Clare was similar. The tastes, affiliation or knowledge of the publican dictated the ethos of each, but indoors activity was dominated by, and prioritised, conversation. The oasis-like aspect of 'the pub' did of course render it ideal to be a hub in traditional music revival when that movement began, for its secretive intimacy was a relief to step into, a licence to temporarily ignore responsibility and time constraints, and, for those so afflicted, hide from the maelstrom of music modernity. The relative silence, dark interior and neutral resonance contributed too to the venue's seduction as a haven for acoustic music-making, and so, where the owner had appropriate knowledge and taste and compliant personal demeanour, pubs across the island welcomed and became synonymous with music.[4] Among these were Paddy and Maureen O'Donoghue's and Paddy Slattery's in Dublin; Ted McGowan's Róisín Dubh in Gurteen, County Sligo; Maisie and Thomas Friel's, Marrinan's, Clery's and Queally's in Miltown Malbay, County Clare; Carberry's in Drogheda; Dowling's of Prosperous, County Kildare.

In many London pubs, traditional music developed to a somewhat charismatic level from the 1950s to 1970s, notable here being The Favourite on the Holloway Road.[5] As well as the music-identifying pubs, some more business-oriented bars came to be known, and valued too, for the practicality of their dependable facilitation of music with a regular timeslot. One of those was the Four Seasons in Dublin in the 1970s, where Ceoltóirí Chualann fiddle-player John Kelly led music and consequently attracted a following of like-minded music aesthetes. Such music pubs were as often run by women as by men, and by couples, iconic among these being the Brazen Head and the Four Seasons in Dublin; and Friel's, Cleary's and Queally's in Miltown Malbay. Most pubs of course had no interest in hosting traditional music, but even such proprietors as those typically considered by musicians to be 'philistine' (regarding wealth as superior to artistic cultural expression[6]) could be enticed by the new commercial value of traditional music to accommodate a session. This is expressed with measured understatement in singer Tim Lyons' satire 'The Grisly Murder of Joe Frawley':

> I'll sing of Mike-ey Cleary, Who in this town did dwell
> He worked in Frawley's music lounge – A place you all know well
> Joe Frawley was a councillor, full of wit and rural charm
> With a Mace food store, in the shop next door – and a ninety-acre farm
> When the week it starts, he has cards and darts
> On Tuesdays there's nothing much
> On Wednesday there's a disco bar, with flashing lights and such
> The local Comhaltas meeting goes wild on Thursday nights[7]
> But when the weekend comes around – Man, it's really out of sight.

The anchor-musician pub session

Musicians have always welcomed the fact that a place to perform could be guaranteed, and the most common location for early sessions was in homes and parochial and other halls. But the pub was psychologically attractive, as already described; it also had appropriate space and furniture always in place, so it rapidly became popular for its session-hosting role. Remuneration for musicians – in cash or in kind – had always been normal for house-dance fiddlers and *céilí*-band musicians, and for Traveller players, but in the aesthetics of music revival it was often vehemently repudiated, the common belief being 'I do it for the love of the music, not for money', so this was not initially a factor in casual pub performance.

Awareness of the economic value of music attracting drinks-purchasing listeners to bars did gradually lead to the custom of the bar paying established 'anchor' players. Payment could be token, or frugal, involving a small sum or a few drinks, but a commercial commitment nevertheless. The economic and exchange value came to be marked by a fee for anchor musicians to guarantee the presence of music as an attraction. For musicians, this meant that they had a regular place to play in agreeable company on a certain day or days, and so the session-pub image was founded. The anchor musicians, who attracted other non-paid players and their friends, generally did not need to discuss this; instead, all the company appreciated and valued the casual informality which gave them the freedom to run things as it suited musicians: for instance, they let musicians play in a circle format in which they could hear each other without being intruded on by the public's compulsion to converse. Anchor players are typically players who are better known to the public – this was a major feature of London pub sessions.[8] In the past they were generally male, but women are increasingly seen in this role. The regular players in such pub sessions learned too how to keep spirits up and tunes going, a quite professional ability, if a subaltern one. Not all were happy with the arrangements and from time to time individual players would grumble at their perception of the publican making profit at their expense, or at the shoddy attitude of some landlords; however, the formula generally worked, and so it persists.

The commercial pub session

Parallel with this largely voluntary and quasi-commercial music scene, a pastiche of the session format was developed by more commercial landlords, and that came to

Figure 14.1 Exterior of San Francisco's most famous Irish bar, The Plough and the Stars. Photo by Patricia Chang, featured on sfgate.com.

be the norm in cities, such as in Dublin and Galway. Here, the model is similar to how large bars in the United States – such as The Plough and the Stars in San Francisco, California and McGurk's in St Louis, Missouri – had operated for decades: musicians playing their own selections, but not casually in open-ended tune-sets as one does in the self-entertaining session circle. Instead, they play for set periods of time with breaks, ranged in a crowd-facing line, and use a PA system with which drinkers strive to volubly compete. While in the American model these are actual gigs, played by reputable, respected, advertised, resident performers for whom the audiences often have specially come, this is not always the case in many of Ireland's music pubs. Indeed, one such Dublin venue has performers confined on a cramped, shelf-like platform, their miked sound distributed to multiple rooms in the building.

Regardless of the varying degrees of commercialisation, remuneration and accorded respect, the commercial music pub acted as an introduction to semi-professional and professional performance opportunities and some cash for traditional musicians. This format is now an institution, providing opportunities for entry to music professionalism worldwide: in it, young players learn skills rapidly, on the hoof,

Figure 14.2 The stage of The Plough and the Stars has hosted many musicians over the years, many of whom are trying to help save the bar. Photo by Patricia Chang featured on sfgate.com.

and can move on if or when it suits them. Noisy, rough-house conditions may be a far cry from the ideal of feeling or being part of a tradition, or of the music's glamorised history, and they are quite different to the environment of learning in classes and at private sessions. But they are educative in on-stage demeanour, resilience, sustenance and survival, and can be valuable in the performers' personal development. Trade unionism does not seem to enter the picture, and issues such as physical and personal conditions remain an issue; as in many other unregulated workplaces, they are matters that musicians themselves negotiate or deal with.

The aesthetic side of the commercial music pub might thus seem far from fulfilling. But for younger, eager, developing players it is exciting, having a compelling, showbiz allure and sense of challenge and achievement. The purpose of the presentation of traditional music in such venues is to provide an uplifting, energised background to conversation and conviviality for people who like the sound of the music, among whom are not only Irish people who can play it, or know it well, but also like-minded visitors from abroad. Though this is such venues' raison d'être and economy, the idea is very much at odds with the beliefs of older and more mature musicians who generally consider it to be something of a shame that the music has plunged from its noble status as *ceol na n-uasal* (music of the nobility) to being mere aural wallpaper. The late Tony MacMahon went a step further, regarding it as aural 'carpet' – a superb aesthetic creation being trampled underfoot by ignorance. However, in defence of the pubs' opportune exploitation, it must be said that a lot of music in the world, including Irish traditional, and even classical, has historically had to accommodate the disability of such usage of music, a treatment which is a consequence of the fact that, as well as sophistication, all music types have the additional dimension of being a capitalised form of cultural production.[9]

The rise of the music pub

The 'music pub' is just one manifestation of how bars responded to the challenge presented by expanding stay-at-home recreational spaces and by private entertainment devices and media after the mid-twentieth century. So, by now, pubs have been a

Figure 14.3 Exterior of The Crane bar, Galway. Photo by Moonyoung Hong.

Figure 14.4 Trad music session in Taaffe's bar, Galway. Photo by Sonder Visuals. Courtesy of Fáilte Ireland.

midwife to a range of music formats: cabaret professionalism, the loud background-music bar, the club-style small gig, and the casual 'session' and musical-friends' rendezvous in traditional music. They also generate money via licensing agencies for plays of traditional music on sound systems. Ballad lounges after the late 1950s were the earliest manifestations of this changing function of bars; it was the vintners' first engagement with impromptu music-making.[10] This new direction was propelled by social changes such as improvements in wages, but in particular by women's rejection of stay-at-home invisibility and marginalisation and, later, feminist challenges to misogynistic taboos such as 'no pints served to women'.[11]

Some lounge bars became major entertainment providers, famous among which in County Dublin were the Embankment, Tallaght and the Abbey Tavern, Howth. Parallel with this, the smaller pub, built around a local or CCÉs (Comhaltas Ceoltóirí Éireann session), held its own. Its absence of electronics and the support of a principled proprietor guaranteed its availability as a local base for music-makers and pundits. For the performers, the small pub was aesthetically more acceptable than the faux glamour, PR-driven scale and financial emphasis of audience-facing, professional-entertainment music spaces. Such smaller premises – or dedicated in-house niches in bigger bars – by now are culturally iconic, and nationally known, and cater for a nationally and internationally mobile clientele of music aficionados and music-makers. Among them have been noted establishments in not only the bigger cities – such as Hughes' and the Cobblestone in Dublin, The Corner House and An Spailpín Fánach in Cork, The Crane and Taaffe's in Galway, Madden's in Belfast – but also in smaller towns such as Red Ned's in Armagh, McCollam's in Cushendall, County Antrim, and Paddy Quinn's, P.J. Kelly's and Considine's in Ennis, County Clare.

Indeed, it was the well-established reputation of these which Dublin City Council had to consider when dealing with the decision to spare the city's iconic Cobblestone pub from the developers' demolition ball in 2021.

Emergence from invisibility via the pub session

The nature and circumstances of traditional music being facilitated and hosted by pubs is marked essentially by symbiosis and synergy. This is best illustrated in the *fleadh cheoils*, forty or so of which take place each year, the biggest of them being the All-Ireland. Each one of these events utilises most of the main public houses in the host town or village, regardless of their attitudes to music for the other fifty-one weekends of the year. Competitions, of course, are the major reason for the *fleadh*'s existence, most importantly for the under-twenties. But the pubs are crucial for the casual music-makers and listeners who make up the *fleadh*'s attendees. There have been changes, the main one being that at *fleadhs* in the 1950s and '60s the small size of pubs meant that people generally congregated to play and listen on the street outside, or close to them; it would have seemed odd to play anywhere else.

As pubs grew in scale over the years, the music sessions were able to move inside, shunted too by the weather, so that, by the 1990s, pub interiors had expanded so much that the indoor session has now taken over, particularly for singing. Retreat from the streets was also propelled by the desire to get away from the dense, perambulating crowds at modern *fleadhs*: half a million people participated in the 2019 All-Ireland at Drogheda. In such festival circumstances the individual pub has no artistic commitment beyond being a provider of seating, recreational drinks and sometimes food. It is the music-making and -loving clientele who mark the venue as a cultural space, but (generally) only for that day or weekend, or full week in the case of the All-Ireland *fleadhs*. Such temporary designation is also a feature of certain other year-round music pubs; notable among these was the New York bar Mona's, where, with a long session from Monday night 8 p.m. until the early hours of the following day was

Irish-traditional, and each other weekday a different nationality or genre. Indeed, too, there are parts of Ireland where whole villages have been so 'audiotopically' defined,[12] and are known for their pubs' association with music, year-round, best among them being Miltown Malbay, County Clare, which hosts *Scoil Samhraidh Willie Clancy* each summer,[13] Ennis, County Clare,[14] and Gurteen, County Sligo.

Pandemic is good for the eyesight

The music/pub link is known intimately by all musicians. It is patently visible and attractive to visitors from outside Ireland. Despite this link, the country itself has tended to take it for granted. But in the opening-up after the 2020–2 Covid-19 closures, national news began to pay attention to traditional music, particularly the session. In one of such bulletins, uilleann piper Louise Mulcahy was filmed playing in the street in Dublin's Temple Bar, in support of the message from local pubs that their public, thousands of whom – pre-Covid – had come to the city daily to hear traditional music in pub surroundings, were being denied the satisfaction of hearing such music live, and consequently the bars were in serious economic jeopardy.

It could also be implied from the news clip that musicians who made their living from in-pub sessions now had no work. Emphasising the supremacy of economics in this, the RTÉ commentary asked, 'How could a ticketing system be applied to something like a trad session?'[15] This highlights that traditional music in bars does have an actual economic value as part of daily entertainment. So, the music session of whatever format has been shown to be not just a decorative – if invisible – take-it-or-leave-it pursuit which the insensitive publican could on occasion deign to trivialise. It has now been acknowledged as an ingredient in the fabric and attractiveness of the very concept of the Irish pub.

Evolution not invention?

It seems that certain aspects of Irish-music culture are somewhat superficial. Misassumptions made by the media and by the hospitality and entertainment sectors – and probably as well by most of those under age forty – include the belief that the music pub is a longstanding Irish institution, and that what is loosely termed 'the session' has always been around. As stated earlier, neither is quite the case. First, though all older bars were small, poky places which were suited to intimate music sessions, their managements and clienteles typically were not always interested in hearing traditional music, particularly before its 1950s-on re-popularisation.[16] In fact, the pub customers' primary need has been for conversation space, latterly spiced by input from television sports. So, session music, itself a form of conversation, a dialogue in music, has had to negotiate its own space.

Moreover, the idea of the session is modern, as it is necessarily tied to traditional music revival and to the increase in post-1960s relative prosperity and the attendant culture of 'going out'. But to regard such consequences as 'invention' seems inappropriate, for neither 'the pub' nor 'the session' were consciously invented, in the way that, for instance, the internal combustion engine was. It can be said more accurately that two equivalents – the burger joint and the disco – were actually invented, the former by major commercial caterers, the latter by commercial promoters. But the music pub as we know it, and the session too, have simply evolved: the former from síbíns and hostelries in response to rising levels of prosperity, the latter from socialisation of musicians via collective, re-popularised music-making in the era of the disappearance of traditional social dance.

The clichéd Irish pub

The evolution continues, driven of course by commercial enterprise. A most striking manifestation of this came in the decades around the turn of the twenty-first century when Ireland's new-age cultural strength was so heightened that it could sell national identity as a cultural commodity throughout the year rather than just on St Patrick's Day. It is at this point that 'invention' became more conscious and deliberate. Music was a major feature in this, surpassing even literature,[17] represented by such iconic, internationally appreciable music-talent exports as Rory Gallager, Van Morrison, U2, The Cranberries, Bob Geldof and Sinéad O'Connor. Because these were in the contemporary, trans-national, English-language Anglo-American rock/pop idiom, and obliged to compete for festival- and air-time with many others on both sides of the Atlantic, it can be argued that traditional music performers are likely to have had greater nationality-related visibility.[18] This was not least because they stood out as distinctively Irish within the world music genre's international milieu which has many distinctive languages, styles, underlying melodies, instruments and folk-music idioms.

Just as Italian-ness can be immediately associated with distinctive foods, so too Irishness in the soundscapes of continental Europe and the United States can be seen and appreciated most clearly in the performance of Irish traditional music, in the vanguard of which were Clannad, The Sands Family, Planxty, Dolores Keane, The Bothy Band and The Chieftains. Regardless of this, the result for Ireland is that Irishness is known internationally through music, represented by both its distinctive indigenous vocal, melodic and dance forms, as well as by a wide variety of modern music genres.

These features have come home to roost in the concept of theme-Irish bars which became a popular business trope all over Europe. Some of these are privately owned, some are financed by major European brewers, and others are franchised through deals with the supplier of their iconic drink, Guinness. The names on such premises reflect the connections to music as well as to Ireland, as they are harvested not only from history and literature, but also from among the personnel of nineteenth-century Irish ballad song and even tunes: Dicey Reilly's, The Foggy Dew, The Cuckoo's Nest, The Mason's Apron. Use of those titles mirrors a similar tendency popular in a different economic era, that of the developing tourism industry in pre-1970s, 'holy' Ireland, in which B&B establishments could be confidently named after Latin-titled Christian saints and religious figureheads – San Giovanni, Santiago, Sancta Maria, St Gabriel.

The comfort of antiquity

It has been stated that 'evolution' is a more appropriate term for the rise of the music pub and the session; however, 'invention' does seem accurate for the cliché-Irish bars, as they are a totally new concept. Decor is critical to their image, as explored by Tracey Dalton in this book. This accidental archive is the legacy of utilitarian consumerism, some of it left behind by the emigrants or set aside by those who stayed, a residue which now has value in the past-worshipping boom. This bricolage was retrieved by on-the-road antique merchants and house-clearance wheeler-dealers who quarried the attics and outhouses of urban and rural Ireland for junk for which there was suddenly a new function on the interior designer's palette. Ironically, these objects came to be transported overseas just like many of their one-time owners, this time via the forty-foot container, to populate the new world of 'bar-bliss', the 'pub in a box'.

The designer pubs began life as a cultural cliché, but by now they are an economic concept, traded as an environment that invokes a material experience of 'Irishness', and have become a cultural interface of some importance. They are often run by Irish personnel and so become sites of communication for not only the numerous working Irish exiles, but also the curious, nostalgic, and alternative-lifestyle non-Irish locals. The pastiche-poverty antiques are not so absurd as they are often dismissed as being, for they are familiar to most Irish people anyway, through museums and indeed many Irish pubs in Ireland, if not through direct experience in older family homes: they have an already-significant, accreted meaning. Musicians themselves have had yet more daily familiarity with such artefacts too, through countless music pub window displays, particularly at *fleadhs*, and, often, the furnishings in the bars in which they play in Ireland.

Image aside, what musician does not get a particular kick out of playing seated in a nineteenth-century chair on a flagstone floor in front of an old oak table beneath an oak-beamed, acoustically friendly ceiling surrounded by artefacts which are of a vintage with the music that is being made? So too for listeners, ambience is critically important, especially when the music is being indulged in, and experienced with regard to its place of origin and identity.[19] That is not to say that good music cannot happen in a melamine kitchen with strip lighting and vinyl chairs, but the association with antiquity relaxes the mind, mutes brash sounds and discourages noisy conversation, and assists in transporting the listener to another era. With its matching timeless ethos, traditional music, when played on the Irish pubs' sound systems, adds a leavening which hazes out any cynicism about the eclectic absurdity of the scavenged decors. Due to the clarity of the message displayed by the physical setting, the music that theme-Irish pubs offer – on the air and live – need not always be the traditional, and indeed those venues' daily soundtracks (chosen perhaps by their young Irish staff) carry Irish popular and rock music as well as traditional. But the latter does feature too, typically in a monthly or weekly session. Where, and when, it is used as a feature, it complements the old-world semiology by creating a therapeutic place of escape defined by sound, for the duration of the occasion or night concerned.[20]

All permutations of traditional and rock melodic, rhythmic, percussive and choreographic quality are perpetually peregrinating in mainland Europe, the United States, Australia and Asia – the good, the bad and the rowdy – much of it finding live, piped or casual opportunities in the theme-Irish bars. The performing, broadcast and recorded musicians therein are often the ambassadors who actively attract people to visit Ireland as tourists.[21] As argued, the most influential of the live Irish troubadours are the traditional-music performers, some of them Dubliners/Fureys/Clancys sound-alike balladeers or Christy Moore acolytes. Other are exclusively dance music players, others parade Horslips memorabilia, U2 impressions, mainstream pop and big-name rock covers, as well as modern traditional-based hybrid, singer-songwriter lyrics. Collectively, they are an aural representation of Ireland, and each version of tonal Irishness among them is an emissarial experience with its own distinct and clearly defined constituency, venues and clientele back in Ireland. All can co-exist as comfortable bed-partners in the imperial-Irish institution that is the Irish bar. So, in this way the Irish pub can be seen to have such a solid indigenous footing that it can join the émigrés and, like the tech, construction, medical and hospitality migrant Irish workers, travellers and itchy-feeters, it has the world at its disposal.

The pub has for the last half century thus evolved as a valuable complementary site for traditional-music sharing and exchange, and with it comes 'the session' as its medium of never-ending melodic conversation. Though the formative home base for traditional music in Ireland remains the thousands of local music get-togethers of all kinds which are found in weekly classes and casual sessions, these link inevitably to the network of well-known, local music bars in cities, towns and villages all over Ireland where musicians get the chance to play 'out' to cultural acclaim from appreciative audiences, an experience that incentivises them to appreciate and develop their talents, repertoires and ambitions.

Fintan Vallely's Choice:

FRIEL'S,

Miltown Malbay, County Clare

Figure 14.5 Exterior of Friel's pub (Lynch's). Photo by Johnny Wilson.

Friel's has been a Mecca for traditional music ever since the 1960s, hosting such noble figures as Willie Clancy at a time when pub music was casual and just part of community. Following Clancy's death in 1973 and the setting up of the annual summer school in his honour, the bar evolved as a spot greatly favoured by musicians, not least on account of the tremendous empathy of the proprietors Maisie and Thomas Friel. With the name 'Lynch' over the door on account of the pub having been Maisie's inheritance, it has become known under her married name, Friel, a minor aberration that can be frustrating for visitors but has never curbed the exemplary sessions, three or more of which may be happening simultaneously in its cavernous interior from lunchtime until closing during each *Scoil Samhraidh Willie Clancy* week.

Chapter 15

The Pub as Infrastructure of Musical Exchange in Contemporary Cork and Galway

Katie Young

Introduction

In the cities of Cork and Galway, pubs have become important sites of musical creation, encounter and exchange for Black-and-Irish and Afrodiasporic musicians. This chapter follows five musicians and music collectives in Cork and Galway with diverse musical styles and influences, including a soul and R&B singer, a rapper, several DJs, and an activist music collective, charting their experiences in several historic Irish pubs, including Róisín Dubh, The King's Head, and Áras na nGael in Galway, and Bull McCabe's Pub and the Sextant in Cork.

The chapter weaves together a series of musical moments in these spaces recounted by each musician or musical collective, ranging from activist projects including musical protests, performances and rehearsals relating to direct provision, to moments of musical exchange, exploration and conversation between artists and musicians in the pub. Across each short snapshot of musical exchange, musicians describe encountering new types of music in the pub, as well as experiences introducing new forms of music into Irish pubs, navigating and complicating musical expectations in Irish pub spaces, and bridging musical ideas, sounds and perspectives in the process. In combination, I show how each musician's experience in the select Irish pubs discussed functions as an example of 'infrastructures of musical exchange', dynamic spaces of creative encounter carved out of broader social space.[1]

This chapter draws on research conducted as part of 'Night Spaces: Migration, culture and IntegraTion in Europe' (NITE), a collaborative HERA-funded research project that explores experiences of migration at night across six European countries: Denmark, Portugal, the Netherland, Germany, the United Kingdom and Ireland.[2] The chapter draws from my research on music and night spaces in Cork and Galway. I was based on the west coast of Ireland from January 2020 until September 2021, conducting postdoctoral research on Black and Irish and Afrodiasporic experiences of music in night space in both cities. While the initial methodological approach for the research was solely ethnographic, the research material presented in this chapter draws on a range of methodological approaches taken in the midst of the Covid-19 pandemic lockdowns in Ireland; this includes in-person research conducted between January and February 2020, as well as online research including extended interviews and engagement with materials such as online events and music videos created by musicians during the pandemic lockdowns. Finally, this chapter draws on materials that emerged from a digital research subproject titled 'Music, Memory and the Night'.[3] This subproject explored Black and Irish as well as Afrodiasporic musicians' memories of diverse night spaces in both Cork and Galway through inter-arts collaborative engagements between musicians and visual artists living in Ireland; many of the memories that emerged centred on the pubs explored in this chapter.

The focus of the NITE project was to chart connections between migration in European cities and the emerging interdisciplinary field of night studies, exploring these connections across diverse cultural, economic and socio-political fields. Night scholars examine the distinctness of the night in relation to atmosphere, affect and interpersonal connections. For example, in his manifesto *Dark Matters*, Nick Dunn suggests that the city can be restructured at night, as new maps and narratives emerge.[4] For Robert Shaw, the night is an 'affective atmosphere' that can be generated and that can 'spill out and connect to the rest of the city'.[5] While this chapter does not explicitly focus on night space as a frame, it is not a coincidence that research participants taking part in the NITE project in Ireland frequently discussed and brought us into key historical pubs in both Galway and Cork. Pub spaces were central to experiences of Black and Irish and Afrodiasporic musicians participating in the research in both cities, highlighting the significance of these spaces as not only key sites of traditional music sessions,[6] but also of dynamic musical exchanges across diverse musical expressions, from DJ nights to rumba band performances. In the below vignettes, it is clear that the music, people, and even the physical spaces of these pubs change and adapt within night spaces as Cork and Galway musicians and musical communities converge over time. Pubs are thus a significant part of the fabric of urban night space within Ireland, an aspect that has yet to be explored in research.

Pubs as sites of musical exchange

The five pubs explored in this chapter act as 'infrastructures of musical exchange', physical sites where creative encounters take place between musicians and broader communities who frequent each space. Of course, pubs have an extended history of musical exchange, particularly in relation to Irish traditional music sessions. In her research on traditional musicians in Ireland, Jessica Cawley writes that the pub can be a space where both young musicians 'learn to negotiate their developing identities by engaging with more experienced musicians' while older musicians encounter cultural changes through engagements with younger pub attendees.[7] For traditional musicians, pub encounters can foster creative communities that challenge musical expectations of both the musician and the listeners.[8] As well as being an important space for community engagement,[9] Gallan and Gibson further argue that pub spaces 'foster the development of unique styles of local live musical production and consumption'.[10] In the Irish pub, there is a history of traditional musicians engaging with new musical styles, repertoires and social behaviours; for many, the pub thus acts as an important space not only to perform, but also to listen and learn from others, to hear 'new music and observe a different way of being in the world'.[11]

In this context, the pub not only acts as an infrastructure of musical exchange, but it also serves as a space where musical communities develop, broaden out and change through new musical encounters. At times in the vignettes below, the pub acts as a space open to transition, as well as being a space for communities in transition.[12] However, it is important to acknowledge the complexities of the pub as a site of musical exchange in these vignettes, too. Research has shown that in Ireland Black and Irish and Afrodiasporic people experience racism within pub spaces.[13] These experiences have been well-established from early research, including Casey and O'Connell's early study, which found that African and Afro-Caribbean people in Ireland had experiences of being discriminated against in entering pubs, and had further experienced verbal harassment as well as actual physical violence within pub spaces.[14] Lucy Michael's research on Afrophobia in Ireland details extended individual experiences of racism and discrimination in pubs, including a Black student in Cork being asked to leave a pub, or a self-identified mixed race woman in Newbridge not being served a drink in a pub, while hearing other patrons say that 'their kind isn't welcome here'.[15] Michael is clear to assert that, 'given the established centrality of pubs and bars in Irish social life, it is essential to see their inaccessibility to Black people as deeply problematic'.[16]

Other factors influence how some individuals might access or feel excluded from pub spaces, including the presence of alcohol and how this might influence or inform attendance in pubs for religious or other reasons; in this case, feelings of inclusion can be inhibited by socio-spatial dynamics of community spaces.[17] As Fathi and Ní Laoire suggest of their research participants, many of whom were refugees in Ireland:

> The cultural hegemony of Irish society and Cork city is intertwined with practices and places that many of the participants do not approve of, or feel belonging to, such as drinking in pubs.[18]

The following vignettes provide complex experiences of pub spaces that both reflect on and pause at experiences of reshaping as well as inhabiting pub spaces, navigating and bending expectations of musical practice within these spaces. It is important to note that the pub spaces discussed in this chapter are inevitably siloed; the chapter does not explore the spaces where Afrodiasporic and Black and Irish musicians did not feel welcome to enter, or were blocked from or unable to hold their musical events, gigs or practices.[19] The diverse recollections and experiences of each musician below reveal a multiplicity of experiences of pub spaces in Cork and Galway for Black and Irish and Afrodiasporic musicians, centred on moments of musical exchange.

Róisín Dubh, Galway city

Róisín Dubh (translated loosely as 'black rose') in Galway is a live music and comedy venue situated in the centre of the city. The space hosts international comedians and musicians on tour as well as emerging artists living in Galway. During my research as part of the NITE project, Róisín Dubh arose twice as a central venue for two different musicians involved in the research.

As part of the 'Music, Memory and the Night' subproject (detailed above), we asked Afro-Irish singer-songwriter Tolü Makay about her musical memories of the night in Galway, and to record these memories in an audio diary. Tolü Makay is a well-known vocalist in Ireland, born in Nigeria and raised in the midlands of Ireland, subsequently moving from Tullamore to Galway for university. Makay has in recent years grown to international recognition as a pop and R&B musician. For the 'Music, Memory and the Night' project, Makay recollected a series of musical experiences during her time living in Galway for university; she then sent her recorded recollection to visual artist Somto Amadi-Obi to use as inspiration for a commissioned artwork.

Figure 15.1 Exterior of Róisín Dubh, Galway. Courtesy of *Hot Press*.

In her recorded memory, Makay wove between memories of diverse spaces with divergent experiences, ranging from experiences of leading her church choir, to a nightclub where she experienced 'something racial face-to-face' for the first time, to everyone converging at Supermac's in Galway city centre at the end of a gig. In this interwoven tapestry of night spaces that shaped her musical experiences of Galway, Makay pauses to reflect on Róisín Dubh:

> I remember a night I was in, I think, is it called Róisín Dubh? I think it was one of the most famous places for music in Galway. I didn't know that at the time. I just went to go visit a friend of mine who was also studying psychology. He had a band and he was doing pretty well. Yeah, it was kind of like a rock, rock band. And one thing I noticed is that with rock bands, they never have a keyboardist. It's always a guitarist, a bassist, a singer and a drummer. And I found that so fascinating because in the church you always need a keys player. That was like, so fundamental. So, it was so different seeing that kind of, like, dynamic and seeing music could be played that way. There was just something so electrifying about it.[20]

Figure 15.2 Commissioned artwork for 'Music, Memory and the Night' by Somto Amadi-Obi, featuring depictions of Róisín Dubh on the right of the artwork.

Makay's recollection reflects an important aspect of Róisín Dubh as an 'infrastructure of musical exchange'; she notes the 'dynamic' and 'electrifying' aspects of encountering a different musical makeup of performance in this setting. The recollection speaks to different kinds of musical expressions found in different spaces throughout Galway city (for example, the differing musical textures of church choir in comparison to a rock band in a pub), but also makes clear the importance of Makay moving between these spaces as a central part of her musical journey in Galway and subsequently in Ireland and internationally. The significance of this moment was subsequently captured in the commissioned artwork for the subproject, created by Somto Amadi-Obi. Based in Offaly, Amadi-Obi draws on Nigerian/African influences in his artwork. In the artwork commissioned for this subproject, Makay's moment of encountering a friend perform live at Róisín Dubh is depicted on the right-hand side, layered onto a line-drawn map of County Galway in combination with her musical memories in the church choir on the left-hand side.[21]

While Makay's experience of music within Róisín Dubh was encountering new musical arrangements different to her experience of church music performance, Theo Ndlovu's experiences of this venue involved introducing new sounds and developing community around his music within this pub.[22] Ndlovu is a Zimbabwean-born rapper and DJ who has lived in Galway for eight years, and has lived in the direct provision system.[23] Ndlovu's initial experience of Róisín Dubh began with attending open mic nights, where he would rap in front of a new audience each week. The open mic night, which has been running since the mid-1990s, has been predominantly attended by White-Irish 'singer-songwriters'. In this instance, Ndlovu's performances in the open mic space at Róisín Dubh highlight the pub space as an infrastructure of musical exchange, where Ndlovu introduces rapping (including those highlighting his experiences of living in direct provision), offering new musical style and sound into the space, but also new lyrical content that connects experiences of asylum-seeking in Galway to those who may not share this experience.

Ndlovu's continued performances within Róisín Dubh over time were met by a diverse group of musicians who regularly frequented the pub. When Ndlovu was given an order for deportation in January 2020 by the Irish government, Róisín Dubh became a site of activism and protest, where funds were raised for Ndlovu's case through a series of musical performances by diverse musicians who attended open mic nights at the venue, including a zydeco group, an experimental one-man-

Figure 15.3 Ndlovu performing at the 'Save Theo' event in Róisín Dubh. Photo by Katie Young.

band, several singer-songwriters, a rock band, and another rapper, as well as Ndlovu performing at the end of the night.[24] At the 'Save Theo' night, Ndlovu spoke about his experiences living in direct provision, while other musicians who frequent Róisín Dubh talked about their musical interactions and experiences with Ndlovu. Róisín Dubh became a space where diverse musical communities interacted and performed in support of Ndlovu's valuable role as a Galwegian musician and member of the musical community. In many ways, this event developed precisely *because* of Ndlovu's ongoing engagement with and bending of the musical boundaries of the space through regular attendance at the open mic nights.

Throughout the NITE project, Róisín Dubh was a site of multiple experiences for Black and Irish musicians living in Galway. For Makay, the venue was a site for encountering new musical arrangements and possibilities while attending a gig, while Ndlovu's experiences show how an artist steps into and reframes the musical boundaries of music within a pub space in Galway over time, ultimately reflecting new forms of musical communities in the process. Both instances reflect the pub environment as an infrastructure of musical exchange, shaping and reshaping musical communities and musical expression in the city.

Bull McCabe's, Kinsale Road, Cork

In Cork's Kinsale Road direct provision centre there is a musical group called Citadel, made up of musicians living in the centre. Together, they bring diverse musical expertise from global perspectives, and draw on their musical practices in collective weekly sessions where they jam and explore new songs and musical possibilities together. In January and February 2020, I began to attend these music sessions as a central part of music and night space for migrant musicians living in Cork. While my time at these sessions was cut short due to the onset of the Covid-19 pandemic, I witnessed important collaborations that were soon brought into Bull McCabe's on Kinsale Road.

Citadel is a group that emerged as one of the creative projects of Roos Demol and Norbert Nkengurutse, who initially began collecting guitars for those living in direct provision in 2017. A key aim of the group is to provide access to music for those living in direct provision, but also to bring residents together through regular musical sessions that take place within the centre. As the group has grown and taken on public performances, Citadel also works to raise awareness about living conditions in the centre through public engagement. Musicians bring their own musical influences, languages and instruments to practice sessions, and collaborate in new ways together through music. From an early stage, Bull McCabe's, a pub close to the Kinsale Road direct provision centre in Cork, became a site where Citadel musicians from the centre could perform. While Bull McCabe's regularly hosts trad music nights, it also began to host events run by Demol and Nkengurutse, including World Music Day events and practice nights in preparation for Citadel performances in Cork's city centre. For example, a fundraising music event in August 2018 was advertised on social media as:

> Musicians from across the globe will join the traditional Irish band to entertain you with music in the car park of Bull McCabe's, free entry, but donations are welcome in aid of the Guitars for People in Direct Provisions Project.

The interconnection between the pub space and Citadel is evidenced in the public promotion flyer pictured here:

Figure 15.4 Poster of Citadel performance during World Music Day at Bull McCabe's pub. Photo by Katie Young.

On one of my visits to a Citadel practice in early 2020, I witnessed a musical collaboration that soon migrated from the Kinsale Road direct provision centre to Bull McCabe's pub. A Nigerian musician who was new to the group was encouraged to perform a song of his choice, and he picked 'African Queen' by 2Face, a Nigerian singer-songwriter. As the sakara drummer/singer began to first perform the melody on his Nigerian sakara drum, and subsequently sing the song, Nkengurutse began to improvise on the guitar, playing together with the sakara drummer for the first time. Soon after this meeting, Citadel organised a jam session at Bull McCabe's pub and invited musicians from University College Cork (UCC) to play with them in preparation for upcoming events (ultimately curtailed by the onset of the Covid-19 pandemic). While I was unable to attend this particular gig, videos posted on social media showed how the collaboration that had emerged between the singer and guitarist weeks earlier in the direct provision centre had moved into this pub space, with a full live performance of 'African Queen' accompanied by a range of musicians from University College Cork.[25] The pub became an infrastructure of musical exchange, where artists from Kinsale Road direct provision centre are not only musically collaborating with trad musicians and UCC music students at different points, but are also introducing their musical influences and musical instruments to those who attend Bull McCabe's on a regular basis; this includes trad musicians who perform at Bull McCabe's, who are themselves involved in ongoing musical exchanges in Cork's pub spaces on a regular basis.[26] In doing so, musicians of Citadel reshape the sonic infrastructures of this pub, while also creating connectivity between this pub (including its attendees and trad musicians) and the direct provision centre, both located on Cork's Kinsale Road.

The King's Head, Galway

The King's Head, a historic building with medieval heritage located in the Latin Quarter of Galway city, holds free live music gigs daily; the historic nature of the pub draws in a wide range of tourists who visit Galway city. Theo Ndlovu, known as DJ Touché and introduced earlier in this chapter in relation to Galway's Róisín Dubh venue, regularly DJs at the King's Head in addition to his open mic performances at Róisín Dubh. While rapping in open mics afforded the development of new communities within Róisín Dubh, his experience of taking on gigs at the King's Head offers a different perspective on the pub space as an infrastructure of musical exchange. In a research interview with Ndlovu, he detailed his experiences of 'testing the waters' each night that he DJs at the King's Head, working to navigate the expectations of a crowd of pub-goers, including tourists. When asked how he curates his music at the King's Head, he explained:

> It depends on the crowd. Just for me personally people tell you, 'Okay play this and that and that and that and that.' No. But I always test the waters. If there's a crowd that accepts, the crowd, if they feel new stuff you give them new stuff. If they feel old stuff, if they don't want anything new, you give them what they want. Just read the crowd. That's how it is, that's what I always do. I read the crowd and I give them what they want. And the thing about me is I listen to everything and I always have different categories of that, like genres and all that stuff. Like King's Head, I know this is what they listen to. But I can edit a little bit of flavour in there and then see how they take it. If they like it, that's cool. I'll slowly throw my bass with that, okay, cool … and then there's a time, say maybe ten minutes, I'll be playing something new that they don't know, but they'll still be grooving to it.[27]

DJ Touché has spent enough time DJ-ing at the King's Head to know what patrons listen to, but also to feel out and 'test the waters' as to what can be edited, pushing the boundaries of the sounds of the King's Head pub each weekend. The back-and-forth negotiation between DJ Touché and King's Head audiences further evidences the pub space as an infrastructure of musical exchange, where at times DJ Touché feels there is enough space to play something entirely new, including Afrobeat music, that audiences may not know but will 'groove to'. This historical pub is another space in which Black and Irish as well as those seeking asylum in Galway reframe the sonic environment in dialogue with those who attend the space over time.

The Sextant, Cork

The Sextant in Cork is a historic pub built in 1877 on Albert Quay. As will be clear in this section, the venue played an important role in opening up new performance

Figure 15.5 The Sextant being demolished in 2020. Photo by Owen O'Connor.

spaces for Black and Irish musicians and artists starting out in Cork until its closure in 2019 and its subsequent demolition.

As part of the 'Music, Memory and the Night' subproject, DJ Safarii, a Black and Irish DJ from Cork, reflected on her experiences in this pub.[28] The Sextant pub was one of the first places that DJ Safarii performed, and in her recollections she recalls the vulnerabilities of performing in a venue that drew a range of diverse musicians, dancers and audience members as part of a regular 'reggae night' that took place in the pub. In her memory, DJ Safarii recalled the pub being attended by 'your Rastafarians … hippies … French crowd, all just vibing to the music',[29] and she reflects on becoming more comfortable in the pub space, feeling unsure of introducing Afrobeats and R&B songs into an already established 'reggae night' that centred on reggae music.[30] Ultimately, she reflects on connecting with the vibe of the room, working to play the music that aligned with the movement of people in the space. This memory reveals an invitation of an emerging Black and Irish DJ into a historic pub, as she grapples with navigating the integration of her own musical influences (Afrobeat and R&B) among existing

Figure 15.6 Commissioned artwork for 'Music, Memory and the Night' by Grace Enemaku

expectations of reggae. This experience is reflected in the commissioned artwork by Grace Enemaku, that visually re-imagines DJ Safarii's experiences in the Sextant.

While the site itself has since been demolished, engaging with memories of night spaces from Black and Irish musicians in Ireland reveals important sites of musical exchange that take place within these built environments. While DJ Safarii now performs in larger nightclubs and venues across Ireland, the pub stands as an emergent space of encounter, engagement and navigation between diverse Afrodiasporic and Black and Irish musicians and a broader musical community in Cork.

Áras na nGael, Galway

Wally Nkikita is a multi-genre musician who plays in rumba bands, is a choir leader and a DJ, and is the organiser of Galway African Diaspora, a community group that runs monthly Afromusic nights in Áras na nGael, an Irish-language centre in Galway city with a community pub.[31] Having lived in direct provision in Galway, Nkikita works to develop a space where musicians living in direct provision are able to come, dance and DJ in a space that is decorated with posters from Galway's annual Africa Day events, while also focusing on playing Afrobeat music. In my interview with Nkikita in the summer of 2020, he explained that some patrons of Áras na nGael had written negative things about the inclusion of Afromusic nights in the pub on the Facebook page, including that the Irish culture had been lost by having this event in the space.[32]

Figure 15.7 An Afromusic night in Áras na nGael, Galway, February 2020. Photo by Katie Young.

Figure 15.8 Commissioned artwork for 'Music, Memory and the Night' by Elton Sibanda. Photo by Katie Young.

At the same time, Nkikita reflects on the willingness of many in Galway to attend and take part and dance in the monthly events. Nkikita also attends Irish trad music nights on Sundays, and has worked to collaborate and perform with musicians, mixing the Irish language with multiple African languages in their compositions.

The memories of performing in Áras na nGael were featured in Nkikita's collaboration as part of the 'Music, Memory and the Night' subproject, through which he reflected on the significance of the Afromusic nights in developing a broader musical community in Galway:

> It was so emotional, that night was enjoyable to all who took part. As performers and crowds, we really feel that we need more of that … what we do really in Galway city, promoting African culture with our event, is really helping the local community to understand what is the difference between Irish music and African music, because some people will come and ask you, 'We never heard of that kind of music before, but where is it from?' And you have to explain to them that the music is in an African beat. So, we are there to promote it in that city, so we can let people know that there are Africans living in Galway city too.[33]

Sibanda's commissioned art reflects the significance of Afromusic nights in Áras na nGael, where a tapestry of different posters from Galway's Africa Day events cover the walls while the dimly lit room invites diverse crowds to dance together, engaging with music that may be incredibly significant or may be new, inviting conversation and engagement within the pub space.

Conclusion

This chapter has presented a series of snapshots reflecting diverse experiences of Black and Irish and Afrodiasporic musicians in pub spaces in Galway and Cork, where these musicians have created musical moments of performance, listening and activism. In each instance, musicians reflect on moments of musical exchange, whether it be Tolü Makay's engagement with new ways of arranging music in Róisín Dubh, DJ Touché's testing of waters with diverse crowds, including tourists, in the King's Head in Galway, or DJ Safarii's encounters with reggae night at the Sextant in Cork. Each moment reflects the flexibility and ever-changing state of pub spaces in Ireland, where those who attend hold purpose and the ability to alter and reshape spaces sonically, aesthetically and culturally through their musical input. In the spaces detailed here, pubs act as infrastructures of exchange, affording new possibilities and opportunities for collaboration among urban communities.

The significance of pub spaces here revolves around the dynamic nature of musical genres, activities, and people who attend these spaces. As is clear from the above vignettes, pub spaces are – and have historically been – home to musicians, dancers and revellers who range in age, musical interests and dancing abilities, and who come from diverse backgrounds. As each Afrodiasporic and Black and Irish musician discussed in this chapter entered a pub space, they brought musical interests, insights and influences that ultimately shaped the space, while also being shaped by and influenced by other musicians and communities in the pub space. In this regard, the Irish pub represents a unique infrastructure of musical exchange that has emerged through research on migration in night space in Ireland.

Katie Young's Choice:

Ryan's Irish pub,

Accra, Ghana

Figure 15.9 Ryan's Irish pub. Photo by Hiroo Yamagata.

Ryan's Irish pub in Accra, Ghana is known as a 'traditional Irish pub in the heart of West Africa'. A large yellow and green multi-storey building with a large garden area, it is located in the heart of Accra's trendy and culturally vibrant neighbourhood of Osu. The pub is popular with tourists and residents alike due to being one of the only Irish pubs in Ghana, with its claim to fame being that it is the only pub in the country to have Guinness on draft. As you enter the pub you are met by a range of decorations from across Ireland, as well as Irish music filling the air. The pub was established by Wexford-born Martin Ryan in the 1980s and to this day remains an important stopping-off point for those unwinding after work and for weekend revellers.'

Part 4

The Future of the Irish Pub

The Perfect Pub

Kevin Martin

They'd arrived at the pub, which for Don Fernando was the same as arriving in heaven, where all the wretchedness of the earth comes to an end.

Miguel de Cervantes, *Don Quixote*[1]

There is nothing which has yet been contrived by man, by which so much happiness is produced as by a good tavern or inn.

Samuel Johnson[2]

From the towns all inns have been driven; from the villages most ... Change your hearts, or you will lose your inns, and you will have deserved to have lost them. But when you have lost your inns, drown your empty selves – for you will have lost the last of England.

Hilaire Belloc[3]

Perhaps the most famous description of the 'perfect pub' in literature is that provided by George Orwell in his 1943 treatise on a fictional establishment called the Moon Under Water. In his last ever contribution to the *Evening Standard*, Orwell outlined ten characteristics of his perfect hostelry in his *Saturday Essay* column.[4] In beautifully crafted and economic prose Orwell noted that his ideal pub was in London, located two minutes from the nearest bus stop, on a side street where 'rowdies never seem to find their way there, even on a Saturday night'. Its clientele consisted mostly of 'regulars' who occupied the same chair every evening and went to the pub for conversation as much as for the beer. He noted that many people chose their favourite pub because of the quality of the beer but his primary concern was the 'atmosphere'. He is unequivocal in stating that the Moon Under Water was 'uncompromisingly Victorian':

> It has no glass-topped tables or other modern miseries, and, on the other hand, no sham roof-beams, ingle-nooks or plastic panels masquerading as oak. The grained woodwork, the ornamental mirrors behind the bar, the cast-iron fireplaces, the florid ceiling stained dark yellow by tobacco-smoke, the stuffed bull's head over the mantelpiece – everything has the solid, comfortable ugliness of the nineteenth century.[5]

The Moon Under Water had at least one fire and contained 'a public bar, a saloon bar, a ladies' bar, a bottle-and-jug for those who are too bashful to buy their supper beer publicly, and, upstairs, a dining-room'.[6] He had no truck with darts, music or singing and, even on Christmas Eve, singing should be 'of a decorous kind'. His views on the bar staff were decidedly of his time:

> The barmaids know most of their customers by name and take a personal interest in everyone. They are all middle-aged women – two of them have their hair dyed in quite surprising shades – and they call everyone 'dear', irrespective of age or sex. ('Dear', not 'Ducky': pubs where the barmaid calls you 'ducky' always have a disagreeable raffish atmosphere.)

The Moon Under Water sold tobacco as well as cigarettes, aspirins and stamps, and was obliging about letting customers use the telephone. While no dinner was available, a snack counter provided liver-sausage sandwiches, mussels, cheese, pickles and 'those large biscuits with caraway seeds in them which only seem to exist in public-houses'. Upstairs one could avail of a 'solid lunch' for about three shillings while, most importantly, the pub served a 'type of creamy draught stout' in pewter pots or china mugs. The Moon Over Water had a garden at the back with plane trees, tables and chairs, as well as swings and a 'chute' for children.[7] The latter features made it a place where all the family could go. Orwell concluded that regrettably there was no pub in London with all the requisite characteristics – although he knew of an unnamed establishment that had eight – and would be glad to hear of any from his readers: 'If anyone knows of a pub that has draught stout, open fires, cheap meals, a garden, motherly barmaids and no radio, I should be glad to hear of it, even though its name were something as prosaic as the *Red Lion* or the *Railway Arms.*' While Orwell's biographer D.J. Taylor noted that Orwell tended to sentimentalise his musings on pubs as a symbol of working-class life, they still provide a valuable social document.[8]

Jessica Boak and Ray Bailey, authors of *20th Century Pub*, noted that Orwell had a particular distaste for what they term the 'improved pubs' of the interwar years and reference *The Road to Wigan Pier* to bolster their contention. Here Orwell described such establishments as 'dismal sham-Tudor places fitted out by the big brewery companies and very expensive'.[9] His allusions to pubs did not stop there. In *Nineteen Eighty-Four*, Winston Smith takes a stroll through the 'Prole' neighbourhood, entering a pub to talk to an old man about the pre-war days, while in *Animal Farm* Mr Jones commiserates in the 'Red Lion', thought to be inspired by the Red Lion in Willingdon, East Sussex.[10]

In what might be considered a deep irony by many pub aficionados, the often much-maligned J.D. Wetherspoon pub chain used the name The Moon Under Water for thirteen of its outlets as of 2018.[11] The great man himself might even subscribe to the notion that such cookie-cutter pubs, with their abrasive music, jangling poker machines, questionable food and cheap lager might best be described as dystopian.[12] While it has never been proven, some authorities suggest the pub Orwell had most in mind was The Compton Arms in Highbury, London, a place now at a vast remove from his original conception of the perfect local.[13]

In 2017 You.Gov Omnibus carried out a survey (Fig. 16.1) across Britain to see if the characteristics George Orwell had outlined for his perfect pub had persisted in popular consciousness. As with so much of his brilliant and prescient literature and nonfiction, the overall picture Orwell had painted had largely stood the test of time.

The results highlighted how different men and women's ideal pubs were. Women were more likely than men to want their ideal pub to serve meals (74 per cent versus 60 per cent). When it came to choice of drinks, men were much more likely to say that their ideal pub would serve real ale (46 per cent versus 28 per cent for women), while women were more likely to want it to serve cocktails (31 per cent versus 14 per cent for men). Women were more likely to appreciate the presence of a fireplace (58 per cent versus 45 per cent of men) and background music (39 per cent versus 30 per cent), while men preferred televisions on the walls (22 per cent versus 13 per cent of women). Perhaps inevitably, more men want both televised and pub sports in their ideal establishment. Additionally, they were more likely to want it to show sports (27 per cent versus 9 per cent of women) and to have a snooker/pool table (29

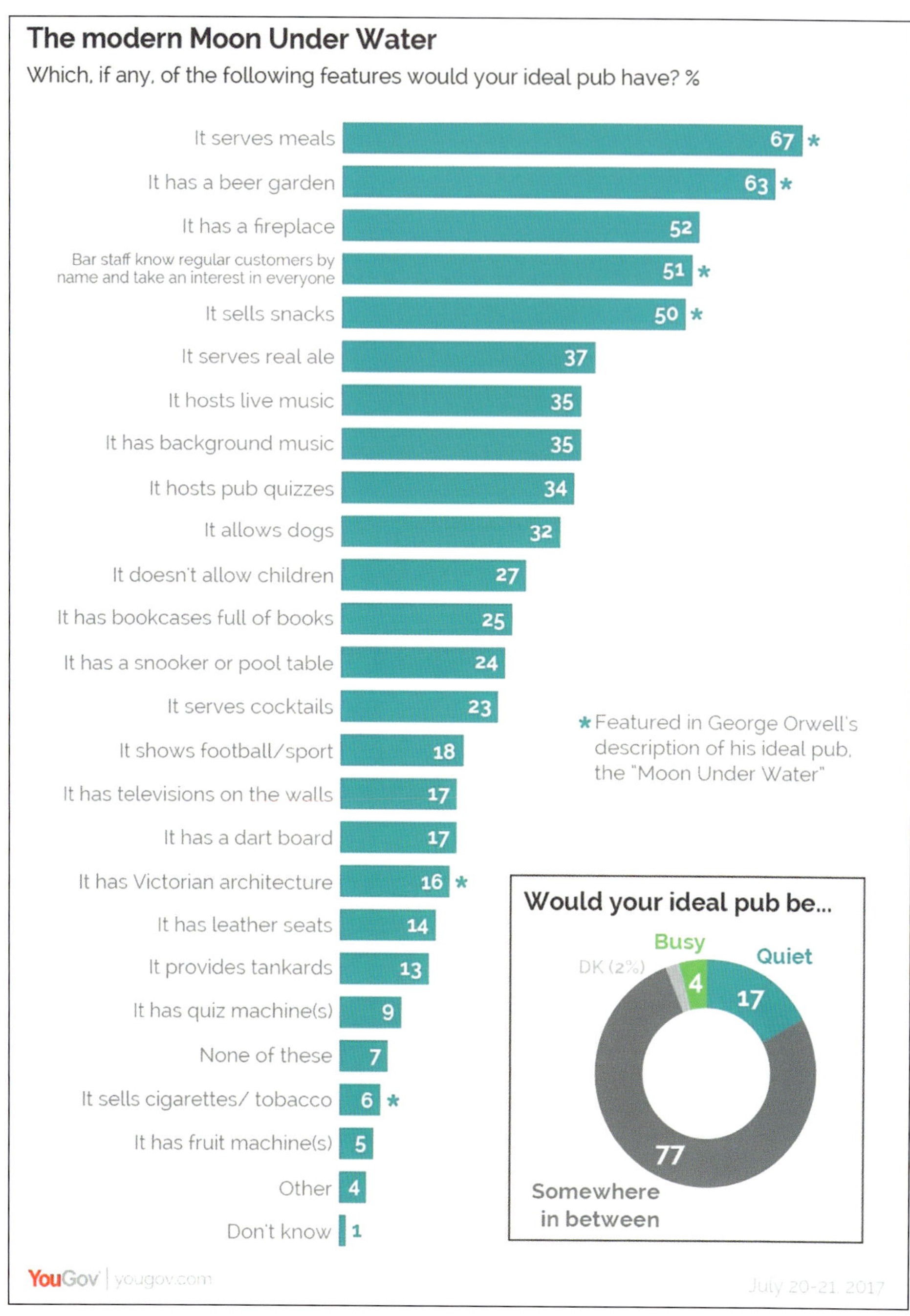

Figure 16.1 Graph of 'Ideal Pub Features'. Matthew Smith, 'What Britain's Ideal Pub Looks Like', 8 August 2017, yougov.co.uk.

per cent versus 19 per cent) and dart board (21 per cent versus 13 per cent). Modern technology, of course, has made the need for an available phone largely redundant but that is not to say there are not clients who may request such. While these statistics are British, it is most likely that they replicate the situation in Ireland, based on the author's experience and interviews with customers and publicans over the years.

If Orwell reached the pinnacle of literary analysis in his description and conception of the perfect pub, then the theory of 'third places' in the work of American sociologist Ray Oldenburg could be viewed as seminal in the academic treatment of drinking establishments. Oldenburg identifies third places as public places on neutral ground where people can gather and interact. His unlikely 1989 bestseller, *The Great Good Place: Cafés, coffee shops, bookstores, bars, hair salons, and other hangouts at the heart of a community*, compared first places (home) and second places (work) to third places like cafés and pubs which, he argued, allow people to put aside their concerns and simply enjoy the company and conversation around them. Third places, Oldenburg wrote, 'host the regular, voluntary, informal, and happily anticipated gatherings of individuals beyond the realms of home and work'.[14]

Oldenburg posited that beer gardens, main streets, pubs, cafés, coffee houses, post offices and other third places are the heart of a community's social vitality. Providing the foundation for a functioning democracy, he contended, these spaces promote social equity by levelling the status of guests, providing a setting for grassroots politics, creating habits of public association and offering psychological support to individuals and communities. Oldenburg believed that functioning third places are characterised by a regular clientele who enjoy themselves in a way that may often be counterpointed by experiences in the home or workplace. The third place may also be similar in some respects to a good home or workplace where psychological comfort is obtained. In its totality, it was an erudite and pithy conception of the role a pub can play when viewed as a nexus of community engagement.

Oldenburg noted that there was a dwindling number of places in American suburbia where people could gather easily, inexpensively, regularly and pleasurably: '"a place on the corner", real life alternatives to television, easy escapes from the cabin fever of marriage and family life that do not necessitate getting into an automobile'. With a diminution of viable third places, he believed life for many was nothing more than a 'home-to-work-and-back-again shuttle'. Oldenburg had a particular distaste for the ubiquitous shopping malls dotting American suburbia with their 'constant, monotonous flow of mall pedestrian traffic' and lack of familiar faces. Reading his work as a social document and a metanarrative of contemporary America is highly instructive and chimes with ideas expressed in the wider body of social and cultural history.[15]

Boiling his work down to its essence, Oldenburg contends that pubs and bars are examples of perfect third places. He wrote of English pubs, but the similarity to Irish pubs is obvious. For Oldenburg the perfect pub is often plain and unpretentious, keeps a low profile and is the perfect locale for providing the degree of playfulness that may not be possible elsewhere. The unique potential of drinking establishments to become ideal third places derives from what he terms the 'fundamental synergism' that arises when alcohol and good company come together. Arguably he could not have put it better. At their best, he contended, these spaces provide citizens a critical opportunity to play, learn, complain, bond and tease one other about their political opinions in a manner not often found in other public spaces.

Oldenburg went on to outline how cafés, beer gardens and tearooms have played critical roles in democratic and revolutionary movements. In fact, he argues, when one grasps the radical freedom these spaces provide it is 'not difficult to understand why coffee houses came under attack by government leaders in England, Scandinavia, and in Saudi Arabia at various points in history'. It was, he notes, 'in coffee houses where people congregated and often, in their discussions, found fault with their countries' rulers'.[16] A codicil that could arguably be added to this strand of his argument might be that Irish pubs, through the centuries of occupation and usurpation by British authorities, were viewed as hotbeds of sedition.

In concluding, Oldenburg bemoans the loss of bars in his native United States: 'The tavern is a failing institution, perhaps even an endangered species … While avoiding few of the problems surrounding alcoholic beverages the nation is losing the socially solidifying rituals of public drinking within inclusive and democratic settings.'[17] Oldenburg's writing on third spaces can be distilled down to eight characteristics, all of which have immediate relevance to pubs. A good third place is a neutral ground, a leveller, a place where conversation is the main activity, is accessible, has regulars, keeps a low profile, has a playful mood and functions as a home away from home.

Perhaps, between the thoughts of George Orwell and Ray Oldenburg, we have arrived at the definition of a perfect pub. However, neither of them had anything to say specifically about Irish pubs, so it may be of benefit to look further in our conception of the perfect Irish hostelry. Various reports over the years have outlined the centrality of pubs to communities in Ireland, with most of them foregrounding their particular importance in rural Ireland. Regardless of the possible inherent bias of some of these documents,[18] they consistently make the point that the pub is a perfect third place in any given rural Irish community. It might not be the perfect pub for many of the inhabitants, but it may be the only one there is and, by default, provides the best option for fulfilling the needs outlined by Oldenburg and Orwell.

In 2014 Dr Ignazio Cabras of the Newcastle Business School, Northumbria University, and Dr Matthew Mount of the Kent Business School at the University of Kent in Canterbury authored an impressive report for the Vintners' Federation of Ireland (VFI) entitled *How Third Places Foster and Shape Community Cohesion, Economic Development and Social Capital: The case of pubs in rural Ireland*.[19] The document inevitably focused on the economic role of the pub in rural Ireland, but also included data drawn from focus groups and interviews with what the authors termed 'pillars' and 'sentinels' of the communities in question, seeking to ascertain their perception and opinions of the roles played by the pub in the participants' respective locales. The report set out to examine three central questions: What was the relationship between pubs as third places and rural communities and economies in the Irish countryside? How was this relationship affecting the level of community cohesion and well-being and the formation of social capital at a local level? And, if the disappearance of these places did represent a threat to rural communities and residents, what solutions might be adopted to address this issue?

The authors note that, among third places, pubs play a pivotal role within local communities and act as incubators for different types of activities, such as the creation of sport teams and events, the organisation of charity and volunteering initiatives, as well as other happenings involving arts, culture and market fairs. These events and initiatives foster socialisation, involvement and engagement among locals, that determine and expand the quality of social networks and enhance the provision of social capital at a local level. Pubs, the authors note, were often pointed to by interviewees as the strongest facilitators of socialisation and engagement in the local community. Respondents also indicated that pubs were preferred places for hosting events, mainly due to the quality of facilities such as kitchens and room size in comparison to other local options.

The authors include examples from interviews where the focus was firmly on the sense of community attached to the local pub. Among the significant array of functions served by the local pubs discussed by participants were the celebrating or commiserating of local sporting results, going there after funerals and other family occasions and rites of passage, hosting local clubs like drama societies, the creation of employment, and providing a locus for the tourist trade and a social outlet for those living in isolated areas and conditions, a drum that has long been beaten by local politicians. It is difficult to argue that the pub does not play a crucial role in the lives of some people in rural communities throughout Ireland, and for many it may indeed be the only suitable third place to interact with others. The cynic might argue that the lily is overgilded in studies of this nature. Notwithstanding these reservations, for these people, then, the local pub may well be, by extrapolation, their idea of the perfect pub.

It is all very well writing about the perfect pub, but what if there were no pubs at all? The decline in the number of pubs in Ireland has garnered the most headlines in the industry for well over a decade. The report *The Irish Pub: Stopping the decline*, released in 2022 and based on the Drinks Industry Group of Ireland analysis of Revenue licence data, including an economic and social analysis by Dublin City University professor and economist Anthony Foley, showed a 21 per cent decline in the number of pubs in Ireland from 2005 to 2021.[20] Overall, twenty-three counties had decreases in the number of pubs of greater than 10 per cent. In 2005, for example, there were 467 pubs in Mayo with 350 remaining in 2021, a drop of 117, or 25 per cent. Laois was worst affected, reporting a 31 per cent decline, while Meath suffered the least with a mere 1.4 per cent decline. The report outlined the role it saw for the pub and why the continuing decline was a worry for rural Irish society.

Echoing Cabras and Mount, Foley noted that public houses contribute to tourism and provide an extensive network of physical facilities and services needed by tourists and locals, particularly in isolated rural areas. These services could include provision of hospitality, food, entertainment, traditional music, a venue for local community events, a pleasant ambience, information and physical facilities. Taken together, these reports are significant evidence of the centrality of the pub to Irish culture, but also highlight the dark hinterland of decreasing numbers and the continuing diminution of third places, particularly in rural Ireland.

Foley was commissioned to update his report in 2023 and noted a continued decline. In 2022 alone over a hundred pubs closed their doors, bringing the total decline since 2005 close to the 2,000 mark.[21] The rate of closure had increased to

22.5 per cent, from 8,617 in 2005 to 6,680 for the most recent period in 2022, a closure of 1,937 public houses across the country since 2005. There were some slight changes over the twenty-six counties. This time Limerick suffered the most with a 32 per cent decline, followed by Roscommon (30 per cent), Cork (30 per cent), Laois (30 per cent), Offaly (29 per cent), Leitrim (29 per cent), Tipperary (29 per cent), Mayo (28 per cent), Longford (27 per cent) and Donegal (26 per cent). This time the lowest decrease was in Dublin at 3.4 per cent. As an aside, there may be an argument that there has been an historical oversupply of pubs in much of Ireland.

On 25 March 2022, Heather Humphreys, then minister for rural and community development, launched a 'Pubs as Community Hubs' pilot programme specifically aimed at supporting rural pubs in Ireland to diversify their facilities for community use.[22] The programme was based on the 'Pub is the Hub' model introduced in England to make pubs viable in areas where they had closed or were in imminent danger of doing so.[23] The essence of the model is straightforward: the pub becomes a venue for a plethora of activities from digital hotdesking to cinema and everything suitable in between. In many cases the pub is owned by the community through a share system and run democratically, based on 'one member, one vote'. Membership is voluntary, affordable and open to all. The Pub is the Hub, the umbrella organisation for participating British pubs, is a not-for-profit venture and offers advice and support to publicans and their communities who are looking to relocate, re-open or introduce vital services and activities in their local pub, as well as to communities considering the options for acquiring their local pub and the range of responsibilities involved. It facilitates projects by encouraging and helping publicans, communities and other interested parties to connect and share their experiences and work together to support and sustain their local services as well as trying to help source local funding opportunities for projects. Even King Charles (then Prince Charles) gave his imprimatur to the project: 'Rural communities, and this country's rural way of life, face unprecedented challenges. The country pub, which has been at the heart of village life for centuries, is disappearing in many areas. Providing services from the pub, such as a post office or a shop, keeps an essential service in the village.'[24] Since its establishment in 2002, when The White Hart, Blythburgh, and The Craven Heifer, Stainforth, came into being as community pubs, it has been remarkably successful and a perfect example of how pubs can be made central to the life of the community again. Two decades later Prince Charles noted in the foreword of the *2023 Good Beer*

Figure 16.2 Exterior of The Keepers Arms, Bawnboy, County Cavan. Photo by John P. Younge Real Estate.

Guide that 'pubs are interwoven in the very fabric of British history, and they are still a much-loved and vital asset of local communities up and down the country'.[25]

Ireland has been slow to follow suit, but there have been encouraging signs. In 2021 Maudie's in Rathgormack, County Waterford was bought by a group of locals to save it from closing.[26] In launching the Irish government initiative in 2022 at The Keepers Arms in Bawnboy, County Cavan, Humphreys suggested that pubs could consider community cinemas, digital hubs, arts and crafts workshops, libraries, marketplaces for local producers and community meeting spaces as possible initiatives under the scheme. The Department of Rural and Community Development provided €50,000 to the Vintners' Federation of Ireland to select five pubs in counties Cavan, Kerry, Donegal, Clare and Cork to participate in the pilot. The VFI's CEO Padraig Cribben welcomed the initiative, stating that he hoped it would provide a roadmap for the organisation's members as they navigate future challenges and opportunities faced by the rural hospitality sector.

At the launch, Sheila and Bryan McKiernan, proprietors of The Keepers Arms, outlined their plans to install a community cinema under the new initiative with the hope of promoting local community integration and assist with combating rural isolation: 'Ireland is changing but through initiatives like this the pub can still be at the heart of rural communities – sometimes it just takes a little bit of thinking outside the box.'[27] It will be of immense interest to publicans and those who frequent pubs to see how these projects fare. If the perfect pub is a crucial third space in any given community, this is a model that may well go some way to reinforce this position.

It is no surprise to learn that Guinness Brewing International/Worldwide (now Diageo) were the originators of the Irish Pub Concept. Based on market research completed between 1985 and 1995 the company observed that each time an Irish pub opened anywhere in the world there was a spike in Guinness sales, and they attributed this to the addition of an Irish pub as well as the provision of the drink itself. The world wanted the Irish pub, the company deduced, and Guinness would bring it to them through the Irish Pub Concept. The genesis of the idea has been attributed to the lack of Irish pubs at the World Cup soccer competition held in Italy in 1990, where Irish fans, used to the intrinsic role of pubs in celebrating sporting competitions of every hue, found no resonances in Italian drinking culture and the type of establishments there.[28]

The 'Guinness Irish Pub Concept' (GIPC) was created in 1992, in partnership with the Irish Pub Company (IPC), a sister company of Dublin-based interior design firm McNally Design (formerly McNally Duffy Design).[29] In 1991, IPC embarked on a countrywide research project on pub types to learn why there was nothing quite like an Irish pub.[30] If they could define the critical factors that made the Irish pub so successful, they could bottle magic for a second time and sell the product to investors across the globe. What then were the desired factors that could make the goose lay the golden egg around the globe? Why was the Irish pub a unique product that could take the world by storm if all the appropriate tropes, motifs and intangibles were put in place?

In 1999 IPC launched its website as part of Guinness and became an entity unto itself in 2002 at the wishes of Diageo. The website exists to this day. The Irish pub, they maintain, is 'always well designed, always buzzing, always cheerful, always welcoming and always serving great Guinness along with great homemade food'.[31] Above all else, authenticity of decor is a primary requisite and there should be a recognisable similarity between these ideal Irish pubs with 'decorative millwork, warm lighting and ornate back bars' to 'effortlessly deliver the same sense of premium comfort, ambiance and timeless conviviality'. This is something other types of establishment find difficult to replicate, they point out, but the Irish pub is a concept that was 'hip and contemporary in 1910 and remains equally relevant in our modern age of social engagement and connectivity'.

As well as the decor, it is essential that the food, drink and music offerings have a similar sense of authenticity. While it might not always be possible to have traditional Irish music, it is essential to carefully select playlists and music acts, as a bad band can hurt business. The Irish Pub Concept also recommends employing Irish people to fill key positions, especially in the opening period of the business. Above all else it is 'critically important' that all employees understand the 'warmth, informality and conviviality' of Irish pubs, regardless of their origins. At the time of writing the Irish Pub Concept website will provide twelve months' unlimited access to its 'Insider's Guide to Opening an Irish Pub' for a one-time fee of US$49.95. For this the prospective entrepreneur will receive guidelines for the selection of suitable premises and locations, along with advice on how to estimate the cost of the project, detailed charts showing the profitability of Irish pubs versus other casual dining concepts, and an 'insightful analysis' of why this is the case. In addition, they will receive a step-by-step guide that outlines what you need to do to plan, develop and open a successful Irish pub, along with suggested timelines and resources.

In summing up the uniqueness of the Irish pub and how to make it work, the company advises the budding entrepreneur 'to make the mundane very special and desirable'. It is imperative, the website notes, 'to distinguish between Irish Pubs that genuinely transport Irish culture, hospitality and tradition … and pubs with Irish names or Irish memorabilia hanging on the walls that deliver nothing other than a generic, sterile bar experience'. In so doing the pub experience can be taken to a 'whole different level of excellence' and become a 'premium environment' that 'can translate into tens of thousands of dollars of incremental revenue and profit'.

The Irish Pub Concept differs from the generic bar experience not just because of its authenticity but because it is 'a robust vehicle for financial success in what is a very challenging industry' and has the potential to realise a 'quantum leap in revenues and profit'. In summary, it notes, a good Irish pub can defy standard industry assumptions, thriving in towns of 25,000 while performing equally well in urban and suburban locations. And so it has proved over the intervening period. The 'Guinness Irish Pub Concept' became a worldwide phenomenon and, by 1998, 1,800 pubs had been completed and were opening at a rate of one per day worldwide.[32] Perhaps they had invented the perfect pub.

As with all things in life, pubs are ultimately a matter of personal taste and choice. Given a choice of establishments, the factors people may consider are myriad: cleanliness, lighting, furnishings, the availability and quality of food, the history and perceived authenticity of the establishment, music, the choice and quality of drink, the clientele, the bar staff and proprietors, and the lack of, or presence of, televisions and facilities for children are just some of the factors that may come into play. Pubs are never just pubs. They intimately reflect the tastes, interests and prejudices of their owners and clientele. Your idea of a perfect pub may be completely different from that of the woman sitting next to you at the bus stop. Essentially, we find in our favourite pub needs that can be fulfilled. Our needs may vary from time to time and we may have different pubs that serve differing needs at different times. As George Orwell wrote, it is a lucky man or woman who finds everything they want in a pub on any given occasion, and indeed for some, like Orwell, it may be an impossible task.

In this regard, pubs are often the locale of specific *communities of interest*: darts players, pool players, card players, lovers of music or in many cases particular music genres, supporters of a particular sport or sports team, those in search of the best televisions and cable television access to watch sport, craft beer aficionados, lovers of cocktails or food and even political allegiances can attract customers to pubs to fulfil their needs at any given time.[33] There is no doubting that class divisions are replicated in some pubs and may also be considered a community of interest.[34]

Sport is often a deciding factor for many people in their choice of pub, for both men and women. On a walk down the street in any provincial town one will encounter pubs where horse racing is particularly popular and where the 'Cheltenham Board' (a betting competition based on the horse-racing festival at that English track) is the highlight of the year for many of the clientele. Often these pubs are located near bookmakers, an ever-growing presence on the streets of towns in Ireland, despite the proliferation of online gambling options. In soccer pubs the proliferation of 'Last Man Standing' (a competition based on selecting winning teams from the English Premiership soccer competition) display boards indicate the dominant sporting interest of the clientele.[35] Pubs frequently sponsor sports teams, although this also seems to be less in evidence as the years go by. Teams and their supporters will most likely drink in the sponsoring pub, creating a symbiotic relationship and enhancing social capital. Most towns in rural Ireland will have pubs favoured by Gaelic games aficionados, with one being held to be the focal point of the sport (as with Mick

Byrne's in Castlebar). The increasing use of paywalls for sports viewing has meant increased business for some pubs, but owners will often argue that the price they must pay for a subscription to these services makes the venture, at best, cost neutral. On balance, more pubs subscribe to these services than not. The inception of cable channel GAAGO (now GAA+) brought this issue into focus when many were critical that the Gaelic Athletic Association, the organisation that administers the Irish sports of hurling and Gaelic football, opted to put some games behind a paywall under their own auspices.[36] The ever-growing popularity of rugby means supporters often have their preferred venue for watching or meeting before and after matches. Anecdotal evidence suggests that sports bars may become increasingly popular as more and more sport gravitates towards a fractured cable television market and not everyone has the means to pay multiple domestic cable subscriptions.[37]

Pub games also have their own following. Anyone who has played or witnessed inter-pub darts or pool competitions will be familiar with the intense rivalry and business they generate. There are many towns in rural Ireland where every pub will have a team in either or both games, although darts would seem to be predominant given that it takes less room and is cheaper to run. While it is true that the demographic attracted to watching sport is predominantly male, there are also female communities of interest. In Castlebar, for example, women's darts is very much part of the pub community, as is ladies' Gaelic football. Where people belong to different communities of interest, so too may they frequent different pubs at different times. As with cable television, pubs in tourist areas tend to have less of an orientation towards darts, pool and other games. It could be ventured that such pubs are conforming to the idealised notion of the Irish pub where there is only conversation and traditional Irish music.

Irish writer Flann O'Brien once noted that 'no genuine Irishman could relax in comfort and feel at home in a pub unless he was sitting in deep gloom on a hard seat with a very sad expression on his face, listening to the drone of bluebottle squadrons carrying out a raid on the yellow cheese sandwich'.[38] Thankfully the days of bluebottles and cheese sandwiches are long gone, but for many the increasing popularity of gastropubs is nothing short of an abomination. Those who hold such a view would argue that pubs are for drinking and socialising, and food should be eaten in restaurants, cafés and so forth. Even if drinking establishments were purveyors of Orwell's liver sausages and crackers with caraway seeds, these purists would look askance. For others they are the perfect third place and they will travel out of their way to try different places and discourse at length on their various merits. The term gastropub (derived from gastronomy) was coined in 1991 when David Eyre and Mike Belben took over The Eagle pub in Clerkenwell, London.[39] Like Irish pubs of old, British pubs were drinking establishments with little emphasis on the serving of food.[40] The growth of gastropubs influenced British dining and pub culture, and has often attracted criticism for potentially removing the character of traditional pubs. Inevitably gastropubs migrated to Ireland and are now a significant part of the industry. Colm Cronin, owner of popular gastropub The Shebeen near Westport, County Mayo, which has consistently featured in the Michelin *Eating Out in Pubs* guide, noted that twenty years ago 80 per cent of his trade was on the alcohol side with the other 20 per cent from food. In recent years the situation had become reversed with the 'dry-led' business model moving ahead of the previously predominant 'wet-led'.[41]

Perhaps it may be possible to isolate some motifs that make the perfect pub for most people. *Conviviality*, ambience, vibe, 'atmosphere' as George Orwell had it, and a plethora of other synonyms are frequently used to describe the essence of the Irish pub and why it has gained such popularity across the world. In Ireland it is often taken for granted that you can enter casual conversation in a pub with people you do not know. In many cultures this simply does not happen. In my experience, Japan is a country where groups of people do not like to be disturbed. While 'craic' is the default word used by many, conviviality is the word which springs most readily to mind when asked to describe the perfect pub. Derived from the Latin *convivium*, meaning banquet, conviviality suggests the sense of fun and joviality associated with a good night in the pub. Albeit with reference to an early version of a gastropub, Charles Dickens aptly captures that sense in his novel *David Copperfield*:

> We had a beautiful little dinner. Quite an elegant dish of fish; the kidney-end of a loin of veal, roasted; fried sausage-meat; a partridge, and a pudding. There was wine, and there was strong ale ... Mr Micawber was uncommonly convivial. I never saw him such good company. He made his face shine with the punch, so that it looked as if it had been varnished all over. He got cheerfully sentimental about the town, and proposed success to it.[42]

Conviviality requires people and, sadly, people are becoming a rarer commodity in many Irish pubs as time goes by. Many people mention the importance of the bar staff or proprietor as a central factor in their choosing of a pub. If you are on your own, the person behind the bar will be your only conversationalist and provider of conviviality. However, it must also be acknowledged that not everyone wants to talk in pubs. Some are seeking solace and want a meditative space.

There is no doubt that the *egalitarian* nature of pubs is a central attraction. As both Orwell and Oldenburg have noted, the pub is a notionally democratic space where all can participate once they adhere to whatever norms are in place. If you have the price of a drink, you can stay in the space. One interviewee in the famous Mass Observation study in the pubs in Bolton noted that he would never have the money to go to a restaurant if invited by someone, but would have the means to go to a pub.[43] As is so often pointed out, pubs are called public houses for a reason: all suitable members of the public can enter what is not a private space (that may be the theory, but it is well known that many pubs throughout Ireland will close their doors when members of the Travelling community are looking for a place to celebrate). In addition, studies like that of Curtin and Ryan in Ennis argue that pubs replicate class systems and social stratification.[44] For what is a perfect pub for one man or woman may be completely opposite for other people. Talking to people about pubs, some will not go to a particular establishment because of the 'type of characters' to be found there. The image of the perfect Irish pub provided by tourism-promoting bodies does not resonate with a large percentage of regular drinkers. They would have no interest in a pub where there was constant traditional music on the soundtrack and no television. For others, microbreweries are the default option.

Closely allied to conviviality for many is the *sine quo non* of the Irish Pub Concept – *authenticity*.[45] When lists of great pubs are drawn up by various authorities there is invariably a preponderance of venerable establishments. For many, the older the pub, the better it is, all other things being equal. Like Orwell, the high Victorian style is frequently the most lauded in urban environments. In rural settings the spirit grocer is often presented as the idyll. Guides to Ireland invariably include lists of the best pubs with both these styles featuring prominently, and it is little surprise that pub design companies are happy to provide facsimiles of both. A further dominant motif in such lists are pubs that carry the surname of the family that own it or, at least, the family who originally did. This nomenclature derives from an old law where the owner could be recognised for taxation purposes.

Anyone who spends any time in an Irish pub will eventually get involved in or hear debates about the *quality of the Guinness* served. For a significant swathe of frequent drinkers, the author included, it is the single most important factor in a drinking establishment. As Flann O'Brien famously had it, 'When things go wrong and will not come right/Though you do the best you can/When life looks black as the hour of night/A pint of plain is your only man'.[46] To outsiders, discussions of temperature, length of draw, shape of glass, glass from the fridge or glass from the shelf, top or bottom of the keg and so forth may seem esoteric, arcane and obscure: to committed Guinness drinkers they are anything but.[47] There can hardly be any other liquid substance that is reputed to vary so much from place to place, time to time, day to day, and, as the connoisseur will be happy to debate, even from keg to keg. At the end of the day, it is always a matter of personal taste. To top it all off, people may have variant ideas as to what makes a good pint of Guinness. One of the most often mentioned is the way the foam moves down the inside of the glass as the pint is consumed; some aficionados posit the theory that seven distinct rings should emerge. Others would argue that this variable depends on the speed at which you drink the pint. In recent times publicans suggest that the stringent standards demanded by Diageo staff mean that the quality of Guinness should be consistent across all purveyors of the product, but not all drinkers are universally in agreement with this thesis.[48]

Whatever of that, there is no doubting the iconic status of Guinness in Irish drinking culture. When Guinness introduced Guinness Light and Guinness Extra Cold, many perceived the moves as sacrilege. The former was unveiled in 1979 at St James' Gate brewery in Dublin with the fate-tempting tagline 'They said it couldn't be done'. At the launch, models emerged from a spaceship dressed in futuristic costumes holding trays replete with pints of Guinness Light which they served to the waiting crowd. The new product was aimed directly at younger drinkers who had turned in increasing numbers to ales and beers. As it transpired, those who said it could not be done were right all along. The demise of Guinness Light was brutal; it disappeared into oblivion two years after its launch.[49] While its abject failure is still frequently a conversation topic among Guinness drinkers and an esoteric interest among cultural historians, there were many other disappearances that went virtually unnoticed over the years, some of whose names would test those with the most recondite knowledge of the subject: Guinness Brite Lager, Guinness Brite Ale, Guinness XXX Extra Strong

Stout, Guinness Cream Stout, Guinness Milk Stout, Guinness Irish Wheat, Guinness Gold, Guinness Pilsner, Guinness Breó (a 'slightly citrusy wheat beer'), Guinness Shandy and Guinness Special Light all ended up being flushed out of the production lines.[50] More successful has been Guinness 0.0, a non-alcoholic version introduced in July 2021. In recent figures released by Diageo, Guinness 0.0 had a 48.7 per cent increase in volume sales between the end of February 2023 and the end of February 2024 across Irish pubs and venues.[51]

Most publicans are aware they will need to cater to as wide a customer base as they can going forward and will thus need to stock as *wide a range of products as possible*. In recent years microbreweries have multiplied and the number of craft beers on the market has expanded exponentially. A 2023 report showed that consumption of beer declined in Ireland by 2.1 per cent since 2017, but that of Irish craft beer rose by 13.5 per cent. The seventy-nine independent microbreweries currently in operation in the Republic of Ireland saw market share of craft beer rise from 2.9 per cent in 2017 to 3.4 per cent in 2022.[52] Many younger people gravitate towards pubs that sell a range of craft beer and spirits in addition to the traditional offerings.[53] Long gone are the days where the customer was limited to a stout, a beer, a couple of lagers on tap and a limited range of spirits. In recent years there has also been a huge increase in the brand of spirits, with whiskey, vodka and gin to the forefront.[54] Now, for example, people will frequently give the specific name of the gin they desire, often paying a high premium for the privilege.

There is a ubiquitous Guinness-related poster that any frequenter of Irish pubs will have seen many times. The poster lists the *price of a pint of Guinness* in 'old money' (pre-decimalisation) and 'new money' (post- decimalisation) and documents the price increase between 1900 and 1992.

John Geraghty of Publin.ie – a (no longer active) website dedicated to all things Dublin pub related – took the poster and calculated the price of a pint of stout from 1900 to 2015 in euro.[55] He used information from the Central Statistics Office (CSO), which provides an index of the average price of certain key consumer goods, one of which is a pint of Guinness. While acknowledging that he was neither professional economist nor statistician, Geraghty concluded that the price of a pint of Guinness has increased over time, taking into account as many variables as possible. For example, he calculated the cost of a pint (at 2015 values) was €3.17 in 1928 while the average cost had reached €4.30 by 2015. While Geraghty's model may not fully stand up to rigorous

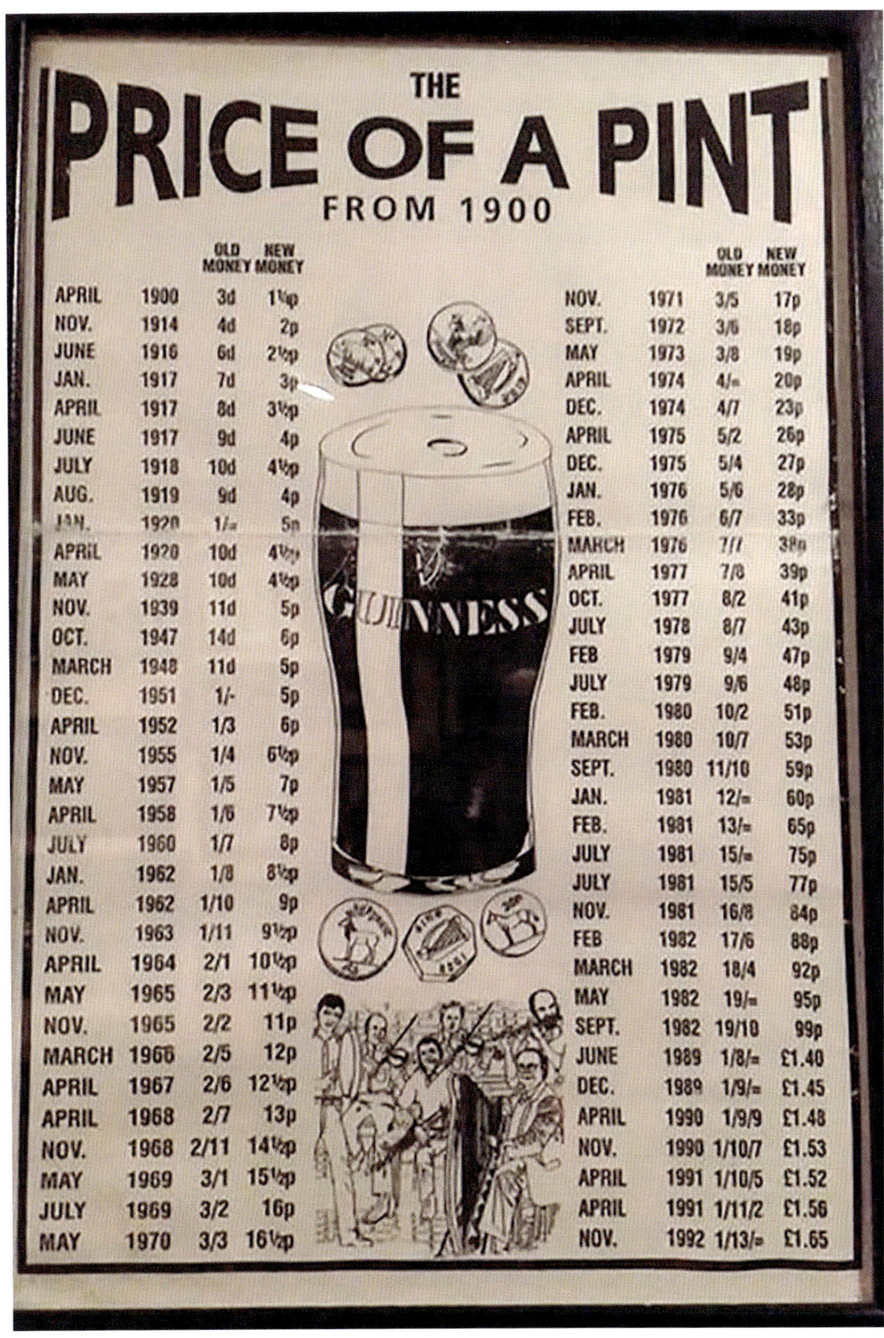

Figure 16.3 Poster of 'The Price of a Pint from 1900'. Photo by Aidan Fleming on Flickr, https://www.flickr.com/photos/25919760@N04/13916293281.

statistical analysis, it does focus on an issue that is often pertinent to people's choice of public house. In January 2023 Diageo blamed 'significant inflation in input costs' as it announced a 12 cent increase – excluding VAT – in its draught beer list prices. The CSO calculated that the average price of a pint of Guinness would top €5.30 while the average price of a pint of lager would jump from €5.57 to €5.72. In March 2024 there was further consternation among members of the Vintners' Federation of Ireland and the Licensed Vintners Association (LVA), the bodies representing rural and Dublin pubs respectively, when Diageo announced a further increase of 6 cent on a pint.[56]

With wearying regularity, the media report on the extortionate prices charged for alcohol in the heavily touristed area of Temple Bar in Dublin. In February 2023, for example, the *Irish Mirror* reported on prices in the Brazen Head, a pub that lays claim to being the oldest in the country, self-identified by a large mural on the outside of the premises which declares its foundation in 1198.[57] The paper noted that a pint of Heineken, Carlsberg, Hop House 13, Bulmers cider and Orchard Thieves cider cost an 'eye-watering' €9.95 while a pint of Guinness or Murphy's cost €8.95.[58] On 3 April 2024, the same newspaper reported that a bill for four drinks at the Oliver St John Gogarty pub came to an 'eye-watering' €47.70 for two pints of Guinness at €9.95 each, a vodka for €10.65 with a Red Bull mixer at €6.20 and a pint of Kilkenny for €10.95. The receipt, which noted that 'all prices include live music from 12 p.m. to 1.45 a.m.', was given to Fine Gael councillor Jim Gildea while out canvassing.[59] Inevitably, he shared it on social media stating his concerns about the tourism industry in Dublin. As with tourist traps all over the world, of course, retailers will charge what the market can bear. A cursory search of newspaper archives, tabloids in particular, will show that the price of the dearest and cheapest drinks in the country is a topic of perennial fascination and the debate has filtered down through the decades, largely centred on the price of a pint of Guinness.[60] In a much publicised case in 1973, for example, the Leicester Arms in Enniskerry, County Wicklow came under fire from regulars incensed at a price hike from 18 to 20 pence[61] for a pint at the 'working man's pub'. Two men addressed around eighty locals one Sunday afternoon, insisting the legal price should be no more than 19 pence, and led fifty of them on a walkout. When the pub reopened after lunch, around fifteen of its morning patrons were outside carrying placards with slogans including 'Pint of stout or pint of flesh'. Its owners were forced to take out a High Court injunction preventing locals from taking further action. In a similar case in 1974, the Jobstown House in Tallaght, County Dublin was picketed over two nights by five men incensed at the 'unauthorised' setting of a pint at 23 pence.[62]

Occasionally there is good news, as when The Crafty Fox, situated off Wexford Street on Camden Row, Dublin, announced in April 2024 it would serve pints of Guinness at €5 going forward. But, sadly, such an establishment is a statistical outlier.[63]

Modern society is one of re-invention, evolution, mutableness. It is inevitable that Irish pubs will need to continue to evolve to stay relevant and to maintain their appeal. Ultimately, it is a buyer's market and each individual will have their own conception of the Holy Grail of drinking establishments. For what it is worth, here is my take on the principles outlined by Orwell in his description, combined with the thoughts of Roy Oldenburg and a lifetime of socialising in Irish pubs here and abroad as well as talking to numerous people on the subject. Inevitably they are idiosyncratic and demonstrate inherent biases, but such was the task put my way for this work. I will call the establishment The Pub at the End of the Rainbow and wish all and sundry 'sláinte':

1. Cleanliness and hygiene (particularly toilets and glasses)
2. Friendly and efficient bar staff and publican
3. A great pint of Guinness at a decent price
4. A television, to see sporting and historical events only
5. No loud music, except in a performative context and in a separate space
6. Convivial company when required, and peace when not
7. Comfortable furniture
8. No food, except that given free by the proprietor
9. A good selection of craft beers and spirits to make the pub democratic and appeal to as wide a demographic as possible
10. A good beer garden.

Unlike Orwell's London, there are still Irish pubs with all these attributes, but it might be best to keep silent about them or they could be overrun.

Kevin Martin's Choice:

Mick Byrne's,

Bridge Street, Castlebar, County Mayo

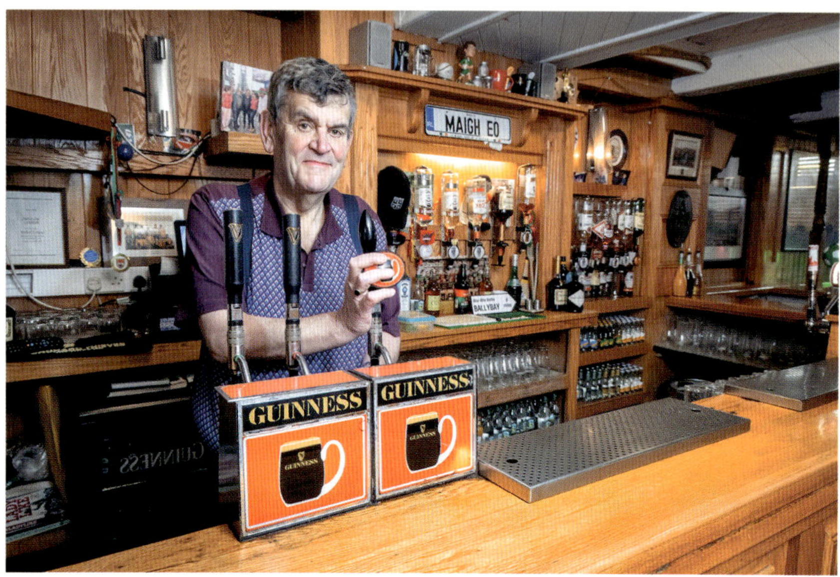

Figure 16.4 Interior of Mick Byrne's. Photo by James Osborne.

If you meet Mick Byrne once, you will never forget his larger-than-life presence and ebullient personality. Entering his cosy premises, established in 1917, Mick will invariably make enquiries as to where you are from and soon you too will be 'auld stock', a term used to describe those native to the town of Castlebar. The pub has long been the focal point of all things GAA in Mayo and it is a rare weekend evening when you will not see a former Mayo star player or some other sporting luminary discussing the intricacies of current sporting events. When the Connacht football final takes place in nearby MacHale Park the pub is a Mecca for fans from far and wide. A famous story goes that Mick once instructed the front and back doors be taken off the hinges to allow a throughflow of people, such were the hordes that had descended on the hostelry.

Mick's grandfather, Michael, a native of Ballyhaunis, bought the premises on Bridge Street in 1917. Mick's father, Michael John Byrne, took over the business in 1949 and ran it until he passed away in 1960. Mick's mother, Margo, ran it for the next eighteen years, until Mick went behind the counter in 1978. If he has a moment to spare, the genial Mick will take the time to ply you with arcane GAA questions and show you some of the memorabilia on the premises. Adding further lustre to the pub's GAA pedigree is the fact that the late, great Roscommon footballer Dermot Earley was born in the pub. His mother was Kitty Byrne, a sister of Mick's father. Additionally, the pub is famous as the launching pad of 'Byrne's Babes', a varied group of people who travel by bus to every away Mayo football match. Mick is also a qualified chef, and if you are lucky to be there on Friday evening his generous trays of free chorizo, black and white puddings and homemade soda bread topped with rosemary sauce, home-cooked ham and pineapple pieces will be doing the rounds. (On Monday you can have the same puddings with crispy bacon.) Above all else it is the quality and hum of conversation which makes the pub stand apart. There are no diversions except for the sport on television. The witty and charismatic Pat Ruane has been Mick's trusty barman since 1978. The only visitor missing from the long roll call of GAA greats who have imbibed in Byrne's is Sam Maguire and, if he ever gets there, Mick will surely have to remove the roof.

Chapter 17

Rural Pubs and Publicans in Contemporary Ireland

James McCauley

Pubs in rural Ireland have traditionally been seen as the focal point of life in their communities. Although these family-owned entities historically occupied a significant role in the fabric of rural Ireland, they have experienced many adverse changes to their commercial prospects since the start of the twenty-first century. Reasons cited for their decline include drink-driving laws, a smoking ban, the increased availability of cheaper alcohol in supermarkets and changing lifestyle habits. Allied to this, the Covid-19 lockdowns in 2020 closed their businesses to the public for almost two years. Considering these ongoing challenges, their transformative journey from latter-day síbíns, taverns and inns to the pubs we know today bears testament to the enduring resilience of the rural pubs that remain.

This chapter sets out to assess two key themes. First it will examine the important role that pubs have historically played within communities in rural Ireland as well as taking a brief look at their present and possible future roles. The second theme discusses the central role of the individual at the heart of these hospitality offerings, the publicans themselves as hosts and key players in the public house edifice.

Rural pubs in a contemporary world

The practice of social drinking in Ireland's public houses is a cultural activity with a distinct pervasiveness deeply entrenched in the Irish psyche. A York University study commissioned by the Vintners' Federation of Ireland in 2015 referenced the significance of pubs to people in rural communities as places where community cohesion and social capital can be fostered – a home away from home.[1] The social historian Kevin C. Kearns once described the Irish pub as the 'epicentre' and 'true microcosm of social life, reflecting the socio-economic ethos of its host community'.[2] Indeed, the public house, particularly in rural Ireland, was sometimes the only site of informal interaction within communities in the absence of sports/social clubs and other activities. The County Leitrim-born writer John McGahern referenced Irish pubs in many of his short stories, including 'The Sky Above Us' where he dealt with aspects of the rural life, citing the pivotal social role of the village pub:

> When the shopping is done, they go to the bars to meet the people they know and to discover the news, each locality to its own bar. If the spire was the epicentre of each of those communities, then local pubs were a tribal gathering point and social mart in which that vital currency of local news could be exchanged.[3]

In a significant 2003 report to the Oireachtas (Ireland's national parliament) titled the *Commission on Liquor Licensing*, the chair, Mr Gordon Holmes, stated that Ireland's pubs 'contribute to the quality-of-life experience of rural residents by serving as a social focal point in villages, providing an informal meeting place for friends and family and a formal meeting place for community groups and associations'.[4] A more recent economic report, *The Irish Pub: Supporting our communities*, by Dublin City University lecturer and economist Anthony Foley, for Drinks Industry Group Ireland, outlined how 'the local pub is so often the heart of social interaction, a space for occasions and events, a cultural heritage site, a place of employment and a buyer of local produce for hundreds of families and businesses'.[5] Both reports make reference to pubs' positive impact on the tourism sector, with traditional Irish pubs contributing to perceptions of Ireland as a tourist destination through providing a uniquely Irish ambience in distinct social settings.

Notwithstanding their historically critical role in the socio-economic landscape, a regrettable fact in recent times is that closures and the consequent loss of social capital has been the reality for too many rural pubs. Every closure is acutely felt, as it represents the continuation of a downward trend over many decades. In 1999, the number of pubs in Ireland was just over 10,000.[6] By 2009, this figure dropped to 9,057 and by 2018 to 8,134. This pattern accelerated following Covid-19, and by 2023 the numbers had fallen to 6,680,[7] with many pubs in rural areas facing into a real fight for survival. Cabras and Mount summarised the social impact of these closures thus:

> The loss of third places appears to hinder an already fragile context in which opportunities for residents to congregate and join together are extremely reduced. Among rural third places, the disappearance of pubs appears to be

> a very significant loss for local communities given the social ties these places bear. Pubs represent interesting sites of social and cultural analysis due to a strong 'rural mythology' placing them at the heart of village social life.[8]

The concept of social capital refers to those all-important elements of human interaction, cohesiveness and networking that occur within a community.[9] In rural areas, outlets like local shops, churches and pubs have helped to accumulate and shape 'social capital' within the communities they serve. Cucchiara observed how 'pubs in Ireland function largely as locales of social significance and cultural reproduction, not just centres of recreational drinking'.[10] When Irish rural publicans themselves were asked what they perceived the role of a 'local' pub to be, most of them mentioned their focus as community hubs for a multitude of recreational and charity activities.[11] The central role that the rural publican plays as the key protagonist in their domain is further explored in the second half of this chapter.

Most rural publicans realise that the nostalgic world of their predecessors has given way to modernity, and this transition has brought many challenges, not least the hard commercial realities of trying to run a viable business. A social history of the pub reveals a place that is in a continuous state of transition, a space showing changes in spatial reconfiguration, décor, products and practices where 'changing social norms such as newly developing tastes in leisure and consumption practices indicate consumer expectations and choices as they evolve over time and according to individual needs'.[12] Such wider cultural trends now mean that the position of the 'traditional' rural pub is seen by many as being increasingly precarious. These trends are actively impacting the bar trade and reshaping the relationship between pubs and current or potential customers. To survive, many pubs have shifted from a 'wet-led' business model where most of the revenue was derived from drinks sales, to a 'dry-led' offering based on food, with other re-invention measures also assisting those that have managed to survive.

Drink-driving laws, a smoking ban, higher local authority rates and insurance costs as well as intermittent cost-of-living crises have all been significant impediments to the survival of rural pubs. Most notably, the increased popularity of home drinking of alcohol bought in supermarkets has seen a step change in consumer behaviour. Cheaper alcohol for home consumption through off-licences and supermarkets now constitutes more than 60 per cent of all alcohol sales by volume. O'Dwyer and colleagues, writing for the Health Research Board, report that:

> Data from Revenue indicate that between 1998 and 2018, the number of pub licences in Ireland decreased by 21.8%, from 10,395 to 8,134. During the same time period, the combined number of wine and spirits off-licences increased by 407%, from 1,063 to 5,389 ... CSO expenditure data indicate that the off-licence share of alcohol market value in 2016 was 27.4%. Because of the lower price per unit of alcohol in the off-licence sector, its share of alcohol volume is much greater than that of the on-trade sector. In 2016, the off-licence sector was estimated to have a 61% volume share of the market.[13]

With these statistics in mind, Robert Connolly's observations were quite salient: 'And so, perhaps, drink in Ireland has come full circle, from the quiet seclusion of a monk oratory to the quiet seclusion of a front sitting room. In particular, pubs have lost their historic role as an integral part of Irish culture and heritage.'[14] These matters are especially compounded in the countryside by spatial remoteness, low population density and infrastructural deficits such as a lack of public transport.

A significant factor for some rural publicans in deciding whether to remain operating is the number of years they have been in business. Many are the long-established, inter-generational pubs, with immense pride in their family pub's history and attachment to its locale. These are publicans whose investment goes beyond the simply financial but is also psychological and emotional. Many examples prevail in rural Ireland of this type of long-term commitment, one being Mellet's Emporium in Swinford, County Mayo whose current proprietors are seventh-generation publicans. The pub has been in the family since 1797. Such examples highlight the deep affinity of these families to their hometowns and villages, leading to a strong sense of 'place'. This is most often symbolised by the family name over the door that has remained in place for decades or centuries in some cases.

This sense of immersion in their communities is a visceral quality unique to many Irish publicans that sees them identify as more than mere service providers. For some, 'letting go' and closing their premises is a difficult decision, emotionally and financially. As the statistics indicate, thousands have closed their doors and simply sold their licences to the ever-growing number of service station and supermarket off-licences. In many other cases, the rising overhead costs and reduced custom have left rural publicans with no other choice but to scale back their opening hours or cease operations altogether. Due to these circumstances, the level of intergenerational transfer is significantly less than in yesteryear, and the long-term survival for many of these establishments remains uncertain.

Rose-tinted memories?

Pubs and their inhabitants have evolved and changed through time. Sometimes, our rose-tinted memories of what they meant to us historically have led us to impose excessive expectations upon them.[15] This proclivity for retrospective nostalgia is not exclusive to Ireland. It is also a facet of the British narrative regarding pub closures where there is a tendency to lament the decline of the 'traditional' British pub.[16] On balance, it is still the case in many parts of rural Ireland that such pubs are still in business and continue to serve as touchstones connecting neighbours and generations. These pubs and their owners can do this because they are distinctly of their place. Pubs in these towns and villages are now fewer in number, but perhaps that is the natural order and evolution of things.

The fact that we were 'over-pubbed' relative to contemporary demand is a matter that many industry voices have amplified in recent years. Such voices argue that pub closures in certain areas are part of an inevitable and natural correction on the supply side. The alternate view of mourning their demise also holds traction, but it is not always entirely clear whether such an idealised, rose-tinted entity ever uniformly existed in all rural Irish towns and villages. In discussing such closures, Smith cautions against catastrophising, emphasising the importance of context and perspective:

> Their closure induces a sense of angst (as tragedies to be mourned) because they illustrate a passed way of life. The decline in viability of rural and village post offices, corner shops and pubs brings about a sense of communal loss in small communities ... Yet, decline and fall is an accepted facet in the emotional and economic order.[17]

Indeed Darmody describes how Irish pubs have been 'romanticised, mythologised, mythicised, and latterly commoditised and commodified'.[18] Fennell and Bunbury proffered what some may deem to be one such overly sentimentalised representation of Irish pubs:

> Traditionally, the pub … encouraged joyful moments, an emigration of the soul from sometimes unhappy realities. But for most people, the pub was there for sheer delight. You never knew who you'd meet, or what strange wisdom someone might pass on. Ideas rebounded from the tobacco-stained walls into every snug and cranny; giddy fiddles and rattling tongues could enliven the darkest corners.[19]

Such idealised views, while perceived as real by some, may not resonate with the reality of the current-day context for all. Irish historian Diarmaid Ferriter dismissed the view that pubs might be 'an emigration of the soul from sometimes unhappy realities' as 'a very deceptive euphemism'.[20] Carrigy, while referring to pubs as 'a refuge from the daily grind', also cautioned against our amplified and unrealistic expectations of what pubs could or should be:

> It can indeed be a locus of happiness and beauty, but if we seek too much from it, if we overload it with excessive expectations and seek from it a fulfilment that it cannot offer, we risk being pushed out of 'real time' and away from a functional place in the greater world, and pulled under into the suffocating temporal space of 'pub time', a place in which we risk drowning.[21]

The lesson therefore may be to appreciate them for what they are: dynamic evolving entities in an ever-changing world and changed Ireland. Observing them as such opens our mind to new possibilities regarding their future.

Future of rural pubs

Being open to the idea that pubs cannot be deemed to be one homogeneous assemblage is an important starting point when contemplating their prospects. A tentative typology of different pub types (Fig. 17.1) shows the diversity of offerings in the Irish pub trade from city-centre tourist venues, large urban outlets, neighbourhood or village pubs, to many more. Their prospects for survival have been based on myriad factors, not least the 'type' of proposition they make.

Historically, many rural publicans also juggled myriad other careers from their pub premises. This saw them operate as undertakers, auctioneers, farmers, grocers,

Large urban pub **or** **Provincial pub**
City-centre/Tourist venue/Late-night entertainment **or** **Suburban-neighbourhood pub**
Large provincial town pub **or** **Small rural village establishment**
Gastropub **or** **'Wet' pub (focus exclusively on beverages)**
Leased premises **or** **Freehold premises**
Highly leveraged business **or** **Business unencumbered by debt** **- the archetypal "cash-rich" publicans of old.**

Figure 17.1 'A Typology of Irish Pubs'. Created by James McCauley for *RTÉ Brainstorm*.

hardware merchants, postmasters and in some instances as local or national politicians. Many industry observers now view the pub trade as a blank canvas, with complete re-invention or significant diversification necessary for survival. Pubs are now as likely to be considered as sites offering co-working spaces, digital hubs, book clubs, as well as providing takeaway food and coffee. The 'Pub is the Hub' initiative for UK rural pubs offers prescription-collection services, arts and crafts sessions, meals on wheels, pop-up shop events, post office collection points and other novelty initiatives to attract custom.[22]

Increasingly, many pubs operate as gastropubs that specialise in a diverse range of craft beers, gins and whiskeys where knowledge of new spirits, wines and other beverage options that appeal to changing demographics is essential. Other successful publicans run businesses that are event-driven, like maximising the benefits of local festivals and big sporting events. They innovate through social media, creating events like themed music weekends, pub 'cinemas', salsa nights, knitting nights, book clubs, table quizzes and small theatre productions. Cork-based publican Michael Droney is a case in point:

> In Crawford & Co., Droney's newest venture, he combined two old Cork pubs to form one warren of activity. In the daytime there's a grocer selling local produce, and a coffee dock that becomes a spot for whiskey tasting and cheese boards in the evening. His jam-packed events line-up includes the usual sports fixtures, along with 'Paint & Prosecco' art classes, salsa dancing, pub quizzes, storytelling, knitting, and writers' meet-ups. 'As people's lifestyle choices and habits are changing, we are trying to go with this flow,' Droney says.[23]

Joe and Caroline O'Leary are the husband-and-wife owners of Levis Corner House in Ballydehob, County Cork which has been in the family for generations. They started growing tomato plants and selling them in the bar, which led to their weekly Wednesday farmers' market where local producers and bakers gather. A local ukulele group meet up to practise in the next room while the market is on. The pub has also endeavoured to differentiate itself in its approach to live music:

> 'There were bars in the village who had been doing music but no one had been doing original music on the level we are,' Joe says. They now host intimate gigs with notable names like Glen Hansard and David Kitt, and even run their own annual Secret Sessions festival in the pub every October. Music and pubs go hand in hand of course, but as Joe points out, 'It's not enough anymore just to "throw someone in the corner and get them to make some noise and talk over them".'[24]

While its pervasiveness has significantly altered, the appeal of the rural pub has not abated entirely. Fundamentally, remaining publicans see the need to become more innovative and entrepreneurial in re-imagining their business to a contemporary Ireland. The possession of requisite character traits to deal with the opportunities and challenges of running a pub will be the hallmark of those that will thrive or merely survive in the pub trade. Many continue to do what they have always done best in spaces designed to promote reciprocity and positive social interaction. The pivotal personal role the publican plays within their pub domain is therefore worthy of elucidation.

The pub owner's personality and presence

> Hosting is not the only consideration in the evolution of a third place, but few factors are more important. A tavern always reflects the personalities behind its bar.[25]

The importance of an Irish publican's inextricable role in the illustrious history of rural pubs within their communities cannot be over-emphasised. Stivers has noted how a publican's role reflects his or her position in the social and economic life of their community, suggesting that the publican was the overseer of two situations – business and pleasure – both as employer and paymaster: 'The publican, then, was provider and procurer of entertainment, a vital link in the dissemination of community news and gossip, and a not unimportant economic influence.'[26] Messenger reflected on the publican's role historically within rural Ireland's hierarchy-based community structure by suggesting that two of the most influential people in communities back then were the head schoolteacher and the owner of the local pub. He observed that both were men [*sic*] who were politically active, with solid business acumen, and were friends to priests, politicians and civil servants.[27]

Kearns described Irish publicans as the central and essential ingredient in the composition of a public house, with their role going far beyond simply that of congenial host behind the bar, suggesting that the publican was seen as a leading figure in the local community, performing vital services for people in times of need. They mostly lived above their shop, knew customers intimately, sometimes mediating family disputes. They generously dispensed advice and guidance on myriad matters and 'customarily provided money and drink for life's great moments … births, christenings, first holy communion, weddings, wakes and burials'.[28] Indeed, pubs are often compared to confession boxes, with publicans being analogous to priests and having the 'patience of saints'.[29] Being good listeners and confidantes with an intimate knowledge of the ins and outs of local affairs remain indispensable qualities to possess.[30] At all times, however, their capacity for discretion and diplomacy, given the eclectic mix of characters that can come through their doors, was vital. As observers of human frailties – like alcoholism and hostile customers – they required the fortitude of referees and peacemakers. Darmody has highlighted how the personal appeal of the Irish pub is 'often composed and constituted through the character of the owner and operator':

> They served as touchstones that linked neighbours and generations and were distinctly of their place. Moreover, these pubs have often tended to be synonymous with their owner(s), whose personality, temperament, and eccentricities (and sometimes idiosyncrasies) were elemental characteristics of each … Much of a pub owner's time was spent interacting with customers and generally making themselves a cornerstone of the pub 'experience'.[31]

To a considerable extent, pubs are about people. They are created and sustained by them, whether that be the customer or the host. The publican's curatorial capacity in managing the sometimes predictable and other times spontaneous activities within their domain can be pivotal to the customers' experience. Their distinctive hosting role in the deft handling of diverse situations within their pubs amplifies their status as custodians of their unique hospitality spaces.

The presence of the publican

> The creation of atmosphere is the achievement of the proprietor, it is a curious and indefinable thing, only understood by feeling its absence or its presence.[32]

One of the kernels of an Irish rural pub's success is the owner's *presence* in the pub. Indeed, at the heart of what makes Irish pubs unique is the origin of its ownership, with the owner's attendance quite often the key anticipated dimension of the customer experience. Most Irish pubs are independently owned by the publican, who is frequently visible and available to the customer. Usually named after the current or previous owner, this sets Irish pubs apart from UK pubs, which are large stock exchange companies or 'pubcos'. The Licensing Act (1872) had it written in statute that the proprietor's name had to be over the front door of the premises:

> Every licensed person shall cause to be painted or fixed, and shall keep painted or fixed on the premises in respect of which his [*sic*] licence is granted, in a conspicuous place and in such form and manner as the [licensing justices] may from time to time direct, his name, with the addition after the name of the word 'licensed'.[33]

The significance and legacy of this is that the family name 'over the door', denoting ownership, past and present, became a ubiquitous sight in rural towns and villages across Ireland. Even when the law permitted them, Irish pub owners were disinclined to follow the English tradition of producing creative and decorative pub names. They continued naming their premises after the current licensee or the family name of the pub's founder, a visual reminder of their immersion in their local communities. The late English-born writer Pete McCarthy described their uniqueness thus:

> Instead of the depressingly corporate environment offered by pubs in the English countryside ... in Ireland you can still find idiosyncratic, family-owned hovels with no food, or décor, that remain temples to hospitality, conversation, and drink. They'd be priceless institutions even if they only served coffee.[34]

The publican in their pivotal role as part of the hospitality edifice is chief protagonist in what Katovich and Reese refer to as 'the detail and drama of the bar milieu'.[35] The capacity to adapt and 'handle' different clientele calls for one of the most important virtues, the trait of discretion. This is referenced by Bill Barich, who described one publican's deft handling of delicate situations in a visit to an Irish hostelry: 'the barmen were rock steady and dedicated to Jack, who'd tutored them well and exercised a control over the place that was somehow both iron-fisted and as light as a feather'.[36] More recent exemplars also exist, and these give hope to those who may still yearn for the person behind the bar to fulfil certain preconceived expectations they have of a 'traditional' Irish pub. The Donegal historian and Michel and Déon Prize winner Breandán Mac Suibhne described his experience of his own 'one consummate barman' thus:

> He was never to be caught gawping at the television or gabbing with cronies, gaming on his phone or giving unsolicited advice. No, like a gun-fighter in a classic western, he was constantly scanning the saloon – not unfriendly but laconic, a strong, silent type. The door would open, his eyes would meet those of an incoming customer, and with an exchange of nods and gestures befitting a veteran auction-goer, he would pull the appropriate pint. He was truly superb, the master and commander of all he surveyed.[37]

The fusion of the traditional space with the leading role of the publican as host is similarly referenced by Aoife Carrigy, who mentions playwright John McGahern's essay on the well-known Enniskillen pub Blakes of the Hollow. He described its beautiful traditional ornate shopfront in the context of the corresponding attraction of those who run it:

> For all the physical impressiveness of Blakes, however, there is a real sense here that, for McGahern, no small part of the pub's inherent happiness and beauty lies within the harmonious balance it achieves between its inner world and the outer world that surrounds it. This is underscored, in no small way, by a real sense that this harmony is fastidiously maintained by the 'extraordinary pair' of characters of Johnny the barman (who 'was kind, but could be sharp') and his boss William Blake (who could assert his authority 'without any obvious word or gesture').[38]

The roles that publicans play as chief protagonist and lead actor are based to a considerable extent on how they manage the traditions, customs and practices of a pub. Many publicans view their primary aim as to provide a space and opportunity for like-minded people to meet while also offering the unpredictable – the broadening experience of chance encounters with random customers – all within their habitus.[39] Whether a publican is idiosyncratically predisposed to do this is often the subject of conjecture and opinion among the pub's patrons. Possessing the desired character traits requires what is described by Polanyi as 'tacit knowledge' – grounded in knowledge and skills acquired through membership of a particular social group and including the taken-for-granted and embodied competence of habitus.[40] How publicans behave and engage with customers within the immediate sphere of influence in their own premises is instructive. Their degree of friendship with customers, old and new, is always an important consideration:

> The publican's role is indeed a complex one, and it may be postulated that the role styles of the publican is a result of the ways both publicans and participants share social interests and a sub-culture forming a social symbiosis, which may say much about the fusion of work and leisure, sociability, and social usage.[41]

Taylor highlighted some character traits that a local (male) Irish publican possesses, describing him as 'a font of story and jest, a diplomat, and a shrewd judge of people. He is a canny businessman with the physical dexterity and memory to serve 200 people well-pulled pints while remembering names and personal quirks'.[42] How hospitality service providers act and perform, whether pub owner or staff, is therefore critically important. For his part, Oldenburg laments the demise of the quality bartender behind the counter:

> The bartender there, like so many these days, was a young fellow with little inclination to socialize and not much to offer when he did consent to speak. He was not that font of local information, that symbol of authority, that arbiter of disputes, or that 'character', which bartenders ought to be.[43]

Carrigy, when writing of McGahern's depictions of rural Irish publicans, captures the essence of their nuanced presence and discretion in guiding conversations towards safe territory:

> It is interesting to note that, once again, it is the barman who is depicted as the master of conversation, in this case being the only local who can be trusted to restrict the limits of conversation to appropriate topics and by all means away from the fraught theme of religion.[44]

In Goffman's seminal dramaturgical work *The Presentation of Self in Everyday Life*, the concept of 'impression management' is put forward, whereby people use their persona as a prism through which they are seen and perceived by others.[45] Social interaction is likened to theatre, whereby individuals adapt roles as performers, audience members, or outsiders that operate on 'stages' or social spaces. To this end, publicans often demonstrate a chameleon capacity to act differently with a diverse clientele, an invaluable character trait:

> A good publican is a man [*sic*] who will listen, not pry, sympathize, not pity. Always the consummate diplomat, a publican should be able to entertain prime ministers and TDs and be on both sides of the political fence. Thus, like a social and political contortionist, he must adapt naturally to every situation he faces.[46]

Taylor suggested that, in Ireland, it is the publican who 'creates the mood and flavour of a pub and therefore draws to his establishment a clientele in sympathy with his personality. The majority of habitués have their favourite haunts and rarely take their patronage elsewhere'.[47] In the words of Billy Keane, son of the late playwright John B., now running the family pub in Listowel, County Kerry, 'a good publican is better than any government official when it comes to keeping our small places alive'.[48] Whether this characterisation of the roles played by individual publicans and rural Irish pubs still holds sway as we approach the next quarter of the twenty-first century remains an open question.

Conclusion

The benefits that emanate from pubs fulfilling their function as institutions for community interaction and social drinking is seen by many as something that is too precious to lose. The ongoing development of innovative strategies for their survival and prosperity will continue to be vital. In all of this, the critically important role of the rural publican at the centre of the endeavour and the fight for their future survival is a key point to bear in mind. Some argue that responsibility for this should not be theirs alone and must also extend to include support from policymakers at local and national levels. The wider societal, as well as local community, benefits that can accrue from pubs' survival go far beyond simply rescuing individual economic business entities. For rural Ireland, this makes it worth fighting for. The rural Irish pub can retain an important presence as a space for cultural and social remission in communities, an invaluable part of 'everyday life', and a quintessential 'third place' for all who may choose to frequent it.

Jim McCauley's Choice:

The Hole in the Wall,

Phoenix Park, Dublin 7

Figure 17.2 The Hole in the Wall. Photo by stjamesofoldcastle on Flickr.

The Hole in the Wall on Blackhorse Avenue, Dublin 7 is nestled against the wall of the Phoenix Park. It dates as far back as 1651 when the medieval inn was then called 'Ye Blackhorse Inn'. English soldiers stationed in the nearby barracks were forbidden to leave the Phoenix Park, so they got their beer through the hole in the wall, hence the name. Now extending over 100 metres in length, it qualifies as the longest pub in Europe, combining the merits of a Dublin cosmopolitan city pub with the pure, fresh air and amenities of the adjoining 1,750-acre Phoenix Park.

It's often said that the story of Dublin's pubs over the last century is one of 'migrants' from Tipperary, Limerick and Cavan coming to the city and buying their own pubs. In 1975 P.J. McCaffrey, a Cavan man, joined the ranks of many other Cavan-born Dublin publicans by purchasing this premises where, through time, the

McCaffrey family acquired over a dozen adjoining cottages and shops, adding to the ever-expanding public house. The premises is now a mixture of antiquity and character throughout, with impeccable attention to detail, making it a unique place to visit.

Known locally as 'The Holer', the pub now produces a craft lager and pale ale with the same name. Throughout the year, it also offers an extensive gastropub menu. Its off-licence with its renowned wine shop has a vast selection of world wines where customers can choose a bottle (with free corkage) to complement their freshly prepared food. Every Christmas, the pub is transformed into a 'winter wonderland' with a dazzling array of Christmas decorations which draws custom from across Dublin and beyond. The pub also boasts roaring fires in the winter months, adding to this atmosphere, with a beer garden in summertime in which to chill and relax. The McCaffreys, never content to sit on their laurels, are now also successfully selling their own branded McCaffrey's whiskey and gin range to such far-flung destination as Canada, India and China. The pub is currently owned and managed by Martin McCaffrey.

Chapter 18

Doing it for Themselves: New promotion realities for the twenty-first-century Irish pubs

Patricia Medcalf and Brian J. Murphy

Introduction

The Irish pub has always been a reservoir of Irish culture. As other chapters in this volume demonstrate, there are many examples of the pub being used as stage and backdrop for performances in drama, music, storytelling and the visual arts. As such it provides a perfect medium for advertising. The pub has frequently benefited from a symbiotic relationship with culture and the arts, including to promote Ireland to tourists, to provide a venue for performance or indeed to create a setting where alcohol itself can be promoted. It also provides an opportunity for the pub to be seen in a cultural context, and promoted as such, among its own customers.

Over time many things, including insurance costs, business rates and changes to licensing laws and consumer behaviour, have contributed to the pub's increasing marginalisation. Perhaps a less obvious factor has been the stringent alcohol advertising laws that have come to the fore. These present a considerable challenge to the modern public house and are likely to lead to the loss of a key strength in how it is perceived within the public sphere. Increasingly, pubs will need to learn how to reach out to audiences through different and innovative means. In future, they will not be able to depend on the traditional promotional benefits that accrued indirectly, as alcohol companies find themselves constrained in terms of their own advertising choices. The option, so often used in the past, of offering the pub as an attractive setting for TV adverts and billboard campaigns is under threat. Public houses now need to consider how their message can be communicated to existing and new audiences in more innovative ways without contravening legislation.

Alcohol advertising and the pub

The idea of setting an ad for an alcoholic beverage in a pub makes sense and, since the 1960s, many companies have embedded this approach into their advertising strategies. Beer brands such as Guinness, Macardles and Phoenix led the way in the early days of

TV advertising in Ireland and provide good examples of congruence theory:

> Recognizing that 'some things go together' while others clash, market researchers and practitioners have long examined how and why congruence can assist marketing strategy … It facilitates the introduction of new products to a market and/or assists consumers' processing of the message.[1]

Another way of describing this phenomenon is associative learning, the premise that 'our brain builds associative connections between signals when they appear at the same time or space and when this simultaneous appearance happens repeatedly over time'.[2] Irish culture, advertising and tourism have all played a significant role in associating alcohol, particularly beer, with the pub.

Phoenix was a popular beer brand in Ireland in the 1960s and left behind a rich legacy of print and TV ads. Fifteen of these form part of the Irish Film Institute's Irish Adverts Project and, in all of them, a pub features.[3] In some ads, the bartender Malachi was portrayed as an expert, extolling the virtues of Phoenix beer to his customers. At all times, as if to emphasise his expertise and lend him gravitas, he wore a bartender's uniform that consisted of a white shirt and tie, waistcoat, black trousers, and a pristine white apron.

The barman as expert is a popular trope in alcohol advertising, and one of the best-known examples of this is central to the 1994 Guinness ad *Anticipation*, sometimes referred to as The Dancing Man.

> The ad features the actor Joe McKinney, who plays the part of a customer. He orders his pint, and then waits for the barman, played by Gordon Winter, to pour it. Winter is in control, like a conductor in charge of an orchestra. He will decide when the pint is ready and he is not prepared to take any shortcuts. Nothing, not even the antics of McKinney, faze him, as he takes pride in his vital role as a master craftsman … Winter refuses to be rushed and appears to enjoy his customer's anticipation. As the pint settles, he teases McKinney and places it in his line of vision, which tantalises him even more. In a scene reminiscent of a young child pleading with a parent, McKinney's facial expression begs with Winter for his waiting to be over. Winter is having none of it and knows that the end result will be worth it.[4]

Many pubs that feature in alcohol ads are fictional, such as Malachi's select bar, but this is not always the case. When an ad showcases a real pub, it can be instrumental in stoking curiosity and introducing new customers to the proprietors. In the 1970s, Bass Ale broadcast its ad *The Dubliners*, which opened with the eponymous traditional music group travelling to O'Donoghue's pub on Merrion Row where they performed the classic ballad 'Rocky Road to Dublin'. At its conclusion, Ronnie Drew, one of the group's singers, took a sip from a pint and uttered the famous slogan, 'Ah ... that's Bass'.[5]

The traditional Irish pub plays an integral role in one of Guinness' most memorable and enduring ads, *Christmas Card*, first aired in 2004. Deliberately understated and in stark contrast to many other festive ads, it wove together a mix of well-known Irish landmarks and cultural triggers. In one scene, there is a shot of J. O'Connell's family pub in Skryne, County Meath, a typical country establishment, complete with a Guinness sign and surrounded by a blanket of virgin snow.

In some ads for alcohol, the image of the pub is a comfort, a reminder of home. One of the most talked about Irish ads was Harp's *Sally O'Brien* in 1983, which gave rise to the memorable line when the male lead reminisced from the Middle East about 'the way she might look at you'. The ad shared excerpts from a letter that he was writing to loved ones at home. It was filled with musings about what he missed most about home and one of those things was a busy pub. The imagery that followed in the ad 'initiates the *promise* of a pint of Harp' in a bar.[6] This suggests that he missed both the pub and Harp (and indeed Sally O'Brien), and that the two were inextricably linked in his mind.

This snapshot of alcohol ads showcases the strong bonds that have been forged between pubs, alcohol brands and consumers. The pub, barmen and customers were often portrayed as triggers for nostalgic musings, a comfort to those who had left Ireland. By being part of such iconic advertisements, there was an amplified interest in the pubs themselves and this helped attract visitors who would not have discovered them otherwise.

Stand by your pub

In 2004, Guinness broadcast what was, on the surface, a very light-hearted, happy ad. *Pat's Bar* was set in a typical, small Irish town. In the opening scene, a man carrying a television led a procession towards a scrapyard. He placed the TV in the boot of a scrapped car and closed the lid. He and his entourage watched happily as the car was grabbed by a mechanical grabber and crushed. Satisfied that their mission had been accomplished, they marched back to Pat's bar. Pints of Guinness were poured and the main character, who turned out to be the barman, gazed up at the empty TV holder on the wall. The backing music stopped, and silence prevailed. He announced: 'Now we've got something to talk about.' A voiceover at the end said, 'Knowing what matters'. In this instance, what mattered was social interaction and not the television schedule.[7]

To understand the sub-text of the ad, it helps to explore the economic and social backdrop against which it was set. In the 1990s, superpubs arrived in Ireland. They could accommodate as many as 1,000 people and attracted customers with food, and big televisions which screened sporting events.[8] In stark contrast to the pub that featured in *Pat's Bar*, superpubs were not conducive to intimate socialising. Often, the booming sound from the televisions drowned out conversations. By 2004, almost 92 per cent of all Irish pubs had televisions, while 61.5 per cent subscribed to Sky Sports/BSkyB. Most pubs in Dublin (90 per cent) had the sports package, compared to just under 58 per cent in pubs outside Dublin.[9]

Pat's Bar was created when the Irish pub sector was in the throes of significant social change. A report commissioned by Drinks Industry Group Ireland reported that, between 2002 and 2008, the number of pub licences on issue fell by 10 per cent, from 9,846 to 8,867.[10] In contrast, there was a surge in the number of licences granted to off-licence outlets, which almost doubled from 2,831 to 5,205. This placed inordinate pressure on sales in pubs and the report notes that, whereas pubs accounted for 83 per cent of alcohol sales in 2001, by 2007 this had fallen to 63 per cent.[11] It suggests that 2003–4 was a tipping point that was triggered by the introduction of penalty points and random breath testing in 2002 and 2003 respectively, and the ban on smoking in public places in 2004. The property boom at the time encouraged many owners of small country pubs to sell their premises to profit from the buoyant market.[12]

The economic and social backdrop against which *Pat's Bar* was set suggests that, despite its comedic, light-hearted feel, its underlying message was far more serious. Most likely, Guinness was taking a stand against these changes by reminding viewers of the importance of the pub as a place for social interaction in many Irish communities.

Raising the bar

Years later, one of the sectors most hit by Covid-19 restrictions in Ireland in 2020 and 2021 was that of hospitality. Pubs remained closed from 15 March 2020 to July 2021. Revenue figures published in March 2021 revealed that per capita alcohol consumption fell by 6.6 per cent in 2020. Beer and cider consumption was worst hit, falling by 17.3 per cent and 11.4 per cent respectively.[13] In 2019, 62.7 per cent of the beer sold was still consumed in pubs, which explains why its consumption levels in 2020 were so adversely affected.[14] This pattern was reflected in Diageo's results for 2020. Overall, their net sales across all products sold in Ireland fell by 20 per cent and beer sales declined by 22 per cent.[15] While the off-trade continued to sell its products, one of its most important partners in the supply chain was removed abruptly from its business model. In recognition of this, Diageo established its 'Raising the Bar' initiative, a US$100 million global programme. Its main remit was to financially support pubs as they reopened, contributing towards the costs of any physical equipment they might need in order to do so.[16]

In June 2021, the *Every Moment Counts* ad was launched across the island of Ireland. The young Irish actor Barry Keoghan assumed centre stage, and his lines were delivered so that they would resonate with an audience who had missed the social aspects of the pub. His opening lines said it all: 'Ah the pub. It's been a while.' The imagery in the ad centred on the pub, filled with friends socialising and drinking Guinness in a manner that took Covid safety measures into account. The closing frame drew attention to Guinness' commitment to pubs in Ireland: 'Guinness has pledged €14 million to support pubs.' When asked about the ad, Alexa Wolff, Guinness Europe Marketing Manager, explained:

> The 'Every Moment Counts' campaign is aiming to support the industry by building awareness of positive and safe socialising so that pubs can remain open for everyone to enjoy this summer and beyond.[17]

As we shall see, increasing restrictions on the advertising of alcohol in Ireland and in particular the role that pubs play in those advertisements will likely mean that many of the examples mentioned above will not be permissible in future.

Countering threats of marketing regulation with self-regulation

According to Alcohol Action Ireland (AAI), per capita annual alcohol consumption in Ireland by those aged fifteen and over rose from 4.9 litres of pure alcohol in 1960 to a record high of 14.3 litres in 2001.[18] There has been a decrease since then but in 2019 a Health Research Board survey found that, while per capita consumption levels had fallen further to 10.8 litres, harmful alcohol-related practices persist. 578,000 adults exhibit alcohol use disorder, and 63 per cent of 15–24-year-old drinkers engage in monthly binge drinking.[19] AAI warned that the health implications of problem drinking are significant, and harmful drinking results in eighty-eight deaths every month in Ireland. Harm to children is well documented and was captured in a 2018 Health Service Executive report, which found that 16 per cent of those surveyed reported that children for whom they were responsible had experienced negative outcomes such as verbal abuse and neglect because of someone else's drinking.[20] Much of the blame for the above problems has been attributed to the way alcohol is advertised in Ireland.

At the start of the twenty-first century the scrutiny visited on the marketing activities of the drinks industry in Ireland and abroad intensified. Diageo's then chairman, Lord Blyth of Rowington, acknowledged this in the 2003 annual report:

> We are investing significantly in a range of initiatives including advertising, focusing on intelligent drinking, education programmes to explain the dangers of underage and binge drinking and server training to ensure that those who run bars have the expertise to stop misuse before it starts.[21]

Ten years later, a desire to be seen to promote responsible alcohol consumption was to the fore, and Diageo's chairman, Franz B. Humer, proclaimed to shareholders in 2013 that:

> As a business engaged in the alcoholic drinks sector, we are acutely aware of the need to meet these [financial and social] obligations in the most responsible way possible. We adhere to an exacting marketing code and we encourage our industry colleagues of all sizes to do the same ... We run responsible drinking programmes which touch millions of lives around the world.[22]

Diageo was not alone among its global peers in this regard.[23] In 2011, Pernod Ricard set out its corporate social responsibility priorities and top of the list was a promise to 'promote responsible drinking of alcoholic beverages'. This was to be the group's 'number 1 priority'.[24]

In Ireland, the advertising regulatory framework mirrored the voluntary approach of the drinks industry. Keeping it in check is the Advertising Standards Authority of Ireland (ASAI). Its objective is to ensure that all marketing communications are 'legal, decent, honest and truthful'.[25] To achieve this, it relies on self-regulation within the parameters of the ASAI Code, now in its seventh edition. Section 9 of the code deals specifically with alcoholic drinks and is 'designed to ensure that the content of alcohol advertising and promotion is consistent with the need for demonstrating responsibility and moderation in consumption, and that it does not encourage consumption by children'.[26] The ASAI welcomes comments and complaints from the public concerning ads and investigates all of them thoroughly. Complaints received about alcohol advertising tend to be low, which suggests that overall compliance with the code is high. In part, this can be attributed to CopyClear, established by the Drinks Industry Group of Ireland (DIGI), the Association of Advertisers in Ireland (AAI) and the Institute of Advertising Practitioners in Ireland (IAPI). Its remit is to be 'an independent pre-vetting service to help ensure the advertising of alcoholic brands in Ireland complies with all relevant Codes of Practice'.[27] In 2019, it pre-vetted more than 9,000 ads and rejected 15 per cent for non-compliance with the codes. This may explain why none of the complaints received by the ASAI about alcohol communications were upheld.[28]

Legislating to reduce the harmful effects of alcohol consumption

Despite the actions of the world's leading drinks companies and their desire to make self-regulation work, it did not placate advocacy groups and lobbyists in Ireland. Legislation was their preferred route and France's 1991 *Loi Évin* (Évin's Law) was held up as a framework that could be followed in Ireland. Its appeal stemmed from its requirement for all alcohol-related packaging and promotional material to contain only factual and objective information. In France, health messages, like those required on tobacco products packaging, are mandatory, and no alcohol marketing activity aimed at those aged under eighteen is permitted.

Following a protracted period of debate and lobbying from interested parties on both sides, the Public Health (Alcohol) Bill was signed into law on 17 October 2018.

The remit of the act is far-reaching and it contains a range of measures designed to reduce the harmful effects of alcohol on Irish adults and children. It is viewed as a first step towards addressing what Dr Geoffrey Shannon, special rapporteur for child protection, refers to as 'our ambivalence towards alcohol'. It should 'offer our children the prospect of a better life; an opportunity to grow up in a confident culture where not every event of their lives must be embarked on by the popping of a bottle or the crack of a can'.[29]

While CopyClear's chairman, Brendan Coyle, acknowledged the act's existence in its 2019 annual report, he surmised that:

> We remain some way away from the full implementation of the Act, if indeed it is fully implemented. As we move forward into 2020, the self-regulatory ASAI code still provides the strictest controls on the marketing communications of alcohol in Ireland. At CopyClear, we remain dedicated to helping our users comply fully with the letter and spirit of that code.[30]

Despite the seeming lack of urgency evident in this statement, some sections relating to out-of-home and cinema advertising have been implemented as of 2019 and are being enforced. If section 13 of the act is enforced, the decades-old relationship between the pub and alcohol brands in ads will be severed. Section 13(7) is very prescriptive in terms of what an advertisement for an alcohol product may or may not contain. At the very least, it must include a warning advising the public of the danger of consuming alcohol. Specifically, it must inform them of the link between alcohol and fatal cancers by directing them to a website that contains more detailed information. The only other images or information that are permitted in an ad for alcohol are some or all of the following:

- An image of an alcohol product, either in a container or glass.
- Details as to whether the product should be diluted with a non-alcoholic drink.
- An image of/reference to the country and region of the product's origin.
- An image of, or reference to, the product's production method and the premises where it was manufactured. The manufacturer's or agent's name and address can be included too.
- The product's price.

- The brand name, trademark and/or brand logo and, if applicable, a corporate name and/or logo.
- The product's flavour, colour and smell may be described in an objective, factual manner.
- The product's alcoholic strength by volume, its quantity of alcohol grams, and its energy value in kilojoules and kilocalories.[31]

Nowhere in the act does it mention pubs or humans. Therefore, it can be deduced that if an ad for alcohol is to comply with the legislation, the days of setting an ad in a pub filled with convivial customers are gone. Such restrictions will potentially place a considerable burden on a pub sector so recently ravaged by the Covid-19 crisis. Not all pub businesses will survive, but those that will must consider alternative engagement strategies to keep them relevant among existing and new audiences. The following sections look at how they might do this.

Engagement through art

'Backward integration' is a term employed by economists to describe 'how a company expands its role to fulfil tasks formerly completed by businesses up the supply chain'.[32] There have been examples in recent years of Irish pubs diversifying into the craft brewing market, in order to supply their own product. According to Bord Bia, the craft beer market has:

> been achieving outstanding growth for the last number of years. It is even more impressive knowing that the broader category has been relatively stagnant. In 2012 we had only 15 breweries in Ireland, now we have over 70 and the range of beers being produced is growing constantly.[33]

Such backward integration not only allows a pub to reduce costs by supplying its own product but also provides an opportunity to reach out to customers through on- and off-sales of its craft beer offering. By selling its own unique product, brewed on site, the pub can establish a strong emotional bond with its customers. In the case of off-trade sales, that bond can extend beyond the pub when the customer brings the beer into their home. It might be likened to the place relationship that some people have

Figure 18.1 Different designs for YellowBelly Beer cans (APA, Unfiltered Lager, Dark Red Ale, Session IPA). From YellowBellyBeer.ie.

with wines from a recognised region. One of the best examples of such innovation is YellowBelly Beer, which was established in 2015 by the Simon Lambert & Sons pub in Wexford.

The beer takes its name from Wexford county's GAA nickname.[34] It is unique in that it has used both story and graphic art (Fig. 18.1) to engage with audiences through both traditional and social media channels:

> Every YellowBelly Beer has been given individual artistic treatment by Creative Director Paul Reck, creating individual stories, illustrations and artwork for every beer release and expanding the YellowBelly Universe through a comic book series and animations.[35]

This in turn has opened both the beer and the Simon Lambert & Sons pub to a wider audience. Their comic book approach centres on the adventures of a character named Yellowbelly (Fig. 18.2) and his many exploits within a created 'Yellowbelly' universe.

Figure 18.2 Cover page of Yellowbelly Comics, *Yellowbelly Tales: Pirate Bay*. Story and art by Paul Reck.

Engagement through literature

An interesting development in food literature has been the phenomenon of people writing books closely associated with one location or business. Many independent fine-dining restaurants already produce books detailing both their recipes and their culinary narrative. *Chapter One: An Irish food story* is a case in point.[36] The book not only includes recipes but also details the people and characters behind the restaurant, key suppliers, equipment, food philosophy, etc. More recently, a similar genre of books is emerging in other food and drink domains such as the traditional Irish butcher shop.[37] Examples include *The Irish Beef Book*[38] and *An Irish Butcher Shop*.[39]

Books based on place-specific Irish pubs are relatively rare but present considerable potential as an alternative way of engaging with a customer base. One book that does this well is *Mulligan's: Grand old pub of Poolbeg Street*, a bestseller that details the history and characters of one of Dublin's most famous pubs.[40]

> Declan Dunne's book … takes the reader from the 1780s when the first Mulligan put his name over the door to the present day, profiling the ordinary drinker as well as the stories of the famous faces who visited including John F. Kennedy, Judy Garland, footballer Eusebio, Sean Penn and Julia Roberts.[41]

Given the rich story that so many traditional Irish pubs have to tell, there is undoubted opportunity for engagement by telling the story of particular places. Books like these can help communicate the attributes that make up the unique identity of the pub in question. While a typical restaurant book is primarily focused on culinary recipes and images, the pub narrative tends to be based on the stories of the place itself through its history, characters and associated anecdotes.

Engagement through performance

Down through the years, pubs have acted as venues for comedy nights, music performances and even theatre performances. Well known whiskey company

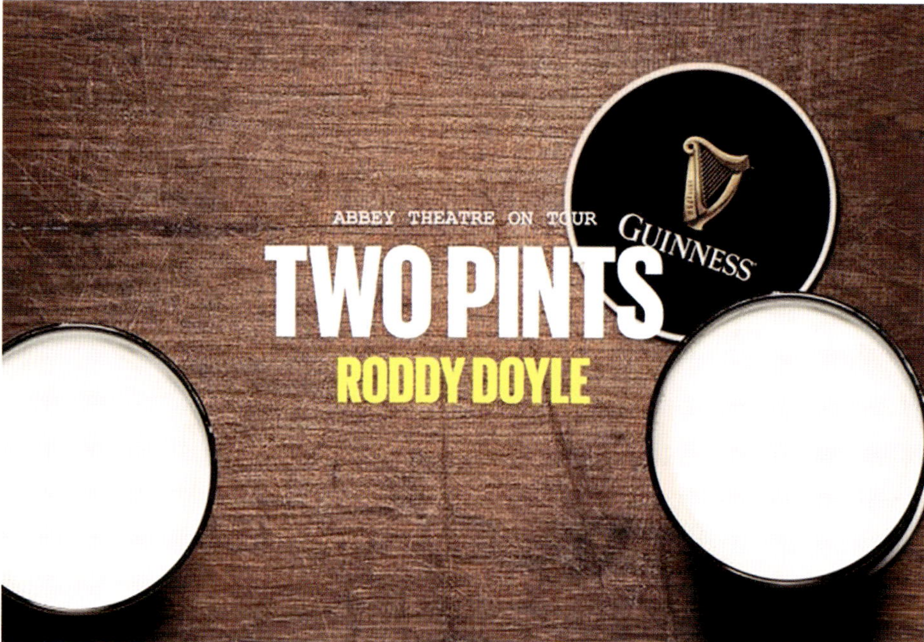

Figure 18.3 Poster of Abbey Theatre production of Roddy Doyle's *Two Pints* in 2017. Courtesy of the Abbey Theatre.

Tullamore Dew presented their 'Tully's Tiny Theatre' project at Toner's pub, Dublin in February 2020. It provides an interesting example of a whiskey company using pub theatre as a vehicle to promote both the pub and the well-known whiskey.[42] Additionally, as referred to in Chapter 13, the Vintners Federation of Ireland (VFI) collaborated with the Abbey Theatre in 2017 to facilitate the performance of Roddy Doyle's show *Two Pints* (Fig. 18.3). Over one month in the summer the play was performed at twenty-two pubs in sixteen counties.[43] Pub collaborations with theatrical performances are not a new phenomenon and there is a long history of that association, particularly in London.[44] Both the Tiny Theatre and *Two Pints* examples clearly demonstrate how sponsored small-scale theatre performance has the potential to be used as a promotion vehicle for the traditional pub sector, at a time when more traditional advertising avenues are becoming somewhat restricted.

Engagement through community work hubs

The Covid-19 pandemic brought considerable challenges in terms of how people engaged with their work environment. One solution proposed was that Irish pubs could act as working hubs where people in rural areas could stay close to home, thus avoiding long commutes. This suggestion was confirmed by the Irish government's *Rural Development Policy 2021–2025*, which committed to 'explor[ing] the potential to develop a pilot scheme to support the use of rural pubs as community spaces and hubs for local services'.[45] Though somewhat radical in terms of approach, particularly in a country that struggles with alcohol, using pubs as work hub spaces provides another opportunity to engage and self-promote in the broader community. The first phase of the pilot scheme was launched by minister for rural and community development Heather Humphreys, with an initial investment of €50,000 to be shared across five rural pubs.[46] A precedent in this area has been set by the innovative Brewdog drinks company in the Untied Kingdom, which now offers its 'Desk Dog Service' across its fifty-one pub locations in England, Scotland and Wales. Their advertising pitch for this innovation is as follows:

> Bored of working from home? Co-work in one of our awesome bars, with unlimited coffee or tea all day, and then a pint at the end of the day when you're done. All for £10. Best part? All our bars are dog friendly, so you can bring your four-legged friend along with you![47]

Engagement through social gastronomy

The term social gastronomy is born out of the idea that food and drink businesses can bring social benefits to communities and often operate beyond the desire for purely mercantile gain. It has become associated with the culinary arts as food projects around the world, frequently directed by well-known chefs and culinary groups, attempt to change lives for the better among communities that need help. In Ireland, prominent examples include FoodCloud, which successfully redistributes surplus food from food businesses to needy causes using their own unique technology platform. Interestingly, in 2021, one of Ireland's premier international food symposia, *Food on the Edge*, shifted its focus towards exploring social gastronomy and how food can be used as a vehicle for social change.[48] The Irish pub also has the potential to engage with its local audience by providing for their social needs in an environment where such services are becoming increasingly diluted.

In recent years we have witnessed the emergence of community café projects in Ireland. Their success could offer the pub sector a path to follow. Supported by government funding, typically these café spaces provide local communities with a meeting place, a small shop and a place for local food and craft businesses to use and display their wares. One of the most prominent examples to date has been Billy's Tea Rooms in Ballyhale, County Kilkenny which has received a lot of media attention. In an article in the *Irish Independent*, Ann Fitzgerald wrote:

> 'I have seen Rock and Roll's future and its name is Bruce Springsteen.' With these rousing words, the world was introduced to 'The Boss' in 1974. Recently, I was struck by a similar feeling, regarding the future of rural Ireland, when I visited Billy's Tea Rooms and Shop in Ballyhale, Co. Kilkenny.[49]

Local initiatives like Billy's Tea Rooms are being developed throughout Ireland with a community focus and social remit in mind. Their true value lies not in monetary terms but in the provision of a social hub where communities can value their own sense of place. The traditional Irish pub has historically fulfilled many of the roles that these new spaces now provide and has the potential to do so again, thus reconnecting with their audience. There are several examples of successful community pubs in the United Kingdom where pub development has been supported by organisations such as the Pub is the Hub[50] and the Plunkett Foundation.[51]

Up until relatively recently, Ireland did not have any structured community pubs but in 2021 a rural pub, Maudie's, in Rathgormack, County Waterford, was saved from closure when a group of nineteen local people moved to ensure that it would remain at the heart of the local community. 'They put up around €12,000 each to buy the popular spot and have been busy putting their various skills to use in renovating it internally and externally over recent months.'[52] It is important to note that the stated purpose of the purchase is not profit, rather the owners have a clear social objective in mind given the pub's central role in the community.

> GAA wins like Rathgormack's 2019 Waterford senior football final triumph, weddings, funerals, card nights, trad sessions, Christmas parties – it all happened at Maudie's ... 'It's the heart of the place. This will be my son's local too when I'm dead and buried. Not one of us [the owners] cares if we make a penny out of it. It's all about keeping this place open and keeping people together.'[53]

Although many contemporary pubs in Ireland are unlikely to take the full community pub route as in the case of Maudie's, there are over one hundred UK examples of pubs that have remained in private ownership with government support to provide an additional much-needed community function. They offer a range of additional services such as cafés, village shops, libraries and more.[54] The previously mentioned government pilot scheme supporting working hubs also makes provision for similar supports in helping pubs develop community-focused activities in Ireland.[55]

Conclusion

In 1959, Guinness launched its first ad created for the Irish market. It precipitated decades of advertising spend by the brewery and its rivals, both domestic and international. This continued unabated throughout the first two decades of the new millennium and, by 2021, promotional expenditure by the alcoholic drinks sector in Ireland, including sponsorship and advertising by supermarket firms, totalled €116 million, as estimated by the lobby group Alcohol Action Ireland.[56] Undoubtedly, the pub sector benefited from this extravagant investment, but clouds had been gathering and lobbying against the promotion of alcohol has been unrelenting. It seems clear that advertising regulation is only going in one direction, confirmed on 17 October 2018 when the Public Health (Alcohol) Act was signed into law. The symbiotic relationship that existed between alcohol advertising and the pub is now threatened.

If the act is fully enforced, public houses will disappear from ads. Cast adrift, they will be forced to promote themselves, but they will have to be smart and do this without the luxury of having millions of euros at their disposal. The examples presented in this chapter have illustrated how the Irish pub can interact with audiences in ways that do not rely on the large advertising budgets of successful alcohol companies. They are presented as innovation and a way to change the narrative of the failing Irish pub.

We have shown how that narrative might in future be influenced through art, literature, performance, community engagement and social gastronomy. If we look a little bit closer, we can see that many of the ideas discussed here are not new and do, in fact, hark back to an older, more romantic notion of our traditional Irish pub. That pub operated in a time before the emergence of the ubiquitous supermarket and petrol station off-licence. Drinking and entertaining at home was much less prevalent then, and the local pub was at the centre of social life. It was a place where you got to know your neighbours, a version of the modern community pub mentioned above. Though less formalised than the performance examples highlighted, these pubs of the past held impromptu sing-songs and music sessions. No one bought tickets but there were local performers on high stools every night, holding court and telling stories to laughing audiences. Even the diversification into craft beer, that we now see as innovation, mimics the fact that up until the 1960s many pubs bottled and labelled their own Guinness stout.[57] And finally, the pubs of the past may not have been designated as official workspaces, in the same vein as Brewdog, but they were definitely places where business was done, labour was sourced and deals were made. So, on closer inspection, perhaps Irish pubs were always 'doing it for themselves'. Now that their over-reliance on alcohol advertising is being removed, they may turn once again to the engagement strategies of the past.

Patricia Medcalf's Choice:

Kennedy's Pub and Restaurant,

Westland Row, Dublin

Figure 18.4 Statue of Oscar Wilde outside Kennedy's. Photo by Lisa Gygax.

Located on the periphery of Trinity College Dublin, Kennedy's has always been a popular and convenient watering hole for the university's students and staff. However, its reputation as a music venue and its rich literary history, which came about due to famous patrons such as James Joyce and Samuel Beckett, place it on the itinerary of many tourists and music enthusiasts. In fact, Joyce liked it so much that he wove it into *Ulysses* as Conway's, an accolade that has cemented its place on the Bloomsday Festival itinerary each June. Kennedy's was established in 1850 and, like so many Irish pubs, it started out as a grocery store, convenient for the residents of nearby Merrion Square. Its most famous employee was Oscar Wilde, who served customers while drawing on their quirks and personalities as inspiration for his literary work. Through the years, Kennedy's has gone through several transformations, not least of which was its footprint, which was reduced in size due to the vagaries of property development during the Celtic Tiger. However, it has weathered the many societal and economic challenges that came its way and continues to be a purveyor of creamy pints, food and convivial company.

Brian Murphy's Choice:

Mel's of Narraghmore,

County Kildare

Figure 18.5 Mel's of Narraghmore. Photo by Melanie Treacy.

Mel's of Narraghmore is situated in the heart of the quaint, attractive village of Narraghmore in south Kildare. This rural Irish pub is owned and managed by Melanie (Mel) Treacy, one of several successful female publicans who have emerged in a sector historically dominated by men. The extended Treacy clan have a long-rooted attachment to the local area and Mel puts her passion for the business down to happy childhood memories of visiting local Kildare pubs on mart days with her father. The pub itself was originally owned by the Kelly family and has been an integral part of village life for generations. It is a pub that is steeped in the GAA, with the local club St Laurence's close by; Mel herself was a renowned senior county camogie player, until recently. In fact, many of the staff are accomplished players, so patrons who dare talk sport from a high stool in the bar better know their stuff! Like many pubs in recent years, Mel has extended the pub's offering to include an extensive menu. While the pub has gained a great reputation for the quality of its food, at its heart this is also a drinker's pub and is fiercely proud of its 'pint of plain'. Above all, Mel's is a place where locals meet, chat and enjoy each other's company. Its infectious combination of welcome and craic is what makes Mel's of Narraghmore that quintessentially Irish pub, so loved by locals and visitors alike.

Chapter 19

Lockdown: The pub as an icon of Irish identity in the Covid-19 pandemic

John O'Brien

Introduction

The Covid-19 pandemic had an unprecedented effect on public houses in the Republic of Ireland. The first lockdown, introduced in March 2020, to stem the spread of the disease was the longest in Europe, and in the subsequent two lockdowns there were comparatively strict restrictions on hospitality. The focus of this chapter is not on the practical effects of the pandemic on licensed premises, but rather how this period of crisis revealed the meanings of the public house as a symbol in Irish society, as it provoked reflection on the meaning of the pub as a social institution and its place in social life, but, more importantly, for collective identity. In times of crisis, change and uncertainty, narratives and symbols are sought that frame and reframe collective identity. Public houses played this role in the pandemic in Ireland. The chapter provides an overview of representations of the pub in Irish print media. It examines the period of the Covid-19 pandemic lockdowns, as well as the period before and after to serve as a contrast. It shows how pubs shifted from a symbolically significant, but mundane, object to a resonant totem of collective identity.

The data source was articles from *The Irish Times*, an established quality broadsheet that is widely considered 'the paper of record' in the Republic of Ireland. It has a socially liberal editorial line, mixing neoliberal and critical commentary with some social and economic conservative voices also.[1] It has been widely used by social scientists to track 'mainstream' opinion.[2] Around 500 articles dealing with public houses were selected in the three months before and the three months after the lockdowns and a further 500 articles were reviewed that were published during the lockdowns. Themes were developed from these to reconstruct the meanings of these texts.[3]

The symbolic resonance of public houses and alcohol

Public houses and drinking are evocative symbols in Irish society, and play an established role in articulating Irishness, notably in tourist and cultural representation.[4]

The centrality of public houses to the public health response to the Covid-19 pandemic multiplied this resonance and increased its profundity. The impact of the lockdowns in terms of extended closures, job losses, risk to the future of premises, the compounding of the existing trend of contraction,[5] the sharp break in everyday life radically changing rituals of sociability, increased the iconic quality of pubs.[6]

Public houses and drinking occasions are important symbols that communicate about identity. The settings for drinking occasions and beverages often operate as symbols of group identities.[7] They are often an important part of sociable rituals that produce the collective effervescence that provides the experiential basis for mutual identification. They act as symbols of class, ethnicity, gender, sexuality and nation, as well as in negative depictions of out-groups.[8] Public morality and discussion about appropriate levels of self-control and loss of control are constructed through public problems associated with drinking culture.[9] An element of this is often the identification of heroes and villains for praise and shaming, whose drinking has variously been constructed as endangering or sustaining the collective body.[10]

A particular association between Irishness, alcohol, drinking and public houses exists not only due to the important social role it has served, but also to colonial stereotypes, which have asserted a link between drinking, pub attendance and Irishness.[11] Stivers argued that the trope of 'the drunken Irish' was a means of placing Irishness at the bottom of the ethnic status hierarchies of the United Kingdom and the United States. It was resisted and reappropriated however through softening the stereotype into a characterisation of the Irish as possessing an inherent love of sociability, rather than a drive to destructive intoxication.[12] On the other hand, abstinence became a symbol of respectability and moral superiority among Protestants and unionists, Catholics and nationalists.[13] It retains powerful metaphorical power, as can be seen from the range of public issues, whether scandals or triumphs, that have been understood through pubs and drinking, from the so-called 'Gargle-gate' scandal[14] to the role of publican Rory O'Neill and his Pantibar premises in the marriage equality referendum.[15] It is consequently not surprising that pubs have served as a metaphor for conjuring the collective identity of 'Irish society' in people's minds in the (Covid-19) pandemic.

The link between crisis, meaning and collective identity

Reviewing the reporting on public houses in the period before, during and after the pandemic and consequent closure of licensed premises revealed it as a time when pubs gained particular symbolic power. It was a period of disruption of the ordinary that interrupted the structure of modern life. Rosa describes modernity as defined by 'dynamic stabilisation', whereby the stability and legitimacy of society is based on continual progress and acceleration.[16] The global closure of meeting places, cancellation of festivities and events, and beer being poured away by breweries signalled a shocking interruption in this fundamental logic of modernity based on accelerating activity. It constituted real-world liminality: an undefined period of in-betweenness breaking with normal certainties. Here, the order of things has collapsed, cannot easily be restored, and thus there is a search for a new order, or at least explanation for what is happening.[17]

During the pandemic, journalism shifted from passively reproducing information received, to direct investigation of pubs. In 'normal' times, there was reliance on press releases and court reports, rather than direct journalistic enquiry. During the pandemic the minds of journalists turned to the topic as it becomes a 'public problem' for which narratives must be constructed to frame events, as their meaning is not evident and a threat to the moral order is addressed.[18] The narrative changed. Non-pandemic stories had a framing of some typical aspect of modernity. There were human interest stories addressing reflexive individualism, a type of selfhood thought to be typical of modern life where a person must continually make choices in a field of risk and possibility, avoiding being constrained by traditional compulsions, for example where a person opened a licensed premises to adopt a different lifestyle out of choice.[19] There were reviews and lifestyle pieces concerning taste and distinction, with drinking and pub attendance used as a signal for social status. There were business stories that framed pubs as rational enterprises and investment opportunities for capital. Finally, there were stories concerning crime and social issues framing pubs in terms of deviance. In contrast, during the pandemic, public houses were represented holistically, treated as a totem of collective identity endangered by radical disruption. With the end of the pandemic, pubs and their role in collective identity faded quickly in stories and reporting returned to the pre-pandemic template.

Normal times: the representation of the pub before and after the pandemic

Before and after the pandemic period, representations of the pub as a place of enchantment were foregrounded. Enchantment, in sociological parlance, refers to the expressive elements of human experience, including what goes beyond the material, desire and emotional collective attachments.[20]

An enchanting place of ecstatic experience

Ecstatic types of experience are shown as taking place in pubs. In this there is a spectrum from collective effervescence to intimacy and a dropping of façades. In journalism, pubs are represented as offering an escape from the heaviness of professional and domestic roles, allowing people to go beyond social structural identities. Honesty is portrayed as being possible in the context of drink, reduced inhibition and a time-out space that encourages the revelation of the real person. Pubs are represented as places where intersubjective being is realised. 'Craic' denotes direct, personalised interaction that is somehow transcendent. To get the craic, and to be craic, is to be inside, partaking in full-flowing intersubjective understanding in personalised interaction. A 'session' implies deep focus on a particular activity, where participants engage in sociability in a determined way. More established forms of collective effervescence in the form of a community ritual cycle are shown as taking place in pubs. There are stories romanticising the wildness of the past and vicarious ecstatic experience through this, with nostalgia about fighting, extreme drinking and the immorality of previous eras. There are also representations of mundane peak experiences, for example in the form of a quiet drink, slipping quickly into a pub for an in-between moment that is savoured.

Ecstatic experience is also shown in pubs through consumer wonder in terms of style and a setting to perform good taste and distinction. Pubs are discussed as prestigious dining places, in reviews of gastropubs, pub-restaurants possessing Michelin stars. They are noted as serving the 'best Guinness', the 'perfect pint', possessing 'cocktail and wine bars', and having their own special atmosphere, whether comfy, quirky or fun. They can be noteworthy appendages to elite hotels and have their own appendages of off-licences that offer the opportunity to explore taste. Only occasionally is bad service noted in the newspaper pieces.

An enchanting place of creativity

Pubs are frequently reported on as a place that facilitates a creative milieu. They are referred to as a haunt of writers and artists, with Grogan's in Dublin standing out as an exemplar. Pub scenes are linked with the chaotic aspect of the creative process, as a place of liminality that facilitates an opening up of self and consciousness. They are thus shown as where creative products are conceived or where inspiration happens and where people are met who spark inspiration. Pubs are shown as where art and culture happen in the form of reading groups, comedy, music, rock gigs, trad music, *sean-nós* and theatre performances. They act as essential side venues alongside the main stage for significant cultural events. They are shown as providing the infrastructure for artistic work, offering residencies, back-rooms for performances and rehearsals, a less pressurised performing space for experimentation and learning one's trade. They are where half-formed or derivative culture can find a place, captured in the phrase 'pub band'. Pubs feature heavily in reports on artistic production, represented in photography series, as a setting for plays, films or writing. Pubs are also the setting where journalism happens, with many interviews taking place there. Pubs are shown as linked with the charisma of celebrity, through celebrity-owned pubs and those that gain a magical aura through their association with a celebrity patron.

An enchanting place where collective identity is (re)produced

Outside of the pandemic, public houses served as a symbol of collective identity. Pubs are represented as institutions associated with an essentialist Irishness to an extent, but more with a dynamic reflexive collective identity that is constantly made and remade, involving a widening of the circle of sociability and identification. Pubs are frequently represented as loci of tradition, embodying an essentialist core of Irish, local and diasporic identity. They are shown as vestiges of peasant society and the pub–church–family–community matrix that composed this.[21] They are sacralised through the invocation of it being in peril but also represented as permanent, with frequent notes that the institution is under threat, combined with the idea that a pub has 'always been there', as the world changes around it.

While the pub is in one sense presented in a static and essentialist manner, it is also shown as a forum for intercultural communication, where 'non-Irish' encounter 'Irish' culture and creative mixing happens. It is used to symbolise the expanding circle of identity, political amity and the settling of historic animosities. It is also a bellwether for social change. On a more local level, pubs are treated as a means of orientation that makes a space legible. They are landmarks, storied locales patronised by storied persons with proprietors who are characters.

An enchanting place where community fabric is spun

The term 'pub' is used frequently as a modifier in articles to describe the popular, semi-rational public sphere of sociable, entertaining, unofficial discourse, for example 'pub talk'. The public house is also represented as a concrete place of 'pub regulars', of mundane sociability. It is painted as a place where social connections are made, with social capital built and drawn on there. It defines the quotidian, with going to the pub / leaving the pub acting as the background where other events intervene. It is where newcomers, such as migrants, returnees, people moving from a different region, successfully establish themselves as locals.

Pubs are represented as having a sect-like as well as a church-like quality. Some are where people who are socially excluded by mainstream society find acceptance in a somewhat closed-in group, within the safety of pub walls that exclude 'normals', as shown in references to gay bars like The George in Dublin or The Kremlin in Belfast. Thus, pubs are shown as where meaningful identities are established, in a setting of comfort, warmth, safety and acceptance. They are where people seek recognition, and the venue for community ritual cycles, such as émigrés returning at Christmas, sport events, or the venue to host celebrations for rites of passage. However, they are also represented as places where marginalisation and exclusion can be confirmed. Organisations representing the Traveller community are reported as noting the lack of protection for human rights and dignity of people who, based on their ethnicity, are refused admission to these quasi-public spaces. Racist incidents of mockery or harassment in pubs are part of reporting, alongside homophobic assaults, and the pub being a place where exclusionary, offensive talk and action can make people unwelcome.

Related to this is the link between pubs and tribal conflict. In the context of commemorations and the fiftieth anniversary of the worst years of the Troubles, there are stories about attacks on pubs by loyalists against Catholics, such as the McGurk's bar massacre, the Birmingham pub bombings, and British soldiers being lured from pubs to be killed by republicans. Davies[22] shows the lingering effects of this period of violence on pub culture. There are more contemporary examples noted, such as a petrol bomb attack on one of the pubs owned by mixed martial arts fighter and celebrity Conor McGregor.[23]

Disenchantment: the pub as a rational target for investment

The charming essence of pubs is balanced by stories where enchantment was broken by disenchantment. Disenchantment, in sociological parlance, refers not to humanistic values but to rational control that makes the world more predictable and manipulable. As Malcolm shows in this volume, the pub is not an intrinsic element of 'Irish culture', but a political creation, shaped by hard-headed considerations like licensing aimed at directing revenue to the state, balanced with the desire to maintain public order and inhibit rebellion and dissent. It is also an institution that serves various social functions, and changes as the demands placed on it by society changes. It involves the dominance of formal means-ends rationalities of science, bureaucracy, the law, and policy-making.[24] The typical image of pubs is of a small proprietor-run business, involving hard work and long hours, that is more than a job. Alongside the traditional image is reporting that shows it as a calculated business with increasing scale, concentrated ownership and a focus of investment.

Pub companies are reported on as chains that make major investments, and expand their position in the sector, with the focus on capital, share price, return on investment, the ups and downs of dividends and profits, acquisitions, and property development and refurbishments. Notable examples are the likes of Press Up (now Eclective), investment companies' portfolios, and UK pub chains with Irish interests, such as Mitchells & Butlers (Britain's largest pub group, which Irish businessmen J.P. McManus and John Magnier own a stake in) and Wetherspoons. Contrasting with this is a theme of vulnerability, and the need for government to support the 'sector' in the form of deregulation, and particularly the extension of hours, to protect what is represented as precarious nightlife and creative scenes. A minor story is the conflict between labour and capital, with it shown as a sector with insecure work and low pay, resulting in labour shortages.

Pubs also feature heavily in stories relating to individual investment in property. They are represented as an indicator of a vibrant area desirable for homeowners. However, alongside positive stories of gentrification around landmark pubs is a discourse about how profit- and rent-seeking results in an erosion of the essence of cultural soul, sociability and liveability for city denizens. Questions are raised of ownership of space, with a lack of (semi-) public amenities in the form of pubs, placed alongside multiple other problems, such as a housing crisis and inadequate public transport. There are stories of vacant pub premises targeted for redevelopment as built-to-let apartments, hotels and student accommodation. A prominent story related to pubs is of cities coming to serve footloose mobile groups and not residents. The potential closure of the Cobblestone pub and its replacement by a hotel became iconic of this, with multiple other prominent cases such as the closure (and ultimate relocation) of the Bernard Shaw, the demolition of Kiely's, or the closure of the Big Tree.

There is a theme regarding the misallocation of investment, appearing as a glut and dearth in different places. There are stories about investment producing commercially driven 'drinktainment' districts (most notoriously Dublin's Temple Bar), with a consequent loss of cultural authenticity and public order problems. Pubs are shown as under threat through the off-trade sales in retail chains, resulting in social isolation. Pub closures are painted as an indicator of community decline due to lack of investment and political neglect. For rural communities closures are shown as linked with depopulation and lack of opportunities. The number of pubs in a place is used as a measure of its significance, and whether it qualifies as a place at all ('a two-pub town').

Disenchantment: consumption

On the consumption side, there is an image of pubs as an aspect of 'Ireland Inc.'. Pubs are represented as a central part of the tourist economy and packaged tourist experience, whereby a commodified notion of Irishness is consumed. Aspects of this include the Guinness Storehouse, literary pubs such as Davy Byrnes, associated alcohol-related festivals like Bloomsday, pubs such as Tom Crean's pub that connect rurality to the global and adventure, and other examples of alco-tourism.

The process of specialisation and functional differentiation is shown in pubs becoming focused on consumption and losing the myriad of functions once associated with them, such as being used to make phone calls before these were a universal domestic convenience, and with food stores, a petrol station and a hardware shop on the same premises. However, they are still shown as incubators of economic and political enterprises before they become free-standing undertakings, for example in the proverbial 'office above a pub'. The spread of drinking beyond pubs is noted also, with them no longer being spaces that drinking is largely contained within, with drinking rather spilling out into homes, streets, football stadiums and other traditionally non-drink-related spaces. The Diageo-created 'Arthur's Day' continues to resonate in reflections as an exemplification of this, when a pub-based event resulted in mass intoxication.

Stories also deal with pubs becoming hyperreal, as in how 'tradition' becomes something for sale, in the form of pub furniture, memorabilia, collectibles and bric-a-brac, sold as lots, to be consciously used to present a premises as characterful. Rather than its design being an organic product of the customs, materials and trade skills of an area, the pub becomes a product of conscious design and carefully planned commercial ends.

Disenchantment: a threat to efficient public administration

The pub appears regularly in reporting as an incidental background to negative incidents in relation to public health, public morality and crime. The most directly made link is with public order problems. The pub is persistently mentioned in the contextualisation of incidents of violence (serious assaults and murder, including gangland assassinations, and interpersonal violence during attendance, outside pubs, and following attendance), sexual harassment, sexual assault, accidents, persons going missing, drink driving resulting in serious injury and death, and theft. Pubs are also mentioned in reference to health and safety violations and quality of life issues such as excessive noise. Public health measures receive some attention, such as the introduction of minimum unit pricing, enforcement of the smoking ban, measures introduced elsewhere. There is minimal focus on licensing, with occasional stories about buildings in homes being turned into bars without permission.

In contrast to this, there is reporting of the demands of a deregulation movement. Their narrative is captured in phrases such as 'pub licences are the taxi plates of the twenty-first century', noting that high profits are caused by a barrier to new entrants, and a failure of policy to adhere to the laws of supply and demand, resulting in market dysfunctions. Opening hours became a particular focus of attention, as a way to provide relief to the sector following the pandemic.

Disenchantment: self-regulation

Public houses are part of the discourse concerning the always moving question of the socially appropriate level of self-control. Stories recur of failures in self-regulation, such as those of alcoholic parents attending pubs rather than to their caring responsibilities, the difficulty of a pub-centred culture for those dealing with addiction, and a trope about how pub attendance encourages non-productiveness. Pubs are represented as loci of decadence and the enervation of civic culture. There are stories of politicians drinking, holding court in pubs, misusing state drivers as rides home, of unwise politically incorrect statements by politicians in pubs made under the influence of an intoxicating atmosphere, of breaches of public health regulations in pubs owned by politicians, politicians failing in caring duties by leaving their children behind in pubs, and assaults by celebrities of other patrons of a pub.

Against this is the reference to pubs in the discussion of new techniques of more precise self-control. There are questions of the appropriate level of disinhibition to produce a good atmosphere. This may come in forms of rational hedonism, such as Dry January, the 'damp lifestyle', or experiments with visiting a pub and not drinking alcohol, the recent boom in alcohol-free beverages, and a fitness culture that counterposes a self-improvement culture of optimisation with a culture of relaxation and indulgence.

Out-of-the-ordinary times: the representation of the pub during the pandemic

In the course of the pandemic, the themes in reporting on public houses changed substantially. The liminal period of the pandemic was one in which technocratic administration driven by the public health crisis greatly intensified and it was thus a period of disenchantment. However, it was equally a period where a sense of control and predictability was suspended as taken-for-granted features of life fell away. Thus, it was also a period of re-enchantment because, as rational control of everyday life spread, so did emotional questioning around the meaning of what was happening.[25] The period was significant in revealing a more atavistic narrative that resurfaced and assumed primacy over the narratives discussed above.

The pandemic was a cultural trauma, causing ontological suffering, stimulating questions around the meaning of what we are going through, and indeed who 'we' are.[26] Articulating that 'we' are part of a greater whole was a source of ontological security. Thus, in periods of cultural trauma, tropes held in collective memory circulate in the form of narratives that combat a sense of chaos and meaninglessness, by reaffirming identity through telling stories about 'us'. Such stories address totems of identity, praising its sacred core and those who sacrifice themselves for the community, obligations of members, real and symbolic boundaries, blame of those who threaten them and contaminate the moral body, and negative characterisations of others and outsiders, especially those who threaten to pierce and rip open the protective boundary of the community. Classifications are established in response to cultural traumas of moral and immoral actors, involving heroes, perpetrators and victims.

Decent folks in pub closure and reopening

Newspapers represented an ideal-type publican who was constructed as representative of post-Land War, small-scale proprietor culture, and was rural and cultural nationalist. This type, viewed as honourable and representative of the nation, was characterised as having 'tradition', an 'older clientele', oriented to the local community or network, and as loyal to staff and customers. The Dublin literary pub Grogan's was particularly iconic, as were small, 'ordinary' rural pubs, and the small and shrinking number of multi-generational family pubs, whose plight served as a warning of the fading soul of 'real' Ireland. The 'good' was portrayed through well-established tropes of Irish identity, such as the rural pub owned by the GAA player, the closure of Irish pubs around the globe resulting in expats returning home, the social isolation of lonely bachelors and widowers in the lockdowns, the threat to sacred watering holes of literary Dublin such as the Palace, Grogan's and Mulligan's, and the loss of 'craic', the *sine qua non* and *je ne sais quoi* of Irishness.

The metaphorical power of publicans came from the scale of the upheaval, shown in the pouring away of beer, images of an empty Temple Bar, and references to how previous crises such as the 'Emergency'[27] or the foot-and-mouth epidemic had not resulted in pub closing. They served as icons of the 'real economy' of locally embedded businesses, in contrast to the multinational sector which suffered minimal disruption. Publicans were prominent in the disorienting early phase of the pandemic, where many made the self-sacrificial act of closing before official instruction was received, in the interest of the public good. Indeed, publicans pushed for government directive for closures due to the unenforceability of social distancing and time limits, though the length of the lockdown was not predicted. They were then reported as being placed in the role of 'schoolteachers' and 'fun police' in enforcing public health protocols during the various partial reopenings.

Publicans were shown as victim-heroes, suffering from the acts of – or neglect by – the perpetrators of the impersonal force of the pandemic, and the inattentive political centre, which connected with the genre of anti-urbanism and the otherness of the political centre and capital.[28] They were constructed as victims of an intensification of the process of rationalisation (the spread of means-ends rationalities characteristic of science, bureaucracy, the law and policy-making), caused by the pandemic. The lockdowns were the latest instance of public health policies such as drink-driving legislation and the smoking ban, which made local practices officially unacceptable in favour of universal protocols based on public health research. The rational basis of public health policy based on the utilitarian calculation – such as epidemiological models for protecting and preserving life – over more intangible goods such as sociability, social capital and leisure that pubs provided was clearly hegemonic. This was exemplified in a story of the taoiseach telling the leader of a group that critiqued the ongoing lockdown of licensed premises to 'cop on and get a bit real', and to end the attempt to 'consistently undermine the public health message'. Thus, publicans were shown as being caught in a purgatory they could not be saved from. Death was a prominent metaphor about such 'real' pubs, as they faced the 'final nail in the coffin'. This was enacted outside the Dáil by Kerry publicans, who staged a protest in which a literal coffin was delivered to the parliament. The term 'wet pub' described those that only served drink, and which were prevented from opening alongside those that served food. 'Wetness' acted as a peculiarly negative descriptor, with connotations of contamination.

Nonetheless, the image of the small owner-proprietor was broken occasionally, for example in the court case between pub businesses and insurers who refused to pay business interruption policies. This case revealed the highly profitable and large scale of many pub businesses. Indeed, one unofficial spokesperson for pub owners began the process of constructing apartments on land beside one of his pubs, which revealed the large assets possessed by some licence holders.

Folk devils in pub closure and reopening: enemies within

Prior to the pandemic, premises and leisure districts associated with neoliberal values and reflexive individualism, such as youth enjoying their freedom, the global, vibrancy, consumer freedom and mixing, were generally positively evaluated. Vibrancy had been the goal for nightlife and pursued by urban policy, exemplified in the redevelopment of Temple Bar in the 1990s as a cultural quarter. This had represented a shift from cultural-nationalist modernist principles, to cosmopolitanism, tapping into global flows of capital and tourists, and seeking to increase the intensity of consumption in districts.[29]

Significantly, Temple Bar was central to how the danger that Irish society faced, in the early and uncertain phase of the pandemic, was represented. The failure to implement or respect government advice on social distancing in premises there by pub staff, patrons or gardaí became a high-profile news story. In response, the minister for health, Simon Harris, described the scenes as an 'insult' to the efforts of the health service to treat and curtail the virus. While the Temple Bar Company days later announced that all licensed premises would be closed, the tone of stories indicated that the opportunity to appear civic-minded or intrinsically motivated by public health concerns had passed, as many premises around the country had already closed voluntarily days before. In the days that followed, the Health (Preservation and Protection and other Emergency Measures in the Public Interest) Bill 2020 was passed, notably accompanied by judgemental comments by parliamentarians about the unsafe and inconsiderate behaviour witnessed in Temple Bar.

Youth-oriented venues were similarly a focus of concern and judgement due to their implications for public health, but also reflected a public morality in how they were represented as involving reckless sociability, where a lack of temperance and civic-mindedness resulted in their fun inflicting damage on Irish society at large. In the early stages of the pandemic prior to lockdown, an article was written about an iconic Dublin nightclub, famous for the amorous mixing that happens there, entitled 'Maintain Social Distancing: How Does that Work in Coppers?' A lack of social distancing and an unconcerned attitude by patrons was reported, with a young woman quizzed in the bathroom responding to the journalist: 'To be honest, I don't give a f**k about the coronavirus.'[30] House parties were represented as nihilistic festivity, and the minister for health was reported as scolding young people, telling them to 'show a bit of cop on and not hold parties', though unlicensed bars established in private dwellings by older people was also a story through the pandemic. In the reopening of pubs there was a series of stories about lack of compliance in youthful and 'trendy' venues, with little similar comment about 'traditional' and 'mature' premises.

A significant running story concerned large gatherings of young people in streets in fashionable quarters of city and town centres, with reports of little social distancing, intoxication and public order incidents. Critical statements from pub bodies against publicans who sold takeaway drinks to people attending such gatherings were published, though a caveat was added that much of the drink had been bought in shops and off-licences, whose alcohol sales had been categorised as an essential service throughout the lockdowns.

There were a small number of stories concerning the difficulties young people faced through the lockdowns, such as their greater reliance on employment in hospitality, the gig-economy, and their more acute need for sociability, which was stifled. The closure of 'third spaces' intensified the inadequacy of the 'first spaces' (accommodation) and 'second spaces' (work) for young adults, who might struggle to gain adequate independent accommodation or non-precarious employment, and who bore more costs than older cohorts in the pandemic.[31] There was reporting of public order incidents that emphasised youthful troublemakers more than aggressive policing. The plight of young people was occasionally framed in utilitarian terms. The 'social recession' was framed as threatening economic recession as lockdowns illustrated the precariousness of the economic model of Ireland's competition state, whose vanguard is a footloose, youthful, highly international workforce. Their attachment to Ireland, and contribution to the tax base, is held by the requirement to be resident and depends on attractions such as the evening and night-time economy. A real and desired flight of this workforce from Ireland to more affordable remote work locations was presented as a warning signal of the precariousness of the economic model of foreign direct investment, property development, a vibrant hospitality and cultural sector and cosmopolitan workforce.

'Different folk': enemies without

There was minor and occasional comment about laxness in regulating licensed premises during the pandemic in close European neighbours such as Sweden or the Netherlands, and lack of collective efficacy and failures of public policy in the United States that saw 'super-spreading' events in bars and nightclubs. However, the frequency and tone of stories about the policy of the UK government and political pronouncements by British politicians regarding licensed premises in the pandemic showed that these went beyond merely factual reporting. Rather, they assumed the role of an 'other' through which identity was constructed. They involved a reversal of the colonial gaze, as Britain was represented as struggling to self-govern, in contrast to the capacity for rational public policy and public support for this shown by Ireland. Policy regarding the closure and reopening of licensed premises in Britain was characterised as driven by symbolic motives rather than rational expedience. Pubs were utilised by British politicians to represent an essentialist British identity grounded in liberalism, which squirms at the constraints of bureaucracy, administration and interdependence, and for which lockdown was particularly chafing. The result was a later closure of licensed premises in the first and second lockdowns and policies that encouraged a return to pubs, such as the 'Eat Out to Help Out' scheme. The essence of the narrative was a binary between responsible and communitarian Ireland and irresponsible and liberal Britain. The policy in relation to licensed premises in the pandemic was on balance represented as involving necessary sacrifice and collective solidarity for a greater good, while UK policy was represented as the opposite.

Pubs were reported on as playing a role in political theatre that distracted from effective management of the pandemic. This was framed by the context of the symbolic use of ale and the pub in the Brexit campaign, with a pint and visit to a pub representing connection to an essential Britishness, defined by the value of liberty. The reporting by the British press of Prime Minister Boris Johnson's statement on the closing of pubs in the United Kingdom was itself reported on, when he stated: 'We are taking away the ancient, inalienable right of the free-born people of the United Kingdom to go to the pub.' This was constructed as representative of the national exceptionalism, the 'fantasy of freedom', and an effort to mobilise particularistic identities for political purposes, while failing in responsible governance. When pubs were re-opened in the United Kingdom there was again reporting of Johnson's statement: 'I do encourage people to take advantage of the freedoms that they are rightly reacquiring, but I must stress that people should act in a responsible way.' Rather than responsible management, the image given was of hasty and disorderly reopening. Johnson was also reported as being guilty of providing misleading descriptions of new restrictions on licensed premises.

The pub chain Wetherspoons and its founder and chairman Tim Martin also represented a negative form of Britishness that Irish identity was constructed against.

They represented McDonaldisation, concentration of ownership, profit-focus, and a foreign influence creeping into the purity of the Irish nation. It was noted how it 'jars with the norms of Irish hospitality', a market constituted by small and medium players, and premises defined by personality. Martin was represented as lacking in care and concern, as when payments were suspended to suppliers until after the end of the lockdown, and for his statements that criticised lockdown restrictions. He was noted as 'virulently pro-Brexit' and 'the selfish British capitalist'. The threat of Wetherspoons is that of a disease agent, both in terms of the pandemic and in infecting the Irish market and cultural body.

Conclusion

Pubs in ordinary times are represented in mainstream newspaper reporting as vehicles for the realisation of the type of reflexive-individualism that is characteristic of contemporary subjectivity. Personal authenticity, experienced as enchantment, is realised through an art of life that the pub serves as a stage for. Pubs are shown as a space of enchantment where attachment, emotion, expression, and the non-material or instrumental prevails. Another picture is of the disenchanted context of rational businesses seeking scale and profits, pursued by utilitarian calculations of acquiring cultural capital, in environments of risk, where health, order and crime threaten the projects carried out in the leisure setting of the pub.

Stories addressing pubs in the pandemic period were markedly different. They were highly stereotypical, articulating established narratives about Irish identity, for which the pub was emblematic. Publicans were portrayed as representatives of the sacred core of Irish collective identity, embodying qualities of age, maturity, rurality, cultural-nationalist identity, and the post-Land War ideal of small, locally oriented owner-proprietors. Irish society has been described as a gerontocracy where the periphery (countryside) dominates the centre (cities and capital), and this is reflected in the stereotypical representation of youth, the urban crowd and mixing as sources of moral and literal infection of the community. Alongside these enemies within is the external other of Britain, represented as embodying the undesirable features of modernity. Thus, it is evident that, while the public house in Irish society is an institution corresponding with the global culture of reflexive individualism, in times of crisis specific and inward-looking characterisations of it leap forth from collective memory, depicting it as an important symbol of 'Irishness'.

John O'Brien's Choice:

Geoff's,

Waterford city

Figure 19.1 Interior of Geoff's. Photo by Hayley Stuart.

Geoff's, situated on John Street, is a Waterford city institution. Its setting has been transformed recently by the redevelopment of the 'Apple Market'. It is no longer off a narrow path on a busy city centre road, but is now set on a pedestrianised square, which has a giant triangular mirror as a roof, giving the impression of an imperial star destroyer from *Star Wars* hovering to protect Waterfordians from the rain. The pub itself has changed over the years. In 1995 it acquired the adjoining premises, considerably increasing its size and, following the smoking ban, it opened the beer garden to the rear, and following the redesign of the Apple Market it opened an on-street terrace, where the theatre of street life can be viewed. It is a pub with a personality, being an intergenerational family pub, in the Power family since 1907, now managed on their behalf. There is an aura of relaxation, and not trying too hard, while food, drink and service remain at a very good standard. It mixes the traditional and the contemporary. The olfactory experience is dominated by a scent mixing varnished wood and stout, typical of any traditional pub. There is classic pub decor with bare planks and old tiled floors, wood-panelled walls and an array of pub bric-a-brac like antique signs and advertising. However, there are also art pieces reminiscent of tribal totems or avant-garde works exploring disturbing aspects of the human condition. The emphasis on good taste in contemporary music has apparently been a feature since Geoff Power took over management in 1977. But there are no televisions. Unlike the traditionally closed view into public houses through raised frosted or stained-glass panels, the frontage is dominated by large single-pane windows. Rather than the reclusiveness and intimacy of traditional pubs, Geoff's is an invitation to people watch within and without.

Chapter 20

Conclusion: Irish Pubs, from the Global to the Personal

Perry Share and Moonyoung Hong

As the first quarter century of the millennium draws to a close, Irish pubs have continued to evolve, reproduce and re-invent themselves. In this concluding chapter, we want to outline some of the more recent developments in the Irish pub scene, from the global to the personal, bringing together the many strands that have emerged in the previous chapters. We also point to some of the compelling questions and issues that will repay further research and enquiry in the future – for the evolution of the Irish pub never stops.

In the summer of 2023, the Vintners' Federation of Ireland (VFI), a representative body for the licensed trade, made a submission to the Department of Culture, Heritage and the Gaeltacht for the Irish pub to be placed on the National Inventory of Intangible Cultural Heritage of Ireland.[1] This is an initial step in attaining broader UNESCO heritage status, where the Irish pub could join other distinctive aspects of Irish cultural patrimony that include uilleann piping, hurling, Irish harping and falconry – with dry stone walling the most recent (2023–4) candidate.[2]

The VFI submission seeks formal international recognition of the phenomenon of the Irish pub – a designation more symbolic than of practical significance. But it also reflects the idea that the Irish pub is in existential peril. According to the *Guardian* newspaper, echoing many other media outlets, pubs in Ireland have 'never been at greater risk'.[3] Much of this recent discourse can be traced to the series of reports compiled by Dublin City University economist Anthony Foley, who has conducted much work funded by Ireland's alcoholic drinks industry. Writing for the sectoral body Drinks Industry Group Ireland in 2023,[4] Foley has noted that since 2005, 1,829 – or one in five – pubs in Ireland have closed, albeit that around 7,000 remain.[5]

This phenomenon is reflected in the experience of one of the authors. His small rural town has seen a reduction in the number of active pubs from eleven to four and a half[6] over a period of two decades since the early 2000s. Similarly, many rural roadside pubs have ceased to function, as wider, faster roads, better vehicles, town and village bypasses and drink-driving legislation have rendered them obsolete. Many country towns have seen significant and well-known pubs disappear from their streetscapes, leaving gaps in the urban fabric that are not always filled by other users.[7] Despite this gloomy prognosis, the Health Research Board has noted that Ireland has the third highest number of pubs per capita in the OECD (after Slovakia and Hungary) and has calculated that three-quarters of Ireland's population lives within just 300 metres of a licensed premises (which could be a bar, pub, supermarket or off-licence).[8]

Cultural change is often experienced as traumatic – even when a person is not directly affected. The loss of pubs, especially but not only in rural areas of Ireland, can be seen as an attack on 'traditional' ways of living. This has resonances when so many other aspects of everyday life can be perceived to be under threat, from the 'traditional family', debated in 2024 in the context of a constitutional referendum, to 'traditional farming practices' – such as slurry-spreading or turf-cutting – that are being challenged by climate breakdown and biodiversity collapse. The disappearance of pubs has meaning for many Irish people in both their psychic and physical space.

In her 2005 book *For Space*, geographer Doreen Massey argues that space is 'an open and ongoing production'.[9] Her argument highlights a dynamic, relational understanding of space and place. To examine the pub from a multidisciplinary angle, as we have attempted in this volume, aligns with Massey's idea of the coexistence of multiple social relations, histories and experiences within a specific space. Places, she argues, are not static or fixed but are formed through a combination of local and global influences. As our contributors have amply demonstrated, the Irish pub is not an entity fixed in aspic, but a product of various historical, economic, social and political forces that have shaped both its interior and its broader location over time, as well as the number and nature of drinking establishments.

Massey's concept of 'thrown togetherness' provides a further valuable framework for understanding Irish pubs. The Irish pub is, first, a product of interrelations, formed through interactions; second, a realm of diverse trajectories and heterogeneous elements; and third, always in the process of being shaped and reshaped by ongoing social, material and cultural dynamics. Our contributors' accounts and understandings of the Irish pub can be 'thrown together' to explore its role as a dynamic space shaped by diverse social interactions, transports, movements, cultural representations, performances, changing economy and contesting ideologies and identities. Focusing on the pub as an assemblage allows us to examine the visible forms and the invisible networks that support them.

This 'thrown togetherness', we further argue, is an aesthetic act. The literary, poetic and musical dimensions that the Irish pub embodies and expresses further animate people's collective acts, desires and will, that are radical and political. As Brian Larkin notes, infrastructures are inherently both imaginative and technical entities, composed of aspirations as much as concrete or steel.[10] Pubs in Ireland constitute a large part of the Irish social infrastructure. They shape our perception of time – whether by creating a sense of detachment from history's flow, anchoring us to the past, isolating us in the present or propelling us toward the future. They interact with their users, evoking emotions such as hope, pessimism, nostalgia, desire, comfort, frustration and anger, which together form the emotive and political dynamics of promise, and its potential failure.

The global: The Irish pub as an exported and cultural commodity

Inevitably the Irish pub is connected to a particular notion of space and place: some notion of 'Ireland' and 'Irishness'. We have seen that even in the archetypal 'non-space' of the international airport, the markers of culture and geography can be deployed to evoke a particular type of feeling and belonging. Pubs have always had a complex relationship to space: associated with the static and rooted notion of 'community' while also originating in human practices of movement and communication.

Elizabeth Malcolm's historical account (chapter 2) shows how the development of public houses in Ireland was closely linked to that of settlements such as villages and towns; conversely there is a strong connection between mobility and pubs. From initially servicing the routes of stagecoaches, canals and steamships, pubs changed in response to road travel and the emergence of the motor vehicle. Most recently air travel and ubiquitous tourism have aided the global spread of Irish pubs. From the hospitality offered to Ireland's medieval travellers to the airport facilities provided for the globally mobile, the provision of drink (and food) for those in transit has always been important.[11]

It is not possible to consider the contemporary Irish pub outside of the context of globalisation. The modern pub within Ireland has increasingly come to form part of the broader tourist and entertainment industry, building on a long exploitation of the charms of the pub as a tourism product. The remarkable global diffusion of the Irish pub[12] has reflected, initially, the impact of Ireland's global diaspora and, more recently, the development of the packaged Irish pub as a global brand, not dissimilar in its ubiquity to the Starbucks coffee shop, the kebab parlour and the pizza restaurant, as described by Tracey Dalton in chapter 7. Like others of these ersatz cultural phenomena, authenticity can lie in being 'Irish enough' to convey a particular set of markers of comfort, safety, predictability and the chance of some 'craic', as Grantham has rather cynically pointed out.[13]

The globalisation of the Irish pub cannot be disconnected from the evolution of Guinness as a global brand. Guinness is currently brewed in fifty countries and consumed in 150. Pilcher describes how the growth of Guinness as a global alcohol brand over three centuries was inextricably linked to the development of the British Empire.[14] Thus, of the current top ten Guinness-consuming countries, four (Nigeria, Cameroon, Ghana and Kenya) are in Africa, three of them former British colonies, along with Malaysia, a former southeast Asian British colony. 'Guinness became globalized by establishing local breweries and shaping drinking cultures in former British colonies around the world, even while retaining the European cachet of its Irish origins.' It could be argued that a similar approach – one that combines an exporting company in a western European country with local and localised entrepreneurial enterprises – has underpinned the global dissemination of the Irish pub. The social media-driven resurgence of Guinness as a cultural phenomenon in global cities such as London and New York in the mid 2020s may have an – as yet unidentified – impact on the development of Irish pubs.[15]

The global Irish pub also functions as a form of 'soft power', shaping international perceptions of Ireland and Irishness through curated symbols of conviviality, music and community, linked to other cultural products such as popular and literary fiction, music videos and St Patrick's Day festivities. Visiting an Irish pub, no matter how 'inauthentic', may be the only connection a person has with the entity of 'Ireland'. Yet this commodification is not without tension. While the pub fosters a sense of cultural connection for diasporic communities and tourists, it also risks perpetuating pernicious and reductive stereotypes, particularly the association of Irish identity with alcohol consumption. Such portrayals have been critiqued in cultural studies and media, from *Punch* cartoons of the nineteenth century to contemporary advertising tropes. These narratives highlight the dual-edged nature of the Irish pub as both a space of cultural pride and a site of contested identity.

Figure 20.1 Bus advertisement for EPIC The Irish Emigration Museum. The character 'Paddy McFlaherty' reflects the stereotypical pint-touting view of Irishness that persists in the output of internet search engines and AI image generators. Courtesy of EPIC The Irish Emigration Museum.

Contemporary social media has amplified the reach and visibility of the Irish pub as a global brand. Platforms like Instagram and TikTok (hashtags include #irishpub and #pintlife) are replete with imagery of 'authentic' Irish pubs in cities ranging from New York to Tokyo, showcasing their unique interiors, cultural performances and connections to the Guinness brand. These visual platforms play a crucial role in constructing and sustaining the mythos of the Irish pub, allowing users to engage in a shared, virtual experience of Irishness. Viral trends, such as virtual pub crawls or Guinness-pouring and drinking challenges, further illustrate how social media both commodifies and democratises the pub experience, extending its cultural resonance to new audiences.

Moreover, the global dissemination of Irish pubs facilitates adaptability to diverse cultural contexts: allowing them to become cultural hybrids. In Copenhagen, we find the Old Irish Pub karaoke bar, while pubs in Hong Kong and Seoul incorporate local culinary and drinking traditions. Global trends such as the craft beer movement, gastropubs, the emergence of alcohol-free pubs, and wellness-oriented spaces – as well as the popularity of karaoke – impact on the development of Irish pubs in Ireland and internationally. While such 'mash-ups' of cultural patterns and practices can be cause

Figure 20.2
The Old Irish Pub karaoke bar, Copenhagen. Photo by Perry Share.

for bemusement and humour,[16] this hybridity reflects the interplay between global branding and local customisation, illustrating Massey's notion of space as continually reshaped by intersecting social and cultural forces.

Irish pubs in texts and on screens: cultural and literary representations

In December 2024, Irish actor Paul Mescal hosted the popular US television show *Saturday Night Live* (SNL). A sketch, 'Irish Americans: What Americans think will happen when they visit Ireland', humorously depicted an American couple visiting an Irish pub, where they are met with exaggerated enthusiasm upon revealing their distant Irish ancestry. The bartender, played by Mescal, and the locals erupt in celebration when the American man mentions he is a quarter Irish and has an Irish grandmother named O'Connor. The bartender joyfully declares, 'Welcome home, lad! Everyone, a son of the soil has returned to us!' before ringing the pub bell to announce his arrival. The sketch satirises American expectations of Ireland, using the pub as the focal setting for this exaggerated fantasy.[17]

While SNL critiques the romanticised portrayal of Irish culture, it also reinforces stereotypes – featuring 'Celtic' designs, Gaelic-style fonts and a final celebratory round of Guinness. This exaggerated yet affectionate rendering reflects how mainstream media often idealises Irish identity, depicting a vision of Ireland – and its pubs – as a land of warm welcomes, community and a sense of belonging tied to ancestry. The sketch, albeit playful, echoes a broader cinematic tradition that has long framed Irish pubs as key cultural and social spaces in both Irish and Irish-American storytelling. Unsurprisingly, it does little to reflect the hybridisation and diversity alluded to above.

The SNL sketch is but one example in a long tradition of Irish pubs serving as significant settings in film and television.[18] A classic instance is *The Quiet Man* (1952),

Figure 20.3 Exterior of Pat Cohan bar, Cong, the location for the film *The Quiet Man*. Photo by Moonyoung Hong.

directed by John Ford, that tells the story of an Irish-American boxer returning to his ancestral home in Cong, County Mayo. The film's enduring appeal has transformed its shooting locations into tourist attractions; in 2008, Pat Cohan's gastropub was established in the very building used as the pub in the film. Now more restaurant than pub, it is unlikely to feature in the type of brawl that was the action centrepiece of the film.

The presence of Irish pubs in popular media extends beyond nostalgic tales. In the quintessential TV crime drama *The Sopranos*, Christopher Moltisanti famously complains about The Emerald Piper, a (fictional) Irish pub described as 'hell' where 'it's St Patrick's Day every day forever', pointing to sharp Italian–Irish ethnic divisions in an American context. Conversely, romantic comedies often utilise the Irish pub as a picturesque setting for meet-cutes and heartfelt moments, as seen in US films *P.S. I Love You* (2007), *Leap Year* (2010) and *Wild Mountain Thyme* (2020).

In *P.S. I Love You*, based on a Cecilia Ahern novel, a pivotal scene takes place in Whelan's pub in Dublin, where the protagonist encounters a singer performing 'Galway Girl', a song tied to her late husband. *Leap Year* pushes the pub trope even further, making the male protagonist a publican. The fictional Caragh's Inn, where Declan works, is represented on film by Conneely's Guesthouse in Kilmurvey, on Inishmore. *Wild Mountain Thyme*, directed by John Patrick Shanley and based on his play *Outside Mullingar*, is another romanticised depiction of a rural west of Ireland.[19] Set in the picturesque landscapes of north Mayo, it tells the story of a local bachelor (Jamie Dornan) and a strong-willed woman (Emily Blunt), featuring a domineering father (Christopher Walken) and a pragmatic widow (Dearbhla Molloy). The film concludes with Emily Blunt singing 'Wild Mountain Thyme' in a traditional Irish pub. However, the film was widely criticised for its inaccurate Irish accents and an overly sentimentalised portrayal of Ireland,[20] with *The Guardian* calling out its 'sublime awfulness and condescension' towards Irish culture.[21]

In contrast to these romanticised portrayals, The *Banshees of Inisherin* (2022), directed by Martin McDonagh, offers a darker, more introspective look at the Irish pub's cultural significance. Set on a remote island, the film follows Pádraic Súilleabháin (Colin Farrell) and Colm Doherty (Brendan Gleeson), whose long-standing friendship fractures when Colm abruptly decides he no longer wants to associate with Pádraic. The pub serves as the stage for this emotional rupture, emphasising its role as a communal gathering place in small rural communities and

Figure 20.4 (right) Exterior of the Hawthorn bar, Belfast. Photo by Rita Kirkpatrick.

Figure 20.5 (below) Exterior of Madden's bar, Belfast. Photo by Rita Kirkpatrick.

as a setting for masculine friendship. Unlike rom-coms that present the Irish pub as a place of charm and serendipity, *Banshees* explores its function as a site of personal identity, darkness, social tension and existential reflection, using the dissolution of friendship as an allegory for Ireland's Civil War.

The pub remains at the centre of much cultural expression from north of the border. The Hawthorn and Madden's bar in Belfast are Kneecap's favourite pubs. Kneecap, a bilingual Irish/English hip-hop trio, blends socialist themes, humour and working-class experiences with references to the Troubles, appealing to younger republicans and others, focused on social issues. They critique authority while resonating across communities, often filming music videos and frequenting local pubs to reflect their roots. This authenticity, alongside their controversial yet nostalgic imagery, mirrors broader generational shifts away from past conflicts. With a global fanbase, international performances and an Oscars-longlisted film, Kneecap embodies the evolving cultural identity of younger Irish nationalists in a post-peace process era. Their music video for the song 'Better Way to Live' was filmed in Madden's bar.[22]

Kneecap creates music that merges local and global influences within their community's physical and cultural spaces, such as the local pubs where they film music videos and engage with fans. Their work highlights the coexistence of historical and modern elements, intertwining memories of the Troubles with present-day issues such as poverty and education. This synthesis mirrors Massey's idea of place as dynamic, shaped by intersecting social relations, histories and identities, and exemplifies how Kneecap uses Irish pubs as vibrant, layered spaces for storytelling and cultural exchange.

Contemporary Irish writing, too, continues to reflect the Irish pub's deep cultural significance. At the end of the last millennium, Roddy Doyle captured, perhaps better than any other writer, the world of the ordinary Dublin pub, notably in his 'Barrytown Trilogy' of novels: *The Commitments*, *The Van* and *The Snapper*.[23] He has continued to excavate the milieu of the pub in later works of fiction and drama. His *Two Pints* series features dialogues between two men in a Dublin pub, discussing world affairs, contemporary issues and personal troubles. The series, which includes *Two Pints* (2011), *Two More Pints* (2014), *Two for the Road* (2019) and *The Zoom Pints* (2020), captures the humour, camaraderie and often meandering conversations typical of Irish pub culture. His novel *Love* (2020), a response to the challenge 'can I make a good novel out of a pub bore?', centres on a night of pint-drinking and conversation, immersing the reader in an unfiltered, stream-of-consciousness dialogue between two old friends reminiscing and arguing over pints.[24]

Doyle's descriptions bring the atmosphere of Dublin pubs to life:

> We'd found a pub that liked us. We'd wandered the city centre for months, every weekend, starting after work on Friday and ending ten minutes before the last bus home on Sunday night. This was after I graduated and had new money in my pocket … I could buy my round. We were peers now and we could become the lifelong friends we hadn't really been before. Getting drunk together, sneering at the world together.[25]

Doyle's writing directs our attention to the gendered identity and dynamics within the pub. The men affirm and navigate their masculinity:

> We were laughing again, chatting. Soaking it in, soaking in it. I could feel myself melting – it was good – flowing slowly into the noise, the accents, the jokes, the stories, the geography. Listening. Hoping someone would say something to me … It was why we'd been coming into town. To make the break. To live up, somehow, to the music we loved, the books we read. To walk streets instead of roads, cross a real river, sit in the pubs that Behan and Flann O'Brien had sat in, find the women who'd see, who'd understand, who'd hold us, who'd do things to us. Who'd come up to us and start it. Let us in. Let us soar.[26]

Doyle's writing explores issues of masculinity, social class and nostalgia, illustrating how Irish pubs serve as spaces of reflection, bonding and, sometimes, existential despair.

Other contemporary depictions, such as Sally Rooney's *Normal People* (2020), showcase the pub as a space for modern Irish social life. In one scene in that novel, characters discuss literature and class dynamics at a well-known Dublin pub, the Stag's Head, highlighting how Irish pubs continue to be sites of intellectual and cultural exchange (a space that enables 'culture as class performance' as the male character Connell remarks). The novel's climax unfolds in Kelleher's, a packed pub on New Year's Eve, reinforcing the enduring role of the Irish pub as a backdrop for both personal and collective emotional experiences.

Paul Murray's *The Bee Sting* (2023), shortlisted for the 2023 Booker Prize, gives a multifaceted picture of the pub. Each section of the novel, narrated from one of the members of the Barnes family, demonstrates the varying experiences of the pub, through diverse lenses of gender, age, sexual orientation and profession. Cass and Elaine, teenage girls about to take their Leaving Cert, spend their time in Doran's pub, which everyone calls 'the Drain'. Murray captures the culture of underage drinking very well:

> The reason was clear as soon as Cass stepped inside. People said that in the days when you could smoke you barely noticed it, but now even with the yard left permanently open, the stink was inescapable … The PA played a non-stop barrage of 1980s metal, the pool table had a rip, and the Guinness

> tap frequently got infested with ants. But the barman never checked ID and so, apart from a handful of genuine rockers with greasy greying locks and upside-down pentagram on their T-shirts, the place was full most nights with underage drinkers.[27]

Later, Cass visits many other pubs with Elaine, to be harassed by other men, while also discovering Cass's parents' secret that it was originally her deceased Uncle Frank (star footballer, town hero and brother of her father Dickie) who got engaged to her mother in Deasy's pub. The pub is a place where they not only celebrate the team's victory, but also debrief after the game:

> The problem was the game didn't end with the final whistle Everyone had an opinion they needed to pass on to him Everyone wanted to buy him a pint or shake his hand In the pub On the street They would come up to him they would crowd round him Everybody wanted a little piece Their share of the magic.[28]

Dickie's experience of studying at Trinity as an undergraduate, navigating his sexuality, also features a pub. He recalls visiting a pub in Dublin near George's Street, 'a pub with purple doors and gilt letters over the windows that spelled out *The Butterfly* [a thinly veiled depiction of Dublin gay bar The George]'.[29] Murray captures the urban, vibrant atmosphere of a contemporary gay bar, so different to the restraint and secretiveness of earlier locations described in chapter 5 of this volume:

> The upper floor of the Butterfly was different to downstairs; very different. He made his way across a dance floor populated by men most of whom had their shirts off, revealing tanned, muscular, hairless chests which rubbed wetly against Dickie as he passed. The walls were black. The air was dense with chemicals, wobbling with lubricious electronic music over which a woman's voice chanted, Ass! Ass! Give me ass! ... Next to them, two men were kissing vigorously; Dickie could see their tongues, like meat-coloured slugs wrestling each other; and now an eye opened, and one of the men was staring right at him – hurriedly he turned in his seat.[30]

Louise Kennedy's novel *Trespasses* (2022) is set during the Troubles in Belfast and revolves around a dangerous affair between a young Catholic woman, Cushla, and a married Protestant barrister, Michael, who advocates for young Catholic men who have been unjustly arrested. Cushla works part time at her family pub, which from the beginning of the novel is foreboding: the others tell Cushla, 'There's hardly any bar left up our way … Most of them have been blown up'.[31] Meanwhile, Cushla contemplates: 'In the pub, Cushla has heard people say it was "very mixed", pursing their mouths in distaste because they had to share the place with Catholics who barely made up ten percent of the population'.[32] However, her involvement with Michael and rising tensions lead to her pub being eventually 'blown up'. At the end of the novel, Cushla is only left with the debris of the pub: 'The bomb had been left in an empty beer keg to the left of the building'.[33] Kennedy's novel suggests how Northern Ireland is still haunted by its past, with the pub space serving as sites of memory, trauma and complex identities.

Set in post-Troubles west Belfast, in Michael Magee's *Close to Home* (2023), Sean, a recent university graduate in his twenties, returns to the city to find that nothing much has changed: the same friends and people are struggling with poverty, unemployment, addiction and violence. Sean works in a club and spends his time drinking and taking drugs. There are many references to various Belfast pubs: 'a wee loyalist bar called Dunmurry Inn'[34] versus 'Kelly's Cellars' where a 'group of tourists … Americans' are 'having a great time watching the long-haired lads playing fiddly-dee music out the front of the bar, but no matter how much they tapped their feet and muttered along to the words of every tune they thought they knew, their hearts weren't in it'.[35] At one point, Sean visits The Laurel Glen, which he frequented as a thirteen-year-old kid. As if frozen in time, but only 'smaller than [he] remembered, and dark', he would watch men he looked up to playing pool: 'John Boy, Buzz, Speedy, Rabbie, Duck and Pigeon. Marty Cafferty. These were names you'd see written on fences and walls all over the estate, and they were famous in that way, for the madness they got up to'.[36] The pubs become symbols of painful lingering trauma, where the Troubles still cast a long shadow on the characters' lives. The novel explores issues of masculinity, violence, substance abuse, friendship and working-class life in post-Troubles Northern Ireland.

Finally, within the field of fine art, the trauma of the Troubles and of broader patterns of division in Northern Ireland were confronted by the Array artists' collective in their 2021 Turner Prize-winning installation *The Druthaib's Ball*.[37] The life-size installation features an imagined *síbín* or unlicensed drinking establishment, of a type common in urban areas of the North during the Troubles. Banners and posters reflective of politics and social movements, and expressions of Ireland's mythic past, surround a commonplace pub setting. The aim is to challenge the sectarian geography of the North – as expressed in its institutions, including pubs. The work also confronts the collective trauma of Northern Irish society and agitates for change, for example in the areas of reproductive rights and mental health services. It makes use of the traditional setting of the pub to raise urgent contemporary issues for Irish society.[38]

Irish Pubs – in Ireland

Within Ireland, the pub continues to occupy a central role as both a cultural institution and a social infrastructure. Unlike its globalised counterparts that, as we have seen, tend to emphasise a curated image of 'Irishness' for international audiences, the Irish pub in its home country largely remains embedded in the rhythms of local life, serving as a locus of community, tradition and memory.[39] Nevertheless, as we have suggested across this volume, the pub has undergone, and continues to undergo, significant transformations, shaped by shifting social, economic and political contexts.

A defining characteristic of the Irish pub is its dual role as a site of memory and re-invention. Historically, it has been closely associated with major life events such as weddings, wakes and community celebrations, offering a space for collective rituals and storytelling. Pubs are integral to the social fabric of Irish towns and villages, serving as both a reflection and a repository of local histories. This role is evident in the cultural nostalgia that surrounds the 'traditional' Irish pub, a construct that combines genuine historical roots with a degree of mythologisation.

The notion of the 'traditional' pub is itself a product of invention and adaptation. As Malcolm notes in chapter 2, the contemporary Irish pub has evolved from a range of earlier establishments such as alehouses, gin palaces and spirit-grocers.[40] Its consolidation as a recognisable institution coincided with multiple legislative and infrastructural changes in the nineteenth century that ultimately standardised licensing laws and reshaped drinking practices. This history complicates the image of the pub as timeless, instead revealing its ability to adapt to changing cultural, economic and technological conditions.[41]

Notwithstanding such fluidity, pubs remain a key component of both Irish self-identity and the Irish tourism and hospitality industry.[42] Expressions of national culture such as literature, music and storytelling synergistically cement the Irish pub as a symbol, as these cross over in phenomena such as literary pub crawls, posters of (predominantly male) writers in pubs, books about pubs and traditional music.

Social media has further transformed the role of Irish pubs in Ireland. Platforms such as Instagram have turned many pubs into visual landmarks, with tourists and locals alike sharing images of their interiors, pints of Guinness and live performances. This visibility reinforces the pub's status as a cultural icon while also creating new pressures to maintain a certain image. Viral trends and digital storytelling have amplified the reach of individual pubs, making them part of a broader narrative about contemporary Irish identity (Table 20.1).

Table 20.1 Ten most Instagrammed pubs in Ireland, from Overland Ireland

Name of Pub	Address	Number of Posts (Geotagged on Instagram)
1. The Temple Bar	47–48 Temple Bar, Dublin	520,313
2. Café en Seine	40 Dawson St, Dublin	39,358
3. The Bernard Shaw	11–12 Richmond St South, Saint Kevin's, Dublin	25,198
4. Lusty Beg Island	Boa Island, Kesh, Northern Ireland	12,157
5. The Oliver Plunkett	116 Oliver Plunkett St, Centre, Cork	11,889
6. Porterhouse Temple Bar	16-18 Parliament St, Temple Bar, Dublin	9,681
7. The Stag's Head	1 Dame Ct, Dublin	8,902
8. Zozimus	Centenary House, Anne's Lane, Anne Street South, Dublin	8,644
9. PantiBar	7-8 Capel Street, North City, Dublin	8,312
10. An Púcán	11 Forster St, Galway	8,276

https://overlandirelandtours.com/blog/these-are-the-50-best-pubs-in-ireland-according-to-instagram/

In recent decades, the decline of rural pubs has emerged as a significant challenge,[43] with economic pressures, changing consumer habits and stricter drink-driving laws contributing to their closure. Rural depopulation has also played a role, as younger generations migrate to urban centres, leaving smaller communities with fewer patrons to sustain their local pubs. This decline is not just an economic issue but a cultural one, as the closure of a pub often signals the loss of a vital social hub. In particular, the decline of pubs has been linked to the rise in feelings of loneliness, an issue explored in the British context by Thomas Furnell-Read and expressed in a celebrated Christmas online advertisement for Charlie's bar in Enniskillen.[44] In response to the decline of rural pubs, some communities have initiated cooperative buyouts or repurposed pubs as multi-functional spaces, combining their traditional role with new uses such as co-working hubs or cultural venues. The state has provided some minimal support to such initiatives.[45]

Urban pubs, meanwhile, have adapted by diversifying their offerings to cater to changing tastes and lifestyles, and many are thriving in line with general economic growth. Gastropubs, craft beer bars and alcohol-free pubs have proliferated, reflecting broader trends in food and drink culture. In cities and towns like Dublin, Cork, Galway and Dingle, pubs have also become key players in the tourism industry, offering literary pub crawls, live music and other experiences that draw on Ireland's cultural heritage. The influence of the Guinness brand is particularly pronounced in this context, with iconic establishments like The Storehouse in Dublin positioning the pub as both a local institution and a global attraction.

Reflective of broader economic trends, pubs are increasingly becoming an object of interest from both domestic and international capital. Sociologists Kuhling and Keohane go so far as to suggest that the pub has become a 'streamlined industrialised space dedicated to maximising of production and consumption of product' through a 'process of economic modernisation', also visible in areas such as the newspaper and agriculture industries.[46] Companies that own multiple pubs, often in conjunction with other entertainment venues, are becoming more prominent, for example the Press Up (now Eclective) group (Workmen's Club, Peruke & Periwig, Mary's Hardware) and Louis Fitzgerald group (the Stag's Head, Dublin; Tigh Neachtain, Galway; Lotts Café Bar, Dublin), both focused primarily on Dublin, and the Benny McCabe chain in Cork (includes The Mutton Lane, the Oval and the Bodega). These companies increasingly involve international investment: thus we have, in recent years, seen the introduction of global equity firms such as the London-based Attestor Capital (involved with a number of Cork pubs), J.P. McManus' Novellus vehicle (financing the redevelopment of the landmark County Meath Tara na Rí pub) and Värde Partners, United States, who financed redevelopment of Moran's Red Cow Hotel.[47] None of these perhaps can vie with the Russian company Harat's Irish Pubs, which claims to be the world's most extensive Irish pub chain, with 102 pubs operating in Russia, Kazakhstan, Croatia, Serbia, Slovenia, Hungary, Cyprus, Kyrgyzstan, Thailand and the United States.[48]

Increasing property values in main urban centres have seen several pubs fall to the wrecker's ball, to be replaced by apartment blocks or hotels.[49] This is a trend also visible in other major cities, such as London. A worrying trend is the failure to develop pubs in 'new' communities. Some of Ireland's fastest-growing urban and suburban communities, such as Celbridge, Carrigaline and Balbriggan, are also those with the fewest pubs per capita. While this is music to the ears of the anti-alcohol community,[50] there is a risk that such neighbourhoods will develop without adequate provision for the community and conviviality that pubs can uniquely provide. This is a topic that merits further exploration and debate, not least among town planners, public health advocates and social scientists.

Finally, the greatest threat to the survival of the pub in Ireland may be long-term shifts in social behaviour. Reflective of broader trends in relation to demography, time-use, working patterns and health concerns, coffee shops, gyms or other 'third spaces' have increasingly come to occupy the role once held by pubs, especially among older patrons.[51] Consciousness of health and well-being has changed attitudes to alcohol consumption, obvious in movements such as 'Dry January' and 'sober curiosity' and reflected in significant successes in the marketing of zero- and low-alcohol beverages such as Guinness 0.0. There is evidence that overall per capita alcohol consumption in Ireland has declined, but such figures are difficult to assess and there are multiple ways to measure consumption. What is clear is that there has been a significant shift towards 'at home' consumption, rather than in the pub setting. This trend, accentuated by regulatory forces, comparatively low supermarket alcohol prices and improvements in domestic facilities, may constitute the biggest threat to the 'traditional' pub.[52]

So, what of the future of the Irish pub? At the international level it appears to have cemented itself as a feature of contemporary hospitality, as ubiquitous and enduring as the Italian pizza restaurant and the Middle Eastern or Turkish kebab shop: also products of extensive global diasporas. No obvious competitor (German *bier keller*, Hungarian *kocsma*, Australian *hotel*?) has yet emerged to challenge this global success story, despite occasional prophecies of doom. That is not to say that the global Irish pub will not evolve and mutate, as it hybridises with the local cultures of Greece, Kazakhstan or Korea. On the home front, the pub continues to thrive in many locations, albeit that an inevitable rationalisation of rural and country town pubs is in evidence, reflective though not as severe as the whittling down of banks, newsagents and hardware stores. Pubs that existed to serve motorists are perhaps the most vulnerable, reduced to a small number of multi-purpose enterprises that are reliant on carvery and other food offerings. The resurgence of such hostelries no doubt awaits the eventual – and much anticipated – development of the self-driving car.

At a public policy level, there are important debates to be had about the relative dearth of pubs in new residential areas, particularly as the country is being urged to engage in extensive home construction. In addition, we know little of the place of pubs in Ireland's increasingly diverse and multicultural community. Should we expect to see a growth in Polish, Brazilian or Indian pubs and, if not, what implications does this have for new and older communities? How can we reconcile the insistent warnings of public health advocates, who call for increasingly stringent controls on alcohol availability, with the needs of pub users, who seek community, conviviality and company in such establishments? How can we justify a pub industry increasingly dependent on tourism, when the planet is experiencing climate breakdown caused at least in part by global travel?

In terms of cultural expression, it is undeniable that our rural and urban built environment is being reshaped by the changes in the pub industry. While some former pubs are successfully repurposed as domestic homes, shops, or for other uses, too many lie forlorn and derelict. As well as the loss to community and craic, there are unique architectural features that may disappear. In our literature, theatre and visual arts, the pub seems secure as a setting, a symbol and a subject. It may be that the static, conversational stage set will give way to the more fluid, dynamic, visual and auditorily vibrant club setting, but drinking establishments will always remain a seductive part of human interaction. We may expect to see Irish pubs popping up in fiction, drama, documentary, graphic design and song – perhaps even in virtual and augmented reality – for many a year to come.

NOTES

Chapter 1 – Introduction: Inventing the Irish Pub

1 The saga of the Cobblestone is described in the 2022 RTÉ film *Athbhaile*, directed by Michael McCormack, https://www.rte.ie/player/series/athbhaile-the-cobblestone/IH10001011-00-0000.

2 Drinks Ireland, the industry body, estimates that Ireland's thirty-plus distillery and brewery visitor centres attracted 2.4 million visitors in 2023 and that this measure is on an upward trajectory, https://www.ibec.ie/drinksireland/our-industry/tourism). For a broader, if dated, industry-sponsored analysis, see Anthony Foley, *The Contribution of the Drinks Industry to Tourism*, https://www.drinksindustry.ie/assets/Documents/The%20Contribution%20of%20the%20Drinks%20Industry%20to%20Tourism%20Report.pdf. For an excellent example of the attractions of such drink tourism, see Sean Muldoon et al., *From Barley to Blarney: A whiskey lover's guide to Ireland* (Kansas City, MI: Andrews McNeel Publishing, 2019).

3 https://www.dublinpubcrawl.com.

4 Comprising 6,680 in the Republic of Ireland (Anthony Foley, *The Irish Pub: Supporting our communities* (Dublin: Drinks Industry Group of Ireland, 2023), https://www.drugsandalcohol.ie/39429/1/The-Irish-Pub-Supporting-Our-Communities2023.pdf); and 770 in NI in 2021 (London, House of Commons Library, Pub Statistics, Briefing Paper Number 8591, 21 May 2021), https://commonslibrary.parliament.uk/research-briefings/cbp-8591/.

5 Perry Share, Mary P. Corcoran and Brian Conway, 'Pubs and Drinking', in *A Sociology of Ireland* (Dublin: Gill & Macmillan, 2012), pp. 311–22.

6 Sam McGrath, 'Major New Map Project of Dublin Gun Murders (1970 to 2022)', Appendix 2 lists twenty-four Dublin pubs where people have been shot dead either outside or within the pub: https://comeheretome.com/2022/04/15/major-new-map-project-of-dublin-gun-murders-1970-to-2022/.

7 Liam Coakley, '"All Over the Place, in Town, in the Pub, Everywhere": A social geography of women's friendship in Cork', *Irish Geography*, vol. 35, no. 1, 2002, pp. 40–50; Matthew Stephens, 'Unpacking Friendship: The impact of friendship practices on Polish migrants' senses of belonging in Cork city, Ireland', unpublished MSc (Research) thesis, Department of Human Geography and Spatial Planning, Utrecht University, 2017, p. 12, https://studenttheses.uu.nl/bitstream/handle/20.500.12932/27571/Thesis%20Matthew%20Stephens%20Final%20Copy%205676088.pdf?sequence=2.

8 Ray Oldenburg, *The Great Good Place: Cafés, coffee shops, bookstores, bars, hair salons, and other hangouts at the heart of a community*, 3rd edn (New York: Marlowe, 1999).

9 Chris Curtin and Colm Ryan, 'Clubs, Pubs and Private Houses in a Clare Town', in Chris Curtin and Tom Wilson (eds), *Ireland from Below: Social change and local communities* (Galway: Galway University Press, 1987); see also Lucy Hastings, 'The Geography of Public Houses in Cork City Centre', *Chimera: UCC geographical journal*, no. 5, 1990, pp. 83–8, https://journals.ucc.ie/index.php/chimera/article/view/4261.

10 Gwen Scarborough, The Irish Pub as a Third Place: A sociological exploration of people, place and identity', unpublished PhD thesis, Institute of Technology Sligo, 2008, https://research.thea.ie/handle/20.500.12065/585.

11 See, for example, Rodhlann Mossop and Alex Pollock, 'Dublin's Remaining Victorian Pubs', *Type* [blog], https://www.type.ie/blog/dublin-sixteen-remaining-victorian-pubs-a-visual-essay.

12 Tom Spalding, '"A Striking Air of Modernity Tempered with Tradition": Vernacular modernism and the design of the public house in Cork and Dublin, 1934–1969', *Journal of Design History*, vol. 35, no. 4, 2022, pp. 346–61, https://doi.org/10.1093/jdh/epab053.

13 Seán Rothery, *The Shops of Ireland* (Dublin: Gill & Macmillan, 1978).

14 Diarmuid Ó Drisceoil and Donal Ó Drisceoil, *The Murphy's Story: The history of Lady's Well Brewery, Cork* (Cork: Murphy Brewery, 1997), pp. 118–21; Tom Spalding, 'Murphy's Brewery, the Development of Corporate Design and Changes to the Irish Pub, 1930–70', in *Designed for Life: Architecture and design in Cork city, 1900–90* (Cork: Cork University Press, 2025), ch. 9.

15 Stephenson designed the interior of the famous Horseshoe Bar in Dublin. Sean Boyd, *Behind the Horseshoe Bar: At Dublin's Shelbourne Hotel* (Dublin: Blackwater Press, 2009), p. 29.

16 Scott designed several premises for distiller and soft drinks manufacturer D.E. Williams in the Irish midlands. Fergal MacCabe, 'Shops and Pubs Designed by Michael Scott in the 1940s for D.E. Williams', *Offaly History* [blog], 3 May 2022, https://offalyhistoryblog.wordpress.com/2022/05/25/emergency-stores-the-1940s-shopfronts-of-michael-scott-by-fergal-maccabe/.

17 Marion McGarry, 'Why Ireland's Older Pubs Are Part of Our Cultural Heritage', *RTÉ Brainstorm*, 19 August 2021, https://www.rte.ie/brainstorm/2021/0316/1204062-ireland-pubs-decor-interiors-heritage/.

18 Foley, *The Irish Pub*.

19 Gail Cotter Buckley and Angela Wright, 'The Domestic Death of a Global Icon? A situational analysis of the Irish public house', *Journal of Social Science for Policy Implications*, vol. 2, no. 1, 2014, pp. 85–99, https://sword.cit.ie/dptopdart/10/.

20 Dominant pub chains include the Louis Fitzgerald Group, which has seventeen pubs, mainly in Dublin, including celebrated pubs such as the Stag's Head and Kehoe's as well as large suburban pubs in centres such as Clondalkin and Maynooth. The Mercantile Group owns the fashionable Café en Seine in Dublin's Dawson Street; The George, Dublin's best-known LGBQTA+ bar; and Whelan's, one of the capital's leading music pubs. Other groups include the Eclective Hospitality Group (formerly Press Up), operators of Mary's Bar and Hardware, in Dublin; Galway Bay Brewery; RHK Group; Wright's; and Benny McCabe (with twelve Cork pubs).

21 Doreen Massey, *Space, Place and Gender* (Cambridge: Polity, 1994), p. 130.

22 For a detailed account of brewing in Ireland see Christina Wade, *Filthy Queens: A history of beer in Ireland* (Dublin: Nine Bean Rows, 2025).

23 Cian Molloy, *The Story of the Irish Pub: An intoxicating history of the licensed trade in Ireland* (Dublin: Liffey Press, 2002), p. 27; Elizabeth Malcolm, 'The Rise of the Pub: A study in the disciplining of popular culture', in James S. Donnelly and Kerby A. Miller (eds), *Irish Popular Culture 1650–1850* (Dublin: Irish Academic Press, 1998), p. 55.

24 Cormac Ó Gráda, *Ireland: A new economic history 1780–1939* (Oxford: Oxford University Press, 1994), p. 304.

25 Dublin-based Cantrell & Cochrane trademarked their 'Club Soda', to be sold across Ireland and the British Empire, somewhat later, in 1877. 'Cantrell & Cochrane: From Belfast's Castle Place to a global brand', *Belfast Entries* [blog], 5 October 2021, https://www.belfastentries.com/places/cantrell-cochrane/.

26 Elizabeth Malcolm, *Ireland Sober, Ireland Free: Drink and temperance in nineteenth-century Ireland* (Dublin: Gill & Macmillan, 1986); Elizabeth Malcolm, 'Temperance and Irish Nationalism', in F.S.L. Lyons (ed.), *Ireland Under the Union: Varieties of tension* (Oxford: Clarendon, 1980); Bradley Kadel, *Drink and Culture in Nineteenth-Century Ireland: The alcohol trade and the politics of the Irish public house* (London: Bloomsbury, 2020).

27 Diarmaid Ferriter, 'Drink and Society in Twentieth-Century Ireland', *Proceedings of the Royal Irish Academy: Archaeology, culture, history, literature*, vol. 115C, Food and Drink in Ireland (Dublin: Royal Irish Academy, 2015), pp. 349–69. The Catholic Church played an important role in the debate, exerting moral control over alcohol consumption.

28 Diarmaid Ferriter, 'There Is Little Middle Ground Debating the Pub Trade in Ireland', *Irish Times*, 4 September 2020; Diarmaid Ferriter, *A Nation of Extremes* (Dublin: Irish Academic Press, 1999).

29 Henri Lefebvre, *The Production of Space*, tr. Donald Nicholson-Smith (Oxford: Blackwell, 1991 [1974]), p. 109.

30 Murphy's of Cork (part of the Heineken company) operated a similar operation.

31 Mark McGovern, 'The "Craic" Market: Irish theme bars and the commodification of Irishness in contemporary Britain', *Irish Journal of Sociology*, vol. 11, no. 2, 2002, p. 79.

32 Lucky's bar on Meath Street in Dublin was known for its 'Bring Your Own Art Art Show' (BYOAAS) (2019), an exhibition where artists could showcase and sell their artwork.

33 Molloy, *The Story of the Irish Pub*, p. 80.

34 Michel de Certeau, *The Practice of Everyday Life*, tr. Steven Rendall (Berkeley: University of California Press, 1984 [1980]), pp. 34–42.

35 Tim Edensor, *National Identity, Popular Culture and Everyday Life* (Oxford: Berg, 2002), p. 49.

36 Michael Billig, *Banal Nationalism* (London: Sage, 1995).

37 Jan Blommaert and Piia Varis, 'Enough Is Enough: The heuristics of authenticity in superdiversity', *Tilburg Papers in Culture Studies*, no. 2 (Tilburg: Tilburg University, 2011), https://research.tilburguniversity.edu/en/publications/enough-is-enough-the-heuristics-of-authenticity-in-superdiversity-3.

38 Eimear Flanagan, 'McGurk's Bar Bombing: "I want justice for my grandparents"', *BBC News*, 12 December 2021, https://www.bbc.com/news/uk-northern-ireland-59569348.

39 This is part of architect Barry Sheehan's broader research project on James Joyce and running: jj21k. See 'James Joyce Run: Nothing happens in the public houses, people drink', TU Dublin, 2018, https://arrow.tudublin.ie/cgi/viewcontent.cgi?article=1017&context=desigpart.

40 Fintan Vallely (ed.), *The Companion to Irish Traditional Music*, 1st edn (Cork: Cork University Press, 2011).

Chapter 2 – From Drink Shops to 'Traditional' Irish Pubs: Laws, Services and Invisible Women, *c.* 1400–1950

1 For such laments see, for example, James Fennell and Turtle Bunbury, *The Irish Pub* (London: Thames & Hudson, 2008); Bill Barich, *A Pint of Plain: Tradition, change and the fate of the Irish pub* (London: Bloomsbury, 2009).

2 For a classic study of how tradition can be manufactured, see Eric Hobsbawm and Terence Ranger (eds), *The Invention of Tradition* (Cambridge: Cambridge University Press, 1983).

3 Peter Clark, *The English Alehouse: A social history, 1200–1830* (London and New York: Longman, 1983), p. 195; Elizabeth Malcolm, 'The Rise of the Pub: A study in the disciplining of popular culture', in James S. Donnelly and Kerby A. Miller (eds), *Irish Popular Culture, 1650–1850* (Dublin: Irish Academic Press, 1999), pp. 71–2.

4 Molloy, *The Story of the Irish Pub*, pp. 8–9, 29–30. Ale made from malted oats and barley had traditionally been drunk in Ireland, but during the sixteenth century hops began to be imported from England. Beer made using hops had a longer shelf-life than ale, and it slowly emerged as the more profitable and popular beverage.

5 Malcolm, 'Ireland Sober, Ireland Free', pp. 12–13.

6 Malcolm, 'The Rise of the Pub', pp. 60–2.

7 Catherine Marie O'Sullivan, *Hospitality in Medieval Ireland, 900–1500* (Dublin: Four Courts Press, 2004), pp. 85–8, 103–5; Fergus Kelly, *A Guide to Early Irish Law* (Dublin: Dublin Institute for Advanced Studies, 1988), pp. 36–8, 139–40, 154.

8 Some male tavern-keepers obviously prospered, as a resident of Winetavern Street named Vincent Taverner was mayor of Dublin in 1264–5. Archaeological excavations undertaken in the street have yielded hundreds of pewter tokens believed to have been used as currency in its many taverns. H.F. Berry, 'Catalogue of the Mayors, Provosts and Bailiffs of Dublin City, AD 1229 to 1447', in Howard Clarke (ed.), *Medieval Dublin: The living city* (Dublin: Irish Academic Press, 1990), pp. 157, 223, n. 60; Breandán Ó Ríordáin, 'Excavations at High Street and Winetavern Street, Dublin', *Medieval Archaeology*, vol. 15, 1971, pp. 73–85.

9 Peadar Slattery, *Social Life in Pre-Reformation Dublin, 1450–1540* (Dublin: Four Courts Press, 2019), pp. 99–101, 112; Margaret Murphy, 'The Economy', in Brendan Smith (ed.), *The Cambridge History of Ireland. Volume 1, 600–1550* (Cambridge: Cambridge University Press, 2018), pp. 395–6, 402–3.

10 Malcolm, 'The Rise of the Pub', pp. 63–4.

11 Seán Réamonn, *History of the Revenue Commissioners* (Dublin: Institute of Public Administration, 1981), pp. 9–19.

12 David A. Fleming, *Politics and Provincial People: Sligo and Limerick, 1691–1761* (Manchester and New York: Manchester University Press, 2010), pp. 162–93.

13 Edward B. McGuire, *Irish Whiskey: A history of distilling, the spirit trade and excise controls in Ireland* (Dublin: Gill & Macmillan, 1973), pp. 64–74, 85–8, 121–2.

14 Timothy D. Watt, *Popular Protest and Policing in Ascendancy Ireland, 1691–1761* (Woodbridge, Suffolk: Boydell Press, 2018), pp. 118–23.

15 David Dickson, 'Taxation and Disaffection in Late Eighteenth-Century Ireland', in Samuel Clark and J.S. Donnelly Jr (eds), *Irish Peasants: Violence and political unrest, 1780–1914* (Manchester: Manchester University Press, 1983), p. 43.

16 Malcolm, 'Ireland Sober, Ireland Free', pp. 21–55; McGuire, *Irish Whiskey*, pp. 110–38; Patrick Lynch and John Vaizey, *Guinness's Brewery in the Irish Economy, 1759–1876* (Cambridge: Cambridge University Press, 1960), pp. 9–77.

17 See Patricia MacCarthy, *Enjoying Claret in Georgian Ireland: A history of amiable excess* (Dublin: Four Courts Press, 2022).

18 Muiris O'Sullivan and Liam Downey, 'Poteen', *Archaeology Ireland*, vol. 35, no. 3, 2021, pp. 38–42; Sinéad Sturgeon, 'The Politics of Poitín: Maria Edgeworth, William Carleton and the battle for the spirit of Ireland', *Irish Studies Review*, vol. 14, no. 4, 2006, pp. 431–45.

19 James Whitelaw, *An Essay on the Population of Dublin, Being the Result of an Actual Survey Taken in 1798* (Dublin: Graisberry & Campbell, 1805), pp. 62–3.

20 For the political context of drink consumption during the eighteenth century, see Martyn J. Powell, *The Politics of Consumption in Eighteenth-Century Ireland* (Basingstoke: Palgrave Macmillan, 2005), pp. 7–42.

21 Malcolm, 'Ireland Sober, Ireland Free', pp. 52–5; Nancy J. Curtin, *The United Irishmen: Popular politics in Ulster and Dublin, 1791–8* (Oxford: Clarendon Press, 1994), p. 137; Kevin Haddick-Flynn, *Orangeism: The making of a tradition* (Dublin: Wolfhound Press, 1999), pp. 138–41.

22 McGuire, *Irish Whiskey*, p. 160.

23 Malcolm, 'The Rise of the Pub', p. 66.

24 Malcolm, 'Ireland Sober, Ireland Free', pp. 27–8, 51–2.

25 Four pints or 2.3 litres.

26 For campaigns mounted by publicans against spirit-grocer shops and also beer-houses, see Bradley Kadel, *Drink and Culture in Nineteenth-Century Ireland: The alcohol trade and the politics of the Irish public house* (London and New York: I.B. Tauris, 2015), pp. 36–67.

27 Malcolm, 'Ireland Sober, Ireland Free', pp. 209–11.

28 Kenneth H. Connell, *Irish Peasant Society* (Oxford: Oxford University Press, 1968), pp. 1–50.

29 McGuire, *Irish Whiskey*, pp. 185, 188, 202–3, 213–25, 279.

30 Lynch and Vaizey, *Guinness's Brewery in the Irish Economy*, p. 230; Stanley R. Dennison and Oliver MacDonagh, *Guinness, 1886–1939: From incorporation to the Second World War* (Cork: Cork University Press, 1998), p. 3.

31 Jim Herlihy, *The Irish Revenue Police: A short history and genealogical guide to the 'poteen hussars'* (Dublin: Four Courts Press, 2018); John McGuffin, *In Praise of Poteen* (Belfast: Appletree Press, 1978), pp. 21–37.

32 Elizabeth Malcolm, *The Irish Policeman, 1822–1922: A life* (Dublin: Four Courts Press, 2006), pp. 115–19.

33 Malcolm, 'The Rise of the Pub', pp. 68–9; McGuire, *Irish Whiskey*, pp. 281–92.

34 Malcolm, 'The Rise of the Pub', p. 70.

35 Molloy, *The Story of the Irish Pub*, pp. 4, 55, 61–2.

36 For a discussion of pubs tied to Murphy's and Beamish & Crawford, Cork breweries that tended to favour employing female publicans, see chapter 3 in this volume.

37 One of the most elaborate of Dublin's 'gin palaces' was the Irish House, built appropriately enough on the corner of Winetavern Street and Wood Quay in 1870, but demolished by Dublin Corporation a century later to make way for office buildings. For photographs of the Irish House's façade, see Mark Girouard, *Victorian Pubs* (New Haven, CT, 1975; London: Yale University Press, 1984), pp. 240–1.

38 For 'traditional' pub designs created for export during 1990–2010, see chapter 7 in this volume.

39 Leslie Dunkling and Gordon Wright, *Dictionary of Pub Names* (Ware, Hertfordshire, 1987; Wentworth, 1994), pp. 64–5, 209, 213.

40 Molloy, *The Story of the Irish Pub*, pp. 274–5, 281–2, 170–3, 212–15.

41 For the 'gendered geography' of Irish pubs from the 1920s to the 1970s, see chapter 3 in this volume.

42 Molloy, *The Story of the Irish Pub*, pp. 78–9.

43 Ibid., pp. 34, 38, 57; Andrew Carpenter (ed.), *Verse in English from Eighteenth-Century Ireland* (Cork: Cork University Press, 1998), pp. 260–4; Brian Ó Dálaigh, *Ennis in the Eighteenth Century: Portrait of an urban community* (Dublin: Irish Academic Press, 1995), pp. 22, 46, 49; Ciara Breathnach, *Ordinary Lives, Death, and Social Class: Dublin city coroner's court, 1876–1902* (Oxford: Oxford University Press, 2022), pp. 44–5.

44 Philip H. Gulliver and Marilyn Silverman, *Merchants and Shopkeepers: A historical anthropology of an Irish market town, 1200–1991* (Toronto: University of Toronto Press, 1995), pp. 59–61.

45 Elizabeth Malcolm, 'Popular Recreation in Nineteenth-Century Ireland', in Oliver MacDonagh, W.E. Mandle and Pauric Travers (eds), *Irish Culture and Nationalism, 1750–1950* (London and Canberra: Macmillan Press, 1983), pp. 40–55; Séamas Ó Maitiú, *The Humours of Donnybrook: Dublin's famous fair and its suppression* (Dublin: Irish Academic Press, 1995); James Kelly, *Sport in Ireland, 1600–1840* (Dublin: Four Courts Press, 2014), pp. 172, 178–9, 225.

46 Malcolm, 'Ireland Sober, Ireland Free', pp. 207–8.

47 Kadel, *Drink and Culture in Nineteenth-Century Ireland*, p. 1; Samuel Clark, *Social Origins of the Irish Land War* (Princeton, NJ: Princeton University Press, 1979), p. 128. For the functions of the pub viewed from the perspectives of anthropology and sociology, see Chapter 4 in this volume.

48 Much information about inns, taverns and hotels can be found in accounts published by travellers and visitors to Ireland. For a guide, see Christopher J. Woods, *Travellers' Accounts as Source-Material for Irish Historians* (Dublin: Four Courts Press, 2009).

49 Kevin C. Kearns, *Dublin Pub Life and Lore: An oral history* (Dublin: Gill & Macmillan, 1996), pp. 53–5.

50 James S. Donnelly Jr, *Captain Rock: The Irish agrarian rebellion of 1821–4* (Cork: Collins Press, 2009), p. 104.

51 John Devoy, *Recollections of an Irish Rebel* (Shannon: Irish University Press, 1969 [1929]), p. 184.

52 Tom Corfe, *The Phoenix Park Murders: Conflict, compromise and tragedy in Ireland, 1879–82* (London: Hodder & Stoughton, 1968), pp. 144, 185.

53 For pubs as male spaces, see Kearns, *Dublin Pub Life and Lore*, pp. 5–6, 40–5, 61–3, 74, 101, 106, 137, 201–3, plates 10, 22–5; Barich, *A Pint of Plain*, pp. 28, 30–1, 59, 89–91, 112. For works examining the relationship between working-class women and pubs, see Susan Martin, *The Shawlies: Cork's women street traders and the 'merchant city', 1901–50* (Dublin: Four Courts Press, 2017); Maria Luddy. *Prostitution and Irish Society, 1800–1940* (Cambridge: Cambridge University Press, 2007), pp. 33–6, 44–6, 209–27. For discussions of gender and the pub, see chapters 3, 4, 8 and 9 in this volume.

54 Mary E. Daly, *Women and Work in Ireland* (Dublin: Economic and Social History Society of Ireland, 1997), pp. 5–8; Diarmaid Ferriter, 'Drink and Society in Twentieth-Century Ireland', *Proceedings of the Royal Irish Academy*, vol. 115C, 2015, p. 356.

55 For an analysis of the perceived 'hegemonic masculinity' of the pub, see Loic Wright, '"A Pint of Plain Is Your Only Man": Masculinities and the pub in twentieth-century Irish fiction', *Estudios Irlandeses*, no. 15, 2020–1, pp. 143–55, https://doi.org/10.24162/EI2020-9371.

56 In 1901, at least a quarter of Australian publicans were women, many of them being of Irish birth or descent. See Clare Wright, *Beyond the Ladies Lounge: Australia's female publicans* (Melbourne: Melbourne University Press, 2003), pp. 30, 43, 161–2; Diane Kirkby, Tanja Luckins and Chris McConville, *The Australian Pub* (Sydney: University of New South Wales Press, 2010), p. 165.

57 For an examination of the spatial development of Cork pubs in terms of gender during the twentieth century, see chapter 3 in this volume.

58 Tanya M. Cassidy, 'Sober for the Sake of the Children: The church, the state and alcohol use amongst women in Ireland', in Anne Byrne and Madeleine Leonard (eds), *Women and Irish Society: A sociological reader* (Belfast: Beyond the Pale Publications, 1997), p. 460.

59 John T. Gilbert (ed.), *Calendar of Ancient Records of Dublin, in Possession of the Municipal Corporation of that City*, 7 vols (Dublin: Joseph Dollard, 1889), pp. i, 342. For similar developments in England, see Judith M. Bennett, *Ale, Beer, and Brewsters in England: Women's work in a changing world, 1300–1600* (New York and Oxford: Oxford University Press, 1996), pp. 3–4, 14–36.

60 Christina Wade, *Filthy Queens: A history of beer in Ireland* (Dublin: Nine Bean Rows, 2025), pp. 150–6, 184–5.

61 Barnabe Rich, *A New Description of Ireland Wherein is Described the Disposition of the Irish Whereunto They Are Inclined* (London: Thomas Adams, 1610), pp. 70–2. For an illustrated history of the Winetavern Street/Wood Quay area, which continued to support many taverns and later public houses into the twentieth century, see Jonathan Bardon and Stephen Conlin, *Dublin: One thousand years of Wood Quay* (Belfast: Blackstaff Press, 1984).

62 Susan Flavin et al., 'Understanding Early Modern Beer: An interdisciplinary case-study', *Historical Journal*, vol. 66, no. 3, 2023, pp. 516–49, https://doi.org/10.1017/S0018246X23000043. This article is the result of a project, led by scholars at Trinity College Dublin, studying food and drink in early modern Ireland. See 'FoodCult: Food, culture and identity in Ireland, *c.* 1550–1650. Exhibition – Brewing Historical Beer', https://foodcult.eu/exhibition/.

63 Clodagh Tait, 'Progress, Challenges and Opportunities in Early Modern Gender History, *c.* 1550–1720', *Irish Historical Studies*, vol. 46, no. 170, 2022, pp. 261–2.

64 Clodagh Tait, 'From Beer and Shoes to Sugar and Slaves: Five Baptist Loobys in Cork and Antigua', in Terence Dooley, Mary Ann Lyons and Salvador Ryan (eds), *The Historian as Detective: Uncovering Irish pasts. Essays in honour of Raymond Gillespie* (Dublin: Four Courts Press, 2021), p. 131.

65 Carpenter, *Verse in English*, pp. 286–7.

66 Madeline Shanahan, '"Whipt with a twig rod": Irish manuscript recipe books as sources for the study of culinary material culture, *c.* 1660 to 1830', *Proceedings of the Royal Irish Academy*, vol. 115C, 2015, pp. 201–2, 204, 209–10.

67 For a female distiller operating in Cork during the 1770s, see James Kelly, 'The Consumption and Sociable Use of Alcohol in Eighteenth-Century Ireland', *Proceedings of the Royal Irish Academy*, vol. 115C, 2015, p. 238.

68 For eighteenth-century women involved in small businesses, including grocer shops selling alcohol, see Mary O'Dowd, *A History of Women in Ireland, 1500–1800* (Harlow: Pearson Longman, 2005), pp. 114–30.

69 Raymond Gillespie, 'Women and Crime in Seventeenth-Century Ireland', in Margaret MacCurtain and Mary O'Dowd (eds), *Women in Early Modern Ireland* (Edinburgh: Edinburgh University Press, 1991), pp. 49–50.

70 Watt, *Popular Protest and Policing in Ascendancy Ireland*, pp. 123–7.

71 Gina Hames, *Alcohol in World History* (London and New York: Routledge, 2012), pp. 39–41.

72 Claudia Kinmonth, *Irish Rural Interiors in Art* (New Haven, CT, and London: Yale University Press, 2006), pp. 201–35; Peter Murray (ed.), *Whipping the Herring: Survival and celebration in nineteenth-century Irish art* (Cork and Kinsale: Crawford Art Gallery and Gandon Editions, 2006), pp. 107, 111, 113, 115–16, 143, 237.

73 For a nineteenth-century Irish-language drinking song about a female beer/ale seller, '*Bean an Leanna*', see Laurence Flanagan (ed.), *Bottle, Draught and Keg: An Irish drinking anthology* (Dublin: Gill & Macmillan, 1995), pp. 51–2. But for middle-class criticism of working-class women frequenting pubs in rural Ireland, see Elizabeth Grant, *The Highland Lady in Ireland: Journals, 1840–50*, eds Patricia Pelly and Andrew Tod (Edinburgh: Canongate, 1991), pp. 19–20.

74 Kinmonth, *Irish Rural Interiors in Art*, figures 207, 210, 211; William Carleton, 'The Geography of an Irish Oath', in William Carleton, *Traits and Stories of the Irish Peasantry* (2nd series, 1834, complete edn, London: George Routledge & Sons, n.d.), p. 4.

75 J.M. Synge, *The Complete Plays*, ed. T.R. Henn (London: Methuen, 1981), pp. 176, 178. See chapter 13 in this volume for a discussion of the pub on stage during the twentieth and early twenty-first centuries, and chapters 11 and 12 for some unflattering treatments of the pub in selected poems and short stories from the same period.

76 Kadel, *Drink and Culture in Nineteenth-Century Ireland*, pp. 46–8.

77 Similarly, wives and daughters working on family farms were rarely counted as employees in censuses. Yet, when they were in 1871, it was revealed that over 30 per cent of the agricultural workforce was female. Daly, *Women and Work in Ireland*, p. 22.

78 For women living and working in Australian family-owned pubs, see Wright, *Beyond the Ladies' Lounge*, pp. 118–26.

79 For many examples of women taking over liquor licences from male relatives, see Molloy, *The Story of the Irish Pub*, pp. 135–6, 188–90, 251–2, 271–2.

80 Habermas originally derived his concept from a study of middle-class gatherings in eighteenth-century English, French and German coffee houses, salons and literary associations. Jürgen Habermas, *The Structural Transformation of the Public Sphere: An inquiry into a category of bourgeois society*, tr. Thomas Burger (Cambridge, MA: MIT Press, 1991). As well as pubs and bars, the concept has been extended in recent decades to include the media and the internet, but it has also been heavily critiqued for its initial limitations in terms of class and gender. See, for example, Fraser, 'Rethinking the Public Sphere: A contribution to the critique of actually existing democracy', *Social Text*, nos. 25–6, 1990, pp. 56–80, https://doi.org/10.2307/466240.

Chapter 3 – Irish Pubs and Gender: Segmentation, containment and integration

1 Doreen Massey, 'Space, Place and Gender', in Jane Rendell, Barbara Penner and Iain Borden (eds), *Gender Space Architecture* (London: Routledge, 2000), p. 129.

2 For a broader historical account of women and pubs in Ireland, see chapter 2 of this volume.

3 Ulf Hannerz, *Transnational Connections* (London: Routledge, 1996).

4 Jeff Malpas, *Place and Experience: A philosophical topography* (Cambridge: Cambridge University Press, 1999), p. 176.

5 Dimitra Gefou-Madianou (ed.), *Alcohol, Gender and Culture* (London: Routledge, 1992).

6 Marja Holmila and Kirsimarja Raitasalo, 'Gender Differences in Drinking: Why do they still exist?', *Addiction*, no. 100, 2005, pp. 1763–9.

7 This cycle of spatialised embodiment reflects Ahmed's observation that bodies 'do not dwell in spaces that are exterior but rather are shaped by their dwellings and take shape by dwelling', in Sara Ahmed, *Queer Phenomenology: Orientations, objects, others* (Durham, NC: Duke University Press, 2006), p. 34.

8 See Gavin Brown, 'Ceramics, Clothing and Other Bodies: Affective geographies of homoerotic cruising encounters', *Social & Cultural Geography*, vol. 9, no. 8, December 2008, pp. 915–32 and Yvette Taylor and Emily Falconer, '"Seedy Bars and Grotty Pints": Close encounters in queer leisure spaces', *Social and Cultural Geography*, vol. 16, no. 1, 2015, pp. 43–57 in relation to understanding how 'material places, geographical imaginaries, and embodied subjects … dialogically construct and reconstruct … sexual geographies' within LGBT spaces (p. 45).

9 Male drinking groups occupying pub spaces remains a contemporary cultural pattern. For example, in his exploration of heavy drinking among fishermen in a small coastal Irish village, anthropologist Adrian Peace, in his *A World of Fine Difference: The social architecture of a modern Irish village* (Dublin: UCD Press, 2001), notes that women are largely absent from both pub social groups and pub-based activities.

10 Jane Rendell, 'Gender, Space: Introduction', in Jane Rendell, Barbara Penner and Iain Borden (eds), *Gender Space Architecture* (London: Routledge, 2000), p. 103.

11 Jos Boys, 'Is There a Feminist Analysis of Architecture?', *Built Environment*, vol. 10, no. 1, 1984, p. 25.

12 There were twelve McArdle's houses in Dundalk. 'Breweries Claim before Rents Commission', *Evening Echo*, 20 March 1951, p. 1.

13 In 1900, of 406 licences in Cork, at least 205 were held by women. Donal Ó Drisceoil and Diarmuid Ó Drisceoil, *Beamish & Crawford: The history of an Irish brewery* (Cork: Collins Press, 2015), Appendix H. The 1961 census reveals that Cork city was the only borough where females outnumbered males. In Dublin only 10 per cent of publicans and 12.5 per cent of staff were female. In Cork, the figures were 61 per cent and 50.5 per cent.

14 'Pubs combined a family home with a business.' Fred Willis, interview, Rochestown, 17 January 2018.

15 Molloy, *The Story of the Irish Pub*, p. 81. Women were not legally guaranteed entry into the pub until the Equal Status Act of 2000.

16 N.L. Smythe, 'Trade Winds of Change', *The Licensed Vintner*, vol. 30, no. 2, July 1964, p. 11.

17 Mary McLeod, 'Everyday and "Other" Spaces', in Jane Rendell, Barbara Penner and Iain Borden (eds), *Gender Space Architecture* (London: Routledge, 2000), p. 193. McLeod is referring to shopping centres.

18 'Elaine': 'The "invasion" of licensed premises by the fairer sex is here to stay', 'A Woman's Eye View of the Lounge Bar', *The Licensed Vintner*, vol. 29, no. 8, January, 1964, p. 11.

19 James Kneale, '"A Problem of Supervision": Moral geographies of nineteenth-century British public houses', *Journal of Historical Geography*, vol. 25, no. 3, 1999, p. 335.

20 Ibid.

21 Charles Dickens, *The Uncommercial Traveller* (Oxford, Chapman & Hall: 1901 [1861]), p. 57.

22 More often women socialised and consumed alcohol at grocery counters, which were common in rural areas. McNabb reports that 'a respectable woman would never set foot inside one of these places unless there is a grocery shop attached. She certainly never drinks in the local bar': Patrick McNabb, 'Social Structure', in Jeremiah Newman (ed.), *The Limerick Rural Survey, 1958–1964* (Tipperary: Muintir na Tíre, 1964), p. 233.

23 Tom Spalding, 'A Striking Air of Modernity Tempered with Tradition': Vernacular modernism and the design of the public house in Cork and Dublin, 1934–1969', *Journal of Design History*, vol. 35, no. 4, 2022, https://doi.org/10.1093/jdh/epab053.

24 Ibid.

25 Kneale, '"A Problem of Supervision"'.

26 Ibid.

27 Some pubs engage in spatial temporalities in their transformation of lounge spaces into family spaces during certain times of the week, such as daytime or weekends. On the creation of 'family friendly' pubs, see Peter Lugosi et al., 'Creating Family-Friendly Pub Experiences: A composite data study', *International Journal of Hospitality Management*, vol. 91, (2020) https://doi.org/10.1016/j.ijhm.2020.102690.

28 Molloy, *The Story of the Irish Pub*, p. 81.

29 'Old-time Public House Almost Extinct', *The Irish National Vintner*, vol. 6, no. 26, November 1966, p. 19.

30 See Oona Brooks' discussion of women's experience of drinking in contemporary pubs: 'Consuming Alcohol in Bars, Pubs and Clubs: A risky freedom for young women?', *Annals of Leisure Research: Cheers! A means-end chain analysis of college students' Bar-Choice Motivations*, vol. 11, nos. 3 & 4, 2008, pp. 331–50; S.L. Holloway et al. explore women's and men's behaviours in different 'drinking landscapes': 'Masculinities, Femininities and the Geographies of Public and Private Drinking Landscapes', *Geoforum*, vol. 40, 2009, pp. 821–31; Helana Darwin discusses the ways in which hybrid-masculinity characterises craft-beer culture in the United States: 'Omnivorous Masculinity: Gender capital and cultural legitimacy in craft beer culture', *Social Currents*, vol. 5, no. 3, 2018, pp. 301–16.

31 See the works of American anthropologists Arensberg and Kimball for ethnographic descriptions on the many uses of the public house by both men and women in rural Ireland in the 1920s and 1930s. Conrad Arensberg, *The Irish Countryman: An anthropological study* (Gloucester, MA: P. Smith, 1959 [1937]), https://archive.org/details/

irishcountrymanaooooaren_z7q4, ch. 5; Conrad Arensberg and Solon Kimball, *Family and Community in Ireland*, 3rd edn (Ennis: CLASP, 2001).

32 There was a strong link between the city's hinterland and the licensees, especially with west Cork.

33 'The Buffet', 30–31 Cook Street, Cork. Interview, Mary Morgan, Glasheen, Cork, 17 January 2018.

34 Interview, Mary Morgan, Glasheen, Cork, 17 January 2018. The pubs: The Gables, Douglas Street (Kathleen); the Green Bough, St Patrick's Quay, (Nora); and the Phoenix, Union Quay (Ellen).

35 The financial expectations of the breweries were modest and the breweries sought female tenants in the belief that they were less likely to turn to drink. Rex Archer, *Tales from the Kiln: A lifetime at Murphy's brewery* (County Cork: Galley Head Press, 2004).

36 Interview, Michael Murphy (b. 1941), by Caroline Cronin, 14 August 1999 (Cork Folklore Project).

37 This was in an 'early house', a pub with a licence to open from 7 a.m., common near docks. Interview, Honor, Derry and Mary O'Shea, by Adrian Roche, 2 September 2010 (Cork Folklore Project).

38 Interview Robert and Collette Crowley, 18 September 2017, Callanan's bar, Cork.

39 This was also common practice in Dublin, Hull and other places. Kneale, '"A Problem of Supervision"', p. 343.

40 Classified advertisement, *Evening Echo*, 16 February 1907, p. 2. Le Château bar, 'the most up-to-date bar in the city', 93 Patrick's Street, had three sections.

41 Such as the Green Bough. Interview, Mary Morgan, Glasheen, Cork, 17 January 2018.

42 For example, Le Château, 93 Patrick's Street, which had a snug, a public bar and two other separate rooms.

43 A '*piscín*' (kitten) was a 'mouthful' and a pony was about 200 ml. Interview Dan Reidy, Le Château bar, Cork, 31 August 2022.

44 Sometimes this was taken medicinally, warmed and with milk. Warm porter was drunk with sugar by children in west Cork in the 1920s and 1930s. Interview, Mary Morgan, Glasheen, Cork, 17 January 2018.

45 Catherine Coffey O'Brien, quoted in Donal O'Keefe, 'Making the Best of a Tight Spot', *Irish Examiner*, 6 February 2019, p. 13.

46 Maura Reidy quoted in ibid.

47 Interview, Mary Morgan, Glasheen, Cork, 17 January 2018.

48 Interview, Michael Reidy Jr, Le Château bar, Cork, 23 February 2022.

49 Interview, Michael O'Donovan, Castle Bar, 99 South Main Street, Cork, 8 February 2018.

50 Such as the characters in Flann O'Brien, 'At Swim-Two-Birds', in *The Complete Novels*, Keith Donohue (ed.) (London: Everyman's Library, 2007 [1939]), p. 17.

51 Valerie Hey, *Patriarchy and Pub Culture* (London: Tavistock Publications, 1985), pp. 44–50.

52 Tom Harrison (ed.), *The Pub and the People* (London: Seven Dials Press, 1943), p. 106.

53 Report of the Royal Commission on Liquor Licensing Laws, 1898, quoted in Ó Drisceoil and Ó Drisceoil, *Beamish & Crawford*, pp. 187–8.

54 Cork had 467 pubs for *c.* 80,000 people in 1925. 'Conditions in Cork Described', *Cork Examiner*, 9 July 1925, p. 7.

55 Frank O'Connor, *Larry Delaney: Lonesome genius* (Cork: Killeen Books, 1996), p. 132.

56 Ibid., p. 60.

57 Interview, Michael Reidy Jr, Le Château bar, Cork, 23 February 2022.

58 They did not 'get on with the snug regulars'. Interview, Mary Morgan, Glasheen, Cork, 17 January 2018.

59 For example, The Green Bough, St Patrick's Quay. Interview, Mary Morgan, Glasheen, Cork, 17 January 2018.

60 The Laurel Bar, Mary Street. Roy Bulson, *Munster Inns and Taverns* (Dublin: Press Associates of Ireland, 1969), p. 45.

61 Griselda Pollock, 'Modernity and the Spaces of Femininity', in Rendell et al., *Gender Space Architecture*, p. 164. See also Kneale, '"A Problem of Supervision"', p. 339.

62 'Mackesy's' [74 Oliver Plunket Street], *Cork Examiner*, 10 January 1957, p. 5.

63 Tommy Maher's, O'Connell Street, Waterford and The White Horse Bar, 1 George's Quay, Dublin are examples of places where a men-only policy was maintained. Maher kept 'a very strict male-only house', Bulson, *Munster Inns and Taverns*, p. 137.

64 There were reasons for this: reduced emigration, new jobs, greater opportunities for travel and the beginnings of a women's liberation movement. See Daly for a discussion of this decade. Mary E. Daly, *Sixties Ireland: Reshaping the economy, state and society, 1957–73* (Cambridge: Cambridge University Press, 2016).

65 Ralph Bossence, 'Dogs Less Trouble than Women in Pubs', *Belfast News-Letter*, 10 September 1968, p. 3.

66 Maurice Gorham, 'The Pub Is in Peril', *Sunday Independent Magazine*, 17 November 1963, pp. 30–1. Gorham was

well known for his books on British pubs, including *Back to the Local* (London: Percival Marshall) published in 1949 and reissued by Faber & Faber in 2024, and (with H. McG. Dunnett) a detailed analysis of pub interiors, *Inside the Pub* (London: The Architectural Press, 1950). Contemporary sexism was strongly present in advertising relating to alcohol and the suggestion that a photo book of 'some of Ulster's comeliest barmaids' be compiled. Ralph Bossence, 'Roy Wants to Bring a Bevy of Barmaids to Book', *Belfast News-Letter*, 29 April 1970, p. 4.

67 Gorham, 'The Pub Is in Peril'.

68 For women, the pub 'usually means more than a drink or two – it is part of a "night out"': 'Elaine', 'A Woman's Eye View of the Lounge Bar', *The Licensed Vintner*, vol. 29, no. 8, January 1964, p. 11.

69 *The Licensed Vintner*, vol. 33, no. 6, November 1967, p.19.

70 'Putting a Name on it', *The Harp* (Arthur Guinness & Co.), spring 1968, p. 15.

71 Cork City Planning application 9922905, http://planning.corkcity.ie/AppFileRefDetails/9922905/0.

72 'If it's Good Enough for the Likes of Miley ...', *Evening Echo*, 27 May 1999, p. 11.

73 'New Pub Is Just so Trendy', *Evening Echo*, 14 December 1996, p. 16.

74 As well as frequent references to dressing up by female journalists, the two trade journals, *The Licensed Vintner* and *The Irish National Vintner*, both had regular columns on ladies' fashions during the 1960s.

75 Donal O'Keefe, 'Making the Best of a Tight Spot', *Irish Examiner*, 6 February 2019, p. 13.

76 Gefou-Madianou, *Alcohol, Gender and Culture*.

77 The exclusion of women from the pub was not always the case, as women drank publicly through the seventeenth century and well into the 1800s. David Pritchard, in *The Irish Pub* (Wicklow: Real Ireland Design Limited, 1985), p. 16, claims that in 'pre-famine times records indicate that women mingled freely with men in Irish drinking places ... However, in the late nineteenth century a strongly moralistic tendency in the Catholic Church imposed new standards of strict behaviour on the Irish people and the idea of women and men drinking together came to be considered improper and even indecent'.

78 John Burnett, *Liquid Pleasures: A social history of drinks in modern Britain* (London: Routledge, 1999), p. 130.

79 See Liam Skelton '"All over the place, in town, in the pub, everywhere": A social geography of women's friendship in Cork', *Irish Geography*, vol. 35, no. 1, 2002, p. 45.

80 Ibid., p. 44.

81 See John Connolly, '"Pints or half-pints": Gender, functional democratization, and the consumption of drink in Ireland', *British Journal of Sociology*, vol. 72, 2021, pp. 1246–59.

82 Some contemporary pubs continue to act as exclusionary spaces and discourage various groups of people from entering or spending any length of time on the premises.

Chapter 4 – The Irish Pub: Views from social science

1 Some key texts include: Elizabeth Malcolm, 'The Rise of the Pub', in James Donnelly and Kerby Miller (eds), *Irish Popular Culture, 1650–1850* (Dublin: Irish Academic Press, 1998); Anthony Cooke, *A History of Drinking: The Scottish pub since 1700* (Edinburgh: Edinburgh University Press, 2015); Paul Jennings, *The Local: A history of the English pub* (Cheltenham: History Press, 2021); Diane Kirkby, Tanja Luckins and Chris McConville, *The Australian Pub* (Sydney: UNSW Press, 2010); Philip Howell, *Pub [Object Lessons]* (London: Bloomsbury, 2025).

2 Kevin Kearns, *Dublin Pub Life and Lore: An oral history* (Dublin: Gill & Macmillan, 1996); Diarmaid Ferriter, *A Nation Of Extremes: The Pioneers in twentieth century Ireland* (Dublin: Irish Academic Press, 1999).

3 Kevin Martin, *Have Ye No Homes To Go To? The history of the Irish pub* (Cork: Collins Press, 2016) and *The Complete Guide to the Best Pubs in Dublin* (Dublin: Orpen Press, 2019); Cian Molloy, *The Story of the Irish Pub* (Dublin: Liffey Press, 2002).

4 Bill Barich, *A Pint of Plain: Tradition, change and the fate of the Irish pub* (London: Bloomsbury, 2009); Pete McCarthy, *McCarthy's Bar: A journey of discovery in Ireland* (London: Hodder & Stoughton, 2000); Sybil Taylor, *Ireland's Pubs: The life and lore of Ireland through its finest pubs* (Harmondsworth: Penguin, 1983).

5 Perry Share, Mary P. Corcoran and Brian Conway, *A Sociology of Ireland* (Dublin: Gill & Macmillan, 2012); Brian Fanning and Andreas Hess, 'Sociology in Ireland: Legacies and challenges', *Irish Journal of Sociology*, vol. 23, no. 1, 2015, pp. 3–21, https://doi.org/10.7227/IJS.23.1.2; Chris Ó Rálaigh, 'A Contribution to a Critique of Irish Sociology', *Irish Journal of Sociology*, vol. 32, nos. 1–2, 2024, pp. 98–114, https://doi.org/10.1177/07916035231208156.

6 Dorren McMahon, '"Which Kind of Paddy?" A survey of the literature on the history, sociology and

anthropology of alcohol and the Irish', UCD Geary Institute discussion paper series, https://www.ucd.ie/geary/static/publications/workingpapers/gearywp200801.pdf (Dublin: University College Dublin, 2008); Alice Mauger, 'A Great Race of Drinkers? Irish interpretations of alcoholism and drinking stereotypes, 1945–1975', *Medical History*, vol. 65, no. 1, 2021, pp. 70–89, https://doi.org/10.1017/mdh.2020.51.

7 Adam Kaul, *Turning the Tune: Traditional music, tourism, and social change in an Irish village* (New York: Berghahn, 2013), p. 2.

8 As observed by Thomas Wilson and Hastings Donnan in *The Anthropology of Ireland* (Oxford: Berg, 2006), p. 33.

9 Anne Byrne, 'Epistolary Research Relations: Correspondences in anthropological research – Arensberg, Kimball, and the Harvard-Irish Survey, 1930–1936', in Diarmuid Ó Giolláin (ed.), *Irish Ethnologies* (South Bend, IN: University of Notre Dame Press, 2017), p. 46, https://aran.library.nuigalway.ie/handle/10379/16351.

10 Conrad Arensberg, *The Irish Countryman: An anthropological study* (Gloucester, MA: P. Smith, 1959 [1937]), https://catalog.hathitrust.org/Record/0001556641959, ch. 5.

11 Adrian Peace, *A World of Fine Difference: The social architecture of a modern Irish village* (Dublin: UCD Press, 2001), p. 9.

12 Shane Butler, *Alcohol, Drugs and Health Promotion in Modern Ireland* (Dublin: Institute of Public Administration, 2002), p.19.

13 John O'Brien, 'The Use of Public Houses as a Collective Representation of the Covid-19 Pandemic in Ireland', *Irish Journal of Sociology*, vol. 29, no. 3, 2021, pp. 353–71, https://doi.org/10.1177/07916035211029202.

14 Hugh Brody, *Inishkillane: Change and decline in the west of Ireland* (Harmondsworth: Penguin, 1973), p. 2.

15 Ibid., p. 159.

16 Ibid., p. 163, note.

17 Ibid., p. 172.

18 Chris Eipper, *The Ruling Trinity: A community study of church, state and business in Ireland* (Aldershot: Gower, 1986), p. 30.

19 Ibid., p. 135.

20 Ibid., pp. 100–1.

21 Peace, *A World of Fine Difference*, p. 57.

22 Ibid., p. 40.

23 Pauline Garvey and David Miller, *Ageing with Smartphones in Ireland* (London: UCL Press, 2021), p. 91, https://www.uclpress.co.uk/products/171340.

24 Ibid., p. 218.

25 Daniel Miller, *The Good Enough Life* (Cambridge: Polity, 2024), p. 58.

26 Ibid., p. 138.

27 Diane Watson, '"Home from Home": The pub and everyday life', in Tony Bennett and Diane Watson (eds), *Understanding Everyday Life* (Oxford: Blackwell/Open University, 2002), p. 190.

28 For relatively recent sociological explorations of the experiences of pubs per se, albeit from a British perspective, see: Thomas Rowell, 'The Pub Experience: A qualitative study of the tangible and intangible aspects of pub-goers' perceptions of pubs', unpublished MPhil thesis, University of Leicester, 2016, https://figshare.le.ac.uk/articles/thesis/The_Pub_Experience_A_Qualitative_Study_of_the_Tangible_and_Intangible_Aspects_of_Pub-goers_Perceptions_of_Pubs/10123304?file=18244457; and Fawn Harrad, 'The Social Ecology of the Public House', unpublished MPhil thesis, University of Leicester, 2016, https://figshare.le.ac.uk/articles/thesis/The_social_ecology_of_the_Public_House/10123271?file=18244379.

29 Watson, '"Home from Home"', pp. 188–9.

30 Ray Oldenburg, *The Great Good Place: Cafés, coffee shops, bookstores, bars, hair salons, and other hangouts at the heart of a community*, 3rd edn (New York: Marlowe, 1999).

31 Gwen Scarbough, 'The Irish Pub as a "Third Place": A sociological exploration of people, place and identity', unpublished PhD thesis, Institute of Technology, Sligo, 2008, https://research.thea.ie/handle/20.500.12065/585.

32 Kearns, *Dublin Pub Life and Lore*, p. 3

33 Ibid., p. 23; Chris Curtin and Colm Ryan, 'Clubs, Pubs and Private Houses in a Clare Town', in Chris Curtin and Tom Wilson (eds), *Ireland from Below: Social change and local communities* (Galway: Galway University Press, 1987).

34 Ignazio Cabras and Matthew Mount, 'How Third Places Foster and Shape Community Cohesion, Economic Development and Social Capital: The case of pubs in rural Ireland', *Journal of Rural Studies*, no. 55, 2017, pp. 71–82, https://doi.org/10.1016/j.jrurstud.2017.07.013.

35 Kearns, *Dublin Pub Life and Lore*, p. 3. See also Trish Murphy, this volume, chapter 6.

36 Thomas Thurnell-Read, '"It's a Small Little Pub, but Everybody Knew Everybody": Pub culture, belonging and social change', *Sociology*, vol. 58, no. 2, 2023, https://doi.org/10.1177/00380385231185936.

37 Cited in Watson, '"Home from home"', p. 201. This, of course, was prior to the widespread development of the shopping centre or mall.

38 John Fiske, Bob Hodge and Graeme Turner (eds), 'The Pub', in *Myths of Oz: Reading Australian popular culture* (Sydney: Allen & Unwin, 1987), p. 5.

39 Patrick McNabb, 'Social Structure', in Jeremiah Newman (ed.), *The Limerick Rural Survey, 1958–1964* (Tipperary: Muintir na Tíre, 1964), p. 233; Curtin and Ryan, 'Clubs, Pubs and Private Houses in a Clare Town', p. 137.

40 Fiske et al., *Myths of Oz*, p. 10.

41 Barry O'Halloran, 'Guinness 0.0 Sales Surge as Diageo Boosts Production to Keep Pace', *Irish Times*, 25 October 2024, https://www.irishtimes.com/business/2024/10/25/diageo-to-double-guinness-00-production-as-taste-for-non-alcoholic-stout-grows/. O'Halloran notes (citing figures from brewer Diageo) that sales of the alcohol-free draught grew by almost 50 per cent in the year to February 2024. Non-alcoholic beer now comprises 2 per cent of the Irish beer market, compared to an EU average of 7 per cent.

42 Ali Dunworth, *A Compendium of Irish Pints: The culture, customs and craic* (Dublin: Nine Bean Rows, 2024).

43 Fiske et al., *Myths of Oz*, p. 16.

44 Robert Shaw, 'The Making of Pub Atmospheres and George Orwell's Moon Under Water', in Sara Asu Schroer and Susanne B. Schmitt (eds), *Exploring Atmospheres Ethnographically* (London: Routledge, 2018), pp. 30–44.

45 George Orwell, 'The Moon Under Water' [Review of *The Pub and the People* by Mass-Observation', *The Listener*, 1943], https://www.orwellfoundation.com/the-orwell-foundation/orwell/essays-and-other-works/the-moon-under-water/. Orwell's essay is analysed in some detail in chapter 16 of this volume.

46 Bill Grantham traces use of the word 'craic' (in its pseudo-Gaeilge spelling) to at least 1968, when it was used in the *Connacht Sentinel* (30 July 1968), 'Teach Furbo ag Oscailt Anocht – Ceol agus Craic' ['Furbo House Open Tonight – Music and Craic']. Cited in his 'Craic in a Box: Commodifying and exporting the Irish pub', *Continuum*, vol. 23, no. 2, pp. 257–67, https://doi.org/10.1080/10304310802710553. British music journalist Colin Irwin describes his pursuit of this elusive quality in his book *In Search of the Craic: One man's pub crawl through Irish music* (London: André Deutsch, 2003).

47 Stefan Engeser, Anje Schiepe-Tiska and Corinna Peifer, 'Historical Lines and an Overview of Current Research on Flow', in Corinna Peifer and Stefan Engeser (eds), *Advances in Flow Research* (Cham: Springer, 2021), https://doi.org/10.1007/978-3-030-53468-4_1.

48 Tom Inglis, *Global Ireland: Same difference* (London: Routledge, 2008), p. 101.

49 Kaul, *Turning the Tune*, p. 98.

50 Ibid.

51 See also Kathleen Heininge, 'Guinness go Leor: Irish pubs and the diaspora', in Catherine Rees (ed.), *Changes in Contemporary Ireland: Texts and contexts* (Newcastle-upon-Tyne: Cambridge Scholars, 2013), https://digitalcommons.georgefox.edu/cgi/viewcontent.cgi?article=1063&context=eng_fac.

52 Aileen Dillane and Sarah Raine, 'Creating Ambiance Through Music in Dublin's Cultural Quarter: Temple Bar TradFest', in Iñigo Sánchez-Fuarros, Daniel Paiva and Daniel Malet Calvo (eds), *Ambiance, Tourism and the City* (London: Routledge, 2023), p. 243.

53 Ibid.

54 Jessica Boak and Ray Bailey, 'Irish Pub: Near and far away', in *20th Century Pub: From beer house to booze bunker* (St Alban's: Homewood Press, 2017), p. 158.

55 Sébastian Tutenges and Frederik Bøhling, 'Designing Drunkenness: How pubs, bars and nightclubs increase alcohol sales', *International Journal of Drug Policy*, no. 70, August 2019, pp. 15–21, https://doi.org/10.1016/j.drugpo.2019.04.009.

56 Mass Observation Library, *The Pub and the People: A Worktown study* (London: Cresset, 1987 [1943]); Scarbrough, 'The Irish Pub as a "Third Place"'; Thurnell-Read, 'It's a Small Little Pub'.

57 Kearns, *Dublin Pub Life and Lore*, p. 24.

58 Fiske et al., *Myths of Oz*.

59 Tom Inglis, *Moral Monopoly: The rise and fall of the Catholic Church in modern Ireland* (Dublin: UCD Press, 1998), pp. 170–2.

60 Scarbrough, 'The Irish Pub as a "Third Place"', p. 161.
61 McNabb, *The Limerick Rural Survey*, p. 236.
62 Inglis, *Moral Monopoly*, p. 172.
63 Kearns, *Dublin Pub Life and Lore*, p. 34.
64 Thomas Thurnell-Read, *Open Arms: The role of pubs in tackling loneliness* [commissioned by the Campaign to End Loneliness] (Loughborough: Loughborough University, 2021), https://hdl.handle.net/2134/13663715.v1.
65 Curtin and Ryan, 'Clubs, Pubs and Private Houses in a Clare Town'; Hastings, 'The Geography of Public Houses in Cork City Centre'.
66 Kearns, *Dublin Pub Life and Lore*, p. 33.
67 Hugh Campbell and Emily Phillips, 'Masculine Hegemony and Leisure Sites', in Perry Share (ed.), *Communication and Culture in Rural Areas* [Key papers 4] (Wagga Wagga: Centre for Rural Research, Charles Sturt University, 1995).
68 Brody, *Inishkillane*, pp. 161, 163.
69 Curtin and Ryan, 'Clubs, Pubs and Private Houses in a Clare Town', p. 137.
70 Ibid., p. 142.
71 Eipper, *The Ruling Trinity*, p. 136.
72 'Pubs and Nightclubs in Ireland: Employment statistics', *Ibis World*, https://www.ibisworld.com/ireland/industry-statistics/pubs-nightclubs/3446.
73 Sarah Burke and Darragh Nolan, 'Trying Times: More than a quarter of Ireland's rural pubs are staffed by as few as two people', *Irish Independent*, 17 March 2024, https://www.independent.ie/irish-news/trying-times-more-than-a-quarter-of-irelands-rural-pubs-are-staffed-by-as-few-as-two-people/a1590920596.html.
74 James Wickham and Alicja Bobek, 'Working in Hospitality', in *Enforced Flexibility? Working in Ireland today* (Dublin: TASC, 2016), https://www.tasc.ie/assets/files/pdf/enforcedflexibilityfinal.pdf.
75 Carmen Kuhling and Kieran Keohane, *Cosmopolitan Ireland: Globalisation and quality of life* (London: Pluto Press, 2007), p. 138.
76 Dino Hadzikadunic, 'Comparison of Job Satisfaction between Irish-born and Immigrant Employees in Non-Supervisory Positions in Dublin's Pubs, Bars and Restaurants', unpublished MA in Human Resources Management thesis, National College of Ireland, August 2020, https://norma.ncirl.ie/4598/1/dinohadzikadunic.pdf.
77 Psychiatrist Patricia Casey, quoted in Butler, *Alcohol, Drugs and Health Promotion in Modern Ireland*, p. 90.
78 Watson, '"Home from home"', pp. 199–200.
79 Ann Whitehead, 'Sexual Antagonism in Herefordshire', in Diana Barker and Sheila Allen (eds), *Dependence and Exploitation in Work and Marriage* (London: Longman, 1976); Curtin and Ryan, 'Clubs, Pubs and Private Houses in a Clare Town'.
80 Taylor, *Ireland's Pubs*, p. 25.
81 Clay Darcy, 'Irish Men, Masculinity and the Cultural Entwinement of Alcohol' (unpublished), University College Dublin, 2014, p. 13, https://www.academia.edu/38544071/_Irish_Men_Masculinity_and_the_Cultural_Entwinement_of_Alcohol_&nav_from=5d359e8e-4cf6-43ca-b343-7c290f783ad7&rw_pos=0.
82 McNabb, *The Limerick Rural Survey, 1958–1964*, p. 236.
83 Curtin and Ryan, 'Clubs, Pubs and Private Houses in a Clare Town', p. 140; Raewyn Connell and James W. Messerschmidt, 'Hegemonic Masculinity: Rethinking the concept', *Gender and Society*, vol. 19, no. 6, 2005, pp. 829–59, https://doi.org/10.1177/0891243205278639.
84 Darcy, 'Irish Men', p. 14.
85 McNabb, *The Limerick Rural Survey, 1958–1964*, p. 233.
86 Eipper, *The Ruling Trinity*, p. 100.
87 Scarbrough, 'The Irish Pub as a "Third Place"', pp. 128–41.
88 Ferriter, *A Nation of Extremes*, p. 168.
89 Jim Atkinson, 'The Bar Bar: What makes a bar a real bar', *Texas Monthly*, May 1983, https://www.texasmonthly.com/food/the-bar-bar.
90 Watson, '"Home from Home"', p. 209.
91 Dunworth, *A Compendium of Irish Pints*, p. 211.
92 Scarbrough, 'The Irish Pub as a "Third Place"'.

93 Claire O'Dwyer, Deirdre Mongan, Anne Doyle and Brian Galvin, *Alcohol Consumption, Alcohol-Related Harm and Alcohol Policy in Ireland*, HRB Overview Series 11 (Dublin: Health Research Board, 2021), https://www.drugsandalcohol.ie/33909.

94 Kristen Hartke, 'Kiss Off, You're Irish: In experiment, Detroit pub bans St Patrick's Day revelers', *The Salt* [NPR], 20 March 2018, https://www.npr.org/sections/thesalt/2018/03/20/595228105/kiss-off-youre-irish-in-experiment-detroit-pub-bans-st-patricks-day-revelers.

95 Inglis, *Moral Monopoly*, p. 100.

96 Boak and Bailey, *20th Century Pub*, p. 160. The allusion is, of course, to a well-known scene from the Channel 4 sitcom, *Father Ted*.

97 Eunice Masson, 'Cape Town Pub Cleared after Police Probe but Racism Case Still before Court', *Mail & Guardian*, 23 August 2023, https://mg.co.za/news/2023-08-28-cape-town-pub-cleared-of-racism/; James O'Brien, 'Boston Irish Pub Refused to Serve Blacks Says Attorney General, *Irish Central*, 16 August 2011, https://www.irishcentral.com/news/boston-irish-pub-refused-to-serve-blacks-says-attorney-general-127820128-237406291.

98 Bianca Giacobone, 'Woodside Pubs Thrive in Diversity', *Irish Echo*, 8 November 2018, https://www.irishecho.com/2018/11/woodside-pubs-thrive-in-diversity.

99 Lucy Michael, *Afrophobia in Ireland: Racism against people of African descent* (Dublin: ENAR Ireland, 2015), pp. 25–6, https://core.ac.uk/download/pdf/287020638.pdf.

100 David Knight and Cristina Montiero (eds), *Public House: A cultural and social history of the London pub* (London: Open City, 2021).

101 Margaret Tierney, 'The Aestheticisation of Pub Culture in Dublin', unpublished MA Sociology thesis, Maynooth University, 1999, https://mural.maynoothuniversity.ie/5260/1/Margaret_Tierney_20140722115658.pdf.

102 'Malwina', resident of Ireland for ten years, cited in Matthew Stephens, 'Unpacking Friendship: The impact of friendship practices on Polish migrants' senses of belonging in Cork City, Ireland', unpublished MSc (Research) thesis, Department of Human Geography and Spatial Planning, Utrecht University, 2017, p. 12, https://studenttheses.uu.nl/bitstream/handle/20.500.12932/27571/Thesis%20Matthew%20Stephens%20Final%20Copy%205676088.pdf?sequence=2.

Chapter 5 – Pubs and Gay Social Life in Dublin, 1923–73

1 John Farrell, *To Live the Impossible Dream* (Dublin: Dubh Linn: 1997), p. 48.

2 Elaine Sission, 'Experiment and the Free State: Mrs Cogley's Cabaret and the founding of the Gate Theatre 1924–1930', in David Clare, Des Lally and Patrick Lonergan (eds), *The Gate Theatre, Dublin: Inspiration and craft* (Oxford: Peter Lang, 2018), pp. 11–28.

3 Ibid.

4 'Humphrey' interviewed by John Farrell and quoted in Paul Condon, 'Reeling in the Years', *Gay Community News* (GCB), February 1996, p. 20.

5 *Evening Herald*, 7 October 1889.

6 *Irish Independent*, 12 September 1938.

7 *Evening Herald*, 16 July 1926.

8 Charles Duff, *Ireland and the Irish* (New York: Putnam's Sons, 1954), p. 164.

9 Liam O'Doherty, *A Tourist's Guide to Ireland* (London: The Mandrake Press, 1929), p. 105.

10 *The Motley*, vol. 2, no. 1, January 1933. Thanks to Maurice Casey for sharing.

11 *Evening Herald*, 16 November 1985.

12 Emails from Sean Leonard to author, 12 and 15 October 2020.

13 Ibid.

14 *Irish Press*, 25 December 1989.

15 *Irish Independent*, 10 March 1967.

16 *Wicklow People*, 17 September 1938.

17 Ibid.

18 Duff, *Ireland and the Irish*, p. 164.

19 *Irish Independent*, 12 September 1938.

20 *Wicklow People*, 17 September 1938.

21 Thomas Campbell of 40 St Peter's Road, Phibsboro died aged sixty-four on 10 March 1927 in Harold's Cross Hospice. The 1901 and 1911 censuses state that he was from County Louth and employed as an outfitter. Thanks to Senan Molony for this information.

22 Byrne was listed as single in the 1901 and 1911 censuses: 1901 census, http://www.census.nationalarchives.ie/pages/1901/Dublin/Rotunda/Dominick_Street/1281754/; 1911 census, http://www.census.nationalarchives.ie/pages/1911/Dublin/Arran_Quay/Rathdown_Road/47498/

23 Buller started as the 'bell stop' on the RMS *Empress of Scotland* ocean liner in the late 1920s and then worked in the Knickerbocker Bar (RMS *Empress of England*) followed by stints in the Savoy Hotel, London and the Berkeley Buttery, London. See *Evening Herald*, 6 August 1935 and James Murphy, *The Bartenders Association of Ireland: A history*, 1997, https://arrow.tudublin.ie/cgi/viewcontent.cgi?article=1013&context=tschafbk.

24 *Irish Times*, 30 November 1956.

25 *Evening Herald*, 6 August 1935.

26 *Irish Press*, 3 August 1938.

27 *Cork Examiner*, 12 December 1939.

28 Kathryn Milligan, 'Temporary Exile: The White Stag Group in Dublin, 1939–1946', in Burcu Dogramaci et al. (eds), *Arrival Cities: Migrating artists and new metropolitan topographies in the 20th century* (Leuven: Leuven University Press, 2020), pp. 317–34.

29 Máirtín Mac Con Iomaire, 'The History of Restaurant Jammet', 2009, https://arrow.tudublin.ie/cgi/viewcontent.cgi?article=1014&context=jamres.

30 Farrell, *To Live the Impossible Dream*, p. 48.

31 Quoted by Christopher Fitz-Simon, *The Boys: A double biography* (Dublin: Gill & Macmillan, 1994), p. 38.

32 Sometimes spelled Wyeman.

33 Hugh Oram, 'An Irishman's Diary', *Irish Times*, 12 March 2007; Liam Collins, 'Counter Culture', *Sunday Independent*, 21 October 2007; Patrick Cooney, 'Bohemian Rhapsody', *Sunday Independent*, 10 March 1996.

34 Quoted by Hugh Oram, *Irish Times*, 12 March 2007.

35 Michael O'Sullivan interview, *The Love that Dare Not Speak Its Name*, documentary film, dir. Bill Hughes (RTÉ, 2000).

36 Charles Gordon Lambert, entry in *Dictionary of Irish Biography* (Dublin: Royal Irish Academy, 2011), https://www.dib.ie/biography/lambert-charles-gordon-a9408.

37 Barry Cassin, *I Never Had a Proper Job: A life in the theatre* (Dublin: Liberties Press, 2014), p. 90.

38 Phyllis Ryan, *The Company I Kept* (Dublin: Town House, 1996), p. 92.

39 Tattens worked in Bewley's from 1948 until 2004. *Irish Times*, 24 February 2007.

40 *Irish Press*, 18 October 1941.

41 Michael J. Carney with Gerald W. Hayes, *From the Great Blasket to America: The last memoir by an islander* (Cork: Collins Press, 2013), p. 105.

42 *Tuam Herald*, 29 November 1941.

43 *Northern Whig*, 15 August 1944.

44 Duff, *Ireland and the Irish*, p. 165.

45 *Holiday*, vol. 19, no. 1, January 1956.

46 Email to author from Brian Ó Catháin, 20 October 2015.

47 Interview with Ian Fox, 2 February 2022.

48 Willie Orr, *The Shepherd and the Morning Star: Two lives apart* (Edinburgh: Birlinn, 2019), p. 79.

49 Email from Willie Orr to author, 22 November 2021.

50 Sometimes known as the Dawson Bar.

51 *Thom's Directory* 1940 and 1941 lists the owner of No. 25 Dawson Street as 'J.J. O'Hanlon & Co., wine & spirit merchants'.

52 Desmond Rushton was also responsible for murals in the Castle Lounge (Grogan's) and the Waterloo Bar.

53 *Irish Independent*, 24 May 1941.

54 Dermod Moore, 'Dublin After Dark', *Hot Press*, 29 March 2001.

55 Ibid.

56 *Irish Press*, 20 January 1951, 5 January 1952.

57 Email from Arthur Gilligan Jr to author, 29 November 2021.

58 J.P. Donleavy, *J.P. Donleavy's Ireland: In all her sins and in some of her graces* (New York: Viking Press, 1986), p. 44.

59 *Sunday Independent*, 24 September 1989; Kevin Monaghan biography, https://whitakerwatercolors.org/eileen-whitaker/monaghans.

60 Eibhear Walsh, 'A Wounded Lynx', *Irish Pages*, vol. 7, no. 2, 2013, pp. 51–62.
61 *Irish Times*, 30 September 1952.
62 Brendan Behan, *The Letters of Brendan Behan*, ed. E.H. Mikhail (Basingstoke: Macmillan, 1992), p. 87.
63 Interview with Ian Fox, 2 February 2022.
64 Head barman Peter Torsney leased the licence from his widow until the Dawson was sold in 1979 to an Irish-American businessman, Frank Cullen. He had it for less than a year. Murt Leonard and family ran it from 1980 for five years. Ron Black bought it in 1985 and was proprietor until 1994.
65 Interview with Ian Fox, 2 February 2022.
66 Moore, 'Dublin After Dark'.
67 *Sunday Independent*, 27 May 1956.
68 Interview with Harold Clarke, 4 December 2021.
69 Eddie Hernon, Facebook message to author, 17 November 2021.
70 Brian Ó Catháin comment on blog article by author, 19 October 2015, https://comeheretome.com/2013/10/06/rices-bartley-dunnes-dublins-first-gay-friendly-bars.
71 Brian Ó Catháin email to author, 20 October 2015.
72 Emails to author from Jeffrey Dudgeon (6 March 2024), Tony O'Connell (7 March 2024), Willie Orr (7 March 2024) and Ian Fox and Jim Harkin (7 March 2024).
73 Bartley Dunne obituary, *Irish Times*, 24 September 2016, https://www.irishtimes.com/life-and-style/people/barry-dunne-all-were-welcome-in-his-family-s-pub-bartley-dunne-s-1.2803432.
74 *Nationalist and Leinster Times*, 23 November 1946.
75 Tony Carey, Facebook message to author, 4 November 2020.
76 Mary Kenny, 'The Ruthless Ulsterman and War Hero – and My Brother's Boozing Pal', 5 December 2016. *Mary Kenny* [blog], https://mary-kenny.com/2016/12/05/the-ruthless-ulsterman-and-war-hero-and-my-brothers-boozing-pal.
77 Brian was employed in Bartley's from about 1962 to 1977.
78 Brian Ó Cáthain comment, 19 October 2015, https://comeheretome.com/2013/10/06/rices-bartley-dunnes-dublins-first-gay-friendly-bars.
79 Email to author from Willie Orr, 7 March 2024.
80 Email to author from Tony O'Connell, 7 March 2024.
81 Email to author from Ian Fox and Jim Harkin, 7 March 2024.
82 Email to author from Jeffrey Dudgeon, 7 March 2024.
83 Ibid.
84 *The Licensed Vintner*, vol. 26, no. 12, May 1961, information supplied by Tom Spalding.
85 Interview with Jim Harkin, 2 February 2022.
86 *Trinity News*, 31 May 1962.
87 *Irish Times*, 7 September 1985.
88 David Norris, *A Kick Against the Pricks: The autobiography* (Dublin: Transworld Ireland, 2012), p. 79.
89 Patrick Fay comment in 'Dublin in the rare old times' Facebook group, 6 July 2014.
90 Phone interview with Jeff Dudgeon, 6 November 2020.
91 Phone interview with Jim Fitzpatrick, 25 November 2020.
92 The pub was known as the Four Provinces before Nolan's.
93 Tom Spalding, '"A Striking Air of Modernity Tempered with Tradition": Vernacular modernism and the design of the public house in Cork and Dublin, 1934–1969', *Journal of Design History*, vol. 35, no. 4, December 2022, pp. 346–61.
94 It is worth noting that Rice's was not listed in the 1962 *Le Guide Gris*.
95 Interview with Ian Fox, 2 February 2022.
96 Email from Tony O'Connell to author, 3 October 2013.
97 David Norris interview, *The Love that Dare Not Speak Its Name*, documentary (RTÉ, 2000).
98 Thanks to Tom Hyde for supplying.
99 Phone interview with Austin MacNally, 25 November 2021.
100 *Dublin Evening News*, 2 July 1942.
101 *Irish Independent*, 15 December 1947.
102 Phone interview with Austin MacNally, 25 November 2021.

103 *Evening Herald*, 17 July 1961.
104 *Irish Independent*, 27 August 1976.
105 Interview with Jim Harkin, 2 February 2022.
106 Interview with Ian Fox, 2 February 2022.
107 Brian Peppard email to author, 30 August 2010.
108 Interview with Jim Harkin, 2 February 2022.
109 John Ryan, *Remembering How We Stood: Bohemian Dublin at the mid-century* (Dublin: Gill & Macmillan, 1975), p. 40.
110 Phone interview with Austin MacNally, 25 November 2021.
111 Email to author from Brian Ó Catháin, 20 October 2015.
112 Maria remained a fixture and friend to the gay community throughout the 1980s and '90s. She died in December 2015.
113 The Manhattan closed in 2007.
114 Phone interview with Tarra Wiggins, 23 November 2020.
115 Ibid.
116 Interview with Ian Fox, 2 February 2022.
117 Phone interview with Harold Clarke, 22 November 2020.
118 Phone interview with Jeff Dudgeon, 6 November 2020.
119 Email to author from Tony O'Connell, 21 November 2020
120 Email to author from Wladek Gaj, 25 November 2020.
121 Ibid.
122 Mrs Gaj's closed in 1980.
123 Phone interview with Harold Clarke, 22 November 2020.
124 B.D. Kelly, 'Homosexuality and Irish Psychiatry: Medicine, law and the changing face of Ireland', *Irish Journal of Psychological Medicine*, vol. 34, no. 3, 2017, pp. 209–15, https://doi.org/10.1017/ipm.2015.72.
125 Orla Ryan, '"Lives were ruined": State moves closer to exonerating men convicted of homosexual "offences"', https://www.thejournal.ie/exoneration-of-gay-men-for-homosexual-convictions-in-ireland-5646248-Jan2022/.
126 Email to author from Brian Ó Catháin, 20 October 2015.
127 Interview with Jim Harkin, 2 February 2022.
128 *Irish Times*, 7 September 1985.
129 The author would like to express his thanks to fellow historians and researchers (Maurice Casey, Averill Earls, Tom Hulme, Páraic Kerrigan, Patrick McDonagh and Kieran Rose), to the men who spoke to him about their memories of the 1950s and 1960s 'scene' (Brian Ó Catháin, Harold Clarke (RIP), Jeffrey Dudgeon, Ian Fox, Jim Harkin, Austin MacNally, Tony O'Connell and Brian Peppard (RIP)) and to others who provided important contextual information (Jim Fitzpatrick, Wladek Gaj, Arthur Gilligan Jr, Sean Leonard, Willie Orr, Michael O'Sullivan and Tara Wiggins).

Chapter 7 – Exporting the Irish Pub: An Interior designer's perspective, 1990–2010

1 Eamonn Slater, 'When the Local Goes Global', in Eamonn Slater and Michel Peillon (eds), *Memories of the Present: A sociological chronicle of Ireland, 1997–1998* (Dublin: Institute of Public Administration, 2000), p. 251.
2 The 'Celtic Tiger' was a term first recorded in a 1994 Morgan Stanley report by Kevin Gardiner. Cited in Peadar Kirby, Luke Gibbons and Michael Cronin, *Reinventing Ireland: Culture, society and the global economy* (London: Pluto Press, 2002), p. 17.
3 This chapter draws from a larger research study of the 'Guinness Irish Pub Concept', focusing of the 'Irish Pub Company', from 1990 to 2009. This is part of a PhD research degree at the Modern Interiors Research Centre, Kingston School of Art, Kingston University, Kingston-Upon-Thames, London, England.
4 By 1999, 'Irish Pub Company' remained the 'preferred' supplier. Other 'approved' suppliers were officially appointed at this time, namely O'Sullivan Interiors, Gemmell Griffin and Dunbar and Sonas Design (Diageo/Guinness press release, 2 June 1999). These companies had been designing and manufacturing Irish pubs for export throughout the 1990s. Other competitors were Murphy's brewery, who collaborated with Heineken to produce their own exported Irish pub concept, with Specialist Joinery Group, the joiners (and partners) for the 'Murphy's Pubs of Ireland' pub concept, in 1997. (Murphy's promotional video, sourced from the Guinness archive, Guinness Storehouse, St James' Gate, Dublin, 21 December 2021.)

5 Bill Grantham, 'Craic in a Box: Commodifying and exporting the Irish pub', *Continuum*, vol. 23, no. 2, 2009, pp. 257–67, https://doi.org/10.1080/10304310802710553; Mark McGovern, 'The "Craic" Market': Irish theme bars and the commodification of Irishness in contemporary Britain', *Irish Journal of Sociology*, vol. 11, no. 2, 2002, https://doi.org/10.1177/079160350201100205; Stephen Brown and Anthony Patterson, 'Knick-Knack Paddy-Whack, Give a Pub a Theme', *Journal of Marketing Management*, vol. 16, no. 6, 2000; Bill Barich, *A Pint of Plain: Tradition, change and the fate of the Irish pub* (London: Bloomsbury, 2009).

6 'From Pizzerias to Pubs: Focus on ... Guinness Italia', *Guinness Globe Magazine*, August 1995, p. 7. Following the success of a replica Victorian pub at the 1989 Milan fair, and the first Irish pub in Italy, 'Matricola' in Milan, hundreds of Irish pubs were opened, due to being thirty times more profitable than an Italian bar, according to Guinness Italia.

7 'The Formation of the Irish Pub Company and the Guinness Irish Pub Concept', Irish Pub Company website, https://irishpubcompany.com/about/the-story-of-the-irish-pub-company.

8 'What Are the Critical Success Factors?', Irish Pub Company website, https://irishpubconcept.com/about/overview/what-are-critical-success-factors.

9 Brown and Patterson, 'Knick-Knack Paddy-Whack', p. 652.

10 Laura Noonan, 'Fears of Last Orders at "Authentic Irish Pub" Firm', *Irish Independent*, 28 October 2009, https://www.independent.ie/business/irish/fears-of-last-orders-at-authentic-irish-pub-firm/26576950.html.

11 Kevin Kearns, *Dublin Pub Life and Lore: An oral history* (Dublin: Gill & Macmillan, 1996) noted 'less than twenty' Victorian pubs still in operation. In 2015 the 'Publin.ie' blog noted 'sixteen remaining pubs worth preserving' (https://www.facebook.com/Publinie/videos/995387563853397) – McDaid's is not a classic Victorian pub, but does share many features. In 2017, a Little Museum of Dublin exhibition, 'A Little History of the Dublin Pub', celebrated these establishments, on the 200th anniversary of the Licensed Vintners Association. For a striking visual record, see Rodhlann Mossop and Alex Pollock 'Dublin's Remaining Victorian Pubs', in *Type* [blog], https://www.type.ie/blog/dublin-sixteen-remaining-victorian-pubs-a-visual-essay.

12 'Guinness Irish Pub Concept' marketing brochure *c.* 1995, p. 15. Accessed in the Guinness archive, Guinness Storehouse, St James' Gate, Dublin, 7 December 2021.

13 Very much the style portrayed in detail in Maurice Gorham and H. McG. Dunnett, *Inside the Pub* (London: The Architectural Press, 1950), pp. 95–110.

14 Ibid.

15 Morrissey's also features as an example of a 'Shop' style pub in several reference and coffee-table books, including James Fennell and Turtle Bunbury, *The Irish Pub* (London: Thames & Hudson, 2008), pp. 32–5.

16 In 1925, travelling through north-west Ireland, writer and poet George Russell commented that 'every third house in Charlestown and Ballaghadereen is licensed to sell liquor' (cited in Diarmaid Ferriter, 'Drink and Society in Twentieth-Century Ireland', *Proceedings of the Royal Irish Academy. Section C: Archaeology, Celtic Studies, History, Linguistics, Literature*, vol. 115, 2015, pp. 349–69.

17 'Guinness Irish Pub Concept' marketing brochure *c.* 2005. Accessed in the Guinness archive, Guinness Storehouse, St James' Gate, Dublin, 7 December 2021.

18 See John Urry, *The Tourist Gaze: Leisure and travel in contemporary societies* (London: Sage, 1990).

19 'The Irish Pub: A Remarkable Business Opportunity': An 'Irish Pub Company' marketing brochure, 1997. Accessed in the McNally Design archive, 7 November 2018. This pub features regularly as an example of the Irish rural pub in a cottage-type structure.

20 'Guinness Irish Pub Concept' marketing brochure *c.* 1995, p. 16. Accessed in the Guinness archive, Guinness Storehouse, St James' Gate, Dublin, 7 December 2021.

21 This pub is photographed as a successful example of the 'Brewery' style pub in the 'Guinness Irish Pub Concept' marketing brochure *c.* 1995, p. 16. Accessed in the Guinness archive, Guinness Storehouse, St James' Gate, Dublin, 7 December 2021.

22 'Guinness Irish Pub Concept' marketing brochure *c.* 1995, p. 17. Accessed in the Guinness archive, Guinness Storehouse, St James' Gate, Dublin, 7 December 2021.

23 Mark McGovern, 'The "Craic" Market': Irish theme bars and the commodification of Irishness in contemporary Britain', *Irish Journal of Sociology*, vol. 11, no. 2, 2002, p. 83, https://doi.org/10.1177/079160350201100205. McGovern notes the Irish Pub Company's 1997 promotional material suggests that Germany and the United States have an interest in 'Gaelicism'.

24 Fadó, meaning 'Long Ago' in Gaelic, was a brand created by John Gilmore of Guinness, Mel McNally, IPC, and Kieran McGill, CEO Fadó USA, in 1996.

25 Irish dancing became a worldwide phenomenon due to 'Riverdance', an interval act at the Eurovision Song Contest, in 1994.

26 Alan Bryman, *The Disneyization of Society* (London: Sage Publications, 2004).

27 The term 'turn-key' is defined as 'of or involving the provision of a complete product or service that is ready for immediate use'. In this case it refers to the provision of a complete service to the client which starts from taking a brief, design, construction, on-site management, without the requirement to engage other external services. The turn-key methodology appears on the Irish Pub Company website, updated in 2019, https://irishpubcompany.com/services/design-and-build.

28 'Agreement between Client and Architect for the Provision of Architectural Services Incorporating Conservation and Restoration Works', Royal Institute of the Architects of Ireland, Dublin, 2019. This is an eight-stage process, from 'Inception' to 'On Site Completion'. This allows for the breakdown of the project process and guides the billing process.

29 Barich, *A Pint of Plain*. Barich is in search of the quintessential Irish 'local' and is consistently critical of the themed pub for export. He also referred to surviving original Victorian Dublin pubs as 'trophy pubs' and 'museum pieces'; Grantham, 'Craic in a Box'. Grantham critiqued the Irish pub for export through an analysis of the US version of the IPC website, breaking down the five criteria for the success of the Irish pub for export.

30 Doreen Massey, *For Space* (London: Sage, 2005).

31 Mike Featherstone, *Consumer Culture and Postmodernism* (London: Sage, 2007), p. 80.

32 Caroline L. Muñoz, Natalie T. Wood and Michael R. Solomon, 'Real or Blarney? A cross-cultural investigation of the perceived authenticity of Irish pubs', *Journal of Consumer Behaviour: An international research review*, vol. 5, no. 3, 2006, pp. 222–34, https://doi.org/10.1002/cb.174.

33 In the 1990s this would be factual. The early 2000s saw the influx of immigrants from central and eastern Europe and the African continent, which changed the demographic of architects and designers in the Irish Pub Company (and in Ireland generally) and had a subsequent effect on design styles and outputs.

34 One such pub is the Ronald Reagan bar, originally in Ballyporeen, County Tipperary, and site of a celebrated US presidential visit in 1984. The pub was subsequently dismantled and now sits underneath an Air Force One aeroplane in the Ronald Reagan Presidential Library in California. The story of this relocation is described in a Publin podcast: 'The Story of the Ronald Reagan Pub: From Tipperary to California' (2023), https://shows.acast.com/publin/episodes/the-story-of-the-ronald-reagan-pub-from-tipperary-to-califor.

35 Jan Blommaert and Piia Varis, 'Enough Is Enough: The heuristics of authenticity in superdiversity', *Tilburg Papers in Culture Studies*, no. 2 (Tilburg: Tilburg University, 2011), https://research.tilburguniversity.edu/en/publications/enough-is-enough-the-heuristics-of-authenticity-in-superdiversity-3.

36 See 'The Insider's Guide to the Guinness Irish Pub Concept', 1998, pp. 9–10. This is a GIPC promotional brochure providing key information on how to build a profitable Irish pub for export. This section advises the potential investor not to 'push for a design that goes too far'. On bric-a-brac it is recommended to 'at all costs avoid leprechauns, quaint Irish sayings, kelly green artefacts and tacky images of Ireland'.

37 This also sits against a backdrop of a private housing boom in Ireland, with house prices escalating by 292 per cent between 1996 and 2006. See Michelle Norris and Dermot Coates, 'How Housing Killed the Celtic Tiger: Anatomy and consequences of Ireland's housing boom and bust', *Journal of Housing and the Built Environment*, vol. 29, no. 2, 2014, p. 30, https://doi.org/10.1007/s10901-013-9384-z.

38 Muñoz et al., 'Real or Blarney?', p. 222.

39 GIPC, 'The Insider's Guide', p. 5.

40 'Irish Pub Concept' website, https://irishpubconcept.com/about/overview/what-are-critical-success-factors/.

41 George Ritzer, *The McDonaldization Thesis: Explorations and extensions* (Thousand Oaks, CA: Sage, 1998).

42 Maurice Gorham, in *Back to the Local* (London: Faber & Faber, 2024 [1949]) defines a 'tied house' as 'a pub in which one brewery has a monopoly of supplying the beer' (p. 121). In practice, Irish pubs (in Ireland) largely serve drinks produced by five leading global drinks corporations – Diageo (e.g. Guinness); Pernod Ricard (e.g. Jameson's); AB-InBev (e.g. Budweiser); Heineken (e.g. Murphy's) and Constellation (e.g. Corona) – and this is also likely to be the case internationally. Alcohol Action Ireland, *Raising the Bar: An examination of the alcohol market in Ireland* (Dublin: Alcohol Action Ireland, 2022), https://alcoholireland.ie/wp-content/uploads/2022/09/21999-AAI-Market-Review-2022_v4screen.pdf.

43 Simon Carswell, 'What Started Fadó, Fadó in Atlanta is Now a $40m Chain of Irish Pubs', *Irish Times*, 10 April 2015, p. 4.

44 Robert Venturi, Denise Scott Brown and Steven Izenour, *Learning from Las Vegas: The forgotten symbolism of architectural form* (Cambridge, MA: MIT Press, 1972). This seminal writing was a major catalyst for the movement, rejecting the 'International' style and embracing eclecticism in architectural style.

45 Bryman, *The Disneyization of Society*.

46 Mel's love of classical architecture and design emerged in the mid-1970s at the School of Architecture, DIT, Bolton Street, Dublin through a successful 'Best Designs within Dublin Pubs' project, exhibited at Dublin's Mansion House (at the height of 'Brutalism'), https://irishpubcompany.com/about/the-story-of-the-irish-pub-company/.

47 McGovern, 'The "Craic" Market', p. 83.

48 Featherstone, *Consumer Culture and Postmodernism*, p. 80.

49 Julian Halevy, 'Disneyland and Las Vegas', *The Nation*, 7 June 1958, pp. 510–12.

50 Jean Baudrillard, *Simulacra and Simulation*, tr. Sheila Faria Glaser (Ann Arbor, MI: University of Michigan Press, 1994).

51 Umberto Eco, *Travels in Hyperreality: Essays*, tr. William Weaver (San Diego: Harcourt Brace Jovanovich, 1990).

52 Mark Gottdiener, *The Theming of America: Dreams, visions, and commercial spaces* (London: Routledge, 1997).

53 James L. Watson, 'McDonald's in Hong Kong: Consumerism, dietary change, and the rise of a children's culture', in James L. Watson (ed.), *Golden Arches East: McDonald's in East Asia* (Redwood City: Stanford University Press, 1997), pp. 110–35.

54 Pierre Bourdieu, *Distinction: A social critique of the judgement of taste* (Cambridge, MA: Harvard University Press, 1979).

55 Eric Hobsbawm and Terence Ranger (eds), *The Invention of Tradition* (Cambridge: Cambridge University Press, 1983). Hobsbawm and Ranger argued that '[m]any of the traditions which we think of as very ancient were not in fact sanctioned by long usage over the centuries, but were invented comparatively recently … This process of invention … addresses the complex interaction of past and present in a fascinating study of ritual and symbolism', https://www.worldcat.org/title/invention-of-tradition/oclc/8763782.

56 Anthony Patterson, Stephen Brown, Lorna Stevens and Pauline MacLaran, 'Casting a Critical "I" over Caffrey's Irish Ale: Soft words, strongly spoken', *Journal of Marketing Management*, vol. 14, no. 7, 1998, pp. 733–48.

57 College of Marketing and Design (now the School of Art and Design at TU Dublin), Griffith College Dublin, and Coláiste Dúlaigh College of Further Education. All were founded in the early 1970s and offered diploma- or degree-level qualifications in interior/spatial design.

58 'The Insider's Guide to the Guinness Irish Pub Concept' (1997, pp. 8–12) provides specific rules for the design of all components of the interior of a GIPC pub. This was provided to clients to encourage a trusting relationship between design firm and client. This was never shown to studio designers but was known to management.

Chapter 8 – How a Home Should Be? Gender identity and belonging in the Irish pubs in London, Dublin and Belfast

1 Edna O'Brien 'The Shovel Kings', in *Saints and Sinners* (London: Faber & Faber, 2011).

2 Kathleen Heininge, 'Guinness go Leor: Irish Pubs and the Diaspora' (Newberg, OR: George Fox University, Faculty Publications – Department of English, 2013), p. 69. [Originally published in *Changes in Contemporary Ireland: Texts and contexts*, edited by Catherine Rees], https://digitalcommons.georgefox.edu/eng_fac/64/.

3 Cited in Tony Murray, *London Irish Fictions: Narrative, diaspora and identity* (Liverpool: Liverpool University Press, 2003), p. 233.

4 Loic Wright, '"A Pint of Plain Is Your Only Man": Masculinities and the pub in twentieth-century Irish fiction', *Estudios Irlandeses: Journal of Irish Studies*, no. 15, 2021, pp. 143–55, https://doi.org/10.24162/EI2020-9371.

5 Valerie Hey, *Patriarchy and Pub Culture* (London: Tavistock, 1986), p. 14.

6 Murray, *London Irish Fictions*, p. 48.

7 Claire Finney, 'Can a Pub Be Feminist? These entrepreneurs say yes', *Vogue*, 20 February 2022, https://www.vogue.co.uk/arts-and-lifestyle/article/feminist-pubs.

8 Paul Chatterton and Robert Hollands, *Urban Nightscapes: Youth cultures, pleasure spaces and corporate power* (London: Routledge, 2003), p. 152.

9 With the benefit of hindsight and a more nuanced view of gender and space, I now see that venues like All Bar One did much to open up pub and bar culture to those who did not feel comfortable in more male-dominated venues. They were, nevertheless, in my view, reliant on certain limiting ideas of gender.

10 O'Brien, 'The Shovel Kings', p. 11.

11 Ibid., p. 18.

12 The final provisions of the Official Languages (Amendment) Act 2021 in Northern Ireland, which granted new language rights for Irish speakers and increased obligations on public bodies regarding the Irish language, came into effect on 21 December 2024. Implementation of the act has led to controversies, such as that over signage at Belfast's new public transport hub.

13 Teresa García Alcaraz, 'Belfast Has More Peace Walls Now than 25 Years Ago: Removing them will be a complex challenge', *The Conversation*, 26 April 2023, https://theconversation.com/belfast-has-more-peace-walls-now-than-25-years-ago-removing-them-will-be-a-complex-challenge-203975.

14 Graham Dawson, *Making Peace with the Past: Memory, trauma and the Irish troubles* (Manchester: Manchester University Press, 2007), p. xx (Preface).

15 Rosie Schapp, 'The John Hewitt, Belfast, Northern Ireland', in Sean Manning (ed.), *Come Here Often? 53 writers raise a glass to their favorite bar* (New York: Catapult, 2014), reproduced in Meredith Turits, 'Hey, Writers: What's Your Favorite Bar?', *Bustle*, 30 September 2014, https://www.bustle.com/articles/41392-in-come-here-often-rosie-schaap-and-52-other-writers-share-their-favorite-bars.

16 Ciaran Carson, *Belfast Confetti* (Oldcastle: Gallery Press, 1989).

17 In addition to these sectarian attacks, pubs have been the site of inter-community violence as part of feuds within republican and loyalist paramilitaries. See 'Paramilitary Feuds in Northern Ireland: A chronology of events', https://cain.ulster.ac.uk/issues/violence/feudchron.htm.

18 Luke Moffett et al., '"No Longer Neighbours": The impact of violence on land, housing and redress in the Northern Ireland conflict', Queen's University Belfast, 2022, p. 37, https://pureadmin.qub.ac.uk/ws/portalfiles/portal/213711196/Land_Report_ENG_Red.pdf.

19 *Maeve* [film], dir. Pat Murphy (London: British Film Institute Production Board, 1981).

20 Nell McCafferty, *Peggy Deery: An Irish family at war* (Jersey City, NJ: Cleis Press, 1989).

21 More recent fictional representations of the pub's politics – gendered and otherwise – in Northern Ireland can be found in Louise Kennedy's *Trespasses* and Michelle Gallen's *Factory Girls*, both published in 2022.

22 Charlotte Higgins, 'The 11-Strong Array Collective on Winning the Turner Prize: "We'll have to have a meeting about this!"', *Guardian*, 2 December 2021, https://www.theguardian.com/artanddesign/2021/dec/02/array-collective-winning-turner-prize-belfast-bar-drinking-den.

23 Deirdre Falvey, 'Síbín Comes to Galway: "It's one thing inside another inside another"', *Irish Times*, 23 August 2022, https://www.irishtimes.com/culture/art/2022/08/23/sibin-comes-to-galway-its-one-thing-inside-another-inside-another/.

24 For an exploration of navigating queer identities in Belfast public spaces, including its bars, see Padraig Regan's essay 'Glitch City' in the collection *Some Integrity* (Manchester: Carcanet, 2022). For more on queer identities in Irish pubs, see Allison Macleod, 'The Contested Space of the Irish Pub', in *Irish Queer Cinema* (Edinburgh: Edinburgh University Press, 2018), pp. 48–66.

25 Quoted in Falvey, 'Síbín Comes to Galway'.

Chapter 9 – Discourses of Inclusion and Exclusion: Gender, race and point of origin in Irish pubs

1 This chapter is a summary of, and revisitation of, work that was first published in my *Brewing Identities: Globalisation, Guinness and the production of Irishness* (New York: Peter Lang, 2015).

2 Valerie Hey, *Patriarchy and Pub Culture* (London: Tavistock, 1986), p. 13.

3 The Madonna-Whore Dichotomy (MWD) denotes polarised perceptions of women in general as either 'good', chaste and pure Madonnas or as 'bad', promiscuous and seductive whores. Whereas prior theories focused on unresolved sexual complexes or evolved psychological tendencies, feminist theory suggests the MWD stems from a desire to reinforce patriarchy born out of benevolent and hostile sexism, sexual objectification of women, and sexual double standards. Orly Bareket et al., 'The Madonna-Whore Dichotomy: Men who perceive women's nurturance and sexuality as mutually exclusive endorse patriarchy and show lower relationship satisfaction', *Sex Roles*, no. 79, 2018. pp. 519–32, https://doi.org/10.1007/s11199-018-0895-7.

4 Sybil Taylor, *Ireland's Pubs: The life and lore of Ireland through its finest pubs* (Harmondsworth: Penguin, 1983), p. 15.
5 For further discussion on the snug see Chapter 3 this volume.
6 A 'glass' of beer = a half pint.
7 Hey, *Patriarchy and Pub Culture*, p. 30.
8 Respondents' reports and quotes are based on research conducted for the book *Brewing Identities*.
9 Famous 'Guinness' pub in Dublin. Renowned as one of the few remaining historical pubs and for its high standards surrounding the storing and serving of Guinness.
10 Interviewed in The Step Inn, Dublin, Ireland, 1996.
11 Interviewed in the Starting Gate pub, Queens, New York, 1997.
12 David Bell and Gill Valentine, *Consuming Geographies: We are where we eat* (London: Routledge, 1997), p. 91.
13 Bronwyn Walter, *Outsiders Inside: Whiteness, place and Irish women* (London: Routledge, 2001).
14 Máirtín Mac an Ghaill, *Contemporary Racisms and Ethnicities: Social and cultural transformations* (London: Open University Press, 1999), p. 4.
15 Interviewed in the Parkway Inn, north London, 1996.
16 Máirtín Mac an Ghaill, 'Young (Male) Irelanders' Postcolonial Ethnicities: Expanding the nation and Irishness', *European Journal of Cultural* Studies, vol. 6, no. 3, 2003, p. 388, https://doi.org/10.1177/13675494030063007.
17 Interviewed in McCormack's bar, Manhattan, New York, 1997.
18 Máirtín Mac an Ghaill and Chris Haywood, 'Nothing to Write Home About: Troubling concepts of home, racialization and self in theories of Irish male (e)migration', *Cultural Sociology*, vol. 5, no. 3, 2010, p. 395, https://doi.org/10.1177/1749975510378196.
19 Interviewed in McCormack's bar, Manhattan, New York, 1997.
20 Frantz Fanon, *Black Skin, White Masks*, tr. Charles Lam Markmann (London: Pluto Press, 1986 [1951]).
21 Liam Greenslade, 'White Skin, White Masks: Psychological distress among the Irish in Britain', in Patrick O'Sullivan (ed.), *The Irish in the New Communities* (Leicester: Leicester University Press, 1992), p. 216.
22 Monica McDermott and Frank Samson, 'White Racial and Ethnic Identity in the United States', *Annual Review of Sociology*, vol. 31, 2005, p. 246, https://www.jstor.org/stable/29737719.
23 Noel Ignatiev, *How the Irish Became White* (London: Routledge, 2008), p. 1.
24 Ronit Lentin and Robbie McVeigh, *After Optimism? Ireland, racism and globalization* (Dublin: Metro Publications, 2006), pp. 22–4.
25 Ibid., p. 23.
26 Interviewed in the Starting Gate pub, Queens, New York, 1997.
27 Ibid.
28 Mac an Ghaill, *Contemporary Racisms*, p. 58.
29 Lentin and McVeigh, *After Optimism?*, p. 22.
30 Binary oppositions can be found in the pub space in Ireland, London and New York. Many implicit examples of inclusion and exclusion can be traced. For example, in Ireland, the status of 'regular' drinker suggests that there is an opposite group of 'non-regulars'. To be a 'regular' brings with it benefits that non-regulars are not even aware of, such as being allowed to stay on drinking after official closing time.
31 Murphy, *Brewing Identities*.
32 Mac an Ghaill, *Contemporary Racisms*, pp. 6–7.
33 Gerald Mars, 'Longshore Drinking, Economic Security and Union Politics in Newfoundland', in Mary Douglas (ed.), *Constructive Drinking: Perspectives on drinking from anthropology* (Cambridge: Cambridge University Press, 1987), pp. 91–101.
34 Bell and Valentine, *Consuming Geographies*, p. 91.

Chapter 10 – The Road to *McCarthy's Bar*: Travel, translation and the Irish pub

1 Eimear Ryan, *Holding Her Breath* (London: Penguin, 2022), p. 102.
2 Kevin Martin, *Have Ye No Homes To Go To? The history of the Irish pub* (Cork: Collins Press, 2016).
3 Martin Heidegger, *The Question Concerning Technology and Other Essays*, tr. William Lovitt (New York: Harper, 1977), p. 134.
4 David Michael Levin (ed.), *Modernity and the Hegemony of Vision* (Berkeley: University of California Press, 1993).

5 Walter Ong, *Orality and Literacy*, 3rd edn (London: Routledge, 2012).

6 Jonathan Culler, 'Semiotics of Tourism', in *Framing the Sign: Criticism and its institutions* (Norman, OK: University of Oklahoma Press, 1990), p. 2, https://web.mit.edu/allanmc/www/culler1.pdf.

7 Michael Cronin, 'Next to Being There: Ireland of the welcomes and the tourism of the word', in Michael Cronin and Barbara O'Connor (eds), *Irish Tourism: Image, culture and identity* (Clevedon: Channel View Publications, 2003), pp. 179–95.

8 Irene Furlong, *Irish Tourism 1880–1980* (Dublin: Irish Academic Press, 2008).

9 George Bernard Shaw, 'Bernard Shaw's Irish Holidays', *Ireland of the Welcomes*, vol. 12, no. 4, 1963, pp. 13–5. Reprinted from *Collier's Magazine*, 10 June 1916 and first published in *The Car*, 5 April 1916.

10 Cited in Diarmaid Ferriter, 'Drink and Society in Twentieth-Century Ireland', in Elizabeth Fitzpatrick and James Kelly (eds), *Food and Drink in Ireland* (Dublin: Royal Irish Academy, 2016), pp. 349–70.

11 Donal S. Connery, *The Irish* (New York: Simon & Schuster, 1970), pp. 97–8.

12 Charles Graves, *Ireland Revisited* (London: Hutchinson, 1949), pp. 35, 112, 129.

13 Ibid., p. 24.

14 Eric Newby, *Round Ireland in Low Gear* (London: Viking, 1987), p. 34.

15 Ibid., p. 85.

16 Ibid., p. 95.

17 Ibid., p. 268.

18 Paul Smethurst, *Travel Writing and the Natural World, 1760–1840* (Basingstoke: Palgrave Macmillan, 2013).

19 Newby, *Round Ireland in Low Gear*, p. 221.

20 Pete McCarthy, *McCarthy's Bar* (London: Hodder & Stoughton, 2001), p. 3.

21 Ibid., pp. 61–2.

22 Ibid., p. 122.

23 Ibid., p. 47.

24 Ibid., p. 40.

25 Ibid., p. 10.

26 Ibid., p. 92.

27 Ibid., p. 123.

28 Kobus Marais, *A (Bio)Semiotic Theory of Translation: The emergence of socio-cultural reality* (London: Routledge, 2019).

29 Roman Jakobson, 'On Linguistic Aspects of Translation', in Lawrence Venuti (ed.), *The Translation Studies Reader* (London: Routledge, 2004), p. 139.

30 Charles Sanders Peirce, *Writings of Charles S. Peirce: A chronological edition*, vol. 4 (Bloomington, IN: Indiana University Press, 1989), p. 127.

31 Marais, *A (Bio)Semiotic Theory of Translation*, p. 141.

32 McCarthy, *McCarthy's Bar*, p. 119.

33 Ibid., p. 171.

34 Ibid., p. 16.

35 Ibid., p. 355.

36 James Buzard, *The Beaten Track: European tourism, literature, and the ways to 'culture', 1800–1918* (Oxford: Oxford University Press, 1993).

37 Paul Fussell, *Abroad: British literary travelling between the wars* (Oxford: Oxford University Press, 1980), p. 37.

38 McCarthy, *McCarthy's Bar*, p. 152.

39 Ibid., p. 163.

40 Ibid., p. 264.

41 Ibid., p. 11.

42 Ibid., p. 365.

43 Ibid., p. 367.

44 Ibid., p. 105.

45 Koh Buck Song, *Brand Singapore: Nation branding after Lee Kuan Yew, in a divisive world* (Singapore: Marshall Cavendish International, 2017).

46 Clay Risen, 'Re-branding America', *Boston Globe*, 13 March 2005, https://universityofleeds.github.io/philtaylorpapers/vp018174.html.

47 Zala Volcic and Mark Andrejevic, 'Nation Branding in the Era of Commercial Nationalism', *International Journal of Communications*, no. 5, 2011, p. 604, https://ijoc.org/index.php/ijoc/article/view/849/544.
48 McCarthy, *McCarthy's Bar*, p. 367.
49 Rebecca Solnit, *A Book of Migrations: Some passages in Ireland* (London: Verso, 1997), p. 44.
50 Ibid., p. 112.
51 Ibid., p. 114.
52 Helen O'Shea, 'Getting to the Heart of the Music: Idealizing musical community and Irish traditional music sessions', *Journal of the Society for Musicology in Ireland*, no. 2, 2006, pp. 1–18, https://doi.org/10.35561/JSMI02061; Adam Kaul, *Turning the Tune: Traditional music, tourism, and social change in an Irish village* (Oxford: Berghahn, 2013).

Chapter 11 – Grim Days in the Pub

1 See Healthline, among many others: https://www.healthline.com/nutrition/is-alcohol-a-stimulant.
2 See Devin A. Garrity (ed.), *44 Irish Short Stories* (Old Greenwich, CT: Devin-Adair, 1955); William Trevor (ed.), *Oxford Book of Irish Short Stories* (Oxford: Oxford University Press, 1984); Dermot Bolger (ed.), *The New Picador Book of Contemporary Irish Fiction* (London: Picador, 2000).
3 Letter to Grant Richards, 5 May 1906, in Richard Ellmann (ed.), *The Letters of James Joyce*, II (London: Faber & Faber, 1966), p. 134.
4 James Joyce, *Dubliners*, ed. Terence Brown (London: Penguin, 1992), p. 28.
5 Ibid., pp. 68–9, 80.
6 Ibid., notes, p. 274.
7 Ibid., p. 86.
8 Ibid., p. 85.
9 Ibid., notes, p. 275.
10 http://www.census.nationalarchives.ie/pages/1901/Dublin/Rathmines___Rathgar_East/Ormond_Road/1293673/
11 Joyce, *Dubliners*, p. 82.
12 Ibid., p. 83.
13 Ibid.
14 Ibid., p. 86.
15 Ibid., p. 87.
16 Ibid., p. 89.
17 Ibid., p. 86.
18 Paul Delaney, '"Tailors of Malt, Hot, All Round": Homosocial consumption in *Dubliners*', *Studies in Short Fiction*, vol. 32, no. 3, 1995, pp. 381–93.
19 Ibid., p. 385.
20 Joyce, *Dubliners*, p. 90.
21 Ibid., p. 91.
22 Ibid., p. 92.
23 Ellmann, *Letters of James Joyce*, II, p. 106.
24 Joyce, *Dubliners*, pp. 92–3.
25 Ibid., p. 93.
26 The pathetic appeal of the boy, 'I'll say a *Hail Mary* for you, pa, if you don't beat me', was taken from the outcry of a child of Joyce's uncle William Murray: see Richard Ellmann, *James Joyce* (London: Oxford University Press, 1966 [1959]), p. 18.
27 John McGahern, *Creatures of the Earth* (London: Faber & Faber, 2006), p. 154.
28 Ibid., p. 152.
29 Ibid., p. 152.
30 Denis Sampson, 'John McGahern and Irish Writing: From *The Dark* to *Amongst Women*', in Derek Hand and Eamon Maher (eds), *Essays on John McGahern: Assessing a literary legacy* (Cork: Cork University Press, 2019), p. 19.
31 McGahern, *Creatures of the Earth*, p. 152.
32 Ibid., p. 158.
33 Ibid., p. 155.

34 Ibid., p. 156.
35 Ibid., p. 154.
36 Ibid., p. 156.
37 Ibid.
38 Ibid., p. 157.
39 Ibid., p. 159.
40 Ibid., p. 162.
41 Ibid., p. 163.
42 Ibid., p. 164.
43 Claire Keegan, 'Dark Horses', in *Walk the Blue Fields* (London: Faber, 2007), pp. 41–8.
44 Ibid., p. 42.
45 Ibid., p. 41.
46 Ibid., pp. 41–2.
47 Any number of Irish country towns have such hotel/bars, generally named after a local landowner, sometimes originally coaching inns: see, for example, the Powerscourt Arms in Enniskerry, the Conyngham Arms in Slane and the Londonderry Arms in Carnlough.
48 Keegan, 'Dark Horses', p. 44.
49 Ibid., p. 43.
50 Ibid., p. 45.
51 Ibid., p. 46.
52 Ibid.
53 Ibid., p. 41.
54 Ibid., p. 48.
55 Ibid., pp. 45–6.
56 Ibid., p. 47.
57 Kevin Barry, *There Are Little Kingdoms* (Edinburgh: Canongate, 2007).
58 Ibid., pp. 102–3.
59 Ibid., p. 97.
60 Ibid., pp. 100–1.
61 Jennifer O'Connell, 'Irish Pub Closures: The slow death of the local bar', *Irish Times*, 14 September 2019, https://www.irishtimes.com/life-and-style/food-and-drink/irish-pub-closures-the-slow-death-of-the-local-bar-1.4016286.
62 To reduce the speed of through traffic in towns and villages without a bypass, Transport Infrastructure Ireland introduced speed bumps and other 'traffic-calming' measures first in 1998: https://www.tii.ie/technical-services/safety/road-safety/traffic-calming/.
63 Kevin Barry, *There Are Little Kingdoms* (Edinburgh: Canongate, 2007), p. 95.
64 Ibid., p. 96.
65 Ibid., p. 97.
66 Ibid., p. 99.
67 Ibid., p. 100. Ironically, it was just such an effect that the printer and publisher would not allow Joyce in his original draft of 'Counterparts' where the woman from the Tivoli 'continued to throw bold glances at [Farrington] and changed the position of her legs often'. See Ellman, *Letters of James Joyce*, II, p. 133.
68 Kevin Barry, *There Are Little Kingdoms* (Edinburgh: Canongate, 2007), p. 106.
69 Ibid.
70 Keegan, 'Dark Horses', p. 48.

Chapter 12 – Paula Meehan's Pubs: From pub counter to counter-public sphere

1 Paula Meehan was born in Dublin and published her first collection of poetry, *Return and No Blame*, in 1984. Other collections include *Reading the Sky* (1986), *The Man Who Was Marked by Winter* (1991), *Pillow Talk* (1994), *Mysteries of the Home* (1996), *Dharmakaya* (2000), *Painting Rain* (2009) *Geomantic* (2016) and *The Solace of Artemis* (2023). Her plays include radio dramas published as *Music for Dogs* (2008).

2 Luz Mar González-Arias and Paula Meehan, '"Playing with the Ghosts of Words": An interview with Paula Meehan', *Atlantis*, vol. 22, no. 1, 2000, pp. 187–204 (p. 189), https://www.jstor.org/stable/41054978.

3 Theo Dorgan, 'An Interview with Paula Meehan', *Colby Quarterly*, vol. 28, no. 4, 1992, pp. 265–9 (p. 269), https://digitalcommons.colby.edu/cgi/viewcontent.cgi?article=2941&context=cq.

4 Andrew J. Auge, *A Chastened Communion: Modern Irish poetry and Catholicism* (Syracuse, NY: Syracuse University Press, 2013), p. 194. The poem was one of ten shortlisted for RTÉ's 'A Poem for Ireland' (2015), nominated by the members of the public as their favourite poem of the past 100 years, before being shortlisted by a panel, https://apoemforireland.rte.ie/.

5 Fintan O'Toole, 'Modern Ireland in 100 Artworks: 1986 – *Reading the Sky*, by Paula Meehan', *Irish Times*, 26 March 2016, https://www.irishtimes.com/culture/modern-ireland-in-100-artworks-1986-reading-the-sky-by-paula-meehan-1.2586029.

6 Luz Mar González-Arias, '*In Dublin's Fair City*: Citified embodiments in Paula Meehan's urban landscapes', *An Sionnach: A journal of literature, culture, and the arts*, vol. 5, nos. 1–2, 2009, pp. 34–49.

7 As Habermas notes (but does not fully explore), the institutions of the public sphere have long had a gendered dynamic: coffee-house society was dominated by men, while *salons* were generally run by women. Jürgen Habermas, *The Structural Transformation of the Public Sphere: An inquiry into a category of bourgeois society*, tr. Thomas Burger with the assistance of Frederick Lawrence (Cambridge, MA: MIT Press, 1991), p. 33.

8 Moonyoung Hong, 'Theatre and Everyday Space: The case of Tom Murphy', unpublished PhD thesis, Trinity College Dublin, 2021, p. 138, n. 21.

9 Valerie Hey, *Patriarchy and Pub Culture* (London: Tavistock Publications, 1986). For a detailed analysis of the gender dynamics of the Irish pub, see chapter 3 of this volume.

10 Kevin C. Kearns, *Dublin Pub Life and Lore: An oral history* (Dublin: Gill & Macmillan, 1996); Nell McCafferty, 'Women Want Liberation in the Local', *Irish Times*, 19 October 1977, p. 12.

11 Rita Felski, *Beyond Feminist Aesthetics: Feminist literature and social change* (Cambridge, MA: Harvard University Press, 1989), p. 166.

12 Nancy Fraser, 'Rethinking the Public Sphere: A contribution to the critique of actually existing democracy', *Social Text*, nos. 25–6, 1990, pp. 56–80 (p. 63), https://doi.org/10.2307/466240.

13 For a response of Meehan's to feminist readings of her work, see Tracy Brain, 'Dry Socks and Floating Signifiers: Paula Meehan's poems', *Critical Survey*, vol. 8, no. 1, 1996, pp. 110–17 (p. 114), https://www.jstor.org/stable/41555980.

14 The inscription on the pub clock which gives the poem its name suggests the bar is Madigan's on North Earl Street.

15 Paula Meehan, *Return and No Blame* (Dublin: Beaver Row Press, 1984), p. 15.

16 Ibid., p. 14.

17 Ibid. In the later toilet scene, she moves 'deftly' and steps 'gingerly' (p. 15), suggesting a strategic, even timid negotiation of public space that will later be discussed in my analysis of 'Buying Winkles'.

18 Meehan, *Return and No Blame*, p. 14.

19 Ibid., p. 15.

20 'Latin. The next one. Shut your eyes and open your mouth. What? *Corpus*: body. Corpse. Good idea the Latin. Stupefies them first.' James Joyce, *Ulysses*, ed. Hans Walter Gabler, Wolfhard Steppe and Claus Melchior (New York: Vintage Books), p. 66.

21 Virgil, *Georgics*, tr. Peter Fallon (Oxford: Oxford University Press, 2006), p. 60.

22 Meehan, *Return and No Blame*, p. 15.

23 Ibid., p. 57.

24 Brian Girvin, 'Ireland Transformed? Modernisation, secularisation and conservatism since 1973', in Thomas Bartlett (ed.), *The Cambridge History of Ireland. Vol. 4: 1880 to the Present* (Cambridge: Cambridge University Press, 2018), pp. 407–40 (p. 421). The Eighth Amendment was repealed by referendum in 2018.

25 Meehan, *Return and No Blame*, p. 15.

26 Auge, *A Chastened Communion*, p. 202.

27 Meehan, *Return and No Blame*, p. 15.

28 Paula Meehan, *The Man Who Was Marked by Winter* (Oldcastle: Gallery Press, 1994 [1991]), p. 31.

29 Ibid., p. 15.

30 Mona Domosh and Joni Seager, *Putting Women in Place: Feminist geographers make sense of the world* (New York: Guilford Press, 2001), p. 100, quoted in Kathryn Kirkpatrick, 'Paula Meehan and the Public Poem', in Ailbhe Darcy and David Wheatley (eds), *A History of Irish Women's Poetry* (Cambridge: Cambridge University Press, 2021), pp. 377–89 (p. 382).
31 Kirkpatrick, 'Meehan and the Public Poem', p. 382.
32 Elisabeth Mahoney, 'Citizens of Its Hiding Place: Gender and urban space in Irish women's poetry', in Scott Brewster, Virginia Crossman, Fiona Becket and David Alderson (eds), *Ireland in Proximity: History, gender, space* (London: Routledge, 2002 [1999]), pp. 145–56 (p. 149).
33 Paula Meehan, *Pillow Talk* (Oldcastle: Gallery Press, 1994), p. 20.
34 Meehan, *The Man Who Was Marked by Winter*, p. 15. Mahoney interprets these 'lingering' women as prostitutes. Mahoney, 'Citizens of Its Hiding Place', p. 149.
35 Meehan, *The Man Who Was Marked by Winter*, p. 15.
36 Gonzalez, 'Citified Embodiments', p. 40.
37 Meehan, *The Man Who Was Marked by Winter*, p. 15.
38 Ibid., p. 16.
39 Ibid. This may be a reference to the goddess Hecate, who is often depicted with a pair of torches and associated with doorways and crossroads, key aspects of this poem.
40 Meehan, *The Man Who Was Marked by Winter*, p. 55.
41 Meehan, *Pillow Talk*, pp. 19, 40.
42 Paula Meehan, *Painting Rain* (Manchester: Carcanet Press, 2009), p. 79.
43 Ibid., p. 57.
44 Ibid., p. 74.
45 Paula Meehan, *Dharmakaya* (Manchester: Carcanet Press, 2000), p. 19.
46 Seán Kennedy, '"I Only Know I Must": Transfiguring Irish shame in Paula Meehan's "Troika"', *Estudios Irlandeses*, no. 14, 2019, pp. 96–108 (pp. 98–9).
47 Meehan, *Dharmakaya*, p. 19.
48 Ibid.
49 Ibid., p. 20.
50 Ibid.
51 Ibid.
52 Ibid.
53 Ibid., emphasis added.
54 Ibid.
55 Ibid.
56 Ibid., p. 21.
57 Ibid.
58 Ibid.
59 Kirkpatrick, 'Meehan and the Public Poem', p. 381.
60 Meehan, *Pillow Talk*, p. 71.
61 For a detailed analysis of trad music economics in the Irish pub, see chapter 14 of this volume.
62 Kevin Kearns, *Dublin Pub Life and Lore: An oral history* (Dublin: Gill & Macmillan, 1996), p. 45.

Chapter 13 – The Stage Irish Pub: Irish pub drama, 1900–2020

1 Mark McGovern, 'The "Craic" Market: Irish theme bars and the commodification of Irishness in contemporary Britain', *Irish Journal of Sociology*, vol. 11, no. 2, 2002, p. 3.
2 Chris Morash and Shaun Richards, *Mapping Irish Theatre: Theories of space and place* (Cambridge: Cambridge University Press, 2013), pp. 47–54.
3 Lady Gregory, *Our Irish Theatre: A chapter of autobiography* (New York: G.P. Putnam's Sons, 1913), p. 112.
4 For further discussion on the trope of the 'stranger in the house', see Nicholas Grene's *The Politics of Irish Drama: Plays in context from Boucicault to Friel* (Cambridge: Cambridge University Press, 1999).
5 This is one of the most famous lines from the play delivered by Pegeen: 'there's a great gap between a gallous

story and a dirty deed' (J.M. Synge, *The Playboy of the Western World: A comedy in three acts* [Project Gutenberg, ebook, 2008])

6 For further information on the performance history of *Playboy* and its relationship to Irish cultural realities, see Charlotte McIvor's 'Playboy of the Western World and Old/New Interculturalisms', in *Migration and Performance in Contemporary Ireland* (London: Palgrave, 2016), pp. 39–83. See also Patrick Lonergan's *Irish Drama and Theatre Since 1950* (London: Bloomsbury, 2019).

7 'History of Sibins', http://sibin.ie/index.php/about.

8 Declan Kiberd, 'The Riotous History of *The Playboy of the Western World*', *Guardian*, 23 September 2011, https://www.theguardian.com/stage/2011/sep/23/playboy-western-world-old-vic.

9 'Riot Over Tricolour at the Abbey' [radio broadcast from 1984], RTÉ Archives, https://www.rte.ie/archives/2016/0329/778151-riot-at-the-plough-and-the-stars.

10 Kiberd, 'The Riotous History'.

11 Marie Hubert Kealy, 'Spirit of Place: A context for social criticism in John B. Keane's *The Field* and *Big Maggie*', *Irish University Review*, vol. 19, no. 2, 1989, pp. 287–301.

12 Ibid., p. 291.

13 John B. Keane, *The Field and Other Irish Plays* (Colorado: Roberts Rinehart, 1994), p. 93.

14 This incident is based on a real unsolved murder, that of Moss Moore, that occurred in 1958 in Reamore. For more discussion on how Keane developed his play from this incident, see Brian Devaney, *Social, Cultural and Psychological Resonance in John B. Keane's* The Field*: What lies beneath* (Newcastle-upon-Tyne, Cambridge Scholars Publishing, 2017).

15 Keane, *The Field*, p. 110.

16 Ibid., p. 122.

17 Ibid., p. 157.

18 Colm Tóibín, 'Interview with Tom Murphy', *DruidMurphy Programme*, 2012, pp. 5–6.

19 Tom Murphy, *Conversations on a Homecoming*, in *Plays: 2* (London: Methuen, 1997), p. 54.

20 Fintan O'Toole, *The Politics of Magic* (Dublin: New Island, 1994), p. 181.

21 Ibid., p. 182.

22 Murphy, *Conversations*, p. 20.

23 Ibid., p. 22.

24 I have discussed Murphy's play in depth in an article elsewhere, comparing the Irish pub to the African barber shop in their engagement with ideas of 'diaspora'. See Moonyoung Hong, '"Home Away from Home": Diasporic consciousness and everyday third places in Tom Murphy's *Conversations on a Homecoming* (1985) and Inua Ellams' *Barber Shop Chronicles* (2017)', *Comparative Drama*, vol. 56, no. 3, 2022, pp. 256–82, http://dx.doi.org/10.1353/cdr.2022.0012.

25 Shane Butler et al., *Alcohol, Power and Public Health: A comparative study of alcohol policy* (New York: Routledge, 2017), p. 86.

26 David Harvey, *Consciousness and the Urban Experience* (Oxford: Blackwell, 1985), p. 250.

27 Another example of a play set in a disco is Jim Sheridan's *Where All Your Dreams Come True* (Dublin: Hell's Kitchen, 1978).

28 O'Toole, *Politics of Magic*, p. 144.

29 John Boland, 'Back to Broad Strokes', *Hibernia*, 6 March 1980; *The Blue Macushla* [press cuttings], Abbey Theatre Digital Archive at National University of Ireland, Galway, 0780_PC_0001, p. 9.

30 Tom Murphy, *The Blue Macushla*, in *Plays: 1* (London: Methuen, 2004), pp. 159–60; emphasis added.

31 Ibid., p. 178.

32 Gerald C. Wood, *Conor McPherson: Imagining mischief* (Dublin: Liffey Press, 2003), p. 16.

33 Conor McPherson, *The Weir and Other Plays* (New York: Theatre Communications Group, 2008), p. 29.

34 Ben Brantley, 'Theatre Review; Dark Yarns Casting Light', *New York Times*, 2 April 1999, https://www.nytimes.com/1999/04/02/movies/theater-review-dark-yarns-casting-light.html.

35 Marie Jones, *The Blind Fiddler: A play* (London: Samuel French, 2008), p. 4.

36 Ibid., p. 5.

37 Ibid., p. 6.

38 Ibid., p. 8.

39 Ibid., pp. 23–4.

40 Mark Phelan, 'From Troubles to Post-Conflict Theatre in Northern Ireland', in Nicholas Grene and Christopher Morash (eds), *The Oxford Handbook of Modern Irish Theatre* (Oxford: Oxford University Press, 2005), p. 385.

41 'McGurk's Bar Massacre Victim Confronts Killer', *Belfast Telegraph*, 1 March 2005, https://www.belfasttelegraph.co.uk/news/northern-ireland/mcgurks-bar-massacre-victim-confronts-killer/28593468.html.

42 Mark Phelan argues that Northern Ireland has 'no state mechanism or apparatus in place for dealing with the past, or to undertake any form of truth recovery … It was not part of the 1998 Good Friday Agreement and there is still precious little political consensus as to how best to deal with the legacies of violence and sectarian division': 'Introduction', in *Owen McCafferty: Plays 1* (London: Faber & Faber, 2013), p. x.

43 Owen McCafferty, *Quietly* (London: Faber & Faber, 2014), p. 28.

44 Ibid., p. 21.

45 Ibid., p. 23.

46 Ibid., p. 30.

47 Ibid., p. 31.

48 Ibid., p. 32.

49 Ibid., p. 32–40.

50 Ibid., p. 35.

51 Ibid., p. 40.

52 Ibid., p. 42.

53 Ibid., p. 41.

54 Perry Share, 'A Genuine "Third Place"? Towards an understanding of the pub in contemporary Irish society', p. 12. Paper presented at the SAI Annual Conference, Cavan, 26 April 2003.

55 Bisi Adigun, *The Paddies of Parnell Street* (Dublin: Arambe Productions, 2013), p. 2.

56 See Jason King's 'Contemporary Irish Theatre, the New *Playboy* Controversy, and the Economic Crisis', *Irish Studies Review*, vol. 24 no. 1, 2016, pp. 67–78.

Chapter 14 – Traditional Music and the Appeal of 'the Pub'

1 Young people from Catholic backgrounds were automatically sworn into the Pioneer Total Abstinence Association. Membership of it demanded partaking of no alcohol, a self-denial virtuously flagged in a quasi-proselytising manner by the wearing of a 'Pioneer pin' lapel badge. For social and economic reasons, it was not unreasonably considered that one should be kept off drink for as long as possible, and, while some stuck with that for life, many fell off the wagon in the excitement of the 1960s. One-time alcoholics who joined up were said to 'take the pledge'; those who abandoned it 'broke the pledge'.

2 Pre-Famine, Kohl describes the public practice of song and music: '… Kilkenny … I had a sight of life in an Irish town, on the eve of a great horse-race … half the population of the surrounding country had streamed in on account of the races, the number was increased to about 40,000 during the three days they lasted. This great crowd of people wandered about … standing, sauntering, singing, and performing music in the streets … the most remarkable objects are the ballad-singers, who are in no country so numerous as here. In Kilkenny there were literally twice as many ballad-singers as lamp-posts standing in the street … crowds of poor people, beggars and rabble, perseveringly swarm around them, follow them step by step, and listen to them with a degree of eagerness, which may partly be attributed to the fact that the singers proclaim their own misfortunes, which they have turned into verse, but still more to the great delight which the Irish take in music and singing, and in everything new that passes in the streets … In every corner of the great main street … bagpipes were snuffling, violins squeaking, melancholy flutes blowing, and ragged Paddies dancing' (Johann Georg Kohl, *Travels in Ireland* (London: Bruce and Wyld, 1844), pp. 195–6), https://celt.ucc.ie/published/T840000-001/index.html.

3 Vincent McGrath, *John McGrath: The musical bridge* (Mayo: Vincent McGrath, 2022).

4 Fintan Vallely, *The Companion to Irish Traditional Music*, 1st edn (Cork: Cork University Press, 2011), p. 554.

5 Reg Hall, *A Few Tunes of Good Music: A history of Irish music and dance in London, 1800–1980 & beyond* (Croydon: Reg Hall, 2016), pp. 633–51.

6 In the word's usage as defined by Matthew Arnold in 'Culture and Anarchy', *Cornhill Magazine*, 1868, pp. 28–9.

7 A Comhaltas Ceoltóirí Éireann branch session which often did not involve alcohol, and may have a preponderance of older, more conservative, participants.
8 Hall, *A Few Tunes*, pp. 141–73.
9 Joe Cleary, *Outrageous Fortune: Capital and culture in modern Ireland* (Dublin: Field Day, 2007), p. 4.
10 Susan H. Motherway, *The Globalization of Irish Traditional Song Performance* (Farnham: Ashgate, 2013), pp. 8–12; P.J. Curtis, *Notes from the Heart: A celebration of traditional Irish music* (Dublin: Torc, 1994), pp. 18–23.
11 Numerous pubs had this rule until its gradual disappearance in the 1990s. The problem was solved by groups of aware women repairing to such bars of a winter's night and ordering numerous hot whiskies. When these were prepared the purchaser would then add '… and one pint of Guinness …', to which the reply was, 'Sorry, we don't serve women pints.' So the customers had to leave, and the barman's consequent economic problem became a political one.
12 Josh Kun, *Audiotopia: Music, race and America* (Berkeley: UCLA Press, 2005).
13 Vallely, *Companion*, pp. 754–6.
14 Geraldine Cotter, *Transforming Tradition: Irish traditional music in Ennis, County Clare 1950–1980* (Ennis: Geraldine Cotter, 2016).
15 RTÉ News, 22 October 2021, https://www.rte.ie/news/ireland/2021/1022/1255246-restrictions-entertainment.
16 Vallely, *Companion*, p. 554.
17 Cleary, *Outrageous Fortune*, pp. 111–79.
18 Ibid.
19 Kun, *Audiotopia*; Ray Pratt, *Rhythm and Resistance: The political uses of American popular music* (Washington: Smithsonian, 1994), pp. 36–40.
20 Pratt, *Rhythm and Resistance*, pp. 26–7.
21 In 1995, Bord Fáilte, the then Irish Tourist Board, conferred honorary ambassadorship on The Chieftains at a ceremony in Dublin.

Chapter 15 – The Pub as Infrastructure of Musical Exchange in Contemporary Cork and Galway

1 John Connell and Chris Gibson, *Sound Tracks: Popular music, identity and place* (London: Routledge, 2003), p. 102.
2 HERA is Humanities in the European Research Area, an EU research funding stream. More information about NITE can be found at https://heranet.info/2022/01/27/project-of-the-month-nite.
3 The 'Music, Memory and the Night' subproject website is available at www.musicmemorynight.com.
4 Nick Dunn, *Dark Matters: A manifesto for the nocturnal* city (Winchester: Zero Books, 2016).
5 Robert Shaw, 'Beyond Night-Time Economy: Affective atmospheres of the urban night', *Geoforum*, vol. 51, no. 1, 2016, p. 87.
6 Jessica Cawley, *Becoming an Irish Traditional Musician: Learning and embodying musical culture* (London: Routledge, 2020).
7 Ibid., p. 65. See also Chapter 14 of this volume.
8 Connell and Gibson, *Sound Tracks*, p. 102.
9 Ben Gallan and Chris Gibson, 'Mild-Mannered Bistro by Day, Eclectic Freak-Land at Night: Memories of an Australian music venue', *Journal of Australian Studies*, vol. 37 no. 2, 2013, p. 174; Allan Watson, *Cultural Production in and beyond the Recording Studio* (London: Routledge, 2015), p. 91.
10 Gallan and Gibson, 'Mild-Mannered Bistro by Day', p. 174.
11 Cawley, *Becoming an Irish Traditional Musician*, pp. 68–9.
12 Gallan and Gibson, 'Mild-Mannered Bistro by Day', p. 176.
13 While this chapter focuses on pub spaces, other research has shown similar patterns of discrimination and racism in nightclub spaces and venues in Ireland. For example, see Katie Young, 'Producing Locality at Night: From Lagos hometown meetings to Galway's G Afro Vibez', *Crossings: Journal of migration and culture*, vol. 13, 2022, pp. 11–26, https://doi.org/10.1386/cjmc_00052_1.
14 Michael O'Connell and Sinead Casey, 'Pain and Prejudice: Assessing the experience of racism in Ireland', in Malcolm MacLachlan and Michael O'Connell (eds), *Cultivating Pluralism: Psychological, social and cultural perspectives on a changing Ireland* (Dublin: Oaktree Press, 2000), p. 31.
15 Lucy Michael, *Afrophobia in Ireland: Racism against people of African descent* (Dublin: ENAR Ireland, 2015), p. 25, https://core.ac.uk/download/pdf/287020638.pdf.

16 Ibid.
17 Ibid., p. 26; Fathi Mastoureh and Caitríona Ní Laoire, 'Urban Home: Young male migrants constructing home in the city', *Journal of Ethnic and Migration Studies*, vol. 49, no. 3, 2023, p. 823.
18 Mastoureh and Ní Laoire, 'Urban Home', p. 826.
19 For examples of exclusion from holding Afromusic nights in Galway, see Katie Young, 'Producing Locality at Night', pp. 11–26.
20 Excerpt from Tolü Makay's recorded audio memory from the 'Music, Memory and the Night' project, December 2020, available in full here: https://www.musicmemorynight.com/tolu-makay.
21 See Katie Young and Ailbhe Kenny, 'Music, Memory and Migration at Night: Relational ways of knowing through arts-based collaborations', in Derek Pardue, Ailbhe Kenny and Katie Young (eds), *Sonic Signatures: Music, migration and the city at night* (London: Intellect Books, 2023), pp. 19–37.
22 A more extensive exploration of this event is available in Ailbhe Kenny and Katie Young, '"The House of the Irish": African migrant musicians and the creation of diasporic space at night', *Ethnomusicology Forum*, vol. 31, no. 3, 2022, pp. 332–52, https://doi.org/10.1080/17411912.2021.1938623.
23 Direct provision is a state system of housing for those seeking international protection while in the asylum-seeking process. Residents have a weekly allowance in addition to food and board. The system was set up in Ireland in 2000 and has continued to be the focus of protests and activist work around living conditions as well as educational and economic opportunities for those living in direct provision spaces.
24 Kenny and Young, 'The House of the Irish', p. 347.
25 A video of this performance is available on Citadel's Facebook page: https://www.facebook.com/citadeleire/videos/498478847727721.
26 Cawley, *Becoming an Irish Traditional Musician*, pp. 68–9.
27 Phone interview with DJ Touché on 5 June 2020.
28 For more on DJ Safarii's experiences of being a DJ, see Ailbhe Kenny, 'Becoming and Being a DJ: Black female experiences in Ireland', *Journal of Popular Music Education*, vol. 6, 2022, pp. 235–46.
29 For more on DJ Safarii's involvement in this subproject, see Young and Kenny, 'Music, Memory and Migration at Night', pp. 19–37.
30 DJ Safarii's memory is available to listen to here: https://www.musicmemorynight.com/dj-safarii.
31 For more on Wally Nkikita's work in Áras na nGael, see Kenny and Young, 'The House of the Irish', pp. 332–52.
32 Ibid., p. 344.
33 Nkikita's full memory is available here: https://www.musicmemorynight.com/wally-nkikita.

Chapter 16 – The Perfect Pub

1 Cited in Pat McMahon, 'What Makes the Perfect Pub?', *Honi Soit*, 25 May 2022, https://honisoit.com/2022/05/what-makes-the-perfect-pub.
2 James Boswell, *The Life of Samuel Johnson* (London: Charles Dilley, 1791), p. 251.
3 'Hilaire Belloc championed the great inns of Sussex', *Sussex Express*, 27 April 2017.
4 George Orwell, 'The Moon Under Water' [Review of *The Pub and the People* by Mass-Observation, *The Listener*, 1943], https://www.orwellfoundation.com/the-orwell-foundation/orwell/essays-and-other-works/the-moon-under-water.
5 Ibid.
6 'Bottle-and-jug' is an old term for an off-licence. For further detail, see Maurice Gorham and Edward Ardizzone, *Back to the Local* (London: Faber & Faber, 2024 [1949]), pp. 42–5. This book, a study of London pubs of the early 1940s, is an extended, and slightly more critical, study of the milieu being described by Orwell.
7 'Chute' is an old word for a playground slide. See Jon Winder, 'Revisiting the Playground: Charles Wicksteed, play equipment and public spaces for children in early twentieth-century Britain', *Urban History*, vol. 50, no. 1, 2021, pp. 1–18, https://doi.org/10.1017/S0963926821000687.
8 Andre Anthony, 'In Search of the Perfect Pub: What makes a great British boozer?', *Observer*, 30 June 2019, https://www.theguardian.com/lifeandstyle/2019/jun/30/in-search-of-the-perfect-pub-great-british-boozer.
9 Orwell, cited in Jessica Boak and Ray Bailey, *20th Century Pub: From beer house to booze bunker* (St Alban's: Homewood Press, 2017), p. 70.

10 Tomé Morrissy-Swan, 'George Orwell Created the Template for the Perfect Pub in 1946 – But Does It Still Exist?', *Telegraph*, 21 January 2010, https://www.telegraph.co.uk/food-and-drink/features/george-orwell-created-template-perfect-pub-1946-does-still.

11 Nathan Smith, 'History in the Pub: The historiography of J.D. Wetherspoon', *Endeavour*, vol. 48, no. 1, 2024, https://doi.org/10.1016/j.endeavour.2023.100889.

12 Peter Jones et al., 'Customer Perceptions of Services Brands: A case study of J.D. Wetherspoons', *British Food Journal*, vol. 104, no. 10, 2002, pp. 845–54, https://doi.org/10.1108/00070700210448935.

13 Ed Cummings, 'The Compton Arms: Orwellian dream or nightmare, depending on how you look at it', *Independent*, 9 August 2019; Emily Finch, 'History Society Moves to Protect George Orwell Pub The Compton Arms', *Islington Tribune*, 10 November 2017.

14 Ray Oldenburg, *The Great Good Place: Cafés, coffee shops, bookstores, bars, hair salons, and other hangouts at the heart of a community*, 3rd edn (New York: Marlowe, 1999).

15 It should be noted that Oldenburg's work has not been without critique, particularly in terms of the idealisation of particular types of 'third places' and a blindness to the potential for such places to be exclusionary and discriminatory, either overtly or inadvertently. See Joanne Dolley and Caryl Bosman (eds), *Rethinking Third Places: Informal public spaces and community building* (Cheltenham: Edward Elgar, 2019).

16 Oldenburg, *The Great Good Place*, p. 22.

17 Ibid., p. 169.

18 Much of the commentary on Irish pubs and their role in the local community is funded directly by the drinks industry.

19 Ignazio Cabras and Matthew P. Mount, 'How Third Places Foster and Shape Community Cohesion, Economic Development and Social Capital: The case of pubs in rural Ireland', *Journal of Rural Studies*, no. 55, 2017, pp. 71–82, https://doi.org/10.1016/j.jrurstud.2017.07.013.

20 Anthony Foley, *The Irish Pub: Stopping the decline. Reduce excise tax, protect the Irish pub*, a Drinks Industry Group of Ireland report, August 2022, Dublin City University Business School, https://www.drinksindustry.ie/assets/Media/DIGI-REPORT-The-Irish-Pub-Stopping-the-Decline.pdf.

21 Anthony Foley, *The Irish Pub: Supporting our communities*, August 2023, a Drinks Industry Group of Ireland report, Dublin City University Business School, https://www.drinksindustry.ie/assets/Documents/The-Irish-Pub-Supporting-Our-Communities2023.pdf.

22 'Our Rural Future: Minister Humphreys launches new "Pubs as Community Hubs" pilot programme', press release by Department of Rural and Community Development, 25 March 2022.

23 For a full account of the history of the 'The Pub is the Hub', see https://www.pubisthehub.org.uk.

24 'Foreword' to Countryside Agency, *The Pub Is the Hub: A good practice guide* (CA 95) (Wetherby: Countryside Agency, 2001).

25 'Pubs Highlighted as "Incredible Force for Good" by HRH in CAMRA's *Good Beer Guide 2023*', https://www.pubisthehub.org.uk/news/community-pubs.

26 Ann Fitzgerald, 'After Losing Five Shops, Three Pubs and the Post Office, How This Rural Community Is Revitalising Itself', *Farming Independent*, 24 March 2019, https://www.independent.ie/farming/agri-business/after-losing-five-shops-three-pubs-and-the-post-office-how-this-rural-community-is-revitalising-itself/37926624.html.

27 'Curtains up for New Pilot Scheme in Bawnboy Pub', *Anglo Celt*, 25 March 2022. The proprietors noted that the nearest cinema to the village was 40 kilometres away in Cavan town.

28 'From Pizzerias to Pubs: Focus on … Guinness Italia', *Guinness Globe Magazine*, August 1995, p. 7.

29 For a full insider's comprehensive account of the development of the Irish Pub Concept see Chapter 7 of this volume.

30 Irish Pub Company website (1990s): 'The Formation of the Irish Pub Company & the Guinness Irish Pub Concept', https://irishpubcompany.com/about/the-story-of-the-irish-pub-company.

31 Kevin Martin, *Have Ye No Homes To Go To? The history of the Irish pub* (Cork: Collins Press, 2016), p. 242.

32 Stephen Brown and Anthony Patterson, 'Knick-Knack Paddy-Whack, Give a Pub a Theme', *Journal of Marketing Management*, vol. 16, no. 6, 2000, p. 652.

33 There are still rural pubs where political representatives hold their clinics in line with the political allegiance of the proprietor and where political opinions at odds with the dominant persuasion are not held in particularly high regard.

34 Chris Curtin and Colm Ryan, 'Clubs, Pubs and Private Houses in a Clare Town', in Chris Curtin and Tom Wilson (eds), *Ireland from Below: Social change and local communities* (Galway: Galway University Press, 1987).

35 In 'Last Man Standing', each entrant picks one English Premier League soccer team competing on any given weekend. If the entrant's selection wins, they progress to the next round. If the team lose or draw, the entrant is out. The last entrant to stay in the game is thus the 'Last Man Standing'.

36 Gordon Manning, 'Championship Coverage on Saturdays to be Dominated by GAAGO', *Irish Times*, 27 April 2023; 'Not Realistic to Expect all GAA Matches To Be Televised, says Taoiseach', *The Journal*, 9 May 2023, https://www.thejournal.ie/gaa-go-paywall-hurling-matches-taoiseach-6063760-May2023/; Robert Hynes, 'GAAGO Blasted as Fans Slam Lack of Hurling Fixtures on Free-To-Air TV', *Irish Mirror*, 7 May 2024.

37 Jordan Whyte, 'Ireland's First Women's Sports Bar Arrives this Weekend Thanks to Carlsberg 0.0', balls.ie, 11 May 2023, https://www.balls.ie/news/irelands-first-womens-sports-bar-arrives-this-weekend-thanks-to-carlsberg- 0-0-553565; Nick Rabbits, 'American-Style Sports Bar to Create 40 Jobs in Limerick City Centre', *Limerick Leader*, 12 December, 2021 Aakanksha Surve, 'New Places Dublin: A trendy sports bar has opened its doors in the city centre just in time for the Six Nations', dublinlive.ie, 30 January 2020, https://www.dublinlive.ie/whats-on/food-drink-news/restaurant-sports-bars-in-dublin-17656429; Kate DeMolder, 'Dublin Has a Brand New Sports Bar – and it Makes for an Amazing Night Out', lovindublin.com, 20 December 2016, https://lovindublin.com/feature/pics-dublin-has-a-brand-new-sports-bar-and-its-a-dream.

38 Jessica Strelitz, 'No Blarney', *Arlington Magazine*, 4 March 2013, https://www.arlingtonmagazine.com/no-blarney.

39 Nicholas Robinson, '30 Years of the Eagle: The UK's first gastropub', *Morning Advertiser*, 12 January 2021, https://www.morningadvertiser.co.uk/Article/2021/01/12/Is-the-Eagle-the-first-Gastropub-in-the-UK.

40 For a discussion of food in Irish pubs, see Brian J. Murphy, '"If it's Eatin' and Drinkin' You Want, Take a Spoon and Fork to a Pint of Stout": A brief history of food and the Irish pub', ch. 27 in Máirtín Mac Con Iomaire and Dorothy Cashman (eds), *Irish Food History: A companion* (Dublin: Royal Irish Academy, 2024), https://arrow.tudublin.ie/irishfoodhist/1.

41 Kevin Martin, interview with Colm Cronin, 11 December 2015. The concept of 'wet pubs' serving alcohol only and 'dry pubs' serving food and alcohol was a dominant motif in discussions pertaining to the industry during the Covid-19 pandemic.

42 Charles Dickens, *David Copperfield* (London: Bradbury & Evans, 1850).

43 Tom Harrison, *The Pub and the People: A Worktown study* (Mass Observation social surveys) (London: Faber & Faber, 2015), cited in Martin, *Have Ye No Homes To Go To?*, p. 165.

44 See Perry Share, Mary P. Corcoran and Brian Conway, 'Pubs and Drinking', in *A Sociology of Ireland* (Dublin: Gill & Macmillan, 2012), pp. 311–22 for a detailed study of this topic. Chapter 4 of this volume contains a considered account of the work of Curtin and Ryan on the pubs and nightclubs of Ennis, County Clare.

45 For a detailed discussion of the concept of 'authenticity', see chapter 7 of this volume.

46 Flann O'Brien (Brian O'Nolan), 'The Workman's Friend', *At Swim-Two-Birds* (London: Penguin Classics, 2000, reprint). In the novel the poem is attributed to Jem Casey, a fictional character who ostensibly represented the voice of the working class.

47 For some examples from the printed press see Lilly Subbotin, 'Where To Find the Best Guinness in London – and How To Spot a Bad One', *Independent*, 18 April 2024; Joe Rogers, 'What Makes the Perfect Pint?', *Spectator*, 22 March 2022; Tim McKirdy, 'Every Factor that Affects the Quality of Your Guinness, Explained', 15 March 2019, https://vinepair.com/articles/guinness-perfect-pint-explainer; Suze Kundu, 'The Science Behind Pouring the Perfect Pint of Guinness', *Forbes*, 11 March 2016.

48 Interviews carried out with publicans and customers for Martin, *Have Ye No Homes to Go To?* (Cork: Collins Press, 2016).

49 David Gluckman, 'Guinness Light: "They said it couldn't be done and they were right"', *Irish Times*, 3 October 2017, https://www.irishtimes.com/culture/books/guinness-light-they-said-it-couldn-t-be-done-and-they-were-right-1.3242416.

50 Kirsty Blake Knox, 'Wanted: Sweden's Museum of Failure is appealing to people of Ireland to track down a "Guinness Light" bottle', *Irish Independent*, 1 May 2017, https://www.independent.ie/irish-news/wanted-swedens-museum-of-failure-is-appealing-to-people-of-ireland-to-track-down-a-guinness-light-bottle/35671545.html.

51 Sean Pollock, 'Zero Dark Thirsty: Diageo aims to have its Guinness 0.0 stout in 2,000 Irish pubs, hotels and restaurants', *Irish Independent*, 11 February 2024, https://www.independent.ie/business/zero-dark-thirsty-diageo-

aims-to-have-its-guinness-00-stout-in 2000-irish-pubs-hotels-and-restaurants/a174732180.html; Andrew Walsh, 'Zero to Hero: Guinness 0.0 sees growing sales as Irish drinkers embrace non-alcohol products', *Limerick Leader*, 30 April 2024.

52 'Craft Beer and Cider Report 2023', Bord Bia (Irish Food Board), https://www.bordbia.ie/industry/insights/publications/craft-beer-and-cider-report.

53 Conor Pope, 'Craft Brewers Buck Trend of Declining Beer Sales', *Irish Times*, 9 September 2023.

54 'Most Dublin Pubs Expect to Grow in 2019 as Gin Trend Continues, but They're Worried about Brexit', thejournal.ie, 19 March 2019, https://www.thejournal.ie/pubs-in-dublin-4549345-Mar2019/; Yvonne Gordon, 'In Ireland, Pubs Now Offer More Than Just a Pint', 15 March 2024, https://www.bbc.com/worklife/article/20240314-changing-irish-pub-culture.

55 John Geraghty, 'The Price of a Pint from 1928–2015 in Today's Money', publin.ie [blog], http://publin.ie/2015/the-price-of-a-pint-from-1928-2015-in-todays-money.

56 Darragh Nolan, '"Hammer Blow" for Pubs as Diageo to Increase Price of Guinness again Next Month', *Irish Independent*, 26 March 2024.

57 This honour is contested by Sean's bar, Athlone, which would appear to have a more genuine claim, as building materials at the site can be dated to its claimed foundation of AD 900. There are so many variables in the equation, however, that a definitive answer will never be possible. For a comprehensive discussion, again we can turn to publin.ie, 'Ireland's Oldest Pubs: The contenders', 2023, https://podcasts.apple.com/ie/podcast/irelands-oldest-pubs-the-contenders/id1647608427?i=1000601230121.

58 Danny De Vaal, 'Temple Bar Punters Floored by Dublin Pub Charging €9.95 for a Pint', *Irish Mirror*, 16 February 2023.

59 Anita McSorley and Laura Lyne, 'Irish Pub Receipt Shows Outrageous Price for Just Four Drinks in Temple Bar in Dublin', *Irish Mirror*, 3 April 2024.

60 For some examples see Jowena Riley, 'Tourists Hit Out at "Barbaric" Prices at Dublin's Popular Temple Bar Pub after Guest Shares Receipt for One Round', *Irish Daily Mail*, 29 August 2023; Danny De Vaal, 'Pubs in Dublin's Temple Bar Area Slammed for "Extortionate" Prices with Pints Near €10', *Irish Star*, 16 February 2023; Clare McCarthy, 'We Bought a Pint of Heineken in an Irish Pub With a Tenner and the Change was Minuscule – Is it Ireland's Most Expensive?', *Irish Mirror*, 13 April 2023.

61 20 pence was equivalent to 25.4 euro cents.

62 Neil Cotter, 'Reeling in the Beers: Inside Ireland's relationship with Guinness over the decades', *Irish Sun*, 14 August 2023.

63 Ruairi Scott Byrne, 'Dublin City Centre Pub Reduces Price of a Pint of Guinness to €5 amid Latest Diageo Price Hike', *Irish Mirror*, 16 April 2024.

Chapter 17 – Rural Pubs and Publicans in Contemporary Ireland

1 Ignazio Cabras and Matthew P. Mount, 'How Third Places Foster and Shape Community Cohesion, Economic Development and Social Capital: The case of pubs in rural Ireland', *Journal of Rural Studies*, no. 55, 2017, pp. 71–82, https://doi.org/10.1016/j.jrurstud.2017.07.013.

2 Kevin Kearns, *Dublin Pub Life and Lore: An oral history* (Dublin: Gill & Macmillan, 1996), p. 3.

3 John McGahern, 'County Leitrim: The sky above us', in *Love of the World: Essays* (London: Faber & Faber, 2010), p. 26.

4 Gordon Holmes, *Commission on Liquor Licensing: Final report* (Dublin: Department of Justice, 2003), pp. 92–3, https://www.drugsandalcohol.ie/5432/1/1683-1588.pdf.

5 Anthony Foley, *The Irish Pub: Supporting our communities*, August 2023, a Drinks Industry Group of Ireland report, Dublin City University Business School, https://www.drinksindustry.ie/assets/Documents/The-Irish-Pub-Supporting-Our-Communities2023.pdf.

6 Cian Molloy, *The Story of the Irish Pub* (Dublin: Liffey Press, 2002).

7 Ibid.

8 Cabras and Mount, 'How Third Places Foster and Shape Community Cohesion', pp. 72–3.

9 Robert Putnam, *Bowling Alone: The collapse and revival of American community* (New York: Simon & Schuster, 2000).

10 Jason Cucchiara, 'Pubs, Punters, and Pints: Anthropological reflections on pub life In Ireland', unpublished master's thesis, Department of Anthropology in the College of Sciences, University of Central Florida, Orlando, FL, 2006, p. 2, https://stars.library.ucf.edu/cgi/viewcontent.cgi?article=5024&context=etd.

11 Cabras and Mount, 'How Third Places Foster and Shape Community Cohesion'.

12 Bridget M. Cunningham, 'A Case-study of Alcohol Consumption and of the Irish Public House in Late Modernity', unpublished PhD thesis, Department of Sociology, NUI Maynooth, 2013, p. 100, https://mural.maynoothuniversity.ie/id/eprint/5391.

13 Claire O'Dwyer, Deirdre Mongan, Anne Doyle and Brian Galvin, *Alcohol Consumption, Alcohol-Related Harm and Alcohol Policy in Ireland*, HRB Overview Series 11 (Dublin: Health Research Board, 2021), p. 21, https://www.drugsandalcohol.ie/33909.

14 Robert Connolly, *The Rise and Fall of the Irish Pub* (Dublin: Liffey Press, 2010), p. 19.

15 Aoife Carrigy, 'Powerful Puzzles: Mapping the symbiosis between two great signifiers of Irishness, the writer and the pub', Dublin Gastronomy Symposium, 2018, https://arrow.tudublin.ie/cgi/viewcontent.cgi?article=1160&context=dgs.

16 For example, Ignazio Cabras and Carlo Reggiani, 'Village Pubs as a Social Propellant in Rural Areas: An econometric study', *Journal of Environmental Planning and Management*, vol. 53, no. 7, pp. 947–62, https://doi.org/10.1080/09640568.2010.495488; Claire Markham, 'The Public House in the Rural Community', unpublished PhD thesis, University of Lincoln, 2014, https://core.ac.uk/download/pdf/42585558.pdf; SIRC, *The Enduring Appeal of the Local*, a report of research conducted by the Social Issues Research Centre, commissioned by Greene King, 1998, https://www.cabidigitallibrary.org/doi/pdf/10.5555/20103083104.

17 Robert Smith, 'Zzzz ... Some reflections on the dynamics of village entrepreneurship', *International Journal of Entrepreneurship and Small Business*, vol. 6, no. 3, 2008, p. 372, https://doi.org/10.1504/IJESB.2008.019133.

18 Aron Darmody, 'Place, Meaning and Sociality: Exploring fullness in the themed retail environment', unpublished PhD thesis, Faculty of Graduate Studies, York University, Toronto, 2013, p. 18.

19 James Fennell and Turtle Bunbury, *The Irish Pub* (London: Thames & Hudson, 2008), p. i.

20 Diarmaid Ferriter, 'Drink and Society in Twentieth-Century Ireland', *Proceedings of the Royal Irish Academy: Archaeology, culture, history, literature*, vol. 115C, Food and Drink in Ireland, 2015, p. 366.

21 Carrigy, 'Powerful Puzzles', p. 12.

22 www.pubisthehub.org.uk.

23 Quoted in Ali Dunworth, 'Games, Craft Beer and Food Trucks: How the Irish pub is changing', *Irish Times*, 9 April 2019, https://www.irishtimes.com/life-and-style/food-and-drink/games-craft-beer-and-food-trucks-how-the-irish-pub-is-changing-1.3835506.

24 Ibid.

25 Ray Oldenburg, *The Great Good Place: Cafés, coffee shops, bookstores, bars, hair salons and other hangouts at the heart of a community*, 2nd edn (Philadelphia: De Capo Press, 1999), p. 171.

26 Richard Stivers, *Hair of the Dog: Irish drinking and its American stereotype* (New York: Continuum, 2000), p. 20.

27 John Messenger, 'Sex and Repression in an Irish Folk Community', in Donald S. Marshall and Robert C. Suggs (eds), *Human Sexual Behavior: Variations in the ethnographic spectrum* (New York: Basic Books, 1971).

28 Kearns, *Dublin Pub Life and Lore*, p. 3.

29 Kevin Martin, *Have Ye No Homes To Go To? The history of the Irish pub* (Cork: Collins Press, 2016).

30 Andrew O'Gorman, *A Handbook for the Licensed Trade* (Dublin: Andrew O'Gorman, 1994).

31 Darmody, 'Place, Meaning and Sociality', p. 18.

32 Kevin Myers, 'An Irishman's Diary', *Irish Times*, 9 March 1994, quoted in *The Hole in the Wall, Phoenix Park: A history of a Tudor inn* (Dublin: Hole in the Wall, 1997), p. 29.

33 Licensing Act (1872), www.irishstatutebook.ie.

34 Pete McCarthy, *McCarthy's Bar: A journey of discovery in Ireland* (London: Hodder & Stoughton, 2000), pp. 61–2.

35 Michael Katovich and William Reese, 'The Regular: Full-time identities and memberships in an urban bar', *Journal of Contemporary Ethnography*, vol. 16, no. 3, 1987, p. 313, https://doi.org/10.1177/0891241687163005.

36 Bill Barich, *A Pint of Plain: Tradition, change and the fate of the Irish pub* (London: Bloomsbury, 2009), p. 23.

37 Breandan Mac Suibhne, 'Let's Drink to Our Pubs' Prospects of Managing a Happy Return', *Sunday Independent*, 9 April 2020.

38 Aoife Carrigy, 'A Place Apart, in Its Own Time: The Irish pub as portrayed in John McGahern's short stories', *Journal of Franco-Irish Studies*, vol. 5, no. 1, 2019, p. 8.

39 Derived from the work of French sociologist Pierre Bourdieu, 'habitus' refers to how people perceive and respond to the social world they inhabit, by way of their personal habits, skills, and disposition of character.

40 Michael Polanyi, *Personal Knowledge: Towards a post-critical philosophy* (Chicago: University of Chicago Press, 1958).
41 M.A. Smith, 'The Publican: Role conflict and aspects of social control', *The Service Industries Journal*, vol. 5, no. 1, 1985, p. 35, https://doi.org/10.1080/02642068500000003.
42 Sybil Taylor, *Ireland's Pubs: The life and lore of Ireland through its finest pubs* (Harmondsworth: Penguin, 1983), p. 17.
43 Oldenburg, *The Great Good Place*, p. 171.
44 Carrigy, 'A Place Apart', p. 7.
45 Erving Goffman, *The Presentation of Self in Everyday Life* (New York: Doubleday Anchor Books, 1971).
46 Kearns, *Dublin Pub Life and Lore*, p. 29.
47 Taylor, *Ireland's Pubs*, p. 20.
48 Billy Keane, 'Jim Was Like the Mayor: He Loved Dunhill and Dunhill Loved Him Back' ['Keane's Kingdom' column], *Irish Independent*, 23 June 2018.

Chapter 18 – Doing it for Themselves: New promotion realities for the twenty-first-century Irish pub

1 Nathalie Fleck and Pascale Quester, 'Birds of a Feather Flock Together … Definition, Role and Measure of Congruence: An application to sponsorship', *Psychology and Marketing*, vol 24, no. 11, 2007, pp. 975–1000, https://doi.org/10.1002/mar.20192.
2 Phil Barden, *Decoded: The science behind why we buy* (Chichester: Wiley, 2013), p. 17.
3 https://ifiarchiveplayer.ie/adverts.
4 Patricia Medcalf, *Advertising the Black Stuff in Ireland 1959–1999: Increments of change* (Oxford: Peter Lang, 2020), p. 163.
5 Roy Bulson, *Irish Pubs of Character* (Dublin: Bruce Spicer, 1969), p. 112. O'Donoghue's is renowned as a venue for traditional music, and it made it into Bulson's guide: 'It was one of the first to introduce what have now become the popular Irish ballads. Many ballad groups which started singing in this pub have now become household names. The host ensures a warm, friendly atmosphere and serves one of the best pints pulled anywhere. Impromptu singing and music is allowed, and this is one of the best pubs in Dublin in which to hear traditional Irish music in a genuine atmosphere.'
6 Peter Corrigan, 'The Sally O'Brien Phenomenon: What price a pint of lager?', *The Crane Bag*, vol. 7, no. 2, 1983, pp. 197–202.
7 'Pat's Bar, Knowing What Matters' [video], https://www.youtube.com/watch?v=jeW7kZKYn1k.
8 Cian Molloy, *The Story of the Irish Pub* (Dublin: Liffey Press, 2002).
9 Anthony Foley, *Survey of Licensed Premises in Ireland 2004*, a report commissioned by the Drinks Industry Group of Ireland (Dublin: Drinks Industry Group Ireland, 2004).
10 Mary Lambkin, 'The Irish Pub and the New Market Realities', *Drinks Industry Ireland*, 27 October 2010, http://www.drinksindustryireland.ie/the-irish-pub-and-the-new-market-realities.
11 Ibid.
12 Ibid.
13 Checkout.ie, 'Figures Show that Per Capita Alcohol Consumption Fell by 6.6% in 2020', https://www.checkout.ie/drinks/per-capita-alcohol-consumption-fell-6-6-2020-125030.
14 Ibid.
15 Diageo, 'Diageo Annual Report 2020' (London: Diageo, 2020), https://www.diageo.com/PR1346/aws/media/11293/annual-report-2020.pdf.
16 Ibid.
17 Jack Beresford, 'Barry Keoghan Stars in Poignant Guinness Advert Celebrating Reopening of Pubs in Ireland', *Irish Post*, 5 June 2021, https://www.irishpost.com/news/barry-keoghan-stars-in-poignant-guinness-advert-celebrating-reopening-of-pubs-in-ireland-213794.
18 Alcohol Action Ireland, https://alcoholireland.ie/facts/how-much-do-we-drink. Alcohol Action Ireland was founded in 2003 and is a national independent advocate for reducing alcohol harm. It does not work with the alcohol industry or any of its funded groups.
19 Deirdre Mongan, Seán Millar and Brian Galvin, *The 2019–20 Irish National Drug and Alcohol Survey: Main findings* (Dublin: Health Research Board, 2021), https://www.drugsandalcohol.ie/34287.

20 Ann Hope, Joe Barry and Seán Byrne, 'The Untold Story: Harms experienced in the Irish population due to others' drinking', Health Service Executive, Dublin, 2018, https://www.drugsandalcohol.ie/28839/1/untold-story-harms-experienced-in-the-irish-population-due-to-others-drinking.pdf.

21 Diageo Guinness, *Diageo Annual Report and Accounts 2003: Delivering results* (London: Diageo, 2003), p. 2.

22 Diageo Guinness, *Diageo Annual Report 2013* (London: Diageo, 2013), p. 8, https://cdn-cf.cfo.com/content/uploads/2013/12/Diageo_AR_2013_Lo-Res_MASTER_FINAL.pdf.

23 Since 2016, Heineken has opened its annual reports with a page headed 'We Are HEINEKEN' on which it lists the key pillars of its corporate ethos. One of those boldly states, 'We always advocate responsible consumption. We are committed to our communities and strive to consistently improve the impact we make on the planet.' *Heineken Annual Report 2016* (Amsterdam: Heineken, 2016), p. 1, https://www.annualreports.com/HostedData/AnnualReportArchive/h/OTC_HEIN_2016.pdf.

24 Pernod Ricard, *Connected: Annual Report 2011/12* (Paris: Pernod Ricard, 2012), p. 3, https://assets.pernod-ricard.com/annual_report_2011-2012_uk.pdf.

25 ASAI, https://www.asai.ie/about-us.

26 ASAI, https://www.asai.ie/asaicode/section-9-alcoholic-drinks.

27 CopyClear, https://copyclear.ie/about-us.html.

28 CopyClear, *CopyClear Annual Report 2019* (Dublin: Central Copy Clearance Ireland, 2019), p. 2.

29 Frank Murray, 'Why Banning Alcohol Advertising for Young People is the Right Move', *Irish Times*, 17 July 2017, https://www.irishtimes.com/opinion/why-banning-alcohol-advertising-for-young-people-is-the-right-move-1.3156702.

30 CopyClear, *Annual Report 2019*, p. 3.

31 Public Health (Alcohol) Act 2018, http://www.irishstatutebook.ie/eli/2018/act/24/enacted/en/html.

32 Will Kinton 'Backward Integration', investopedia.com, 2021, https://www.investopedia.com/terms/b/backwardintegration.asp.

33 Steven Spillane, 'The Irish Craft Beer Industry' (2020), https://www.bordbia.ie/industry/news/food-alerts/2020/the-irish-craft-beer-industry.

34 In GAA circles hurlers from Wexford are referred to as 'yellowbellies', a name reputed to have come from a famous mid-eighteenth-century game of hurling that took place in Cornwall, England when the men from Wexford wore yellow sashes to distinguish them from the opposition, as reported by Eamon Doyle 'The "Yellow Bellies" and the Hurling Men of Cornwall', historyireland.com, no date, https://www.historyireland.com/18th-19th-century-history/the-yellow-bellies-and-the-hurling-men-of-cornwall.

35 Yellowbelly Beer, https://www.distillery.news/places/ireland/wexford-1/wexford-2/breweries/yellowbelly-beer.

36 Ross Lewis, *Chapter One: An Irish food story* (Dublin: Gill & Macmillan, 2013).

37 Brian Murphy, 'A Traditional Irish Family Butcher Shop: Harnessing the power of *patrimoine*', in Eamon Maher and Eugene O'Brien (eds), *Patrimoine/Cultural Heritage in France and Ireland* (Oxford: Peter Lang, 2018), p. 183.

38 Pat Whelan and Katy McGuinness, *The Irish Beef Book* (Dublin: Gill & Macmillan, 2013).

39 Pat Whelan, *An Irish Butcher Shop* (Dublin: Gill & Macmillan, 2010).

40 Declan Dunne, *Mulligan's: Grand old pub of Poolbeg Street* (Dublin: Mercier, 2015).

41 'Crowds at the Bar as Mulligan's Celebrates Book Launch', *Irish Times*, 2 June 2015, https://www.irishtimes.com/culture/books/crowds-at-the-bar-as-mulligan-s-celebrates-book-launch-1.2233907.

42 Brian Dillon, 'A "Tiny Theatre" is Coming to this Iconic Dublin Pub' [sponsored article], lovindublin.com, 20 February 2020, https://lovindublin.com/sponsored/a-tiny-theatre-is-coming-to-this-iconic-dublin-pub.

43 Vintners Federation of Ireland, 'Roddy Doyle's Two Pints Play on Tour in VFI Pubs' [video], https://www.youtube.com/watch?v=6gzuR2iVigc.

44 Matt Trueman, 'Time for Another Round: The rebirth of pub theatre', *Guardian*, 11 May 2017, https://www.theguardian.com/stage/2017/may/11/rebirth-pub-theatre-old-red-lion-gate-finborough-fringe-productions-audiences.

45 Shane Harrison, 'Irish Pubs Could Become Work Hubs in Post-Pandemic Plan', bbc.com, 30 March 2021, https://www.bbc.com/news/world-europe-56575266.

46 Marese McDonagh, 'Rural Pubs to take on New Functions in Quiet Times Under Pilot Scheme', *Irish Times*, 25 March 2022, https://www.irishtimes.com/news/ireland/irish-news/rural-pubs-to-take-on-new-functions-in-quiet-times-under-pilot-scheme-1.4836154.

47 Brewdog.com, 'Bored of Working from Home? Desk Dog', https://www.brewdog.com/uk/locations/bar-experience/desk-dog.

48 J.P. McMahon, 'Food Can Be a Real Vehicle for Cultural Change', *Sunday Independent Life Magazine*, 25 July 2021, p. 21.

49 Ann Fitzgerald, 'After Losing Five Shops, Three Pubs and the Post Office, How this Rural Community is Revitalising Itself', *Farming Independent*, 24 March 2019, https://www.independent.ie/business/farming/rural-life/after-losing-five-shops-three-pubs-and-the-post-office-how-this-rural-community-is-revitalising-itself-37926624.html.

50 The Pub is the Hub, https://www.pubisthehub.org.uk.

51 The Plunkett Foundation, https://plunkett.co.uk.

52 Caroline Allen, 'Rural Pub Saved by Actions of "Village" People', *Agriland*, 24 July 2021, https://www.agriland.ie/farming-news/rural-pub-saved-by-actions-of-village-people.

53 Michelle Fleming, 'Iconic Irish Bar Undergoing Major Changes to Make it "Lady-Friendly" after Being Bought by Regulars', *Irish Mirror*, 25 July 2021, https://www.irishmirror.ie/lifestyle/iconic-irish-bar-undergoing-major-24611775.

54 The Pub is the Hub case studies, https://www.pubisthehub.org.uk/case-studies/.

55 'Pubs as Community Hubs: Pubs encouraged to diversify', podcast from 'The Last Word with Matt Cooper', Today FM, 25 March 2022, https://www.todayfm.com/podcasts/the-last-word-with-matt-cooper/pubs-as-community-hubs-rural-pubs-encouraged-to-diversify.

56 Alcohol Action Ireland, *Raising the Bar: An examination of the alcohol market in Ireland*, Alcohol Market Review 2022 (Dublin: Alcohol Action Ireland, 2022), p. 8, https://alcoholireland.ie/wp-content/uploads/2022/09/21999-AAI-Market-Review-2022_v4screen.pdf.

57 'Caps to Replace Corks', RTÉ broadcast, 1969, https://www.rte.ie/archives/2019/0122/1024760-changes-to-bottled-stout.

Chapter 19 – Lockdown: The pub as an icon of Irish identity in the Covid-19 pandemic

1 Terence Brown, *The Irish Times: 150 years of influence* (London: Bloomsbury, 2015); Caleb Richardson, 'Transforming Anglo-Ireland: R.M. Smyllie and *The Irish Times*', *New Hibernia Review*, vol. 11, no. 4, 2007, pp. 17–36, https://www.jstor.org/stable/20558202.

2 Brian Conway, 'Who Do We Think We Are? Immigration and the discursive construction of national identity in an Irish daily mainstream newspaper, 1996–2004', *Translocations: The Irish migration, race and social transformation review*, vol. 1, no. 1, 2006, p. 82, https://mural.maynoothuniversity.ie/id/eprint/751/1/conway.pdf.

3 Barney Glaser and Anselm Strauss, *The Discovery of Grounded Theory: Strategies for qualitative research* (Mill Valley: Sociology Press, 1967).

4 Michael Cronin and Barbara O'Connor (eds), *Irish Tourism: Image, culture and identity* (Clevedon: Channel View Publications, 2003).

5 Deirdre Mongan, 'Overview of Alcohol Consumption, Alcohol-Related Harm and Alcohol Policy in Ireland', *Drugnet Ireland*, no. 59, 2016, pp. 1–3.

6 Domini Conroy and Emily Nicholls, 'All in this Together?', *The Psychologist*, 11 May 2020, https://thepsychologist.bps.org.uk/all-together; John O'Brien, 'The Use of Public Houses as a Collective Representation of the Covid-19 Pandemic in Ireland', *Irish Journal of Sociology*, vol. 29, no. 3, pp. 353–71, https://doi.org/10.1177/07916035211029202.

7 Elizabeth Malcolm, *Ireland Sober, Ireland Free: Drink and temperance in nineteenth-century Ireland* (Dublin: Gill & Macmillan, 1986); James Nicholls, *The Politics of Alcohol: A history of the drink question in England* (Manchester: Manchester University Press, 2011).

8 Thomas Wilson, 'Drinking Cultures: Sites and practices in the production and expression of meaning', in Thomas Wilson (ed.), *Drinking Cultures* (Oxford: Berg, 2005).

9 Jan-Willem Gerritsen, *The Control of Fuddle and Flash: A sociological history of the regulation of alcohol and opiates* (Boston: Brill, 2000); Joseph Gusfield, *The Culture of Public Problems: Drinking-driving and the symbolic order* (Chicago: University of Chicago Press, 1984).

10 Joseph Gusfield, *Symbolic Crusade: Status politics and the American temperance movement* (Chicago: University of Illinois Press, 1986).

11 Richard Stivers, *Hair of the Dog: Irish drinking and its American stereotype* (New York: Continuum, 2000); Mark McGovern, 'The "Craic" Market: Irish theme bars and the commodification of Irishness in contemporary Britain', *Irish Journal of Sociology*, vol. 11, no. 2, 2002, https://doi.org/10.1177/079160350201100205.

12 Stivers, *Hair of the Dog*.

13 Malcolm, *Ireland Sober, Ireland Free*.

14 Ryle Dwyer, 'Forget all about Garglegate in Galway – it's the Economy, Stupid', *Irish Examiner*, 18 September 2010, https://www.irishexaminer.com/opinion/columnists/arid-20131133.html.

15 John O'Brien, 'Formal Generations of Drinkers: Generational change in Irish drinking culture to 1950', in Thomas Thurnell-Read and Laura Fenton (eds), *Alcohol, Age, Generation and the Life Course* (London: Palgrave, 2022).

16 Hartmut Rosa, *Social Acceleration: A new theory of modernity* (New York: Columbia University Press, 2013).

17 Árpád Szakolczai, *Reflexive Historical Sociology* (London: Routledge, 2000).

18 Gusfield, *The Culture of Public Problems*.

19 Anthony Giddens, *Modernity and Self-Identity: Self and identity in the late modern age* (Cambridge: Polity Press, 1991).

20 Richard Jenkins, 'Disenchantment, Enchantment and Re-Enchantment: Max Weber at the millennium', *Max Weber Studies*, vol. 1, no. 1, 2000, pp. 11–32, https://www.jstor.org/stable/24579711.

21 Tom Inglis, *Moral Monopoly: The rise and fall of the Catholic Church in modern Ireland* (Dublin: UCD Press, 1998).

22 Chapter 8 of this volume.

23 'Conor McGregor's Dublin Pub Targeted in "Petrol Bomb" Attack', *Irish Times*, 13 January 2022, https://www.irishtimes.com/news/crime-and-law/conor-mcgregor-s-dublin-pub-targeted-in-petrol-bomb-attack-1.4775647.

24 Jenkins, *Disenchantment, Enchantment and Re-Enchantment*.

25 Ibid.

26 Jeffrey C. Alexander, Ron Eyerman, Bernhard Giesen, Neil J. Smelser and Piotr Sztompka, *Cultural Trauma and Collective Identity* (Berkeley: University of California Press, 2004).

27 Irish term for the Second World War.

28 Tom Garvin, *Preventing the Future: Why was Ireland so poor for so long?* (Dublin: Gill & Macmillan, 2004); Mervyn Horgan, 'Anti-Urbanism as a Way of Life: Disdain for Dublin in the nationalist imaginary', *Canadian Journal of Irish Studies*, vol. 30, no. 2, pp. 38–47, http://dx.doi.org/10.2307/25515532.

29 Kieran Bonner, 'Exciting, Intoxicating and Dangerous: Some Tiger effects on Ireland and the culture of Dublin', *Canadian Journal of Irish Studies*, vol. 37, nos. 1–2, pp. 50–75, https://www.jstor.org/stable/41955739.

30 Jade Wilson '"Maintain social distancing": How does that work in Coppers?', *Irish Times*, 8 March 2020, https://www.irishtimes.com/news/ireland/irish-news/maintain-social-distancing-how-does-that-work-in-coppers-1.4196768.

31 Mary P. Murphy, 'Will Ireland's Youth Once Again Pay for Their Elders' Crisis?', *Irish Journal of Sociology*, vol. 28, no. 2, 2020, pp. 231–6, https://doi.org/10.1177/0791603520939858.

Chapter 20 – Conclusion: Irish Pubs, from the Global to the Personal

1 Una Mulally, 'Since 2005 Nearly 2,000 Irish Pubs Have Closed. It's Time To Declare Them a Cultural Asset', *Irish Times*, 22 January 2024, https://www.irishtimes.com/opinion/2024/01/22/una-mullally-why-dont-we-declare-our-pubs-a-cultural-asset.

2 UNESCO, Intangible Cultural Heritage: Ireland, https://ich.unesco.org/en/state/ireland-IE.

3 Vic O'Sullivan, 'Six of Ireland's Best Traditional Pubs', *Guardian*, 16 March 2023, https://www.theguardian.com/travel/2023/mar/16/six-of-irelands-best-traditional-pubs.

4 Anthony Foley, *The Irish Pub: Supporting our communities*, August 2023, a Drinks Industry Group of Ireland report, Dublin City University Business School, https://www.drinksindustry.ie/assets/Documents/The-Irish-Pub-Supporting-Our-Communities2023.pdf.

5 See Anne Doyle, Deidre Mongan and Brian Galvin, *Alcohol: Availability, affordability, related harm, and policy in Ireland* [HRB Overview Series 13] (Dublin: Health Research Board, 2024), pp. 51–3, https://www.drugsandalcohol.ie/40465.

6 The 'half pub' now has highly restricted opening hours, is strictly cash only, and has a limited number of beers on tap. See Gemma Tipton on Heraghty's pub, Manorhamilton in 'From Pints to Property and Beyond:

Irish shops are multitasking to make ends meet', *Irish Times*, 6 April 2024, https://www.irishtimes.com/lifestyle/2024/04/06/from-pints-to-property-and-beyond-irish-shops-are-multitasking-to-make-ends-meet.

7 'This building is of a type that was, until recently, a ubiquitous feature of the streetscapes of small Irish towns and villages but is now becoming increasingly rare due to insensitive alteration and/or demolition': McGonagle's bar, Market Place, Churchland Quarters, Carndonagh, County Donegal. National Inventory of Architectural Heritage, https://www.buildingsofireland.ie/buildings-search/building/40805029/mcgonagles-bar-market-place-churchland-quarters-carndonagh-co-donegal.

8 Doyle et al., *Alcohol: Availability, affordability, related harm*, p. 4. Geographer Ronan Foley of Maynooth University indicates that if we focus on pubs only, then 56 per cent of Irish people live within 300 metres of a pub (pers. comm., 26 June 2024). Thank you to Dr Foley for the provision of this data.

9 Doreen Massey, *For Space* (London: Sage, 2005), p. 55.

10 Brian Larkin, 'Promising Forms: The political aesthetics of infrastructure', in Nikhil Anand et al. (eds), *The Promise of Infrastructure* (Durham, NC: Duke University Press, 2018), pp. 176–202.

11 Catherine Marie O'Sullivan, *Hospitality in Medieval Ireland 900–1500* (Dublin: Four Courts Press, 2004).

12 Kerryman Colm Dalton has made it his (impossible?) mission to 'visit every Irish pub on earth'. His web and Instagram sites constitute a repository of Irish pubs across the globe, https://publicanenemy.com.

13 Bill Grantham, 'Craic in a Box: Commodifying and exporting the Irish pub', *Continuum*, vol. 23, no. 2, pp. 257–67, https://doi.org/10.1080/10304310802710553.

14 Jeffrey M. Pilcher, 'The Globalization of Guinness: Marketing taste, transferring technology', *Jahrbuch für Wirtschaftsgeschichte/Economic History Yearbook*, vol. 65, no. 1, 2024, pp. 17–35, https://doi.org/10.1515/jbwg-2024-0004.

15 'Everybody is Drinking Guinness: We know why', *New York Times*, 3 December 2024, https://www.nytimes.com/2024/12/03/dining/drinks/guinness.html; 'Guinness Raids Its Irish Reserves to Ease UK Shortages amid Gen Z Demand', https://www.theguardian.com/business/2024/dec/22/guinness-shortages-uk-irish-reserves.

16 See the discussion by comedy duo The Two Johnnies on their culturally confused experience of Irish pubs in European resorts, specifically Murphy's Irish Bar in Santorini and the Danny Boy in Salou: *The Two Johnnies Podcast*, ep. 53, 21 February 2019, https://www.youtube.com/watch?v=pvPMeXjINog.

17 'Irish Americans – SNL' [YouTube video], https://youtu.be/xzlMME_sekI?si=4cTqHCfUi_3nx5rB.

18 Ruth Barton (ed.), *Screening Irish-America: Representing Irish-America in film and television* (Dublin: Irish Academic Press, 2009).

19 *P.S. I Love You* (2007) dir. Richard LaGravenese; *Leap Year* (2010) dir. Anand Tucker; *Wild Mountain Thyme* (2020) dir. John Patrick Shanley.

20 Dan Barry, 'Down the Rabbit Hole in Search of a Few Frames of Irish American History', *New York Times*, 15 March 2024, https://www.nytimes.com/2024/03/15/movies/silent-film-irish-callahans-muphys.html.

21 Peter Bradshaw, '*Wild Mountain Thyme* review – Emily Blunt Is an Awful Irish Stew', *Guardian*, 30 April 2021.

22 Kneecap, 'Better Way to Live' [music video], https://www.youtube.com/watch?v=KSnF7RaeoXE.

23 John Geraghty, 'A Pint in Barrytown: Pubs in the work of Roddy Doyle, parts 1 & 2', publin.ie [podcast], https://youtu.be/1_W9sLpRo5I?si=tUjeLJwvCg49wWxM and https://www.youtube.com/watch?v=aUOocaS9FKA&t=15s.

24 Barney Norris, '*Love* by Roddy Doyle Review – Profundity Down the Pub', *Guardian*, 15 October 2020, https://www.theguardian.com/books/2020/oct/15/love-by-roddy-doyle-review-profundity-down-the-pub.

25 Roddy Doyle, *Love* (London: Viking, 2020), p. 7.

26 Ibid., p. 37.

27 Paul Murray, *The Bee Sting* (London: Macmillan, 2023), pp. 42–3.

28 Ibid., p. 223.

29 Ibid., p. 366.

30 Ibid., p. 373.

31 Louise Kennedy, *Trespasses* (New York: Riverhead Books, 2022), p. 36.

32 Ibid.

33 Ibid., p. 283.

34 Michael Magee, *Close to Home* (London: Hamish Hamilton, 2023), p. 35.

35 Ibid., p. 9.

36 Ibid., p. 51.

37 'Array Collective Win Turner Prize 2021', Tate Gallery, 1 December 2021 [media release], https://www.tate.org.uk/press/press-releases/array-collective-win-turner-prize-2021. See also Chapter 8 of this volume for a more extensive discussion by Eli Davies.

38 Liz Gorny, 'Winner Array Collective Brings Political Charge to Turner Prize Conversation', *It's Nice That* [blog], 8 December 2021, https://www.itsnicethat.com/news/array-collective-turner-prize-art-081221.

39 *The Irish Pub* (2013), a documentary film directed by Alex Fegan, is based on interviews with owners of traditional Irish pubs across Ireland. It captures the heritage, atmosphere and deep-rooted community connections of the pub. It highlights how traditional pubs are perceived both within and outside Ireland, with commentary on the export of Irish pub culture.

40 For further historical information on the making and selling of beer in Ireland, see Christina Wade, *Filthy Queens: A history of beer in Ireland* (Dublin: Nine Bean Rows, 2025).

41 Indeed, it was with something of a shock that one of these (pint-drinking) authors discovered that the contemporary form of Guinness draught was developed as recently as 1959, based on new storage and pouring technologies: https://www.guinness.com/en-ie/beers/guinness-draught.

42 Bord Fáilte, 'Irish Pubs: A core tourism experience' (Dublin, Bord Fáilte, 2014), https://www.itic.ie/itic-pub-docs/2014/Irish_Pubs_A_core_tourism_experience_July_14.pdf; Anthony Foley, *The Contribution of the Drinks Industry to Irish Tourism*, report commissioned by the Drinks Industry Group of Ireland (Dublin: DIGI, 2017), https://vfipubs.ie/wp-content/uploads/2017/09/DIGI-Tourism-Report-2017-1.pdf.

43 Not only in Ireland, but in Hungary, Britain, the United States, the Netherlands, Australia and New Zealand, to list some countries where this trend has been identified. See, for example, Adrián Zoltan, Jennifer Varga and Nagy Gergely Miklós, 'The Reasons Behind the Mass Disappearance of Traditional Hungarian Pubs: Not just a severe crisis, but a systemic transformation', 24.hu, https://24.hu/belfold/2024/10/15/tradional-hungarian-pubs-disappearance-crisis-transformation-drinking-alcoholism.

44 Thomas Thurnell-Read, *Open Arms: The role of pubs in tackling loneliness* [commissioned by the Campaign to End Loneliness] (Loughborough: Loughborough University, 2021), https://hdl.handle.net/2134/13663715.v1; Charlie's bar Christmas Advertisement, https://www.youtube.com/watch?v=fMdWN2bQvsA.

45 Marese McDonagh, 'Rural Pubs to Take on New Functions in Quiet Times under Pilot Scheme', *Irish Times*, 25 March 2022, https://www.irishtimes.com/news/ireland/irish-news/rural-pubs-to-take-on-new-functions-in-quiet-times-under-pilot-scheme-1.4836154.

46 Carmen Kuhling and Kieran Keohane, *Cosmopolitan Ireland: Globalisation and quality of life* (London: Pluto Press, 2007), pp. 137–8.

47 On the Attestor merger, see Competition and Consumer Protection Commission at https://www.ccpc.ie/business/wp-content/uploads/sites/3/2024/04/M.24.025-Merger-Announcement.pdf; on the activities of Novellus, see https://thecurrency.news/articles/144628/inside-the-bank-of-jp-mcmanus-how-novellus-is expanding-into-ireland; for Värde, see https://varde.com/varde-provides-e70-million-refinancing-loan-for-dublin-multifamily-and-hospitalityproperties-2.

48 'Harats Press Release: Results 2024', https://harats.com/news/press-reliz-harats-itogi-2024/.

49 Such proposals (averted as of early 2025) have threatened celebrated Dublin pubs such as Nealon's of Capel Street and the Cobblestone of Smithfield, perhaps Dublin's best-known traditional music pub. The Marble Arch pub in Drimnagh has been purchased for conversion to a six-storey apartment complex by former mixed martial arts star Conor McGregor: *Irish Independent*, 5 February 2024, https://www.independent.ie/irish-news/conor-mcgregorproposes-new-six-storey-apartment-block-at-marble-arch-pub-site-in-dublin-after-earlier-plan-rejected/a2031460665.html.

50 Anne Doyle, Deirdre Mongan and Brian Galvin, *Alcohol: Availability, affordability, related harm, and policy in Ireland* [HRB Overview Series 13] (Dublin: Health Research Board, 2024), https://www.drugsandalcohol.ie/40465.

51 See the recent anthropological reports on the town of 'Cuan' (Swords, County Dublin), in Daniel Miller, *The Good Enough Life* (London: Polity, 2023) and Daniel Miller and Pauline Garvey, *Ageing with Smartphones in Ireland* (London: UCL Press, 2021), https://discovery.ucl.ac.uk/id/eprint/10126928/1/Ageing-with-Smartphones-in-Ireland.pdf.

52 Drink Aware, 'Alcohol Consumption in Ireland', 5 July 2024, https://drinkaware.ie/research/alcohol-consumption-in-ireland.

Select Bibliography

Archer, Rex, *Tales from the Kiln: A lifetime at Murphy's Brewery* (Co. Cork: Galley Head Press, 2004)

Arensberg, Conrad, and Solon Kimball, *Family and Community in Ireland*, 3rd edn (Ennis: CLASP, 2001)

Arensberg, Conrad, *The Irish Countryman: An anthropological study* (Gloucester, MA: P. Smith, 1959 [1937]), https://archive.org/details/irishcountrymana0000aren_z7q4

Barich, Bill, *A Pint of Plain: Tradition, change and the fate of the Irish pub* (London: Bloomsbury, 2009)

Barry, Kevin, *There Are Little Kingdoms* (Edinburgh: Canongate, 2007)

Barton, Ruth (ed.), *Screening Irish-America: Representing Irish-America in film and television* (Dublin: Irish Academic Press, 2009)

Bell, David, and Gill Valentine, *Consuming Geographies: We are where we eat* (London: Routledge, 1997)

Bennett, Judith M., *Ale, Beer, and Brewsters in England: Women's work in a changing world, 1300–1600* (New York and Oxford: Oxford University Press, 1996)

Billig, Michael, *Banal Nationalism* (London: Sage, 1995)

Blommaert, Jan, and Piia Varis, 'Enough Is Enough: The heuristics of authenticity in superdiversity', *Tilburg Papers in Culture Studies*, no. 2 (Tilburg: Tilburg University, 2011), https://research.tilburguniversity.edu/en/publications/enough-is-enough-the-heuristics-of-authenticity-in-superdiversity-3

Boak, Jessica, and Ray Bailey, 'Irish Pub: Near and far away', in *20th Century Pub: From beer house to booze bunker* (St Alban's: Homewood Press, 2017)

Bonner, Kieran, 'Exciting, Intoxicating and Dangerous: Some Tiger effects on Ireland and the culture of Dublin', *Canadian Journal of Irish Studies*, vol. 37, nos. 1–2, 2011, pp. 50–75

Boyd, Sean, *Behind the Horseshoe Bar: At Dublin's Shelbourne Hotel* (Dublin: Blackwater Press, 2009)

Brody, Hugh, *Inishkillane: Change and decline in the west of Ireland* (Harmondsworth: Penguin, 1973)

Brooks, Oona, 'Consuming Alcohol in Bars, Pubs and Clubs: A risky freedom for young women?', *Annals of Leisure Research: Cheers! A means-end chain analysis of college students' Bar-Choice Motivations*, vol. 11, nos. 3 & 4, 2008, pp. 331–50

Brown, Gavin, 'Ceramics, Clothing and Other Bodies: Affective geographies of homoerotic cruising encounters', *Social & Cultural Geography*, vol. 9, no. 8, December 2008, pp. 915–32.

Brown, Stephen, and Anthony Patterson, 'Knick-Knack Paddy-Whack, Give a Pub a Theme', *Journal of Marketing Management*, vol. 16, no. 6, 2000, pp. 647–62

Bulson, Roy, *Irish Pubs of Character* (Dublin: Bruce Spicer, 1969)

———, *Munster Inns and Taverns* (Dublin: Press Associates of Ireland, 1969)

Burnett, John, *Liquid Pleasures: A social history of drinks in modern Britain* (London: Routledge, 1999)

Butler, Shane, *Alcohol, Drugs and Health Promotion in Modern Ireland* (Dublin: Institute of Public Administration, 2002)

Cabras, Ignazio, and Matthew Mount, 'How Third Places Foster and Shape Community Cohesion, Economic Development and Social Capital: The case of pubs in rural Ireland', *Journal of Rural Studies*, no. 55, 2017, pp. 71–82, https://doi.org/10.1016/j.jrurstud.2017.07.013

Carrigy, Aoife, 'Powerful Puzzles: Mapping the symbiosis between two great signifiers of Irishness, the writer and the pub', Dublin Gastronomy Symposium, 2018, https://arrow.tudublin.ie/cgi/viewcontent.cgi?article=1160&context=dgs

———, 'A Place Apart, in Its Own Time: The Irish pub as portrayed in John McGahern's short stories', *Journal of Franco-Irish Studies*, vol. 5, no. 1, 2019

Carson, Ciaran, *Belfast Confetti* (Oldcastle: Gallery Press, 1989)

Cassidy, Tanya M., 'Sober for the Sake of the Children: The church, the state and alcohol use amongst women in Ireland', in Anne Byrne and Madeleine Leonard (eds), *Women and Irish Society: A sociological reader* (Belfast: Beyond the Pale Publications, 1997)

Cawley, Jessica, *Becoming an Irish Traditional Musician: Learning and embodying musical culture* (London: Routledge, 2020)

Chatterton, Paul, and Robert Hollands, *Urban Nightscapes: Youth cultures, pleasure spaces and corporate power* (London: Routledge, 2003)

Clark, Peter, *The English Alehouse: A social history, 1200–1830* (London and New York: Longman, 1983)

Coakley, Liam, '"All Over the Place, in Town, in the Pub, Everywhere": A social geography of women's friendship in Cork', *Irish Geography*, vol. 35, no. 1, 2002, pp. 40–50

Connell, Kenneth H., *Irish Peasant Society* (Oxford: Oxford University Press, 1968)

Connolly, Robert, *The Rise and Fall of the Irish Pub* (Dublin: Liffey Press, 2010)

Cooke, Anthony, *A History of Drinking: The Scottish pub since 1700* (Edinburgh: Edinburgh University Press, 2015)

Corrigan, Peter, 'The Sally O'Brien Phenomenon: What price a pint of lager?', *The Crane Bag*, vol. 7, no. 2, 1983, pp. 197–202

Cotter Buckley, Gail, and Angela Wright, 'The Domestic Death of a Global Icon? A situational analysis of the Irish public house', *Journal of Social Science for Policy Implications*, vol. 2, no. 1, 2014, pp. 85–99, https://sword.cit.ie/dptopdart/10/

Cotter, Geraldine, *Transforming Tradition: Irish traditional music in Ennis, County Clare 1950–1980* (Ennis: Geraldine Cotter, 2016)

Cronin, Michael, and Barbara O'Connor (eds), *Irish Tourism: Image, culture and identity* (Clevedon: Channel View Publications, 2003)

Cucchiara, Jason, 'Pubs, Punters, and Pints: Anthropological reflections on pub life In Ireland', unpublished master's thesis, Department of Anthropology in the College of Sciences, University of Central Florida, Orlando, FL, 2006, p. 2, https://stars.library.ucf.edu/cgi/viewcontent.cgi?article=5024&context=etd

Cunningham, Bridget M., 'A Case-study of Alcohol Consumption and of the Irish Public House in Late Modernity', unpublished PhD thesis, Department of Sociology, NUI Maynooth, 2013, p. 100, https://mural.maynoothuniversity.ie/id/eprint/5391/

Curtin, Chris, and Colm Ryan, 'Clubs, Pubs and Private Houses in a Clare town', in Chris Curtin and Tom Wilson (eds), *Ireland from Below: Social change and local communities* (Galway: Galway University Press, 1987)

Darcy, Clay, 'Irish Men, Masculinity and the Cultural Entwinement of Alcohol', University College

Dublin, unpublished, 2014, https://www.academia.edu/38544071/_Irish_Men_Masculinity_and_the_Cultural_Entwinement_of_Alcohol_&nav_from=5d359e8e-4cf6-43ca-b343-7c290f783ad7&rw_pos=0
Darwin Helana, 'Omnivorous Masculinity: Gender capital and cultural legitimacy in craft beer culture', *Social Currents*, vol. 5, no. 3, 2018, pp. 301–16
Dawson, Graham, *Making Peace with the Past: Memory, trauma and the Irish trouble* (Manchester: Manchester University Press, 2007), p. xx (Preface)
de Certeau, Michel, *The Practice of Everyday Life*, tr. Steven Rendall (Berkeley: University of California Press, 1984 [1980])
Delaney, Paul, '"Tailors of Malt, Hot, all Round": Homosocial consumption in *Dubliners*', *Studies in Short Fiction*, vol. 32, no. 3, 1995, pp. 381–93
Dennison, Stanley R., and Oliver MacDonagh, *Guinness, 1886–1939: From incorporation to the Second World War* (Cork: Cork University Press, 1998)
Doyle, Anne, Deirdre Mongan and Brian Galvin, *Alcohol: Availability, affordability, related harm, and policy in Ireland* (HRB Overview Series 13) (Dublin: Health Research Board, 2024)
Doyle, Roddy, *Love* (London: Jonathan Cape, 2020)
———, *The Complete Two Pints* (London: Vintage, 2021)
Dunne, Declan, *Mulligan's: Grand Old Pub of Poolbeg Street* (Dublin: Mercier, 2015)
Dunworth, Ali, *A Compendium of Irish Pints: The culture, customs and craic* (Dublin: Nine Bean Rows, 2024)
Edensor, Tim, *National Identity, Popular Culture and Everyday Life* (Oxford: Berg, 2002)
Eipper, Chris, *The Ruling Trinity: A community study of church, state and business in Ireland* (Aldershot: Gower, 1986)
Featherstone, Mike, *Consumer Culture and Postmodernism* (London: Sage, 2007)
Fegan, Alex (dir.), *The Irish Pub* (Dublin: Atom Films, 2013)
Felski, Rita, *Beyond Feminist Aesthetics: Feminist literature and social change* (Cambridge, MA: Harvard University Press, 1989)
Fennell, James, and Turtle Bunbury, *The Irish Pub* (London: Thames & Hudson, 2008)
Ferriter, Diarmaid, *A Nation of Extremes* (Dublin: Irish Academic Press, 1999)
———, 'Drink and Society in Twentieth-Century Ireland', in Elizabeth Fitzpatrick and James Kelly (eds), *Food and Drink in Ireland* (Dublin: Royal Irish Academy, 2016), pp. 349–70
Fiske, John, Bob Hodge and Graeme Turner, 'The Pub', in Fiske, Hodge and Turner (eds), *Myths of Oz: Reading Australian popular culture* (Sydney: Allen & Unwin, 1987)
Flanagan, Laurence (ed.), *Bottle, Draught and Keg: An Irish drinking anthology* (Dublin: Gill & Macmillan, 1995)
Flavin, Susan, et al., 'Understanding Early Modern Beer: An interdisciplinary case-study', *Historical Journal*, vol. 66, no. 3, 2023, pp. 516–49, https://doi.org/10.1017/S0018246X23000043
Foley, Anthony, *The Contribution of the Drinks Industry to Tourism* (Dublin: Drinks Ireland (IBEC), 2014), https://www.drinksindustry.ie/assets/Documents/The%20Contribution%20of%20the%20Drinks %20Industry%20to%20Tourism%20Report.pdf

———, *The Irish Pub: Stopping the decline. Reduce excise tax, protect the Irish pub*, a Drinks Industry Group of Ireland report, August 2022, Dublin City University Business School, https://www.drinksindustry.ie/assets/Media/DIGI-REPORT-The-Irish-Pub-Stopping-the-Decline.pdf

———, *The Irish Pub: Supporting our communities* (Dublin: Drinks Industry Group of Ireland, 2023), https://www.drugsandalcohol.ie/39429/1/The-Irish-Pub-Supporting-Our-Communities2023.pdf

Fraser, Nancy, 'Rethinking the Public Sphere: A contribution to the critique of actually existing democracy', *Social Text*, vols 25–6, 1990, pp. 56–80, https://doi.org/10.2307/466240

Furlong, Irene, *Irish Tourism 1880–1980* (Dublin: Irish Academic Press, 2008)

Gallen, Michelle, *Factory Girls* (New York: Hachette, 2022)

Garvey, Pauline, and David Miller, *Ageing with Smartphones in Ireland* (London: UCL Press, 2021), https://www.uclpress.co.uk/products/171340

Gefou-Madianou, Dimitra (ed.), *Alcohol, Gender and Culture* (London: Routledge, 1992)

Geraghty, John, 'A Pint in Barrytown: Pubs in the work of Roddy Doyle, parts 1 & 2', Publin (podcast), https://youtu.be/1_W9sLpRo5I?si=tUjeLJwvCg49wWxM and https://www.youtube.com /watch?v=aUOocaS9FKA&t=15s

Gerritsen, Jan-Willem, *The Control of Fuddle and Flash: A sociological history of the regulation of alcohol and opiates* (Boston: Brill, 2000)

Girouard, Mark, *Victorian Pubs* (New Haven, CT, and London: Yale University Press, 1984 [1975])

Gorham, Maurice, *Back to the Local* (London: Faber & Faber, 2024, originally published by Percival Marshall, London, in 1949)

———, and Harding McGregor Dunnett, *Inside the Pub* (London: The Architectural Press, 1950)

Grantham, Bill, 'Craic in a Box: Commodifying and exporting the Irish pub', *Continuum*, vol. 23, no. 2, 2009, pp. 257–67, https://doi.org/10.1080/10304310802710553

Graves, Charles, *Ireland Revisited* (London: Hutchinson, 1949)

Gulliver, Philip H., and Marilyn Silverman, *Merchants and Shopkeepers: A historical anthropology of an Irish market town, 1200–1991* (Toronto: University of Toronto Press, 1995)

Gusfield, Joseph, *The Culture of Public Problems: Drinking-driving and the symbolic order* (Chicago: University of Chicago Press, 1984)

———, *Symbolic Crusade: Status politics and the American temperance movement* (Chicago: University of Illinois Press, 1986)

Hames, Gina, *Alcohol in World History* (London and New York: Routledge, 2012)

Harrison, Tom (ed.), *The Pub and the People* (London: Seven Dials Press, 1943)

Hastings, Lucy, 'The Geography of Public Houses in Cork City Centre', *Chimera: UCC Geographical Journal*, no. 5, 1990, pp. 83–8, https://journals.ucc.ie/index.php/chimera/article/view/4261.

Heininge, Kathleen, 'Guinness go Leor: Irish pubs and the diaspora', in Catherine Rees (ed.), *Changes in Contemporary Ireland: Texts and contexts* (Cambridge: Cambridge Scholars Publishing, 2013), pp. 68–79

Herlihy, Jim, *The Irish Revenue Police: A short history and genealogical guide to the 'poteen hussars'* (Dublin: Four Courts Press, 2018)

Hey, Valerie, *Patriarchy and Pub Culture* (London: Tavistock, 1986)

Hobsbawm, Eric, and Terence Ranger (eds), *The Invention of Tradition* (Cambridge: Cambridge University Press, 1983)

Holloway, S.L, G. Valentine and M. Jayne, 'Masculinities, Femininities and the Geographies of Public and Private Drinking Landscapes', *Geoforum*, vol. 40, 2009, pp. 821–31

Holmes, Gordon, *Commission on Liqueur Licensing: Final report* (Dublin: Department of Justice, Equality and Law Reform, 2003)

Holmila, Marja, and Kirsimarja Raitasalo, 'Gender Differences in Drinking: Why do they still exist?', *Addiction*, no. 100, 2005, pp. 1763–9

Hong, Moonyoung, '"Home Away from Home": Diasporic consciousness and everyday third places in Tom Murphy's *Conversations on a Homecoming* (1985) and Inua Ellams' *Barber Shop Chronicles* (2017)', *Comparative Drama*, vol. 56, no. 3, 2022, pp. 256–82, http://dx.doi.org/10.1353/cdr.2022.0012

———, *Tom Murphy's Theatre of Everyday Space* (London: Routledge, 2025)

Hope, Ann, Joe Barry and Seán Byrne, *The Untold Story: Harms experienced in the Irish population due to others' drinking* (Dublin: Health Service Executive, 2018), https://www.drugsandalcohol.ie/28839/1/untold-story-harms-experienced-in-the-irish-population-due-to-others-drinking.pdf

Howell, Philip, *Pub* [Object Lessons series] (London: Bloomsbury, 2025)

Inglis, Tom, *Moral Monopoly: The rise and fall of the Catholic Church in modern Ireland* (Dublin: UCD Press, 1998)

Irish Pub Concept, The, https://irishpubconcept.com/resources-tools/the-insiders-guide-download/

Irwin, Colin, *In Search of the Craic: One man's pub crawl through Irish music* (London: André Deutsch, 2003)

Jennings, Paul, *The Local: A history of the English pub* (Cheltenham: History Press, 2021)

Jones, Marie, *The Blind Fiddler: A play* (London: Samuel French, 2008)

Joyce, James, *Ulysses*, eds Hans Walter Gabler, Wolfhard Steppe and Claus Melchior (New York: Vintage Books, 1986)

———, *Dubliners*, ed. Terence Brown (London: Penguin, 1992)

Kadel, Bradley, *Drink and Culture in Nineteenth-Century Ireland: The alcohol trade and the politics of the Irish public house* (London: Bloomsbury, 2020)

Katovich, Michael, and William Reese, 'The Regular: Full-time identities and memberships in an urban bar', *Journal of Contemporary Ethnography*, vol. 16, no. 3, 1987, https://doi.org/10.1177/0891241687163005

Kaul, Adam, *Turning the Tune: Traditional music, tourism, and social change in an Irish village* (Oxford: Berghahn, 2013)

Keane, John B., *The Field and Other Irish Plays* (Colorado: Roberts Rinehart, 1994)

Kearns, Kevin, *Dublin Pub Life and Lore: An oral history* (Dublin: Gill & Macmillan, 1996)

Keegan, Claire, 'Dark Horses', in *Walk the Blue Fields* (London: Faber, 2007), pp. 41–8

Kelly, Fergus, *A Guide to Early Irish Law* (Dublin: Dublin Institute for Advanced Studies, 1988)

Kelly, James, 'The Consumption and Sociable Use of Alcohol in Eighteenth-Century Ireland', *Proceedings of the Royal Irish Academy*, vol. 115C, 2015

Kennedy, Louise, *Trespasses* (New York: Riverhead Books, 2022)

Kenny, Ailbhe, and Katie Young, '"The House of the Irish": African migrant musicians and the creation of diasporic space at night', *Ethnomusicology Forum*, vol. 31, no. 3, 2022, pp. 332–52, https://doi.org/10.1080/17411912.2021.1938623

Kirkby, Diane, Tanja Luckins and Chris McConville, *The Australian Pub* (Sydney: University of New South Wales Press, 2010)

Kneale, James, '"A Problem of Supervision": Moral geographies of nineteenth-century British public houses', *Journal of Historical Geography*, vol. 25, no. 3, 1999

Knight, David, and Cristina Montiero (eds), *Public House: A cultural and social history of the London pub* (London: Open City, 2021)

Kuhling, Carmen, and Kieran Keohane, 'Binge drinking and overeating: globalisation and insatiability', Chapter 6 in *Cosmopolitan Ireland: Globalisation and quality of life* (London: Pluto Press, 2007)

Lefebvre, Henri, *The Production of Space*, tr. Donald Nicholson-Smith (Oxford: Blackwell, 1991 [1974])

Lentin, Ronit, and Robbie McVeigh, *After Optimism? Ireland, racism and globalization* (Dublin: Metro Publications, 2006)

Lugosi, Peter, et al., 'Creating Family-Friendly Pub Experiences: A composite data study', *International Journal of Hospitality Management*, vol. 91, https://doi.org/10.1016/j.ijhm.2020.102690

Lynch, Patrick, and John Vaizey, *Guinness's Brewery in the Irish Economy, 1759–1876* (Cambridge: Cambridge University Press, 1960)

Mac Con Iomaire, Máirtín, 'The History of Restaurant Jammet', 2009, https://arrow.tudublin.ie/cgi/viewcontent.cgi?article=1014&context=jamres

MacCabe, Fergal, 'Shops and Pubs Designed by Michael Scott in the 1940s for D.E. Williams', *Offaly History* [blog], 3 May 2022, https://offalyhistoryblog.wordpress.com/2022/05/25/emergency-stores-the-1940s-shopfronts-of-michael-scott-by-fergal-maccabe/

MacCarthy, Patricia, *Enjoying Claret in Georgian Ireland: A history of amiable excess* (Dublin: Four Courts Press, 2022)

Macleod, Allison, 'The Contested Space of the Irish Pub', in *Irish Queer Cinema* (Edinburgh: Edinburgh University Press, 2018)

Magee, Michael, *Close to Home* (London: Hamish Hamilton, 2023)

Malcolm, Elizabeth, 'Temperance and Irish Nationalism', in F.S.L. Lyons (ed.), *Ireland Under the Union: Varieties of tension* (Oxford: Clarendon, 1980)

———, 'Popular Recreation in Nineteenth-Century Ireland', in Oliver MacDonagh, W.E. Mandle and Pauric Travers (eds), *Irish Culture and Nationalism, 1750–1950* (London and Canberra: Macmillan Press, 1983)

———, *Ireland Sober, Ireland Free: Drink and temperance in nineteenth-century* Ireland (Dublin: Gill & Macmillan, 1986)

———, 'The Rise of the Pub: A study in the disciplining of popular culture', in James S. Donnelly and Kerby A. Miller (eds), *Irish Popular Culture 1650–1850* (Dublin: Irish Academic Press, 1998)

Malpas, Jeff, *Place and Experience: A philosophical topography* (Cambridge: Cambridge University Press, 1999)

Marais, Kobus, *A (Bio)Semiotic Theory of Translation: The emergence of socio-cultural reality* (London: Routledge, 2019)

Markham, Claire, 'The Public House in the Rural Community', unpublished PhD thesis, University of Lincoln, 2014, https://core.ac.uk/download/pdf/42585558.pdf

Mars, Gerald, 'Longshore Drinking, Economic Security and Union Politics in Newfoundland', in Mary Douglas (ed.), *Constructive Drinking: Perspectives on drinking from anthropology* (Cambridge: Cambridge University Press, 1987), pp. 91–101

Martin, Kevin, *Have Ye No Homes To Go To? The History of the Irish pub* (Cork: Collins Press, 2016)

———, *The Complete Guide to the Best Pubs in Dublin* (Dublin: Orpen Press, 2019)

Mass Observation Library, *The Pub and the People: A Worktown study* (London: Cresset, 1987 [originally published 1943])

Massey, Doreen, *Space, Place and Gender* (Cambridge: Polity, 1994)

———, 'Space, Place and Gender', in Jane Rendell, Barbara Penner and Iain Borden (eds), *Gender Space Architecture* (London: Routledge, 2000)

———, *For Space* (London: Sage, 2005)

Mauger, Alice, 'A Great Race of Drinkers? Irish interpretations of alcoholism and drinking stereotypes, 1945–1975', *Medical History*, vol. 65, no. 1, 2021, pp. 70–89, https://doi.org/10.1017/mdh.2020.51

McCafferty, Nell, *Peggy Deery: An Irish family at war* (Jersey City, NJ: Cleis Press, 1989)

McCafferty, Owen, *Plays 1* (London: Faber, 2013)

———, *Quietly* (London: Faber, 2014)

McCarthy, Pete, *McCarthy's Bar* (London: Hodder & Stoughton, 2001)

McCormack, Michael (dir.), *Athbhaile*, RTÉ, 2022, https://www.rte.ie/player/series/athbhaile-the-cobblestone/IH10001011-00-0000

McGahern, John, *Creatures of the Earth* (London: Faber, 2006)

McGarry, Marion, 'Why Ireland's Older Pubs Are Part of Our Cultural Heritage', *RTÉ Brainstorm*, 19 August 2021, https://www.rte.ie brainstorm/2021/0316/1204062-ireland-pubs-decor-interiors-heritage/

McGovern, Mark, 'The "Craic" Market: Irish theme bars and the commodification of Irishness in contemporary Britain', *Irish Journal of Sociology*, vol. 11, no. 2, 2002, pp. 77–98, https://doi.org/10.1177/079160350201100205

McGuffin, John, *In Praise of Poteen* (Belfast: Appletree Press, 1978)

McGuire, Edward B., *Irish Whiskey: A history of distilling, the spirit trade and excise controls in Ireland* (Dublin: Gill & Macmillan, 1973)

McMahon, Dorren, '"Which Kind of Paddy?" A survey of the literature on the history, sociology and anthropology of alcohol and the Irish', UCD Geary Institute discussion paper series, University College Dublin, 2008, https://www.ucd.ie/geary/static/publications/workingpapersgearywp200801.pdf

McNabb, Patrick, 'Social Structure', in Jeremiah Newman (ed.), *The Limerick Rural Survey, 1958–1964* (Tipperary: Muintir na Tíre, 1964)

McPherson, Conor, *The Weir and Other Plays* (New York: Theatre Communications Group, 2008)

Medcalf, Patricia, *Advertising the Black Stuff in Ireland 1959–1999: Increments of change* (Oxford: Peter Lang, 2020)

Meehan, Paula, *Return and No Blame* (Dublin: Beaver Row Press, 1984)

———, *The Man Who Was Marked by Winter* (Oldcastle: Gallery Press, 1994 [1991])

———, *Pillow Talk* (Oldcastle: Gallery Press, 1994)

———, *Dharmakaya* (Manchester: Carcanet Press, 2000)

———, *Painting Rain* (Manchester: Carcanet Press, 2009)

———, *Geomantic* (Dublin: Dedalus Press, 2016)

———, *The Solace of Artemis* (Dublin: Dedalus Press, 2023)

Michael, Lucy, *Afrophobia in Ireland: Racism against people of African descent* (Dublin: ENAR Ireland, 2015), https://core.ac.uk/download/pdf/287020638.pdf

Miller, Daniel, *The Good Enough Life* (Cambridge: Polity, 2024)

Molloy, Cian, *The Story of the Irish Pub: An intoxicating history of the licensed trade in Ireland* (Dublin: Liffey Press, 2002)

Mossop, Rodhlann, and Alex Pollock, 'Dublin's Remaining Victorian Pubs', Type [blog], https://www.type.ie/blog/dublin-sixteen-remaining-victorian-pubs-a-visual-essay

Motherway, Susan H., *The Globalization of Irish Traditional Song Performance* (Farnham: Ashgate, 2013)

Muldoon, Sean, et al., *From Barley to Blarney: A whiskey lover's guide to Ireland* (Kansas City, MI: Andrews McNeel Publishing, 2019)

Muñoz, Caroline L., Natalie T. Wood and Michael R. Solomon, 'Real or Blarney? A cross-cultural investigation of the perceived authenticity of Irish pubs', *Journal of Consumer Behaviour: An international research review*, vol. 5, no. 3, 2006, pp. 222–34, https://doi.org/10.1002/cb.174

Murphy, Brenda, *Brewing Identities: Globalisation, Guinness and the production of Irishness* (New York: Peter Lang, 2015)

Murphy, Brian J., '"If it's Eatin' and Drinkin' You Want, Take a Spoon and Fork to a Pint of Stout": A brief history of food and the Irish pub', in Máirtín Mac Con Iomaire and Dorothy Cashman (eds), *Irish Food History: A companion* (Dublin: Royal Irish Academy, 2024), https://arrow.tudublin.ie/irishfoodhist/1/

Murphy, James, *The Bartenders Association of Ireland: A History*, 1997, https://arrow.tudublin.ie/cgi/viewcontent.cgi?article=1013&context=tschafbk

Murphy, Pat (dir.), *Maeve* (London: British Film Institute Production Board, 1981)

Murphy, Tom, *Plays: 1* (London: Methuen, 1992)

———, *Plays: 2* (London: Methuen, 1997)

Murray, Paul, *The Bee Sting* (London: Macmillan, 2023)

Newby, Eric, *Round Ireland in Low Gear* (London: Viking, 1987)

Nicholls, James, *The Politics of Alcohol: A history of the drink question in England* (Manchester: Manchester University Press, 2011)

Ó Drisceoil, Diarmuid, and Donal Ó Drisceoil, *The Murphy's Story: The history of Lady's Well Brewery, Cork* (Cork: Murphy Brewery, 1997)

Ó Drisceoil, Donal, and Diarmuid Ó Drisceoil, *Beamish & Crawford: The history of an Irish brewery* (Cork: Collins Press, 2015)

O'Brien, Edna, *Saints and Sinners* (London: Faber, 2011)

O'Brien, John, 'The Use of Public Houses as a Collective Representation of the Covid-19 Pandemic in Ireland', *Irish Journal of Sociology*, vol. 29, no. 3, 2021, pp. 353–71, https://doi.org/10.1177/07916035211029202

———, 'Formal Generations of Drinkers: Generational change in Irish drinking culture to 1950', in Thomas Thurnell-Read and Laura Fenton (eds), *Alcohol, Age, Generation and the Life Course* (London: Palgrave, 2022)

O'Gorman, Andrew, *A Handbook for the Licensed Trade* (Dublin: Andrew O'Gorman, 1994)

O'Shea, Helen, 'Getting to the Heart of the Music: Idealizing musical community and Irish traditional music sessions', *Journal of the Society for Musicology in Ireland*, no. 2, 2006, pp. 1–18, https://doi.org/10.35561/JSMI02061

O'Sullivan, Catherine Marie, *Hospitality in Medieval Ireland, 900–1500* (Dublin: Four Courts Press, 2004)

O'Sullivan, Muiris, and Liam Downey, 'Poteen', *Archaeology Ireland*, vol. 35, no. 3, 2021, pp. 38–42

Oldenburg, Ray, *The Great Good Place: Cafés, coffee shops, bookstores, bars, hair salons, and other hangouts at the heart of a community*, 3rd edn (New York: Marlowe, 1999)

Orwell, George, 'The Moon Under Water' [Review of *The Pub and the People* by Mass-Observation, *The Listener*, 1943], https://www orwellfoundation.com/the-orwell-foundation/orwell/essays-and-other-works/the-moon-under-water/

Peace, Adrian, *A World of Fine Difference: The social architecture of a modern Irish village* (Dublin: UCD Press, 2001)

Pilcher, Jeffrey M., 'The Globalization of Guinness: Marketing taste, transferring technology', *Jahrbuch für Wirtschaftsgeschichte/Economic History Yearbook*, vol. 65, no. 1, 2024, pp. 17–35, https://doi.org/10.1515/jbwghttps://doi.org/10.1515/jbwg-2024-00042024-0004

Powell, Martyn J., *The Politics of Consumption in Eighteenth-Century Ireland* (Basingstoke: Palgrave Macmillan, 2005)

Pritchard, David, *The Irish Pub* (Wicklow: Real Ireland Design Limited, 1985)

Ritzer, George, *The McDonaldization Thesis: Explorations and extensions* (London: Sage, 1998)

Ryan, Eimear, *Holding Her Breath* (London: Penguin, 2022)

Scarborough, Gwen, 'The Irish Pub as a Third Place: A sociological exploration of people, place and identity', unpublished PhD thesis, Institute of Technology Sligo, 2008, https://research.thea.ie/handle/20.500.12065/585

Share, Perry, Mary P. Corcoran and Brian Conway, 'Pubs and Drinking', in *A Sociology of Ireland* (Dublin: Gill & Macmillan, 2012), pp. 311–22

Shaw, Robert, 'The Making of Pub Atmospheres and George Orwell's Moon Under Water', in Sara Asu Schroer and Susanne B. Schmitt (eds), *Exploring Atmospheres Ethnographically* (London: Routledge, 2018), pp. 30–44

SIRC [Social Issues Research Centre], *The Enduring Appeal of the Local*. A report of research conducted by the Social Issues Research Centre, Commissioned by Greene King, 1998, https://www.cabidigitallibrary.org/doi/pdf/10.5555/20103083104

Slater, Eamonn, 'When the Local Goes Global', in Eamonn Slater and Michel Peillon (eds), *Memories of the Present: A sociological chronicle of Ireland, 1997–1998* (Dublin: Institute of Public Administration, 2000)

Slattery, Peadar, *Social Life in Pre-Reformation Dublin, 1450–1540* (Dublin: Four Courts Press, 2019)

Smith, M.A., 'The Publican: Role conflict and aspects of social control', *The Service Industries Journal*, vol. 5, no. 1, 1985, https://doi.org/10.1080/02642068500000003

Solnit, Rebecca, *A Book of Migrations: Some passages in Ireland* (London: Verso, 1997)

Spalding, Tom, '"A Striking Air of Modernity Tempered with Tradition": Vernacular modernism and the design of the public house in Cork and Dublin, 1934–1969', *Journal of Design History*, vol. 35, no. 4, 2022, pp. 346–61, https://doi.org/10.1093/jdh/epab053

———, 'Murphy's Brewery, the Development of Corporate Design and Changes to the Irish Pub, 1930–70', in *Designed for Life: Architecture and design in Cork city, 1900–90* (Cork: Cork University Press, 2025), ch. 9

Stivers, Richard, *Hair of the Dog: Irish drinking and Its American Stereotype* (New York: Continuum, 2000)

Sturgeon, Sinéad, 'The Politics of Poitín: Maria Edgeworth, William Carleton and the battle for the spirit of Ireland', *Irish Studies Review*, vol. 14, no. 4, 2006, pp. 431–45, https://doi.org/10.1080/09670880600984400

Synge, J.M., *The Playboy of the Western World: A comedy in three acts*, Project Gutenberg, 2008, https://www.gutenberg.org/ebooks/1240

Taylor, Sybil, *Ireland's Pubs: The life and lore of Ireland through its finest pubs* (London: Penguin, 1983)

Taylor, Yvette and Emily Falconer, '"Seedy Bars and Grotty Pints": Close encounters in queer leisure spaces', *Social and Cultural Geography*, vol. 16, no. 1, 2015, pp. 43–57.

Thurnell-Read, Thomas, *Open Arms: The role of pubs in tackling loneliness* [commissioned by the Campaign to End Loneliness] (Loughborough: Loughborough University, 2021)

———, '"It's a Small Little Pub, but Everybody Knew Everybody": Pub culture, belonging and social change', *Sociology*, vol. 58, no. 2, 2023, https://doi.org/10.1177/00380385231185936

Tierney, Margaret, 'The Aestheticisation of Pub Culture in Dublin', unpublished MA sociology thesis, Maynooth University, 1999, https://mural.maynoothuniversity.ie/5260/1/Margaret_Tierney_20140722115658.pdf

Vallely, Fintan, *The Companion to Irish Traditional Music*, 1st edn (Cork: Cork University Press, 2011)

Wade, Christina, *Filthy Queens: A history of beer in Ireland* (Dublin: Nine Bean Rows, 2025)

Walter, Bronwyn, *Outsiders Inside: Whiteness, place and Irish women* (London: Routledge, 2001)

Watson, Diane, '"Home from Home": The pub and everyday life', in Tony Bennett and Diane Watson (eds), *Understanding Everyday Life* (Oxford: Blackwell/Open University, 2002)

Wilson, Thomas, 'Drinking Cultures: Sites and practices in the production and expression of meaning', in Thomas Wilson (ed.), *Drinking Cultures* (Oxford: Berg, 2005)

Wright, Clare, *Beyond the Ladies Lounge: Australia's female publicans* (Melbourne: Melbourne University Press, 2003)

Wright, Loic, '"A Pint of Plain Is Your Only Man": Masculinities and the pub in twentieth-century Irish fiction', *Estudios Irlandeses: Journal of Irish Studies*, vol. 15, 2020, pp. 143–55, https://doi.org/10.24162/EI2020-9371

Young, Katie, 'Producing Locality at Night: From Lagos hometown meetings to Galway's G Afro Vibez', *Crossings: Journal of Migration and Culture*, vol. 13, 2022, pp. 11–26, https://doi.org/10.1386/cjmc_00052_1

INDEX

Illustrations are indicated by page numbers in bold.

GUINNESS
SOUTH POLE INN
LORD EDWARD
The Lord E
BAR
KENNEDYS
WESTLAND ROW
GUINNESS
NEARY'S
THE CRANE
ABSOLUT VODKA
AULD SHILLELAGH
THE HAWTHORN BAR
WINE & SPIRIT STORE
The Hawthorn Bar
THE TEMPLE BAR
DUBLIN
James Joyce
1882 - 1941
THE TEMPLE BAR